AN INTRODUCTION TO
GAME THEORY

AN INTRODUCTION TO
GAME THEORY

MARTIN J. OSBORNE
University of Toronto

NEW YORK   OXFORD
OXFORD UNIVERSITY PRESS
2004

Oxford University Press

Oxford   New York
Auckland   Bangkok   Buenos Aires   Cape Town   Chennai
Dar es Salaam   Delhi   Hong Kong   Istanbul   Karachi   Kolkata
Kuala Lumpur   Madrid   Melbourne   Mexico City   Mumbai
Nairobi   São Paolo   Shanghai   Taipei   Tokyo   Toronto

Published by Oxford University Press, Inc.
198 Madison Avenue, New York, New York, 10016
http://www.oup-usa.org

Oxford is a registered trademark of Oxford University Press

Library of Congress Cataloging-in-Publication Data
Osborne, Martin J.
    An introduction to game theory / Martin J. Osborne.
        p. cm.
    Includes bibliographical references and index.
    ISBN 0-19-512895-8 (cloth : acid-free paper)
    1. Game Theory. I. Title.

QA269.O78 2004
519.3–dc21   2003042981

Photograph of John von Neumann on page 3 kindly supplied by the
Los Alamos National Laboratory, New Mexico, U.S.A.
Photograph of John Nash on page 23 copyright © The Nobel Foundation.

This book was typeset by the author, who is greatly indebted to
Donald Knuth (TeX), Leslie Lamport (LaTeX), Diego Puga (mathpazo),
Christian Schenk (MiKTeX), Ed Sznyter (ppctr), Timothy van Zandt (PSTricks),
Vincent Zoonekynd (boites), and others, for generously making superlative
software freely available. The main font is 10pt Palatino.

Printing number: 9 8 7 6 5 4 3

Printed in the United States of America
on acid-free paper

Contents

Preface   xi

1   **Introduction**   **1**
   1.1   What is game theory?   1
           An outline of the history of game theory   2
           John von Neumann   3
   1.2   The theory of rational choice   4
   1.3   Coming attractions: interacting decision-makers   7
        Notes   9

I   **Games with Perfect Information**   **11**

2   **Nash Equilibrium: Theory**   **13**
   2.1   Strategic games   13
   2.2   Example: the *Prisoner's Dilemma*   14
   2.3   Example: *Bach or Stravinsky?*   18
   2.4   Example: *Matching Pennies*   19
   2.5   Example: the *Stag Hunt*   20
   2.6   Nash equilibrium   21
           John F. Nash, Jr.   23
           Studying Nash equilibrium experimentally   24
   2.7   Examples of Nash equilibrium   26
           Experimental evidence on the Prisoner's Dilemma   28
           Focal points   32
   2.8   Best response functions   35
   2.9   Dominated actions   45
   2.10 Equilibrium in a single population: symmetric games and symmetric equilibria   50
        Notes   53

3   **Nash Equilibrium: Illustrations**   **55**
   3.1   Cournot's model of oligopoly   55
   3.2   Bertrand's model of oligopoly   63
           Cournot, Bertrand, and Nash: some historical notes   69
   3.3   Electoral competition   70
   3.4   The *War of Attrition*   77

3.5   Auctions   80
       Auctions from Babylonia to eBay   81
3.6   Accident law   91
       Notes   97

4   Mixed Strategy Equilibrium   99
4.1   Introduction   99
              Some evidence on expected payoff functions   104
4.2   Strategic games in which players may randomize   106
4.3   Mixed strategy Nash equilibrium   107
4.4   Dominated actions   120
4.5   Pure equilibria when randomization is allowed   122
4.6   Illustration: expert diagnosis   123
4.7   Equilibrium in a single population   128
4.8   Illustration: reporting a crime   131
              Reporting a crime: social psychology and game theory   133
4.9   The formation of players' beliefs   134
4.10   Extension: finding all mixed strategy Nash equilibria   137
4.11   Extension: games in which each player has a continuum of actions   142
4.12   Appendix: representing preferences by expected payoffs   146
       Notes   150

5   Extensive Games with Perfect Information: Theory   153
5.1   Extensive games with perfect information   153
5.2   Strategies and outcomes   159
5.3   Nash equilibrium   161
5.4   Subgame perfect equilibrium   164
5.5   Finding subgame perfect equilibria of finite horizon games:
       backward induction   169
              Ticktacktoe, chess, and related games   178
       Notes   179

6   Extensive Games with Perfect Information: Illustrations   181
6.1   The ultimatum game, the holdup game, and agenda control   181
              Experiments on the ultimatum game   183
6.2   Stackelberg's model of duopoly   187
6.3   Buying votes   192
6.4   A race   197
       Notes   203

7   Extensive Games with Perfect Information: Extensions and Discussion   205
7.1   Allowing for simultaneous moves   205
              More experimental evidence on subgame perfect equilibrium   211
7.2   Illustration: entry into a monopolized industry   213
7.3   Illustration: electoral competition with strategic voters   215

7.4   Illustration: committee decision-making   217
7.5   Illustration: exit from a declining industry   221
7.6   Allowing for exogenous uncertainty   225
7.7   Discussion: subgame perfect equilibrium and backward induction   231
            Experimental evidence on the centipede game   234
        Notes   236

8   Coalitional Games and the Core   239
8.1   Coalitional games   239
8.2   The core   243
8.3   Illustration: ownership and the distribution of wealth   247
8.4   Illustration: exchanging homogeneous horses   251
8.5   Illustration: exchanging heterogeneous houses   256
8.6   Illustration: voting   260
8.7   Illustration: matching   263
            Matching doctors with hospitals   268
8.8   Discussion: other solution concepts   269
        Notes   270

II   Games with Imperfect Information   271

9   Bayesian Games   273
9.1   Motivational examples   273
9.2   General definitions   278
9.3   Two examples concerning information   282
9.4   Illustration: Cournot's duopoly game with imperfect information   285
9.5   Illustration: providing a public good   289
9.6   Illustration: auctions   291
            Auctions of the radio spectrum   300
9.7   Illustration: juries   301
9.8   Appendix: auctions with an arbitrary distribution of valuations   307
        Notes   311

10   Extensive Games with Imperfect Information   313
10.1   Extensive games with imperfect information   313
10.2   Strategies   317
10.3   Nash equilibrium   318
10.4   Beliefs and sequential equilibrium   323
10.5   Signaling games   331
10.6   Illustration: conspicuous expenditure as a signal of quality   336
10.7   Illustration: education as a signal of ability   340
10.8   Illustration: strategic information transmission   343
10.9   Illustration: agenda control with imperfect information   351
        Notes   357

III   Variants and Extensions   359

11   Strictly Competitive Games and Maxminimization   361
11.1   Maxminimization   361
11.2   Maxminimization and Nash equilibrium   364
11.3   Strictly competitive games   365
11.4   Maxminimization and Nash equilibrium in strictly competitive games   367
    Maxminimization: some history   370
    Empirical tests: experiments, tennis, and soccer   373
    Notes   375

12   Rationalizability   377
12.1   Rationalizability   377
12.2   Iterated elimination of strictly dominated actions   385
12.3   Iterated elimination of weakly dominated actions   388
12.4   Dominance solvability   391
    Notes   392

13   Evolutionary Equilibrium   393
13.1   Monomorphic pure strategy equilibrium   394
    Evolutionary game theory: some history   399
13.2   Mixed strategies and polymorphic equilibrium   400
13.3   Asymmetric contests   406
    Side-blotched lizards   407
    Explaining the outcomes of contests in nature   409
13.4   Variation on a theme: sibling behavior   411
13.5   Variation on a theme: the nesting behavior of wasps   414
13.6   Variation on a theme: the evolution of the sex ratio   416
    Notes   417

14   Repeated Games: The *Prisoner's Dilemma*   419
14.1   The main idea   419
14.2   Preferences   421
14.3   Repeated games   423
14.4   Finitely repeated *Prisoner's Dilemma*   424
14.5   Infinitely repeated *Prisoner's Dilemma*   426
14.6   Strategies in an infinitely repeated *Prisoner's Dilemma*   426
14.7   Some Nash equilibria of an infinitely repeated *Prisoner's Dilemma*   428
14.8   Nash equilibrium payoffs of an infinitely repeated *Prisoner's Dilemma*   431
    Experimental evidence   436
14.9   Subgame perfect equilibria and the one-deviation property   437
    Axelrod's tournaments   439

14.10 Some subgame perfect equilibria of an infinitely repeated
        Prisoner's Dilemma   441
                Reciprocal altruism among sticklebacks   445
14.11 Subgame perfect equilibrium payoffs of an infinitely repeated
        Prisoner's Dilemma   446
                Medieval trade fairs   448
14.12 Concluding remarks   449
        Notes   449

15 Repeated Games: General Results   451
15.1   Nash equilibria of general infinitely repeated games   451
15.2   Subgame perfect equilibria of general infinitely repeated games   455
15.3   Finitely repeated games   460
15.4   Variation on a theme: imperfect observability   461
        Notes   463

16 Bargaining   465
16.1   Bargaining as an extensive game   465
16.2   Illustration: trade in a market   477
16.3   Nash's axiomatic model   481
16.4   Relation between strategic and axiomatic models   489
        Notes   491

17 Appendix: Mathematics   493
17.1   Numbers   493
17.2   Sets   494
17.3   Functions   495
17.4   Profiles   498
17.5   Sequences   499
17.6   Probability   499
17.7   Proofs   505

References   507

Index   525

Preface

GAME-THEORETIC REASONING pervades economic theory and is used widely in other social and behavioral sciences. This book presents the main ideas of game theory and shows how they can be used to understand economic, social, political, and biological phenomena. It assumes no knowledge of economics, political science, or any other social or behavioral science. It emphasizes the ideas behind the theory rather than their mathematical expression and assumes no specific mathematical knowledge beyond that typically taught in U.S. and Canadian high schools. (Chapter 17 reviews the mathematical concepts used in the book.) In particular, calculus is not used, except in the appendix of Chapter 9 (Section 9.8). Nevertheless, all concepts are defined precisely, and logical reasoning is used throughout. My aim is to explain the main ideas of game theory as simply as possible while maintaining complete precision; the more comfortable you are with tight logical analysis, the easier you will find the arguments.

The only way to appreciate the theory is to see it in action, or better still to put it into action. So the book includes a wide variety of illustrations from the social and behavioral sciences, and over 280 exercises.

The structure of the book is illustrated in the figure on the next page. The gray boxes indicate core chapters (the darker gray, the more important). A black arrow from Chapter i to Chapter j means that Chapter j depends on Chapter i. The gray arrow from Chapter 4 to Chapter 9 means that the latter depends weakly on the former; for all but Section 9.7 only an understanding of expected payoffs (Section 4.1.3) is required, not a knowledge of mixed strategy Nash equilibrium. (Two chapters are not included in this figure: Chapter 1 reviews the theory of a single rational decision-maker, and Chapter 17 reviews the mathematical concepts used in the book.)

Each topic is presented with the aid of "Examples", which highlight theoretical points, and "Illustrations", which demonstrate how the theory may be used to understand social, economic, political, and biological phenomena. The "Illustrations" introduce no new theoretical points, and any or all of them may be skipped without loss of continuity. The "Illustrations" for the key models of strategic and extensive games are grouped in separate chapters (3 and 6).

The limited dependencies between chapters mean that several routes may be taken through the book.

- At a minimum, you should study Chapters 2 (Nash Equilibrium: Theory) and 5 (Extensive Games with Perfect Information: Theory).

- Optionally you may sample some sections of Chapters 3 (Nash Equilibrium: Illustrations) and 6 (Extensive Games with Perfect Information: Illustrations).

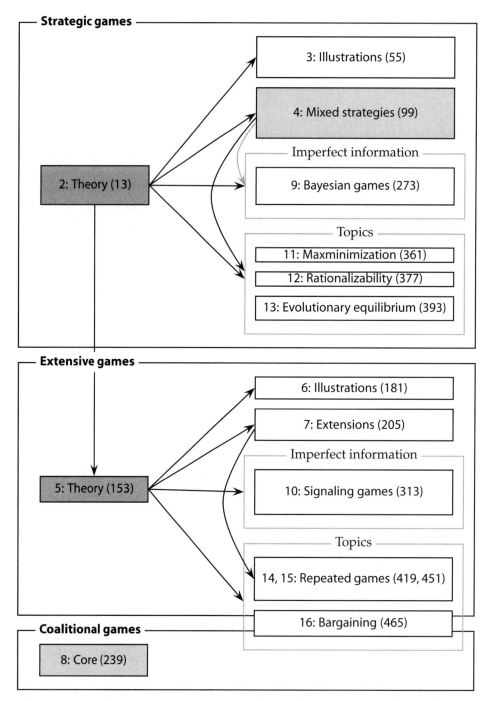

The structure of the book. Each chapter is represented by a box whose area is proportional to the length of the chapter; the number in parentheses is the page on which the chapter begins. Boxes shaded gray correspond to core chapters; dark gray chapters are more central than light gray ones. An arrow from Chapter *i* to Chapter *j* means that Chapter *i* is a prerequisite for Chapter *j*. The gray arrow from Chapter 4 to Chapter 9 means that the latter depends only weakly on the former.

- You may add to this plan any combination of Chapters 4 (Mixed Strategy Equilibrium), 9 (Bayesian Games, except Section 9.7, which requires Chapter 4), 7 (Extensive Games with Perfect Information: Extensions and Discussion), 8 (Coalitional Games and the Core), and 16 (Bargaining).

- If you read Chapter 4 (Mixed Strategy Equilibrium), then you may in addition study any combination of the remaining chapters covering strategic games, and if you study Chapter 7 (Extensive Games with Perfect Information: Extensions and Discussion), then you are ready to tackle Chapters 14 and 15 (Repeated Games).

Whichever route you take, you can choose the examples and illustrations to fit one of several themes. You can, for instance, study all the economic examples, or all the political or biological ones. Alternatively, you can build a course around all the examples on a more narrow topic; two possibilities are auction theory and oligopoly theory.

All the material is intended to be accessible to undergraduate students. A one-semester course for third or fourth year North American economics majors (who have been exposed to a few of the main ideas in first and second year courses) could cover up to about half the material in the book in moderate detail.

Osborne and Rubinstein (1994), a graduate text, offers a more advanced treatment of the field. With few exceptions, the two books use the same notation and terminology. The exceptions are noted on the website for this book (see the end of the preface).

Examples modeling economic, political, and biological phenomena

The main examples that involve economic, political, or biological phenomena are listed below. (Examples used to make a primarily game-theoretic point are omitted.)

Economic phenomena

Accident law: Section 3.6
Adverse selection: Exercise 282.3
Auctions: Section 3.5 (perfect information), Example 143.1 (all-pay), Section 9.6 (imperfect information), Section 9.8 (imperfect information)
Bertrand's model of oligopoly: Section 3.2, Exercise 136.2, Exercise 146.1, Exercise 192.1, Exercise 214.1, Exercise 392.1 (dominance solvability), Exercise 454.3 (repeated game), Exercise 459.1, Exercise 459.2, Section 15.4 (repeated game with imperfectly observable actions)
Chain-store game: Example 231.1
Collective decision-making: Section 2.9.4
Common property: Section 3.1.5

Competition in product characteristics: Exercise 76.1

Cournot's model of oligopoly: Section 3.1, Exercise 136.1, Section 9.4 (imperfect
        information), Exercise 388.2 (rationalizability)

Entry into an industry by a financially-constrained challenger: Exercise 174.2

Entry into a monopolized industry: Section 7.2

Exit from a declining industry: Section 7.5

Expert diagnosis: Section 4.6

Firm–union bargaining: Exercise 177.1, Exercise 227.2, Exercise 489.1

Holdup game: Section 6.1.2

Market games: Exercise 211.2, Example 245.5, Section 8.4, Section 8.5, Section 16.2

Matching: Example 242.2, Section 8.7

Ownership and the distribution of wealth: Example 240.2, Example 244.2,
        Section 8.3

Price competition between sellers: Exercise 128.1, Exercise 212.1

Provision of a public good: Exercise 33.1, Section 2.8.4, Exercise 44.1,
        Exercise 132.3, Section 9.5, Exercise 388.1 (rationalizability)

Reporting a crime (private provision of a public good): Section 4.8

"Rotten kid theorem": Exercise 177.2

Signaling ability with education: Section 10.7

Signaling quality with conspicuous expenditure: Section 10.6

Stackelberg's model of duopoly: Section 6.2

Strategic information transmission: Section 10.8

Timing product release: Exercise 80.1

Political phenomena

Agenda control: Section 6.1.3 (perfect information), Section 10.9 (imperfect
        information)

Allocating resources in election campaigns: Exercise 141.3

Approval voting: Exercise 49.2

Buying votes in a legislature: Section 6.3

Cohesion of governing coalitions in legislatures: Exercise 228.1

Collective decision-making: Section 2.9.4

Committee decision-making: Section 7.4

Electoral competition between citizen-candidates: Exercise 75.2

Electoral competition between policy-motivated candidates: Exercise 75.1

Hotelling's model of electoral competition: Section 3.3, Exercise 196.3,
        Exercise 196.4, Section 7.3 (strategic voters), Exercise 387.5 (rationalizability),
        Exercise 454.2 (repeated game)

Juries: Section 9.7

Lobbying as an auction: Exercise 91.1

Majority game: Example 240.3, Exercise 245.1

Vote trading: Exercise 247.1

Voter participation: Exercise 34.2, Exercise 118.2

Voting: Section 2.9.3 (strategic game), Section 8.6 (coalitional game),
    Exercise 307.1 (swing voter's curse), Exercise 391.3 (dominance solvability)
Voting by alternating veto: Exercise 173.3

Biological phenomena

Evolution of sex ratio: Section 13.6
Hawk–Dove: Example 398.2, Example 404.2, Example 409.1
Hermaphroditic fish: Exercise 18.1
Nesting behavior of wasps: Section 13.5
Reciprocal altruism: Box on page 445
Sibling competition: Section 13.4
Signaling hunger (Sir Philip Sydney game): Exercise 335.2
War of Attrition: Section 3.4

Personal pronouns

The English language lacks a third person singular pronoun widely interpreted
to be sex neutral. In particular, many experiments have shown that "he" is not
neutral[1], a finding consistent with the observation that whereas people may say
"when an airplane pilot is working, he needs to concentrate", they do not usually
say "when a flight attendant is working, he needs to concentrate" or "when a secre-
tary is working, he needs to concentrate". To quote the *American Heritage Dictionary*
(third edition, page 831), "Thus *he* is not really a gender-neutral pronoun; rather
it refers to a male who is to be taken as the representative member of the group
referred to by its antecedent. The traditional usage, then, is not simply a gram-
matical convention; it also suggests a particular pattern of thought." Like many
writers, I regard as unacceptable the bias implicit in the use of "he" for individuals of unspecified sex. The *New Oxford Dictionary of English* states the case clearly:
"[the use of *he* to refer to a person of unspecified sex] has become ... a hallmark of
old-fashioned language or sexism in language." Writers have become sensitive to
this issue in the last fifty years, but the lack of a sex-neutral pronoun "has been felt
since at least as far back as Middle English" (*Webster's Dictionary of English Usage*,
Merriam-Webster Inc. 1989, 499). A common solution has been to use "they",[2] a
usage that the *New Oxford Dictionary of English* endorses (and employs). In some
contexts this usage sounds natural, but in others it does not; it can also create am-
biguity when the pronoun follows references to more than one person. I choose a
different solution: I use "she" exclusively. Obviously this usage, like that of "he",

---

[1]See, for example, Janice Moulton, George M. Robinson, and Cherin Elias, "Sex bias in language
use: 'neutral' pronouns that aren't", *American Psychologist* **33** (1978), 1032–1036; Janet Shibley Hyde,
"Children's understanding of sexist language", *Development Psychology* **20** (1984), 697–706; and John
Gastil, "Generic pronouns and sexist language: the oxymoronic character of masculine generics", *Sex
Roles* **23** (1990), 629–643.

[2]For a discussion of the history of the use of "they", see Ann Bodine, "Androcentrism in prescriptive
grammar: singular 'they', sex-indefinite 'he', and 'he or she' ", *Language in Society* **4** (1975), 129–146.

is not sex neutral, but it may help to counterbalance the widespread use of "he", and seems unlikely to do any harm.

References

The "Notes" section at the end of each chapter attempts to assign credit for the ideas discussed. Several cases present difficulties. In some cases, ideas evolved over a long period of time, with contributions by many people, making their origins hard to summarize in a sentence or two. In a few cases, my research has led to a conclusion about the origins of an idea different from the standard one. In all cases, I cite the relevant papers without regard to their difficulty.

Over the years, I have taken exercises from many sources. I have attempted to remember the origins of the ones I use in this book, and give credit appropriately.

Conventions, numbering, and nomenclature

I use the term "dollar" for a unit of money because it is probably recognizable as such to a majority of readers of this book, even if they pay their bills in rupees, yuan, or pa'anga.

In formal definitions, the terms being defined are set in **boldface**. Terms set in *italics* are informal definitions.

Definitions, propositions, lemmas, examples, exercises, and equations are numbered according to the page on which they appear. If the first such object on page n is an exercise, for example, it is called Exercise $n.1$; if the next object on that page is a definition, it is called Definition $n.2$. For example, the definition of a strategic game with ordinal preferences on page 13 is Definition 13.1. Figures are numbered separately, using the same page-based system. The scheme allows numbered items to be found rapidly and enhances the precision of index entries.

Symbol/term	Meaning
⑦	Exercise, with solution on website
⑦	Hard exercise, with solution on website
⑦	Exercise, with solution available only to instructors (see website for conditions)
⑦	Hard exercise, with solution available only to instructors (see website for conditions)
▶	Definition
■	Result
◆	Example: a game that illustrates a game-theoretic point
Illustration	A game, or family of games, that shows how the theory can illuminate observed phenomena

Acknowledgments

I owe a huge debt to Ariel Rubinstein. I have learned, and continue to learn, vastly from him about game theory. His influence on this book will be clear to anyone familiar with our jointly authored book *A course in game theory*. Had we not written that book and our previous book *Bargaining and markets*, I doubt that I would have embarked on this project.

I was privileged as a graduate student at Stanford University to learn game theory from Robert Aumann, Sergiu Hart, Mordecai Kurz, Al Roth, and Robert Wilson. Discussions over the years with Jean-Pierre Benoît, Haruo Imai, Vijay Krishna, Michael Peters, and Carolyn Pitchik have improved my understanding of many game-theoretic topics.

Many people have generously commented on all or parts of drafts of the book. I am particularly grateful to Peter McCabe for many very thoughtful comments. I am very grateful also to Gian Luigi Albano, Jeffrey Banks, Nikolaos Benos, Ted Bergstrom, Tilman Börgers, Randy Calvert, Vu Cao, In-Koo Cho, Rachel Croson, Eddie Dekel, Marina De Vos, Laurie Duke, Patrick Elias, Mukesh Eswaran, Xinhua Gu, Costas Halatsis, Joe Harrington, Hiroyuki Kawakatsu, Lewis Kornhauser, Jack Leach, Tao Li, Simon Link, Bart Lipman, Kin Chung Lo, Massimo Marinacci, Massimo Morelli, Nathan Nunn, Barry O'Neill, Robin G. Osborne, Marco Ottaviani, Carolyn Pitchik, Marie Rekkas, Bob Rosenthal, Al Roth, Matthew Shum, Branislav L. Slantchev, Giora Slutzki, Michael Smart, Nick Vriend, Charles A. Wilson, Luís Zemborain, and several anonymous reviewers.

My editors at Oxford University Press, Kenneth MacLeod and Stephen McGroarty, offered much encouragement and advice. Their enthusiasm for the project was a great help in keeping the book on track. The many suggestions of Oxford's production editor Brian Kinsey greatly improved the appearance of the book.

The book has its origins in a course I taught at Columbia University in the early 1980s. My experience in that course, and in courses at McMaster University and the University of Toronto, brought the book to its current form. The Kyoto Institute of Economic Research at Kyoto University and the School of Economics at the Australian National University provided me with splendid environments in which to work on the book during visits in 1999 and 2001.

I maintain a website for the book. The current URL is
`http://www.economics.utoronto.ca/osborne/igt/`

MARTIN J. OSBORNE
`martin.osborne@utoronto.ca`
`http://www.economics.utoronto.ca/osborne/`
Department of Economics, University of Toronto
150 St. George Street, Toronto, Canada, M5S 3G7
May 2003

AN INTRODUCTION TO
GAME THEORY

1 Introduction

1.1 What is game theory?   1
1.2 The theory of rational choice   4
1.3 Coming attractions: interacting decision-makers   7

1.1 What is game theory?

GAME THEORY aims to help us understand situations in which decision-makers interact. A game in the everyday sense—"a competitive activity ... in which players contend with each other according to a set of rules", in the words of a dictionary—is an example of such a situation, but the scope of game theory is very much larger. Indeed, I devote very little space to games in the everyday sense; my main focus is the use of game theory to illuminate economic, political, and biological phenomena.

A list of some of the applications I discuss will give you an idea of the range of situations to which game theory can be applied: firms competing for business, political candidates competing for votes, jury members deciding on a verdict, animals fighting over prey, bidders competing in an auction, the evolution of siblings' behavior towards each other, competing experts' incentives to correctly diagnose a problem, legislators' voting behavior under pressure from interest groups, and the role of threats and punishment in long-term relationships.

Like other sciences, game theory consists of a collection of models. A model is an abstraction we use to understand our observations and experiences. What "understanding" entails is not clear-cut. Partly, at least, it entails our perceiving relationships between situations, isolating principles that apply to a range of problems, so that we can fit into our thinking new situations that we encounter. For example, we may fit our observation of the path taken by a lobbed tennis ball into a model that assumes the ball moves forward at a constant velocity and is pulled towards the ground by the constant force of "gravity". This model enhances our understanding because it fits well, no matter how hard or in which direction the ball is hit, and applies also to the paths taken by baseballs, cricket balls, and a wide variety of other missiles, launched in any direction.

A model is unlikely to help us understand a phenomenon if its assumptions are wildly at odds with our observations. At the same time, a model derives power from its simplicity; the assumptions upon which it rests should capture the essence of the situation, not irrelevant details. For example, when considering the path

AN OUTLINE OF THE HISTORY OF GAME THEORY

Some game-theoretic ideas can be traced to the 18th century, but the major development of the theory began in the 1920s with the work of the mathematician Émile Borel (1871–1956) and the polymath John von Neumann (1903–57). A decisive event in the development of the theory was the publication in 1944 of the book *Theory of games and economic behavior* by von Neumann and Oskar Morgenstern, which established the foundations of the field. In the early 1950s, John F. Nash (see the box on page 23) developed a key concept (Nash equilibrium) and initiated the game-theoretic study of bargaining. Soon after Nash's work, game-theoretic models began to be used in economic theory and political science, and psychologists began studying how human subjects behave in experimental games. In the 1970s game theory was first used as a tool in evolutionary biology. Subsequently, game-theoretic methods have come to dominate microeconomic theory and are used also in many other fields of economics and a wide range of other social and behavioral sciences. The 1994 Nobel Prize in Economic Sciences was awarded to the game theorists John C. Harsanyi (1920–2000), John F. Nash (1928–), and Reinhard Selten (1930–).

taken by a lobbed tennis ball we should ignore the dependence of the force of gravity on the distance of the ball from the surface of the earth.

Models cannot be judged by an absolute criterion: they are neither "right" nor "wrong". Whether a model is useful or not depends, in part, on the purpose for which it is used. For example, when I determine the shortest route from Florence to Venice, I do not worry about the projection of the map I am using; I work under the assumption that the earth is flat. When I determine the shortest route from Beijing to Havana, however, I pay close attention to the projection—I assume that the earth is spherical. And were I to climb the Matterhorn I would assume that the earth is neither flat nor spherical!

One reason for improving our understanding of the world is to enhance our ability to mold it to our desires. The understanding that game-theoretic models give is particularly relevant in the social, political, and economic arenas. Studying game-theoretic models (or other models that apply to human interaction) may also suggest ways in which an individual's behavior may be modified to improve her own welfare. By analyzing the incentives faced by negotiators locked in battle, for example, we may see the advantages and disadvantages of various strategies.

The models of game theory are precise expressions of ideas that can be presented verbally. Verbal descriptions tend to be long and imprecise; in the interest of conciseness and precision, I frequently employ mathematical symbols. Although I use the language of mathematics, I use few of its concepts; the ones I use are described in Chapter 17. I aim to take advantage of the precision and conciseness of a mathematical formulation without losing sight of the underlying ideas.

JOHN VON NEUMANN

John von Neumann, the most important figure in the early development of game theory, was born in Budapest, Hungary, in 1903. He displayed exceptional mathematical ability as a child (he had mastered calculus by the age of 8), but his father, concerned about his son's financial prospects, did not want him to become a mathematician. As a compromise he enrolled in mathematics at the University of Budapest in 1921, but immediately left to study chemistry, first at the University of Berlin and subsequently at the Swiss Federal Institute of Technology in Zurich, from which he earned a degree in chemical engineering in 1925. During his time in Germany and Switzerland he returned to Budapest to write examinations, and in 1926 obtained a Ph.D. in mathematics from the University of Budapest. He taught in Berlin and Hamburg, and, from 1930 to 1933, at Princeton University. In 1933 he became the youngest of the first six professors of the School of Mathematics at the Institute for Advanced Study in Princeton (Einstein was another).

Von Neumann's first published scientific paper appeared in 1922, when he was 19 years old. In 1928 he published a paper that establishes a key result on strictly competitive games, a result that had eluded Borel. He made many major contributions in pure and applied mathematics and in physics—enough, according to Halmos (1973), "for about three ordinary careers, in pure mathematics alone". While at the Institute for Advanced Study he collaborated with the Princeton economist Oskar Morgenstern in writing *Theory of games and economic behavior*, the book that established game theory as a field. In the 1940s he became increasingly involved in applied work. In 1943 he became a consultant to the Manhattan Project, which was developing an atomic bomb, and in 1944 he became involved with the development of the first electronic computer, to which he made major contributions. He stayed at Princeton until 1954, when was appointed to the U.S. Atomic Energy Commission. He died in 1957.

Game-theoretic modeling starts with an idea related to some aspect of the interaction of decision-makers. We express this idea precisely in a model, incorporating features of the situation that appear to be relevant. This step is an art. We wish to put enough ingredients into the model to obtain nontrivial insights, but not so many that we are led into irrelevant complications; we wish to lay bare the underlying structure of the situation as opposed to describing its every detail. The next step is to analyze the model—to discover its implications. At this stage we need to adhere to the rigors of logic; we must not introduce extraneous considerations absent from the model. Our analysis may confirm our idea, or suggest it is wrong. If it is wrong, the analysis should help us to understand why it is wrong. We may see that an assumption is inappropriate, or that an important element is missing from the model; we may conclude that our idea is invalid, or that we need to investigate it further by studying a different model. Thus, the interaction between our ideas and models designed to shed light on them runs in two directions: the implications of models help us determine whether our ideas make sense, and these ideas, in the light of the implications of the models, may show us how the assumptions of our models are inappropriate. In either case, the process of formulating and analyzing a model should improve our understanding of the situation we are considering.

1.2   The theory of rational choice

The theory of rational choice is a component of many models in game theory. Briefly, this theory is that a decision-maker chooses the best action according to her preferences, among all the actions available to her. No qualitative restriction is placed on the decision-maker's preferences; her "rationality" lies in the consistency of her decisions when faced with different sets of available actions, not in the nature of her likes and dislikes.

1.2.1   Actions

The theory is based on a model with two components: a set A consisting of all the actions that, under some circumstances, are available to the decision-maker, and a specification of the decision-maker's preferences. In any given situation, the decision-maker is faced with a subset[1] of A, from which she must choose a single element. The decision-maker knows this subset of available choices, and takes it as given; in particular, the subset is not influenced by the decision-maker's preferences. The set A could, for example, be the set of bundles of goods that the decision-maker can possibly consume; given her income at any time, she is restricted to choose from the subset of A containing the bundles she can afford.

1.2.2   Preferences and payoff functions

As to preferences, we assume that the decision-maker, when presented with any pair of actions, knows which of the pair she prefers, or knows that she regards both actions as equally desirable (in which case she is "indifferent between the actions"). We assume further that these preferences are consistent in the sense that if the decision-maker prefers the action a to the action b, and the action b to the action c, then she prefers the action a to the action c. No other restriction is imposed on preferences. In particular, we allow a person's preferences to be altruistic in the sense that how much she likes an outcome depends on some other person's welfare. Theories that use the model of rational choice aim to derive implications that do not depend on any qualitative characteristic of preferences.

---

[1]See Chapter 17 for a description of mathematical terminology.

How can we describe a decision-maker's preferences? One way is to specify, for each possible pair of actions, the action the decision-maker prefers, or to note that the decision-maker is indifferent between the actions. Alternatively we can "represent" the preferences by a *payoff function*, which associates a number with each action in such a way that actions with higher numbers are preferred. More precisely, the payoff function u represents a decision-maker's preferences if, for any actions a in A and b in A,

$$u(a) > u(b) \text{ if and only if the decision-maker prefers } a \text{ to } b. \tag{5.1}$$

(A better name than payoff function might be "preference indicator function". In economic theory a payoff function that represents a consumer's preferences is often called a "utility function".)

◆ EXAMPLE 5.2 (Payoff function representing preferences) A person is faced with the choice of three vacation packages, to Havana, Paris, and Venice. She prefers the package to Havana to the other two, which she regards as equivalent. Her preferences between the three packages are represented by any payoff function that assigns the same number to Paris and Venice and a higher number to Havana. For example, we can set $u(\text{Havana}) = 1$ and $u(\text{Paris}) = u(\text{Venice}) = 0$, or $u(\text{Havana}) = 10$ and $u(\text{Paris}) = u(\text{Venice}) = 1$, or $u(\text{Havana}) = 0$ and $u(\text{Paris}) = u(\text{Venice}) = -2$.

⑦ EXERCISE 5.3 (Altruistic preferences) Person 1 cares about both her income and person 2's income. Precisely, the value she attaches to each unit of her own income is the same as the value she attaches to any two units of person 2's income. For example, she is indifferent between a situation in which her income is 1 and person 2's is 0, and one in which her income is 0 and person 2's is 2. How do her preferences order the outcomes $(1, 4)$, $(2, 1)$, and $(3, 0)$, where the first component in each case is her income and the second component is person 2's income? Give a payoff function consistent with these preferences.

A decision-maker's preferences, in the sense used here, convey only *ordinal* information. They may tell us that the decision-maker prefers the action a to the action b to the action c, for example, but they do not tell us "how much" she prefers a to b, or whether she prefers a to b "more" than she prefers b to c. Consequently a payoff function that represents a decision-maker's preferences also conveys only ordinal information. It may be tempting to think that the payoff numbers attached to actions by a payoff function convey intensity of preference—that if, for example, a decision-maker's preferences are represented by a payoff function u for which $u(a) = 0, u(b) = 1$, and $u(c) = 100$, then the decision-maker likes c a lot more than b but finds little difference between a and b. *A payoff function contains no such information!* The *only* conclusion we can draw from the fact that $u(a) = 0, u(b) = 1$, and $u(c) = 100$ is that the decision-maker prefers c to b to a. Her preferences are represented equally well by the payoff function v for which $v(a) = 0, v(b) = 100$, and $v(c) = 101$, for example, or any other function w for which $w(a) < w(b) < w(c)$.

From this discussion we see that a decision-maker's preferences are represented by many different payoff functions. Looking at (5.1), we see that if u represents a decision-maker's preferences and the payoff function v assigns a higher number to the action a than to the action b if and only if the payoff function u does so, then v also represents these preferences. Stated more compactly, if u represents a decision-maker's preferences and v is another payoff function for which

$$v(a) > v(b) \text{ if and only if } u(a) > u(b),$$

then v also represents the decision-maker's preferences. Or, more succinctly, if u represents a decision-maker's preferences, then any increasing function of u also represents these preferences.

(?) EXERCISE 6.1 (Alternative representations of preferences) A decision-maker's preferences over the set $A = \{a, b, c\}$ are represented by the payoff function u for which $u(a) = 0$, $u(b) = 1$, and $u(c) = 4$. Are they also represented by the function v for which $v(a) = -1$, $v(b) = 0$, and $v(c) = 2$? How about the function w for which $w(a) = w(b) = 0$ and $w(c) = 8$?

Sometimes it is natural to formulate a model in terms of preferences and then find payoff functions that represent these preferences. In other cases it is natural to start with payoff functions, even if the analysis depends only on the underlying preferences, not on the specific representation we choose.

1.2.3 The theory of rational choice

The theory of rational choice may be stated simply: in any given situation the decision-maker chooses the member of the available subset of A that is best according to her preferences. Allowing for the possibility that there are several equally attractive best actions, **the theory of rational choice** is

> the action chosen by a decision-maker is at least as good, according to her preferences, as every other available action.

For any action, we can design preferences with the property that no other action is preferred. Thus if we have no information about a decision-maker's preferences, and make no assumptions about their character, any *single* action is consistent with the theory. However, if we assume that a decision-maker who is indifferent between two actions sometimes chooses one action and sometimes the other, not every *collection* of choices for different sets of available actions is consistent with the theory. Suppose, for example, we observe that a decision-maker chooses a whenever she faces the set $\{a, b\}$, but sometimes chooses b when facing the set $\{a, b, c\}$. The fact that she always chooses a when faced with $\{a, b\}$ means that she prefers a to b (if she were indifferent, she would sometimes choose b). But then when she faces the set $\{a, b, c\}$, she must choose either a or c, never b. Thus her choices are inconsistent with the theory. (More concretely, if you choose the same dish from the menu of your favorite bistro whenever there are no specials, then, regardless of your preferences, it is inconsistent for you to choose some other item *from the menu* on a day when there is an off-menu special.)

If you have studied the standard economic theories of the consumer and the firm, you have encountered the theory of rational choice before. In the economic theory of the consumer, for example, the set of available actions is the set of all bundles of goods that the consumer can afford. In the theory of the firm, the set of available actions is the set of all input–output vectors, and the action a is preferred to the action b if and only if a yields a higher profit than does b.

1.2.4 Discussion

The theory of rational choice is enormously successful; it is a component of countless models that enhance our understanding of social phenomena. It pervades economic theory to such an extent that arguments are classified as "economic" as much because they involve rational choices as because they involve particularly "economic" variables.

Nevertheless, under some circumstances its implications are at variance with observations of human decision-making. To take a small example, adding an undesirable action to a set of actions sometimes significantly changes the action chosen (see Rabin 1998, 38). The significance of such discordance with the theory depends upon the phenomenon being studied. If we are considering how the markup of price over cost in an industry depends on the number of firms, for example, this sort of weakness in the theory may be unimportant. But if we are studying how advertising, designed specifically to influence peoples' preferences, affects consumers' choices, then the inadequacies of the model of rational choice may be crucial.

No general theory currently challenges the supremacy of rational choice theory. But you should bear in mind as you read this book that the theory has its limits, and some of the phenomena that you may think of explaining by using a game-theoretic model may lie beyond these limits. As always, the proof of the pudding is in the eating: if a model enhances our understanding of the world, then it serves its purpose.

1.3 Coming attractions: interacting decision-makers

In the model of the previous section, the decision-maker chooses an action from a set A and cares only about this action. A decision-maker in the world often does not have the luxury of controlling all the variables that affect her. If some of the variables that affect her are the actions of *other* decision-makers, her decision-making problem is altogether more challenging than that of an isolated decision-maker. The study of such situations, which we may model as *games*, occupies the remainder of the book.

Consider, for example, firms competing for business. Each firm controls its price, but not the other firms' prices. Each firm cares, however, about all the firms' prices, because these prices affect its sales. How should a firm choose its price in these circumstances? Or consider a candidate for political office choosing a policy platform. She is likely to care not only about her own platform, but those of her rivals, which affect her chance of being elected. How should she choose her platform, knowing that every other candidate faces the same problem? Or suppose you are negotiating a purchase. You care about the price, which depends on both your behavior and that of the seller. How should you decide what price to offer?

Part I presents the main models of game theory: a strategic game, an extensive game, and a coalitional game. These models differ in two dimensions. A strategic game and an extensive game focus on the actions of individuals, whereas a coalitional game focuses on the outcomes that can be achieved by groups of individuals; a strategic game and a coalitional game consider situations in which actions are chosen once and for all, whereas an extensive game allows for the possibility that plans may be revised as they are carried out.

The model within which rational choice theory is cast is tailor-made for the theory. If we want to develop another theory of a single decision-maker, we need to add elements to the model in addition to actions and preferences. The same is not true of most models in game theory: strategic interaction is sufficiently complex that even a relatively simple model can admit more than one theory of the outcome. We refer to a theory that specifies a set of outcomes for a model as a "solution". Chapter 2 describes the model of a strategic game and the solution of Nash equilibrium for such games. The theory of Nash equilibrium in a strategic game has been applied to a vast variety of situations; a few of the most significant applications are discussed in Chapter 3.

Chapter 4 extends the notion of Nash equilibrium in a strategic game to allow for the possibility that a decision-maker, when indifferent between actions, may not always choose the same action.

The model of an extensive game, which adds a temporal dimension to the description of strategic interaction captured by a strategic game, is studied in Chapters 5, 6, and 7. Part I concludes with Chapter 8, which discusses the model of a coalitional game and a solution for such a game, the core.

Part II extends the models of a strategic game (Chapter 9) and an extensive game (Chapter 10) to situations in which the players do not know the other players' characteristics or past actions.

The chapters in Part III cover topics outside the basic theory. Chapters 11 and 12 examine two theories of the outcome in a strategic game that are alternatives to the theory of Nash equilibrium. Chapter 13 discusses how a variant of the notion of Nash equilibrium in a strategic game can be used to model behavior that is the outcome of evolutionary pressure rather than conscious choice. Chapters 14 and 15 use the model of an extensive game to study long-term relationships, in which the same group of players repeatedly interact. Finally, Chapter 16 uses extensive and coalitional models to gain an understanding of the outcome of bargaining.

Notes

Von Neumann and Morgenstern (1944) established game theory as a field. The information about John von Neumann in the box on page 3 is drawn from Ulam (1958), Halmos (1973), Thompson (1987), Poundstone (1992), and Leonard (1995). Aumann (1985), on which I draw in the opening section, contains a very readable discussion of the aims and achievements of game theory. Two papers that discuss the limitations of rational choice theory are Rabin (1998) and Elster (1998).

Games with Perfect Information

2   Nash Equilibrium: Theory   13
3   Nash Equilibrium: Illustrations   55
4   Mixed Strategy Equilibrium   99
5   Extensive Games with Perfect Information:
     Theory   153
6   Extensive Games with Perfect Information:
     Illustrations   181
7   Extensive Games with Perfect Information:
     Extensions and Discussion   205
8   Coalitional Games and the Core   239

2 Nash Equilibrium: Theory

2.1 Strategic games 13
2.2 Example: the *Prisoner's Dilemma* 14
2.3 Example: *Bach or Stravinsky?* 18
2.4 Example: *Matching Pennies* 19
2.5 Example: the *Stag Hunt* 20
2.6 Nash equilibrium 21
2.7 Examples of Nash equilibrium 26
2.8 Best response functions 35
2.9 Dominated actions 45
2.10 Equilibrium in a single population: symmetric games and symmetric equilibria 50
Prerequisite: Chapter 1

2.1 Strategic games

A STRATEGIC GAME is a model of interacting decision-makers. In recognition of the interaction, we refer to the decision-makers as *players*. Each player has a set of possible *actions*. The model captures interaction between the players by allowing each player to be affected by the actions of *all* players, not only her own action. Specifically, each player has *preferences* about the action *profile*—the list of all the players' actions. (See Section 17.4, in the mathematical appendix, for a discussion of profiles.)

More precisely, a strategic game is defined as follows. (The qualification "with ordinal preferences" distinguishes this notion of a strategic game from a more general notion studied in Chapter 4.)

▶ DEFINITION 13.1 (*Strategic game with ordinal preferences*) A **strategic game** (with ordinal preferences) consists of

- a set of **players**
- for each player, a set of **actions**
- for each player, **preferences** over the set of action profiles.

A very wide range of situations may be modeled as strategic games. For example, the players may be firms, the actions prices, and the preferences a reflection of the firms' profits. Or the players may be candidates for political office, the actions

campaign expenditures, and the preferences a reflection of the candidates' probabilities of winning. Or the players may be animals fighting over some prey, the actions concession times, and the preferences a reflection of whether an animal wins
or loses. In this chapter I describe some simple games designed to capture funda-
mental conflicts present in a variety of situations. The next chapter is devoted to
more detailed applications to specific phenomena.

As in the model of rational choice by a single decision-maker (Section 1.2), it is
frequently convenient to specify the players' preferences by giving *payoff functions*
that represent them. Suppose, for example, that a player prefers the action profile
a to the profile b, and prefers b to c. We may specify these preferences by assigning
the payoffs 3 to a, 2 to b, and 1 to c. Or, alternatively, we may specify the preferences
by assigning the payoffs 100 to a, 0 to b, and -2 to c. The two specifications are
equally good; in particular, the latter does *not* imply that the player's preference
between a and b is stronger than her preference between b and c. The point is that a
strategic game with ordinal preferences is defined by the players' preferences, not
by payoffs that represent these preferences.

Time is absent from the model. The idea is that each player chooses her action once and for all, and the players choose their actions "simultaneously" in the
sense that no player is informed, when she chooses her action, of the action chosen
by any other player. (For this reason, a strategic game is sometimes referred to
as a "simultaneous-move game".) Nevertheless, an action may involve activities
that extend over time, and may take into account an unlimited number of contingencies. An action might specify, for example, "if company X's stock falls below
$10, buy 100 shares; otherwise, do not buy any shares". (For this reason, an action
is sometimes called a "strategy".) However, the fact that time is absent from the
model means that when analyzing a situation as a strategic game, we abstract from
the complications that may arise if a player is allowed to change her plan as events
unfold: we assume that actions are chosen once and for all.

2.2 Example: the *Prisoner's Dilemma*

One of the most well-known strategic games is the *Prisoner's Dilemma*. Its name
comes from a story involving suspects in a crime; its importance comes from the
huge variety of situations in which the participants face incentives similar to those
faced by the suspects in the story.

◆ EXAMPLE 14.1 (*Prisoner's Dilemma*) Two suspects in a major crime are held in separate cells. There is enough evidence to convict each of them of a minor offense,
but not enough evidence to convict either of them of the major crime unless one of
them acts as an informer against the other (finks). If they both stay quiet, each will
be convicted of the minor offense and spend one year in prison. If one and only
one of them finks, she will be freed and used as a witness against the other, who
will spend four years in prison. If they both fink, each will spend three years in
prison.

This situation may be modeled as a strategic game:

Players The two suspects.

Actions Each player's set of actions is $\{Quiet, Fink\}$.

Preferences Suspect 1's ordering of the action profiles, from best to worst, is $(Fink, Quiet)$ (she finks and suspect 2 remains quiet, so she is freed), $(Quiet, Quiet)$ (she gets one year in prison), $(Fink, Fink)$ (she gets three years in prison), $(Quiet, Fink)$ (she gets four years in prison). Suspect 2's ordering is $(Quiet, Fink)$, $(Quiet, Quiet)$, $(Fink, Fink)$, $(Fink, Quiet)$.

We can represent the game compactly in a table. First choose payoff functions that represent the suspects' preference orderings. For suspect 1 we need a function u_1 for which

$$u_1(Fink, Quiet) > u_1(Quiet, Quiet) > u_1(Fink, Fink) > u_1(Quiet, Fink).$$

A simple specification is $u_1(Fink, Quiet) = 3$, $u_1(Quiet, Quiet) = 2$, $u_1(Fink, Fink) = 1$, and $u_1(Quiet, Fink) = 0$. For suspect 2 we can similarly choose the function u_2 for which $u_2(Quiet, Fink) = 3$, $u_2(Quiet, Quiet) = 2$, $u_2(Fink, Fink) = 1$, and $u_2(Fink, Quiet) = 0$. Using these representations, the game is illustrated in Figure 15.1. In this figure the two rows correspond to the two possible actions of player 1, the two columns correspond to the two possible actions of player 2, and the numbers in each box are the players' payoffs to the action profile to which the box corresponds, with player 1's payoff listed first.

		Suspect 2	
		Quiet	*Fink*
Suspect 1	*Quiet*	2, 2	0, 3
	Fink	3, 0	1, 1

Figure 15.1 The *Prisoner's Dilemma* (Example 14.1).

The *Prisoner's Dilemma* models a situation in which there are gains from cooperation (each player prefers that both players choose *Quiet* than they both choose *Fink*) but each player has an incentive to "free ride" (choose *Fink*) whatever the other player does. The game is important not because we are interested in understanding the incentives for prisoners to confess, but because many other situations have similar structures. Whenever each of two players has two actions, say C (corresponding to *Quiet*) and D (corresponding to *Fink*), player 1 prefers (D, C) to (C, C) to (D, D) to (C, D), and player 2 prefers (C, D) to (C, C) to (D, D) to (D, C), the *Prisoner's Dilemma* models the situation that the players face. Some examples follow.

2.2.1 Working on a joint project

You are working with a friend on a joint project. Each of you can either work hard or goof off. If your friend works hard, then you prefer to goof off (the outcome of

the project would be better if you worked hard too, but the increment in its value
to you is not worth the extra effort). You prefer the outcome of your both working
hard to the outcome of your both goofing off (in which case nothing gets accomplished), and the worst outcome for you is that you work hard and your friend
goofs off (you hate to be "exploited"). If your friend has the same preferences,
then the game that models the situation you face is given in Figure 16.1, which, as
you can see, differs from the *Prisoner's Dilemma* only in the names of the actions.

	Work hard	Goof off
Work hard	2, 2	0, 3
Goof off	3, 0	1, 1

Figure 16.1 Working on a joint project.

I am *not* claiming that a situation in which two people pursue a joint project
necessarily has the structure of the *Prisoner's Dilemma*, only that the players' preferences in such a situation *may* be the same as in the *Prisoner's Dilemma*! If, for
example, each person prefers to work hard than to goof off when the other person
works hard, then the *Prisoner's Dilemma* does *not* model the situation: the players'
preferences are different from those given in Figure 16.1.

⑦ EXERCISE 16.1 (Working on a joint project) Formulate a strategic game that models
a situation in which two people work on a joint project in the case that their preferences are the same as those in the game in Figure 16.1 except that each person
prefers to work hard than to goof off when the other person works hard. Present
your game in a table like the one in Figure 16.1.

2.2.2 Duopoly

In a simple model of a duopoly, two firms produce the same good, for which each
firm charges either a low price or a high price. Each firm wants to achieve the
highest possible profit. If both firms choose *High*, then each earns a profit of $1000.
If one firm chooses *High* and the other chooses *Low*, then the firm choosing *High*
obtains no customers and makes a loss of $200, whereas the firm choosing *Low*
earns a profit of $1200 (its unit profit is low, but its volume is high). If both firms
choose *Low*, then each earns a profit of $600. Each firm cares only about its profit,
so we can represent its preferences by the profit it obtains, yielding the game in
Figure 16.2.

	High	Low
High	1000, 1000	−200, 1200
Low	1200, −200	600, 600

Figure 16.2 A simple model of a price-setting duopoly.

Bearing in mind that what matters are the players' preferences, not the particular payoff functions that we use to represent them, we see that this game, like the previous one, differs from the *Prisoner's Dilemma* only in the names of the actions. The action *High* plays the role of *Quiet*, and the action *Low* plays the role of *Fink*; firm 1 prefers (*Low, High*) to (*High, High*) to (*Low, Low*) to (*High, Low*), and firm 2 prefers (*High, Low*) to (*High, High*) to (*Low, Low*) to (*Low, High*).

⑦ EXERCISE 17.1 (Games equivalent to the *Prisoner's Dilemma*) Determine whether each of the games in Figure 17.1 differs from the *Prisoner's Dilemma* only in the names of the players' actions, or whether it differs also in one or both of the players' preferences.

	X	Y
X	3,3	1,5
Y	5,1	0,0

	X	Y
X	2,1	0,5
Y	3,−2	1,−1

Figure 17.1 The strategic games for Exercise 17.1.

As in the previous example, I do not claim that the incentives in a duopoly are *necessarily* those in the *Prisoner's Dilemma*; different assumptions about the relative sizes of the profits in the four cases generate a different game. Further, in this case one of the abstractions incorporated into the model—that each firm has only two prices to choose between—may not be harmless. If the firms may choose among many prices, then the structure of the interaction may change. (A richer model is studied in Section 3.2.)

2.2.3 The arms race

Under some assumptions about the countries' preferences, an arms race can be modeled as the *Prisoner's Dilemma*. (The *Prisoner's Dilemma* was first studied in the early 1950s, when the United States and the Soviet Union were involved in a nuclear arms race, so you might suspect that U.S. nuclear strategy was influenced by game theory; the evidence suggests that it was not.) Assume that each country can build an arsenal of nuclear bombs, or can refrain from doing so. Assume also that each country's favorite outcome is that it has bombs and the other country does not; the next best outcome is that neither country has any bombs; the next best outcome is that both countries have bombs (what matters is relative strength, and bombs are costly to build); and the worst outcome is that only the other country has bombs. In this case the situation is modeled by the *Prisoner's Dilemma*, in which the action *Don't build bombs* corresponds to *Quiet* in Figure 15.1 and the action *Build bombs* corresponds to *Fink*. However, once again the assumptions about preferences necessary for the *Prisoner's Dilemma* to model the situation may not be satisfied: a country may prefer *not* to build bombs if the other country does not, for example (bomb-building may be very costly), in which case the situation is modeled by a different game.

2.2.4   Common property

Two farmers are deciding how much to allow their sheep to graze on the village common. Each farmer prefers that her sheep graze a lot rather than a little, regardless of the other farmer's action, but prefers that both sets of sheep graze a little rather than a lot (in which case the common is ruined for future use). Under these assumptions the game is the *Prisoner's Dilemma*. (A richer model is studied in Section 3.1.5.)

2.2.5   Other situations modeled as the Prisoner's Dilemma

A huge number of other situations have been modeled as the *Prisoner's Dilemma*, from mating hermaphroditic fish to tariff wars between countries.

? EXERCISE 18.1 (Hermaphroditic fish) Members of some species of hermaphroditic fish choose, in each mating encounter, whether to play the role of a male or a female. Each fish has a preferred role, which uses up fewer resources and hence allows more future mating. A fish obtains a payoff of H if it mates in its preferred role and L if it mates in the other role, where $H > L$. (Payoffs are measured in terms of number of offspring, which fish are evolved to maximize.) Consider an encounter between two fish whose preferred roles are the same. Each fish has two possible actions: mate in either role or insist on its preferred role. If both fish offer to mate in either role, the roles are assigned randomly, and each fish's payoff is $\frac{1}{2}(H + L)$ (the average of H and L). If each fish insists on its preferred role, the fish do not mate; each goes off in search of another partner, and obtains the payoff S. The higher the chance of meeting another partner, the larger is S. Formulate this situation as a strategic game and determine the range of values of S, for any given values of H and L, for which the game differs from the *Prisoner's Dilemma* only in the names of the actions.

2.3   Example: *Bach or Stravinsky?*

In the *Prisoner's Dilemma* the main issue is whether the players will cooperate (choose *Quiet*). In the following game the players agree that it is better to cooperate than not to cooperate, but they disagree about the best outcome.

◆ EXAMPLE 18.2 (*Bach or Stravinsky?*) Two people wish to go out together. Two concerts are available: one of music by Bach, and one of music by Stravinsky. One person prefers Bach and the other prefers Stravinsky. If they go to different concerts, each of them is equally unhappy listening to the music of either composer.

We may model this situation as the two-player strategic game in Figure 19.1, in which the person who prefers Bach chooses a row and the person who prefers Stravinsky chooses a column.

This game is also referred to as the "Battle of the Sexes" (though the conflict it models surely occurs no more frequently between people of the opposite sex

	Bach	*Stravinsky*
Bach	2, 1	0, 0
Stravinsky	0, 0	1, 2

Figure 19.1 *Bach or Stravinsky? (BoS) (Example 18.2).*

than it does between people of the same sex). I call the game *BoS*, an acronym that fits both names. (I assume that each player is indifferent between listening to Bach and listening to Stravinsky when she is alone only for consistency with the standard specification of the game. As we shall see, the analysis of the game remains the same in the absence of this indifference.)

Like the *Prisoner's Dilemma*, *BoS* models a wide variety of situations. Consider, for example, two officials of a political party deciding the stand to take on an issue. Suppose that they disagree about the best stand, but are both better off if they take the same stand than if they take different stands; the cases in which they take different stands, leading voters to be confused, are equally bad. Then *BoS* captures the situation they face. Or consider two merging firms that currently use different computer technologies. As two divisions of a single firm they will both be better off if they both use the same technology; each firm prefers that the common technology be the one it used in the past. *BoS* models the choices the firms face.

2.4   Example: *Matching Pennies*

Aspects of both conflict and cooperation are present in both the *Prisoner's Dilemma* and *BoS*. The next game is purely conflictual.

◆ EXAMPLE 19.1 (*Matching Pennies*) Two people choose, simultaneously, whether to show the head or the tail of a coin. If they show the same side, person 2 pays person 1 a dollar; if they show different sides, person 1 pays person 2 a dollar. Each person cares only about the amount of money she receives, and (naturally!) prefers to receive more than less. A strategic game that models this situation is shown in Figure 19.2. (In this representation of the players' preferences, the payoffs are equal to the amounts of money involved. We could equally well work with another representation—for example, 2 could replace each 1, and 1 could replace each −1.)

In this game the players' interests are diametrically opposed (such a game is called "strictly competitive"): player 1 wants to take the same action as the other player, whereas player 2 wants to take the opposite action.

	Head	*Tail*
Head	1, −1	−1, 1
Tail	−1, 1	1, −1

Figure 19.2 *Matching Pennies (Example 19.1).*

This game may, for example, model the choices of appearances for new products by an established producer and a new firm in a market of fixed size. Suppose that each firm can choose one of two different appearances for the product. The established producer prefers the newcomer's product to look different from its own (so that its customers will not be tempted to buy the newcomer's product), whereas the newcomer prefers that the products look alike. Or the game could model a relationship between two people in which one person wants to be like the other, whereas the other wants to be different.

(?) EXERCISE 20.1 (Games without conflict) Give some examples of two-player strategic games in which each player has two actions and the players have the same preferences, so that there is no conflict between their interests. (Present your games as tables like the one in Figure 19.2.)

2.5 Example: the *Stag Hunt*

A sentence in *Discourse on the origin and foundations of inequality among men* (1755) by the philosopher Jean-Jacques Rousseau discusses a group of hunters who wish to catch a stag. (See Rousseau 1988, 36.) They will succeed if they all remain sufficiently attentive, but each is tempted to desert her post and catch a hare. One interpretation of the sentence is that the interaction between the hunters may be modeled as the following strategic game.

◆ EXAMPLE 20.2 (*Stag Hunt*) Each of a group of hunters has two options: she may remain attentive to the pursuit of a stag, or she may catch a hare. If all hunters pursue the stag, they catch it and share it equally; if any hunter devotes her energy to catching a hare, the stag escapes, and the hare belongs to the defecting hunter alone. Each hunter prefers a share of the stag to a hare.
   The strategic game that corresponds to this specification is:

Players The hunters.

Actions Each player's set of actions is {*Stag*, *Hare*}.

Preferences For each player, the action profile in which all players choose *Stag* (resulting in her obtaining a share of the stag) is ranked highest, followed by any profile in which she chooses *Hare* (resulting in her obtaining a hare), followed by any profile in which she chooses *Stag* and one or more of the other players chooses *Hare* (resulting in her leaving empty-handed).

   Like other games with many players, this game cannot easily be presented in a table like that in Figure 19.2. For the case in which there are two hunters, the game is shown in the left panel of Figure 21.1.
   The variant of the two-player *Stag Hunt* shown in the right panel of Figure 21.1 has been suggested as an alternative to the *Prisoner's Dilemma* as a model of an arms race, or, more generally, of the "security dilemma" faced by a pair of countries. The game differs from the *Prisoner's Dilemma* in that a country prefers the outcome in

	Stag	Hare
Stag	2,2	0,1
Hare	1,0	1,1

	Refrain	Arm
Refrain	3,3	0,2
Arm	2,0	1,1

Figure 21.1 Left panel: The *Stag Hunt* (Example 20.2) for the case of two hunters. Right panel: A variant of the two-player *Stag Hunt* that models the "security dilemma".

which both countries refrain from arming themselves to the one in which it alone arms itself: the cost of arming outweighs the benefit if the other country does not arm itself.

2.6 Nash equilibrium

What actions will be chosen by the players in a strategic game? We wish to assume, as in the theory of a rational decision-maker (Section 1.2), that each player chooses the best available action. In a game, the best action for any given player depends, in general, on the other players' actions. So when choosing an action a player must have in mind the actions the other players will choose. That is, she must form a *belief* about the other players' actions.

On what basis can such a belief be formed? The assumption underlying the analysis in this chapter and the next two chapters is that each player's belief is derived from her past experience playing the game, and that this experience is sufficiently extensive that she *knows* how her opponents will behave. No one tells her the actions her opponents will choose, but her previous involvement in the game leads her to be sure of these actions. (The question of *how* a player's experience can lead her to the correct beliefs about the other players' actions is addressed briefly in Section 4.9.)

Although we assume that each player has experience playing the game, we assume that she views each play of the game in isolation. She does not become familiar with the behavior of specific opponents and consequently does not condition her action on the opponent she faces; nor does she expect her current action to affect the other players' future behavior.

It is helpful to think of the following idealized circumstances. For each player in the game there is a population of many decision-makers who may, on any occasion, take that player's role. In each play of the game, players are selected randomly, one from each population. Thus each player engages in the game repeatedly, against ever-varying opponents. Her experience leads her to beliefs about the actions of "typical" opponents, not any specific set of opponents.

As an example, think of the repeated interaction of buyers and sellers. To a first approximation, many of the pairings may be modeled as random; in many cases a buyer transacts only once with any given seller, or interacts anonymously (when the seller is a large store, for example).

In summary, the solution theory we study has two components. First, each player chooses her action according to the model of rational choice, given her belief about the other players' actions. Second, every player's belief about the other players' actions is correct. These two components are embodied in the following definition.

> A *Nash equilibrium* is an action profile a^* with the property that no player i can do better by choosing an action different from a_i^*, given that every other player j adheres to a_j^*.

In the idealized setting in which the players in any given play of the game are drawn randomly from a collection of populations, a Nash equilibrium corresponds to a *steady state*. If, whenever the game is played, the action profile is the same Nash equilibrium a^*, then no player has a reason to choose any action different from her component of a^*; there is no pressure on the action profile to change. Expressed differently, a Nash equilibrium embodies a stable "social norm": if everyone else adheres to it, no individual wishes to deviate from it.

The second component of the theory of Nash equilibrium—that the players' beliefs about each other's actions are correct—implies, in particular, that two players' beliefs about a third player's action are the same. For this reason, the condition is sometimes referred to as the requirement that the players' "expectations are coordinated".

The situations to which we wish to apply the theory of Nash equilibrium do not in general correspond exactly to the idealized setting described above. For example, in some cases the players do not have much experience with the game; in others they do not view each play of the game in isolation. Whether the notion of Nash equilibrium is appropriate in any given situation is a matter of judgment. In some cases, a poor fit with the idealized setting may be mitigated by other considerations. For example, inexperienced players may be able to draw conclusions about their opponents' likely actions from their experience in other situations, or from other sources. (One aspect of such reasoning is discussed in the box on page 32). Ultimately, the test of the appropriateness of the notion of Nash equilibrium is whether it gives us insights into the problem at hand.

With the aid of an additional piece of notation, we can state the definition of a Nash equilibrium precisely. Let a be an action profile, in which the action of each player i is a_i. Let a_i' be any action of player i (either equal to a_i, or different from it). Then (a_i', a_{-i}) denotes the action profile in which every player j *except* i chooses her action a_j as specified by a, whereas player i chooses a_i'. (The $-i$ subscript on a stands for "except i".) That is, (a_i', a_{-i}) is the action profile in which all the players other than i adhere to a while i "deviates" to a_i'. (If $a_i' = a_i$, then of course $(a_i', a_{-i}) = (a_i, a_{-i}) = a$.) If there are three players, for example, then (a_2', a_{-2}) is the action profile in which players 1 and 3 adhere to a (player 1 chooses a_1, player 3 chooses a_3) and player 2 deviates to a_2'.

Using this notation, we can restate the condition for an action profile a^* to be a Nash equilibrium: no player i has any action a_i for which she prefers (a_i, a_{-i}^*) to a^*. Equivalently, for every player i and every action a_i of player i, the action profile a^* is at least as good for player i as the action profile (a_i, a_{-i}^*).

JOHN F. NASH, JR.

A few of the ideas John F. Nash, Jr., developed while he was a graduate student at Princeton from 1948 to 1950 transformed game theory. Nash was born in 1928 in Bluefield, West Virginia, where he grew up. He was an undergraduate mathematics major at Carnegie Institute of Technology from 1945 to 1948. In 1948 he obtained both a B.S. and an M.S., and began graduate work in the Department of Mathematics at Princeton University. (One of his letters of recommendation, from a professor at Carnegie Institute of Technology, was a single sentence: "This man is a genius" (Kuhn et al. 1995, 282).) A paper containing the main result of his thesis was submitted to the *Proceedings of the National Academy of Sciences* in November 1949, fourteen months after he started his graduate work. ("A fine goal to set ... graduate students", to quote Harold Kuhn! (See Kuhn et al. 1995, 282.)) He completed his Ph.D. the following year, graduating on his twenty-second birthday. His thesis (Nash 1950b), 28 pages in length, introduces the equilibrium notion now known as "Nash equilibrium" and delineates a class of strategic games that have Nash equilibria (Proposition 119.1 in this book). The notion of Nash equilibrium vastly expanded the scope of game theory, which had previously focused on two-player "strictly competitive" games (in which the players' interests are directly opposed). While a graduate student at Princeton, Nash also wrote the seminal paper in bargaining theory, Nash (1950c) (the ideas of which originated in an elective class in international economics he took as an undergraduate). He went on to take an academic position in the Department of Mathematics at MIT, where he produced "a remarkable series of papers" (Milnor 1995, 15); he has been described as "one of the most original mathematical minds of [the twentieth] century" (Kuhn 1996). He shared the 1994 Nobel Prize in Economic Sciences with the game theorists John C. Harsanyi and Reinhard Selten.

▶ DEFINITION 23.1 (*Nash equilibrium of strategic game with ordinal preferences*) The action profile a^* in a strategic game with ordinal preferences is a **Nash equilibrium** if, for every player i and every action a_i of player i, a^* is at least as good according to player i's preferences as the action profile (a_i, a^*_{-i}) in which player i chooses a_i while every other player j chooses a^*_j. Equivalently, for every player i,

$$u_i(a^*) \geq u_i(a_i, a^*_{-i}) \text{ for every action } a_i \text{ of player } i, \tag{23.2}$$

where u_i is a payoff function that represents player i's preferences.

This definition implies neither that a strategic game necessarily has a Nash equilibrium, nor that it has at most one. Examples in the next section show that some games have a single Nash equilibrium, some possess no Nash equilibrium, and others have many Nash equilibria.

The definition of a Nash equilibrium is designed to model a steady state among experienced players. An alternative approach to understanding players' actions in strategic games assumes that the players know each others' preferences, and considers what each player can deduce about the other players' actions from their rationality and their knowledge of each other's rationality. This approach is studied in Chapter 12. For many games, it leads to a conclusion different from that of Nash equilibrium. For games in which the conclusion is the same, the approach offers us an alternative interpretation of a Nash equilibrium, as the outcome of rational calculations by players who do not necessarily have any experience playing the game.

STUDYING NASH EQUILIBRIUM EXPERIMENTALLY

The theory of strategic games lends itself to experimental study: arranging for subjects to play games and observing their choices is relatively straightforward. A few years after game theory was launched by von Neumann and Morgenstern's (1944) book, reports of laboratory experiments began to appear. Subsequently a huge number of experiments have been conducted, illuminating many issues relevant to the theory. I discuss selected experimental evidence throughout the book.

The theory of Nash equilibrium, as we have seen, has two components: the players act in accordance with the theory of rational choice, given their beliefs about the other players' actions, and these beliefs are correct. If every subject understands the game she is playing and faces incentives that correspond to the preferences of the player whose role she is taking, then a divergence between the observed outcome and a Nash equilibrium can be blamed on a failure of one or both of these two components. Experimental evidence has the potential of indicating the types of games for which the theory works well and, for those in which the theory does not work well, of pointing to the faulty component and giving us hints about the characteristics of a better theory. In designing an experiment that cleanly tests the theory, however, we need to confront several issues.

The model of rational choice takes preferences as given. Thus to test the theory of Nash equilibrium experimentally, we need to ensure that each subject's preferences are those of the player whose role she is taking in the game we are examining. The standard way of inducing the appropriate preferences is to pay each subject an amount of money directly related to the payoff given by a payoff function that represents the preferences of the player whose role the subject is taking. Such remuneration works if each subject likes money and cares only about the amount of money she receives, ignoring the amounts received by her opponents. The assumption that people like receiving money is reasonable in many cultures, but the assumption that people care only about their own monetary rewards— are "selfish"—may, in some contexts at least, not be reasonable. Unless we check whether our subjects are selfish in the context of our experiment, we will jointly test two hypotheses: that humans are selfish—a hypothesis not part of game theory—and that the notion of Nash equilibrium models their behavior. In some cases we may indeed wish to test these hypotheses jointly. But to test the theory of Nash equilibrium alone we need to ensure that we induce the preferences we wish to study.

Assuming that better decisions require more effort, we need also to ensure that each subject finds it worthwhile to put in the extra effort required to obtain a higher payoff. If we rely on monetary payments to provide incentives, the amount of money a subject can obtain must be sufficiently sensitive to the quality of her decisions to compensate her for the effort she expends (paying a flat fee, for example, is inappropriate). In some cases, monetary payments may not be necessary: under some circumstances, subjects drawn from a highly competitive culture like that of the United States may be sufficiently motivated by the possibility of obtaining a high score, even if that score does not translate into a monetary payoff.

The notion of Nash equilibrium models action profiles compatible with steady states. Thus to study the theory experimentally we need to collect observations of subjects' behavior when they have experience playing the game. But they should not have obtained that experience while knowingly facing the same opponents repeatedly, for the theory assumes that the players consider each play of the game in isolation, not as part of an ongoing relationship. One option is to have each subject play the game against many different opponents, gaining experience about how the other subjects on average play the game, but not about the choices of any other given player. Another option is to describe the game in terms that relate to a situation in which the subjects already have experience. A difficulty with this second approach is that the description we give may connote more than simply the payoff numbers of our game. If we describe the *Prisoner's Dilemma* in terms of cooperation on a joint project, for example, a subject may be biased toward choosing the action she has found appropriate when involved in joint projects, even if the structures of those interactions were significantly different from that of the *Prisoner's Dilemma*. As she plays the experimental game repeatedly she may come to appreciate how it differs from the games in which she has been involved previously, but her biases may disappear only slowly.

Whatever route we take to collect data on the choices of subjects experienced in playing the game, we confront a difficult issue: how do we know when the outcome has converged? Nash's theory concerns only equilibria; it has nothing to say about the path players' choices will take on the way to an equilibrium, and so provides no guidance about whether 10, 100, or 1,000 plays of the game are enough to give a chance for the subjects' expectations to become coordinated.

Finally, we can expect the theory of Nash equilibrium to correspond to reality only approximately: like all useful theories, it definitely is not *exactly* correct. How do we tell whether the data are close enough to the theory to support it? One possibility is to compare the theory of Nash equilibrium with some other theory. But for many games there is no obvious alternative theory—and certainly not one with the generality of Nash equilibrium. Statistical tests can sometimes aid in deciding whether the data are consistent with the theory, though ultimately we remain the judge of whether our observations persuade us that the theory enhances our understanding of human behavior in the game.

2.7   Examples of Nash equilibrium

2.7.1   Prisoner's Dilemma

By examining the four possible pairs of actions in the *Prisoner's Dilemma* (reproduced in Figure 26.1), we see that (*Fink*, *Fink*) is the unique Nash equilibrium.

	Quiet	*Fink*
Quiet	2, 2	0, 3
Fink	3, 0	1, 1

Figure 26.1 The *Prisoner's Dilemma*.

The action pair (*Fink*, *Fink*) is a Nash equilibrium because (*i*) given that player 2 chooses *Fink*, player 1 is better off choosing *Fink* than *Quiet* (looking at the right column of the table we see that *Fink* yields player 1 a payoff of 1 whereas *Quiet* yields her a payoff of 0), and (*ii*) given that player 1 chooses *Fink*, player 2 is better off choosing *Fink* than *Quiet* (looking at the bottom row of the table we see that *Fink* yields player 2 a payoff of 1 whereas *Quiet* yields her a payoff of 0).

No other action profile is a Nash equilibrium:

- (*Quiet*, *Quiet*) does not satisfy (23.2) because when player 2 chooses *Quiet*, player 1's payoff to *Fink* exceeds her payoff to *Quiet* (look at the first components of the entries in the left column of the table). (Further, when player 1 chooses *Quiet*, player 2's payoff to *Fink* exceeds her payoff to *Quiet*: player 2, as well as player 1, wants to deviate. To show that a pair of actions is not a Nash equilibrium, however, it is not necessary to study player 2's decision once we have established that player 1 wants to deviate: it is enough to show that *one* player wishes to deviate to show that a pair of actions is not a Nash equilibrium.)

- (*Fink*, *Quiet*) does not satisfy (23.2) because when player 1 chooses *Fink*, player 2's payoff to *Fink* exceeds her payoff to *Quiet* (look at the second components of the entries in the bottom row of the table).

- (*Quiet*, *Fink*) does not satisfy (23.2) because when player 2 chooses *Fink*, player 1's payoff to *Fink* exceeds her payoff to *Quiet* (look at the first components of the entries in the right column of the table).

In summary, in the only Nash equilibrium of the *Prisoner's Dilemma* both players choose *Fink*. In particular, the incentive to free ride eliminates the possibility that the mutually desirable outcome (*Quiet, Quiet*) occurs. In the other situations discussed in Section 2.2 that may be modeled as the *Prisoner's Dilemma*, the outcomes predicted by the notion of Nash equilibrium are thus as follows: both people goof off when working on a joint project; both duopolists charge a low price; both countries build bombs; both farmers graze their sheep a lot. (The overgrazing of a common thus predicted is sometimes called the "tragedy of the commons". The intuition that some of these dismal outcomes may be avoided if the same pair of people play the game repeatedly is explored in Chapter 14.)

In the *Prisoner's Dilemma*, the Nash equilibrium action of each player (*Fink*) is the best action for each player not only if the other player chooses her equilibrium action (*Fink*), but also if she chooses her other action (*Quiet*). The action pair (*Fink, Fink*) is a Nash equilibrium because if a player believes that her opponent will choose *Fink*, then it is optimal for her to choose *Fink*. But in fact it is optimal for a player to choose *Fink regardless* of the action she expects her opponent to choose. In most of the games we study, a player's Nash equilibrium action does not satisfy this condition: the action is optimal if the other players choose their Nash equilibrium actions, but some other action is optimal if the other players choose nonequilibrium actions.

(?) EXERCISE 27.1 (Variant of *Prisoner's Dilemma* with altruistic preferences) Each of two players has two possible actions, *Quiet* and *Fink*; each action pair results in the players' receiving amounts of *money* equal to the numbers corresponding to that action pair in Figure 26.1. (For example, if player 1 chooses *Quiet* and player 2 chooses *Fink*, then player 1 receives nothing, whereas player 2 receives $3.) The players are not "selfish"; rather, the preferences of each player i are represented by the payoff function $m_i(a) + \alpha m_j(a)$, where $m_i(a)$ is the amount of money received by player i when the action profile is a, j is the other player, and α is a given nonnegative number. Player 1's payoff to the action pair (*Quiet, Quiet*), for example, is $2 + 2\alpha$.

    a. Formulate a strategic game that models this situation in the case $\alpha = 1$. Is this game the *Prisoner's Dilemma*?

    b. Find the range of values of α for which the resulting game is the *Prisoner's Dilemma*. For values of α for which the game is not the *Prisoner's Dilemma*, find the Nash equilibria.

(?) EXERCISE 27.2 (Selfish and altruistic social behavior) Two people enter a bus. Two adjacent cramped seats are free. Each person must decide whether to sit or stand. Sitting alone is more comfortable than sitting next to the other person, which is more comfortable than standing.

    a. Suppose that each person cares only about her own comfort. Model the situation as a strategic game. Is this game the *Prisoner's Dilemma*? Find its Nash equilibrium (equilibria?).

b. Suppose that each person is altruistic, ranking the outcomes according to the *other* person's comfort, but, out of politeness, prefers to stand than to sit if the other person stands. Model the situation as a strategic game. Is this game the *Prisoner's Dilemma*? Find its Nash equilibrium (equilibria?).

c. Compare the people's comfort in the equilibria of the two games.

EXPERIMENTAL EVIDENCE ON THE *Prisoner's Dilemma*

The *Prisoner's Dilemma* has attracted a great deal of attention by economists, psychologists, sociologists, and biologists. A huge number of experiments have been conducted with the aim of discovering how people behave when playing the game. Almost all these experiments involve each subject's playing the game repeatedly against an unchanging opponent, a situation that calls for an analysis significantly different from the one in this chapter (see Chapter 14).

The evidence on the outcome of isolated plays of the game is inconclusive. No experiment of which I am aware carefully induces the appropriate preferences and is specifically designed to elicit a steady state action profile (see the box on page 24). Thus in each case the choice of *Quiet* by a player could indicate that she is not "selfish" or that she is not experienced in playing the game, rather than providing evidence against the notion of Nash equilibrium.

In two experiments with very low payoffs, each subject played the game a small number of times against different opponents; between 50 and 94% of subjects chose *Fink*, depending on the relative sizes of the payoffs and some details of the design (Rapoport, Guyer, and Gordon 1976, 135–137, 211–213, and 223–226). In a more recent experiment, 78% of subjects chose *Fink* in the last 10 of 20 rounds of play against different opponents (Cooper, DeJong, Forsythe, and Ross 1996). In face-to-face games in which communication is allowed, the incidence of the choice of *Fink* tends to be lower: from 29 to 70% depending on the nature of the communication allowed (Deutsch 1958, and Frank, Gilovich, and Regan 1993, 163–167). (In all these experiments, the subjects were college students in the United States or Canada.)

One source of the variation in the results seems to be that some designs induce preferences that differ from those of the *Prisoner's Dilemma*; no clear answer emerges to the question of whether the notion of Nash equilibrium is consistent with humans' choices in the *Prisoner's Dilemma*. If, nevertheless, one interprets the evidence as showing that some subjects in the *Prisoner's Dilemma* systematically choose *Quiet* rather than *Fink*, one must fault the rational choice component of Nash equilibrium, not the coordinated expectations component. Why? Because, as noted in the text, *Fink* is optimal *no matter* what a player thinks her opponent will choose, so that any model in which the players act according to the model of rational choice, regardless of whether their expectations are coordinated, predicts that each player chooses *Fink*.

2.7.2 BoS

To find the Nash equilibria of *BoS* (Figure 19.1), we can examine each pair of actions in turn:

- (*Bach, Bach*): If player 1 switches to *Stravinsky*, then her payoff decreases from 2 to 0; if player 2 switches to *Stravinsky*, then her payoff decreases from 1 to 0. Thus a deviation by either player decreases her payoff. Thus (*Bach, Bach*) is a Nash equilibrium.

- (*Bach, Stravinsky*): If player 1 switches to *Stravinsky*, then her payoff increases from 0 to 1. Thus (*Bach, Stravinsky*) is not a Nash equilibrium. (Player 2 can increase her payoff by deviating, too, but to show that the pair is not a Nash equilibrium, it suffices to show that one player can increase her payoff by deviating.)

- (*Stravinsky, Bach*): If player 1 switches to *Bach*, then her payoff increases from 0 to 2. Thus (*Stravinsky, Bach*) is not a Nash equilibrium.

- (*Stravinsky, Stravinsky*): If player 1 switches to *Bach*, then her payoff decreases from 1 to 0; if player 2 switches to *Bach*, then her payoff decreases from 2 to 0. Thus a deviation by either player decreases her payoff. Thus (*Stravinsky, Stravinsky*) is a Nash equilibrium.

We conclude that *BoS* has two Nash equilibria: (*Bach, Bach*) and (*Stravinsky, Stravinsky*). That is, both of these outcomes are compatible with a steady state; both outcomes are stable social norms. If, in every encounter, both players choose *Bach*, then no player has an incentive to deviate; if, in every encounter, both players choose *Stravinsky*, then no player has an incentive to deviate. If we use the game to model the choices of men when matched with women, for example, then the notion of Nash equilibrium shows that two social norms are stable: both players choose the action associated with the outcome preferred by women, and both players choose the action associated with the outcome preferred by men.

2.7.3 Matching Pennies

By checking each of the four pairs of actions in *Matching Pennies* (Figure 19.2) we see that the game has no Nash equilibrium. For the pairs of actions (*Head, Head*) and (*Tail, Tail*), player 2 is better off deviating; for the pairs of actions (*Head, Tail*) and (*Tail, Head*), player 1 is better off deviating. Thus for this game the notion of Nash equilibrium isolates no steady state. In Chapter 4 we return to this game; an extension of the notion of a Nash equilibrium gives us an understanding of the likely outcome.

2.7.4 The Stag Hunt

Inspection of the left panel of Figure 21.1 shows that the two-player *Stag Hunt* has two Nash equilibria: (*Stag, Stag*) and (*Hare, Hare*). If one player remains attentive to the pursuit of the stag, then the other player prefers to remain attentive; if one player chases a hare, the other one prefers to chase a hare (she cannot catch a stag alone). (The equilibria of the variant of the game in the right panel of Figure 21.1 are analogous: (*Refrain, Refrain*) and (*Arm, Arm*).)

Unlike the Nash equilibria of *BoS*, one of these equilibria is better for both players than the other: each player prefers (*Stag, Stag*) to (*Hare, Hare*). This fact has no bearing on the equilibrium status of (*Hare, Hare*), since the condition for an equilibrium is that a *single* player cannot gain by deviating, *given* the other player's behavior. Put differently, an equilibrium is immune to any *unilateral* deviation; coordinated deviations by groups of players are not contemplated. However, the existence of two equilibria raises the possibility that one equilibrium might more likely be the outcome of the game than the other. I return to this issue in Section 2.7.6.

I argue that the many-player *Stag Hunt* (Example 20.2) also has two Nash equilibria: the action profile (*Stag, . . . , Stag*) in which every player joins in the pursuit of the stag, and the profile (*Hare, . . . , Hare*) in which every player catches a hare.

- (*Stag, . . . , Stag*) is a Nash equilibrium because each player prefers this profile to that in which she alone chooses *Hare*. (A player is better off remaining attentive to the pursuit of the stag than running after a hare if all the other players remain attentive.)

- (*Hare, . . . , Hare*) is a Nash equilibrium because each player prefers this profile to that in which she alone pursues the stag. (A player is better off catching a hare than pursuing the stag if no one else pursues the stag.)

- No other profile is a Nash equilibrium, because in any other profile at least one player chooses *Stag* and at least one player chooses *Hare*, so that any player choosing *Stag* is better off switching to *Hare*. (A player is better off catching a hare than pursing the stag if at least one other person chases a hare, since the stag can be caught only if everyone pursues it.)

❓ EXERCISE 30.1 (Variants of the *Stag Hunt*) Consider variants of the *n*-hunter *Stag Hunt* in which only *m* hunters, with $2 \leq m < n$, need to pursue the stag in order to catch it. (Continue to assume that there is a single stag.) Assume that a captured stag is shared only by the hunters who catch it. Under each of the following assumptions on the hunters' preferences, find the Nash equilibria of the strategic game that models the situation.

   a. As before, each hunter prefers the fraction $1/n$ of the stag to a hare.

   b. Each hunter prefers the fraction $1/k$ of the stag to a hare, but prefers a hare to any smaller fraction of the stag, where k is an integer with $m \leq k \leq n$.

The following more difficult exercise enriches the hunters' choices in the *Stag Hunt*. This extended game has been proposed as a model that captures Keynes' basic insight about the possibility of multiple economic equilibria, some of which are undesirable (Bryant 1983, 1994).

⑦ EXERCISE 31.1 (*Extension of the Stag Hunt*) Extend the n-hunter *Stag Hunt* by giving each hunter K (a positive integer) units of effort, which she can allocate between pursuing the stag and catching hares. Denote the effort hunter i devotes to pursuing the stag by e_i, a nonnegative integer equal to at most K. The chance that the stag is caught depends on the smallest of all the hunters' efforts, denoted $\min_j e_j$. ("A chain is as strong as its weakest link.") Hunter i's payoff to the action profile $(e_1, \ldots, e_n)$ is $2 \min_j e_j - e_i$. (She is better off the more likely the stag is caught, and worse off the more effort she devotes to pursuing the stag, which means she catches fewer hares.) Is the action profile $(e, \ldots, e)$, in which every hunter devotes the same effort to pursuing the stag, a Nash equilibrium for any value of e? (What is a player's payoff to this profile? What is her payoff if she deviates to a lower or higher effort level?) Is any action profile in which not all the players' effort levels are the same a Nash equilibrium? (Consider a player whose effort exceeds the minimum effort level of all players. What happens to her payoff if she reduces her effort level to the minimum?)

2.7.5 Hawk–Dove

The game in the next exercise captures a basic feature of animal conflict.

⑦ EXERCISE 31.2 (*Hawk–Dove*) Two animals are fighting over some prey. Each can be passive or aggressive. Each prefers to be aggressive if its opponent is passive, and passive if its opponent is aggressive; given its own stance, it prefers the outcome in which its opponent is passive to that in which its opponent is aggressive. Formulate this situation as a strategic game and find its Nash equilibria.

2.7.6 A coordination game

Consider two people who wish to go out together, but who, unlike the dissidents in *BoS*, agree on the more desirable concert—say they both prefer *Bach*. A strategic game that models this situation is shown in Figure 31.1; it is an example of a *coordination game*. By examining the four action pairs, we see that the game has two Nash equilibria: (*Bach, Bach*) and (*Stravinsky, Stravinsky*). In particular, the action pair (*Stravinsky, Stravinsky*) in which both people choose their less-preferred concert is a Nash equilibrium.

Is the equilibrium in which both people choose *Stravinsky* plausible? People who argue that the technology of Apple computers originally dominated that of IBM computers, and that the Beta format for video recording is better than VHS, would say "yes". In both cases users had a strong interest in adopting the same

	Bach	Stravinsky
Bach	2, 2	0, 0
Stravinsky	0, 0	1, 1

Figure 31.1 A *coordination game*.

FOCAL POINTS

In games with many Nash equilibria, the theory isolates more than one pattern of behavior compatible with a steady state. In some games, some of these equilibria seem more likely to attract the players' attentions than others. To use the terminology of Schelling (1960), some equilibria are *focal*. In the coordination game in Figure 31.1, where the players agree on the more desirable Nash equilibrium and obtain the same payoff to every nonequilibrium action pair, the preferable equilibrium seems more likely to be focal (though two examples are given in the text of steady states involving the inferior equilibrium). In the variant of this game in which the two equilibria are equally good (i.e. $(2,2)$ is replaced by $(1,1)$), nothing in the structure of the game gives any clue to which steady state might occur. In such a game, the names or nature of the actions, or other information, may predispose the players to one equilibrium rather than the other.

Consider, for example, voters in an election. Pre-election polls may give them information about each other's intended actions, pointing them to one of many Nash equilibria. Or consider a situation in which two players independently divide $100 into two piles, each receiving $10 if they choose the same divisions and nothing otherwise. The strategic game that models this situation has many Nash equilibria, in each of which both players choose the same division. But the equilibrium in which both players choose the $(\$50, \$50)$ division seems likely to command the players' attentions, possibly for esthetic reasons (it is an appealing division), and possibly because it is a steady state in an unrelated game in which the chosen division determines the players' payoffs.

The theory of Nash equilibrium is neutral about the equilibrium that will occur in a game with many equilibria. If features of the situation not modeled by the notion of a strategic game make some equilibria focal, then those equilibria may be more likely to emerge as steady states, and the rate at which a steady state is reached may be higher than it otherwise would have been.

standard, and one standard was better than the other; in the steady state that emerged in each case, the inferior technology was adopted by a large majority of users.

If two people played this game in a laboratory it seems likely that the outcome would be (*Bach, Bach*). Nevertheless, (*Stravinsky, Stravinsky*) also corresponds to a steady state: if either action pair is reached, there is no reason for either player to deviate from it.

2.7.7 Provision of a public good

The model in the next exercise captures an aspect of the provision of a "public good", like a park or a swimming pool, whose use by one person does not diminish

	L	M	R
T	1,1	1,0	0,1
B	1,0	0,1	1,0

Figure 33.1 A game with a unique Nash equilibrium, which is not a strict equilibrium.

its value to another person (at least, not until it is overcrowded). (Other aspects of public good provision are studied in Section 2.8.4.)

? EXERCISE 33.1 (Contributing to a public good) Each of n people chooses whether to contribute a fixed amount toward the provision of a public good. The good is provided if and only if at least k people contribute, where $2 \leq k \leq n$; if it is not provided, contributions are not refunded. Each person ranks outcomes from best to worst as follows: (*i*) any outcome in which the good is provided and she does not contribute, (*ii*) any outcome in which the good is provided and she contributes, (*iii*) any outcome in which the good is not provided and she does not contribute, (*iv*) any outcome in which the good is not provided and she contributes. Formulate this situation as a strategic game and find its Nash equilibria. (Is there a Nash equilibrium in which more than k people contribute? One in which k people contribute? One in which fewer than k people contribute? (Be careful!))

2.7.8 Strict and nonstrict equilibria

In all the Nash equilibria of the games we have studied so far, a deviation by a player leads to an outcome *worse* for that player than the equilibrium outcome. The definition of Nash equilibrium (23.1), however, requires only that the outcome of a deviation be *no better* for the deviant than the equilibrium outcome. And, indeed, some games have equilibria in which a player is indifferent between her equilibrium action and some other action, given the other players' actions.

Consider the game in Figure 33.1. This game has a unique Nash equilibrium, namely (T, L). (For every other pair of actions, one of the players is better off changing her action.) When player 2 chooses L, as she does in this equilibrium, player 1 is equally happy choosing T or B (her payoff is 1 in each case); if she deviates to B, then she is no worse off than she is in the equilibrium. We say that the Nash equilibrium (T, L) is not a *strict equilibrium*.

For a general game, an equilibrium is strict if each player's equilibrium action is *better* than all her other actions, given the other players' actions. Precisely, an action profile a^* is a **strict Nash equilibrium** if for every player i we have $u_i(a^*) > u_i(a_i, a^*_{-i})$ for every action $a_i \neq a^*_i$ of player i. (Contrast the strict inequality in this definition with the weak inequality in (23.2).)

2.7.9 Additional examples

The following exercises are more difficult than most of the previous ones. In the first two, the number of actions of each player is arbitrary, so you cannot mechanically examine each action profile individually, as we did for games in which each player has two actions. Instead, you can consider groups of action profiles that have features in common, and show that all action profiles in any given group are or are not equilibria. Deciding how best to group the profiles into types calls for some intuition about the character of a likely equilibrium; the exercises contain suggestions on how to proceed.

⑦ EXERCISE 34.1 (Guessing two-thirds of the average) Each of three people announces an integer from 1 to K. If the three integers are different, the person whose integer is closest to $\frac{2}{3}$ of the average of the three integers wins \$1. If two or more integers are the same, \$1 is split equally between the people whose integer is closest to $\frac{2}{3}$ of the average integer. Is there any integer k such that the action profile (k,k,k), in which every person announces the same integer k, is a Nash equilibrium? (If $k \geq 2$, what happens if a person announces a smaller number?) Is any other action profile a Nash equilibrium? (What is the payoff of a person whose number is the highest of the three? Can she increase this payoff by announcing a different number?)

Game theory is used widely in political science, especially in the study of elections. The game in the following exercise explores citizens' costly decisions to vote.

⑦ EXERCISE 34.2 (Voter participation) Two candidates, A and B, compete in an election. Of the n citizens, k support candidate A and $m\,(=n-k)$ support candidate B. Each citizen decides whether to vote, at a cost, for the candidate she supports, or to abstain. A citizen who abstains receives the payoff of 2 if the candidate she supports wins, 1 if this candidate ties for first place, and 0 if this candidate loses. A citizen who votes receives the payoffs $2-c$, $1-c$, and $-c$ in these three cases, where $0 < c < 1$.

a. For $k = m = 1$, is the game the same (except for the names of the actions) as any considered so far in this chapter?

b. For $k = m$, find the set of Nash equilibria. (Is the action profile in which everyone votes a Nash equilibrium? Is there any Nash equilibrium in which the candidates tie and not everyone votes? Is there any Nash equilibrium in which one of the candidates wins by one vote? Is there any Nash equilibrium in which one of the candidates wins by two or more votes?)

c. What is the set of Nash equilibria for $k < m$?

If, when sitting in a traffic jam, you have ever thought about the time you might save if another road were built, the next exercise may lead you to think again.

⑦ EXERCISE 34.3 (Choosing a route) Four people must drive from A to B at the same time. Each of them must choose a route. Two routes are available, one via X and one via Y. (Refer to the left panel of Figure 35.1.) The roads from A to X, and from Y to B are both short and narrow; in each case, one car takes 6 minutes, and each

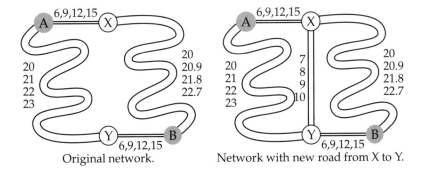

Figure 35.1 Getting from A to B: the road networks in Exercise 34.3. The numbers beside each road are the travel times *per car* when 1, 2, 3, or 4 cars take that road.

additional car increases the travel time *per car* by 3 minutes. (If two cars drive from A to X, for example, *each car* takes 9 minutes.) The roads from A to Y, and from X to B are long and wide; on A to Y one car takes 20 minutes, and each additional car increases the travel time *per car* by 1 minute; on X to B one car takes 20 minutes, and each additional car increases the travel time *per car* by 0.9 minutes. Formulate this situation as a strategic game and find the Nash equilibria. (If all four people take one of the routes, can any of them do better by taking the other route? What if three take one route and one takes the other route, or if two take each route?)

Now suppose that a relatively short, wide road is built from X to Y, giving each person four options for travel from A to B: A–X–B, A–Y–B, A–X–Y–B, and A–Y–X–B. Assume that a person who takes A–X–Y–B travels the A–X portion at the same time as someone who takes A–X–B, and the Y–B portion at the same time as someone who takes A–Y–B. (Think of there being constant flows of traffic.) On the road between X and Y, one car takes 7 minutes and each additional car increases the travel time *per car* by 1 minute. Find the Nash equilibria in this new situation. Compare each person's travel time with her travel time in the equilibrium before the road from X to Y was built.

2.8 Best response functions

2.8.1 Definition

We can find the Nash equilibria of a game in which each player has only a few actions by examining each action profile in turn to see if it satisfies the conditions for equilibrium. In more complicated games, it is often better to work with the players' "best response functions".

Consider a player, say player i. For any given actions of the players other than i, player i's actions yield her various payoffs. We are interested in the best actions—those that yield her the highest payoff. In *BoS*, for example, *Bach* is the best action for player 1 if player 2 chooses *Bach*; *Stravinsky* is the best action for player 1 if player 2 chooses *Stravinsky*. In particular, in *BoS*, player 1 has a single best action for each action of player 2. By contrast, in the game in Figure 33.1, both T and B are best actions for player 1 if player 2 chooses L: they both yield the payoff of 1, and player 1 has no action that yields a higher payoff (in fact, she has no other action).

We denote the set of player i's best actions when the list of the other players' actions is a_{-i} by $B_i(a_{-i})$. Thus in *BoS* we have $B_1(Bach) = \{Bach\}$ and $B_1(Stravinsky) = \{Stravinsky\}$; in the game in Figure 33.1 we have $B_1(L) = \{T, B\}$.

Precisely, we define the function B_i by

$$B_i(a_{-i}) = \{a_i \text{ in } A_i : u_i(a_i, a_{-i}) \geq u_i(a_i', a_{-i}) \text{ for all } a_i' \text{ in } A_i\} :$$

any action in $B_i(a_{-i})$ is at least as good for player i as every other action of player i when the other players' actions are given by a_{-i}. We call B_i the **best response function** of player i.

The function B_i is *set-valued*: it associates a set of actions with any list of the other players' actions. Every member of the set $B_i(a_{-i})$ is a **best response** of player i to a_{-i}: if each of the other players adheres to a_{-i}, then player i can do no better than choose a member of $B_i(a_{-i})$. In some games, like *BoS*, the set $B_i(a_{-i})$ consists of a single action for every list a_{-i} of actions of the other players: no matter what the other players do, player i has a *single* optimal action. In other games, like the one in Figure 33.1, $B_i(a_{-i})$ contains more than one action for some lists a_{-i} of actions of the other players.

2.8.2 Using best response functions to define Nash equilibrium

A Nash equilibrium is an action profile with the property that no player can do better by changing her action, given the other players' actions. Using the terminology just developed, we can alternatively define a Nash equilibrium to be an action profile for which every player's action is a best response to the other players' actions. That is, we have the following result.

▪ PROPOSITION 36.1 *The action profile a^* is a Nash equilibrium of a strategic game with ordinal preferences if and only if every player's action is a best response to the other players' actions:*

$$a_i^* \text{ is in } B_i(a_{-i}^*) \text{ for every player } i. \tag{36.2}$$

If each player i has a single best response to each list a_{-i} of the other players' actions, we can write the conditions in (36.2) as equations. In this case, for each player i and each list a_{-i} of the other players' actions, denote the single member of $B_i(a_{-i})$ by $b_i(a_{-i})$ (that is, $B_i(a_{-i}) = \{b_i(a_{-i})\}$). Then (36.2) is equivalent to

$$a_i^* = b_i(a_{-i}^*) \text{ for every player } i, \tag{36.3}$$

a collection of n equations in the n unknowns a_i^*, where n is the number of players in the game. For example, in a game with two players, say 1 and 2, these equations are

$$a_1^* = b_1(a_2^*)$$
$$a_2^* = b_2(a_1^*).$$

	L	C	R
T	1 ,2*	2*,1	1*,0
M	2*,1*	0 ,1*	0 ,0
B	0 ,1	0 ,0	1*,2*

Figure 37.1 Using best response functions to find Nash equilibria in a two-player game in which each player has three actions.

That is, in a two-player game in which each player has a single best response to every action of the other player, (a_1^*, a_2^*) is a Nash equilibrium if and only if player 1's action a_1^* is her best response to player 2's action a_2^*, and player 2's action a_2^* is her best response to player 1's action a_1^*.

2.8.3 Using best response functions to find Nash equilibria

The definition of a Nash equilibrium in terms of best response functions suggests a method for finding Nash equilibria:

- find the best response function of each player

- find the action profiles that satisfy (36.2) (which reduces to (36.3) if each player has a single best response to each list of the other players' actions).

To illustrate this method, consider the game in Figure 37.1. First find the best response of player 1 to each action of player 2. If player 2 chooses L, then player 1's best response is M (2 is the highest payoff for player 1 in this column); indicate the best response by attaching a star to player 1's payoff to (M, L). If player 2 chooses C, then player 1's best response is T, indicated by the star attached to player 1's payoff to (T, C). And if player 2 chooses R, then both T and B are best responses for player 1; both are indicated by stars. Second, find the best response of player 2 to each action of player 1 (for each row, find highest payoff of player 2); these best responses are indicated by attaching stars to player 2's payoffs. Finally, find the boxes in which both players' payoffs are starred. Each such box is a Nash equilibrium: the star on player 1's payoff means that player 1's action is a best response to player 2's action, and the star on player 2's payoff means that player 2's action is a best response to player 1's action. Thus we conclude that the game has two Nash equilibria: (M, L) and (B, R).

⑦ EXERCISE 37.1 (Finding Nash equilibria using best response functions)

a. Find the players' best response functions in the *Prisoner's Dilemma* (Figure 15.1), *BoS* (Figure 19.1), *Matching Pennies* (Figure 19.2), and the two-player *Stag Hunt* (left panel of Figure 21.1) (and verify the Nash equilibria of each game).

b. Find the Nash equilibria of the game in Figure 38.1 by finding the players' best response functions.

	L	C	R
T	2,2	1,3	0,1
M	3,1	0,0	0,0
B	1,0	0,0	0,0

Figure 38.1 The game in Exercise 37.1b.

The players' best response functions for the game in Figure 37.1 are presented in a different format in Figure 38.2. In this figure, player 1's actions are on the horizontal axis and player 2's are on the vertical axis. (Thus the columns correspond to choices of player 1, and the rows correspond to choices of player 2, whereas the reverse is true in Figure 37.1. I choose this orientation for Figure 38.2 for consistency with the convention for figures of this type.) Player 1's best responses are indicated by circles, and player 2's by dots. Thus the circle at (T, C) reflects the fact that T is player 1's best response to player 2's choice of C, and the circles at (T, R) and (B, R) reflect the fact that T and B are both best responses of player 1 to player 2's choice of R. Any action pair marked by both a circle and a dot is a Nash equilibrium: the circle means that player 1's action is a best response to player 2's action, and the dot indicates that player 2's action is a best response to player 1's action.

ⓘ EXERCISE 38.1 (Constructing best response functions) Draw the analogue of Figure 38.2 for the game in Exercise 37.1b.

ⓘ EXERCISE 38.2 (Dividing money) Two people have $10 to divide between themselves. They use the following procedure. Each person names a number of dollars (a nonnegative integer), at most equal to 10. If the sum of the amounts that the people name is at most 10, then each person receives the amount of money she named (and the remainder is destroyed). If the sum of the amounts that the people name exceeds 10 and the amounts named are different, then the person who

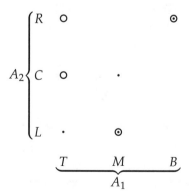

Figure 38.2 The players' best response functions for the game in Figure 37.1. Player 1's best responses are indicated by circles, and player 2's by dots. The action pairs for which there is both a circle and a dot are the Nash equilibria.

named the smaller amount receives that amount and the other person receives the remaining money. If the sum of the amounts that the people name exceeds 10 and the amounts named are the same, then each person receives $5. Determine the best response of each player to each of the other player's actions, plot them in a diagram like Figure 38.2, and thus find the Nash equilibria of the game.

A diagram like Figure 38.2 is a convenient representation of the players' best response functions also in a game in which each player's set of actions is an interval of numbers, as the next example illustrates.

◆ EXAMPLE 39.1 (A synergistic relationship) Two individuals are involved in a synergistic relationship. If both individuals devote more effort to the relationship, they are both better off. For any given effort of individual j, the return to individual i's effort first increases, then decreases. Specifically, an effort level is a nonnegative number, and individual i's preferences (for $i = 1, 2$) are represented by the payoff function $a_i(c + a_j - a_i)$, where a_i is i's effort level, a_j is the other individual's effort level, and $c > 0$ is a constant.

The following strategic game models this situation.

Players The two individuals.

Actions Each player's set of actions is the set of effort levels (nonnegative numbers).

Preferences Player i's preferences are represented by the payoff function $a_i(c + a_j - a_i)$, for $i = 1, 2$.

In particular, each player has infinitely many actions, so that we cannot present the game in a table like those used previously (Figure 38.1, for example).

To find the Nash equilibria of the game, we can construct and analyze the players' best response functions. Given a_j, individual i's payoff is a quadratic function of a_i that is zero when $a_i = 0$ and when $a_i = c + a_j$, and reaches a maximum in between. The symmetry of quadratic functions (see Section 17.3) implies that the best response of each individual i to a_j is

$$b_i(a_j) = \tfrac{1}{2}(c + a_j).$$

(If you know calculus, you can reach the same conclusion by setting the derivative of player i's payoff with respect to a_i equal to zero.)

The best response functions are shown in Figure 40.1. Player 1's actions are plotted on the horizontal axis and player 2's actions are plotted on the vertical axis. Player 1's best response function associates an action for player 1 with every action for player 2. Thus to interpret the function b_1 in the diagram, take a point a_2 on the vertical axis, and go across to the line labeled b_1 (the steeper of the two lines), then read down to the horizontal axis. The point on the horizontal axis that you reach is $b_1(a_2)$, the best action for player 1 when player 2 chooses a_2. Player 2's best response function, on the other hand, associates an action for player 2 with every action of player 1. Thus to interpret this function, take a point a_1 on the horizontal

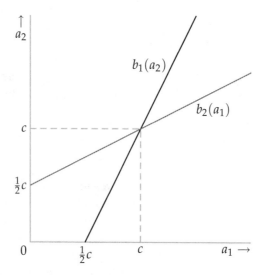

Figure 40.1 The players' best response functions for the game in Example 39.1. The game has a unique Nash equilibrium, $(a_1^*, a_2^*) = (c, c)$.

axis, and go up to b_2, then across to the vertical axis. The point on the vertical axis that you reach is $b_2(a_1)$, the best action for player 2 when player 1 chooses a_1.

At a point (a_1, a_2) where the best response functions intersect in the figure, we have $a_1 = b_1(a_2)$, because (a_1, a_2) is on the graph of b_1, player 1's best response function, and $a_2 = b_2(a_1)$, because (a_1, a_2) is on the graph of b_2, player 2's best response function. Thus any such point (a_1, a_2) is a Nash equilibrium. In this game the best response functions intersect at a single point, so there is one Nash equilibrium. In general, they may intersect more than once; every point at which they intersect is a Nash equilibrium.

To find the point of intersection of the best response functions precisely, we can solve the two equations in (36.3):

$$a_1 = \tfrac{1}{2}(c + a_2)$$
$$a_2 = \tfrac{1}{2}(c + a_1).$$

Substituting the second equation in the first, we get $a_1 = \tfrac{1}{2}(c + \tfrac{1}{2}(c + a_1)) = \tfrac{3}{4}c + \tfrac{1}{4}a_1$, so that $a_1 = c$. Substituting this value of a_1 into the second equation, we get $a_2 = c$. We conclude that the game has a unique Nash equilibrium $(a_1, a_2) = (c, c)$. (To reach this conclusion, it suffices to solve the two equations; we do not have to draw Figure 40.1. However, the diagram shows us at once that the game has a unique equilibrium, in which both players' actions exceed $\tfrac{1}{2}c$, facts that serve to check the results of our algebra.)

In the game in this example, each player has a unique best response to every action of the other player, so that the best response functions are lines. If a player has many best responses to some of the other players' actions, then her best response function is "thick" at some points; several examples in the next chapter have this

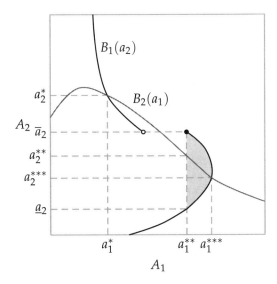

Figure 41.1 An example of the best response functions of a two-player game in which each player's set of actions is an interval of numbers. The set of Nash equilibria of the game consists of the pairs of actions (a_1^*, a_2^*) and (a_1^{***}, a_2^{***}), and all the pairs of actions on player 2's best response function between (a_1^{**}, a_2^{**}) and (a_1^{***}, a_2^{***}).

property (see, for example, Figure 66.1). The game in Example 39.1 is special also because it has a unique Nash equilibrium—the best response functions cross once. As we have seen, some games have more than one equilibrium, and others have none. Figure 41.1 shows a pair of best response functions that illustrates some of the possibilities. The shaded area of player 1's best response function indicates that for a_2 between $\bar{a}_2$ and $\underline{a}_2$, player 1 has a range of best responses. For example, all actions of player 1 greater than a_1^{**} and at most a_1^{***} are best responses to the action a_2^{**} of player 2. For a game with these best response functions, the set of Nash equilibria consists of the pairs of actions (a_1^*, a_2^*) and (a_1^{***}, a_2^{***}), and all the pairs of actions on player 2's best response function between (a_1^{**}, a_2^{**}) and (a_1^{***}, a_2^{***}).

? EXERCISE 41.1 (Strict and nonstrict Nash equilibria) Which of the Nash equilibria of the game whose best response functions are given in Figure 41.1 are strict (see the definition on page 33)?

Another feature that differentiates the best response functions in Figure 41.1 from those in Figure 40.1 is that the best response function b_1 of player 1 is not continuous. When player 2's action is $\bar{a}_2$, player 1's best response is a_1^{**} (indicated by the small disk at $(a_1^{**}, \bar{a}_2)$), but when player 2's action is slightly greater than $\bar{a}_2$, player 1's best response is significantly less than a_1^{**}. (The small circle indicates a point excluded from the best response function.) Again, several examples in the next chapter have this feature. From Figure 41.1 we see that if a player's best response function is discontinuous, then depending on where the discontinuity occurs, the best response functions may not intersect—the game may, like *Matching Pennies*, have no Nash equilibrium.

⊘ EXERCISE 42.1 (Finding Nash equilibria using best response functions) Find the Nash equilibria of the two-player strategic game in which each player's set of actions is the set of nonnegative numbers and the players' payoff functions are $u_1(a_1, a_2) = a_1(a_2 - a_1)$ and $u_2(a_1, a_2) = a_2(1 - a_1 - a_2)$.

⊘ EXERCISE 42.2 (A joint project) Two people are engaged in a joint project. If each person i puts in the effort x_i, a nonnegative number equal to at most 1, which costs her $c(x_i)$, the outcome of the project is worth $f(x_1, x_2)$. The worth of the project is split equally between the two people, regardless of their effort levels. Formulate this situation as a strategic game. Find the Nash equilibria of the game when (a) $f(x_1, x_2) = 3x_1x_2$ and $c(x_i) = x_i^2$ for $i = 1, 2$, and (b) $f(x_1, x_2) = 4x_1x_2$ and $c(x_i) = x_i$ for $i = 1, 2$. In each case, is there a pair of effort levels that yields higher payoffs for both players than do the Nash equilibrium effort levels?

2.8.4 Illustration: contributing to a public good

Exercise 33.1 models decisions on whether to contribute to the provision of a "public good". We now study a model in which two people decide not only whether to contribute, but also *how much* to contribute.

Denote person i's wealth by w_i, and the amount she contributes to the public good by c_i ($0 \leq c_i \leq w_i$); she spends her remaining wealth $w_i - c_i$ on "private goods" (like clothes and food, whose consumption by one person precludes their consumption by anyone else). The amount of the public good is equal to the sum of the contributions. Each person cares both about the amount of the public good and her consumption of private goods.

Suppose that person i's preferences are represented by the payoff function $v_i(c_1 + c_2) + w_i - c_i$. Because w_i is a constant, person i's preferences are alternatively represented by the payoff function

$$u_i(c_1, c_2) = v_i(c_1 + c_2) - c_i. \tag{42.3}$$

This situation is modeled by the following strategic game.

Players The two people.

Actions Player i's set of actions is the set of her possible contributions (nonnegative numbers less than or equal to w_i), for $i = 1, 2$.

Preferences Player i's preferences are represented by the payoff function u_i given in (42.3), for $i = 1, 2$.

To find the Nash equilibria of this strategic game, consider the players' best response functions. Player 1's best response to the contribution c_2 of player 2 is the value of c_1 that maximizes $v_1(c_1 + c_2) - c_1$. Without specifying the form of the function v_1 we cannot explicitly calculate this optimal value. However, we can determine how it varies with c_2.

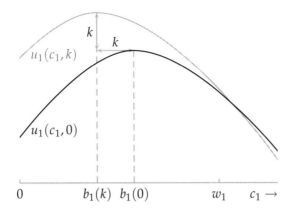

Figure 43.1 The relation between player 1's best responses $b_1(0)$ and $b_1(k)$ to $c_2 = 0$ and $c_2 = k$ in the game of contributing to a public good.

First consider player 1's best response to $c_2 = 0$. Suppose that the form of the function v_1 is such that the function $u_1(c_1, 0)$ increases up to its maximum, then decreases (as in Figure 43.1). Then player 1's best response to $c_2 = 0$, which I denote $b_1(0)$, is unique. This best response is the value of c_1 that maximizes $u_1(c_1, 0) = v_1(c_1) - c_1$ subject to $0 \le c_1 \le w_1$. Assume that $0 < b_1(0) < w_1$: player 1's optimal contribution to the public good when player 2 makes no contribution is positive and less than her entire wealth.

Now consider player 1's best response to $c_2 = k > 0$. This best response is the value of c_1 that maximizes $u_1(c_1, k) = v_1(c_1 + k) - c_1$. Now, we have $u_1(c_1 + k, 0) = v_1(c_1 + k) - c_1 - k$ by the definition of u_1, so that

$$u_1(c_1, k) = u_1(c_1 + k, 0) + k.$$

That is, the graph of $u_1(c_1, k)$ as a function of c_1 is the translation to the left k units and up k units of the graph of $u_1(c_1, 0)$ as a function of c_1 (refer to Figure 43.1). Thus if $k \le b_1(0)$, then $b_1(k) = b_1(0) - k$: if player 2's contribution increases from 0 to k, then player 1's best response decreases by k. If $k > b_1(0)$, then, given the form of $u_1(c_1, 0)$, we have $b_1(k) = 0$.

We conclude that if player 2 increases her contribution by k, then player 1's best response is to reduce her contribution by k (or to zero, if k is larger than player 1's original contribution)!

The same analysis applies to player 2: for every unit more that player 1 contributes, player 2 contributes a unit less, so long as her contribution is nonnegative. The function v_2 may be different from the function v_1, so that player 1's best contribution $b_1(0)$ when $c_2 = 0$ may be different from player 2's best contribution $b_2(0)$ when $c_1 = 0$. But both best response functions have the same character: the slope of each function is -1 where the value of the function is positive. They are shown in Figure 44.1 for a case in which $b_1(0) > b_2(0)$.

We deduce that if $b_1(0) > b_2(0)$, then the game has a unique Nash equilibrium, $(b_1(0), 0)$: player 2 contributes nothing. Similarly, if $b_1(0) < b_2(0)$, then the unique

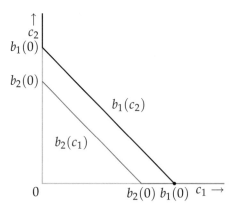

Figure 44.1 The best response functions for the game of contributing to a public good in a case in which $b_1(0) > b_2(0)$. The best response function of player 1 is the black line; that of player 2 is the gray line.

Nash equilibrium is $(0, b_2(0))$: player 1 contributes nothing. That is, the person who contributes more when the other person contributes nothing is the only one to make a contribution in a Nash equilibrium. Only if $b_1(0) = b_2(0)$, which is not likely if the functions v_1 and v_2 differ, is there an equilibrium in which both people contribute. In this case the downward-sloping parts of the best response functions coincide, so that any pair of contributions (c_1, c_2) with $c_1 + c_2 = b_1(0)$ and $c_i \geq 0$ for $i = 1, 2$ is a Nash equilibrium.

In summary, the notion of Nash equilibrium predicts that, except in unusual circumstances, only one person contributes to the provision of the public good when each person's payoff function takes the form $v_i(c_1 + c_2) + w_i - c_i$, each function $v_i(c_i) - c_i$ increases to a maximum, then decreases, and each person optimally contributes less than her entire wealth when the other person does not contribute. The person who contributes is the one who wishes to contribute more when the other person does not contribute. In particular, the identity of the person who contributes does not depend on the distribution of wealth; any distribution in which each person optimally contributes less than her entire wealth when the other person does not contribute leads to the same outcome.

The next exercise asks you to consider a case in which the amount of the public good affects each person's enjoyment of the private good. (The public good might be clean air, which improves each person's enjoyment of her free time.)

⍰ EXERCISE 44.1 (Contributing to a public good) Consider the model in this section when $u_i(c_1, c_2)$ is the sum of three parts: the amount $c_1 + c_2$ of the public good provided, the amount $w_i - c_i$ person i spends on private goods, and a term $(w_i - c_i)(c_1 + c_2)$ that reflects an interaction between the amount of the public good and her private consumption—the greater the amount of the public good, the more she values her private consumption. In summary, suppose that person i's payoff is $c_1 + c_2 + w_i - c_i + (w_i - c_i)(c_1 + c_2)$, or

$$w_i + c_j + (w_i - c_i)(c_1 + c_2),$$

where j is the other person. Assume that $w_1 = w_2 = w$, and that each player i's contribution c_i may be any number (positive or negative, possibly larger than w). Find the Nash equilibrium of the game that models this situation. (You can calculate the best responses explicitly. Imposing the sensible restriction that c_i lie between 0 and w complicates the analysis but does not change the answer.) Show that in the Nash equilibrium both players are worse off than they are when both contribute half of their wealth to the public good. If you can, extend the analysis to the case of n people. As the number of people increases, how does the total amount contributed in a Nash equilibrium change? Compare the players' equilibrium payoffs with their payoffs when each contributes half her wealth to the public good, as n increases without bound. (The game is studied further in Exercise 388.1.)

2.9 Dominated actions

2.9.1 Strict domination

You drive up to a red traffic light. The left lane is free; in the right lane there is a car that may turn right when the light changes to green, in which case it will have to wait for a pedestrian to cross the side street. Assuming you wish to progress as quickly as possible, the action of pulling up in the left lane "strictly dominates" that of pulling up in the right lane. If the car in the right lane turns right, then you are much better off in the left lane, where your progress will not be impeded; and even if the car in the right lane does not turn right, you are still better off in the left lane, rather than behind the other car.

In any game, a player's action "strictly dominates" another action if it is superior, *no matter what the other players do*.

▶ DEFINITION 45.1 (*Strict domination*) In a strategic game with ordinal preferences, player i's action a_i'' **strictly dominates** her action a_i' if

$$u_i(a_i'', a_{-i}) > u_i(a_i', a_{-i}) \text{ for every list } a_{-i} \text{ of the other players' actions,}$$

where u_i is a payoff function that represents player i's preferences. We say that the action a_i' is **strictly dominated**.

In the *Prisoner's Dilemma*, for example, the action *Fink* strictly dominates the action *Quiet*: regardless of her opponent's action, a player prefers the outcome when she chooses *Fink* to the outcome when she chooses *Quiet*. In *BoS*, on the other hand, neither action strictly dominates the other: *Bach* is better than *Stravinsky* if the other player chooses *Bach*, but is worse than *Stravinsky* if the other player chooses *Stravinsky*.

A strictly dominated action is not a best response to any actions of the other players: whatever the other players do, some other action is better. Since a player's Nash equilibrium action is a best response to the other players' Nash equilibrium actions,

a strictly dominated action is not used in any Nash equilibrium.

	L	R
T	1	0
M	2	1
B	1	3

	L	R
T	1	0
M	2	1
B	3	2

Figure 46.1 Two games in which player 1's action T is strictly dominated by M. (Only player 1's payoffs are given.) In the left-hand game, B is better than M if player 2 chooses R; in the right-hand game, M itself is strictly dominated, by B.

When looking for the Nash equilibria of a game, we can thus eliminate from consideration all strictly dominated actions. For example, in the *Prisoner's Dilemma* we can eliminate *Quiet* for each player, leaving (*Fink*, *Fink*) as the only action pair that can possibly be a Nash equilibrium. (As we know, this action pair is indeed a Nash equilibrium.)

The fact that the action a_i'' strictly dominates the action a_i' of course does *not* imply that a_i'' strictly dominates *all* actions. Indeed, a_i'' may itself be strictly dominated. In the left-hand game in Figure 46.1, for example, M strictly dominates T, but B is better than M if player 2 chooses R. (I give only the payoffs of player 1 in the figure, because those of player 2 are not relevant.) Since T is strictly dominated, the game has no Nash equilibrium in which player 1 uses it; but the game may also not have any equilibrium in which player 1 uses M. In the right-hand game, M strictly dominates T, but is itself strictly dominated by B. In this case, in any Nash equilibrium player 1's action is B (her only action that is not strictly dominated).

A strictly dominated action is incompatible not only with a steady state, but also with rational behavior by a player who confronts a game for the first time. This fact is the first step in a theory different from Nash equilibrium, explored in Chapter 12.

2.9.2 Weak domination

As you approach the red light in the situation at the start of the previous section (2.9.1), there is a car in *each* lane. The car in the right lane may, or may not, be turning right; if it is, it may be delayed by a pedestrian crossing the side street. The car in the left lane cannot turn right. In this case your pulling up in the left lane "weakly dominates", though does not strictly dominate, your pulling up in the right lane. If the car in the right lane does not turn right, then both lanes are equally good; if it does, then the left lane is better.

In any game, a player's action "weakly dominates" another action if the first action is at least as good as the second action, no matter what the other players do, and is better than the second action for some actions of the other players.

▷ DEFINITION 46.1 (*Weak domination*) In a strategic game with ordinal preferences, player i's action a_i'' **weakly dominates** her action a_i' if

$$u_i(a_i'', a_{-i}) \geq u_i(a_i', a_{-i}) \text{ for every list } a_{-i} \text{ of the other players' actions}$$

$$
\begin{array}{c|cc}
 & L & R \\
\hline
T & 1 & 0 \\
M & 2 & 0 \\
B & 2 & 1 \\
\end{array}
$$

Figure 47.1 A game illustrating weak domination. (Only player 1's payoffs are given.) The action M weakly dominates T; B weakly dominates M. The action B strictly dominates T.

and

$$u_i(a_i'', a_{-i}) > u_i(a_i', a_{-i}) \text{ for some list } a_{-i} \text{ of the other players' actions,}$$

where u_i is a payoff function that represents player i's preferences. We say that the action a_i' is **weakly dominated**.

For example, in the game in Figure 47.1 (in which, once again, only player 1's payoffs are given), M weakly dominates T, and B weakly dominates M; B strictly dominates T.

In a *strict* Nash equilibrium (Section 2.7.8) no player's equilibrium action is weakly dominated: for every player, the payoff to each nonequilibrium action is less than her equilibrium payoff, so that no nonequilibrium action weakly dominates her equilibrium action.

Can an action be weakly dominated in a nonstrict Nash equilibrium? Definitely. Consider the games in Figure 47.2. In both games B weakly (but not strictly) dominates C for both players. But in both games (C, C) is a Nash equilibrium: *given* that player 2 chooses C, player 1 cannot do better than choose C, and *given* that player 1 chooses C, player 2 cannot do better than choose C. Both games also have a Nash equilibrium, (B, B), in which neither player's action is weakly dominated. In the left-hand game this equilibrium is better for both players than the equilibrium (C, C) in which both players' actions are weakly dominated, whereas in the right-hand game it is worse for both players than (C, C).

? EXERCISE 47.1 (Strict equilibria and dominated actions) For the game in Figure 48.1, determine, for each player, whether any action is strictly dominated or weakly dominated. Find the Nash equilibria of the game; determine whether any equilibrium is strict.

? EXERCISE 47.2 (Nash equilibrium and weakly dominated actions) Give an example of a two-player strategic game in which each player has finitely many actions and in the only Nash equilibrium both players' actions are weakly dominated.

$$
\begin{array}{c|cc}
 & B & C \\
\hline
B & 1,1 & 0,0 \\
C & 0,0 & 0,0 \\
\end{array}
\qquad
\begin{array}{c|cc}
 & B & C \\
\hline
B & 1,1 & 2,0 \\
C & 0,2 & 2,2 \\
\end{array}
$$

Figure 47.2 Two strategic games with a Nash equilibrium (C, C) in which both players' actions are weakly dominated.

$$
\begin{array}{c|c|c|c|}
 & L & C & R \\
\hline
T & 0,0 & 1,0 & 1,1 \\
\hline
M & 1,1 & 1,1 & 3,0 \\
\hline
B & 1,1 & 2,1 & 2,2 \\
\hline
\end{array}
$$

Figure 48.1 The game in Exercise 47.1.

2.9.3 Illustration: voting

Two candidates, A and B, vie for office. Each of an odd number of citizens may vote for either candidate. (Abstention is not possible.) The candidate who obtains the most votes wins. (Because the number of citizens is odd, a tie is impossible.) A majority of citizens prefer A to win.

The following strategic game models the citizens' voting decisions in this situation.

> *Players* The citizens.

> *Actions* Each player's set of actions consists of voting for A and voting for B.

> *Preferences* All players are indifferent among all action profiles in which a majority of players vote for A; all players are also indifferent among all action profiles in which a majority of players vote for B. Some players (a majority) prefer an action profile of the first type to one of the second type, and the others have the reverse preference.

I claim that a citizen's voting for her less preferred candidate is weakly dominated by her voting for her favorite candidate. Suppose that citizen i prefers candidate A; fix the votes of all citizens other than i. If citizen i switches from voting for B to voting for A, then, depending on the other citizens' votes, either the outcome does not change, or A wins rather than B; such a switch cannot cause the winner to change from A to B. That is, citizen i's switching from voting for B to voting for A either has no effect on the outcome, or makes her better off; it cannot make her worse off.

The game has Nash equilibria in which some, or all, citizens' actions are weakly dominated. For example, the action profile in which all citizens vote for B is a Nash equilibrium (no citizen's switching her vote has any effect on the outcome).

? EXERCISE 48.1 (Voting) Find all the Nash equilibria of the game. (First consider action profiles in which the winner obtains one more vote than the loser and at least one citizen who votes for the winner prefers the loser to the winner, then profiles in which the winner obtains one more vote than the loser and all citizens who vote for the winner prefer the winner to the loser, and finally profiles in which the winner obtains three or more votes more than the loser.) Is there any equilibrium in which no player uses a weakly dominated action?

Consider a variant of the game in which the number of candidates is greater than two. A variant of the argument above shows that a citizen's action of voting for her least preferred candidate is weakly dominated by her other two actions. The next exercise asks you to show that no other action is weakly dominated.

? EXERCISE 49.1 (Voting between three candidates) Suppose there are three candidates, A, B, and C, and no citizen is indifferent between any two of them. A tie for first place is possible in this case; assume that a citizen who prefers a win by x to a win by y ranks a tie between x and y between an outright win for x and an outright win for y. Show that a citizen's only weakly dominated action is a vote for her least preferred candidate. Find a Nash equilibrium in which some citizen does not vote for her favorite candidate, but the action she takes is not weakly dominated.

? EXERCISE 49.2 (Approval voting) In the system of "approval voting", a citizen may vote for as many candidates as she wishes. If there are two candidates, say A and B, for example, a citizen may vote for neither candidate, for A, for B, or for both A and B. As before, the candidate who obtains the most votes wins. Show that any action that includes a vote for a citizen's least preferred candidate is weakly dominated, as is any action that does not include a vote for her most preferred candidate. More difficult: show that if there are k candidates, then for a citizen who prefers candidate 1 to candidate 2 to ... to candidate k, the action that consists of votes for candidates 1 and $k - 1$ is *not* weakly dominated.

2.9.4   Illustration: collective decision-making

The members of a group of people are affected by a policy, modeled as a number. Each person i has a favorite policy, denoted x_i^*; she prefers the policy y to the policy z if and only if y is closer to x_i^* than is z. The number n of people is odd. The following mechanism is used to choose a policy: each person names a policy, and the policy chosen is the median of those named. (That is, the policies named are put in order, and the one in the middle is chosen. If, for example, there are five people, and they name the policies -2, 0, 0.6, 5, and 10, then the policy 0.6 is chosen.)

What outcome does this mechanism induce? Does anyone have an incentive to name her favorite policy, or are people induced to distort their preferences? We can answer these questions by studying the following strategic game.

Players The n people.

Actions Each person's set of actions is the set of policies (numbers).

Preferences Each person i prefers the action profile a to the action profile a' if and only if the median policy named in a is closer to x_i^* than is the median policy named in a'.

I claim that for each player i, the action of naming her favorite policy x_i^* weakly dominates *all* her other actions. The reason is that relative to the situation in which she names x_i^*, she can change the median only by naming a policy *further* from her favorite policy than the current median; no change in the policy she names moves the median closer to her favorite policy.

Precisely, I show that for each action $x_i \neq x_i^*$ of player i, (a) for *all* actions of the other players, player i is at least as well off naming x_i^* as she is naming x_i, and (b) for *some* actions of the other players she is better off naming x_i^* than she is naming x_i. Take $x_i > x_i^*$.

a. For any list of actions of the players *other than* player i, denote the value of the $\frac{1}{2}(n-1)$th highest action by $\underline{a}$ and the value of the $\frac{1}{2}(n+1)$th highest action by $\bar{a}$ (so that half of the remaining players' actions are at most $\underline{a}$ and half of them are at least $\bar{a}$).

   • If $\bar{a} \leq x_i^*$ or $\underline{a} \geq x_i$, then the median policy is the same whether player i names x_i^* or x_i.
   • If $\bar{a} > x_i^*$ and $\underline{a} < x_i$, then when player i names x_i^* the median policy is at most the greater of x_i^* and $\underline{a}$ and when player i names x_i the median policy is at least the lesser of x_i and $\bar{a}$. Thus player i is worse off naming x_i than she is naming x_i^*.

b. Suppose that half of the remaining players name policies less than x_i^* and half of them name policies greater than x_i. Then the outcome is x_i^* if player i names x_i^*, and x_i if she names x_i. Thus she is better off naming x_i^* than she is naming x_i.

A symmetric argument applies when $x_i < x_i^*$.

If we think of the mechanism as asking the players to name their favorite policies, then the result is that telling the truth weakly dominates all other actions.

An implication of the fact that player i's naming her favorite policy x_i^* weakly dominates *all* her other actions is that the action profile in which every player names her favorite policy is a Nash equilibrium. That is, truth-telling is a Nash equilibrium, in the interpretation of the previous paragraph.

? EXERCISE 50.1 (Other Nash equilibria of the game modeling collective decision-making) Find two Nash equilibria in which the outcome is the median favorite policy, and one in which it is not.

? EXERCISE 50.2 (Another mechanism for collective decision-making) Consider the variant of the mechanism for collective decision-making in which the policy chosen is the *mean*, rather than the median, of the policies named by the players. Does a player's action of naming her favorite policy weakly dominate all her other actions?

2.10 Equilibrium in a single population: symmetric games and symmetric equilibria

A Nash equilibrium of a strategic game corresponds to a steady state of an interaction between the members of several populations, one for each player in the

	A	B
A	w,w	x,y
B	y,x	z,z

	Quiet	Fink
Quiet	2,2	0,3
Fink	3,0	1,1

	Stag	Hare
Stag	2,2	0,1
Hare	1,0	1,1

Figure 51.1 The general form of a two-player symmetric game (left), and two examples, the *Prisoner's Dilemma* (middle) and the two-player *Stag Hunt* (right).

game; each play of the game involves one member of each population. Sometimes we want to model an interaction in which the members of a *single* homogeneous population are involved anonymously and symmetrically. Consider, for example, pedestrians approaching each other on a sidewalk or car drivers arriving simultaneously at an intersection from different directions. In each case, the members of an encounter (pairs of pedestrians who meet each other, groups of car drivers who simultaneously approach intersections) are drawn from a single population and have the same role.

I restrict attention here to cases in which each interaction involves two participants. Define a two-player game to be "symmetric" if each player has the same set of actions and each player's evaluation of an outcome depends only on her action and that of her opponent, not on whether she is player 1 or player 2. That is, player 1 feels the same way about the outcome (a_1, a_2), in which her action is a_1 and her opponent's action is a_2, as player 2 feels about the outcome (a_2, a_1), in which *her* action is a_1 and her opponent's action is a_2. In particular, the players' preferences may be represented by payoff functions in which both players' payoffs are the same whenever the players choose the same action: $u_1(a, a) = u_2(a, a)$ for every action a.

▶ DEFINITION 51.1 (*Symmetric two-player strategic game with ordinal preferences*) A two-player strategic game with ordinal preferences is **symmetric** if the players' sets of actions are the same and the players' preferences are represented by payoff functions u_1 and u_2 for which $u_1(a_1, a_2) = u_2(a_2, a_1)$ for every action pair (a_1, a_2).

A two-player game in which each player has two actions is symmetric if the players' preferences are represented by payoff functions that take the form shown in the left panel of Figure 51.1, where w, x, y, and z are arbitrary numbers. Several of the two-player games we have considered are symmetric, including the *Prisoner's Dilemma* and the two-player *Stag Hunt* (given again in the middle and right panels of Figure 51.1), and the game in Exercise 38.2. *BoS* (Figure 19.1) and *Matching Pennies* (Figure 19.2) are not symmetric.

⑦ EXERCISE 51.2 (Symmetric strategic games) Which of the games in Exercises 31.2 and 42.1, Example 39.1, Section 2.8.4, and Figure 47.2 are symmetric?

When the players in a symmetric two-player game are drawn from a single population, nothing distinguishes one of the players in any given encounter from the other. We may call them "player 1" and "player 2", but these labels are only for our convenience. There is only one role in the game, so that a steady state

	Left	Right
Left	1,1	0,0
Right	0,0	1,1

Figure 52.1 Approaching pedestrians.

is characterized by a *single* action used by every participant whenever she plays the game. An action a^* corresponds to such a steady state if no player can do better by using any other action, given that all the other players use a^*. An action a^* has this property if and only if (a^*, a^*) is a Nash equilibrium of the game. In other words, the solution that corresponds to a steady state of pairwise interactions between the members of a single population is "symmetric Nash equilibrium": a Nash equilibrium in which both players take the same action. The idea of this notion of equilibrium does not depend on the game's having only two players, so I give a definition for a game with any number of players.

▶ DEFINITION 52.1 (*Symmetric Nash equilibrium*) An action profile a^* in a strategic game with ordinal preferences in which each player has the same set of actions is a **symmetric Nash equilibrium** if it is a Nash equilibrium and a_i^* is the same for every player i.

As an example, consider a model of approaching pedestrians. Each participant in any given encounter has two possible actions—to step to the right, and to step to the left—and is better off when participants both step in the same direction than when they step in different directions (in which case a collision occurs). The resulting symmetric strategic game is given in Figure 52.1. The game has two symmetric Nash equilibria, namely (*Left, Left*) and (*Right, Right*). That is, there are two steady states, in one of which every pedestrian steps to the left as she approaches another pedestrian, and in another of which both participants step to the right. (The latter steady state seems to prevail in the United States and Canada.)

A symmetric game may have no symmetric Nash equilibrium. Consider, for example, the game in Figure 52.2. This game has two Nash equilibria, (X, Y) and (Y, X), neither of which is symmetric. You may wonder if, in such a situation, there is a steady state in which each player does not always take the same action in every interaction. This question is addressed in Section 4.7.

? EXERCISE 52.2 (Equilibrium for pairwise interactions in a single population) Find all the Nash equilibria of the game in Figure 53.1. Which of the equilibria, if any, correspond to a steady state if the game models pairwise interactions between the members of a single population?

	X	Y
X	0,0	1,1
Y	1,1	0,0

Figure 52.2 A symmetric game with no symmetric Nash equilibrium.

	A	B	C
A	1,1	2,1	4,1
B	1,2	5,5	3,6
C	1,4	6,3	0,0

Figure 53.1 The game in Exercise 52.2.

Notes

The notion of a strategic game originated in the work of Borel (1921) and von Neumann (1928). The notion of Nash equilibrium (and its interpretation) is due to Nash (1950a). (The idea that underlies it goes back at least to Cournot 1838, Ch. 7.)

The *Prisoner's Dilemma* appears to have first been considered by Melvin Dresher and Merrill Flood, who used it in an experiment at the RAND Corporation in January 1950 (Flood 1958/59, 11–17); it is an example in Nash's Ph.D. thesis (Nash 1950b), submitted in May 1950. The story associated with it is due to Tucker (1950) (see Straffin 1980). O'Neill (1994, 1010–1013) argues that there is no evidence that game theory (and in particular the *Prisoner's Dilemma*) influenced U.S. nuclear strategists in the 1950s. The precise analysis of the idea that common property will be overused was initiated by Gordon (1954). Hardin (1968) coined the phrase "tragedy of the commons".

BoS, like the *Prisoner's Dilemma*, is an example in Nash's Ph.D. thesis; Luce and Raiffa (1957, 90–91) name it and associate a story with it. *Matching Pennies* was first considered by von Neumann (1928). Rousseau's sentence about hunting stags is interpreted as a description of a game by Ullmann-Margalit (1977, 121) and Jervis (1977/78), following discussion by Waltz (1959, 167–169) and Lewis (1969, 7, 47).

The information about John Nash in the box on page 23 comes from Leonard (1994), Kuhn et al. (1995), Kuhn (1996), Myerson (1996), Nasar (1998), and Nash (1995). *Hawk–Dove* is known also as "Chicken" (two drivers approach each other on a narrow road; the one who pulls over first is "chicken"). It was first suggested (in a more complicated form) as a model of animal conflict by Maynard Smith and Price (1973). The discussion of focal points in the box on page 32 draws on Schelling (1960, 54–58).

Games modeling voluntary contributions to a public good were first considered by Olson (1965, Section I.D). The game in Exercise 33.1 is studied in detail by Palfrey and Rosenthal (1984). The result in Section 2.8.4 is due to Warr (1983) and Bergstrom, Blume, and Varian (1986).

Game theory was first used to study voting behavior by Farquharson (1969) (whose book was completed in 1958; see also Niemi 1983). The system of "approval voting" in Exercise 49.2 was first studied formally by Brams and Fishburn (1978, 1983).

Exercise 18.1 is based on Leonard (1990). Exercise 27.2 is based on Ullmann-Margalit (1977, 48). The game in Exercise 31.1 is taken from Van Huyck, Battalio, and Beil (1990). The game in Exercise 34.1 is taken from Moulin (1986b, 72). The game in Exercise 34.2 was first studied by Palfrey and Rosenthal (1983). Exercise 34.3 is based on Braess (1968); see also Murchland (1970). The game in Exercise 38.2 is taken from Brams, Kilgour, and Davis (1993).

3 Nash Equilibrium: Illustrations

3.1 Cournot's model of oligopoly 55
3.2 Bertrand's model of oligopoly 63
3.3 Electoral competition 70
3.4 The *War of Attrition* 77
3.5 Auctions 80
3.6 Accident law 91
Prerequisite: Chapter 2

IN THIS CHAPTER I discuss in detail a few key models that use the notion of Nash equilibrium to study economic, political, and biological phenomena. The discussion shows how the notion of Nash equilibrium improves our understanding of a wide variety of phenomena. It also illustrates some of the many forms strategic games and their Nash equilibria can take. The models in Sections 3.1 and 3.2 are related to each other, whereas those in each of the other sections are independent of each other.

3.1 Cournot's model of oligopoly

3.1.1 Introduction

How does the outcome of competition among the firms in an industry depend on the characteristics of the demand for the firms' output, the nature of the firms' cost functions, and the number of firms? Will the benefits of technological improvements be passed on to consumers? Will a reduction in the number of firms generate a less desirable outcome? To answer these questions we need a model of the interaction between firms competing for the business of consumers. In this section and the next I analyze two such models. Economists refer to them as models of "oligopoly" (competition between a small number of sellers), though they involve no restriction on the number of firms; the label reflects the strategic interaction they capture. Both models were studied first in the 19th century, before the notion of Nash equilibrium was formalized for a general strategic game. The first is due to the economist Cournot (1838).

3.1.2 General model

A single good is produced by n firms. The cost to firm i of producing q_i units of the good is $C_i(q_i)$, where C_i is an increasing function (more output is more costly to produce). All the output is sold at a single price, determined by the demand for the good and the firms' total output. Specifically, if the firms' total output is Q, then the market price is $P(Q)$; P is called the "inverse demand function". Assume that P is a decreasing function when it is positive: if the firms' total output increases, then the price decreases (unless it is already zero). If the output of each firm i is q_i, then the price is $P(q_1 + \cdots + q_n)$, so that firm i's revenue is $q_i P(q_1 + \cdots + q_n)$. Thus firm i's profit, equal to its revenue minus its cost, is

$$\pi_i(q_1, \ldots, q_n) = q_i P(q_1 + \cdots + q_n) - C_i(q_i). \tag{56.1}$$

Cournot suggested that the industry be modeled as the following strategic game, which I refer to as **Cournot's oligopoly game**.

Players   The firms.

Actions   Each firm's set of actions is the set of its possible outputs (nonnegative numbers).

Preferences   Each firm's preferences are represented by its profit, given in (56.1).

3.1.3   Example: duopoly with constant unit cost and linear inverse demand function

For specific forms of the functions C_i and P we can compute a Nash equilibrium of Cournot's game. Suppose there are two firms (the industry is a "duopoly"), each firm's cost function is the same, given by $C_i(q_i) = cq_i$ for all q_i ("unit cost" is constant, equal to c), and the inverse demand function is linear where it is positive, given by

$$P(Q) = \begin{cases} \alpha - Q & \text{if } Q \le \alpha \\ 0 & \text{if } Q > \alpha, \end{cases} \tag{56.2}$$

where $\alpha > 0$ and $c \ge 0$ are constants. This inverse demand function is shown in Figure 57.1. (Note that the price $P(Q)$ cannot be equal to $\alpha - Q$ for *all* values of Q, for then it would be negative for $Q > \alpha$.) Assume that $c < \alpha$, so that there is some value of total output Q for which the market price $P(Q)$ is greater than the firms' common unit cost c. (If c were to exceed α, there would be no output for the firms at which they could make any profit, because the market price never exceeds α.)

To find the Nash equilibria in this example, we can use the procedure based on the firms' best response functions (Section 2.8.3). First we need to find the firms' payoffs (profits). If the firms' outputs are q_1 and q_2, then the market price $P(q_1 + q_2)$ is $\alpha - q_1 - q_2$ if $q_1 + q_2 \le \alpha$ and zero if $q_1 + q_2 > \alpha$. Thus firm 1's profit is

$$\begin{aligned} \pi_1(q_1, q_2) &= q_1(P(q_1 + q_2) - c) \\ &= \begin{cases} q_1(\alpha - c - q_1 - q_2) & \text{if } q_1 + q_2 \le \alpha \\ -cq_1 & \text{if } q_1 + q_2 > \alpha. \end{cases} \end{aligned}$$

To find firm 1's best response to any given output q_2 of firm 2, we need to study firm 1's profit as a function of its output q_1 for given values of q_2. If $q_2 = 0$, then

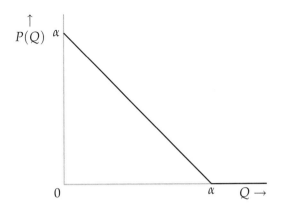

Figure 57.1 The inverse demand function in the example of Cournot's game studied in Section 3.1.3.

firm 1's profit is $\pi_1(q_1, 0) = q_1(\alpha - c - q_1)$ for $q_1 \le \alpha$, a quadratic function that is zero when $q_1 = 0$ and when $q_1 = \alpha - c$. This function is the black curve in Figure 58.1. Given the symmetry of quadratic functions (Section 17.3), the output q_1 of firm 1 that maximizes its profit is $q_1 = \frac{1}{2}(\alpha - c)$. (If you know calculus, you can reach the same conclusion by setting the derivative of firm 1's profit with respect to q_1 equal to zero and solving for q_1.) Thus firm 1's best response to an output of zero for firm 2 is $b_1(0) = \frac{1}{2}(\alpha - c)$.

As the output q_2 of firm 2 increases, the profit firm 1 can obtain at any given output decreases, because more output of firm 2 means a lower price. The gray curve in Figure 58.1 is an example of $\pi_1(q_1, q_2)$ for $q_2 > 0$ and $q_2 < \alpha - c$. Again this function is a quadratic up to the output $q_1 = \alpha - q_2$ that leads to a price of zero. Specifically, the quadratic is $\pi_1(q_1, q_2) = q_1(\alpha - c - q_2 - q_1)$, which is zero when $q_1 = 0$ and when $q_1 = \alpha - c - q_2$. From the symmetry of quadratic functions (or some calculus), we conclude that the output that maximizes $\pi_1(q_1, q_2)$ is $q_1 = \frac{1}{2}(\alpha - c - q_2)$. (When $q_2 = 0$, this is equal to $\frac{1}{2}(\alpha - c)$, the best response to an output of zero that we found in the previous paragraph.)

When $q_2 > \alpha - c$, the value of $\alpha - c - q_2$ is negative. Thus for such a value of q_2, we have $q_1(\alpha - c - q_2 - q_1) < 0$ for all positive values of q_1: firm 1's profit is negative for any positive output, so that its best response is to produce no output.

We conclude that the best response of firm 1 to the output q_2 of firm 2 depends on the value of q_2: if $q_2 \le \alpha - c$, then firm 1's best response is $\frac{1}{2}(\alpha - c - q_2)$, whereas if $q_2 > \alpha - c$, then firm 1's best response is 0. Or, more compactly,

$$b_1(q_2) = \begin{cases} \frac{1}{2}(\alpha - c - q_2) & \text{if } q_2 \le \alpha - c \\ 0 & \text{if } q_2 > \alpha - c. \end{cases}$$

Because firm 2's cost function is the same as firm 1's, its best response function b_2 is also the same: for any number q, we have $b_2(q) = b_1(q)$. Of course, firm 2's best response function associates a value of firm 2's output with every output of firm 1, whereas firm 1's best response function associates a value of firm 1's output with every output of firm 2, so we plot them relative to different axes. They

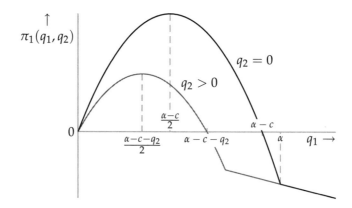

Figure 58.1 Firm 1's profit as a function of its output, given firm 2's output. The black curve shows the case $q_2 = 0$, whereas the gray curve shows a case in which $q_2 > 0$.

are shown in Figure 59.1 (b_1 is black; b_2 is gray). As for a general game (see Section 2.8.3), b_1 associates each point on the vertical axis with a point on the horizontal axis, and b_2 associates each point on the horizontal axis with a point on the vertical axis.

A Nash equilibrium is a pair (q_1^*, q_2^*) of outputs for which q_1^* is a best response to q_2^*, and q_2^* is a best response to q_1^*:

$$q_1^* = b_1(q_2^*) \quad \text{and} \quad q_2^* = b_2(q_1^*)$$

(see (36.3)). The set of such pairs is the set of points at which the best response functions in Figure 59.1 intersect. From the figure we see that there is exactly one such point, which is given by the solution of the two equations

$$q_1 = \tfrac{1}{2}(\alpha - c - q_2)$$
$$q_2 = \tfrac{1}{2}(\alpha - c - q_1).$$

Solving these two equations (by substituting the second into the first and then isolating q_1, for example) we find that $q_1^* = q_2^* = \tfrac{1}{3}(\alpha - c)$.

In summary, when there are two firms, the inverse demand function is given by $P(Q) = \alpha - Q$ for $Q \leq \alpha$, and the cost function of each firm is $C_i(q_i) = cq_i$, Cournot's oligopoly game has a unique Nash equilibrium $(q_1^*, q_2^*) = (\tfrac{1}{3}(\alpha - c), \tfrac{1}{3}(\alpha - c))$. The total output in this equilibrium is $\tfrac{2}{3}(\alpha - c)$, so that the price at which output is sold is $P(\tfrac{2}{3}(\alpha - c)) = \tfrac{1}{3}(\alpha + 2c)$. As α increases (meaning that consumers are willing to pay more for the good), the equilibrium price and the output of each firm increases. As c (the unit cost of production) increases, the output of each firm falls and the price rises; each unit increase in c leads to a two-thirds of a unit increase in the price.

❓ EXERCISE 58.1 (Cournot's duopoly game with linear inverse demand and different unit costs) Find the Nash equilibrium of Cournot's game when there are two firms, the inverse demand function is given by (56.2), the cost function of each firm i is

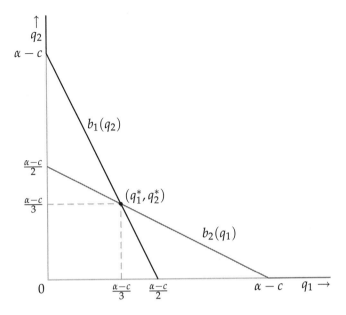

Figure 59.1 The best response functions in Cournot's duopoly game when the inverse demand function is given by (56.2) and the cost function of each firm is cq. The unique Nash equilibrium is $(q_1^*, q_2^*) = (\frac{1}{3}(\alpha - c), \frac{1}{3}(\alpha - c))$.

$C_i(q_i) = c_i q_i$, where $c_1 > c_2$, and $c_1 < \alpha$. (There are two cases, depending on the size of c_1 relative to c_2.) Which firm produces more output in an equilibrium? What is the effect of technical change that lowers firm 2's unit cost c_2 (while not affecting firm 1's unit cost c_1) on the firms' equilibrium outputs, the total output, and the price?

⁇ EXERCISE 59.1 (Cournot's duopoly game with linear inverse demand and a quadratic cost function) Find the Nash equilibrium of Cournot's game when there are two firms, the inverse demand function is given by (56.2), and the cost function of each firm i is $C_i(q_i) = q_i^2$.

In the next exercise each firm's cost function has a component that is independent of output. You will find in this case that Cournot's game may have more than one Nash equilibrium.

⁇ EXERCISE 59.2 (Cournot's duopoly game with linear inverse demand and a fixed cost) Find the Nash equilibria of Cournot's game when there are two firms, the inverse demand function is given by (56.2), and the cost function of each firm i is given by

$$C_i(q_i) = \begin{cases} 0 & \text{if } q_i = 0 \\ f + c q_i & \text{if } q_i > 0, \end{cases}$$

where $c \geq 0$, $f > 0$, and $c < \alpha$. (Note that the fixed cost f affects only the firm's decision of whether to operate; it does not affect the output a firm wishes to produce *if it wishes to operate*.)

So far we have assumed that each firm's objective is to maximize its profit. The next exercise asks you to consider a case in which one firm's objective is to maximize its market share.

? EXERCISE 60.1 (Variant of Cournot's duopoly game with market-share-maximizing firms) Find the Nash equilibrium (equilibria?) of a variant of the example of Cournot's duopoly game that differs from the one in this section (linear inverse demand, constant unit cost) only in that one of the two firms chooses its output to maximize its market share subject to not making a loss, rather than to maximize its profit. What happens if *each* firm maximizes its market share?

3.1.4 Properties of Nash equilibrium

Two economically interesting properties of a Nash equilibrium of Cournot's game concern the relation between the firms' equilibrium profits and the profits they could obtain if they acted collusively, and the character of an equilibrium when the number of firms is large.

Comparison of Nash equilibrium with collusive outcomes   In Cournot's game with two firms, is there any pair of outputs at which *both* firms' profits exceed their levels in a Nash equilibrium? The next exercise asks you to show that the answer is "yes" in the example considered in the previous section (3.1.3). Specifically, both firms can increase their profits relative to their equilibrium levels by reducing their outputs.

? EXERCISE 60.2 (Nash equilibrium of Cournot's duopoly game and collusive outcomes) Find the total output (call it Q^*) that maximizes the firms' *total* profit in Cournot's game when there are two firms and the inverse demand function and cost functions take the forms assumed Section 3.1.3. Compare $\frac{1}{2}Q^*$ with each firm's output in the Nash equilibrium, and show that each firm's equilibrium profit is less than its profit in the "collusive" outcome in which each firm produces $\frac{1}{2}Q^*$. Why is this collusive outcome not a Nash equilibrium?

The same is true more generally. For nonlinear inverse demand functions and cost functions, the shapes of the firms' best response functions differ, in general, from those in the example studied in the previous section. But for many inverse demand functions and cost functions, the game has a Nash equilibrium and, for any equilibrium, there are pairs of outputs in which each firm's output is less than its equilibrium level and each firm's profit exceeds its equilibrium level.

To see why, suppose that (q_1^*, q_2^*) is a Nash equilibrium and consider the set of pairs (q_1, q_2) of outputs at which firm 1's profit is at least its equilibrium profit. The assumption that P is decreasing (higher total output leads to a lower price) implies that if (q_1, q_2) is in this set and $q_2' < q_2$, then (q_1, q_2') is also in the set. (We have $q_1 + q_2' < q_1 + q_2$, and hence $P(q_1 + q_2') > P(q_1 + q_2)$, so that firm 1's profit at (q_1, q_2') exceeds its profit at (q_1, q_2).) Thus in Figure 61.1 the set of pairs of outputs at which firm 1's profit is at least its equilibrium profit lies on or below the line $q_2 = q_2^*$; an example of such a set is shaded light gray. Similarly, the set of pairs of

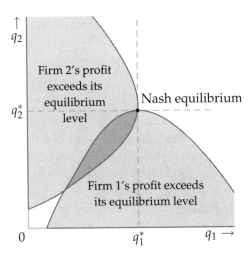

Figure 61.1 The pair (q_1^*, q_2^*) is a Nash equilibrium; along each gray curve one of the firm's profits is constant, equal to its profit at the equilibrium. The area shaded dark gray is the set of pairs of outputs at which both firms' profits exceed their equilibrium levels.

outputs at which firm 2's profit is at least its equilibrium profit lies on or to the left of the line $q_1 = q_1^*$, and an example is shaded light gray.

We see that if the parts of the boundaries of these sets indicated by the gray lines in Figure 61.1 are smooth, then the two sets must intersect; in the figure the intersection is shaded dark gray. At every pair of outputs in this area, each firm's output is less than its equilibrium level ($q_i < q_i^*$ for $i = 1, 2$) and each firm's profit is higher than its equilibrium profit. That is, *both* firms are better off by restricting their outputs.

Dependence of Nash equilibrium on number of firms   How does the equilibrium outcome in Cournot's game depend on the number of firms? If each firm's cost function has the same constant unit cost c, the best outcome for consumers compatible with no firm's making a loss has a price of c and a total output of $\alpha - c$. The next exercise asks you to show that if, for this cost function, the inverse demand function is linear (as in Section 3.1.3), then the price in the Nash equilibrium of Cournot's game decreases as the number of firms increases, approaching c. That is, from the viewpoint of consumers, the outcome is better the larger the number of firms, and when the number of firms is very large, the outcome is close to the best one compatible with nonnegative profits for the firms.

⑦ EXERCISE 61.1 (Cournot's game with many firms) Consider Cournot's game in the case of an arbitrary number n of firms; retain the assumptions that the inverse demand function takes the form (56.2) and the cost function of each firm i is $C_i(q_i) = cq_i$ for all q_i, with $c < \alpha$. Find the best response function of each firm and set up the conditions for $(q_1^*, \ldots, q_n^*)$ to be a Nash equilibrium (see (36.3)), assuming that there is a Nash equilibrium in which all firms' outputs are positive. Solve these equations to find the Nash equilibrium. (For $n = 2$ your answer should be $\left(\frac{1}{3}(\alpha - c), \frac{1}{3}(\alpha - c)\right)$, the equilibrium found in Section 3.1.3. First show that in an equilibrium all firms produce the same output, then solve for that output. If you cannot show that all firms produce the same output, simply assume that they do.) Find the price at which output is sold in a Nash equilibrium and show that this price decreases as n increases, approaching c as the number of firms increases without bound.

The main idea behind this result does not depend on the assumptions about the inverse demand function and the firms' cost functions. Suppose, more generally, that the inverse demand function is any decreasing function, that each firm's cost function is the same, denoted by C, and that there is a single output, say $\underline{q}$, at which the average cost of production $C(q)/q$ is minimal. In this case, any given total output is produced most efficiently by each firm's producing $\underline{q}$, and the lowest price compatible with the firms' not making losses is the minimal value of the average cost. The next exercise asks you to show that in a Nash equilibrium of Cournot's game in which the firms' total output is large relative to $\underline{q}$, this is the price at which the output is sold.

⁇ EXERCISE 62.1 (Nash equilibrium of Cournot's game with small firms) Suppose that there are infinitely many firms, all of which have the same cost function C. Assume that $C(0) = 0$, and for $q > 0$ the function $C(q)/q$ has a unique minimizer $\underline{q}$; denote the minimum of $C(q)/q$ by $\underline{p}$. Assume that the inverse demand function P is decreasing. Show that in any Nash equilibrium the firms' total output Q^* satisfies

$$P(Q^* + \underline{q}) \leq \underline{p} \leq P(Q^*).$$

(That is, the price is at least the minimal value $\underline{p}$ of the average cost, but is close enough to this minimum that increasing the total output of the firms by $\underline{q}$ would reduce the price to at most $\underline{p}$.) To establish these inequalities, show that if $P(Q^*) < \underline{p}$ or $P(Q^* + \underline{q}) > \underline{p}$, then Q^* is not the total output of the firms in a Nash equilibrium, because in each case at least one firm can deviate and increase its profit.

3.1.5 A generalization of Cournot's game: using common property

In Cournot's game, the payoff function of each firm i is $q_i P(q_1 + \cdots + q_n) - C_i(q_i)$. In particular, each firm's payoff depends only on its output and the sum of all the firm's outputs, not on the distribution of the total output among the firms, and decreases when this sum increases (given that P is decreasing). That is, the payoff of each firm i may be written as $f_i(q_i, q_1 + \cdots + q_n)$, where the function f_i is decreasing in its second argument (given the value of its first argument, q_i).

This general payoff function captures many situations in which players compete in using a piece of common property whose value to any one player diminishes as total use increases. The property might, for example, be a village green that is less valuable to any given farmer the higher the total number of sheep that graze on it.

The first property of a Nash equilibrium in Cournot's model discussed in Section 3.1.3 applies to this general model: common property is "overused" in a Nash equilibrium in the sense that every player's payoff increases when every player reduces her use of the property from its equilibrium level. For example, all farmers' payoffs increase if each farmer reduces her use of the village green from its equilibrium level: in an equilibrium the green is "overgrazed". The argument is the same as the one illustrated in Figure 61.1 in the case of two players, because this argument depends only on the fact that each player's payoff function is smooth and is decreasing in the other player's action. (In Cournot's model, the "common property" that is overused is the demand for the good.)

⑦ EXERCISE 63.1 (Interaction among resource users) A group of n firms uses a common resource (a river or a forest, for example) to produce output. As more of the resource is used, any given firm can produce less output. Denote by x_i the amount of the resource used by firm i ($= 1, \ldots, n$). Assume specifically that firm i's output is $x_i(1 - (x_1 + \cdots + x_n))$ if $x_1 + \cdots + x_n \leq 1$, and zero otherwise. Each firm i chooses x_i to maximize its output. Formulate this situation as a strategic game. Find values of α and c such that the game is the same as the one studied in Exercise 61.1, and hence find its Nash equilibria. Find an action profile $(x_1, \ldots, x_n)$ at which each firm's output is higher than it is at the Nash equilibrium.

3.2 Bertrand's model of oligopoly

3.2.1 General model

In Cournot's game, each firm chooses an output; the price is determined by the demand for the good in relation to the total output produced. In an alternative model of oligopoly, associated with a review of Cournot's book by Bertrand (1883), each firm chooses a price, and produces enough output to meet the demand it faces, given the prices chosen by all the firms. The model is designed to shed light on the same questions that Cournot's game addresses; as we shall see, some of the answers it gives are different.

The economic setting for the model is similar to that for Cournot's game. A single good is produced by n firms; each firm can produce q_i units of the good at a cost of $C_i(q_i)$. It is convenient to specify demand by giving a "demand function" D, rather than an inverse demand function as we did for Cournot's game. The interpretation of D is that if the good is available at the price p, then the total amount demanded is $D(p)$.

Assume that if the firms set different prices, then all consumers purchase the good from the firm with the lowest price, which produces enough output to meet this demand. If more than one firm sets the lowest price, all the firms doing so share the demand at that price equally. A firm whose price is not the lowest price receives no demand and produces no output. (Note that a firm does not choose its output strategically; it simply produces enough to satisfy all the demand it faces, given the prices, even if its price is below its unit cost, in which case it makes a loss. This assumption can be modified at the price of complicating the model.)

In summary, **Bertrand's oligopoly game** is the following strategic game.

Players The firms.

Actions Each firm's set of actions is the set of possible prices (nonnegative numbers).

Preferences Firm i's preferences are represented by its profit, which is equal to $p_i D(p_i)/m - C_i(D(p_i)/m)$ if firm i is one of m firms setting the lowest price ($m = 1$ if firm i's price p_i is lower than every other price), and equal to zero if some firm's price is lower than p_i.

3.2.2 Example: duopoly with constant unit cost and linear demand function

Suppose, as in Section 3.1.3, that there are two firms, each of whose cost function has constant unit cost c (that is, $C_i(q_i) = cq_i$ for $i = 1, 2$). Assume that the demand function is $D(p) = \alpha - p$ for $p \leq \alpha$ and $D(p) = 0$ for $p > \alpha$, and that $c < \alpha$.

Because the cost of producing each unit is the same, equal to c, firm i makes the profit of $p_i - c$ on every unit it sells. Thus its profit is

$$
\pi_i(p_1, p_2) = \begin{cases} (p_i - c)(\alpha - p_i) & \text{if } p_i < p_j \\ \frac{1}{2}(p_i - c)(\alpha - p_i) & \text{if } p_i = p_j \\ 0 & \text{if } p_i > p_j, \end{cases}
$$

where j is the other firm ($j = 2$ if $i = 1$, and $j = 1$ if $i = 2$).

As before, we can find the Nash equilibria of the game by finding the firms' best response functions. If firm j charges p_j, what is the best price for firm i to charge? We can reason informally as follows. If firm i charges p_j, it shares the market with firm j; if it charges slightly less, it sells to the entire market. Thus if p_j exceeds c, so that firm i makes a positive profit selling the good at a price slightly below p_j, firm i is definitely better off serving all the market at such a price than serving half of the market at the price p_j. If p_j is very high, however, firm i may be able to do even better: by reducing its price significantly below p_j it may increase its profit, because the extra demand engendered by the lower price may more than compensate for the lower revenue per unit sold. Finally, if p_j is less than c, then firm i's profit is negative if it charges a price less than or equal to p_j, whereas this profit is zero if it charges a higher price. Thus in this case firm i would like to charge any price greater than p_j, to make sure that it gets no customers. (Remember that if customers arrive at its door it is obliged to serve them, regardless of whether it makes a profit by so doing.)

We can make these arguments precise by studying firm i's payoff as a function of its price p_i for various values of the price p_j of firm j. Denote by p^m the value of p (price) that maximizes $(p - c)(\alpha - p)$. This price would be charged by a firm with a monopoly of the market (because $(p - c)(\alpha - p)$ is the profit of such a firm).

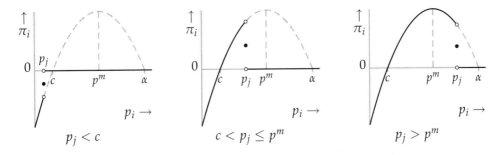

Figure 65.1 Three cross sections (in black) of firm i's payoff function in Bertrand's duopoly game. Where the payoff function jumps, its value is given by the small disk; the small circles indicate points that are excluded as values of the functions.

Three cross sections of firm i's payoff function, for different values of p_j, are shown in black in Figure 65.1. (The gray dashed line is the function $(p_i - c)(\alpha - p_i)$.)

- If $p_j < c$ (firm j's price is below the unit cost), then firm i's profit is negative if $p_i \leq p_j$ and zero if $p_i > p_j$ (see the left panel of Figure 65.1). Thus *any* price greater than p_j is a best response to p_j. That is, the set of firm i's best responses is $B_i(p_j) = \{p_i : p_i > p_j\}$.

- If $p_j = c$, then the analysis is similar to that of the previous case except that p_j, as well as any price greater than p_j, yields a profit of zero, and hence is a best response to p_j: $B_i(p_j) = \{p_i : p_i \geq p_j\}$.

- If $c < p_j \leq p^m$, then firm i's profit increases as p_i increases to p_j, then drops abruptly at p_j (see the middle panel of Figure 65.1). Thus there is no best response: firm i wants to choose a price less than p_j, but is better off the closer that price is to p_j. For any price less than p_j there is a higher price that is also less than p_j, so there is no best price. (I have assumed that a firm can choose *any* number as its price; in particular, it is not restricted to charge an integral number of cents.) Thus $B_i(p_j)$ is empty (has no members).

- If $p_j > p^m$, then p^m is the unique best response of firm i (see the right panel of Figure 65.1): $B_i(p_j) = \{p^m\}$.

In summary, firm i's best response function is given by

$$B_i(p_j) = \begin{cases} \{p_i : p_i > p_j\} & \text{if } p_j < c \\ \{p_i : p_i \geq p_j\} & \text{if } p_j = c \\ \varnothing & \text{if } c < p_j \leq p^m \\ \{p^m\} & \text{if } p^m < p_j, \end{cases}$$

where $\varnothing$ denotes the set with no members (the "empty set"). Note the respects in which this best response function differs qualitatively from a firm's best response function in Cournot's game: for some actions of its opponent, a firm has no best response, and for some actions it has multiple best responses.

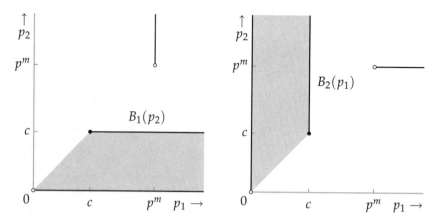

Figure 66.1 The firms' best response functions in Bertrand's duopoly game. Firm 1's best response function is in the left panel; firm 2's is in the right panel.

The fact that firm i has *no* best response when $c < p_j < p^m$ is an artifact of modeling price as a continuous variable (a firm can choose its price to be any non-negative number). If instead we assume that each firm's price must be a multiple of some indivisible unit ϵ (e.g. price must be an integral number of cents), then firm i's optimal response to a price p_j with $c < p_j < p^m$ is $p_j - \epsilon$. I model price as a continuous variable because doing so simplifies some of the analysis; in Exercise 67.2 you are asked to study the case of discrete prices.

When $p_j < c$, firm i's set of best responses is the set of all prices greater than p_j. In particular, prices between p_j and c are best responses. You may object that setting a price less than c is not very sensible. Such a price exposes firm i to the risk of posting a loss (if firm j chooses a higher price) and has no advantage over the price of c, regardless of firm j's price. That is, such a price is *weakly dominated* (Definition 46.1) by the price c. Nevertheless, such a price *is* a best response! That is, it is optimal for firm i to choose such a price, *given* firm j's price: there is no price that yields firm i a higher profit, *given* firm j's price. The point is that when asking if a player's action is a best response to her opponent's action, we do not consider the "risk" that the opponent will take some other action.

Figure 66.1 shows the firms' best response functions (firm 1's on the left, firm 2's on the right). The shaded gray area in the left panel indicates that for a price p_2 less than c, *any* price greater than p_2 is a best response for firm 1. The absence of a black line along the sloping left boundary of this area indicates that only prices p_1 *greater than* (not equal to) p_2 are included. The black line along the top of the area indicates that for $p_2 = c$ any price greater than *or equal* to c is a best response. As before, the dot indicates a point that is included, whereas the small circle indicates a point that is excluded. Firm 2's best response function has a similar interpretation.

A Nash equilibrium is a pair (p_1^*, p_2^*) of prices such that p_1^* is a best response to p_2^*, and p_2^* is a best response to p_1^*—that is, p_1^* is in $B_1(p_2^*)$ and p_2^* is in $B_2(p_1^*)$ (see (36.2)). If we superimpose the two best response functions, any such pair is in the intersection of their graphs. If you do so, you will see that the graphs have a single point of intersection, namely $(p_1^*, p_2^*) = (c, c)$. That is, the game has a single Nash equilibrium, in which each firm charges the price c.

The method of finding the Nash equilibria of a game by constructing the players' best response functions is systematic. As long as these functions may be computed, the method straightforwardly leads to the set of Nash equilibria. However, in some games we can make a direct argument that avoids the need to construct the entire best response functions. Using a combination of intuition and trial and error, we find the action profiles that seem to be equilibria; then we show precisely that any such profile is an equilibrium and every other profile is not an equilibrium. To show that a pair of actions is not a Nash equilibrium we need only find a *better* response for one of the players—not necessarily the *best* response.

In Bertrand's game we can argue as follows. (*i*) First we show that $(p_1, p_2) = (c, c)$ is a Nash equilibrium. If one firm charges the price c, then the other firm can do no better than charge the price c also, because if it raises its price it sells no output, and if it lowers its price it posts a loss. (*ii*) Next we show that no other pair (p_1, p_2) is a Nash equilibrium, as follows.

- If $p_i < c$ for either $i = 1$ or $i = 2$, then the profit of the firm whose price is lowest (or the profit of both firms, if the prices are the same) is negative, and this firm can increase its profit (to zero) by raising its price to c.

- If $p_i = c$ and $p_j > c$, then firm i is better off increasing its price slightly, making its profit positive rather than zero.

- If $p_i > c$ and $p_j > c$, suppose that $p_i \geq p_j$. Then firm i can increase its profit by lowering p_i to slightly below p_j if $D(p_j) > 0$ (i.e. if $p_j < \alpha$) and to p^m if $D(p_j) = 0$ (i.e. if $p_j \geq \alpha$).

In conclusion, both arguments show that when the unit cost of production is a constant c, the same for both firms, and demand is linear, Bertrand's game has a unique Nash equilibrium, in which each firm's price is equal to c.

⊘ EXERCISE 67.1 (Bertrand's duopoly game with constant unit cost) Consider the extent to which the analysis depends upon the demand function D taking the specific form $D(p) = \alpha - p$. Suppose that D is any function for which $D(p) \geq 0$ for all p and there exists $\overline{p} > c$ such that $D(p) > 0$ for all $p \leq \overline{p}$. Is (c, c) still a Nash equilibrium? Is it still the only Nash equilibrium?

⊘ EXERCISE 67.2 (Bertrand's duopoly game with discrete prices) Consider the variant of the example of Bertrand's duopoly game in this section in which each firm is restricted to choose a price that is an integral number of cents. Take the monetary unit to be a cent, and assume that c is an integer and $\alpha > c + 1$. Is (c, c) a Nash equilibrium of this game? Is there any other Nash equilibrium?

3.2.3 Discussion

For a duopoly in which both firms have the same constant unit cost and the demand function is linear, the Nash equilibria of Cournot's and Bertrand's games generate different economic outcomes. The equilibrium price in Bertrand's game is equal to the common unit cost c, whereas the price associated with the equilibrium of Cournot's game is $\frac{1}{3}(\alpha + 2c)$, which exceeds c because $c < \alpha$. In particular, the equilibrium price in Bertrand's game is the lowest price compatible with the firms' not posting losses, whereas the price at the equilibrium of Cournot's game is higher. In Cournot's game, the price decreases toward c as the number of firms increases (Exercise 61.1), whereas in Bertrand's game it is c even if there are only two firms. In the next exercise you are asked to show that as the number of firms increases in Bertrand's game, the price remains c.

⊘ EXERCISE 68.1 (Bertrand's oligopoly game) Consider Bertrand's oligopoly game when the cost and demand functions satisfy the conditions in Section 3.2.2 and there are n firms, with $n \geq 3$. Show that the set of Nash equilibria is the set of profiles $(p_1, \ldots, p_n)$ of prices for which $p_i \geq c$ for all i and at least two prices are equal to c. (Show that any such profile is a Nash equilibrium, and that every other profile is not a Nash equilibrium.)

What accounts for the difference between the Nash equilibria of Cournot's and Bertrand's games? The key point is that different strategic variables (output in Cournot's game, price in Bertrand's game) imply different types of strategic reasoning by the firms. In Cournot's game a firm changes its behavior if it can increase its profit by changing its output, on the assumption that the other firms' outputs will remain the same and the price will adjust to clear the market. In Bertrand's game a firm changes its behavior if it can increase its profit by changing its price, on the assumption that the other firms' prices will remain the same and their outputs will adjust to clear the market. Which assumption makes more sense depends on the context. For example, the wholesale market for agricultural produce may fit Cournot's game better, whereas the retail market for food may fit Bertrand's game better.

Under some variants of the assumptions in the previous section (3.2.2), Bertrand's game has no Nash equilibrium. In one case the firms' cost functions have constant unit costs, and these costs are different; in another case the cost functions have a fixed component. In both these cases, as well as in some other cases, an equilibrium is restored if we modify the way in which consumers are divided between the firms when the prices are the same, as the following exercises show. (We can think of the division of consumers between firms charging the same price as being determined as part of the equilibrium. Note that we retain the assumption that if the firms charge different prices, then the one charging the lower price receives all the demand.)

⊘ EXERCISE 68.2 (Bertrand's duopoly game with different unit costs) Consider Bertrand's duopoly game under a variant of the assumptions of Section 3.2.2 in which the firms' unit costs are different, equal to c_1 and c_2, where $c_1 < c_2$. Denote by p_1^m the price that maximizes $(p - c_1)(\alpha - p)$, and assume that $c_2 < p_1^m$ and that the function $(p - c_1)(\alpha - p)$ is increasing in p up to p_1^m.

a. Suppose that the rule for splitting up consumers when the prices are equal assigns all consumers to firm 1 when both firms charge the price c_2. Show that $(p_1, p_2) = (c_2, c_2)$ is a Nash equilibrium and that no other pair of prices is a Nash equilibrium.

b. Show that no Nash equilibrium exists if the rule for splitting up consumers when the prices are equal assigns some consumers to firm 2 when both firms charge c_2.

? EXERCISE 69.1 (Bertrand's duopoly game with fixed costs) Consider Bertrand's game under a variant of the assumptions of Section 3.2.2 in which the cost function of each firm i is given by $C_i(q_i) = f + cq_i$ for $q_i > 0$, and $C_i(0) = 0$, where f is positive and less than the maximum of $(p - c)(\alpha - p)$ with respect to p. Denote by $\bar{p}$ the price p that satisfies $(p - c)(\alpha - p) = f$ and is less than the maximizer of $(p - c)(\alpha - p)$ (see Figure 69.1). Show that if firm 1 gets all the demand when both firms charge the same price, then $(\bar{p}, \bar{p})$ is a Nash equilibrium. Show also that no other pair of prices is a Nash equilibrium. (First consider cases in which the firms charge the same price, then cases in which they charge different prices.)

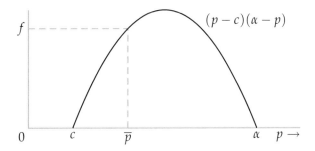

Figure 69.1 The determination of the price $\bar{p}$ in Exercise 69.1.

COURNOT, BERTRAND, AND NASH: SOME HISTORICAL NOTES

Associating the names of Cournot and Bertrand with the strategic games in Sections 3.1 and 3.2 invites two conclusions. First, that Cournot, writing in the first half of the 19th century, developed the concept of Nash equilibrium in the context of a model of oligopoly. Second, that Bertrand, dissatisfied with Cournot's game, proposed an alternative model in which price rather than output is the strategic variable. On both points the history is much less straightforward.

Cournot presented his "equilibrium" as the outcome of a dynamic adjustment process in which, in the case of two firms, the firms alternately choose best responses to each other's outputs. During such an adjustment process, each firm, when choosing an output, acts on the assumption that the other firm's output will remain the same, an assumption shown to be incorrect when the other firm subsequently adjusts its output. The fact that the adjustment process rests on the firms' acting on assumptions constantly shown to be false was the subject of criticism in a leading presentation of Cournot's model (Fellner 1949) available at the time Nash was developing his idea.

Certainly Nash did not literally generalize Cournot's idea: the evidence suggests that he was completely unaware of Cournot's work when developing the notion of Nash equilibrium (Leonard 1994, 502–503). In fact, only gradually, as Nash's work was absorbed into mainstream economic theory, was Cournot's solution interpreted as a Nash equilibrium (Leonard 1994, 507–509).

The association of the price-setting model with Bertrand (a mathematician) rests on a paragraph he wrote in 1883 in a review of Cournot's book. (The book, published in 1838, had previously been largely ignored.) The review is confused. Bertrand is under the impression that in Cournot's model the firms compete in prices, undercutting each other to attract more business! He argues that there is "no solution" because there is no limit to the fall in prices, a result he says that Cournot's formulation conceals (Bertrand 1883, 503). In brief, Bertrand's understanding of Cournot's work is flawed; he sees that price competition leads each firm to undercut the other, but his conclusion about the outcome is incorrect.

Through the lens of modern game theory we see that the models associated with Cournot and Bertrand are strategic games that differ only in the strategic variable, the solution in both cases being a Nash equilibrium. Until Nash's work, the picture was much murkier.

3.3 Electoral competition

What factors determine the number of political parties and the policies they propose? How is the outcome of an election affected by the electoral system and the voters' preferences among policies? A model that is the foundation for many theories of political phenomena addresses these questions. In the model, each of several candidates chooses a policy; each citizen has preferences over policies and votes for one of the candidates.

A simple version of this model is a strategic game in which the players are the candidates and a policy is a number, referred to as a "position". (The compression of all policy differences into one dimension is a major abstraction, though political positions are often categorized on a left–right axis.) After the candidates have chosen positions, each of a set of citizens votes (nonstrategically) for the candidate whose position she likes best. The candidate who obtains the most votes wins. Each candidate cares only about winning; no candidate has an ideological attachment to any position. Specifically, each candidate prefers to win than to tie for first place (in which case perhaps the winner is determined randomly), and prefers to tie for first place than to lose; if she ties for first place, she prefers to do so with as few other candidates as possible.

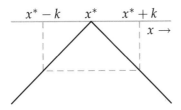

Figure 71.1 The payoff of a voter whose favorite position is x^*, as a function of the winning position, x.

There is a continuum of voters, each with a favorite position. The distribution of these favorite positions over the set of all possible positions is arbitrary. In particular, this distribution may not be uniform: a large fraction of the voters may have favorite positions close to one point, while few voters have favorite positions close to some other point. A position that turns out to have special significance is the *median* favorite position: the position m with the property that exactly half of the voters' favorite positions are at most m, and half of the voters' favorite positions are at least m. (I assume that the distribution of favorite positions is such that there is only one position with this property.)

Each voter's distaste for any position is given by the distance between that position and her favorite position. In particular, for any value of k, a voter whose favorite position is x^* is indifferent between the positions $x^* - k$ and $x^* + k$. (Refer to Figure 71.1.)

Under this assumption, each candidate attracts the votes of all citizens whose favorite positions are closer to her position than to the position of any other candidate. An example is shown in Figure 71.2. In this example there are three candidates, with positions x_1, x_2, and x_3. Candidate 1 attracts the votes of every citizen whose favorite position is in the interval, labeled "Votes for 1", up to the midpoint $\frac{1}{2}(x_1 + x_2)$ of the line segment from x_1 to x_2; candidate 2 attracts the votes of every citizen whose favorite position is in the interval from $\frac{1}{2}(x_1 + x_2)$ to $\frac{1}{2}(x_2 + x_3)$; and candidate 3 attracts the remaining votes. I assume that citizens whose favorite position is $\frac{1}{2}(x_1 + x_2)$ divide their votes equally between candidates 1 and 2, and those whose favorite position is $\frac{1}{2}(x_2 + x_3)$ divide their votes equally between candidates 2 and 3. If two or more candidates take the same position, then they share equally the votes that the position attracts.

In summary, I consider the following strategic game, which, in honor of its originator, I call **Hotelling's model of electoral competition**.

Players The candidates.

Actions Each candidate's set of actions is the set of positions (numbers).

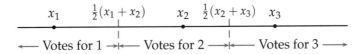

Figure 71.2 The allocation of votes between three candidates, with positions x_1, x_2, and x_3.

Preferences   Each candidate's preferences are represented by a payoff function that assigns n to every action profile in which she wins outright, k to every action profile in which she ties for first place with $n - k$ other candidates (for $1 \leq k \leq n - 1$), and 0 to every action profile in which she loses, where positions attract votes in the way described in the previous paragraph.

Suppose there are two candidates. We can find a Nash equilibrium of the game by studying the players' best response functions. Fix the position x_2 of candidate 2 and consider the best position for candidate 1. First suppose that $x_2 < m$. If candidate 1 takes a position to the left of x_2, then candidate 2 attracts the votes of all citizens whose favorite positions are to the right of $\frac{1}{2}(x_1 + x_2)$, a set that includes the 50% of citizens whose favorite positions are to the right of m, and more. Thus candidate 2 wins, and candidate 1 loses. If candidate 1 takes a position to the right of x_2, then she wins as long as the dividing line between her supporters and those of candidate 2 is less than m (see Figure 72.1). If she is so far to the right that this dividing line lies to the right of m, then she loses. She prefers to win than to lose, and is indifferent between all the outcomes in which she wins, so her set of best responses to x_2 is the set of positions that causes the midpoint $\frac{1}{2}(x_1 + x_2)$ of the line segment from x_2 to x_1 to be less than m. (If this midpoint is *equal* to m, then the candidates tie.) The condition $\frac{1}{2}(x_1 + x_2) < m$ is equivalent to $x_1 < 2m - x_2$, so candidate 1's set of best responses to x_2 is the set of all positions between x_2 and $2m - x_2$ (excluding the points x_2 and $2m - x_2$).

A symmetric argument applies to the case in which $x_2 > m$. In this case candidate 1's set of best responses to x_2 is the set of all positions between $2m - x_2$ and x_2.

Finally consider the case in which $x_2 = m$. In this case candidate 1's unique best response is to choose the *same* position, m! If she chooses any other position, then she loses, whereas if she chooses m, then she ties for first place.

In summary, candidate 1's best response function is defined by

$$B_1(x_2) = \begin{cases} \{x_1 : x_2 < x_1 < 2m - x_2\} & \text{if } x_2 < m \\ \{m\} & \text{if } x_2 = m \\ \{x_1 : 2m - x_2 < x_1 < x_2\} & \text{if } x_2 > m. \end{cases}$$

Candidate 2 faces exactly the same incentives as candidate 1, and hence has the same best response function. The candidates' best response functions are shown in Figure 73.1.

If you superimpose the two best response functions, you will see that the game has a unique Nash equilibrium, in which both candidates choose the position m,

Figure 72.1 An action profile (x_1, x_2) for which candidate 1 wins.

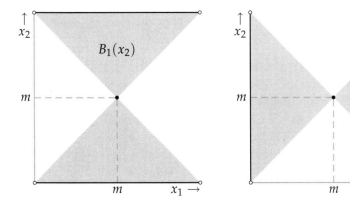

Figure 73.1 The candidates' best response functions in Hotelling's model of electoral competition with two candidates. Candidate 1's best response function is in the left panel; candidate 2's is in the right panel. (The edges of the shaded areas are excluded.)

the voters' median favorite position. (Remember that the edges of the shaded area, which correspond to pairs of positions that result in ties, are excluded from the best response functions.) The outcome is that the election is a tie.

As in the case of Bertrand's duopoly game in the previous section, we can make a direct argument that (m, m) is the unique Nash equilibrium of the game, without constructing the best response functions. First, (m, m) is an equilibrium: it results in a tie, and if either candidate chooses a position different from m, then she loses. Second, no other pair of positions is a Nash equilibrium, by the following argument.

- If one candidate loses, then she can do better by moving to m, where she either wins outright (if her opponent's position is different from m) or ties for first place (if her opponent's position is m).

- If the candidates tie (because their positions are either the same or symmetric about m), then either candidate can do better by moving to m, where she wins outright.

Our conclusion is that the competition between the candidates to secure a majority of the votes drives them to select the same position, equal to the median of the citizens' favorite positions. Hotelling (1929, 54), the originator of the model, writes that this outcome is "strikingly exemplified." He continues, "The competition for votes between the Republican and Democratic parties [in the United States] does not lead to a clear drawing of issues, an adoption of two strongly contrasted positions between which the voter may choose. Instead, each party strives to make its platform as much like the other's as possible."

? EXERCISE 73.1 (Electoral competition with asymmetric voters' preferences) Consider a variant of Hotelling's model in which voters' preferences are asymmetric. Specifically, suppose that each voter cares twice as much about policy differences to the left of her favorite position than about policy differences to the right of her favorite position. How does this affect the Nash equilibrium?

In the model considered so far, no candidate has the option of staying out of the race. Suppose that we give each candidate this option; assume that it is better than losing and worse than tying for first place. Then the Nash equilibrium remains as before: both players enter the race and choose the position m. The direct argument differs from the one before only in that in addition we need to check that there is no equilibrium in which one or both of the candidates stay out of the race. If one candidate stays out, then, given the other candidate's position, she can enter and either win outright or tie for first place. If both candidates stay out, then either candidate can enter and win outright.

The next exercise asks you to consider the Nash equilibria of this variant of the model when there are three candidates.

? EXERCISE 74.1 (Electoral competition with three candidates) Consider a variant of Hotelling's model in which there are three candidates and each candidate has the option of staying out of the race, which she regards as better than losing and worse than tying for first place. Use the following arguments to show that the game has no Nash equilibrium. First, show that there is no Nash equilibrium in which a single candidate enters the race. Second, show that in any Nash equilibrium in which more than one candidate enters, all candidates that enter tie for first place. Third, show that there is no Nash equilibrium in which two candidates enter the race. Fourth, show that there is no Nash equilibrium in which all three candidates enter the race and choose the same position. Finally, show that there is no Nash equilibrium in which all three candidates enter the race and do not all choose the same position.

? EXERCISE 74.2 (U.S. presidential election) Consider a variant of Hotelling's model that captures features of a U.S. presidential election. Voters are divided between two states. State 1 has more electoral college votes than does state 2. The winner is the candidate who obtains the most electoral college votes. Denote by m_i the median favorite position among the citizens of state i, for $i = 1, 2$; assume that $m_2 < m_1$. Each of two candidates chooses a single position. Each citizen votes (nonstrategically) for the candidate whose position is closest to her favorite position. The candidate who wins a majority of the votes in a state obtains all the electoral college votes of that state; if for some state the candidates obtain the same number of votes, they each obtain half of the electoral college votes of that state. Find the Nash equilibrium (equilibria?) of the strategic game that models this situation.

So far we have assumed that the candidates care only about winning; they are not at all concerned with the winner's position. The next exercise asks you to consider the case in which each candidate cares *only* about the winner's position, and not at all about winning. (You may be surprised by the equilibrium.)

❓ EXERCISE 75.1 (Electoral competition between candidates who care only about the winning position) Consider the variant of Hotelling's model in which the candidates (like the citizens) care about the winner's position, and not at all about winning per se. There are two candidates. Each candidate has a favorite position; her dislike for other positions increases with their distance from her favorite position. Assume that the favorite position of one candidate is less than m and the favorite position of the other candidate is greater than m. Assume also that if the candidates tie when they take the positions x_1 and x_2, then the outcome is the compromise policy $\frac{1}{2}(x_1 + x_2)$. Find the set of Nash equilibria of the strategic game that models this situation. (First consider pairs (x_1, x_2) of positions for which either $x_1 < m$ and $x_2 < m$, or $x_1 > m$ and $x_2 > m$. Next consider pairs (x_1, x_2) for which either $x_1 < m < x_2$, or $x_2 < m < x_1$, then those for which $x_1 = m$ and $x_2 \neq m$, or $x_1 \neq m$ and $x_2 = m$. Finally consider the pair (m, m).)

The set of candidates in Hotelling's model is given. The next exercise asks you to analyze a model in which the set of candidates is generated as part of an equilibrium.

❓ EXERCISE 75.2 (Citizen-candidates) Consider a game in which the players are the citizens. Any citizen may, at some cost $c > 0$, become a candidate. Assume that the only position a citizen can espouse is her favorite position, so that a citizen's only decision is whether to stand as a candidate. After all citizens have (simultaneously) decided whether to become candidates, each citizen votes for her favorite candidate, as in Hotelling's model. Citizens care about the position of the winning candidate; a citizen whose favorite position is x loses $|x - x^*|$ if the winning candidate's position is x^*. (For any number z, $|z|$ denotes the absolute value of z: $|z| = z$ if $z > 0$ and $|z| = -z$ if $z < 0$.) Winning confers the benefit b. Thus a citizen who becomes a candidate and ties with $k - 1$ other candidates for first place obtains the payoff $b/k - c$; a citizen with favorite position x who becomes a candidate and is not one of the candidates tied for first place obtains the payoff $-|x - x^*| - c$, where x^* is the winner's position; and a citizen with favorite position x who does not become a candidate obtains the payoff $-|x - x^*|$, where x^* is the winner's position. Assume that for every position x there is a citizen for whom x is the favorite position. Show that if $b \leq 2c$, then the game has a Nash equilibrium in which one citizen becomes a candidate. Is there an equilibrium (for any values of b and c) in which two citizens, each with favorite position m, become candidates? Is there an equilibrium in which two citizens with favorite positions different from m become candidates?

Hotelling's model assumes a basic agreement among the voters about the ordering of the positions. For example, if one voter prefers x to y to z and another voter prefers y to z to x, no voter prefers z to x to y. The next exercise asks you to study a model that does not so restrict the voters' preferences.

❓ EXERCISE 75.3 (Electoral competition for more general preferences) Suppose that there is a finite number of positions and a finite, odd, number of voters. For any positions x and y, each voter either prefers x to y or prefers y to x. (That is, no voter regards any two positions as equally desirable.) We say that a position x^* is a *Condorcet winner* if for every position y different from x^*, a majority of voters prefer x^* to y.

a. Show that for any configuration of preferences there is at most one Condorcet winner.

b. Give an example in which no Condorcet winner exists. (Suppose that there are three positions (x, y, and z) and three voters. Assume that voter 1 prefers x to y to z. Construct preferences for the other two voters with the properties that one voter prefers x to y and the other prefers y to x, one prefers x to z and the other prefers z to x, and one prefers y to z and the other prefers z to y. The preferences you construct must, of course, satisfy the condition that a voter who prefers a to b and b to c also prefers a to c, where a, b, and c are any positions.)

c. Consider the strategic game in which two candidates simultaneously choose positions, as in Hotelling's model. If the candidates choose different positions, each voter endorses the candidate whose position she prefers, and the candidate who receives the most votes wins. If the candidates choose the same position, they tie. Show that this game has a unique Nash equilibrium if the voters' preferences are such that there is a Condorcet winner, and has no Nash equilibrium if the voters' preferences are such that there is no Condorcet winner.

A variant of Hotelling's model of electoral competition can be used to analyze the choices of product characteristics by competing firms in situations in which price is not a significant variable. (Think of radio stations that offer different styles of music, for example.) The set of positions is the range of possible characteristics for the product, and the citizens are consumers rather than voters. Consumers' tastes differ; each consumer buys (at a fixed price, possibly zero) one unit of the product she likes best. The model differs substantially from Hotelling's model of electoral competition in that each firm's objective is to maximize its market share, rather than to obtain a market share larger than that of any other firm. In the next exercise you are asked to show that the Nash equilibria of this game in the case of two or three firms are the same as those in Hotelling's model of electoral competition.

? EXERCISE 76.1 (Competition in product characteristics) In the variant of Hotelling's model that captures competing firms' choices of product characteristics, show that when there are two firms the unique Nash equilibrium is (m, m) (both firms offer the consumers' median favorite product), and when there are three firms there is no Nash equilibrium. (Start by arguing that when there are two firms whose products differ, either firm is better off making its product more similar to that of its rival.)

3.4 The *War of Attrition*

The game known as the *War of Attrition* elaborates on the ideas captured by the game *Hawk–Dove* (Exercise 31.2). It was originally posed as a model of a conflict between two animals fighting over prey. Each animal chooses the time at which it intends to give up. When an animal gives up, its opponent obtains all the prey (and the time at which the winner intended to give up is irrelevant). If both animals give up at the same time, then each has an equal chance of obtaining the prey. Fighting is costly: each animal prefers as short a fight as possible.

The game models not only such a conflict between animals, but also many other disputes. The "prey" can be any indivisible object, and "fighting" can be any costly activity—for example, simply waiting.

To define the game precisely, let time be a continuous variable that starts at 0 and runs indefinitely. Assume that the value party i attaches to the object in dispute is $v_i > 0$ and the value it attaches to a 50% chance of obtaining the object is $v_i/2$. Each unit of time that passes before the dispute is settled (i.e. one of the parties concedes) costs each party one unit of payoff. Thus if player i concedes first, at time t_i, her payoff is $-t_i$ (she spends t_i units of time and does not obtain the object). If the other player concedes first, at time t_j, player i's payoff is $v_i - t_j$ (she obtains the object after t_j units of time). If both players concede at the same time, player i's payoff is $\frac{1}{2}v_i - t_i$, where t_i is the common concession time. The **War of Attrition** is the following strategic game.

Players The two parties to a dispute.

Actions Each player's set of actions is the set of possible concession times (non-negative numbers).

Preferences Player i's preferences are represented by the payoff function

$$u_i(t_1, t_2) = \begin{cases} -t_i & \text{if } t_i < t_j \\ \frac{1}{2}v_i - t_i & \text{if } t_i = t_j \\ v_i - t_j & \text{if } t_i > t_j, \end{cases}$$

where j is the other player.

To find the Nash equilibria of this game, we start, as before, by finding the players' best response functions. Intuitively, if player j's intended concession time is early enough (t_j is small), then it is optimal for player i to wait for player j to concede. That is, in this case player i should choose a concession time later than t_j; any such time is as good as any other. By contrast, if player j intends to hold out for a long time (t_j is large), then player i should concede immediately. Because player i values the object at v_i, the length of time it is worth her waiting is v_i.

To make these ideas precise, we can study player i's payoff function for various fixed values of t_j, the concession time of player j. The three cases that the intuitive argument suggests are qualitatively different are shown in Figure 78.1: $t_j < v_i$ in

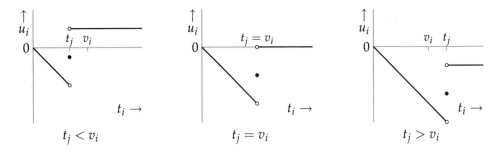

Figure 78.1 Three cross sections of player i's payoff function in the *War of Attrition*.

the left panel, $t_j = v_i$ in the middle panel, and $t_j > v_i$ in the right panel. Player i's best responses in each case are her actions for which her payoff is highest: the set of times after t_j if $t_j < v_i$, 0 and the set of times after t_j if $t_j = v_i$, and 0 if $t_j > v_i$.

In summary, player i's best response function is given by

$$B_i(t_j) = \begin{cases} \{t_i : t_i > t_j\} & \text{if } t_j < v_i \\ \{t_i : t_i = 0 \text{ or } t_i > t_j\} & \text{if } t_j = v_i \\ \{0\} & \text{if } t_j > v_i. \end{cases}$$

For a case in which $v_1 > v_2$, this function is shown in the left panel of Figure 78.2 for $i = 1$ and $j = 2$ (player 1's best response function), and in the right panel for $i = 2$ and $j = 1$ (player 2's best response function).

Superimposing the players' best response functions, we see that there are two areas of intersection: the vertical axis at and above v_1 and the horizontal axis at and to the right of v_2. Thus (t_1, t_2) is a Nash equilibrium of the game if and only if either

$$t_1 = 0 \text{ and } t_2 \geq v_1$$

or

$$t_2 = 0 \text{ and } t_1 \geq v_2.$$

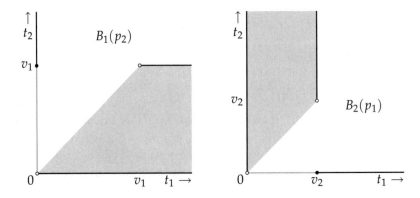

Figure 78.2 The players' best response functions in the *War of Attrition* (for a case in which $v_1 > v_2$). Player 1's best response function is in the left panel; player 2's is in the right panel. (The sloping edges are excluded.)

In words, in every equilibrium either player 1 concedes immediately and player 2 concedes at time v_1 or later, or player 2 concedes immediately and player 1 concedes at time v_2 or later.

? EXERCISE 79.1 (Direct argument for Nash equilibria of *War of Attrition*) Give a direct argument, not using information about the entire best response functions, for the set of Nash equilibria of the *War of Attrition*. (Argue that if $t_1 = t_2$, $0 < t_i < t_j$, or $0 = t_i < t_j < v_i$ (for $i = 1$ and $j = 2$, or $i = 2$ and $j = 1$), then the pair (t_1, t_2) is not a Nash equilibrium. Then argue that any remaining pair is a Nash equilibrium.)

Three features of the equilibria are notable. First, in no equilibrium is there any fight: one player always concedes immediately. Second, either player may concede first, regardless of the players' valuations. In particular, there are always equilibria in which the player who values the object more highly concedes first. Third, the equilibria are *asymmetric* (the players' actions are different), even when $v_1 = v_2$, in which case the game is symmetric—the players' sets of actions are the same and player 1's payoff to (t_1, t_2) is the same as player 2's payoff to (t_2, t_1) (Definition 51.1). Given this asymmetry, to interpret the Nash equilibria as action profiles compatible with steady states, the populations from which the two players are drawn must be distinct. One player might be the current owner of the object in dispute and the other a challenger, for example. In this case the equilibria correspond to the two conventions that a challenger always gives up immediately and an owner always does so. (Some evidence is discussed in the box on page 409.) If all players—those in the role of player 1 as well as those in the role of player 2—are drawn from a single population, then only symmetric equilibria are relevant (see Section 2.10). The *War of Attrition* has no such equilibria, so the notion of Nash equilibrium makes no prediction about the outcome in such a situation.

? EXERCISE 79.2 (Variant of *War of Attrition*) Consider the variant of the *War of Attrition* in which each player attaches no value to the time spent waiting for the other player to concede, but the object in dispute loses value as time passes. (Think of a rotting animal carcass or a melting ice cream cone.) Assume that the value of the object to each player i after t units of time is $v_i - t$ (and the value of a 50% chance of obtaining the object is $\frac{1}{2}(v_i - t)$). Specify the strategic game that models this situation (take care with the payoff functions). Construct the analogue of Figure 78.1, find the players' best response functions, and hence find the Nash equilibria of the game.

The *War of Attrition* is an example of a "game of timing", in which each player's action is a number and each player's payoff depends sensitively on whether her action is greater or less than the other player's action. In many such games, each player's strategic variable is the time at which to act, hence the name "game of timing". The next two exercises are further examples of such games. (In the first the strategic variable is time, whereas in the second it is not.)

❔ EXERCISE 80.1 (Timing product release)   Two firms are developing competing products for a market of fixed size. The longer a firm spends on development, the better its product. But the first firm to release its product has an advantage: the customers it obtains will not subsequently switch to its rival. (Once a person starts using a product, the cost of switching to an alternative, even one significantly better, is too high to make a switch worthwhile.) A firm that releases its product first, at time t, captures the share $h(t)$ of the market, where h is a function that increases from time 0 to time T, with $h(0) = 0$ and $h(T) = 1$. The remaining market share is left for the other firm. If the firms release their products at the same time, each obtains half of the market. Each firm wishes to obtain the highest possible market share. Model this situation as a strategic game and find its Nash equilibrium (equilibria?). (When finding firm i's best response to firm j's release time t_j, there are three cases: that in which $h(t_j) < \frac{1}{2}$ (firm j gets less than half of the market if it is the first to release its product), that in which $h(t_j) = \frac{1}{2}$, and that in which $h(t_j) > \frac{1}{2}$.)

❔ EXERCISE 80.2 (A fight) Each of two people has one unit of a resource. Each person chooses how much of the resource to use in fighting the other individual and how much to use productively. If each person i devotes y_i to fighting, then the total output is $f(y_1, y_2) \geq 0$ and person i obtains the fraction $p_i(y_1, y_2)$ of the output, where

$$p_i(y_1, y_2) = \begin{cases} 1 & \text{if } y_i > y_j \\ \frac{1}{2} & \text{if } y_i = y_j \\ 0 & \text{if } y_i < y_j. \end{cases}$$

The function f is continuous (small changes in y_1 and y_2 cause small changes in $f(y_1, y_2)$), is decreasing in both y_1 and y_2 (the more each player devotes to fighting, the less output is produced), and satisfies $f(1, 1) = 0$ (if each player devotes all her resource to fighting, then no output is produced). (If you prefer to deal with a specific function f, take $f(y_1, y_2) = 2 - y_1 - y_2$.) Each person cares only about the amount of output she receives, and prefers to receive as much as possible. Specify this situation as a strategic game and find its Nash equilibrium (equilibria?). (Use a direct argument: first consider pairs (y_1, y_2) with $y_1 \neq y_2$, then those with $y_1 = y_2 < 1$, then those with $y_1 = y_2 = 1$.)

3.5   Auctions

3.5.1   Introduction

In an "auction", a good is sold to the party who submits the highest bid. Auctions, broadly defined, are used to allocate significant economic resources, from works of art to short-term government bonds to offshore tracts for oil and gas exploration to the radio spectrum. They take many forms. For example, bids may be called out sequentially (as in auctions for works of art) or may be submitted in sealed envelopes; the price paid may be the highest bid, or some other price; if more than one unit of a good is being sold, bids may be taken on all units simultaneously, or the units may be sold sequentially. A game-theoretic analysis helps us to understand the consequences of various auction designs; it suggests, for example, the design likely to be the most effective at allocating resources, and the one likely to raise the most revenue. In this section I discuss auctions in which every buyer knows her own valuation and every other buyer's valuation of the item being sold. Chapter 9 develops tools that allow us to study, in Section 9.6, auctions in which buyers are not perfectly informed of each other's valuations.

AUCTIONS FROM BABYLONIA TO EBAY

Auctioning has a very long history. Herodotus, a Greek writer of the fifth century B.C. who, together with Thucydides, created the intellectual field of history, describes auctions in Babylonia. He writes that the Babylonians' "most sensible" custom was an annual auction in each village of the women of marriageable age. The women most attractive to the men were sold first; they commanded positive prices, whereas men were paid to be matched with the least desirable women. In each auction, bids appear to have been called out sequentially, the man who bid the most winning and paying the price he bid.

Auctions were used also in Athens in the fifth and fourth centuries B.C. to sell the rights to collect taxes, to dispose of confiscated property, and to lease land and mines. The evidence on the nature of the auctions is slim, but some interesting accounts survive. For example, the Athenian politician Andocides (c. 440–391 B.C.) reports collusion in an auction of tax-collection rights (see Langdon 1994, 260).

Auctions were frequent in ancient Rome, and continued to be used in medieval Europe after the end of the Roman empire (tax-collection rights were annually auctioned by the towns of the medieval and early modern Low Countries, for example). The earliest use of the English word "auction" given by the *Oxford English Dictionary* dates from 1595 and concerns an auction "when will be sold Slaves, household goods, etc." Rules surviving from the auctions of this era show that in some cases, at least, bids were called out sequentially, with the bidder remaining at the end obtaining the object at the price she bid (Cassady 1967, 30–31). A variant of this mechanism, in which a time limit is imposed on the bids, is reported by the English diarist and naval administrator Samuel Pepys (1633–1703). The auctioneer lit a short candle, and bids were valid only if made before the flame went out. Pepys reports that a flurry of bidding occurred at the last moment. At an auction on September 3, 1662, a bidder "cunninger than the rest" told him that just as the flame goes out, "the smoke descends", signaling the moment at which one should bid, an observation Pepys found "very pretty" (Pepys 1970, 185–186).

The auction houses of Sotheby's and Christie's were founded in the mid-18th century. At the beginning of the 21st century, they are being eclipsed, at least in the value of the goods they sell, by online auction companies. For example, eBay, founded in September 1995, sold U.S.$1.3 billion of merchandise in 62 million auctions during the second quarter of 2000, roughly double the numbers for the second quarter of the previous year; Sotheby's and Christie's together sold around U.S.$1 billion of art and antiques each quarter.

The mechanism used by eBay shares a feature with the ones Pepys observed: all bids must be received before some fixed time. The way in which the price is determined differs. In an eBay auction, a bidder submits a "proxy bid" that is not revealed; the prevailing price is a small increment above the second-highest proxy bid. As in the 17th-century auctions Pepys observed, many bidders on eBay act at the last moment—a practice known as "sniping" in the argot of cyberspace. Other online auction houses use different termination rules. For example, Amazon waits ten minutes after a bid before closing an auction. The fact that last-minute bidding is much less common in Amazon auctions than it is in eBay auctions has attracted the attention of game theorists; Roth and Ockenfels (2002) explain it in terms of the difference in the auctions' termination rules.

In recent years, many countries have auctioned the rights to the radio spectrum, used for wireless communication. These auctions have been much studied by game theorists; they are discussed in the box on page 300.

3.5.2 Second-price sealed-bid auctions

In a common form of auction, people sequentially submit increasing bids for an object. (The word "auction" comes from the Latin *augere*, meaning "to increase".) When no one wishes to submit a bid higher than the current bid, the person making the current bid obtains the object at the price she bid.

Given that every person is certain of her valuation of the object before the bidding begins, during the bidding no one can learn anything relevant to her actions. Thus we can model the auction by assuming that each person decides, before bidding begins, the most she is willing to bid—her "maximal bid". When the players carry out their plans, the winner is the person whose maximal bid is highest. How much does she need to bid? Eventually only she and the person with the second highest maximal bid will be left competing against each other. To win, she therefore needs to bid slightly more than the *second highest* maximal bid. If the bidding increment is small, we can take the price the winner pays to be *equal* to the second highest maximal bid.

Thus we can model such an auction as a strategic game in which each player chooses an amount of money, interpreted as the *maximal* amount she is willing to bid, and the player who chooses the highest amount obtains the object and pays a price equal to the second highest amount.

This game models also a situation in which the people simultaneously put bids in sealed envelopes, and the person who submits the highest bid wins and pays a price equal to the *second* highest bid. For this reason the game is called a *second-price sealed-bid* auction.

To define the game precisely, denote by v_i the value player i attaches to the object; if she obtains the object at the price p her payoff is $v_i - p$. Assume that the players' valuations of the object are all different and all positive; number the players 1 through n in such a way that $v_1 > v_2 > \cdots > v_n > 0$. Each player i submits a (sealed) bid b_i. If player i's bid is higher than every other bid, she obtains the object at a price equal to the second-highest bid, say b_j, and hence receives the payoff $v_i - b_j$. If some other bid is higher than player i's bid, player i does not obtain the object and receives the payoff of zero. If player i is in a tie for the highest bid, her payoff depends on the way in which ties are broken. A simple (though arbitrary) assumption is that the winner is the player among those submitting the highest bid whose number is smallest (i.e. whose valuation of the object is highest). (If the highest bid is submitted by players 2, 5, and 7, for example, the winner is player 2.) Under this assumption, player i's payoff when she bids b_i and is in a tie for the highest bid is $v_i - b_i$ if her number is lower than that of any other player submitting the bid b_i, and 0 otherwise.

In summary, a **second-price sealed-bid auction** (with complete information) is the following strategic game.

Players   The n bidders, where $n \geq 2$.

Actions   The set of actions of each player is the set of possible bids (nonnegative numbers).

Preferences   The payoff of any player i is $v_i - b_j$, where b_j is the highest bid submitted by a player other than i if either b_i is higher than every other bid, or b_i is at least as high as every other bid and the number of every other player who bids b_i is greater than i. Otherwise player i's payoff is 0.

This game has many Nash equilibria. One equilibrium is $(b_1, \ldots, b_n) = (v_1, \ldots, v_n)$: each player's bid is equal to her valuation of the object. Because $v_1 > v_2 > \cdots > v_n$, the outcome is that player 1 obtains the object at the price b_2; her payoff is $v_1 - b_2$ and every other player's payoff is zero. This profile is a Nash equilibrium by the following argument.

- If player 1 changes her bid to some other price at least equal to b_2, then the outcome does not change (recall that she pays the *second* highest bid, not the highest bid). If she changes her bid to a price less than b_2, then she loses and obtains the payoff of zero.

- If some other player lowers her bid or raises it to some price at most equal to b_1, then she remains a loser; if she raises her bid above b_1, then she wins but, in paying the price b_1, makes a loss (because her valuation is less than b_1).

Another equilibrium is $(b_1, \ldots, b_n) = (v_1, 0, \ldots, 0)$. In this equilibrium, player 1 obtains the object and pays the price of zero. The profile is an equilibrium because if player 1 changes her bid, then the outcome remains the same, and if any of the remaining players—say player i—raises her bid, then either the outcome remains the same (if player i's new bid is at most v_1) or causes player i to obtain the object at a price that exceeds her valuation (if her bid exceeds v_1). (The auctioneer obviously has an incentive for the price to be bid up, but she is not a player in the game!)

In both of these equilibria, player 1 obtains the object. But there are also equilibria in which player 1 does not obtain the object. Consider, for example, the action profile $(v_2, v_1, 0, \ldots, 0)$, in which player 2 obtains the object at the price v_2 and every player (including player 2) receives the payoff of zero. This action profile is a Nash equilibrium by the following argument.

- If player 1 raises her bid to v_1 or more, she wins the object but her payoff remains zero (she pays the price v_1, bid by player 2). Any other change in her bid has no effect on the outcome.

- If player 2 changes her bid to some other price greater than v_2, the outcome does not change. If she changes her bid to v_2 or less she loses, and her payoff remains zero.

- If any other player raises her bid to at most v_1, the outcome does not change. If she raises her bid above v_1, then she wins, but in paying the price v_1 (bid by player 2) she obtains a negative payoff.

? EXERCISE 84.1 (Nash equilibrium of second-price sealed-bid auction) Find a Nash equilibrium of a second-price sealed-bid auction in which player n obtains the object.

Player 2's bid in this equilibrium exceeds her valuation, and thus may seem a little rash: if player 1 were to increase her bid to any value less than v_1, player 2's payoff would be negative (she would obtain the object at a price greater than her valuation). This property of the action profile does not affect its status as an equilibrium, because in a Nash equilibrium a player does not consider the "risk" that another player will take an action different from her equilibrium action; each player simply chooses an action that is optimal, *given* the other players' actions. But the property does suggest that the equilibrium is less plausible as the outcome of the auction than the equilibrium in which every player bids her valuation.

The same point takes a different form when we interpret the strategic game as a model of events that unfold over time. Under this interpretation, player 2's action v_1 means that she will continue bidding until the price reaches v_1. If player 1 is *sure* that player 2 will continue bidding until the price is v_1, then player 1 rationally stops bidding when the price reaches v_2 (or, indeed, when it reaches any other level at most equal to v_1). But there is little reason for player 1 to believe that player 2 will in fact stay in the bidding if the price exceeds v_2: player 2's action is not credible, because if the bidding were to go above v_2, player 2 would rationally withdraw.

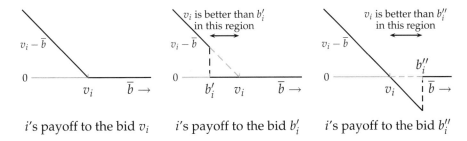

Figure 85.1 Player i's payoffs in a second-price sealed-bid auction as a function of the highest of the other players' bids, denoted $\bar{b}$, for bids of v_i (left panel), $b'_i < v_i$ (middle panel), and $b''_i > v_i$ (right panel).

The weakness of the equilibrium is reflected in the fact that player 2's bid v_1 is weakly dominated by the bid v_2. More generally,

> in a second-price sealed-bid auction (with complete information), a player's bid equal to her valuation weakly dominates all her other bids.

That is, for any bid $b_i \neq v_i$, player i's bid v_i is at least as good as b_i, *no matter what the other players bid*, and is better than b_i for some actions of the other players. (See Definition 46.1.) A player who bids less than her valuation stands not to win in some cases in which she could profit by winning (when the highest of the other bids is between her bid and her valuation), and never stands to gain relative to the situation in which she bids her valuation; a player who bids more than her valuation stands to win in some cases in which she obtains a negative payoff by doing so (when the highest of the remaining bids is between her valuation and her bid), and never stands to gain relative to the situation in which she bids her valuation. The key point is that in a second-price auction, a player who changes her bid does not lower the price she pays, but only possibly changes her status from that of a winner into that of a loser, or vice versa.

A precise argument is illustrated in Figure 85.1, which compares player i's payoffs to the bid v_i (left panel) with her payoffs to a bid $b'_i < v_i$ (middle panel), and with her payoffs to a bid $b''_i > v_i$ (right panel), as a function of the highest of the other players' bids, denoted $\bar{b}$. We see that for all values of the highest of the other players' bids, player i's payoffs to v_i are at least as large as her payoffs to any other bid and, for any bid $b_i \neq v_i$, there are some values of the highest of the other players' bids for which her payoffs to v_i exceed her payoffs to b_i. Thus player i's bid v_i weakly dominates all her other bids.

In summary, a second-price auction has many Nash equilibria, but the equilibrium $(b_1, \ldots, b_n) = (v_1, \ldots, v_n)$, in which every player's bid is equal to her valuation of the object, is distinguished by the fact that every player's action weakly dominates all her other actions.

⊘ EXERCISE 85.1 (*Second-price sealed-bid auction with two bidders*) Find *all* the Nash equilibria of a second-price sealed-bid auction with two bidders. (Construct the players' best response functions. Apart from a difference in the tie-breaking rule, the game is the same as the one in Exercise 79.2.)

? EXERCISE 86.1 (Auctioning the right to choose) An action affects each of two people. The right to choose the action is sold in a second-price auction. That is, the two people simultaneously submit bids, and the one who submits the higher bid chooses her favorite action and pays (to a third party) the amount bid by the *other* person, who pays nothing. (Assume that if the bids are the same, person 1 is the winner.) For $i = 1, 2$, the payoff of person i when the action is a and person i pays m is $u_i(a) - m$. In the game that models this situation, find for each player a bid that weakly dominates all the player's other bids (and thus find a Nash equilibrium in which each player's equilibrium action weakly dominates all her other actions).

3.5.3 First-price sealed-bid auctions

A first-price auction differs from a second-price auction only in that the winner pays the price she bids, not the second highest bid. Precisely, a **first-price sealed-bid auction** (with complete information) is defined as follows.

Players The n bidders, where $n \geq 2$.

Actions The set of actions of each player is the set of possible bids (nonnegative numbers).

Preferences The payoff of any player i is $v_i - b_i$ if either (a) b_i is higher than every other bid or (b) b_i is at least as high as every other bid and the number of every other player who bids b_i is greater than i. Otherwise player i's payoff is 0.

This game models an auction in which people submit sealed bids and the highest bid wins. (You conduct such an auction when you solicit offers for a car you wish to sell, or, as a buyer, get estimates from contractors to fix your leaky basement, assuming in both cases that you do not inform potential bidders of existing bids.) The game models also a dynamic auction in which the auctioneer begins by announcing a high price, which she gradually lowers until someone indicates her willingness to buy the object. (Flowers are sold in this way in the Netherlands.) A bid in the strategic game is interpreted as the price at which the bidder will indicate her willingness to buy the object in the dynamic auction.

One Nash equilibrium of a first-price sealed-bid auction is $(b_1, \ldots, b_n) = (v_2, v_2, v_3, \ldots, v_n)$, in which player 1's bid is player 2's valuation v_2 and every other player's bid is her own valuation. The outcome of this equilibrium is that player 1 obtains the object at the price v_2.

? EXERCISE 86.2 (Nash equilibrium of first-price sealed-bid auction) Show that $(b_1, \ldots, b_n) = (v_2, v_2, v_3, \ldots, v_n)$ is a Nash equilibrium of a first-price sealed-bid auction.

A first-price sealed-bid auction has many other equilibria, but in all equilibria the winner is the player who values the object most highly (player 1), by the following argument. In any action profile $(b_1, \ldots, b_n)$ in which some player $i \neq 1$ wins, we have $b_i > b_1$. If $b_i > v_2$, then i's payoff is negative, so that she can do better by reducing her bid to 0; if $b_i \leq v_2$, then player 1 can increase her payoff from 0 to $v_1 - b_i$ by bidding b_i, in which case she wins. Thus no such action profile is a Nash equilibrium.

? EXERCISE 87.1 (First-price sealed-bid auction) Show that in a Nash equilibrium of a first-price sealed-bid auction the two highest bids are the same, one of these bids is submitted by player 1, and the highest bid is at least v_2 and at most v_1. Show also that any action profile satisfying these conditions is a Nash equilibrium.

In any equilibrium in which the winning bid exceeds v_2, at least one player's bid exceeds her valuation. As in a second-price sealed-bid auction, such a bid seems "risky" because it would yield the bidder a negative payoff if it were to win. In the equilibrium there is no risk, because the bid does not win; but, as before, the fact that the bid has this property reduces the plausibility of the equilibrium.

As in a second-price sealed-bid auction, the potential "riskiness" to player i of a bid $b_i > v_i$ is reflected in the fact that it is weakly dominated by the bid v_i, as shown by the following argument.

- If the other players' bids are such that player i loses when she bids b_i, then the outcome is the same whether she bids b_i or v_i.

- If the other players' bids are such that player i wins when she bids b_i, then her payoff is negative when she bids b_i and zero when she bids v_i (regardless of whether this bid wins).

However, in a first-price auction, unlike a second-price auction, a bid $b_i < v_i$ of player i is *not* weakly dominated by the bid v_i. In fact, such a bid is not weakly dominated by *any* bid. It is not weakly dominated by a bid $b_i' < b_i$ because if the other players' highest bid is between b_i' and b_i, then b_i' loses, whereas b_i wins and yields player i a positive payoff. And it is not weakly dominated by a bid $b_i' > b_i$ because if the other players' highest bid is less than b_i, then both b_i and b_i' win and b_i yields a lower price.

Further, even though the bid v_i weakly dominates higher bids, this bid is itself weakly dominated, by a lower bid! If player i bids v_i her payoff is 0 regardless of the other players' bids, whereas if she bids less than v_i her payoff is either 0 (if she loses) or positive (if she wins).

In summary,

> in a first-price sealed-bid auction (with complete information), a player's bid of at least her valuation is weakly dominated, and a bid of less than her valuation is not weakly dominated.

An implication of this result is that in *every* Nash equilibrium of a first-price sealed-bid auction at least one player's action is weakly dominated. However, this property of the equilibria depends on the assumption that a bid may be any number. In the variant of the game in which bids and valuations are restricted to be multiples of some discrete monetary unit ϵ (e.g. a cent), an action profile $(v_2 - \epsilon, v_2 - \epsilon, b_3, \ldots, b_n)$ for any $b_j \leq v_j - \epsilon$ for $j = 3, \ldots, n$ is a Nash equilibrium in which no player's bid is weakly dominated. Further, every equilibrium in which no player's bid is weakly dominated takes this form. When ϵ is small, each such equilibrium is close to an equilibrium $(v_2, v_2, b_3, \ldots, b_n)$ (with $b_j \leq v_j$ for $j = 3, \ldots, n$) of the game with unrestricted bids. On this (somewhat *ad hoc*) basis, I select action profiles $(v_2, v_2, b_3, \ldots, b_n)$ with $b_j \leq v_j$ for $j = 3, \ldots, n$ as "distinguished" equilibria of a first-price sealed-bid auction.

One conclusion of this analysis is that while both second-price and first-price auctions have many Nash equilibria, yielding a variety of outcomes, their distinguished equilibria yield the *same* outcome. (Recall that the distinguished equilibrium of a second-price sealed-bid auction is the action profile in which every player bids her valuation.) In every distinguished equilibrium of each game, the object is sold to player 1 at the price v_2. In particular, the auctioneer's revenue is the same in both cases. Thus if we restrict attention to the distinguished equilibria, the two auction forms are "revenue equivalent". The rules are different, but the players' equilibrium bids adjust to the difference and lead to the same outcome:

> the single Nash equilibrium in which no player's bid is weakly dominated in a second-price auction yields the same outcome as the distinguished equilibria of a first-price auction.

⊙ EXERCISE 88.1 (Third-price auction) Consider a *third*-price sealed-bid auction, which differs from a first- and a second-price auction only in that the winner (the person who submits the highest bid) pays the third highest price. (Assume that there are at least three bidders.)

    a. Show that for any player i the bid of v_i weakly dominates any lower bid but does not weakly dominate any higher bid. (To show the latter, for any bid $b_i > v_i$, find bids for the other players such that player i is better off bidding b_i than bidding v_i.)

    b. Show that the action profile in which each player bids her valuation is not a Nash equilibrium.

    c. Find a Nash equilibrium. (There are ones in which every player submits the same bid.)

3.5.4 Variants

Uncertain valuations   The models in this section depart from reality with respect to the assumption that each bidder is certain of both her own valuation and every other bidder's valuation. In most, if not all, actual auctions, information is surely less complete. The case in which the players are uncertain about each other's valuations has been thoroughly explored and is discussed in Section 9.6. The result that a player's bidding her valuation weakly dominates all her other actions in a second-price auction survives when players are uncertain about each other's valuations, as does the revenue equivalence of first- and second-price auctions under some conditions on the players' preferences.

Common valuations   In some auctions the main difference between the bidders is not that they value the object differently but that they have different information about its value. For example, the bidders for an oil tract who put similar values on any given amount of oil may have different information about how much oil is in the tract. Such auctions involve informational considerations that do not arise in the model we have studied in this section; they are studied in Section 9.6.3.

All-pay auctions   Some situations may be modeled as *all-pay auctions* in which *every* bidder, not only the winner, pays. An example is competition between lobby groups for government attention: each group spends resources in attempt to win favor; the one that spends the most is successful. (Other models that cast lobbying as an auction are considered on page 91.) You are asked to study both first- and second-price versions of an all-pay auction in the following exercise.

(?) EXERCISE 89.1 (All-pay auctions)   Consider variants of the sealed-bid auctions in Sections 3.5.2 and 3.5.3 in which *all* bidders pay the winning price. Show that for two bidders the variant of a second-price auction differs from the *War of Attrition* studied in Section 3.4 only in the payoffs when the players' bids are equal, a difference that does not affect the set of Nash equilibria. Show also that the variant of a first-price auction has no Nash equilibrium.

Multiunit auctions   In some auctions, like those for U.S. Treasury bills (short-term government bonds), many units of an object are available, and each bidder may value positively more than one unit. In each of the types of auction described in the following list, each bidder submits a bid for each unit of the good. That is, an action is a list of bids $(b^1, \ldots, b^k)$, where b^1 is the player's bid for the first unit of the good, b^2 is her bid for the second unit, and so on. The player who submits the highest bid for any given unit obtains that unit. The auctions differ in the prices paid by the winners. (The first type of auction generalizes a first-price auction, whereas the next two generalize a second-price auction.)

Discriminatory auction   The price paid for each unit is the winning bid for that unit.

Uniform-price auction   The price paid for each unit is the same, equal to the highest rejected bid among all the bids for all units.

Vickrey auction   A bidder who wins k objects pays the sum of the k highest rejected bids submitted by the *other* bidders.

The next exercise asks you to study these auctions when two units of an object are available.

⑦ EXERCISE 90.1 (Multiunit auctions) Two units of an object are available. There are n bidders. Bidder i values the first unit that she obtains at v_i and the second unit at w_i, where $v_i > w_i > 0$. Each bidder submits two bids; the two highest bids win. Retain the tie-breaking rule in the text. Show that in discriminatory and uniform-price auctions, player i's action of bidding v_i and w_i does not dominate all her other actions, whereas in a Vickrey auction it does. (In the case of a Vickrey auction, consider separately the cases in which the other players' bids are such that player i wins no units, one unit, and two units when her bids are v_i and w_i.)

Goods for which the demand exceeds the supply at the going price are sometimes sold to the people who are willing to wait longest in line. We can model such situations as multiunit auctions in which each person's bid is the amount of time she is willing to wait.

⑦ EXERCISE 90.2 (Waiting in line) Two hundred people are willing to wait in line to see a movie at a theater whose capacity is one hundred. Denote person i's valuation of the movie in excess of the price of admission, expressed in terms of the amount of time she is willing to wait, by v_i. That is, person i's payoff if she waits for t_i units of time is $v_i - t_i$. Each person attaches no value to a second ticket, and cannot buy tickets for other people. Assume that $v_1 > v_2 > \cdots > v_{200}$. Each person chooses an arrival time. If several people arrive at the same time, then their order in line is determined by their index (lower-numbered people go first). If a person arrives to find 100 or more people already in line, her payoff is zero. Model the situation as a variant of a discriminatory multiunit auction, in which each person submits a bid for only one unit, and find its Nash equilibria. (Look at your answer to Exercise 87.1 before seeking the Nash equilibria.) Arrival times for people at movies do not in general seem to conform with a Nash equilibrium. What feature missing from the model could explain the pattern of arrivals?

The next exercise is another application of a multiunit auction. As in the previous exercise each person wants to buy only one unit, but in this case the price paid by the winners is the highest losing bid.

⑦ EXERCISE 90.3 (Internet pricing) A proposal to deal with congestion on electronic message pathways is that each message should include a field stating an amount of money the sender is willing to pay for the message to be sent. Suppose that during some time interval, each of n people wants to send one message and the capacity of the pathway is k messages, with $k < n$. The k messages whose bids are highest are the ones sent, and each of the persons sending these messages pays a price equal to the $(k+1)$st highest bid. Model this situation as a multiunit auction. (Use the same tie-breaking rule as the one in the text.) Does a person's action of bidding the value of her message weakly dominate all her other actions? (Note that the auction differs from those considered in Exercise 90.1 because each person submits only one bid. Look at the argument in the text that in a second-price sealed-bid auction a player's action of bidding her value weakly dominates all her other actions.)

Lobbying as an auction   Variants of the models in this section can be used to understand some situations that are not explicitly auctions. An example, illustrated in the next exercise, is the competition between groups pressuring a government to follow certain policies. This exercise shows also that the outcome of an auction may depend significantly (and perhaps counterintuitively) on the form the auction takes.

? EXERCISE 91.1 (Lobbying as an auction) A government can pursue three policies, x, y, or z. The monetary values attached to these policies by two interest groups, A and B, are given in Figure 91.1. The government chooses a policy in response to the payments the interest groups make to it. Consider the following two mechanisms.

First-price auction   Each interest group chooses a policy and an amount of money it is willing to pay. The government chooses the policy proposed by the group willing to pay the most. This group makes its payment to the government, and the losing group makes no payment.

Menu auction   Each interest group states, for each policy, the amount it is willing to pay to have the government implement that policy. The government chooses the policy for which the sum of the payments the groups are willing to make is the highest, and *each* group pays the government the amount of money it is willing to pay for that policy.

In each case each interest group's payoff is the value it attaches to the policy implemented minus the payment it makes. Assume that a tie is broken by the government's choosing the policy, among those tied, whose name is first in the alphabet.

	x	y	z
Interest group A	0	3	-100
Interest group B	0	-100	3

Figure 91.1 The values of the interest groups for the policies x, y, and z in Exercise 91.1.

Show that the first-price auction has a Nash equilibrium in which lobby A says it will pay 103 for y, lobby B says it will pay 103 for z, and the government's revenue is 103. Show that the menu auction has a Nash equilibrium in which lobby A announces that it will pay 3 for x, 6 for y, and 0 for z, and lobby B announces that it will pay 3 for x, 0 for y, and 6 for z, and the government chooses x, obtaining a revenue of 6. (In each case the pair of actions given is in fact the unique equilibrium.)

3.6   Accident law

3.6.1   Introduction

In some situations, laws influence the participants' payoffs and hence their actions. For example, a law may provide for the victim of an accident to be compensated by a party who was at fault, and the size of the compensation may affect the care that each party takes. What laws can we expect to produce socially desirable outcomes? A game-theoretic analysis is useful in addressing this question.

3.6.2 The game

Consider the interaction between an *injurer* (player 1) and a *victim* (player 2). The victim suffers a loss that depends on the amounts of care taken by both her and the injurer. (How badly you hurt yourself when you fall down on the sidewalk in front of my house depends on both how well I have cleared the ice and how carefully you tread.) Denote by a_i the amount of care player i takes, measured in monetary terms, and by $L(a_1, a_2)$ the loss, also measured in monetary terms, suffered by the victim, as a function of the amounts of care. (In many cases the victim does not suffer a loss with certainty, but only with probability less than one. In such cases we can interpret $L(a_1, a_2)$ as the expected loss—the average loss suffered over many occurrences.) Assume that $L(a_1, a_2) > 0$ for all values of (a_1, a_2), and that more care taken by either player reduces the loss: L is decreasing in a_1 for any fixed value of a_2, and decreasing in a_2 for any fixed value of a_1.

A legal rule determines the fraction of the loss borne by the injurer, as a function of the amounts of care taken. Denote this fraction by $\rho(a_1, a_2)$. If $\rho(a_1, a_2) = 0$ for all (a_1, a_2), for example, the victim bears the entire loss, regardless of how much care she takes or how little care the injurer takes. At the other extreme, $\rho(a_1, a_2) = 1$ for all (a_1, a_2) means that the victim is fully compensated by the injurer no matter how careless she is or how careful the injurer is.

If the amounts of care are (a_1, a_2), then the injurer bears the cost a_1 of taking care and suffers the loss of $L(a_1, a_2)$, of which she bears the fraction $\rho(a_1, a_2)$. Thus the injurer's payoff is

$$-a_1 - \rho(a_1, a_2)L(a_1, a_2).$$

Similarly, the victim's payoff is

$$-a_2 - (1 - \rho(a_1, a_2))L(a_1, a_2).$$

For any given legal rule, embodied in ρ, we can model the interaction between the injurer and victim as the following strategic game.

Players The injurer and the victim.

Actions The set of actions of each player is the set of possible levels of care (nonnegative numbers).

Preferences The injurer's preferences are represented by the payoff function $-a_1 - \rho(a_1, a_2)L(a_1, a_2)$ and the victim's preferences are represented by the payoff function $-a_2 - (1 - \rho(a_1, a_2))L(a_1, a_2)$, where a_1 is the injurer's level of care and a_2 is the victim's level of care.

How do the equilibria of this game depend upon the legal rule? Do any legal rules lead to socially desirable equilibrium outcomes?

I restrict attention to a class of legal rules known as *negligence with contributory negligence*. (This class was established in the United States in the mid-19th century, and prevailed until the mid-1970s.) Each rule in this class requires the injurer to compensate the victim for a loss if and only if *both* the victim is sufficiently careful *and* the injurer is sufficiently careless; the required compensation is the total loss. Rules in the class differ in the standards of care they specify for each party. The rule that specifies the standards of care X_1 for the injurer and X_2 for the victim requires the injurer to pay the victim the entire loss $L(a_1, a_2)$ when $a_1 < X_1$ (the injurer is insufficiently careful) and $a_2 \geq X_2$ (the victim is sufficiently careful), and nothing otherwise. That is, under this rule the fraction $p(a_1, a_2)$ of the loss borne by the injurer is

$$p(a_1, a_2) = \begin{cases} 1 & \text{if } a_1 < X_1 \text{ and } a_2 \geq X_2 \\ 0 & \text{if } a_1 \geq X_1 \text{ or } a_2 < X_2. \end{cases}$$

Included in this class of rules are those for which X_1 is a positive finite number and $X_2 = 0$ (the injurer has to pay if she is not sufficiently careful, even if the victim takes no care at all), known as rules of *pure negligence*, and that for which X_1 is infinite and $X_2 = 0$ (the injurer has to pay regardless of how careful she is and how careless the victim is), known as the rule of *strict liability*.

3.6.3   Nash equilibrium

Suppose we decide that the pair $(\hat{a}_1, \hat{a}_2)$ of actions is socially desirable. We wish to answer the question: Are there values of X_1 and X_2 such that the game generated by the rule of negligence with contributory negligence for (X_1, X_2) has $(\hat{a}_1, \hat{a}_2)$ as its unique Nash equilibrium? If the answer is affirmative, then, assuming that the solution concept of Nash equilibrium is appropriate for the situation we are considering, we have found a legal rule that induces the socially desirable outcome.

Specifically, suppose that we select as socially desirable the pair $(\hat{a}_1, \hat{a}_2)$ of actions that maximizes the sum of the players' payoffs. That is,

$$(\hat{a}_1, \hat{a}_2) \text{ maximizes } -a_1 - a_2 - L(a_1, a_2).$$

(For some functions L, this pair $(\hat{a}_1, \hat{a}_2)$ may be a reasonable candidate for a socially desirable outcome; in other cases it may induce a very inequitable distribution of payoff between the players, and thus be an unlikely candidate.)

I claim that the unique Nash equilibrium of the game induced by the legal rule of negligence with contributory negligence for $(X_1, X_2) = (\hat{a}_1, \hat{a}_2)$ is $(\hat{a}_1, \hat{a}_2)$. That is, if the standards of care are equal to their socially desirable levels, then these are the levels chosen by an injurer and a victim in the only equilibrium of the game. The outcome is that the injurer pays no compensation: her level of care is $\hat{a}_1$, just high enough that $p(a_1, a_2) = 0$. At the same time the victim's level of care is $\hat{a}_2$,

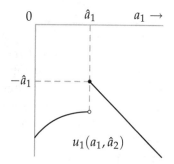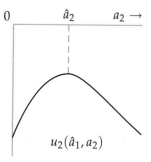

Figure 94.1 The left panel show the injurer's payoff as a function of her level of care a_1 when the victim's level of care is $a_2 = \hat{a}_2$ (see (94.1)). The right panel shows the victim's payoff as a function of her level of care a_2 when the injurer's level of care is $a_1 = \hat{a}_1$ (see (94.2)).

high enough that if the injurer reduces her level of care even slightly, then she has to pay full compensation.

I first argue that $(\hat{a}_1, \hat{a}_2)$ is *a* Nash equilibrium of the game, then show that it is the *only* equilibrium. To show that $(\hat{a}_1, \hat{a}_2)$ is a Nash equilibrium, I need to show that the injurer's action $\hat{a}_1$ is a best response to the victim's action $\hat{a}_2$ and *vice versa*.

Injurer's action Given that the victim's action is $\hat{a}_2$, the injurer has to pay compensation if and only if $a_1 < \hat{a}_1$. Thus the injurer's payoff is

$$u_1(a_1, \hat{a}_2) = \begin{cases} -a_1 - L(a_1, \hat{a}_2) & \text{if } a_1 < \hat{a}_1 \\ -a_1 & \text{if } a_1 \geq \hat{a}_1. \end{cases} \qquad (94.1)$$

For $a_1 = \hat{a}_1$, this payoff is $-\hat{a}_1$. If she takes more care than $\hat{a}_1$, she is worse off, because care is costly and, beyond $\hat{a}_1$, does not reduce her liability for compensation. If she takes less care, then, given the victim's level of care, she has to pay compensation, and we need to compare the money saved by taking less care with the size of the compensation. The argument is a little tricky. First, by definition,

$$(\hat{a}_1, \hat{a}_2) \text{ maximizes } -a_1 - a_2 - L(a_1, a_2).$$

Hence

$$\hat{a}_1 \text{ maximizes } -a_1 - \hat{a}_2 - L(a_1, \hat{a}_2)$$

(given $\hat{a}_2$). Because $\hat{a}_2$ is a constant, it follows that

$$\hat{a}_1 \text{ maximizes } -a_1 - L(a_1, \hat{a}_2).$$

But from (94.1) we see that $-a_1 - L(a_1, \hat{a}_2)$ is the injurer's payoff $u_1(a_1, \hat{a}_2)$ when her action is $a_1 < \hat{a}_1$ and the victim's action is $\hat{a}_2$. We conclude that the injurer's payoff takes a form like that in the left panel of Figure 94.1. In particular, $\hat{a}_1$ maximizes $u_1(a_1, \hat{a}_2)$, so that $\hat{a}_1$ is a best response to $\hat{a}_2$.

Victim's action Given that the injurer's action is $\hat{a}_1$, the victim never receives compensation. Thus her payoff is

$$u_2(\hat{a}_1, a_2) = -a_2 - L(\hat{a}_1, a_2). \qquad (94.2)$$

We can argue as we did for the injurer. By definition, $(\hat{a}_1, \hat{a}_2)$ maximizes $-a_1 - a_2 - L(a_1, a_2)$, so

$$\hat{a}_2 \text{ maximizes } -\hat{a}_1 - a_2 - L(\hat{a}_1, a_2)$$

(given $\hat{a}_1$). Because $\hat{a}_1$ is a constant, it follows that

$$\hat{a}_2 \text{ maximizes } -a_2 - L(\hat{a}_1, a_2), \tag{95.1}$$

which is the victim's payoff (see (94.2) and the right panel of Figure 94.1). That is, $\hat{a}_2$ maximizes $u_2(\hat{a}_1, a_2)$, so that $\hat{a}_2$ is a best response to $\hat{a}_1$.

We conclude that $(\hat{a}_1, \hat{a}_2)$ is a Nash equilibrium of the game induced by the legal rule of negligence with contributory negligence when the standards of care are $\hat{a}_1$ for the injurer and $\hat{a}_2$ for the victim.

To show that $(\hat{a}_1, \hat{a}_2)$ is the *only* Nash equilibrium of the game, first consider the injurer's best response function. Her payoff function is

$$u_1(a_1, a_2) = \begin{cases} -a_1 - L(a_1, a_2) & \text{if } a_1 < \hat{a}_1 \text{ and } a_2 \geq \hat{a}_2 \\ -a_1 & \text{if } a_1 \geq \hat{a}_1 \text{ or } a_2 < \hat{a}_2. \end{cases}$$

We can split the analysis into three cases, according to the victim's level of care.

$a_2 < \hat{a}_2$: In this case the injurer does not have to pay any compensation, regardless of her level of care; her payoff is $-a_1$, so that her best response is $a_1 = 0$.

$a_2 = \hat{a}_2$: In this case the injurer's best response is $\hat{a}_1$, as I argued when I showed that $(\hat{a}_1, \hat{a}_2)$ is a Nash equilibrium.

$a_2 > \hat{a}_2$: In this case the injurer's best response is at most $\hat{a}_1$, because her payoff for larger values of a_1 is equal to $-a_1$, a decreasing function of a_1.

We conclude that the injurer's best response function takes a form like that shown in the left panel of Figure 96.1.

Now, given that the injurer's best response to any value of a_2 is never greater than $\hat{a}_1$, in any equilibrium we have $a_1 \leq \hat{a}_1$: any point (a_1, a_2) at which the victim's best response function crosses the injurer's best response function must have $a_1 \leq \hat{a}_1$. (Draw a few possible best response functions for the victim in the left panel of Figure 96.1.) We know that the victim's best response to $\hat{a}_1$ is $\hat{a}_2$ (because $(\hat{a}_1, \hat{a}_2)$ is a Nash equilibrium), so we need to worry only about the victim's best responses to values of a_1 with $a_1 < \hat{a}_1$ (i.e. for cases in which the injurer takes insufficient care).

Let $a_1 < \hat{a}_1$. Then if the victim takes insufficient care she bears the loss; otherwise she is compensated for the loss, and hence bears only the cost a_2 of her taking care. Thus the victim's payoff is

$$u_2(a_1, a_2) = \begin{cases} -a_2 - L(a_1, a_2) & \text{if } a_2 < \hat{a}_2 \\ -a_2 & \text{if } a_2 \geq \hat{a}_2. \end{cases} \tag{95.2}$$

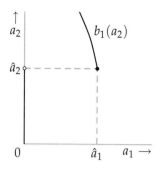 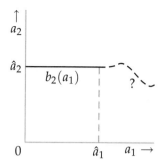

Figure 96.1 The players' best response functions under the rule of negligence with contributory negligence when $(X_1, X_2) = (\hat{a}_1, \hat{a}_2)$. The injurer's best response function b_1 is in the left panel. The victim's best response function b_2 is in the right panel. (The position of the victim's best response function for $a_1 > \hat{a}_1$ is not significant and is not determined in the text.)

Now, by (95.1) the level of care $\hat{a}_2$ maximizes $-a_2 - L(\hat{a}_1, a_2)$, so that

$$-a_2 - L(\hat{a}_1, a_2) \le -\hat{a}_2 - L(\hat{a}_1, \hat{a}_2) \text{ for all } a_2.$$

Further, the loss is nonnegative, so $-\hat{a}_2 - L(\hat{a}_1, \hat{a}_2) \le -\hat{a}_2$. We conclude that

$$-a_2 - L(\hat{a}_1, a_2) \le -\hat{a}_2 \text{ for all } a_2. \tag{96.1}$$

Finally, the loss increases as the injurer takes less care, so that given $a_1 < \hat{a}_1$ we have $L(a_1, a_2) > L(\hat{a}_1, a_2)$ for all a_2. Thus $-a_2 - L(a_1, a_2) < -a_2 - L(\hat{a}_1, a_2)$ for all a_2, and hence, using (96.1), we conclude that

$$-a_2 - L(a_1, a_2) < -\hat{a}_2 \text{ for all } a_2.$$

From (95.2) it follows that the victim's best response to any $a_1 < \hat{a}_1$ is $\hat{a}_2$, as shown in the right panel of Figure 96.1.

Combining the two best response functions, we see that $(\hat{a}_1, \hat{a}_2)$, the pair of levels of care that maximizes the sum of the players' payoffs, is the unique Nash equilibrium of the game. That is, the rule of negligence with contributory negligence for standards of care equal to $\hat{a}_1$ and $\hat{a}_2$ induces the players to choose these levels of care. If legislators can determine the values of $\hat{a}_1$ and $\hat{a}_2$, then by writing these levels into law they will induce a game that has as its unique Nash equilibrium the socially optimal actions.

Other standards also induce a pair of levels of care equal to $(\hat{a}_1, \hat{a}_2)$, as you are asked to show in the following exercise.

⑦ EXERCISE 96.2 (Alternative standards of care under negligence with contributory negligence) Show that $(\hat{a}_1, \hat{a}_2)$ is the unique Nash equilibrium for the rule of negligence with contributory negligence for any value of (X_1, X_2) for which *either* $X_1 = \hat{a}_1$ and $X_2 \le \hat{a}_2$ (including the pure negligence case of $X_2 = 0$), *or* $X_1 \ge M$ and $X_2 = \hat{a}_2$ for sufficiently large M. (Use the lines of argument in the text.)

? EXERCISE 97.1 (Equilibrium under strict liability) Study the Nash equilibrium (equilibria?) of the game studied in the text under the rule of strict liability, in which X_1 is infinite and $X_2 = 0$ (i.e. the injurer is liable for the loss no matter how careful she is and how careless the victim is). How are the equilibrium actions related to $\hat{a}_1$ and $\hat{a}_2$?

Notes

The model in Section 3.1 was developed by Cournot (1838). The model in Section 3.2 is widely credited to Bertrand (1883). The box on page 69 is based on Leonard (1994) and Magnan de Bornier (1992). The models are discussed in more detail by Shapiro (1989).

The model in Section 3.3 is due to Hotelling (1929) (though the focus of his paper is a model in which the players are firms that choose not only locations, but also prices). Downs (1957, especially Chapter 8) popularized Hotelling's model, using it to gain insights about electoral competition. Shepsle (1991) and Osborne (1995) survey work in the field.

The *War of Attrition* studied in Section 3.4 is due to Maynard Smith (1974); it is a variant of the *Dollar Auction* presented by Shubik (1971) (see Example 175.1).

Vickrey (1961) initiated the formal modeling of auctions, as studied in Section 3.5. The literature is surveyed by Wilson (1992). The box on page 81 draws on Herodotus' *Histories* (Book 1, paragraph 196; see, for example, Herodotus 1998, 86), Langdon (1994), Cassady (1967, Chapter 3), Shubik (1983), Andreau (1999, 38–39), the website www.eBay.com, Roth and Ockenfels (2002), and personal correspondence with Robin G. Osborne (on ancient Greece and Rome) and John H. Munro (on medieval Europe).

The model of accident law in Section 3.6 originated with Brown (1973) and Diamond (1974); the result about negligence with contributory negligence is due to Brown (1973, 340–341). The literature is surveyed by Benoît and Kornhauser (2002).

Novshek and Sonnenschein (1978) study, in a general setting, the issue addressed in Exercise 62.1. A brief summary of the early work on common property is given in the Notes to Chapter 2. The idea of the tie-breaking rule being determined by the equilibrium, used in Exercises 68.2 and 69.1, is due to Simon and Zame (1990). The result in Exercise 75.1 is due to Wittman (1977). Exercise 75.2 is based on Osborne and Slivinski (1996). The notion of a Condorcet winner defined in Exercise 75.3 is associated with Marie-Jean-Antoine-Nicolas de Caritat, marquis de Condorcet (1743–94), an early student of voting procedures. The game in Exercise 80.1 is a variant of a game studied by Blackwell and Girschick (1954, Example 5 in Chapter 2). It is an example of a *noisy duel* (which models the situation of duelists, each of whom chooses when to fire a single bullet, which her opponent hears, as she gradually approaches her rival). Duels were first modeled as games in the late 1940s by members of the RAND Corporation in the United States; see Karlin (1959b, Chapter 5). Exercise 91.1 is based on Boylan (2000). The situation considered in Exercise 90.2, in which people decide when to join a queue, is studied by Holt and Sherman (1982). Exercise 90.3 is based on MacKie-Mason and Varian (1995).

4 Mixed Strategy Equilibrium

4.1   Introduction   99
4.2   Strategic games in which players may randomize   106
4.3   Mixed strategy Nash equilibrium   107
4.4   Dominated actions   120
4.5   Pure equilibria when randomization is allowed   122
4.6   Illustration: expert diagnosis   123
4.7   Equilibrium in a single population   128
4.8   Illustration: reporting a crime   131
4.9   The formation of players' beliefs   134
4.10   Extension: finding all mixed strategy Nash equilibria   137
4.11   Extension: games in which each player has a
       continuum of actions   142
4.12   Appendix: representing preferences by
       expected payoffs   146
       Prerequisite: Chapter 2

4.1 Introduction

4.1.1 Stochastic steady states

A NASH EQUILIBRIUM of a strategic game is an action profile in which every player's action is optimal given every other player's action (Definition 23.1). Such an action profile corresponds to a steady state of the idealized situation in which for each player in the game there is a population of individuals, and whenever the game is played, one player is drawn randomly from each population (see Section 2.6). In a steady state, every player's behavior is the same whenever she plays the game, and no player wishes to change her behavior, knowing (from her experience) the other players' behavior. In a steady state in which each player's "behavior" is simply an action and within each population all players choose the same action, the outcome of every play of the game is the same Nash equilibrium.

More general notions of a steady state allow the players' choices to vary, as long as the pattern of choices remains constant. For example, different members of a given population may choose different actions, each player choosing the same action whenever she plays the game. Or each individual may, on each occasion she plays the game, choose her action probabilistically according to the same, unchanging distribution. These two more general notions of a steady state are equivalent: a steady state of the first type in which the fraction p of the population representing player i chooses the action a corresponds to a steady state of the second type in which each member of the population representing player i chooses a with probability p. In both cases, in each play of the game the probability that the individual in the role of player i chooses a is p. Both these notions of steady state are modeled by a mixed strategy Nash equilibrium, a generalization of the notion of Nash equilibrium. For expository convenience, in most of this chapter I interpret such an equilibrium as a model of the second type of steady state, in which each player chooses her actions probabilistically; such a steady state is called *stochastic* ("involving probability").

4.1.2 Example: Matching Pennies

An analysis of the game *Matching Pennies* (Example 19.1) illustrates the idea of a stochastic steady state. My discussion focuses on the outcomes of this game, given in Figure 100.1, rather than payoffs that represent the players' preferences, as before.

	Head	*Tail*
Head	$1, −$1	−$1, $1
Tail	−$1, $1	$1, −$1

Figure 100.1 The outcomes of *Matching Pennies*.

As we saw previously, this game has no Nash equilibrium: no pair of actions is compatible with a steady state in which each player's action is the same whenever the game is played. I claim, however, that the game has a *stochastic* steady state in which each player chooses each of her actions with probability $\frac{1}{2}$. To establish this result, I need to argue that if player 2 chooses each of her actions with probability $\frac{1}{2}$, then player 1 optimally chooses each of her actions with probability $\frac{1}{2}$, and vice versa.

Suppose that player 2 chooses each of her actions with probability $\frac{1}{2}$. If player 1 chooses *Head* with probability p and *Tail* with probability $1 − p$, then each outcome (*Head, Head*) and (*Head, Tail*) occurs with probability $\frac{1}{2}p$, and each outcome (*Tail, Head*) and (*Tail, Tail*) occurs with probability $\frac{1}{2}(1 − p)$. Thus the probability that the outcome is either (*Head, Head*) or (*Tail, Tail*), in which case player 1 gains $1, is $\frac{1}{2}p + \frac{1}{2}(1 − p)$, which is equal to $\frac{1}{2}$. In the other two outcomes, (*Head, Tail*) and (*Tail, Head*), she loses $1, so the probability of her losing $1 is also $\frac{1}{2}$. In particular, the probability distribution over outcomes is independent of p! Thus *every* value of p is optimal. In particular, player 1 can do no better than choose *Head* with probability $\frac{1}{2}$ and *Tail* with probability $\frac{1}{2}$. A similar analysis shows that player 2 optimally chooses each action with probability $\frac{1}{2}$ when player 1 does so. We conclude that the game has a stochastic steady state in which each player chooses each action with probability $\frac{1}{2}$.

I further claim that, under a reasonable assumption on the players' preferences, the game has no other steady state. This assumption is that each player wants the probability of her gaining \$1 to be as large as possible. More precisely, if $p > q$, then each player prefers to gain \$1 with probability p and lose \$1 with probability $1 - p$ than to gain \$1 with probability q and lose \$1 with probability $1 - q$.

To show that under this assumption there is no steady state in which the probability of each player's choosing *Head* is different from $\frac{1}{2}$, denote the probability with which player 2 chooses *Head* by q (so that she chooses *Tail* with probability $1 - q$). If player 1 chooses *Head* with probability p, then she gains \$1 with probability $pq + (1 - p)(1 - q)$ (the probability that the outcome is either (*Head*, *Head*) or (*Tail*, *Tail*)) and loses \$1 with probability $(1 - p)q + p(1 - q)$. The first probability is equal to $1 - q + p(2q - 1)$ and the second is equal to $q + p(1 - 2q)$. Thus if $q < \frac{1}{2}$ (player 2 chooses *Head* with probability less than $\frac{1}{2}$), the first probability is decreasing in p and the second is increasing in p, so that the lower is p, the better is the outcome for player 1; the value of p that induces the best probability distribution over outcomes for player 1 is 0. That is, if player 2 chooses *Head* with probability less than $\frac{1}{2}$, then the uniquely best policy for player 1 is to choose *Tail* with certainty. A similar argument shows that if player 2 chooses *Head* with probability greater than $\frac{1}{2}$, the uniquely best policy for player 1 is to choose *Head* with certainty.

Now, if player 1 chooses an action with certainty, a similar analysis leads to the conclusion that the optimal policy of player 2 is to choose an action with certainty (*Head* if player 1 chooses *Tail* and *Tail* if player 1 chooses *Head*).

We conclude that there is no steady state in which the probability that player 2 chooses *Head* differs from $\frac{1}{2}$. A symmetric argument shows that there is no steady state in which the probability that player 1 chooses *Head* differs from $\frac{1}{2}$. Thus in the only stochastic steady state each player chooses each action with probability $\frac{1}{2}$.

As discussed in the opening section (4.1.1), the stable pattern of behavior we have found can be alternatively interpreted as a steady state in which no player randomizes. Instead, half the players in the population of individuals who take the role of player 1 in the game choose *Head* whenever they play the game and half of them choose *Tail* whenever they play the game; similarly half of those who take the role of player 2 choose *Head* and half choose *Tail*. Given that the individuals involved in any given play of the game are chosen randomly from the populations, in each play of the game each individual faces with probability $\frac{1}{2}$ an opponent who chooses *Head*, and with probability $\frac{1}{2}$ an opponent who chooses *Tail*.

? EXERCISE 101.1 (*Variant of Matching Pennies*) Find the steady state(s) of the game that differs from *Matching Pennies* only in that the outcomes of (*Head*, *Head*) and of (*Tail*, *Tail*) are that player 1 gains \$2 and player 2 loses \$1.

4.1.3 Generalizing the analysis: expected payoffs

The fact that *Matching Pennies* has only two outcomes for each player (gain \$1, lose \$1) makes the analysis of a stochastic steady state particularly simple because it allows us to deduce, under a weak assumption, the players' preferences regarding *lotteries* (probability distributions) over outcomes from their preferences regarding deterministic outcomes (outcomes that occur with certainty). If a player prefers the deterministic outcome a to the deterministic outcome b, it is very plausible that if $p > q$, then she prefers the lottery in which a occurs with probability p (and b occurs with probability $1 - p$) to the lottery in which a occurs with probability q (and b occurs with probability $1 - q$).

In a game with more than two outcomes for some player, we cannot extrapolate in this way from preferences regarding deterministic outcomes to preferences regarding lotteries over outcomes. Suppose, for example, that a game has three possible outcomes, a, b, and c, and that a player prefers a to b to c. Does she prefer the deterministic outcome b to the lottery in which a and c each occur with probability $\frac{1}{2}$, or vice versa? The information about her preferences over deterministic outcomes gives us no clue about the answer to this question. She may prefer b to the lottery in which a and c each occur with probability $\frac{1}{2}$, or she may prefer this lottery to b; both preferences are consistent with her preferring a to b to c. To study her behavior when she is faced with choices between lotteries, we need to add to the model a description of her preferences regarding lotteries over outcomes.

A standard assumption in game theory restricts attention to preferences regarding lotteries over outcomes that may be represented by the expected value of a payoff function over deterministic outcomes. (See Section 17.6.3 if you are unfamiliar with the notion of "expected value".) That is, for every player i there is a payoff function u_i with the property that player i prefers one lottery over outcomes to another if and only if, according to u_i, the expected value of the first lottery exceeds the expected value of the second lottery.

For example, suppose that there are three outcomes, a, b, and c, and lottery P yields a with probability p_a, b with probability p_b, and c with probability p_c, whereas lottery Q yields these three outcomes with probabilities q_a, q_b, and q_c. Then the assumption is that for each player i there are numbers $u_i(a)$, $u_i(b)$, and $u_i(c)$ such that player i prefers lottery P to lottery Q if and only if $p_a u_i(a) + p_b u_i(b) + p_c u_i(c) > q_a u_i(a) + q_b u_i(b) + q_c u_i(c)$. (I discuss the representation of preferences by the expected value of a payoff function in more detail in Section 4.12, an appendix to this chapter.)

The first systematic investigation of preferences regarding lotteries represented by the expected value of a payoff function over deterministic outcomes was undertaken by von Neumann and Morgenstern (1944). Accordingly such preferences are called **vNM preferences**. A payoff function over deterministic outcomes (u_i in the previous paragraph) whose expected value represents such preferences is called a **Bernoulli payoff function** (in honor of Daniel Bernoulli (1700–1782), who appears to have been one of the first persons to use such a function to represent preferences).

The restrictions on preferences regarding deterministic outcomes required for them to be represented by a payoff function are relatively innocuous (see Section 1.2.2). The same is not true of the restrictions on preferences regarding lotteries over outcomes required for them to be represented by the expected value of a payoff function. (I do not discuss these restrictions, but the box at the end of this section gives an example of preferences that violate them.) Nevertheless, we obtain many insights from models that assume that preferences take this form; following standard game theory (and standard economic theory), I maintain the assumption throughout the book.

The assumption that a player's preferences are represented by the expected value of a payoff function does not restrict her attitudes to risk: a person whose preferences are represented by such a function may have an arbitrarily strong liking or dislike for risk.

Suppose, for example, that a, b, and c are three outcomes, and a person prefers a to b to c. If the person is very averse to risky outcomes, then she prefers to obtain b for sure rather than to face the lottery in which a occurs with probability p and c occurs with probability $1 - p$, even if p is relatively large. Such preferences may be represented by the expected value of a payoff function u for which $u(a)$ is close to $u(b)$, which is much larger than $u(c)$. For a case in which a, b, and c are numbers, such payoffs are illustrated in the left panel of Figure 103.1.

If the person is not at all averse to risky outcomes, then she prefers the lottery to the certain outcome b, even if p is relatively small. Such preferences are represented by the expected value of a payoff function u for which $u(a)$ is much larger than $u(b)$, which is close to $u(c)$. For a case in which a, b, and c are numbers, such payoffs are illustrated in the right panel of Figure 103.1. If $u(a) = 10$, $u(b) = 9$, and $u(c) = 0$, for example, then the person prefers the certain outcome b to any lottery between a and c that yields a with probability less than $\frac{9}{10}$. But if $u(a) = 10$, $u(b) = 1$, and $u(c) = 0$, she prefers any lottery between a and c that yields a with probability greater than $\frac{1}{10}$ to the certain outcome b.

Suppose that the outcomes are amounts of money, and a person's preferences are represented by the expected value of a payoff function in which the payoff of each outcome is equal to the amount of money involved. Then we say the person is *risk neutral*. Such a person compares lotteries according to the expected amount of

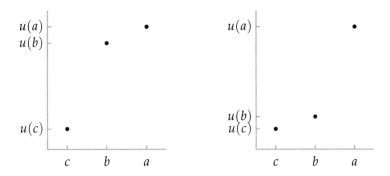

Figure 103.1 The Bernoulli payoffs for the outcomes a, b, and c for persons who prefer a to b to c and are very averse to risk (left panel) and not at all averse to risk (right panel).

money involved. (For example, she is indifferent between receiving $100 for sure and the lottery that yields $0 with probability $\frac{9}{10}$ and $1000 with probability $\frac{1}{10}$.) On the one hand, the fact that people buy insurance suggests that in some circumstances preferences are *risk averse*: people prefer to obtain $z with certainty than to receive the outcome of a lottery that yields $z on average. On the other hand, the fact that people buy lottery tickets that pay, on average, much less than their purchase price, suggests that in other circumstances preferences are *risk preferring*. In both cases, preferences over lotteries are not represented by expected *monetary* values, though they still may be represented by the expected value of a *payoff* function (in which the payoffs to outcome are different from the monetary values of the outcomes).

Any given preferences over deterministic outcomes are represented by many different payoff functions (see Section 1.2.2). The same is true of preferences over lotteries; the relation between payoff functions whose expected values represent the same preferences is discussed in Section 4.12.2 in the appendix to this chapter. In particular, we may choose arbitrary payoffs for the outcomes that are best and worst according to the preferences, as long as the payoff to the best outcome exceeds the payoff to the worst outcome. Suppose, for example, that there are three outcomes, a, b, and c, and a person prefers a to b to c, and is indifferent between b and the lottery that yields a with probability $\frac{1}{2}$ and c with probability $\frac{1}{2}$. Then we may choose $u(a) = 3$ and $u(c) = 1$, in which case $u(b) = 2$; or, for example, we may choose $u(a) = 10$ and $u(c) = 0$, in which case $u(b) = 5$, or $u(a) = 1$ and $u(c) = -1$, in which case $u(b) = 0$.

SOME EVIDENCE ON EXPECTED PAYOFF FUNCTIONS

Consider the following two lotteries (the first of which is, in fact, deterministic):

Lottery 1 You receive $2 million with certainty.

Lottery 2 You receive $10 million with probability 0.1, $2 million with probability 0.89, and nothing with probability 0.01.

Which do you prefer? Now consider two more lotteries:

Lottery 3 You receive $2 million with probability 0.11 and nothing with probability 0.89.

Lottery 4 You receive $10 million with probability 0.1 and nothing with probability 0.9.

Which do you prefer? A significant fraction of experimental subjects say they prefer lottery 1 to lottery 2, and lottery 4 to lottery 3. (See, for example, Conlisk 1989 and Camerer 1995, 622–623.)

These preferences cannot be represented by an expected payoff function! If they could be, there would exist a payoff function u for which the expected payoff of lottery 1 exceeds that of lottery 2:

$$u(2) > 0.1u(10) + 0.89u(2) + 0.01u(0),$$

where the amounts of money are expressed in millions. Subtracting $0.89u(2)$ and adding $0.89u(0)$ to each side we obtain

$$0.11u(2) + 0.89u(0) > 0.1u(10) + 0.9u(0).$$

But this inequality says that the expected payoff of lottery 3 exceeds that of lottery 4! Thus preferences represented by an expected payoff function that yield a preference for lottery 1 over lottery 2 must also yield a preference for lottery 3 over lottery 4.

Preferences represented by the expected value of a payoff function *are*, however, consistent with a person's being indifferent between lotteries 1 and 2, and between lotteries 3 and 4. Suppose we assume that when a person is almost indifferent between two lotteries, she may make a "mistake". Then a person's expressed preference for lottery 1 over lottery 2 and for lottery 4 over lottery 3 is not directly inconsistent with her preferences' being represented by the expected value of a payoff function in which she is almost indifferent between lotteries 1 and 2 and between lotteries 3 and 4. If, however, we add the assumption that mistakes are distributed symmetrically, then the frequency with which people express a preference for lottery 2 over lottery 1 and for lottery 4 over lottery 3 (also inconsistent with preferences represented by the expected value of a payoff function) should be similar to that with which people express a preference for lottery 1 over lottery 2 and for lottery 3 over lottery 4. In fact, however, the second pattern is significantly more common than the first (Conlisk 1989), so that a more significant modification of the theory is needed to explain the observations.

A limitation of the evidence is that it is based on the preferences expressed by people faced with *hypothetical* choices; understandably (given the amounts of money involved), no experiment has been run in which subjects were paid according to the lotteries they chose! Experiments with stakes consistent with normal research budgets show few choices inconsistent with preferences represented by the expected value of a payoff function (Conlisk 1989). This evidence, however, does not contradict the evidence based on hypothetical choices with large stakes: with larger stakes subjects might make choices in line with the preferences they express when asked about hypothetical choices.

In summary, the evidence for an inconsistency with preferences compatible with an expected payoff function is, at a minimum, suggestive. It has spurred the development of alternative theories. Nevertheless, the vast majority of models in game theory (and also in economics) that involve choice under uncertainty currently assume that each decision-maker's preferences are represented by the expected value of a payoff function. I maintain this assumption throughout the book, although many of the ideas I discuss appear not to depend on it.

4.2   Strategic games in which players may randomize

To study stochastic steady states, we extend the notion of a strategic game given in Definition 13.1 by endowing each player with vNM preferences about lotteries over the set of action profiles.

▶ DEFINITION 106.1 (*Strategic game with vNM preferences*) A **strategic game** (with vNM preferences) consists of

- a set of **players**
- for each player, a set of **actions**
- for each player, **preferences** regarding lotteries over action profiles that may be represented by the expected value of a ("Bernoulli") payoff function over action profiles.

A two-player strategic game with vNM preferences in which each player has finitely many actions may be presented in a table like those in Chapter 2. Such a table looks exactly the same as it did before, though the interpretation of the numbers in the boxes is different. In Chapter 2 these numbers are values of payoff functions that represent the players' preferences over deterministic outcomes; here they are the values of (Bernoulli) payoff functions whose expected values represent the players' preferences over lotteries.

Given the change in the interpretation of the payoffs, two tables that represent the same strategic game with ordinal preferences no longer necessarily represent the same strategic game with vNM preferences. For example, the two tables in Figure 107.1 represent the same game with ordinal preferences—namely the *Prisoner's Dilemma* (Section 2.2). In both cases the best outcome for each player is that in which she chooses F and the other player chooses Q, the next best outcome is (Q, Q), then comes (F, F), and the worst outcome is that in which she chooses Q and the other player chooses F. However, the tables represent *different* strategic games with vNM preferences. For example, in the table on the left, player 1's payoff to (Q, Q) is the *same* as her expected payoff to the lottery that yields (F, Q) with probability $\frac{1}{2}$ and (F, F) with probability $\frac{1}{2}$ ($\frac{1}{2}u_1(F, Q) + \frac{1}{2}u_1(F, F) = \frac{1}{2} \cdot 3 + \frac{1}{2} \cdot 1 = 2 = u_1(Q, Q)$), whereas in the table on the right, her payoff to (Q, Q) is *greater than* her expected payoff to this lottery ($3 > \frac{1}{2} \cdot 4 + \frac{1}{2} \cdot 1$). Thus the left-hand table represents a situation in which player 1 is indifferent between the deterministic outcome (Q, Q) and the lottery in which (F, Q) occurs with probability $\frac{1}{2}$ and (F, F) occurs with probability $\frac{1}{2}$. In the right-hand table, however, she prefers the deterministic outcome (Q, Q) to the lottery.

To show, as in this example, that two tables represent different strategic games with vNM preferences, we need only find a pair of lotteries whose expected payoffs are ordered differently by the two tables. To show that they represent the *same* strategic game with vNM preferences is more difficult; see Section 4.12.2.

② EXERCISE 106.2 (Extensions of *BoS* with vNM preferences) Construct a table of payoffs for a strategic game with vNM preferences in which the players' prefer-

	Q	F
Q	2,2	0,3
F	3,0	1,1

	Q	F
Q	3,3	0,4
F	4,0	1,1

Figure 107.1 Two tables that represent the same strategic game with ordinal preferences but different strategic games with vNM preferences.

ences over deterministic outcomes are the same as they are in *BoS* (Example 18.2), and their preferences over lotteries satisfy the following condition. Each player is indifferent between (*i*) going to her less preferred concert in the company of the other player, and (*ii*) the lottery in which with probability $\frac{1}{2}$ she and the other player go to different concerts and with probability $\frac{1}{2}$ they both go to her more preferred concert. Do the same in the case that each player is indifferent between (*i*) going to her less preferred concert in the company of the other player and (*ii*) the lottery in which with probability $\frac{3}{4}$ she and the other player go to different concerts and with probability $\frac{1}{4}$ they both go to her more preferred concert. (In each case set each player's payoff to the outcome that she least prefers equal to 0 and her payoff to the outcome that she most prefers equal to 2.)

Despite the importance of saying how the numbers in a payoff table should be interpreted, users of game theory sometimes fail to make the interpretation clear. When one interprets discussions of Nash equilibrium in the literature, a reasonably safe assumption is that if the players are not allowed to choose their actions randomly, then the numbers in payoff tables are payoffs that represent the players' ordinal preferences, whereas if the players are allowed to randomize, then the numbers are payoffs whose expected values represent the players' preferences regarding lotteries over outcomes.

4.3 Mixed strategy Nash equilibrium

4.3.1 Mixed strategies

In the generalization of the notion of Nash equilibrium that models a stochastic steady state of a strategic game with vNM preferences, we allow each player to choose a probability distribution over her set of actions rather than restricting her to choose a single deterministic action. We refer to such a probability distribution as a *mixed strategy*.

▶ DEFINITION 107.1 (*Mixed strategy*) A **mixed strategy** of a player in a strategic game is a probability distribution over the player's actions.

I usually use α to denote a profile of mixed strategies; $\alpha_i(a_i)$ is the probability assigned by player i's mixed strategy α_i to her action a_i. To specify a mixed strategy of player i we need to give the probability it assigns to each of player i's actions. For example, the strategy of player 1 in *Matching Pennies* that assigns probability $\frac{1}{2}$ to each action is the strategy α_1 for which $\alpha_1(Head) = \frac{1}{2}$ and $\alpha_1(Tail) = \frac{1}{2}$. Because this way of describing a mixed strategy is cumbersome, I often use a shorthand for a game that is presented in a table like those in Figure 107.1: I write a mixed strategy as a list of probabilities, one for each action, *in the order the actions are given in the table*. For example, the mixed strategy $(\frac{1}{3}, \frac{2}{3})$ for player 1 in either of the games in Figure 107.1 assigns probability $\frac{1}{3}$ to Q and probability $\frac{2}{3}$ to F.

A mixed strategy may assign probability 1 to a single action: by *allowing* a player to choose probability distributions, we do not prohibit her from choosing deterministic actions. We refer to such a mixed strategy as a **pure strategy**. Player i's choosing the pure strategy that assigns probability 1 to the action a_i is equivalent to her simply choosing the action a_i, and I denote this strategy simply by a_i.

4.3.2 Equilibrium

The notion of equilibrium that we study is called "mixed strategy Nash equilibrium". The idea behind it is the same as the idea behind the notion of Nash equilibrium for a game with ordinal preferences: a mixed strategy Nash equilibrium is a mixed strategy profile α^* with the property that no player i has a mixed strategy α_i such that she prefers the lottery over outcomes generated by the strategy profile $(\alpha_i, \alpha^*_{-i})$ to the lottery over outcomes generated by the strategy profile α^*. The following definition states this condition using payoff functions whose expected values represent the players' preferences.

▶ DEFINITION 108.1 (*Mixed strategy Nash equilibrium of strategic game with vNM preferences*) The mixed strategy profile α^* in a strategic game with vNM preferences is a **(mixed strategy) Nash equilibrium** if, for each player i and every mixed strategy α_i of player i, the expected payoff to player i of α^* is at least as large as the expected payoff to player i of $(\alpha_i, \alpha^*_{-i})$ according to a payoff function whose expected value represents player i's preferences over lotteries. Equivalently, for each player i,

$$U_i(\alpha^*) \geq U_i(\alpha_i, \alpha^*_{-i}) \text{ for every mixed strategy } \alpha_i \text{ of player } i, \qquad (108.2)$$

where $U_i(\alpha)$ is player i's expected payoff to the mixed strategy profile α.

The technique of constructing the players' best response functions (Section 2.8), useful in finding Nash equilibria of some strategic games with ordinal preferences, is useful too in finding mixed strategy Nash equilibria of some strategic games with vNM preferences, especially very simple ones. I discuss this technique in the next section. In Section 4.3.4 I discuss a characterization of mixed strategy Nash equilibrium that is an invaluable tool for studying the equilibria of any game.

4.3.3 Best response functions

General definition   As before, I denote player i's best response function by B_i. For a strategic game with ordinal preferences, $B_i(a_{-i})$ is the set of player i's best actions when the list of the other players' actions is a_{-i}. For a strategic game with vNM preferences, $B_i(\alpha_{-i})$ is the set of player i's best mixed strategies when the list of the other players' mixed strategies is α_{-i}. From the definition of a mixed strategy equilibrium, a profile α^* of mixed strategies is a mixed strategy Nash equilibrium if and only if every player's mixed strategy is a best response to the other players' mixed strategies (cf. Proposition 36.1):

> the mixed strategy profile α^* is a mixed strategy Nash equilibrium if and only if α_i^* is in $B_i(\alpha_{-i}^*)$ for every player i.

Two-player two-action games The analysis of *Matching Pennies* in Section 4.1.2 shows that each player's set of best responses to a mixed strategy of the other player is either a single pure strategy or the set of *all* mixed strategies. (For example, if player 2's mixed strategy assigns probability less than $\frac{1}{2}$ to *Head*, then player 1's unique best response is the pure strategy *Tail*, if player 2's mixed strategy assigns probability greater than $\frac{1}{2}$ to *Head*, then player 1's unique best response is the pure strategy *Head*, and if player 2's mixed strategy assigns probability $\frac{1}{2}$ to *Head*, then all of player 1's mixed strategies are best responses.)

The character of each player's set of best responses in any two-player game in which each player has two actions is similar to the character of each player's set of best responses in *Matching Pennies*: it consists either of a single pure strategy or of all mixed strategies. The reason lies in the form of the payoff functions.

Consider a two-player game in which each player has two actions, T and B for player 1 and L and R for player 2. Denote by u_i, for $i = 1, 2$, a Bernoulli payoff function for player i. (That is, u_i is a payoff function over action pairs whose expected value represents player i's preferences regarding lotteries over action pairs.) Player 1's mixed strategy α_1 assigns probability $\alpha_1(T)$ to her action T and probability $\alpha_1(B)$ to her action B (with $\alpha_1(T) + \alpha_1(B) = 1$). For convenience, let $p = \alpha_1(T)$, so that $\alpha_1(B) = 1 - p$. Similarly, denote the probability $\alpha_2(L)$ that player 2's mixed strategy assigns to L by q, so that $\alpha_2(R) = 1 - q$.

We take the players' choices to be independent, so that when the players use the mixed strategies α_1 and α_2, the probability of any action pair (a_1, a_2) is the product of the probability player 1's mixed strategy assigns to a_1 and the probability player 2's mixed strategy assigns to a_2. (See Section 17.6.2 in the mathematical appendix if you are not familiar with the idea of independence.) Thus the probability distribution generated by the mixed strategy pair (α_1, α_2) over the four possible outcomes of the game has the form given in Figure 109.1: (T, L) occurs with probability pq, (T, R) occurs with probability $p(1 - q)$, (B, L) occurs with probability $(1 - p)q$, and (B, R) occurs with probability $(1 - p)(1 - q)$.

	$L\ (q)$	$R\ (1-q)$
$T\ (p)$	pq	$p(1-q)$
$B\ (1-p)$	$(1-p)q$	$(1-p)(1-q)$

Figure 109.1 The probabilities of the four outcomes in a two-player two-action strategic game when player 1's mixed strategy is $(p, 1 - p)$ and player 2's mixed strategy is $(q, 1 - q)$.

From this probability distribution we see that player 1's expected payoff to the mixed strategy pair (α_1, α_2) is

$$pq \cdot u_1(T,L) + p(1-q) \cdot u_1(T,R) + (1-p)q \cdot u_1(B,L) + (1-p)(1-q) \cdot u_1(B,R),$$

which we can alternatively write as

$$p[q \cdot u_1(T,L) + (1-q) \cdot u_1(T,R)] + (1-p)[q \cdot u_1(B,L) + (1-q) \cdot u_1(B,R)].$$

The first term in square brackets is player 1's expected payoff when she uses a *pure* strategy that assigns probability 1 to T and player 2 uses her mixed strategy α_2; the second term in square brackets is player 1's expected payoff when she uses a *pure* strategy that assigns probability 1 to B and player 2 uses her mixed strategy α_2. Denote these two expected payoffs $E_1(T, \alpha_2)$ and $E_1(B, \alpha_2)$. Then player 1's expected payoff to the mixed strategy pair (α_1, α_2) is

$$pE_1(T, \alpha_2) + (1-p)E_1(B, \alpha_2).$$

That is, player 1's expected payoff to the mixed strategy pair (α_1, α_2) is a weighted average of her expected payoffs to T and B when player 2 uses the mixed strategy α_2, with weights equal to the probabilities assigned to T and B by α_1.

In particular, player 1's expected payoff, given player 2's mixed strategy, is an *linear* function of p—when plotted in a graph, it is a straight line.[1] A case in which $E_1(T, \alpha_2) > E_1(B, \alpha_2)$ is illustrated in Figure 110.1.

⑦ EXERCISE 110.1 (Expected payoffs) Construct diagrams like Figure 110.1 for *BoS* (Figure 19.1) and the game in the left panel of Figure 21.1 (in each case treating the numbers in the tables as Bernoulli payoffs). In each diagram, plot player 1's expected payoff as a function of the probability p that she assigns to her top action in three cases: when the probability q that player 2 assigns to her left action is 0, $\frac{1}{2}$, and 1.

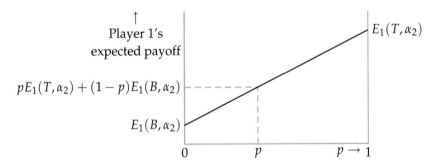

Figure 110.1 Player 1's expected payoff as a function of the probability p she assigns to T in the game in which her actions are T and B, when player 2's mixed strategy is α_2 and $E_1(T, \alpha_2) > E_1(B, \alpha_2)$.

---

[1]See Section 17.3 (in particular Figure 496.2) for my usage of the term "linear".

A significant implication of the linearity of player 1's expected payoff is that there are three possibilities for her best response to a given mixed strategy of player 2:

- player 1's unique best response is the pure strategy T (if $E_1(T, \alpha_2) > E_1(B, \alpha_2)$, as in Figure 110.1)

- player 1's unique best response is the pure strategy B (if $E_1(B, \alpha_2) > E_1(T, \alpha_2)$, in which case the line representing player 1's expected payoff as a function of p in the analogue of Figure 110.1 slopes down)

- all mixed strategies of player 1 yield the same expected payoff, and hence all are best responses (if $E_1(T, \alpha_2) = E_1(B, \alpha_2)$, in which case the line representing player 1's expected payoff as a function of p in the analogue of Figure 110.1 is horizontal).

In particular, a mixed strategy $(p, 1 - p)$ for which $0 < p < 1$ is never the *unique* best response; either it is not a best response or *all* mixed strategies are best responses.

⑦ EXERCISE 111.1 (Best responses) For each game and each value of q in Exercise 110.1, use the graphs you drew in that exercise to find player 1's set of best responses.

Example: Matching Pennies   The argument in Section 4.1.2 establishes that *Matching Pennies* has a unique mixed strategy Nash equilibrium, in which each player's mixed strategy assigns probability $\frac{1}{2}$ to *Head* and probability $\frac{1}{2}$ to *Tail*. I now describe an alternative route to this conclusion that uses the method described in Section 2.8.3, which involves explicitly constructing the players' best response functions; this method may be used in other games.

Represent each player's preferences by the expected value of a payoff function that assigns the payoff 1 to a gain of \$1 and the payoff -1 to a loss of \$1. The resulting strategic game with vNM preferences is shown in Figure 111.1.

	Head	*Tail*
Head	1, −1	−1, 1
Tail	−1, 1	1, −1

Figure 111.1 *Matching Pennies.*

Denote by p the probability that player 1's mixed strategy assigns to *Head*, and by q the probability that player 2's mixed strategy assigns to *Head*. Then, given player 2's mixed strategy, player 1's expected payoff to the pure strategy *Head* is

$$q \cdot 1 + (1 - q) \cdot (-1) = 2q - 1$$

and her expected payoff to *Tail* is

$$q \cdot (-1) + (1 - q) \cdot 1 = 1 - 2q.$$

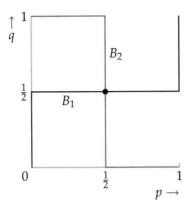

Figure 112.1 The players' best response functions in *Matching Pennies* (Figure 111.1) when randomization is allowed. The probabilities assigned by players 1 and 2 to *Head* are p and q, respectively. The best response function of player 1 is black and that of player 2 is gray. The disk indicates the unique Nash equilibrium.

Thus if $q < \frac{1}{2}$, then player 1's expected payoff to *Tail* exceeds her expected payoff to *Head*, and hence exceeds also her expected payoff to every mixed strategy that assigns a positive probability to *Head*. (Recall the discussion in the previous section.) Similarly, if $q > \frac{1}{2}$, then her expected payoff to *Head* exceeds her expected payoff to *Tail*, and hence exceeds her expected payoff to every mixed strategy that assigns a positive probability to *Tail*. If $q = \frac{1}{2}$, then both *Head* and *Tail*, and hence all her mixed strategies, yield the same expected payoff. We conclude that player 1's best responses to player 2's strategy are her mixed strategy that assigns probability 0 to *Head* if $q < \frac{1}{2}$, her mixed strategy that assigns probability 1 to *Head* if $q > \frac{1}{2}$, and all her mixed strategies if $q = \frac{1}{2}$. That is, denoting by $B_1(q)$ the set of probabilities player 1 assigns to *Head* in best responses to q, we have

$$B_1(q) = \begin{cases} \{0\} & \text{if } q < \frac{1}{2} \\ \{p : 0 \leq p \leq 1\} & \text{if } q = \frac{1}{2} \\ \{1\} & \text{if } q > \frac{1}{2}. \end{cases}$$

The best response function of player 2 is similar: $B_2(p) = \{1\}$ if $p < \frac{1}{2}$, $B_2(p) = \{q : 0 \leq q \leq 1\}$ if $p = \frac{1}{2}$, and $B_2(p) = \{0\}$ if $p > \frac{1}{2}$. Both players' best response functions are illustrated in Figure 112.1 (the best response function of player 1 is black and that of player 2 is gray).

The set of mixed strategy Nash equilibria of the game corresponds (as before) to the set of intersections of the best response functions in this figure; we see that there is one intersection, corresponding to the equilibrium we found previously, in which each player assigns probability $\frac{1}{2}$ to *Head*.

Matching Pennies has no Nash equilibrium if the players are not allowed to randomize. If a game has a Nash equilibrium when randomization is not allowed, is it possible that it has additional equilibria when randomization is allowed? The following example shows that the answer is positive.

$$
\begin{array}{c|cc}
 & B & S \\
\hline
B & 2,1 & 0,0 \\
S & 0,0 & 1,2 \\
\end{array}
$$

Figure 113.1 A version of the game *BoS* with vNM preferences.

Example: BoS   Consider the two-player game with vNM preferences in which the players' preferences over deterministic action profiles are the same as in *BoS* and their preferences over lotteries are represented by the expected value of the payoff functions specified in Figure 113.1. What are the mixed strategy equilibria of this game?

First construct player 1's best response function. Suppose that player 2 assigns probability q to B. Then player 1's expected payoff to B is $2 \cdot q + 0 \cdot (1 - q) = 2q$ and her expected payoff to S is $0 \cdot q + 1 \cdot (1 - q) = 1 - q$. Thus if $2q > 1 - q$, or $q > \frac{1}{3}$, then her unique best response is B, while if $q < \frac{1}{3}$, then her unique best response is S. If $q = \frac{1}{3}$, then both B and S, and hence all player 1's mixed strategies, yield the same expected payoffs, so that every mixed strategy is a best response. In summary, player 1's best response function is

$$
B_1(q) = \begin{cases} \{0\} & \text{if } q < \frac{1}{3} \\ \{p : 0 \le p \le 1\} & \text{if } q = \frac{1}{3} \\ \{1\} & \text{if } q > \frac{1}{3}. \end{cases}
$$

Similarly we can find player 2's best response function. The best response functions of both players are shown in Figure 113.2.

We see that the game has three mixed strategy Nash equilibria, in which $(p, q) = (0, 0)$, $(\frac{2}{3}, \frac{1}{3})$, and $(1, 1)$. The first and third equilibria correspond to the Nash equilibria of the ordinal version of the game when the players were not allowed to randomize (Section 2.7.2). The second equilibrium is new. In this equilibrium each

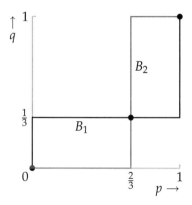

Figure 113.2 The players' best response functions in *BoS* (Figure 113.1) when randomization is allowed. The probabilities assigned by players 1 and 2 to B are p and q, respectively. The best response function of player 1 is black and that of player 2 is gray. The disks indicate the Nash equilibria (two pure, one mixed).

player chooses both B and S with positive probability (so that each of the four outcomes (B, B), (B, S), (S, B), and (S, S) occurs with positive probability).

? EXERCISE 114.1 (Mixed strategy equilibria of *Hawk–Dove*) Consider the two-player game with vNM preferences in which the players' preferences over deterministic action profiles are the same as in *Hawk–Dove* (Exercise 31.2) and their preferences over lotteries satisfy the following two conditions. Each player is indifferent between (*i*) the outcome (*Passive, Passive*) and (*ii*) the lottery that assigns probability $\frac{1}{2}$ to (*Aggressive, Aggressive*) and probability $\frac{1}{2}$ to the outcome in which she is aggressive and the other player is passive; each player is indifferent also between (*i*) the outcome in which she is passive and the other player is aggressive and (*ii*) the lottery that assigns probability $\frac{2}{3}$ to the outcome (*Aggressive, Aggressive*) and probability $\frac{1}{3}$ to the outcome (*Passive, Passive*). Find payoffs whose expected values represent these preferences (take each player's payoff to (*Aggressive, Aggressive*) to be 0 and each player's payoff to the outcome in which she is passive and the other player is aggressive to be 1). Find the mixed strategy Nash equilibrium of the resulting strategic game.

Both *Matching Pennies* and *BoS* have finitely many mixed strategy Nash equilibria: the players' best response functions intersect at a finite number of points (one for *Matching Pennies*, three for *BoS*). One of the games in the next exercise has a continuum of mixed strategy Nash equilibria because segments of the players' best response functions coincide.

? EXERCISE 114.2 (Games with mixed strategy equilibria) Find all the mixed strategy Nash equilibria of the strategic games in Figure 114.1.

? EXERCISE 114.3 (A coordination game) Two people can perform a task if, and only if, they both exert effort. They are both better off if they both exert effort and perform the task than if neither exerts effort (and nothing is accomplished); the worst outcome for each person is that she exerts effort and the other person does not (in which case again nothing is accomplished). Specifically, the players' preferences are represented by the expected value of the payoff functions in Figure 115.1, where c is a positive number less than 1 that can be interpreted as the cost of exerting effort. Find all the mixed strategy Nash equilibria of this game. How do the equilibria change as c increases? Explain the reasons for the changes.

? EXERCISE 114.4 (Swimming with sharks) You and a friend are spending two days at the beach; you both enjoy swimming. Each of you believes that with probabil-

	L	R
T	6,0	0,6
B	3,2	6,0

	L	R
T	0,1	0,2
B	2,2	0,1

Figure 114.1 Two strategic games with vNM preferences.

	No effort	Effort
No effort	$0,0$	$0,-c$
Effort	$-c,0$	$1-c,1-c$

Figure 115.1 The coordination game in Exercise 114.3.

ity π the water is infested with sharks. If sharks are present, a swimmer will surely be attacked. Each of you has preferences represented by the expected value of a payoff function that assigns $-c$ to being attacked by a shark, 0 to sitting on the beach, and 1 to a day's worth of undisturbed swimming (where $c > 0$!). If a swimmer is attacked by sharks on the first day, then you both deduce that a swimmer will surely be attacked the next day, and hence do not go swimming the next day. If at least one of you swims on the first day and is not attacked, then you both know that the water is shark-free. If neither of you swims on the first day, each of you retains the belief that the probability of the water's being infested is π, and hence on the second day swims if $-\pi c + 1 - \pi > 0$ and sits on the beach if $-\pi c + 1 - \pi < 0$, thus receiving an expected payoff of $\max\{-\pi c + 1 - \pi, 0\}$. Model this situation as a strategic game in which you and your friend each decide whether to go swimming on your first day at the beach. If, for example, you go swimming on the first day, you (and your friend, if she goes swimming) are attacked with probability π, in which case you stay out of the water on the second day; you (and your friend, if she goes swimming) swim undisturbed with probability $1 - \pi$, in which case you swim on the second day. Thus your expected payoff if you swim on the first day is $\pi(-c + 0) + (1 - \pi)(1 + 1) = -\pi c + 2(1 - \pi)$, independent of your friend's action. Find the mixed strategy Nash equilibria of the game (depending on c and π). Does the existence of a friend make it more or less likely that you decide to go swimming on the first day? (Penguins diving into water where seals may lurk are sometimes said to face the same dilemma; Court (1996) argues that they do not.)

4.3.4 A useful characterization of mixed strategy Nash equilibrium

The method we have used so far to study the set of mixed strategy Nash equilibria of a game involves constructing the players' best response functions. This method is useful in simple games, but is of limited use in more complicated ones. I now present a characterization of mixed strategy Nash equilibrium that is invaluable in the study of general games. The characterization gives us an easy way to check whether a mixed strategy profile is an equilibrium; it is also the basis of a procedure (described in Section 4.10) for finding all equilibria of a game.

The key point is an observation made in Section 4.3.3 for two-player two-action games: a player's expected payoff to a mixed strategy profile is a weighted average of her expected payoffs to her pure strategies, where the weight attached to each pure strategy is the probability assigned to that strategy by the player's mixed strategy. This property holds for any game (with any number of players) in which each player has finitely many actions. We can state it more precisely as follows.

> *A player's expected payoff to the mixed strategy profile α is a weighted aver-*
> *age of her expected payoffs to all mixed strategy profiles of the type (a_i, α_{-i}),*
> *where the weight attached to (a_i, α_{-i}) is the probability $\alpha_i(a_i)$ assigned to*
> *a_i by player i's mixed strategy α_i.* (116.1)

Symbolically we have

$$U_i(\alpha) = \sum_{a_i \in A_i} \alpha_i(a_i) E_i(a_i, \alpha_{-i}),$$

where A_i is player i's set of actions (pure strategies) and $E_i(a_i, \alpha_{-i})$ is (as before) her expected payoff when she uses the pure strategy that assigns probability 1 to a_i and every other player j uses her mixed strategy α_j. (See the end of Section 17.2 in the appendix on mathematics for an explanation of the $\sum$ notation.)

This property leads to a useful characterization of mixed strategy Nash equilibrium. Let α^* be a mixed strategy Nash equilibrium and denote by E_i^* player i's expected payoff in the equilibrium (i.e. $E_i^* = U_i(\alpha^*)$). Because α^* is an equilibrium, player i's expected payoff, given α_{-i}^*, to all her strategies, including all her pure strategies, is at most E_i^*. Now, by (116.1), E_i^* is a weighted average of player i's expected payoffs to the pure strategies to which α_i^* assigns positive probability. Thus player i's expected payoffs to these pure strategies are all equal to E_i^*. (If any were smaller, then the weighted average would be smaller.) We conclude that the expected payoff to each action to which α_i^* assigns positive probability is E_i^*, and the expected payoff to every other action is at most E_i^*. Conversely, if these conditions are satisfied for every player i, then α^* is a mixed strategy Nash equilibrium: the expected payoff to α_i^* is E_i^*, and the expected payoff to any other mixed strategy is at most E_i^*, because by (116.1) it is a weighted average of E_i^* and numbers that are at most E_i^*.

This argument establishes the following result.

■ PROPOSITION 116.2 (Characterization of mixed strategy Nash equilibrium of finite game) *A mixed strategy profile α^* in a strategic game with vNM preferences in which each player has finitely many actions is a mixed strategy Nash equilibrium if and only if, for each player i,*

- *the expected payoff, given α_{-i}^*, to every action to which α_i^* assigns positive probability is the same*

- *the expected payoff, given α_{-i}^*, to every action to which α_i^* assigns zero probability is at most the expected payoff to any action to which α_i^* assigns positive probability.*

Each player's expected payoff in an equilibrium is her expected payoff to any of her actions that she uses with positive probability.

The significance of this result is that it gives conditions for a mixed strategy Nash equilibrium in terms of each player's expected payoffs only to her *pure* strategies. For games in which each player has finitely many actions, it allows us easily

	$L\,(0)$	$C\,(\frac{1}{3})$	$R\,(\frac{2}{3})$
$T\,(\frac{3}{4})$	$\cdot,2$	$3,3$	$1,1$
$M\,(0)$	$\cdot,\cdot$	$0,\cdot$	$2,\cdot$
$B\,(\frac{1}{4})$	$\cdot,4$	$5,1$	$0,7$

Figure 117.1 A partially specified strategic game, illustrating a method of checking whether a mixed strategy profile is a mixed strategy Nash equilibrium. The dots indicate irrelevant payoffs.

to check whether a mixed strategy profile is an equilibrium. For example, in *BoS* (Section 4.3.3) the strategy pair $((\frac{2}{3},\frac{1}{3}),(\frac{1}{3},\frac{2}{3}))$ is a mixed strategy Nash equilibrium because given player 2's strategy $(\frac{1}{3},\frac{2}{3})$, player 1's expected payoffs to B and S are both equal to $\frac{2}{3}$, and given player 1's strategy $(\frac{2}{3},\frac{1}{3})$, player 2's expected payoffs to B and S are both equal to $\frac{2}{3}$.

The next example is slightly more complicated.

◆ EXAMPLE 117.1 (Checking whether a mixed strategy profile is a mixed strategy Nash equilibrium) I claim that for the game in Figure 117.1 (in which the dots indicate irrelevant payoffs), the indicated pair of strategies, $(\frac{3}{4},0,\frac{1}{4})$ for player 1 and $(0,\frac{1}{3},\frac{2}{3})$ for player 2, is a mixed strategy Nash equilibrium. To verify this claim, it suffices, by Proposition 116.2, to study each player's expected payoffs to her three pure strategies. For player 1 these payoffs are

$$T\ :\ \tfrac{1}{3}\cdot 3+\tfrac{2}{3}\cdot 1=\tfrac{5}{3}$$
$$M\ :\ \tfrac{1}{3}\cdot 0+\tfrac{2}{3}\cdot 2=\tfrac{4}{3}$$
$$B\ :\ \tfrac{1}{3}\cdot 5+\tfrac{2}{3}\cdot 0=\tfrac{5}{3}.$$

Player 1's mixed strategy assigns positive probability to T and B and probability zero to M, so the two conditions in Proposition 116.2 are satisfied for player 1. The expected payoff to each of player 2's pure strategies is $\frac{5}{2}$ ($\frac{3}{4}\cdot 2+\frac{1}{4}\cdot 4=\frac{3}{4}\cdot 3+\frac{1}{4}\cdot 1=\frac{3}{4}\cdot 1+\frac{1}{4}\cdot 7=\frac{5}{2}$), so the two conditions in Proposition 116.2 are satisfied also for her.

Note that the expected payoff to player 2's action L, which she uses with probability zero, is the *same* as the expected payoff to her other two actions. This equality is consistent with Proposition 116.2, the second part of which requires only that the expected payoffs to actions used with probability zero be *no greater than* the expected payoffs to actions used with positive probability (not that they necessarily be less). Note also that the fact that player 2's expected payoff to L is the same as her expected payoffs to C and R does *not* imply that the game has a mixed strategy Nash equilibrium in which player 2 uses L with positive probability—it may, or it may not, depending on the unspecified payoffs.

⑦ EXERCISE 117.2 (Choosing numbers) Players 1 and 2 each choose a positive integer up to K. If the players choose the same number, then player 2 pays \$1 to player 1; otherwise no payment is made. Each player's preferences are represented by her expected monetary payoff.

a. Show that the game has a mixed strategy Nash equilibrium in which each player chooses each positive integer up to K with probability $1/K$.

b. (More difficult.) Show that the game has no other mixed strategy Nash equilibria. (Deduce from the fact that player 1 assigns positive probability to some action k that player 2 must do so; then look at the implied restriction on player 1's equilibrium strategy.)

? EXERCISE 118.1 (Silverman's game) Each of two players chooses a positive integer. If player i's integer is greater than player j's integer and less than three times this integer, then player j pays \$1 to player i. If player i's integer is at least three times player j's integer, then player i pays \$1 to player j. If the integers are equal, no payment is made. Each player's preferences are represented by her expected monetary payoff. Show that the game has no Nash equilibrium in pure strategies and that the pair of mixed strategies in which each player chooses 1, 2, and 5 each with probability $\frac{1}{3}$ is a mixed strategy Nash equilibrium. (In fact, this pair of mixed strategies is the unique mixed strategy Nash equilibrium.) (You cannot appeal to Proposition 116.2 because the number of actions of each player is not finite. However, you can use the argument for the "if" part of this result.)

? EXERCISE 118.2 (Voter participation) Consider the game of voter participation in Exercise 34.2. Assume that $k \leq m$ and that each player's preferences are represented by the expectation of her payoffs given in Exercise 34.2. Show that there is a value of p between 0 and 1 such that the game has a mixed strategy Nash equilibrium in which every supporter of candidate A votes with probability p, k supporters of candidate B vote with certainty, and the remaining $m - k$ supporters of candidate B abstain. How do the probability p that a supporter of candidate A votes and the expected number of voters ("turnout") depend upon c? (Note that if every supporter of candidate A votes with probability p, then the probability that exactly $k - 1$ of them vote is $kp^{k-1}(1 - p)$.)

? EXERCISE 118.3 (Defending territory) General A is defending territory accessible by two mountain passes against an attack by General B. General A has three divisions at her disposal, and general B has two divisions. Each general allocates her divisions between the two passes. General A wins the battle at a pass if and only if she assigns at least as many divisions to the pass as does General B; she successfully defends her territory if and only if she wins the battle at both passes. Formulate this situation as a strategic game and find all its mixed strategy equilibria. (First argue that in every equilibrium B assigns probability zero to the action of allocating one division to each pass. Then argue that in any equilibrium she assigns probability $\frac{1}{2}$ to each of her other actions. Finally, find A's equilibrium strategies.) In an equilibrium, do the generals concentrate all their forces at one pass, or spread them out?

An implication of Proposition 116.2 is that a nondegenerate mixed strategy equilibrium (a mixed strategy equilibrium that is not also a pure strategy equilibrium) is never a *strict* Nash equilibrium: every player whose mixed strategy assigns positive probability to more than one action is indifferent between her equilibrium mixed strategy and every action to which this mixed strategy assigns positive probability.

Any equilibrium (in mixed strategies or not) that is not strict has less appeal than a strict equilibrium because some (or all) of the players lack a positive incentive to choose their equilibrium strategies, given the other players' behavior. There is no reason for them *not* to choose their equilibrium strategies, but at the same time there is no reason for them not to choose another strategy that is equally good. Many pure strategy equilibria—especially in complex games—are also not strict, but among mixed strategy equilibria the problem is pervasive.

Given that in a mixed strategy equilibrium no player has a positive incentive to choose her equilibrium strategy, what determines how she randomizes in equilibrium? From the examples studied in Section 4.3.3 (e.g. *Matching Pennies* and *BoS*) we see that a player's equilibrium mixed strategy in a two-player game keeps the *other* player indifferent between a set of her actions, so that *she* is willing to randomize. In the mixed strategy equilibrium of *BoS*, for example, player 1 chooses B with probability $\frac{2}{3}$ so that player 2 is indifferent between B and S, and hence is willing to choose each with positive probability. Note, however, that the theory is *not* that the players consciously choose their strategies with this goal in mind! Rather, the conditions for equilibrium are designed to ensure that it is consistent with a steady state. In *BoS*, for example, if player 1 chooses B with probability $\frac{2}{3}$ and player 2 chooses B with probability $\frac{1}{3}$, then neither player has any reason to change her action. We have not yet studied how a steady state might come about, but have rather simply looked for strategy profiles consistent with steady states. In Section 4.9 I briefly discuss some theories of how a steady state might be reached.

4.3.5 Existence of equilibrium in finite games

Every game we have examined has at least one mixed strategy Nash equilibrium. In fact, every game in which each player has *finitely* many actions has at least one such equilibrium.

■ PROPOSITION 119.1 (Existence of mixed strategy Nash equilibrium in finite games) *Every strategic game with vNM preferences in which each player has finitely many actions has a mixed strategy Nash equilibrium.*

This result is of no help in *finding* equilibria. But it is a useful fact: your quest for an equilibrium of a game in which each player has finitely many actions in principle may succeed! Note that the finiteness of the number of actions of each player is only *sufficient* for the existence of an equilibrium, not *necessary*; many games in which the players have infinitely many actions possess mixed strategy Nash equilibria. Note also that a player's strategy in a mixed strategy Nash equilibrium may assign probability 1 to a single action; if every player's strategy does so, then the equilibrium corresponds to a ("pure strategy") equilibrium of the associated game with ordinal preferences. Relatively advanced mathematical tools are needed to prove the result; see, for example, Osborne and Rubinstein (1994, 19–20).

4.4 Dominated actions

In a strategic game with ordinal preferences, one action of a player strictly dominates another action if it is superior, no matter what the other players do (see Definition 45.1). In a game with vNM preferences in which players may randomize, we extend this definition to allow an action to be dominated by a *mixed strategy*.

▶ DEFINITION 120.1 (*Strict domination*) In a strategic game with vNM preferences, player i's mixed strategy α_i **strictly dominates** her action a_i' if

$$U_i(\alpha_i, a_{-i}) > u_i(a_i', a_{-i}) \text{ for every list } a_{-i} \text{ of the other players' actions,}$$

where u_i is a payoff function whose expected value represents player i's preferences over lotteries and $U_i(\alpha_i, a_{-i})$ is player i's expected payoff under u_i when she uses the mixed strategy α_i and the actions chosen by the other players are given by a_{-i}. We say that the action a_i' is **strictly dominated**.

Figure 120.1 (in which only player 1's payoffs are given) shows that an action not strictly dominated by any pure strategy (i.e. is not strictly dominated in the sense of Definition 45.1) may be strictly dominated by a mixed strategy. The action T of player 1 is not strictly (or weakly) dominated by either M or B, but it is strictly dominated by the mixed strategy that assigns probability $\frac{1}{2}$ to M and probability $\frac{1}{2}$ to B, because if player 2 chooses L, then the mixed strategy yields player 1 the payoff of 2, whereas the action T yields her the payoff of 1, and if player 2 chooses R, then the mixed strategy yields player 1 the payoff of $\frac{3}{2}$, whereas the action T yields her the payoff of 1.

⑦ EXERCISE 120.2 (Strictly dominating mixed strategies) In Figure 120.1, the mixed strategy that assigns probability $\frac{1}{2}$ to M and probability $\frac{1}{2}$ to B is not the only mixed strategy that strictly dominates T. Find all the mixed strategies that do so.

⑦ EXERCISE 120.3 (Strict domination for mixed strategies) Determine whether each of the following statements is true or false. (*a*) A mixed strategy that assigns positive probability to a strictly dominated action is strictly dominated. (*b*) A mixed strategy that assigns positive probability only to actions that are not strictly dominated is not strictly dominated.

In a Nash equilibrium of a strategic game with ordinal preferences, no player uses a strictly dominated action (Section 2.9.1). I now argue that the same is true of

	L	R
T	1	1
M	4	0
B	0	3

Figure 120.1 Player 1's payoffs in a strategic game with vNM preferences. The action T of player 1 is strictly dominated by the mixed strategy that assigns probability $\frac{1}{2}$ to M and probability $\frac{1}{2}$ to B.

a mixed strategy Nash equilibrium of a strategic game with vNM preferences. In fact, I argue that a strictly dominated action is not a best response to any collection of mixed strategies of the other players.

Suppose that player i's action a_i' is strictly dominated by her mixed strategy α_i. Player i's expected payoff $U_i(\alpha_i, \alpha_{-i})$ when she uses the mixed strategy α_i and the other players use the mixed strategies α_{-i} is a weighted average of her payoffs $U_i(\alpha_i, a_{-i})$ as a_{-i} varies over all the collections of actions for the other players, with the weight on each a_{-i} equal to the probability with which it occurs when the other players' mixed strategies are α_{-i}. Player i's expected payoff when she uses the action a_i' and the other players use the mixed strategies α_{-i} is a similar weighted average; the weights are the same, but the terms take the form $u_i(a_i', a_{-i})$ rather than $U_i(\alpha_i, a_{-i})$. The fact that a_i' is strictly dominated by α_i means that $U_i(\alpha_i, a_{-i}) > u_i(a_i', a_{-i})$ for *every* collection a_{-i} of the other players' actions. Hence player i's expected payoff when she uses the mixed strategy α_i exceeds her expected payoff when she uses the action a_i', given α_{-i}. Consequently,

> a strictly dominated action is not used with positive probability in any mixed strategy Nash equilibrium.

Thus when looking for mixed strategy equilibria we can eliminate from consideration every strictly dominated action.

As before, we can define the notion of weak domination (see Definition 46.1).

▶ DEFINITION 121.1 (*Weak domination*) In a strategic game with vNM preferences, player i's mixed strategy α_i **weakly dominates** her action a_i' if

$$U_i(\alpha_i, a_{-i}) \geq u_i(a_i', a_{-i}) \text{ for every list } a_{-i} \text{ of the other players' actions}$$

and

$$U_i(\alpha_i, a_{-i}) > u_i(a_i', a_{-i}) \text{ for some list } a_{-i} \text{ of the other players' actions,}$$

where u_i is a payoff function whose expected value represents player i's preferences over lotteries and $U_i(\alpha_i, a_{-i})$ is player i's expected payoff under u_i when she uses the mixed strategy α_i and the actions chosen by the other players are given by a_{-i}. We say that the action a_i' is **weakly dominated**.

We saw that a weakly dominated action may be used in a Nash equilibrium (see Figure 47.2). Thus a weakly dominated action may be used with positive probability in a mixed strategy equilibrium, so that we *cannot* eliminate *weakly* dominated actions from consideration when finding mixed strategy equilibria.

? EXERCISE 121.2 (Eliminating dominated actions when finding equilibria) Find all the mixed strategy Nash equilibria of the game in Figure 122.1 by first eliminating any strictly dominated actions and then constructing the players' best response functions.

	L	M	R
T	2,2	0,3	1,2
B	3,1	1,0	0,2

Figure 122.1 The strategic game with vNM preferences in Exercise 121.2.

The fact that a player's strategy in a mixed strategy Nash equilibrium may be weakly dominated raises the question of whether a game necessarily has a mixed strategy Nash equilibrium in which no player's strategy is weakly dominated. The following result (which is not easy to prove) shows that the answer is affirmative for a finite game.

■ PROPOSITION 122.1 (Existence of mixed strategy Nash equilibrium with no weakly dominated strategies in finite games) *Every strategic game with vNM preferences in which each player has finitely many actions has a mixed strategy Nash equilibrium in which no player's strategy is weakly dominated.*

4.5 Pure equilibria when randomization is allowed

The analysis in Section 4.3.3 shows that the mixed strategy Nash equilibria of *BoS* in which each player's strategy is pure correspond precisely to the Nash equilibria of the version of the game (considered in Section 2.3) in which the players are not allowed to randomize. The same is true for a general game: equilibria when the players are not allowed to randomize remain equilibria when they are allowed to randomize, and any pure equilibria that exist when the players are allowed to randomize are equilibria when they are not allowed to randomize.

To establish this claim, let N be a set of players and let A_i, for each player i, be a set of actions. Consider the following two games.

G: the strategic game with ordinal preferences in which the set of players is N, the set of actions of each player i is A_i, and the preferences of each player i are represented by the payoff function u_i

G':   the strategic game with vNM preferences in which the set of players is N, the set of actions of each player i is A_i, and the preferences of each player i are represented by the expected value of u_i.

First I argue that any Nash equilibrium of G corresponds to a mixed strategy Nash equilibrium (in which each player's strategy is pure) of G'. Let a^* be a Nash equilibrium of G, and for each player i let α_i^* be the mixed strategy that assigns probability 1 to a_i^*. Since a^* is a Nash equilibrium of G, we know that in G' no player i has an action that yields her a payoff higher than does a_i^* when all the other players adhere to α_{-i}^*. Thus α^* satisfies the two conditions in Proposition 116.2, so that it is a mixed strategy equilibrium of G', establishing the following result.

■ PROPOSITION 122.2 (Pure strategy equilibria survive when randomization is allowed) *Let a^* be a Nash equilibrium of G and for each player i let α_i^* be the mixed strategy* *of player i that assigns probability one to the action a_i^*. Then α^* is a mixed strategy Nash equilibrium of G'.*

Next I argue that any mixed strategy Nash equilibrium of G' in which each player's strategy is pure corresponds to a Nash equilibrium of G. Let α^* be a mixed strategy Nash equilibrium of G' in which every player's mixed strategy is pure; for each player i, denote by a_i^* the action to which α_i assigns probability one. Then no mixed strategy of player i yields her a payoff higher than does α_i^* when the other players' mixed strategies are given by α_{-i}^*. Hence, in particular, no *pure* strategy of player i yields her a payoff higher than does α_i^*. Thus a^* is a Nash equilibrium of G. In words, if a pure strategy is optimal for a player when she is allowed to randomize, then it remains optimal when she is prohibited from randomizing. (More generally, prohibiting a decision-maker from taking an action that is not optimal does not change the set of actions that are optimal.)

■ PROPOSITION 123.1 (Pure strategy equilibria survive when randomization is prohibited) *Let α^* be a mixed strategy Nash equilibrium of G' in which the mixed strategy of each player i assigns probability one to the single action a_i^*. Then a^* is a Nash equilibrium of G.*

4.6 Illustration: expert diagnosis

I seem to confront the following predicament all too frequently. Something about which I am relatively ill informed (my car, my computer, my body) stops working properly. I consult an expert, who makes a diagnosis and recommends an action. I am not sure that the diagnosis is correct—the expert, after all, has an interest in selling her services. I have to decide whether to follow the expert's advice or to try to fix the problem myself, put up with it, or consult another expert.

4.6.1 Model

A simple model that captures the main features of this situation starts with the assumption that there are two types of problem, *major* and *minor*. Denote the fraction of problems that are major by r, and assume that $0 < r < 1$. An expert knows, on seeing a problem, whether it is *major* or *minor*; a consumer knows only the probability r. (The diagnosis is costly neither to the expert nor to the consumer.) An expert may recommend either a major or a minor repair (regardless of the true nature of the problem), and a consumer may either accept the expert's recommendation or seek another remedy. A major repair fixes both a major problem and a minor one.

Assume that a consumer always accepts an expert's advice to obtain a minor repair—there is no reason for her to doubt such a diagnosis—but may either accept or reject advice to obtain a major repair. Further assume that an expert always recommends a major repair for a major problem—a minor repair does not fix a major problem, so there is no point in an expert's recommending one for a major problem—but may recommend either repair for a minor problem. Suppose that an expert obtains the same profit $\pi > 0$ (per unit of time) from selling a minor repair to a consumer with a minor problem as she does from selling a major repair to a consumer with a major problem, but obtains the profit $\pi' > \pi$ from selling a major repair to a consumer with a minor problem. (The rationale is that in the last case the expert does not in fact perform a major repair, at least not in its entirety.) A consumer pays an expert E for a major repair and $I < E$ for a minor one; the cost she effectively bears if she chooses some other remedy is $E' > E$ if her problem is major and $I' > I$ if it is minor. (Perhaps she consults other experts before proceeding, or works on the problem herself, in either case spending valuable time.) I assume throughout that $E > I'$.

Under these assumptions we can model the situation as a strategic game in which the expert has two actions (recommend a minor repair for a minor problem; recommend a major repair for a minor problem), and the consumer has two actions (accept the recommendation of a major repair; reject the recommendation of a major repair). I name the actions as follows.

Expert *Honest* (recommend a minor repair for a minor problem and a major repair for a major problem) and *Dishonest* (recommend a major repair for both types of problem).

Consumer *Accept* (buy whatever repair the expert recommends) and *Reject* (buy a minor repair but seek some other remedy if a major repair is recommended)

Assume that each player's preferences are represented by the player's expected monetary payoff. Then the players' payoffs to the four action pairs are as follows (the strategic game is given in Figure 125.1).

(H, A): With probability r the consumer's problem is major, so she pays E, and with probability $1 - r$ it is minor, so she pays I. Thus her expected payoff is $-rE - (1 - r)I$. The expert's profit is π.

(D, A): The consumer's payoff is $-E$. The consumer's problem is major with probability r, yielding the expert π, and minor with probability $1 - r$, yielding the expert π', so that the expert's expected payoff is $r\pi + (1 - r)\pi'$.

(H, R): The consumer's cost is E' if her problem is major (in which case she rejects the expert's advice to get a major repair) and I if her problem is minor, so that her expected payoff is $-rE' - (1 - r)I$. The expert obtains a payoff only if the consumer's problem is minor, in which case she gets π; thus her expected payoff is $(1 - r)\pi$.

(D, R): The consumer never accepts the expert's advice, and thus obtains the expected payoff $-rE' - (1 - r)I'$. The expert does not get any business, and thus obtains the payoff of 0.

		Consumer	
		Accept (q)	*Reject (1 − q)*
Expert	*Honest (p)*	$\pi, -rE - (1-r)I$	$(1-r)\pi, -rE' - (1-r)I$
	Dishonest (1 − p)	$r\pi + (1-r)\pi', -E$	$0, -rE' - (1-r)I'$

Figure 125.1 A game between an expert and a consumer with a problem.

4.6.2 Nash equilibrium

To find the Nash equilibria of the game we can construct the best response functions, as before. Denote by p the probability the expert assigns to H and by q the probability the consumer assigns to A.

Expert's best response function If $q = 0$ (i.e. the consumer chooses R with probability one), then the expert's best response is $p = 1$ (since $(1-r)\pi > 0$). If $q = 1$ (i.e. the consumer chooses A with probability one), then the expert's best response is $p = 0$ (since $\pi' > \pi$, so that $r\pi + (1-r)\pi' > \pi$). For what value of q is the expert indifferent between H and D? Given q, the expert's expected payoff to H is $q\pi + (1-q)(1-r)\pi$ and her expected payoff to D is $q[r\pi + (1-r)\pi']$, so she is indifferent between the two actions if

$$q\pi + (1-q)(1-r)\pi = q[r\pi + (1-r)\pi'].$$

Upon simplification, this yields $q = \pi/\pi'$. We conclude that the expert's best response function takes the form shown in both panels of Figure 126.1.

Consumer's best response function If $p = 0$ (i.e. the expert chooses D with probability one), then the consumer's best response depends on the relative sizes of E and $rE' + (1-r)I'$. If $E < rE' + (1-r)I'$, then the consumer's best response is $q = 1$, whereas if $E > rE' + (1-r)I'$, then her best response is $q = 0$; if $E = rE' + (1-r)I'$, then she is indifferent between R and A.

If $p = 1$ (i.e. the expert chooses H with probability one), then the consumer's best response is $q = 1$ (given $E < E'$).

We conclude that if $E < rE' + (1-r)I'$, then the consumer's best response to every value of p is $q = 1$, as shown in the left panel of Figure 126.1. If $E > rE' + (1-r)I'$, then the consumer is indifferent between A and R if

$$p[rE + (1-r)I] + (1-p)E = p[rE' + (1-r)I] + (1-p)[rE' + (1-r)I'],$$

which reduces to

$$p = \frac{E - [rE' + (1-r)I']}{(1-r)(E-I')}.$$

In this case the consumer's best response function takes the form shown in the right panel of Figure 126.1.

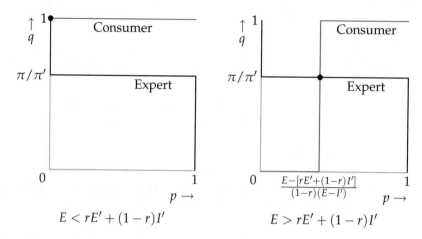

Figure 126.1 The players' best response functions in the game of expert diagnosis. The probability assigned by the expert to H is p and the probability assigned by the consumer to A is q.

Equilibrium   Given the best response functions, if $E < rE' + (1-r)I'$, then the pair of pure strategies (D, A) is the unique Nash equilibrium. The condition $E < rE' + (1-r)I'$ says that the cost of a major repair by an expert is less than the *expected* cost of an alternative remedy; the only equilibrium yields the dismal outcome for the consumer in which the expert is always dishonest and the consumer always accepts her advice.

If $E > rE' + (1-r)I'$, then the unique equilibrium of the game is in mixed strategies, with $(p, q) = (p^*, q^*)$, where

$$p^* = \frac{E - [rE' + (1-r)I']}{(1-r)(E - I')} \quad \text{and} \quad q^* = \frac{\pi}{\pi'}.$$

In this equilibrium the expert is sometimes honest, sometimes dishonest, and the consumer sometimes accepts her advice to obtain a major repair and sometimes ignores such advice.

As discussed in the introduction to the chapter, a mixed strategy equilibrium can be given more than one interpretation as a steady state. In the game we are studying, and the games studied earlier in the chapter, I have focused on the interpretation in which each player chooses her action randomly, with probabilities given by her equilibrium mixed strategy, every time she plays the game. In the game of expert diagnosis a different interpretation fits well: among the population of individuals who may play the role of each given player, every individual chooses the same action whenever she plays the game, but different individuals choose different actions; the fraction of individuals who choose each action is equal to the equilibrium probability that that action is used in a mixed strategy equilibrium. Specifically, if $E > rE' + (1-r)I'$, then the fraction p^* of experts is honest (recommending minor repairs for minor problems) and the fraction $1 - p^*$ is dishonest (recommending major repairs for minor problems), while the fraction q^* of consumers is credulous (accepting any recommendation) and the fraction $1 - q^*$ is wary (accepting only a recommendation of a minor repair). Honest and dishonest experts obtain the same expected payoff, as do credulous and wary consumers.

? EXERCISE 127.1 (Equilibrium in the expert diagnosis game) Find the set of mixed strategy Nash equilibria of the game when $E = rE' + (1 - r)I'$.

4.6.3 Properties of the mixed strategy Nash equilibrium

Studying how the equilibrium is affected by changes in the parameters of the model helps us understand the nature of the strategic interaction between the players. I consider the effects of three changes.

Suppose that major problems become less common (cars become more reliable, more resources are devoted to preventive health care). If we rearrange the expression for p^* to

$$p^* = 1 - \frac{r(E' - E)}{(1 - r)(E - I')},$$

we see that p^* increases as r decreases (the numerator of the fraction decreases and the denominator increases). Thus in a mixed strategy equilibrium, the experts are more honest when major problems are less common. Intuitively, if a major problem is less likely, a consumer has less to lose from ignoring an expert's advice, so the probability of an expert's being honest has to rise for her advice to be heeded. The value of q^* is not affected by the change in r: the probability of a consumer's accepting an expert's advice remains the same when major problems become less common. *Given* the expert's behavior, a decrease in r increases the consumer's payoff to rejecting the expert's advice more than it increases her payoff to accepting this advice, so that she prefers to reject the advice. But this partial analysis is misleading: in the equilibrium that exists after r decreases, the consumer is exactly as likely to accept the expert's advice as she was before the change.

Now suppose that major repairs become less expensive relative to minor ones (technological advances reduce the cost of complex equipment). We see that p^* decreases as E decreases (with E' and I' constant): when major repairs are less costly, experts are less honest. As major repairs become less costly, a consumer has more potentially to lose from ignoring an expert's advice, so that she heeds the advice even if experts are less likely to be honest.

Finally, suppose that the profit π' from an expert's fixing a minor problem with an alleged major repair falls (the government requires experts to return replaced parts to the consumer, making it more difficult for an expert to fraudulently claim to have performed a major repair). Then q^* increases—consumers become less wary. Experts have less to gain from acting dishonestly, so that consumers can be more confident of their advice.

? EXERCISE 127.2 (Incompetent experts) Consider a (realistic?) variant of the model, in which the experts are not entirely competent. Assume that each expert always correctly recognizes a major problem but correctly recognizes a minor problem with probability $s < 1$: with probability $1 - s$ she mistakenly thinks that a minor problem is major, and, if the consumer accepts her advice, performs a major repair and obtains the profit π. Maintain the assumption that each consumer believes (correctly) that the probability her problem is major is r, and assume that a consumer who does not give the job of fixing her problem to an expert bears the cost E' if it is major and I' if it is minor.

Suppose, for example, that an expert is honest and a consumer rejects advice to obtain a major repair. With probability r the consumer's problem is major, so that the expert recommends a major repair, which the consumer rejects; the consumer bears the cost E'. With probability $1 - r$ the consumer's problem is minor. In this case with probability s the expert correctly diagnoses it as minor, and the consumer accepts her advice and pays I; with probability $1 - s$ the expert diagnoses it as major, and the consumer rejects her advice and bears the cost I'. Thus the consumer's expected payoff in this case is $-rE' - (1 - r)[sI + (1 - s)I']$.

Construct the payoffs for every pair of actions and find the mixed strategy equilibrium in the case $E > rE' + (1 - r)I'$. Does incompetence breed dishonesty? More wary consumers?

⁇ EXERCISE 128.1 (Choosing a seller) Each of two sellers has available one indivisible unit of a good. Seller 1 posts the price p_1 and seller 2 posts the price p_2. Each of two buyers would like to obtain one unit of the good; they simultaneously decide which seller to approach. If both buyers approach the same seller, each trades with probability $\frac{1}{2}$; the disappointed buyer does not subsequently have the option to trade with the other seller. (This assumption models the risk faced by a buyer that a good is sold out when she patronizes a seller with a low price.) Each buyer's preferences are represented by the expected value of a payoff function that assigns the payoff 0 to not trading and the payoff $1 - p$ to purchasing one unit of the good at the price p. (Neither buyer values more than one unit.) For any pair (p_1, p_2) of prices with $0 \leq p_i \leq 1$ for $i = 1, 2$, find the Nash equilibria (in pure and in mixed strategies) of the strategic game that models this situation. (There are three main cases: $p_2 < 2p_1 - 1$, $2p_1 - 1 < p_2 < \frac{1}{2}(1 + p_1)$, and $p_2 > \frac{1}{2}(1 + p_1)$.)

4.7 Equilibrium in a single population

In Section 2.10 I discussed deterministic steady states in situations in which the members of a single population interact. I now discuss stochastic steady states in such situations.

First extend the definitions of a symmetric strategic game and a symmetric Nash equilibrium (Definitions 51.1 and 52.1) to a game with vNM preferences. Recall that a two-player strategic game with ordinal preferences is symmetric if each player has the same set of actions and each player's evaluation of an outcome depends only on her action and that of her opponent, not on whether she is player 1 or player 2. A symmetric game with vNM preferences satisfies the same conditions; its definition differs from Definition 51.1 only because a player's evaluation of an outcome is given by her expected payoff rather than her ordinal preferences.

	Left	*Right*
Left	1, 1	0, 0
Right	0, 0	1, 1

Figure 129.1 Approaching pedestrians.

▶ DEFINITION 129.1 (*Symmetric two-player strategic game with vNM preferences*) A two-player strategic game with vNM preferences is **symmetric** if the players' sets of actions are the same and the players' preferences are represented by the expected values of payoff functions u_1 and u_2 for which $u_1(a_1, a_2) = u_2(a_2, a_1)$ for every action pair (a_1, a_2).

A Nash equilibrium of a strategic game with ordinal preferences in which every player's set of actions is the same is symmetric if all players take the same action. This notion of equilibrium extends naturally to strategic games with vNM preferences. (As before, it does not depend on the game's having only two players, so I define it for a game with any number of players.)

▶ DEFINITION 129.2 (*Symmetric mixed strategy Nash equilibrium*) A profile α^* of mixed strategies in a strategic game with vNM preferences in which each player has the same set of actions is a **symmetric mixed strategy Nash equilibrium** if it is a mixed strategy Nash equilibrium and α_i^* is the same for every player i.

Now consider again the game of approaching pedestrians (Figure 52.1, reproduced in Figure 129.1), interpreting the payoff numbers as Bernoulli payoffs whose expected values represent the players' preferences over lotteries. We found that this game has two deterministic steady states, corresponding to the two symmetric Nash equilibria in pure strategies, (*Left, Left*) and (*Right, Right*). The game also has a symmetric mixed strategy Nash equilibrium, in which each player assigns probability $\frac{1}{2}$ to *Left* and probability $\frac{1}{2}$ to *Right*. This equilibrium corresponds to a steady state in which half of all encounters result in collisions! (Player 1 chooses *Left* and player 2 chooses *Right* with probability $\frac{1}{4}$, and player 1 chooses *Right* and player 2 chooses *Left* with probability $\frac{1}{4}$.)

In this example not only is the game symmetric, but the players' interests coincide. The game in Figure 129.2 is symmetric, but the players prefer to take different actions rather than the same actions. This game has no pure symmetric equilibrium, but has a symmetric mixed strategy equilibrium, in which each player chooses each action with probability $\frac{1}{2}$.

These examples show that a symmetric game may have no symmetric *pure* strategy equilibrium. But both games have a symmetric mixed strategy Nash

	X	Y
X	0, 0	1, 1
Y	1, 1	0, 0

Figure 129.2 A symmetric game.

	Stop	Continue
Stop	1, 1	$1 - \epsilon, 2$
Continue	$2, 1 - \epsilon$	0, 0

Figure 130.1 The game in Exercise 130.2.

equilibrium, as does any symmetric game in which each player has finitely many actions, by the following result (the proof of which requires relatively advanced mathematical tools).

■ PROPOSITION 130.1 (Existence of symmetric mixed strategy Nash equilibrium in symmetric finite games) *Every strategic game with vNM preferences in which each player has the same finite set of actions has a symmetric mixed strategy Nash equilibrium.*

? EXERCISE 130.2 (Approaching cars) Members of a single population of car drivers are randomly matched in pairs when they simultaneously approach intersections from different directions. In each interaction, each driver can either stop or continue. The drivers' preferences are represented by the expected value of the payoff functions given in Figure 130.1; the parameter ϵ, with $0 < \epsilon < 1$, reflects the fact that each driver dislikes being the only one to stop. Find the symmetric Nash equilibrium (equilibria?) of the game (find both the equilibrium strategies and the equilibrium payoffs).

Now suppose that drivers are (re)educated to feel guilty about choosing *Continue*, with the consequence that their payoffs when choosing *Continue* fall by $\delta > 0$. That is, the entry $(2, 1 - \epsilon)$ in Figure 130.1 is replaced by $(2 - \delta, 1 - \epsilon)$, the entry $(1 - \epsilon, 2)$ is replaced by $(1 - \epsilon, 2 - \delta)$, and the entry $(0, 0)$ is replaced by $(-\delta, -\delta)$. Show that all drivers are *better off* in the symmetric equilibrium of this game than they are in the symmetric equilibrium of the original game. Why is the society better off if everyone feels guilty about being aggressive? (The equilibrium of this game, like that of the equilibrium of the game of expert diagnosis in Section 4.6, may attractively be interpreted as representing a steady state in which some members of the population always choose one action and other members always choose the other action.)

? EXERCISE 130.3 (Bargaining) Pairs of players from a single population bargain over the division of a pie of size 10. The members of a pair simultaneously make demands; the possible demands are the nonnegative *even* integers up to 10. If the demands sum to 10, then each player receives her demand; if the demands sum to less than 10, then each player receives her demand plus half of the pie that remains after both demands have been satisfied; if the demands sum to more than 10, then neither player receives any payoff. Find all the symmetric mixed strategy Nash equilibria in which each player assigns positive probability to at most two demands. (Many situations in which each player assigns positive probability to two actions, say a' and a'', can be ruled out as equilibria because when one player uses such a strategy, some action yields the other player a payoff higher than does one or both of the actions a' and a''.)

4.8 Illustration: reporting a crime

A crime is observed by a group of n people. Each person would like the police to be informed but prefers that someone else make the phone call. Specifically, suppose that each person attaches the value v to the police being informed and bears the cost c if she makes the phone call, where $v > c > 0$. Then the situation is modeled by the following strategic game with vNM preferences.

Players The n people.

Actions Each player's set of actions is {*Call, Don't call*}.

Preferences Each player's preferences are represented by the expected value of a payoff function that assigns 0 to the profile in which no one calls, $v - c$ to any profile in which she calls, and v to any profile in which at least one person calls, but she does not.

This game is a variant of the one in Exercise 33.1, with $k = 1$. It has n pure Nash equilibria, in each of which exactly one person calls. (If that person switches to not calling, her payoff falls from $v - c$ to 0; if any other person switches to calling, her payoff falls from v to $v - c$.) If the members of the group differ in some respect, then these asymmetric equilibria may be compelling as steady states. For example, the social norm in which the oldest person in the group makes the phone call is stable.

If the members of the group either do not differ significantly or are not aware of any differences among themselves—if they are drawn from a single homogeneous population—then there is no way for them to coordinate, and a symmetric equilibrium, in which every player uses the same strategy, is more compelling.

The game has no symmetric pure Nash equilibrium. (If everyone calls, then any person is better off switching to not calling. If no one calls, then any person is better off switching to calling.)

However, it has a symmetric mixed strategy equilibrium in which each person calls with positive probability less than one. In any such equilibrium, each person's expected payoff to calling is equal to her expected payoff to not calling. Each person's payoff to calling is $v - c$, and her payoff to not calling is 0 if no one else calls and v if at least one other person calls, so the equilibrium condition is

$$v - c = 0 \cdot \Pr\{\text{no one else calls}\} + v \cdot \Pr\{\text{at least one other person calls}\},$$

or

$$v - c = v \cdot (1 - \Pr\{\text{no one else calls}\}),$$

or

$$c/v = \Pr\{\text{no one else calls}\}. \tag{131.1}$$

Denote by p the probability with which each person calls. The probability that no one else calls is the probability that every one of the other $n - 1$ people does not call, namely $(1 - p)^{n-1}$. Thus the equilibrium condition is $c/v = (1 - p)^{n-1}$, or

$$p = 1 - (c/v)^{1/(n-1)}.$$

This number p is between 0 and 1, so we conclude that the game has a unique symmetric mixed strategy equilibrium, in which each person calls with probability $1 - (c/v)^{1/(n-1)}$. That is, there is a steady state in which whenever a person is in a group of n people facing the situation modeled by the game, she calls with probability $1 - (c/v)^{1/(n-1)}$.

How does this equilibrium change as the size of the group increases? We see that as n increases, the probability p that any given person calls decreases. (As n increases, $1/(n-1)$ decreases, so that $(c/v)^{1/(n-1)}$ increases.) What about the probability that *at least* one person calls? Fix any player i. Then the event "no one calls" is the same as the event "i does not call and no one *other than* i calls". Thus

$$\Pr\{\text{no one calls}\} = \Pr\{i \text{ does not call}\} \cdot \Pr\{\text{no one else calls}\}. \qquad (132.1)$$

Now, the probability that any given person calls decreases as n increases, or equivalently the probability that she does not call increases as n increases. Further, from the equilibrium condition (131.1), $\Pr\{\text{no one else calls}\}$ is equal to c/v, *independent of n*. We conclude that the probability that no one calls *increases* as n increases. That is, the larger the group, the *less* likely the police are informed of the crime!

The condition defining a mixed strategy equilibrium is responsible for this result. For any given person to be indifferent between calling and not calling, this condition requires that the probability that no one else calls be independent of the size of the group. Thus each person's probability of not calling is larger in a larger group, and hence, by the laws of probability reflected in (132.1), the probability that no one calls is larger in a larger group.

The result that the larger the group, the less likely any given person calls is not surprising. The result that the larger the group, the less likely at least one person calls is a more subtle implication of the notion of equilibrium. In a larger group no individual is any less concerned that the police should be called, but in a steady state the behavior of the group drives down the chance that the police are notified of the crime.

⊘ EXERCISE 132.2 (Reporting a crime when the witnesses are heterogeneous) Consider a variant of the model studied in this section in which n_1 witnesses incur the cost c_1 to report the crime, and n_2 witnesses incur the cost c_2, where $0 < c_1 < v$, $0 < c_2 < v$, and $n_1 + n_2 = n$. Show that if c_1 and c_2 are sufficiently close, then the game has a mixed strategy Nash equilibrium in which every witness's strategy assigns positive probabilities to both reporting and not reporting.

⊘ EXERCISE 132.3 (Contributing to a public good) Consider an extension of the analysis in this section to the game in Exercise 33.1 for $k \geq 2$. (In this case a player may contribute even though the good is not provided; the player's payoff in this case is $-c$.) Denote by $Q_{n-1,m}(p)$ the probability that exactly m of a group of $n - 1$ players contribute when each player contributes with probability p. What condition must be satisfied by $Q_{n-1,k-1}(p)$ in a symmetric mixed strategy equilibrium (in which each player contributes with the same probability)? (When does a player's contribution make a difference to the outcome?) For the case $v = 1$, $n = 4, k = 2$, and $c = \frac{3}{8}$, find the equilibria explicitly. (You need to use the fact that $Q_{3,1}(p) = 3p(1 - p)^2$, and do a bit of algebra.)

REPORTING A CRIME: SOCIAL PSYCHOLOGY AND GAME THEORY

Thirty-eight people witnessed the brutal murder of Catherine ("Kitty") Genovese over a period of half an hour in New York City in March 1964. During this period, no one significantly responded to her screams for help; no one even called the police. Journalists, psychiatrists, sociologists, and others subsequently struggled to understand the witnesses' inaction. Some ascribed it to apathy engendered by life in a large city: "Indifference to one's neighbor and his troubles is a conditioned reflex of life in New York as it is in other big cities" (Rosenthal 1964, 81–82).

The event particularly interested social psychologists. It led them to try to understand the circumstances under which a bystander would help someone in trouble. Experiments quickly suggested that, contrary to the popular theory, people— even those living in large cities—are not in general apathetic to others' plights. An experimental subject who is the lone witness of a person in distress is very likely to try to help. But as the size of the group of witnesses increases, there is a decline not only in the probability that any given one of them offers assistance, but also in the probability that at least one of them offers assistance. Social psychologists hypothesize that three factors explain these experimental findings. First, "diffusion of responsibility": the larger the group, the lower the psychological cost of not helping. Second, "audience inhibition": the larger the group, the greater the embarrassment suffered by a helper in case the event turns out to be one in which help is inappropriate (because, for example, it is not in fact an emergency). Third, "social influence": a person infers the appropriateness of helping from others' behavior, so that in a large group everyone else's lack of intervention leads any given person to think intervention is less likely to be appropriate.

In terms of the model in Section 4.8, these three factors raise the expected cost and/or reduce the expected benefit of a person's intervening. They all seem plausible. However, they are not needed to explain the phenomenon: our game-theoretic analysis shows that even if the cost and benefit are *independent* of group size, a decrease in the probability that at least one person intervenes is an implication of equilibrium. This game-theoretic analysis has an advantage over the socio-psychological one: it derives the conclusion from the same principles that underlie all the other models studied so far (oligopoly, auctions, voting, and elections, for example), rather than positing special features of the specific environment in which a group of bystanders may come to the aid of a person in distress.

The critical element missing from the socio-psychological analysis is the notion of an *equilibrium*. Whether any given person intervenes depends on the probability she assigns to some other person's intervening. In an equilibrium each person must be indifferent between intervening and not intervening, and as we have seen this condition leads inexorably to the conclusion that an increase in group size reduces the probability that at least one person intervenes.

4.9 The formation of players' beliefs

In a Nash equilibrium, each player chooses a strategy that maximizes her expected payoff, *knowing* the other players' strategies. So far we have not considered how players may acquire such information. Informally, the idea underlying the previous analysis is that the players have learned each other's strategies from their experience playing the game. In the idealized situation to which the analysis corresponds, for each player in the game there is a large population of individuals who may take the role of that player; in any play of the game, one participant is drawn randomly from each population. In this situation, a new individual who joins a population that is in a steady state (i.e. is using a Nash equilibrium strategy profile) can learn the other players' strategies by observing their actions over many plays of the game. As long as the turnover in players is small enough, existing players' encounters with neophytes (who may use nonequilibrium strategies) will be sufficiently rare that their beliefs about the steady state will not be disturbed, so that a new player's problem is simply to learn the other players' actions.

This analysis leaves open the question of what might happen if new players simultaneously join more than one population in sufficient numbers that they have a significant chance of facing opponents who are themselves new. In particular, can we expect a steady state to be reached when no one has experience playing the game?

4.9.1   Eliminating dominated actions

In some games the players may reasonably be expected to choose their Nash equilibrium actions from an introspective analysis of the game. At an extreme, each player's best action may be independent of the other players' actions, as in the *Prisoner's Dilemma* (Example 14.1). In such a game no player needs to worry about the other players' actions. In a less extreme case, some player's best action may depend on the other players' actions, but the actions the other players will choose may be clear because each of these players has an action that strictly dominates all others. For example, in the game in Figure 135.1, player 2's action R strictly dominates L, so that no matter what player 2 thinks player 1 will do, she should choose R. Consequently, player 1, who can deduce by this argument that player 2 will choose R, may reason that she should choose B. That is, even inexperienced players may be led to the unique Nash equilibrium (B, R) in this game.

This line of argument may be extended. For example, in the game in Figure 135.2, player 1's action T is strictly dominated, so player 1 may reason that

$$
\begin{array}{c|cc}
 & L & R \\
\hline
T & 1,2 & 0,3 \\
B & 0,0 & 1,1
\end{array}
$$

Figure 135.1 A game in which player 2 has a strictly dominant action and player 1 does not.

$$
\begin{array}{c|cc}
 & L & R \\
\hline
T & 0,2 & 0,0 \\
M & 2,1 & 1,2 \\
B & 1,1 & 2,2
\end{array}
$$

Figure 135.2 A game in which player 1 may reason that she should choose B because player 2 will reason that player 1 will not choose T, so that player 2 will choose R.

player 2 will deduce that player 1 will not choose T. Consequently player 1 may deduce that player 2 will choose R, making B a better action for her than M.

The set of action profiles that remain at the end of such a reasoning process contains all Nash equilibria; for many games (unlike these examples) the set contains many other action profiles as well. In fact, in many games no action profiles are eliminated, because no player has a strictly dominated action. Nevertheless, in some classes of games the process is powerful; its logical consequences are explored in Chapter 12.

4.9.2 Learning

Another approach to the question of how a steady state might be reached assumes that each player starts with an unexplained "prior" belief about the other players' actions, and changes these beliefs—"learns"—in response to information she receives. She may learn, for example, from observing the fortunes of other players like herself, from discussing the game with such players, or from her own experience playing the game. Here I briefly discuss two theories in which the same set of participants repeatedly play a game, each participant changing her beliefs about the others' strategies in response to her observations of their actions.

Best response dynamics   A particularly simple theory assumes that in each period after the first, each player believes that the other players will choose the actions they chose in the previous period. In the first period, each player chooses a best response to an arbitrary deterministic belief about the other players' actions. In every subsequent period, each player chooses a best response to the other players' actions in the *previous* period. This process is known as *best response dynamics*. An action profile that remains the same from period to period is a pure Nash equilibrium of the game. Further, a pure Nash equilibrium in which each player's action is her only best response to the other players' actions is an action profile that remains the same from period to period.

In some games the sequence of action profiles generated best response dynamics converges to a pure Nash equilibrium, regardless of the players' initial beliefs. The example of Cournot's duopoly game studied in Section 3.1.3 is such a game. Looking at the best response functions in Figure 59.1, you can convince yourself that from arbitrary initial actions, the players' actions approach the Nash equilibrium (q_1^*, q_2^*).

? EXERCISE 136.1 (Best response dynamics in Cournot's duopoly game) Find the sequence of pairs of outputs chosen by the firms in Cournot's duopoly game under the assumptions of Section 3.1.3 if both firms initially choose 0. (If you know how to solve a first-order difference equation, find a formula for the outputs in each period; if not, find the outputs in the first few periods.)

? EXERCISE 136.2 (Best response dynamics in Bertrand's duopoly game) Consider Bertrand's duopoly game in which the set of possible prices is discrete, under the assumptions of Exercise 67.2. Does the sequences of prices under best response dynamics converge to a Nash equilibrium when both prices initially exceed $c + 1$? What happens when both prices are initially equal to c?

For other games there are initial beliefs for which the sequence of action profiles generated by the process does not converge. In *BoS* (Example 18.2), for example, if player 1 initially believes that player 2 will choose *Stravinsky* and player 2 initially believes that player 1 will choose *Bach*, then the players' choices will subsequently alternate indefinitely between the action pairs (*Bach, Stravinsky*) and (*Stravinsky, Bach*). This example highlights the limited extent to which a player is assumed to reason in the model, which does not consider the possibility that she cottons on to the fact that her opponent's action is always a best response to her own previous action.

Fictitious play   Under best response dynamics, the players' beliefs are continually revealed to be incorrect unless the starting point is a Nash equilibrium: the players' actions change from period to period. Further, each player believes that every other player is using a pure strategy: a player's belief does not admit the possibility that her opponents' actions are realizations of mixed strategies.

Another theory, known as *fictitious play*, assumes that players consider actions in all the previous periods when forming a belief about their opponents' strategies. They treat these actions as realizations of mixed strategies. Consider a two-player game. Each player begins with an arbitrary probabilistic belief about the other player's action. In the first play of the game she chooses a best response to this belief and observes the other player's action, say A. She then changes her belief to one that assigns probability 1 to A; in the second period, she chooses a best response to this belief and observes the other player's action, say B. She then changes her belief to one that assigns probability $\frac{1}{2}$ to both A and B, and chooses a best response to this belief. She continues to change her belief each period; in any period she adopts the belief that her opponent is using a mixed strategy in

	Head	*Tail*
Head	1, −1	−1, 1
Tail	−1, 1	1, −1

Figure 137.1 *Matching Pennies.*

which the probability of each action is proportional to the frequency with which her opponent chose that action in the previous periods. (If, for example, in the first six periods player 2 chooses A twice, B three times, and C once, player 1's belief in period 7 assigns probability $\frac{1}{3}$ to A, probability $\frac{1}{2}$ to B, and probability $\frac{1}{6}$ to C.)

In the game *Matching Pennies* (Example 19.1), reproduced in Figure 137.1, this process works as follows. Suppose that player 1 begins with the belief that player 2's action will be *Tail*, and player 2 begins with the belief that player 1's action will be *Head*. Then in period 1 both players choose *Tail*. Thus in period 2 both players believe that their opponent will choose *Tail*, so that player 1 chooses *Tail* and player 2 chooses *Head*. Consequently in period 3, player 1's belief is that player 2 will choose *Head* with probability $\frac{1}{2}$ and *Tail* with probability $\frac{1}{2}$, and player 2's belief is that player 1 will definitely choose *Tail*. Thus in period 3, both *Head* and *Tail* are best responses of player 1 to her belief, so that she may take either action; the unique best response of player 2 is *Head*. The process continues similarly in subsequent periods.

In two-player games like *Matching Pennies*, in which the players' interests are directly opposed, and in any two-player game in which each player has two actions, this process converges to a mixed strategy Nash equilibrium from any initial beliefs. That is, after a sufficiently large number of periods, the frequencies with which each player chooses her actions are close to the frequencies induced by her mixed strategy in the Nash equilibrium. For other games there are initial beliefs for which the process does not converge. (The simplest example is too complicated to present compactly.)

The people involved in an interaction that we model as a game may form beliefs about their opponents' strategies from an analysis of the structure of the players' payoffs, from their observations of their opponents' actions, and from information they obtain from other people involved in similar interactions. The models I have outlined in this section explore the logical implications of two ways in which players may draw inferences from their opponents' actions. Models that assume the players to be more sophisticated may give more insights into the circumstances in which a Nash equilibrium is likely to be attained; this topic is an active area of current research.

4.10 Extension: finding all mixed strategy Nash equilibria

We can find all the mixed strategy Nash equilibria of a two-player game in which each player has two actions by constructing the players' best response functions, as we have seen. In more complicated games, this method is usually not practical.

The following systematic method of finding all mixed strategy Nash equilibria of a game is suggested by the characterization of an equilibrium in Proposition 116.2.

- For each player i, choose a subset S_i of her set A_i of actions.

- Check whether there exists a mixed strategy profile α such that (*i*) the set of actions to which each strategy α_i assigns positive probability is S_i and (*ii*) α satisfies the conditions in Proposition 116.2.

- Repeat the analysis for every collection of subsets of the players' sets of actions.

The following example illustrates this method for a two-player game in which each player has two actions.

⬥ EXAMPLE 138.1 (Finding all mixed strategy equilibria of a two-player game in which each player has two actions) Consider a two-player game in which each player has two actions. Denote the actions and payoffs as in Figure 139.1. Each player's set of actions has three nonempty subsets: two each consisting of a single action, and one consisting of both actions. Thus there are nine (3×3) pairs of subsets of the players' action sets. For each pair (S_1, S_2), we check if there is a pair (α_1, α_2) of mixed strategies such that each strategy α_i assigns positive probability only to actions in S_i and the conditions in Proposition 116.2 are satisfied.

- Checking the four pairs of subsets in which each player's subset consists of a single action amounts to checking whether any of the four pairs of actions is a pure strategy equilibrium. (For each player, the first condition in Proposition 116.2 is automatically satisfied because there is only one action in each subset.)

- Consider the pair of subsets $\{T, B\}$ for player 1 and $\{L\}$ for player 2. The second condition in Proposition 116.2 is automatically satisfied for player 1, who has no actions to which she assigns probability 0, and the first condition is automatically satisfied for player 2, because she assigns positive probability to only one action. Thus for there to be a mixed strategy equilibrium in which player 1's probability of using T is p we need $u_{11} = u_{21}$ (player 1's payoffs to her two actions must be equal) and

$$pv_{11} + (1 - p)v_{21} \geq pv_{12} + (1 - p)v_{22}$$

(*L* must be at least as good as *R*, given player 1's mixed strategy). If $u_{11} \neq u_{21}$, or if there is no probability p satisfying the inequality, then there is no equilibrium of this type. A similar argument applies to the three other pairs of subsets in which one player's subset consists of both her actions and the other player's subset consists of a single action.

- To check whether there is a mixed strategy equilibrium in which the subsets are $\{T, B\}$ for player 1 and $\{L, R\}$ for player 2, we need to find a pair of

$$
\begin{array}{c|cc}
 & L & R \\
\hline
T & u_{11}, v_{11} & u_{12}, v_{12} \\
B & u_{21}, v_{21} & u_{22}, v_{22}
\end{array}
$$

Figure 139.1 A two-player strategic game.

mixed strategies that satisfies the first condition in Proposition 116.2 (the second condition is automatically satisfied because both players assign positive probability to both their actions). That is, we need to find probabilities p and q (if any such exist) for which

$$
qu_{11} + (1-q)u_{12} = qu_{21} + (1-q)u_{22}
$$
$$
pv_{11} + (1-p)v_{21} = pv_{12} + (1-p)v_{22}.
$$

For example, in *BoS* we find the two pure equilibria when we check pairs of subsets in which each subset consists of a single action, we find no equilibria when we check pairs in which one subset consists of a single action and the other consists of both actions, and we find the mixed strategy equilibrium when we check the pair $(\{B, S\}, \{B, S\})$.

⊘ EXERCISE 139.1 (Finding all mixed strategy equilibria of two-player games) Use the method described in Example 138.1 to find all of the mixed strategy equilibria of the games in Figure 114.1.

In a game in which each player has two actions, for any subset of any player's set of actions at most one of the two conditions in Proposition 116.2 is relevant (the first if the subset contains both actions and the second if it contains only one action). When a player has three or more actions and we consider a subset of her set of actions that contains two actions, both conditions are relevant, as the next example illustrates.

◆ EXAMPLE 139.2 (Finding all mixed strategy equilibria of a variant of *BoS*) Consider the variant of *BoS* given in Figure 139.2. First, by inspection we see that the game has two pure strategy Nash equilibria, namely (B, B) and (S, S).

Now consider the possibility of an equilibrium in which player 1's strategy is pure whereas player 2's strategy assigns positive probability to two or more actions. If player 1's strategy is B, then player 2's payoffs to her three actions (2, 0, and 1) are all different, so the first condition in Proposition 116.2 is not satisfied. Thus there is no equilibrium of this type. Similar reasoning rules out an equilibrium in which player 1's strategy is S and player 2's strategy assigns positive

$$
\begin{array}{c|ccc}
 & B & S & X \\
\hline
B & 4,2 & 0,0 & 0,1 \\
S & 0,0 & 2,4 & 1,3
\end{array}
$$

Figure 139.2 A variant of the game *BoS*.

probability to more than one action, and also an equilibrium in which player 2's strategy is pure and player 1's strategy assigns positive probability to both of her actions.

Next consider the possibility of an equilibrium in which player 1's strategy assigns positive probability to both her actions and player 2's strategy assigns positive probability to two of her three actions. Denote by p the probability player 1's strategy assigns to B. There are three possibilities for the pair of player 2's actions that have positive probability.

B and S: For the conditions in Proposition 116.2 to be satisfied we need player 2's expected payoff to B to be equal to her expected payoff to S and at least her expected payoff to X. That is, we need

$$2p = 4(1-p) \geq p + 3(1-p).$$

The equation implies that $p = \frac{2}{3}$, which does not satisfy the inequality. (That is, if p is such that B and S yield the same expected payoff, then X yields a higher expected payoff.) Thus there is no equilibrium of this type.

B and X: For the conditions in Proposition 116.2 to be satisfied we need player 2's expected payoff to B to be equal to her expected payoff to X and at least her expected payoff to S. That is, we need

$$2p = p + 3(1-p) \geq 4(1-p).$$

The equation implies that $p = \frac{3}{4}$, which satisfies the inequality. For the first condition in Proposition 116.2 to be satisfied for player 1 we need player 1's expected payoffs to B and S to be equal: $4q = 1 - q$, where q is the probability player 2 assigns to B, or $q = \frac{1}{5}$. Thus the pair of mixed strategies $((\frac{3}{4}, \frac{1}{4}), (\frac{1}{5}, 0, \frac{4}{5}))$ is a mixed strategy equilibrium.

S and X: For every strategy of player 2 that assigns positive probability only to S and X, player 1's expected payoff to S exceeds her expected payoff to B. Thus there is no equilibrium of this sort.

The final possibility is that there is an equilibrium in which player 1's strategy assigns positive probability to both her actions and player 2's strategy assigns positive probability to all three of her actions. Let p be the probability player 1's strategy assigns to B. Then for player 2's expected payoffs to her three actions to be equal we need

$$2p = 4(1-p) = p + 3(1-p).$$

For the first equality we need $p = \frac{2}{3}$, violating the second equality. That is, there is no value of p for which player 2's expected payoffs to her three actions are equal, and thus no equilibrium in which she chooses each action with positive probability.

We conclude that the game has three mixed strategy equilibria: $((1,0), (1,0,0))$ (i.e. the pure strategy equilibrium (B, B)), $((0,1), (0,1,0))$ (i.e. the pure strategy equilibrium (S, S)), and $((\frac{3}{4}, \frac{1}{4}), (\frac{1}{5}, 0, \frac{4}{5}))$.

	L	M	R
T	2,2	0,3	1,3
B	3,2	1,1	0,2

Figure 141.1 The strategic game with vNM preferences in Exercise 141.1.

⟨?⟩ EXERCISE 141.1 (Finding all mixed strategy equilibria of a two-player game) Use the method described in Example 139.2 to find all the mixed strategy Nash equilibria of the strategic game in Figure 141.1.

As you can see from the examples, this method has the disadvantage that for games in which each player has several strategies, or in which there are several players, the number of possibilities to examine is huge. Even in a two-player game in which each player has three actions, each player's set of actions has seven nonempty subsets (three each consisting of a single action, three consisting of two actions, and the entire set of actions), so that there are 49 (7×7) possible collections of subsets to check. In a symmetric game, like the one in the next exercise, many cases involve the same argument, reducing the number of distinct cases to be checked.

⟨?⟩ EXERCISE 141.2 (*Rock, Paper, Scissors*) Each of two players simultaneously announces either *Rock*, or *Paper*, or *Scissors*. *Paper* beats (wraps) *Rock*, *Rock* beats (blunts) *Scissors*, and *Scissors* beats (cuts) *Paper*. The player who names the winning object receives $1 from her opponent; if both players make the same choice, then no payment is made. Each player's preferences are represented by the expected amount of money she receives. (An example of the variant of Hotelling's model of electoral competition considered in Exercise 75.3 has the same payoff structure. Suppose there are three possible positions, A, B, and C, and three citizens, one of whom prefers A to B to C, one of whom prefers B to C to A, and one of whom prefers C to A to B. Two candidates simultaneously choose positions. If the candidates choose different positions, each citizen votes for the candidate whose position she prefers; if both candidates choose the same position, they tie for first place.)

   a. Formulate this situation as a strategic game and find all its mixed strategy equilibria (give both the equilibrium strategies and the equilibrium payoffs).

   b. Find all the mixed strategy equilibria of the modified game in which player 1 is prohibited from announcing *Scissors*.

⟨?⟩ EXERCISE 141.3 (Election campaigns) A new political party, A, is challenging an established party, B. The race involves three localities of different sizes. Party A can wage a strong campaign in only one locality; B must commit resources to defend its position in one of the localities, without knowing which locality A has targeted. If A targets district i and B devotes its resources to some other district, then A gains a_i votes at the expense of B; let $a_1 > a_2 > a_3 > 0$. If B devotes

	A	B
A	1, 1, 1	0, 0, 0
B	0, 0, 0	0, 0, 0

A

	A	B
A	0, 0, 0	0, 0, 0
B	0, 0, 0	4, 4, 4

B

Figure 142.1 The three-player game in Exercise 142.1.

resources to the district that A targets, then A gains no votes. Each party's preferences are represented by the expected number of votes it gains. (Perhaps seats in a legislature are allocated proportionally to vote shares.) Formulate this situation as a strategic game and find its mixed strategy equilibria.

Although games with many players cannot in general be conveniently represented in tables like those we use for two-player games, three-player games can be accommodated. We construct one table for each of player 3's actions; player 1 chooses a row, player 2 chooses a column, and player 3 chooses a *table*. The next exercise is an example of such a game.

? EXERCISE 142.1 (A three-player game) Find the mixed strategy Nash equilibria of the three-player game in Figure 142.1, in which each player has two actions.

4.11 Extension: games in which each player has a continuum of actions

In all the games studied so far in this chapter each player has finitely many actions. In Chapter 3 we saw that many situations may conveniently be modeled as games in which each player has a continuum of actions. (For example, in Cournot's model the set of possible outputs for a firm is the set of nonnegative numbers, and in Hotelling's model the set of possible positions for a candidate is the set of nonnegative numbers.) The principles involved in finding mixed strategy equilibria of such games are the same as those involved in finding mixed strategy equilibria of games in which each player has finitely many actions, though the techniques are different.

Proposition 116.2 says that a strategy profile in a game in which each player has finitely many actions is a mixed strategy Nash equilibrium if and only if, for each player, (a) every action to which her strategy assigns positive probability yields the same expected payoff, and (b) no action yields a higher expected payoff. Now, a mixed strategy of a player who has a continuum of actions is determined by the probabilities it assigns to sets of actions, not by the probabilities it assigns to single actions (all of which may be zero, for example). Thus (a) does not fit such a game. However, the following restatement of the result, equivalent to Proposition 116.2 for a game in which each player has finitely many actions, does fit.

■ PROPOSITION 142.2 (Characterization of mixed strategy Nash equilibrium) *A mixed strategy profile α^* in a strategic game with vNM preferences is a mixed strategy Nash equilibrium if and only if, for each player i,*

- α_i^* assigns probability zero to the set of actions a_i for which the action profile (a_i, α_{-i}^*) yields player i an expected payoff less than her expected payoff to α^*

- for no action a_i does the action profile (a_i, α_{-i}^*) yield player i an expected payoff greater than her expected payoff to α^*.

A significant class of games in which each player has a continuum of actions consists of games in which each player's set of actions is a one-dimensional interval of numbers. Consider such a game with two players; let player i's set of actions be the interval from $\underline{a}_i$ to $\bar{a}_i$, for $i = 1, 2$. Identify each player's mixed strategy with a *cumulative* probability distribution on this interval. (See Section 17.6.4 in the appendix on mathematics if you are not familiar with this notion.) That is, the mixed strategy of each player i is a nondecreasing function F_i for which $0 \leq F_i(a_i) \leq 1$ for every action a_i; the number $F_i(a_i)$ is the probability that player i's action is at most a_i.

The form of a mixed strategy Nash equilibrium in such a game may be very complex. Some such games, however, have equilibria of a particularly simple form, in which each player's equilibrium mixed strategy assigns probability zero except in an interval. Specifically, consider a pair (F_1, F_2) of mixed strategies that satisfies the following conditions for $i = 1, 2$.

- There are numbers x_i and y_i such that player i's mixed strategy F_i assigns probability zero except in the interval from x_i to y_i: $F_i(z) = 0$ for $z < x_i$, and $F(z) = 1$ for $z \geq y_i$.

- Player i's expected payoff when her action is a_i and the other player uses her mixed strategy F_j takes the form

$$\begin{cases} = c_i & \text{for } x_i \leq a_i \leq y_i \\ \leq c_i & \text{for } a_i < x_i \text{ and } a_i > y_i, \end{cases}$$

where c_i is a constant.

(The second condition is illustrated in Figure 144.1.) By Proposition 142.2, such a pair of mixed strategies, if it exists, is a mixed strategy Nash equilibrium of the game, in which player i's expected payoff is c_i, for $i = 1, 2$.

The next example illustrates how a mixed strategy equilibrium of such a game may be found. The example is designed to be very simple; be warned that in most such games an analysis of the equilibria is, at a minimum, somewhat more complex. Further, my analysis is not complete: I merely find an equilibrium, rather than studying all equilibria. (In fact, the game has no other equilibria.)

◆ EXAMPLE 143.1 (All-pay auction) Two people submit sealed bids for an object worth $\$K$ to each of them. Each person's bid may be any nonnegative number up to $\$K$. The winner is the person whose bid is higher; in the event of a tie each person receives half of the object, which she values at $\$K/2$. (Note that this tie-breaking rule differs from the one considered in Section 3.5.) Each person pays her

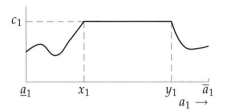 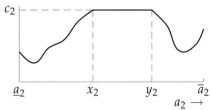

Player 1's expected payoff given F_2 Player 2's expected payoff given F_1

Figure 144.1 If (i) F_1 assigns positive probability only to actions in the interval from x_1 to y_1, (ii) F_2 assigns positive probability only to the actions in the interval from x_2 to y_2, (iii) given player 2's mixed strategy F_2, player 1's expected payoff takes the form shown in the left panel, and (iv) given player 1's mixed strategy F_1, player 2's expected payoff takes the form shown in the right panel, then (F_1, F_2) is a mixed strategy equilibrium.

bid, *regardless of whether she wins*, and has preferences represented by the expected amount of money she receives.

This situation may be modeled by the following strategic game, known as an **all-pay auction**. (Variants of this game are considered in Exercise 89.1.)

Players The two bidders.

Actions Each player's set of actions is the set of possible bids (nonnegative numbers up to K).

Payoff functions Each player i's preferences are represented by the expected value of the payoff function given by

$$u_i(a_1, a_2) = \begin{cases} -a_i & \text{if } a_i < a_j \\ K/2 - a_i & \text{if } a_i = a_j \\ K - a_i & \text{if } a_i > a_j, \end{cases}$$

where j is the other player.

One situation that may be modeled as such an auction is a lobbying process in which each of two interest groups spends resources to persuade a government to carry out the policy it prefers, and the group that spends the most wins. Another situation that may be modeled as such an auction is the competition between two firms to develop a new product by some deadline, where the firm that spends the most develops a better product, which captures the entire market.

An all-pay auction has no pure strategy Nash equilibrium, by the following argument.

- No pair of actions (x, x) with $x < K$ is a Nash equilibrium because either player can increase her payoff by slightly increasing her bid.

- (K, K) is not a Nash equilibrium because either player can increase her payoff from $-K/2$ to 0 by reducing her bid to 0.

- No pair of actions (a_1, a_2) with $a_1 \neq a_2$ is a Nash equilibrium because the player whose bid is higher can increase her payoff by reducing her bid (and the player whose bid is lower can, if her bid is positive, increase her payoff by reducing her bid to 0).

Consider the possibility that the game has a mixed strategy Nash equilibrium. Denote by F_i the mixed strategy (i.e. cumulative probability distribution over the interval of possible bids) of player i. I look for an equilibrium in which neither mixed strategy assigns positive probability to any *single* bid. (Remember that there are infinitely many possible bids.) In this case $F_i(a_i)$ is both the probability that player i bids at most a_i and the probability that she bids less than a_i. I further restrict attention to strategy pairs (F_1, F_2) for which, for $i = 1, 2$, there are numbers x_i and y_i such that F_i assigns positive probability only to the interval from x_i to y_i.

To investigate the possibility of such an equilibrium, consider player 1's expected payoff when she uses the action a_1, given player 2's mixed strategy F_2.

- If $a_1 < x_2$, then a_1 is less than player 2's bid with probability one, so that player 1's payoff is $-a_1$.

- If $a_1 > y_2$, then a_1 exceeds player 2's bid with probability one, so that player 1's payoff is $K - a_1$.

- If $x_2 \leq a_1 \leq y_2$, then player 1's expected payoff is calculated as follows. With probability $F_2(a_1)$ player 2's bid is less than a_1, in which case player 1's payoff is $K - a_1$; with probability $1 - F_2(a_1)$ player 2's bid exceeds a_1, in which case player 1's payoff is $-a_1$; and, by assumption, the probability that player 2's bid is exactly equal to a_1 is zero. Thus player 1's expected payoff is

$$(K - a_1)F_2(a_1) + (-a_1)(1 - F_2(a_1)) = KF_2(a_1) - a_1.$$

We need to find values of x_2 and y_2 and a strategy F_2 such that player 1's expected payoff satisfies the condition illustrated in the left panel of Figure 144.1: it is constant on the interval from x_1 to y_1, and less than this constant for $a_1 < x_1$ and $a_1 > y_1$. The constancy of the payoff on the interval from x_1 to y_1 requires that $KF_2(a_1) - a_1 = c_1$ for $x_1 \leq a_1 \leq y_1$, for some constant c_1. We also need $F_2(x_2) = 0$ and $F_2(y_2) = 1$ (because I am restricting attention to equilibria in which neither player's strategy assigns positive probability to any single action), and F_2 must be nondecreasing (so that it is a cumulative probability distribution). Analogous conditions must be satisfied by x_2, y_2, and F_1.

We see that if $x_1 = x_2 = 0$, $y_1 = y_2 = K$, and $F_1(z) = F_2(z) = z/K$ for all z with $0 \leq z \leq K$, then all these conditions are satisfied. Each player's expected payoff is constant, equal to 0 for all her actions a_1.

Thus the game has a mixed strategy Nash equilibrium in which each player randomizes "uniformly" over all her actions. In this equilibrium each player's expected payoff is 0: on average, the amount a player spends is exactly equal to the value of the object. (A more involved argument shows that this equilibrium is the *only* mixed strategy Nash equilibrium of the game.)

⑦ EXERCISE 145.1 (All-pay auction with many bidders) Consider the generalization of the game considered in the previous example in which there are $n \geq 2$ bidders.

Find a mixed strategy Nash equilibrium in which each player uses the same mixed strategy. (If you know how, find each player's mean bid in the equilibrium.)

? EXERCISE 146.1 (Bertrand's duopoly game) Consider Bertrand's oligopoly game (Section 3.2) when there are two firms. Assume that each firm's preferences are represented by its expected profit. Show that if the function $(p - c)D(p)$ is increasing in p, and increases without bound as p increases without bound, then for every $p > c$, the game has a mixed strategy Nash equilibrium in which each firm uses the same mixed strategy F, with $F(\underline{p}) = 0$ and $F(p) > 0$ for $p > \underline{p}$.

In the games in the example and exercises, each player's payoff depends only on her action and whether this action is greater than, equal to, or less than the other players' actions. The limited dependence of each player's payoff on the other players' actions makes the calculation of a player's expected payoff straightforward. In many games, each player's payoff is affected more substantially by the other players' actions, making the calculation of expected payoff more complex; more sophisticated mathematical tools are required to analyze such games.

4.12   Appendix: representing preferences by expected payoffs

4.12.1   Expected payoffs

Suppose that a decision-maker has preferences over a set of deterministic outcomes, and that each of her actions results in a *lottery* (probability distribution) over these outcomes. To determine the action she chooses, we need to know her preferences over these lotteries. As argued in Section 4.1.3, we cannot *derive* these preferences from her preferences over deterministic outcomes; rather, we must specify them as part of the model.

So assume that we are given the decision-maker's preferences over lotteries. As in the case of preferences over deterministic outcomes, under some fairly weak assumptions we can represent these preferences by a payoff function. (Refer to Section 1.2.2.) That is, when there are K deterministic outcomes we can find a function, say U, over lotteries such that

$$U(p_1, \ldots, p_K) > U(p'_1, \ldots, p'_K)$$

if and only if the decision-maker prefers the lottery $(p_1, \ldots, p_K)$ to the lottery $(p'_1, \ldots, p'_K)$ (where $(p_1, \ldots, p_K)$ is the lottery in which outcome 1 occurs with probability p_1, outcome 2 occurs with probability p_2, and so on).

For many purposes, however, we need more structure: we cannot get very far without restricting ourselves to preferences for which there is a more specific representation. The standard approach, developed by von Neumann and Morgenstern (1944), is to impose an additional assumption—the "independence axiom"—that allows us to conclude that the decision-maker's preferences can be represented by an *expected payoff function*. More precisely, the independence axiom (which I do not describe) allows us to conclude that there is a payoff function

u over *deterministic* outcomes such that the decision-maker's preference relation over lotteries is represented by the function $U(p_1, \ldots, p_K) = \sum_{k=1}^{K} p_k u(a_k)$, where a_k is the kth outcome of the lottery:

$$\sum_{k=1}^{K} p_k u(a_k) > \sum_{k=1}^{K} p'_k u(a_k) \tag{147.1}$$

if and only if the decision-maker prefers the lottery $(p_1, \ldots, p_K)$ to the lottery $(p'_1, \ldots, p'_K)$. That is, the decision-maker evaluates a lottery by its *expected payoff* according to the function u, which is known as the decision-maker's *Bernoulli payoff function*.

Suppose, for example, that there are three possible deterministic outcomes: the decision-maker may receive \$0, \$1, or \$5, and naturally she prefers \$5 to \$1 to \$0. Suppose that she prefers the lottery $(\frac{1}{2}, 0, \frac{1}{2})$ to the lottery $(0, \frac{3}{4}, \frac{1}{4})$ (where the first number in each list is the probability of \$0, the second number is the probability of \$1, and the third number is the probability of \$5). This preference is consistent with preferences represented by the expected value of a payoff function u for which $u(0) = 0$, $u(1) = 1$, and $u(5) = 4$ because

$$\tfrac{1}{2} \cdot 0 + \tfrac{1}{2} \cdot 4 > \tfrac{3}{4} \cdot 1 + \tfrac{1}{4} \cdot 4.$$

(Many other payoff functions are consistent with a preference for $(\frac{1}{2}, 0, \frac{1}{2})$ over $(0, \frac{3}{4}, \frac{1}{4})$. Among those in which $u(0) = 0$ and $u(5) = 4$, for example, any function for which $u(1) < \frac{4}{3}$ does the job.) Suppose, on the other hand, that the decision-maker prefers the lottery $(0, \frac{3}{4}, \frac{1}{4})$ to the lottery $(\frac{1}{2}, 0, \frac{1}{2})$. This preference is consistent with preferences represented by the expected value of a payoff function u for which $u(0) = 0$, $u(1) = 3$, and $u(5) = 4$ because

$$\tfrac{1}{2} \cdot 0 + \tfrac{1}{2} \cdot 4 < \tfrac{3}{4} \cdot 3 + \tfrac{1}{4} \cdot 4.$$

❓ EXERCISE 147.2 (Preferences over lotteries) There are three possible outcomes; in the outcome a_i a decision-maker gains $\$a_i$, where $a_1 < a_2 < a_3$. The decision-maker prefers a_3 to a_2 to a_1 and she prefers the lottery $(0.3, 0, 0.7)$ to $(0.1, 0.4, 0.5)$ to $(0.3, 0.2, 0.5)$ to $(0.45, 0, 0.55)$. Is this information consistent with the decision-maker's preferences' being represented by the expected value of a payoff function? If so, find a payoff function consistent with the information. If not, show why not. Answer the same questions when, alternatively, the decision-maker prefers the lottery $(0.4, 0, 0.6)$ to $(0, 0.5, 0.5)$ to $(0.3, 0.2, 0.5)$ to $(0.45, 0, 0.55)$.

Preferences represented by the expected value of a (Bernoulli) payoff function have the great advantage that they are completely specified by that payoff function. Once we know $u(a_k)$ for each possible outcome a_k we know the decision-maker's preferences among all lotteries. This significant advantage does, however, carry with it a small price: it is very easy to confuse a Bernoulli payoff function with a payoff function that represents the decision-maker's preferences over deterministic outcomes.

To describe the relation between the two, suppose that a decision-maker's preferences over lotteries are represented by the expected value of the Bernoulli payoff function u. Then certainly u is a payoff function that represents the decision-maker's preferences over deterministic outcomes (which are special cases of lotteries, in which a single outcome is assigned probability 1). However, the converse is *not* true: if the decision-maker's preferences over deterministic outcomes are represented by the payoff function u (i.e. the decision-maker prefers a to a' if and only if $u(a) > u(a')$), then u is *not* necessarily a Bernoulli payoff function whose expected value represents the decision-maker's preferences over lotteries. For instance, suppose that the decision-maker prefers \$5 to \$1 to \$0 and prefers the lottery $(\frac{1}{2}, 0, \frac{1}{2})$ to the lottery $(0, \frac{3}{4}, \frac{1}{4})$. Then her preferences over deterministic outcomes are consistent with the payoff function u for which $u(0) = 0$, $u(1) = 3$, and $u(5) = 4$. However, her preferences over lotteries are *not* consistent with the expected value of this function (since $\frac{1}{2} \cdot 0 + \frac{1}{2} \cdot 4 < \frac{3}{4} \cdot 3 + \frac{1}{4} \cdot 4$). The moral is that you should be careful to determine the type of payoff function with which you are dealing.

4.12.2 Equivalent Bernoulli payoff functions

If a decision-maker's preferences in a deterministic environment are represented by the payoff function u, then they are represented also by any payoff function that is an increasing function of u (see Section 1.2.2). The analogous property is not satisfied by Bernoulli payoff functions. Consider the example discussed above. A Bernoulli payoff function u for which $u(0) = 0$, $u(1) = 1$, and $u(5) = 4$ is consistent with a preference for the lottery $(\frac{1}{2}, 0, \frac{1}{2})$ over $(0, \frac{3}{4}, \frac{1}{4})$, but the function $\sqrt{u}$, for which $u(0) = 0$, $u(1) = 1$, and $u(5) = 2$, is not consistent with such a preference $(\frac{1}{2} \cdot 0 + \frac{1}{2} \cdot 2 < \frac{3}{4} \cdot 1 + \frac{1}{4} \cdot 2)$, though the square root function is increasing (larger numbers have larger square roots).

Under what circumstances do the expected values of two Bernoulli payoff functions represent the same preferences? The next result shows that they do so if and only if one payoff function is an increasing *linear* function of the other.

■ LEMMA 148.1 (Equivalence of Bernoulli payoff functions) *Suppose there are at least three possible outcomes. The expected values of the Bernoulli payoff functions u and v represent the same preferences over lotteries if and only if there exist numbers η and θ with $\theta > 0$ such that $u(x) = \eta + \theta v(x)$ for all x.*

If the expected value of u represents a decision-maker's preferences over lotteries, then so, for example, do the expected values of $2u$, $1 + u$, and $-1 + 4u$; but the expected values of u^2 and of $\sqrt{u}$ do not.

Part of the lemma is easy to establish. Let u be a Bernoulli payoff function whose expected value represents a decision-maker's preferences, and let $v(x) = \eta + \theta u(x)$ for all x, where η and θ are constants with $\theta > 0$. I argue that the expected values of u and of v represent the same preferences. Suppose that the decision-maker prefers the lottery $(p_1, \ldots, p_K)$ to the lottery $(p'_1, \ldots, p'_K)$. Then her expected payoff to $(p_1, \ldots, p_K)$ exceeds her expected payoff to $(p'_1, \ldots, p'_K)$, or, as given in (147.1),

$$\sum_{k=1}^{K} p_k u(a_k) > \sum_{k=1}^{K} p_k' u(a_k). \tag{149.1}$$

Now,

$$\sum_{k=1}^{K} p_k v(a_k) = \sum_{k=1}^{K} p_k \eta + \sum_{k=1}^{K} p_k \theta u(a_k) = \eta + \theta \sum_{k=1}^{K} p_k u(a_k),$$

using the fact that the sum of the probabilities p_k is 1. Similarly,

$$\sum_{k=1}^{K} p_k' v(a_k) = \eta + \theta \sum_{k=1}^{K} p_k' u(a_k).$$

Substituting for u in (149.1) we obtain

$$\frac{1}{\theta} \left(\sum_{k=1}^{K} p_k v(a_k) - \eta \right) > \frac{1}{\theta} \left(\sum_{k=1}^{K} p_k' v(a_k) - \eta \right),$$

which, given $\theta > 0$, is equivalent to

$$\sum_{k=1}^{K} p_k v(a_k) > \sum_{k=1}^{K} p_k' v(a_k):$$

according to v, the expected payoff of $(p_1, \ldots, p_K)$ exceeds the expected payoff of $(p_1', \ldots, p_K')$. We conclude that if u represents the decision-maker's preferences, then so does the function v defined by $v(x) = \eta + \theta u(x)$.

I omit the more difficult argument that if the expected values of the Bernoulli payoff functions u and v represent the same preferences over lotteries, then $v(x) = \eta + \theta u(x)$ for some constants η and $\theta > 0$.

⑦ EXERCISE 149.2 (Normalized Bernoulli payoff functions) Suppose that a decision-maker's preferences can be represented by the expected value of the Bernoulli payoff function u. Find a Bernoulli payoff function whose expected value represents the decision-maker's preferences and assigns a payoff of 1 to the best outcome and a payoff of 0 to the worst outcome.

4.12.3 *Equivalent strategic games with vNM preferences*

Turning to games, consider the three payoff tables in Figure 150.1. All three tables represent the same strategic game with deterministic preferences: in each case, player 1 prefers (B, B) to (S, S) to (B, S), which she regards as indifferent to (S, B), and player 2 prefers (S, S) to (B, B) to (B, S), which she regards as indifferent to (S, B). However, only the left and middle tables represent the same strategic game with vNM preferences. The reason is that the payoff functions in the middle table are linear functions of the payoff functions in the left table, whereas the payoff functions in the right table are not. Specifically, denote the Bernoulli payoff functions of player i in the three games by u_i, v_i, and w_i. Then

$$v_1(a) = 2u_1(a) \text{ and } v_2(a) = -3 + 3u_2(a),$$

	B	S
B	2,1	0,0
S	0,0	1,2

	B	S
B	4, 0	0,−3
S	0,−3	2, 3

	B	S
B	3,2	0,1
S	0,1	1,4

Figure 150.1 All three tables represent the same strategic game with ordinal preferences, but only the left and middle games, not the right one, represent the same strategic game with vNM preferences.

so that the left and middle tables represent the same strategic game with vNM preferences. However, w_1 is not a linear function of u_1. If it were, there would exist constants η and $\theta > 0$ such that $w_1(a) = \eta + \theta u_1(a)$ for each action pair a, or equivalently

$$0 = \eta + \theta \cdot 0$$
$$1 = \eta + \theta \cdot 1$$
$$3 = \eta + \theta \cdot 2.$$

However, these three equations have no solution. Thus the left and right tables represent different strategic games with vNM preferences. (As you can check, w_2 is not a linear function of u_2 either; but for the games not to be equivalent it is sufficient that *one* player's preferences be different.) Another way to see that player 1's vNM preferences in the left and right games are different is to note that in the left table player 1 is indifferent between the certain outcome (S, S) and the lottery in which (B, B) occurs with probability $\frac{1}{2}$ and (S, B) occurs with probability $\frac{1}{2}$ (each yields an expected payoff of 1), whereas in the right table she prefers the latter (since it yields an expected payoff of 1.5).

? EXERCISE 150.1 (Games equivalent to the *Prisoner's Dilemma*) Which of the tables in Figure 150.2 represents the same strategic game with vNM preferences as the *Prisoner's Dilemma* as specified in the left panel of Figure 107.1, when the numbers are interpreted as Bernoulli payoffs?

	C	D
C	3,3	0,4
D	4,0	2,2

	C	D
C	6, 0	0, 2
D	9,−4	3,−2

Figure 150.2 The payoff tables for Exercise 150.1.

Notes

The ideas behind mixed strategies and preferences represented by expected payoffs date back in Western thought at least to the eighteenth century (see Guilbaud (1961) and Kuhn (1968), and Bernoulli (1738), respectively). The modern formulation of a mixed strategy is due to Borel (1921; 1924, 204–221; 1927); the model of the representation of preferences by an expected payoff function is due to von Neumann and Morgenstern (1944, 15–31; 1947, 617–632). The model of a mixed strategy Nash equilibrium and Proposition 119.1 on the existence of a mixed strategy Nash equilibrium in a finite game are due to Nash (1950a, 1951). Proposition 122.1 is an implication of the existence of a "trembling hand perfect equilibrium", due to Selten (1975, Theorem 5).

The example in the box on page 104 is taken from Allais (1953). Conlisk (1989) discusses some of the evidence on the theory of expected payoffs; Machina (1987) and Hey (1997) survey the subject. (The purchasing power of the largest prize in Allais' example was roughly U.S.$6.6 million in 1989 (the date of Conlisk's paper, in which the prize is U.S.$5 million) and roughly U.S.$8 million in 1999.) The model in Section 4.6 is due to Pitchik and Schotter (1987). The model in Section 4.8 is a special case of the one in Palfrey and Rosenthal (1984); the interpretation and analysis that I describe is taken from an unpublished 1984 paper of William F. Samuelson. The box on page 133 draws upon Rosenthal (1964), Latané and Nida (1981), Brown (1986), and Aronson (1995). Best response dynamics were first studied by Cournot (1838, Chapter VII), in the context of his duopoly game. Fictitious play was suggested by Brown (1951). Robinson (1951) shows that the process converges to a mixed strategy Nash equilibrium in any two-player game in which the players' interests are opposed; Shapley (1964, Section 5) exhibits a game outside this class in which the process does not converge. Recent work on learning in games is surveyed by Fudenberg and Levine (1998).

The game in Exercise 118.1 is due to David L. Silverman (see Silverman 1981–82 and Heuer 1995). Exercise 118.2 is based on Palfrey and Rosenthal (1983). Exercise 118.3 is taken from Shubik (1982, 226) (who finds only one of the continuum of equilibria of the game).

The model in Exercise 128.1 is taken from Peters (1984). Exercise 130.2 is a variant of an exercise of Moulin (1986b, 167, 185). Exercise 132.3 is based on Palfrey and Rosenthal (1984). The game *Rock, Paper, Scissors* (Exercise 141.2) was first studied by Borel (1924) and von Neumann (1928). Exercise 141.3 is based on Karlin (1959a, 92–94), who attributes the game to an unpublished paper by Dresher.

Exercise 145.1 is based on a result in Baye, Kovenock, and de Vries (1996). The mixed strategy Nash equilibria of Bertrand's model of duopoly (Exercise 146.1) are studied in detail by Baye and Morgan (1999).

The method of finding all mixed strategy equilibrium described in Section 4.10 is computationally very intense in all but the simplest games. Some computationally more efficient methods are implemented in the freely available computer program GAMBIT.

5 Extensive Games with Perfect Information: Theory

5.1 Extensive games with perfect information   153
5.2 Strategies and outcomes   159
5.3 Nash equilibrium   161
5.4 Subgame perfect equilibrium   164
5.5 Finding subgame perfect equilibria of finite horizon games: backward induction   169
Prerequisite: Chapters 1 and 2

THE MODEL of a strategic game suppresses the sequential structure of decision-making. When applying the model to situations in which decision-makers move sequentially, we assume that each decision-maker chooses her plan of action once and for all; she is committed to this plan, which she cannot modify as events unfold. The model of an extensive game, by contrast, describes the sequential structure of decision-making explicitly, allowing us to study situations in which each decision-maker is free to change her mind as events unfold.

In this chapter and the next two we study a model in which each decision-maker is always fully informed about all previous actions. In Chapter 10 we study a more general model, which allows each decision-maker, when taking an action, to be imperfectly informed about previous actions.

5.1 Extensive games with perfect information

5.1.1 Definition

To describe an extensive game with perfect information, we need to specify the set of players and their preferences, as for a strategic game (Definition 13.1). In addition, we need to specify the order of the players' moves and the actions each player may take at each point. We do so by specifying the set of all sequences of actions that can possibly occur, together with the player who moves at each point in each sequence. We refer to each possible sequence of actions as a *terminal history* and to the function that gives the player who moves at each point in each terminal history as the *player function*. That is, an extensive game has four components:

- players
- terminal histories
- player function
- preferences for the players.

Before giving precise definitions of these components, I give an example that illustrates them informally.

◆ EXAMPLE 154.1 (Entry game) An incumbent faces the possibility of entry by a challenger. (The challenger may, for example, be a firm considering entry into an industry currently occupied by a monopolist, a politician competing for the leadership of a party, or an animal considering competing for the right to mate with a congener of the opposite sex.) The challenger may enter or not. If it enters, the incumbent may either acquiesce or fight.

We may model this situation as an extensive game with perfect information in which the terminal histories are (*In, Acquiesce*), (*In, Fight*), and *Out*, and the player function assigns the challenger to the start of the game and the incumbent to the history *In*.

At the start of an extensive game, and after any sequence of events, a player chooses an action. The sets of actions available to the players are not, however, given explicitly in the description of the game. Instead, the description of the game specifies the set of terminal histories and the player function, from which we can deduce the available sets of actions.

In the entry game, for example, the actions available to the challenger at the start of the game are *In* and *Out*, because these actions (and no others) begin terminal histories, and the actions available to the incumbent are *Acquiesce* and *Fight*, because these actions (and no others) follow *In* in terminal histories. More generally, suppose that (C, D) and (C, E) are terminal histories and the player function assigns player 1 to the start of the game and player 2 to the history C. Then two of the actions available to player 2 after player 1 chooses C at the start of the game are D and E.

The terminal histories of a game are specified as a set of sequences. But not every set of sequences is a legitimate set of terminal histories. If (C, D) is a terminal history, for example, there is no sense in specifying C as a terminal history: the fact that (C, D) is terminal implies that after C is chosen at the start of the game, some player may choose D, so that the action C does not end the game. More generally, a sequence that is a *proper subhistory* of a terminal history cannot itself be a terminal history. This restriction is the only one we need to impose on a set of sequences in order that the set be interpretable as a set of terminal histories.

To state the restriction precisely, define the **subhistories** of a finite sequence $(a^1, a^2, \ldots, a^k)$ of actions to be the empty sequence consisting of no actions, denoted ∅ (the **empty history**, representing the start of the game), and all sequences of the form $(a^1, a^2, \ldots, a^m)$, where $1 \leq m \leq k$. (In particular, the entire sequence is a subhistory of itself.) Similarly, define the **subhistories** of an infinite sequence $(a^1, a^2, \ldots)$ of actions to be the empty sequence ∅, every sequence of the form $(a^1, a^2, \ldots, a^m)$, where m is a positive integer, and the entire sequence $(a^1, a^2, \ldots)$. A subhistory not equal to the entire sequence is called a **proper subhistory**. A sequence of actions that is a subhistory of some terminal history is called simply a **history**.

In the entry game in Example 154.1, the subhistories of $(In, Acquiesce)$ are the empty history $\varnothing$ and the sequences In and $(In, Acquiesce)$; the proper subhistories are the empty history and the sequence In.

▶ DEFINITION 155.1 (*Extensive game with perfect information*) An **extensive game with perfect information** consists of

- a set of **players**

- a set of sequences (**terminal histories**) with the property that no sequence is a proper subhistory of any other sequence

- a function (the **player function**) that assigns a player to every sequence that is a proper subhistory of some terminal history

- for each player, **preferences** over the set of terminal histories.

The set of terminal histories is the set of all sequences of actions that may occur; the player assigned by the player function to any history h is the player who takes an action after h.

As for a strategic game, we may specify a player's preferences by giving a *payoff function* that represents them (see Section 1.2.2). In some situations an outcome is associated with each terminal history, and the players' preferences are naturally defined over these outcomes, rather than directly over the terminal histories. For example, if we are modeling firms choosing prices, then we may think in terms of each firm's caring about its profit—the outcome of a profile of prices—rather than directly about the profile of prices. However, any preferences over outcomes (e.g. profits) may be translated into preferences over terminal histories (e.g. sequences of prices). In the general definition, outcomes are conveniently identified with terminal histories and preferences are defined directly over these histories, avoiding the need for an additional element in the specification of the game.

◆ EXAMPLE 155.2 (Entry game) In the situation described in Example 154.1, suppose that the best outcome for the challenger is that it enters and the incumbent acquiesces, and the worst outcome is that it enters and the incumbent fights, whereas the best outcome for the incumbent is that the challenger stays out, and the worst outcome is that it enters and there is a fight. Then the situation may be modeled as the following extensive game with perfect information.

Players The challenger and the incumbent.

Terminal histories $(In, Acquiesce)$, $(In, Fight)$, and Out.

Player function $P(\varnothing) = Challenger$ and $P(In) = Incumbent$.

Preferences The challenger's preferences are represented by the payoff function u_1 for which $u_1(In, Acquiesce) = 2$, $u_1(Out) = 1$, and $u_1(In, Fight) = 0$, and the incumbent's preferences are represented by the payoff function u_2 for which $u_2(Out) = 2$, $u_2(In, Acquiesce) = 1$, and $u_2(In, Fight) = 0$.

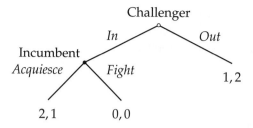

Figure 156.1 The entry game of Example 155.2. The challenger's payoff is the first number in each pair.

This game is readily illustrated in a diagram. The small circle at the top of Figure 156.1 represents the empty history (the start of the game). The label above this circle indicates that the challenger chooses an action at the start of the game ($P(\varnothing) = Challenger$). The two branches labeled *In* and *Out* represent the challenger's choices. The branch labeled *In* leads to a small black disk, the label beside which indicates that the incumbent takes an action after the history *In* (that is, $P(In) = Incumbent$). The two branches emanating from the disk represent the incumbent's choices, *Acquiesce* and *Fight*. The pair of numbers beneath each terminal history gives the players' payoffs to that history, with the challenger's payoff listed first. (The players' payoffs may be given in any order. For games like this one, in which the players move in a well-defined order, I generally list the payoffs in that order. For games in which the players' names are 1, 2, 3, and so on, I list the payoffs in the order of their names.)

Definition 155.1 does not directly specify the sets of actions available to the players at their various moves. As I discussed briefly before the definition, we can deduce these sets from the set of terminal histories and the player function. If, for some nonterminal history h, the sequence (h, a) is a history, then a is one of the actions available to the player who moves after h. Thus the set of all actions available to the player who moves after h is

$$A(h) = \{a \colon (h, a) \text{ is a history}\}. \tag{156.1}$$

For example, for the game in Figure 156.1, the histories are $\varnothing$, *In*, *Out*, (*In*, *Acquiesce*), and (*In*, *Fight*). Thus the set of actions available to the player who moves at the start of the game, namely the challenger, is $A(\varnothing) = \{In, Out\}$, and the set of actions available to the player who moves after the history *In*, namely the incumbent, is $A(In) = \{Acquiesce, Fight\}$.

● EXERCISE 156.2 (Examples of extensive games with perfect information)

    a. Represent in a diagram like Figure 156.1 the two-player extensive game with perfect information in which the terminal histories are (C, E), (C, F), (D, G), and (D, H), the player function is given by $P(\varnothing) = 1$ and $P(C) = P(D) = 2$, player 1 prefers (C, F) to (D, G) to (C, E) to (D, H), and player 2 prefers (D, G) to (C, F) to (D, H) to (C, E).

b. Write down the set of players, set of terminal histories, player function, and players' preferences for the game in Figure 160.1.

c. The political figures Rosa and Ernesto have to choose either Berlin (*B*) or Havana (*H*) as the location for a party congress. They choose sequentially. A third person, Karl, determines who chooses first. Both Rosa and Ernesto care only about the actions they choose, not about who chooses first. Rosa prefers the outcome in which both she and Ernesto choose *B* to that in which they both choose *H*, and prefers this outcome to either of the ones in which she and Ernesto choose different actions; she is indifferent between these last two outcomes. Ernesto's preferences differ from Rosa's in that the roles of *B* and *H* are reversed. Karl's preferences are the same as Ernesto's. Model this situation as an extensive game with perfect information. (Specify the components of the game and represent the game in a diagram.)

Definition 155.1 allows terminal histories to be infinitely long. Thus we can use the model of an extensive game to study situations in which the participants do not consider any particular fixed horizon when making decisions. If the length of the longest terminal history is in fact finite, we say that the game has a **finite horizon**.

Even a game with a finite horizon may have infinitely many terminal histories, because some player has infinitely many actions after some history. If a game has a finite horizon *and* finitely many terminal histories we say it is **finite**. Note that a game that is not finite cannot be represented in a diagram like Figure 156.1, because such a figure allows for only finitely many branches.

An extensive game with perfect information models a situation in which each player, when choosing an action, knows all actions chosen previously (has *perfect information*) and always moves alone (rather than simultaneously with other players). Some economic and political situations that the model encompasses are discussed in the next chapter. The competition between interest groups courting legislators is one example. This situation may be modeled as an extensive game in which the groups sequentially offer payments to induce the legislators to vote for their favorite version of a bill (Section 6.3). A race (between firms developing a new technology, or between directors making competing movies, for instance), is another example. This situation is modeled as an extensive game in which the parties alternately decide how much effort to expend (Section 6.4). Parlor games such as chess, ticktacktoe, and go, in which there are no random events, the players move sequentially, and each player always knows all actions taken previously, may also be modeled as extensive games with perfect information (see the box on page 178).

In Section 7.1 I discuss a more general notion of an extensive game in which players may move simultaneously, though each player, when choosing an action, still knows all previous actions. In Chapter 10 I discuss a much more general notion that allows arbitrary patterns of information. In each case I sometimes refer to the object under consideration simply as an "extensive game".

5.1.2 Solutions

In the entry game in Figure 156.1, it seems clear that the challenger will enter and the incumbent will subsequently acquiesce. The challenger can reason that if it enters then the incumbent will acquiesce, because doing so is better for the incumbent than fighting. Given that the incumbent will respond to entry in this way, the challenger is better off entering.

This line of argument is called *backward induction*. Whenever a player has to move, she deduces, for each of her possible actions, the actions that the players (including herself) will subsequently rationally take, and chooses the action that yields the terminal history she most prefers.

While backward induction may be applied to the game in Figure 156.1, it cannot be applied to every extensive game with perfect information. Consider, for example, the variant of this game shown in Figure 158.1, in which the incumbent's payoff to the terminal history (*In, Fight*) is 1 rather than 0. If, in the modified game, the challenger enters, the incumbent is indifferent between acquiescing and fighting. Backward induction does not tell the challenger what the incumbent will do in this case, and thus leaves open the question of which action the challenger should choose. Games with infinitely long histories present another difficulty for backward induction: they have no end from which to start the induction. The generalization of an extensive game with perfect information that allows for simultaneous moves (studied in Chapter 7) poses yet another problem: when players move simultaneously we cannot in general straightforwardly deduce each player's optimal action. (As in a strategic game, each player's best action depends on the other players' actions.)

Another approach to defining equilibrium takes off from the notion of Nash equilibrium. It seeks to model patterns of behavior that can persist in a steady state. The resulting notion of equilibrium applies to all extensive games with perfect information. Because the idea of backward induction is more limited, and the principles behind the notion of Nash equilibrium have been established in previous chapters, I begin by discussing the steady state approach. In games in which backward induction is well-defined, this approach turns out to lead to the backward induction outcome, so that there is no conflict between the two ideas.

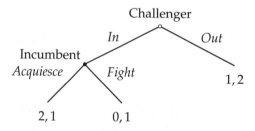

Figure 158.1 A variant of the entry game of Figure 156.1. The challenger's payoff is the first number in each pair.

5.2   Strategies and outcomes

5.2.1   Strategies

A key concept in the study of extensive games is that of a *strategy*. A player's strategy specifies the action the player chooses for *every* history after which it is her turn to move.

▶ DEFINITION 159.1 (*Strategy*) A **strategy** of player i in an extensive game with perfect information is a function that assigns to each history h after which it is player i's turn to move (i.e. $P(h) = i$, where P is the player function) an action in $A(h)$ (the set of actions available after h).

Consider the game in the top panel of Figure 159.1.

- Player 1 moves only at the start of the game (i.e. after the empty history), when the actions available to her are C and D. Thus she has two strategies: one that assigns C to the empty history, and one that assigns D to the empty history.

- Player 2 moves after both the history C and the history D. After the history C the actions available to her are E and F, and after the history D the actions available to her are G and H. Thus a strategy of player 2 is a function that assigns either E or F to the history C, and either G or H to the history D. That is, player 2 has *four* strategies, which are shown in the bottom panel of Figure 159.1.

I refer to the strategies of player 1 in this game simply as C and D, and to the strategies of player 2 simply as EG, EH, FG, and FH. For many other finite games I use a similar shorthand: I write a player's strategy as a list of actions, one for each

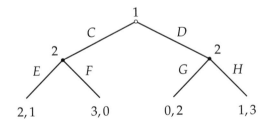

	Action assigned to history C	Action assigned to history D
Strategy 1	E	G
Strategy 2	E	H
Strategy 3	F	G
Strategy 4	F	H

Figure 159.1 An extensive game with perfect information (top panel) and the four strategies of player 2 in this game (bottom panel).

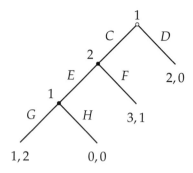

Figure 160.1 An extensive game in which player 1 moves both before and after player 2.

history after which it is the player's turn to move. In general I write the actions in the order in which they occur in the game, and, if they are available at the same "stage", from left to right as they appear in the diagram of the game. When the meaning of a list of actions is unclear, I explicitly give the history after which each action is taken.

Each of player 2's strategies in the game in the top panel of Figure 159.1 may be interpreted as a plan of action or contingency plan: it specifies what player 2 does *if* player 1 chooses C, *and* what she does *if* player 1 chooses D. In every game, a player's strategy provides sufficient information to determine her *plan of action*: the actions she intends to take, *whatever* the other players do. In particular, if a player appoints an agent to play the game for her, and tells the agent her strategy, then the agent has enough information to carry out her wishes, *whatever* actions the other players take.

In some games some players' strategies are *more* than plans of action. Consider the game in Figure 160.1. Player 1 moves both at the start of the game and after the history (C, E). In each case she has two actions, so she has *four* strategies: CG (i.e. choose C at the start of the game and G after the history (C, E)), CH, DG, and DH. In particular, each strategy specifies an action after the history (C, E) *even if it specifies the action D at the beginning of the game*, in which case the history (C, E) does not occur! The point is that Definition 159.1 requires that a strategy of any player *i* specify an action for *every* history after which it is player *i*'s turn to move, *even for histories that, if the strategy is followed, do not occur*.

In view of this point and the fact that "strategy" is a synonym for "plan of action" in everyday language, you may regard the word "strategy" as inappropriate for the concept in Definition 159.1. You are right. You may also wonder why we cannot restrict attention to plans of action.

For the purposes of the notion of Nash equilibrium (discussed in the next section), we *could* in fact work with plans of action rather than strategies. But, as we shall see, the notion of Nash equilibrium for an extensive game is not satisfactory; the concept we adopt depends on the players' full strategies. When discussing this concept (in Section 5.4.4) I elaborate on the interpretation of a strategy. At the moment, you may think of a player's strategy as a plan of what to do, whatever the other players do, both if the player carries out her intended actions and also if she makes mistakes. For example, we can interpret the strategy DG of player 1 in the game in Figure 160.1 to mean "I intend to choose D, but if I make a mistake and choose C instead, then I will subsequently choose G". (Because the notion of Nash equilibrium depends only on plans of action, I could delay the definition of a strategy to the start of Section 5.4. I do not do so because the notion of a strategy is central to the study of extensive games, and its precise definition is much simpler than that of a plan of action.)

? EXERCISE 161.1 (*Strategies in extensive games*) What are the strategies of the players in the entry game (Example 155.2)? What are Rosa's strategies in the game in Exercise 156.2*c*?

5.2.2 Outcomes

A strategy profile determines the terminal history that occurs. Denote the strategy profile by s and the player function by P. At the start of the game player $P(\varnothing)$ moves. Her strategy is $s_{P(\varnothing)}$, and she chooses the action $s_{P(\varnothing)}(\varnothing)$. Denote this action by a^1. If the history a^1 is not terminal, player $P(a^1)$ moves next. Her strategy is $s_{P(a^1)}$, and she chooses the action $s_{P(a^1)}(a^1)$. Denote this action by a^2. If the history (a^1, a^2) is not terminal, then again the player function specifies whose turn it is to move, and that player's strategy specifies the action she chooses. The process continues until a terminal history is constructed. We refer to this terminal history as the **outcome of** s, and denote it $O(s)$.

In the game in Figure 160.1, for example, the outcome of the strategy pair (DG, E) is the terminal history D, and the outcome of (CH, E) is the terminal history (C, E, H).

Note that the outcome $O(s)$ of the strategy profile s depends only on the players' plans of action, not their full strategies. That is, to determine $O(s)$ we do *not* need to refer to any component of any player's strategy that specifies her actions after histories precluded by that strategy.

5.3 Nash equilibrium

As for strategic games, we are interested in notions of equilibrium that model the players' behavior in a steady state. That is, we look for patterns of behavior with the property that if every player knows every other player's behavior, she has no reason to change her own behavior. I start by defining a Nash equilibrium: a strategy profile from which no player wishes to deviate, given the other players' strategies. The definition is an adaptation of that of a Nash equilibrium in a strategic game (23.1).

▷ DEFINITION 161.2 (*Nash equilibrium of extensive game with perfect information*) The strategy profile s^* in an extensive game with perfect information is a **Nash equilibrium** if, for every player i and every strategy r_i of player i, the terminal history

$O(s^*)$ generated by s^* is at least as good according to player i's preferences as the terminal history $O(r_i, s^*_{-i})$ generated by the strategy profile (r_i, s^*_{-i}) in which player i chooses r_i while every other player j chooses s^*_j. Equivalently, for each player i,

$$u_i(O(s^*)) \geq u_i(O(r_i, s^*_{-i})) \text{ for every strategy } r_i \text{ of player } i,$$

where u_i is a payoff function that represents player i's preferences and O is the outcome function of the game.

One way to find the Nash equilibria of an extensive game in which each player has finitely many strategies is to list each player's strategies, find the outcome of each strategy profile, and analyze this information as for a strategic game. That is, we construct the following strategic game, known as the **strategic form** of the extensive game.

Players   The set of players in the extensive game.

Actions   Each player's set of actions is her set of strategies in the extensive game.

Preferences   Each player's payoff to each action profile is her payoff to the terminal history generated by that action profile in the extensive game.

From Definition 161.2 we see that

the set of Nash equilibria of any extensive game with perfect information is the set of Nash equilibria of its strategic form.

◆ EXAMPLE 162.1 (Nash equilibria of the entry game) In the entry game in Figure 156.1, the challenger has two strategies, *In* and *Out*, and the incumbent has two strategies, *Acquiesce* and *Fight*. The strategic form of the game is shown in Figure 162.1. We see that it has two Nash equilibria: $(In, Acquiesce)$ and $(Out, Fight)$. The first equilibrium is the pattern of behavior isolated by backward induction, discussed at the start of Section 5.1.2.

In the second equilibrium the challenger always chooses *Out*. This strategy is optimal given the incumbent's strategy to fight in the event of entry. Further, the incumbent's strategy *Fight* is optimal given the challenger's strategy: the challenger chooses *Out*, so whether the incumbent plans to choose *Acquiesce* or *Fight* makes no difference to its payoff. Thus neither player can increase its payoff by choosing a different strategy, *given the other player's strategy*.

		Incumbent	
		Acquiesce	*Fight*
Challenger	*In*	2,1	0,0
	Out	1,2	1,2

Figure 162.1 The strategic form of the entry game in Figure 156.1.

Thinking about the extensive game in this example raises a question about the Nash equilibrium (*Out*, *Fight*) that does not arise in the strategic form: How does the challenger know that the incumbent will choose *Fight* if it enters? We interpret the strategic game to model a situation in which, whenever the challenger plays the game, it observes the incumbent's action, even if it chooses *Out*. By contrast, we interpret the extensive game to model a situation in which a challenger that always chooses *Out* never observes the incumbent's action, because the incumbent never moves. In a strategic game, the rationale for the Nash equilibrium condition that each player's strategy be optimal given the other players' strategies is that in a steady state, each player's experience playing the game leads her belief about the other players' actions to be correct. This rationale does not apply to the Nash equilibrium (*Out*, *Fight*) of the (extensive) entry game, because a challenger who always chooses *Out* never observes the incumbent's action after the history *In*.

We can escape from this difficulty in interpreting a Nash equilibrium of an extensive game by considering a slightly perturbed steady state in which, on rare occasions, nonequilibrium actions are taken (perhaps players make mistakes, or deliberately experiment), and the perturbations allow each player eventually to observe every other player's action after *every* history. Given such perturbations, each player eventually learns the other players' entire strategies.

Interpreting the Nash equilibrium (*Out*, *Fight*) as such a perturbed steady state, however, we run into another problem. On those (rare) occasions when the challenger enters, the subsequent behavior of the incumbent to fight is not a steady state in the remainder of the game: if the challenger enters, the incumbent is better off acquiescing than fighting. That is, the Nash equilibrium (*Out*, *Fight*) does not correspond to a *robust* steady state of the extensive game.

Note that the extensive game embodies the assumption that the incumbent cannot commit, at the beginning of the game, to fight if the challenger enters; it is free to choose either *Acquiesce* or *Fight* in this event. If the incumbent *could* commit to fight in the event of entry, then the analysis would be different. Such a commitment would induce the challenger to stay out, an outcome that the incumbent prefers. In the absence of the possibility of the incumbent's making a commitment, we might think of its *announcing* at the start of the game that it intends to fight; but such a *threat* is not credible, because after the challenger enters the incumbent's only incentive is to acquiesce.

⑦ EXERCISE 163.1 (Nash equilibria of extensive games) Find the Nash equilibria of the games in Exercise 156.2*a* and Figure 160.1. (When constructing the strategic form of each game, be sure to include *all* the strategies of each player.)

⑦ EXERCISE 163.2 (Voting by alternating veto) Two people select a policy that affects them both by alternately vetoing policies until only one remains. First person 1 vetoes a policy. If more than one policy remains, person 2 then vetoes a policy. If more than one policy still remains, person 1 then vetoes another policy. The process continues until a single policy remains unvetoed. Suppose there are three possible policies, X, Y, and Z, person 1 prefers X to Y to Z, and person 2 prefers Z to Y to X. Model this situation as an extensive game and find its Nash equilibria.

5.4   Subgame perfect equilibrium

5.4.1   Definition

The notion of Nash equilibrium ignores the sequential structure of an extensive game; it treats strategies as choices made once and for all before play begins. Consequently, as we saw in the previous section, the steady state to which a Nash equilibrium corresponds may not be robust.

I now define a notion of equilibrium that models a robust steady state. This notion requires each player's strategy to be optimal, given the other players' strategies, not only at the start of the game but after every possible history.

To define this concept, I first define the notion of a subgame. For any nonterminal history h, the *subgame* following h is the part of the game that remains after h has occurred. For example, the subgame following the history *In* in the entry game (Example 154.1) is the game in which the incumbent is the only player, and there are two terminal histories, *Acquiesce* and *Fight*.

▶ DEFINITION 164.1 (*Subgame of extensive game with perfect information*) Let Γ be an extensive game with perfect information, with player function P. For any nonterminal history h of Γ, the **subgame $\Gamma(h)$ following the history** h is the following extensive game.

    Players   The players in Γ.

    Terminal histories   The set of all sequences h' of actions such that (h, h') is a terminal history of Γ.

    Player function   The player $P(h, h')$ is assigned to each proper subhistory h' of a terminal history.

    Preferences   Each player prefers h' to h'' if and only if she prefers (h, h') to (h, h'') in Γ.

Note that the subgame following the empty history $\varnothing$ is the entire game. Every other subgame is called a *proper subgame*. Because there is a subgame for every nonterminal history, the number of subgames is equal to the number of nonterminal histories.

As an example, the game in the top panel of Figure 159.1 has three nonterminal histories (the empty history, C, and D), and hence three subgames: the whole game (the part of the game following the empty history), the game following the history C, and the game following the history D. The two proper subgames are shown in Figure 165.1.

The game in Figure 160.1 also has three nonterminal histories, and hence three subgames: the whole game, the game following the history C, and the game following the history (C, E). The two proper subgames are shown in Figure 165.2.

? EXERCISE 164.2 (Subgames) Find all the subgames of the game in Exercise 156.2c.

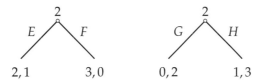

Figure 165.1 The two proper subgames of the extensive game in the top panel of Figure 159.1.

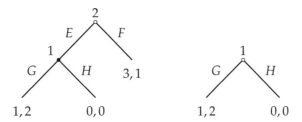

Figure 165.2 The two proper subgames of the extensive game in Figure 160.1.

In an equilibrium that corresponds to a perturbed steady state in which *every* history sometimes occurs, the players' behavior must correspond to a steady state in *every subgame*, not only in the whole game. Interpreting the actions specified by a player's strategy in a subgame to give the player's behavior if, possibly after a series of mistakes, that subgame is reached, this condition is embodied in the following informal definition.

> A *subgame perfect equilibrium* is a strategy profile s^* with the property that in no subgame can any player i do better by choosing a strategy different from s_i^*, given that every other player j adheres to s_j^*.

(Compare this definition with that of a Nash equilibrium of a strategic game given on page 22.)

For example, the Nash equilibrium (*Out*, *Fight*) of the entry game (Example 154.1) is not a subgame perfect equilibrium because in the subgame following the history *In*, the strategy *Fight* is not optimal for the incumbent: *in this subgame*, the incumbent is better off choosing *Acquiesce* than it is choosing *Fight*. The Nash equilibrium (*In*, *Acquiesce*) *is* a subgame perfect equilibrium: each player's strategy is optimal, given the other player's strategy, both in the whole game and in the subgame following the history *In*.

To define the notion of subgame perfect equilibrium precisely, we need a new piece of notation. Let h be a history and s a strategy profile. Suppose that h occurs (even though it is not necessarily consistent with s), and *afterward* the players adhere to the strategy profile s. The resulting terminal history (consisting of h followed by the outcome generated in the subgame following h by the strategy profile induced by s in the subgame) is denoted $O_h(s)$. Note that for any strategy profile s, we have $O_\varnothing(s) = O(s)$ (where $\varnothing$, as always, denotes the empty history).

As an example, consider again the entry game. Let s be the strategy profile (*Out*, *Fight*) and let h be the history *In*. If h occurs, and *afterward* the players adhere to s, the resulting terminal history is $O_h(s) = (In, Fight)$.

▶ DEFINITION 166.1 (*Subgame perfect equilibrium of extensive game with perfect information*) The strategy profile s^* in an extensive game with perfect information is a **subgame perfect equilibrium** if, for every player i, every history h after which it is player i's turn to move (i.e. $P(h) = i$), and every strategy r_i of player i, the terminal history $O_h(s^*)$ generated by s^* after the history h is at least as good according to player i's preferences as the terminal history $O_h(r_i, s^*_{-i})$ generated by the strategy profile (r_i, s^*_{-i}) in which player i chooses r_i while every other player j chooses s^*_j. Equivalently, for every player i and every history h after which it is player i's turn to move,

$$u_i(O_h(s^*)) \geq u_i(O_h(r_i, s^*_{-i})) \text{ for every strategy } r_i \text{ of player } i,$$

where u_i is a payoff function that represents player i's preferences and $O_h(s)$ is the terminal history consisting of h followed by the sequence of actions generated by s after h.

The important point in this definition is that each player's strategy is required to be optimal for *every* history after which it is the player's turn to move, not only at the start of the game as in the definition of a Nash equilibrium (161.2).

5.4.2 Subgame perfect equilibrium and Nash equilibrium

In a subgame perfect equilibrium every player's strategy is optimal, in particular, after the empty history (put $h = \varnothing$ in the definition, and remember that $O_\varnothing(s) = O(s)$). Thus

every subgame perfect equilibrium is a Nash equilibrium.

In fact, a subgame perfect equilibrium generates a Nash equilibrium in every subgame: if s^* is a subgame perfect equilibrium, then, for any history h and player i, the strategy induced by s^*_i in the subgame following h is optimal given the strategies induced by s^*_{-i} in the subgame. Further, any strategy profile that generates a Nash equilibrium in every subgame is a subgame perfect equilibrium, so that we can give the following alternative definition.

A *subgame perfect equilibrium* is a strategy profile that induces a Nash equilibrium in every subgame.

In a Nash equilibrium every player's strategy is optimal, given the other players' strategies, in the whole game. As we have seen, it may *not* be optimal in some subgames. I claim, however, that it *is* optimal in any subgame that is reached when the players follow their strategies. Given this claim, the significance of the requirement in the definition of a subgame perfect equilibrium that each player's strategy be optimal after every history, relative to the requirement in the definition of a Nash equilibrium, is that each player's strategy be optimal after histories that do not occur if the players follow their strategies (like the history *In* when the challenger's action is *Out* at the beginning of the entry game).

To show my claim, suppose that s^* is a Nash equilibrium of a game in which you are player i. Then your strategy s_i^* is optimal given the other players' strategies s_{-i}^*. When the other players follow their strategies, there comes a point (possibly the start of the game) when you have to move for the first time. Suppose that at this point you follow your strategy s_i^*; denote the action you choose by C. Now, after choosing C, should you change your strategy in the rest of the game, given that the other players will continue to adhere to their strategies? No! If you could do better by changing your strategy after choosing C—say by switching to the strategy s_i' in the subgame—then you could have done better at the start of the game by choosing the strategy that chooses C and then follows s_i'. That is, if your plan is optimal, given the other players' strategies, at the start of the game, and you stick to it, then you never want to change your mind after play begins, as long as the other players stick to their strategies. (The general principle is known as the *principle of optimality* in dynamic programming.)

5.4.3 Examples

◆ EXAMPLE 167.1 (Entry game) Consider again the entry game of Example 154.1, which has two Nash equilibria, $(In, Acquiesce)$ and $(Out, Fight)$. The fact that the Nash equilibrium $(Out, Fight)$ is not a subgame perfect equilibrium follows from the formal definition as follows. For $s^* = (Out, Fight)$, $i = $ Incumbent, $r_i = $ Acquiesce, and $h = $ In, we have $O_h(s^*) = (In, Fight)$ and $O_h(r_i, s_{-i}^*) = (In, Acquiesce)$, so that the inequality in the definition is violated: $u_i(O_h(s^*)) = 0$ and $u_i(O_h(r_i, s_{-i}^*)) = 1$.

The Nash equilibrium $(In, Acquiesce)$ *is* a subgame perfect equilibrium because (a) it is a Nash equilibrium, so that at the start of the game the challenger's strategy In is optimal, given the incumbent's strategy $Acquiesce$, and (b) after the history In, the incumbent's strategy $Acquiesce$ in the subgame is optimal. In the language of the formal definition, let $s^* = (In, Acquiesce)$.

- The challenger moves after one history, namely $h = \varnothing$. We have $O_h(s^*) = (In, Acquiesce)$, and hence for $i = $ challenger we have $u_i(O_h(s^*)) = 2$, whereas for the only other strategy of the challenger, $r_i = $ Out, we have $u_i(O_h(r_i, s_{-i}^*)) = 1$.

- The incumbent moves after one history, namely $h = In$. We have $O_h(s^*) = (In, Acquiesce)$, and hence for $i = $ incumbent we have $u_i(O_h(s^*)) = 1$, whereas for the only other strategy of the incumbent, $r_i = $ Fight, we have $u_i(O_h(r_i, s_{-i}^*)) = 0$.

Every subgame perfect equilibrium is a Nash equilibrium, so we conclude that the game has a unique subgame perfect equilibrium, $(In, Acquiesce)$.

◆ EXAMPLE 167.2 (Variant of entry game) Consider the variant of the entry game in which the incumbent is indifferent between fighting and acquiescing if the challenger enters (see Figure 158.1). This game, like the original game, has two Nash equilibria, (*In, Acquiesce*) and (*Out, Fight*). But now *both* of these equilibria are sub-game perfect equilibria, because after the history *In*, both *Fight* and *Acquiesce* are optimal for the incumbent.

In particular, the game has a steady state in which every challenger always chooses *In* and every incumbent always chooses *Acquiesce*. If you, as the challenger, were playing the game for the first time, you would probably regard the action *In* as "risky" because after the history *In* the incumbent is indifferent between *Acquiesce* and *Fight*, and you prefer the terminal history *Out* to the terminal history (*In, Fight*). Indeed, as discussed in Section 5.1.2, backward induction does not yield a clear solution of this game. But the subgame perfect equilibrium (*In, Acquiesce*) corresponds to a perfectly reasonable steady state. If you had played the game hundreds of times against opponents drawn from the same population, and on every occasion your opponent had chosen *Acquiesce*, you could reasonably expect your next opponent to choose *Acquiesce*, and thus optimally choose *In*.

? EXERCISE 168.1 (Checking for subgame perfect equilibria) Which of the Nash equilibria of the game in Figure 160.1 are subgame perfect?

5.4.4 Interpretation

A Nash equilibrium of a strategic game corresponds to a steady state in an idealized setting in which the participants in each play of the game are drawn randomly from a collection of populations (see Section 2.6). The idea is that each player's long experience playing the game leads her to correct beliefs about the other players' actions; given these beliefs, her equilibrium action is optimal.

A subgame perfect equilibrium of an extensive game corresponds to a slightly perturbed steady state in which all players, on rare occasions, take nonequilibrium actions, so that after long experience each player forms correct beliefs about the other players' entire strategies and thus knows how the other players will behave in every subgame. Given these beliefs, no player wishes to deviate from her strategy either at the start of the game or after *any* history.

This interpretation of a subgame perfect equilibrium, like the interpretation of a Nash equilibrium as a steady state, does not require a player to know the other players' preferences, or to think about the other players' rationality. It entails interpreting a strategy as a plan specifying a player's actions not only after histories consistent with the strategy, but also after histories that result when the player chooses arbitrary alternative actions, perhaps because she makes mistakes or deliberately experiments.

The subgame perfect equilibria of some extensive game can be given other interpretations. In some cases, one alternative interpretation is particularly attractive. Consider an extensive game with perfect information in which each player has a unique best action at every history after which it is her turn to move, and the horizon is finite. In such a game, a player who knows the other players' preferences and knows that the other players are rational may use backward induction to deduce her optimal strategy, as discussed in Section 5.1.2. Thus we can interpret a subgame perfect equilibrium as the outcome of the players' rational calculations about each other's strategies.

This interpretation of a subgame perfect equilibrium entails an interpretation of a strategy different from the one that fits the steady state interpretation. Consider, for example, the game in Figure 160.1. When analyzing this game, player 1 must consider the consequences of choosing C. Thus she must think about player 2's action after the history C, and hence must form a belief about what player 2 thinks she (player 1) will do after the history (C, E). The component of her strategy that specifies her action after this history reflects this belief. For instance, the strategy DG means that player 1 chooses D at the start of the game and believes that were she to choose C, player 2 would believe that after the history (C, E) she would choose G. In an arbitrary game, the interpretation of a subgame perfect equilibrium as the outcome of the players' rational calculations about each other's strategies entails interpreting the components of a player's strategy that assign actions to histories inconsistent with other parts of the strategy as specifying the player's belief about the other players' beliefs about what the player will do if one of these histories occurs.

This interpretation of a subgame perfect equilibrium is not free of difficulties, which are discussed in Section 7.7. Further, the interpretation is not tenable in games in which some player has more than one optimal action after some history, or in the more general extensive games considered in Section 7.1 and Chapter 10. Nevertheless, in some of the games studied in this chapter and the next it is an appealing alternative to the steady state interpretation. Further, an extension of the procedure of backward induction can be used to find all subgame perfect equilibria of finite horizon games, as we shall see in the next section. (This extension cannot be given an appealing behavioral interpretation in games in which some player has more than one optimal action after some history.)

5.5 Finding subgame perfect equilibria of finite horizon games: backward induction

We found the subgame perfect equilibria of the games in Examples 167.1 and 167.2 by finding the Nash equilibria of the games and checking whether each of these equilibria is subgame perfect. In a game with a finite horizon the set of subgame perfect equilibria may be found more directly by using an extension of the procedure of backward induction discussed briefly in Section 5.1.2.

Define the *length of a subgame* to be the length of the longest history in the subgame. (The lengths of the subgames in Figure 165.2, for example, are 2 and 1.) The procedure of backward induction works as follows. We start by finding the optimal actions of the players who move in the subgames of length 1 (the "last" subgames). Then, taking these actions as given, we find the optimal actions of the players who move first in the subgames of length 2. We continue working back to

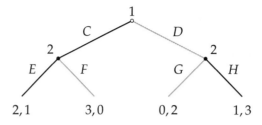

Figure 170.1 A game illustrating the procedure of backward induction. The actions selected by backward induction are indicated in black.

the beginning of the game, at each stage k finding the optimal actions of the players who move at the start of the subgames of length k, given the optimal actions we have found in all shorter subgames.

At each stage k of this procedure, the optimal actions of the players who move at the start of the subgames of length k are easy to determine: they are simply the actions that yield the players the highest payoffs, given the optimal actions in all shorter subgames.

Consider, for example, the game in Figure 170.1.

- First consider subgames of length 1. The game has two such subgames, in both of which player 2 moves. In the subgame following the history C, player 2's optimal action is E, and in the subgame following the history D, her optimal action is H.

- Now consider subgames of length 2. The game has one such subgame, namely the entire game, at the start of which player 1 moves. Given the optimal actions in the subgames of length 1, player 1's choosing C at the start of the game yields her a payoff of 2, whereas her choosing D yields her a payoff of 1. Thus player 1's optimal action at the start of the game is C.

The game has no subgame of length greater than 2, so the procedure of backward induction yields the strategy pair (C, EH).

As another example, consider again the game in Figure 160.1. We first deduce that in the subgame of length 1 following the history (C, E), player 1 chooses G; then that at the start of the subgame of length 2 following the history C, player 2 chooses E; then that at the start of the whole game, player 1 chooses D. Thus the procedure of backward induction in this game yields the strategy pair (DG, E).

In any game in which this procedure selects a single action for the player who moves at the start of each subgame, the strategy profile thus selected is the unique subgame perfect equilibrium of the game. (You should find this result very plausible, though a complete proof is not trivial.)

What happens in a game in which at the start of some subgames more than one action is optimal? In such a game an extension of the procedure of backward induction locates all subgame perfect equilibria. This extension traces back *separately* the implications for behavior in the longer subgames of *every combination* of optimal actions in the shorter subgames.

Consider, for example, the game in Figure 172.1.

- The game has three subgames of length 1, in each of which player 2 moves. In the subgames following the histories C and D, player 2 is indifferent between her two actions. In the subgame following the history E, player 2's unique optimal action is K. Thus there are *four* combinations of player 2's optimal actions in the subgames of length 1: FHK, FIK, GHK, and GIK (where the first component in each case is player 2's action after the history C, the second component is her action after the history D, and the third component is her action after the history E).

- The game has a single subgame of length 2, namely the whole game, in which player 1 moves first. We now consider player 1's optimal action in this game for *every combination* of the optimal actions of player 2 in the subgames of length 1.

    ○ For the combinations FHK and FIK of optimal actions of player 2, player 1's optimal action at the start of the game is C.

    ○ For the combination GHK of optimal actions of player 2, the actions C, D, and E are all optimal for player 1.

    ○ For the combination GIK of optimal actions of player 2, player 1's optimal action at the start of the game is D.

Thus the strategy pairs isolated by the procedure are (C, FHK), (C, FIK), (C, GHK), (D, GHK), (E, GHK), and (D, GIK).

The procedure, which for simplicity I refer to simply as **backward induction**, may be described compactly for an arbitrary game as follows.

- Find, for each subgame of length 1, the set of optimal actions of the player who moves first. Index the subgames by j, and denote by $S_j^*(1)$ the set of optimal actions in subgame j. (If the player who moves first in subgame j has a unique optimal action, then $S_j^*(1)$ contains a single action.)

- For each combination of actions consisting of one from each set $S_j^*(1)$, find, for each subgame of length 2, the set of optimal actions of the player who moves first. The result is a set of strategy profiles for each subgame of length 2. Denote by $S_\ell^*(2)$ the set of strategy profiles in subgame ℓ.

- Continue by examining successively longer subgames until you reach the start of the game. At each stage k, for each combination of strategy profiles consisting of one from each set $S_p^*(k-1)$ constructed in the previous stage, find, for each subgame of length k, the set of optimal actions of the player who moves first, and hence a set of strategy profiles for each subgame of length k.

The set of strategy profiles that this procedure yields for the whole game is the set of subgame perfect equilibria of the game.

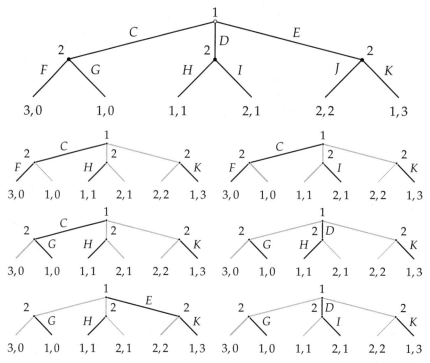

Figure 172.1 A game in which the first-mover in some subgames has multiple optimal actions. The top diagram shows the full game. The six small diagrams illustrate the six subgame perfect equilibria; in each case, the actions specified by the equilibrium strategies are indicated by black lines, and the remaining actions are indicated by gray lines.

■ PROPOSITION 172.1 (Subgame perfect equilibrium of finite horizon games and backward induction) *The set of subgame perfect equilibria of a finite horizon extensive game with perfect information is equal to the set of strategy profiles isolated by the procedure of backward induction.*

You should find this result, like my claim for games in which the player who moves at the start of every subgame has a single optimal action, very plausible, though again a complete proof is not trivial.

In the terminology of my description of the general procedure, the analysis for the game in Figure 172.1 is as follows. Number the subgames of length 1 from left to right. Then we have $S_1^*(1) = \{F, G\}$, $S_2^*(1) = \{H, I\}$, and $S_3^*(1) = \{K\}$. There are four lists of actions consisting of one action from each set: FHK, FIK, GHK, and GIK. For FHK and FIK, the action C of player 1 is optimal at the start of the game; for GHK the actions C, D, and E are all optimal; and for GIK the action D is optimal. Thus the set $S^*(2)$ of strategy profiles consists of (C, FHK), (C, FIK), (C, GHK), (D, GHK), (E, GHK), and (D, GIK). There are no longer subgames, so this set of strategy profiles is the set of subgame perfect equilibria of the game.

Each example I have presented so far in this section is a finite game—that is, a game that has not only a finite horizon but also a finite number of terminal histories. In such a game, the player who moves first in any subgame has finitely many actions; at least one action is optimal. Thus in such a game the procedure of backward induction isolates at least one strategy profile. Using Proposition 172.1, we conclude that every finite game has a subgame perfect equilibrium.

■ PROPOSITION 173.1 (Existence of subgame perfect equilibrium) *Every finite extensive game with perfect information has a subgame perfect equilibrium.*

Note that this result does *not* claim that a finite extensive game has a *single* subgame perfect equilibrium. (As we have seen, the game in Figure 172.1, for example, has more than one subgame perfect equilibrium.)

A finite horizon game in which some player does not have finitely many actions after some history may or may not possess a subgame perfect equilibrium. A simple example of a game that does not have a subgame perfect equilibrium is the trivial game in which a single player chooses a number *less than* 1 and receives a payoff equal to the number she chooses. There is no greatest number less than one, so the single player has no optimal action, and thus the game has no subgame perfect equilibrium.

? EXERCISE 173.2 (Finding subgame perfect equilibria) Find the subgame perfect equilibria of the games in parts *a* and *c* of Exercise 156.2, and in Figure 173.1.

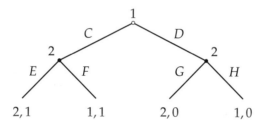

Figure 173.1 One of the games for Exercise 173.2.

? EXERCISE 173.3 (Voting by alternating veto) Find the subgame perfect equilibria of the game in Exercise 163.2. Does the game have any Nash equilibrium that is not a subgame perfect equilibrium? Is any outcome generated by a Nash equilibrium not generated by any subgame perfect equilibrium? Consider variants of the game in which player 2's preferences may differ from those specified in Exercise 163.2. Are there any preferences for which the outcome in a subgame perfect equilibrium of the game in which player 1 moves first differs from the outcome in a subgame perfect equilibrium of the game in which player 2 moves first?

? EXERCISE 173.4 (Burning a bridge) Army 1, of country 1, must decide whether to attack army 2, of country 2, which is occupying an island between the two countries. In the event of an attack, army 2 may fight, or retreat over a bridge to its mainland. Each army prefers to occupy the island than not to occupy it; a fight is the worst outcome for both armies. Model this situation as an extensive game with perfect information and show that army 2 can increase its subgame perfect equilibrium payoff (and reduce army 1's payoff) by burning the bridge to its mainland (assume this act entails no cost), eliminating its option to retreat if attacked.

? EXERCISE 174.1 (Sharing heterogeneous objects) A group of n people have to share k objects that they value differently. Each person assigns values to the objects; no one assigns the same value to two different objects. Each person evaluates a set of objects according to the sum of the values she assigns to the objects in the set. The following procedure is used to share the objects. The players are ordered 1 through n. Person 1 chooses an object, then person 2 does so, and so on; if $k > n$, then after person n chooses an object, person 1 chooses a second object, then person 2 chooses a second object, and so on. Objects are chosen until none remain. (Canadian and U.S. professional sports teams use a similar procedure to choose new players.) Denote by $G(n,k)$ the extensive game that models this procedure. If $k \leq n$, then obviously $G(n,k)$ has a subgame perfect equilibrium in which each player's strategy is to choose her favorite object among those remaining when her turn comes. Show that if $k > n$, then $G(n,k)$ may have no subgame perfect equilibrium in which person 1 chooses her favorite object on the first round. (You can give an example in which $n = 2$ and $k = 3$.) Now fix $n = 2$. Define x_k to be the object least preferred by the person who does *not* choose at stage k (i.e. who does not choose the last object); define x_{k-1} to be the object, among all those except x_k, least preferred by the person who does *not* choose at stage $k - 1$. Similarly, for any j with $2 \leq j \leq k$, given $x_j, \ldots, x_k$, define x_{j-1} to be the object, among all those excluding $\{x_j, \ldots, x_k\}$, least preferred by the person who does *not* choose at stage $j - 1$. Show that the game $G(2,3)$ has a subgame perfect equilibrium in which for every $j = 1, \ldots, k$ the object x_j is chosen at stage j. (This result is true for $G(2,k)$ for all values of k.) If $n \geq 3$, then interestingly a person may be better off in all subgame perfect equilibria of $G(n,k)$ when she comes later in the ordering of players. (An example, however, is difficult to construct; one is given in Brams and Straffin 1979.)

The next exercise shows how backward induction can cause a relatively minor change in the way in which a game ends to reverberate to the start of the game, leading to a very different action for the first-mover.

? EXERCISE 174.2 (An entry game with a financially constrained firm) An incumbent in an industry faces the possibility of entry by a challenger. First the challenger chooses whether to enter. If it does not enter, neither firm has any further action; the incumbent's payoff is TM (it obtains the profit M in each of the following $T \geq 1$ periods) and the challenger's payoff is 0. If the challenger enters, it pays the entry cost $f > 0$, and in each of T periods the incumbent first commits to fight or cooperate with the challenger in that period, then the challenger chooses whether to stay in the industry or to exit. (Note that the order of the firms' moves within a period differs from that in the game in Example 154.1.) If, in any period, the challenger stays in, each firm obtains in that period the profit $-F < 0$ if the incumbent fights and $C > \max\{F, f\}$ if it cooperates. If, in any period, the challenger exits, both firms obtain the profit zero in that period (regardless of the incumbent's action); the incumbent obtains the profit $M > 2C$ and the challenger the profit 0 in every subsequent period. Once the challenger exits, it cannot subsequently reenter. Each firm cares about the sum of its profits.

a. Find the subgame perfect equilibria of the extensive game that models this situation.

b. Consider a variant of the situation in which the challenger is constrained by its financial war chest, which allows it to survive at most $T - 2$ fights. Specifically, consider the game that differs from the one in part a in one respect: the histories in which (i) at the start of the game the challenger enters and (ii) the incumbent fights in $T - 1$ periods are terminal histories (the challenger has to exit). For the terminal history in which the incumbent fights in the first $T - 1$ periods, the incumbent's payoff is $M - (T - 2)F$ and the challenger's payoff is $-f - (T - 2)F$ (in period $T - 1$ the incumbent's payoff is 0, and in the last period its payoff is M). For the terminal history in which the incumbent cooperates in one of the first $T - 1$ periods and fights in the remainder of these periods and in the last period, the incumbent's payoff is $C - (T - 2)F$ and the challenger's payoff is $-f + C - (T - 2)F$. Find the subgame perfect equilibria of this game.

◆ EXAMPLE 175.1 (Dollar auction) Consider an auction in which an object is sold to the highest bidder, but *both* the highest bidder *and* the second-highest bidder pay their bids to the auctioneer. When such an auction is conducted and the object is a dollar, the outcome is sometimes that the object is sold at a price *greater* than a dollar. (Shubik writes: "A total of payments between three and five dollars is not uncommon" (1971, 110).) Obviously such an outcome is inconsistent with a subgame perfect equilibrium of an extensive game that models the auction: every participant has the option of not bidding, so that in no subgame perfect equilibrium can anyone's payoff be negative.

Why, then, do such outcomes occur? Suppose that there are two participants, and both start bidding. If the player making the lower bid thinks that making a bid above the other player's bid will induce the other player to quit, she may be better off doing so than stopping bidding. For example, if the bids are currently $0.50 and $0.51, the player bidding $0.50 is better off bidding $0.52 *if* doing so induces the other bidder to quit, because she then wins the dollar and obtains a payoff of $0.48, rather than losing $0.50. The same logic applies even if the bids are greater than $1.00, as long as they do not differ by more than $1.00. If, for example, they are currently $2.00 and $2.01, then the player bidding $2.00 loses only $1.02 if a bid of $2.02 induces her opponent to quit, whereas she loses $2.00 if she herself quits. That is, in subgames in which bids have been made, the player making the second-highest bid may optimally beat a bid that exceeds $1.00, depending on the other players' strategies and the difference between the top two bids. (When discussing outcomes in which the total payment to the auctioneer exceeds $1, Shubik remarks that "In playing this game, a large crowd is desirable ... the best time is during a party when spirits are high and the propensity to calculate does not settle in until at least two bids have been made" (1971, 109).)

In the next exercise you are asked to find the subgame perfect equilibria of an extensive game that models a simple example of such an auction.

? EXERCISE 176.1 (Dollar auction) An object that two people each value at v, a positive integer, is sold in an auction. In the auction, the people take turns bidding; a bid must be a positive integer greater than the previous bid. (In the situation that gives the game its name, v is 100 cents.) On her turn, a player may pass rather than bid, in which case the game ends and the other player receives the object; *both* players pay their last bids (if any). (If player 1 passes initially, for example, player 2 receives the object and makes no payment; if player 1 bids 1, player 2 bids 3, and then player 1 passes, player 2 obtains the object and pays 3, and player 1 pays 1.) Each person's wealth is w, which exceeds v; neither player may bid more than her wealth. For $v = 2$ and $w = 3$, model the auction as an extensive game and find its subgame perfect equilibria. (A much more ambitious project is to find all subgame perfect equilibria for arbitrary values of v and w.)

In all the extensive games studied so far in this chapter, each player has available finitely many actions whenever she moves. The next examples show how the procedure of backward induction may be used to find the subgame perfect equilibria of games in which a continuum of actions is available after some histories.

◆ EXAMPLE 176.2 (A synergistic relationship) Consider a variant of the situation in Example 39.1, in which two individuals are involved in a synergistic relationship. Suppose that the players choose their effort levels sequentially, rather than simultaneously. First individual 1 chooses her effort level a_1, then individual 2 chooses her effort level a_2. An effort level is a nonnegative number, and individual i's preferences (for $i = 1, 2$) are represented by the payoff function $a_i(c + a_j - a_i)$, where j is the other individual and $c > 0$ is a constant.

To find the subgame perfect equilibria, we first consider the subgames of length 1, in which individual 2 chooses a value of a_2. Individual 2's optimal action after the history a_1 is her best response to a_1, which we found to be $\frac{1}{2}(c + a_1)$ in Example 39.1. Thus individual 2's strategy in any subgame perfect equilibrium is the function that associates with each history a_1 the action $\frac{1}{2}(c + a_1)$.

Now consider individual 1's action at the start of the game. Given individual 2's strategy, individual 1's payoff if she chooses a_1 is $a_1(c + \frac{1}{2}(c + a_1) - a_1)$, or $\frac{1}{2}a_1(3c - a_1)$. This function is a quadratic that is zero when $a_1 = 0$ and when $a_1 = 3c$, and reaches a maximum in between. Thus individual 1's optimal action at the start of the game is $a_1 = \frac{3}{2}c$.

We conclude that the game has a unique subgame perfect equilibrium, in which individual 1's strategy is $a_1 = \frac{3}{2}c$ and individual 2's strategy is the function that associates with each history a_1 the action $\frac{1}{2}(c + a_1)$. The outcome of the equilibrium is that individual 1 chooses $a_1 = \frac{3}{2}c$ and individual 2 chooses $a_2 = \frac{5}{4}c$.

? EXERCISE 177.1 (Firm–union bargaining) A firm's output is $L(100 - L)$ when it uses $L \leq 50$ units of labor, and 2500 when it uses $L > 50$ units of labor. The price of output is 1. A union that represents workers presents a wage demand (a nonnegative number w), which the firm either accepts or rejects. If the firm accepts the demand, it chooses the number L of workers to employ (which you should take to be a continuous variable, not an integer); if it rejects the demand, no production takes place ($L = 0$). The firm's preferences are represented by its profit; the union's preferences are represented by the value of wL.

    a. Formulate this situation as an extensive game with perfect information.

    b. Find the subgame perfect equilibrium (equilibria?) of the game.

    c. Is there an outcome of the game that both parties prefer to any subgame perfect equilibrium outcome?

    d. Find a Nash equilibrium for which the outcome differs from any subgame perfect equilibrium outcome.

? EXERCISE 177.2 (The "rotten kid theorem") A child's action a (a number) affects both her own private income $c(a)$ and her parents' income $p(a)$; for all values of a we have $c(a) < p(a)$. The child is selfish: she cares only about the amount of money she has. Her loving parents care both about how much money they have and how much their child has. Specifically, model the parents as a single individual whose preferences are represented by a payoff equal to the smaller of the amount of money they have and the amount of money the child has. The parents may transfer money to the child. First the child takes an action, then the parents decide how much money to transfer. Model this situation as an extensive game and show that in a subgame perfect equilibrium the child takes an action that maximizes the sum of her private income and her parents' income. (In particular, the child's action does not maximize her own private income. The result is not limited to the specific form of the parents' preferences, but holds for any preferences with the property that the amount of money the child receives in the optimal allocation of a fixed amount x on money between the parents and the child increases with x.)

? EXERCISE 177.3 (Comparing simultaneous and sequential games) The set of actions available to player 1 is A_1; the set available to player 2 is A_2. Player 1's preferences over pairs (a_1, a_2) are represented by the payoff $u_1(a_1, a_2)$, and player 2's preferences are represented by the payoff $u_2(a_1, a_2)$. Compare the Nash equilibria (in pure strategies) of the strategic game in which the players choose actions simultaneously with the subgame perfect equilibria of the extensive game in which player 1 chooses an action, then player 2 does so. (For each history a_1 in the extensive game, the set of actions available to player 2 is A_2.)

    a. Show that if, for every value of a_1, a unique member of A_2 maximizes $u_2(a_1, a_2)$, then in every subgame perfect equilibrium of the extensive game, player 1's payoff is at least equal to her highest payoff in any Nash equilibrium of the strategic game.

  b. Show that player 2's payoff in every subgame perfect equilibrium of the extensive game may be higher than her highest payoff in any Nash equilibrium of the strategic game.

  c. Show that if for some values of a_1 more than one member of A_2 maximizes $u_2(a_1, a_2)$, then the extensive game may have a subgame perfect equilibrium in which player 1's payoff is less than her payoff in all Nash equilibria of the strategic game.

(For parts b and c you can give examples in which both A_1 and A_2 contain two actions. See Example 320.2 for further discussion of the implication of the order of play.)

TICKTACKTOE, CHESS, AND RELATED GAMES

Ticktacktoe, chess, and related games may be modeled as extensive games with perfect information. (A history is a sequence of moves and each player prefers to win than to tie than to lose.) Both ticktacktoe and chess may be modeled as finite games, so by Proposition 173.1 each game has a subgame perfect equilibrium. (The official rules of chess allow indefinitely long sequences of moves, but the game seems to be well modeled by an extensive game in which a draw is declared automatically if a position is repeated three times, rather than a player having the option of declaring a draw in this case, as in the official rules.) The subgame perfect equilibria of ticktacktoe are of course known, whereas those of chess are not (yet).

Ticktacktoe and chess are "strictly competitive" games (Definition 365.2): in every outcome, either one player loses and the other wins, or the players draw. A result in a later chapter implies that for such a game all Nash equilibria yield the same outcome (Corollary 369.1). Further, a player's Nash equilibrium strategy yields *at least* her equilibrium payoff, regardless of the other players' strategies (Proposition 368.1a). (The same is definitely not true for an arbitrary game that is not strictly competitive: look, for example, at the game in Figure 31.1.) Because any subgame perfect equilibrium is a Nash equilibrium, the same is true for subgame perfect equilibrium strategies.

We conclude that in ticktacktoe and chess, either (*a*) one of the players has a strategy that guarantees she wins, or (*b*) each player has a strategy that guarantees at worst a draw.

In ticktacktoe, of course, we know that (*b*) is true. Chess is more subtle. In particular, it is not known whether White has a strategy that guarantees it wins, or Black has a strategy that guarantees it wins, or each player has a strategy that guarantees at worst a draw. The empirical evidence suggests that Black does not have a winning strategy, but this result has not been proved. When will a subgame perfect equilibrium of chess be found? (The answer "never" underestimates human ingenuity!)

⍰ EXERCISE 179.1 (Subgame perfect equilibria of ticktacktoe) Ticktacktoe has subgame perfect equilibria in which the first player puts her first X in a corner. The second player's move is the same in all these equilibria. What is it?

⍰ EXERCISE 179.2 (Toetacktick) Toetacktick is a variant of ticktacktoe in which a player who puts three marks in a line *loses* (rather than wins). Find a strategy of the first-mover that guarantees that she does not lose. (If fact, in all subgame perfect equilibria the game is a draw.)

⍰ EXERCISE 179.3 (Three Men's Morris, or Mill) The ancient game of Three Men's Morris is played on a ticktacktoe board. Each player has three counters. The players move alternately. On each of her first three turns, a player places a counter on an unoccupied square. On each subsequent move, a player may move one of her counters to an adjacent square (vertically or horizontally, but not diagonally). The first player whose counters are in a row (vertically, horizontally, or diagonally) wins. Find a subgame perfect equilibrium strategy of player 1, and the equilibrium outcome.

Notes

The notion of an extensive game is due to von Neumann and Morgenstern (1944). Kuhn (1950b, 1953) suggested the formulation described in this chapter. The description of an extensive game in terms of histories was suggested by Ariel Rubinstein. The notion of subgame perfect equilibrium is due to Selten (1965). Proposition 173.1 is due to Kuhn (1953). The interpretation of a strategy when a subgame perfect equilibrium is interpreted as the outcome of the players' reasoning about each other's rational actions is due to Rubinstein (1991). The principle of optimality in dynamic programming is discussed by Bellman (1957, 83), for example.

The procedure in Exercises 163.2 and 173.3 was first studied by Mueller (1978) and Moulin (1981). The idea in Exercise 173.4 goes back at least to Sun-tzu, who, in *The art of warfare* (probably written between 500 and 300 B.C.), advises "in surrounding the enemy, leave him a way out; do not press an enemy that is cornered" (end of Chapter 7; see, for example, Sun-tzu (1993, 132)). (That is, if no bridge exists in the situation described in the exercise, army 1 should build one.) Schelling (1966, 45) quotes Sun-tzu and gives examples of the strategy's being used in antiquity. My formulation of the exercise comes from Tirole (1988, 316). The model in Exercise 174.1 is studied by Kohler and Chandrasekaran (1971) and Brams and Straffin (1979). The game in Exercise 174.2 is based on Benoît (1984, Section 1). The dollar auction (Exercise 176.1) was introduced into the literature by Shubik (1971). Some of its subgame perfect equilibria, for arbitrary values of v and w, are studied by O'Neill (1986) and Leininger (1989); see also Taylor (1995, Chapters 1 and 6). Poundstone (1992, 257–272) writes informally about the game and its possible applications. The result in Exercise 177.2 is due to Becker (1974); see also Bergstrom (1989). The first formal study of chess is Zermelo (1913); see Schwalbe and Walker (2000) for a discussion of this paper and related work. Exercises 179.1, 179.2, and 179.3 are taken from Gardner (1959, Chapter 4), which includes several other intriguing examples.

6 Extensive Games with Perfect Information: Illustrations

6.1   The ultimatum game, the holdup game, and agenda
       control   181
6.2   Stackelberg's model of duopoly   187
6.3   Buying votes   192
6.4   A race   197
       Prerequisite: Chapter 5

THE first three sections of this chapter illustrate the notion of subgame perfect equilibrium in games in which the longest history has length two or three. The last section studies a game with an arbitrary finite horizon. Some games with infinite horizons are studied in Chapters 14, 15, and 16.

6.1   The ultimatum game, the holdup game, and agenda control

6.1.1   The ultimatum game

Bargaining over the division of a pie may naturally be modeled as an extensive game. Here I analyze a very simple game that is the basis of a richer model studied in Chapter 16. The game is so simple, in fact, that you may not initially think of it as a model of "bargaining".

Two people use the following procedure to split $c. Person 1 offers person 2 an amount of money up to $c. If 2 accepts this offer, then 1 receives the remainder of the $c. If 2 rejects the offer, then *neither* person receives any payoff. Each person cares *only* about the amount of money she receives, and (naturally!) prefers to receive as much as possible.

Assume that the amount person 1 offers can be any number, not necessarily an integral number of cents. Then the following extensive game, known as the **ultimatum game**, models the procedure.

Players   The two people.

Terminal histories   The set of sequences (x, Z), where x is a number with $0 \leq x \leq c$ (the amount of money that person 1 offers to person 2) and Z is either Y ("yes, I accept") or N ("no, I reject").

Player function $P(\varnothing) = 1$ and $P(x) = 2$ for all x.

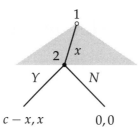

Figure 182.1 An illustration of the ultimatum game. The gray triangle represents the continuum of possible offers of player 1; the black lines indicate the terminal histories that start with the offer x.

Preferences Each person's preferences are represented by payoffs equal to the amounts of money she receives. For the terminal history (x, Y) person 1 receives $c - x$ and person 2 receives x; for the terminal history (x, N) each person receives 0.

This game is illustrated in Figure 182.1, in which the continuum of offers of player 1 is represented by the gray triangle, and the black lines indicate the terminal histories that start with the offer x. The game has a finite horizon, so we can use backward induction to find its subgame perfect equilibria. First consider the subgames of length 1, in which person 2 either accepts or rejects an offer of person 1. For every possible offer of person 1, there is such a subgame. In the subgame that follows an offer x of person 1 for which $x > 0$, person 2's optimal action is to accept (if she rejects, she gets nothing). In the subgame that follows the offer $x = 0$, person 2 is indifferent between accepting and rejecting. Thus in a subgame perfect equilibrium person 2's strategy either accepts all offers (including 0), or accepts all offers $x > 0$ and rejects the offer $x = 0$.

Now consider the whole game. For each possible subgame perfect equilibrium strategy of person 2, we need to find the optimal strategy of person 1.

- If person 2 accepts all offers (including 0), then person 1's optimal offer is 0 (which yields her the payoff $\$c$).

- If person 2 accepts all offers except zero, then *no* offer of person 1 is optimal! No offer $x > 0$ is optimal, because the offer $x/2$ (for example) is better, given that person 2 accept both offers. And an offer of 0 is not optimal because person 2 rejects it, leading to a payoff of 0 for person 1, who is thus better off offering any positive amount less than $\$c$.

We conclude that the only subgame perfect equilibrium of the game is the strategy pair in which person 1 offers 0 and person 2 accepts all offers. In this equilibrium, person 1's payoff is $\$c$ and person 2's payoff is zero.

This one-sided outcome is a consequence of the one-sided structure of the game. If we allow person 2 to make a counteroffer after rejecting person 1's opening offer (and possibly allow further responses by both players), so that the model corresponds more closely to a "bargaining" situation, then under some circumstances the outcome is less one-sided. (An extension of this type is explored in Chapter 16.)

? EXERCISE 183.1 (Nash equilibria of the ultimatum game) Find the values of x for which there is a Nash equilibrium of the ultimatum game in which person 1 offers x.

? EXERCISE 183.2 (Subgame perfect equilibria of the ultimatum game with indivisible units) Find the subgame perfect equilibria of the variant of the ultimatum game in which the amount of money is available only in multiples of a cent.

? EXERCISE 183.3 (Dictator game and impunity game) The "dictator game" differs from the ultimatum game only in that person 2 does not have the option to reject person 1's offer (and thus has no strategic role in the game). The "impunity game" differs from the ultimatum game only in that person 1's payoff when person 2 rejects any offer x is $c - x$, rather than 0. (The game is named for the fact that person 2 is unable to "punish" person 1 for making a low offer.) Find the subgame perfect equilibria of each game.

? EXERCISE 183.4 (Variants of ultimatum game and impunity game with equity-conscious players) Consider variants of the ultimatum game and impunity game in which each person cares not only about the amount of money she receives, but also about the equity of the allocation. Specifically, suppose that person i's preferences are represented by the payoff function given by $u_i(x_1, x_2) = x_i - \beta_i|x_1 - x_2|$, where x_i is the amount of money person i receives, $\beta_i > 0$, and, for any number z, $|z|$ denotes the absolute value of z (i.e. $|z| = z$ if $z > 0$ and $|z| = -z$ if $z < 0$). Assume $c = 1$. Find the set of subgame perfect equilibria of each game and compare them. Are there any values of β_1 and β_2 for which an offer is rejected in equilibrium? (An interesting further variant of the ultimatum game in which person 1 is uncertain about the value of β_2 is considered in Exercise 227.1.)

EXPERIMENTS ON THE ULTIMATUM GAME

The sharp prediction of the notion of subgame perfect equilibrium in the ultimatum game lends itself to experimental testing. The first test was conducted in the late 1970s among graduate students of economics in a class at the University of Cologne (in what was then West Germany). The amount c available varied among the games played; it ranged from 4 DM to 10 DM (around U.S.$2 to U.S.$5 at the time). A group of 42 students was split into two groups and seated on different sides of a room. Each member of one subgroup played the role of player 1 in an ultimatum game. She wrote down on a form the amount (up to c) that she demanded. Her form was then given to a randomly determined member of the other group, who, playing the role of player 2, either accepted what remained of the amount c or rejected it (in which case neither player received any payoff). Each player had 10 minutes to make her decision. The entire experiment was repeated a week later. (Güth, Schmittberger, and Schwarze 1982.)

In the first experiment the average demand by people playing the role of player 1 was $0.65c$, and in the second experiment it was $0.69c$, much less than the amount c or $c - 0.01$ predicted by the notion of subgame perfect equilibrium (0.01 DM was the smallest monetary unit; see Exercise 183.2). Almost 20% of offers were rejected over the two experiments, including one of 3 DM (out of a pie of 7 DM) and five of around 1 DM (out of pies of between 4 DM and 6 DM). Many other experiments, including one in which the amount of money to be divided was much larger (Hoffman, McCabe, and Smith 1996), have produced similar results. In brief, the results do not accord well with the predictions of subgame perfect equilibrium.

Or do they? Each player in the ultimatum game cares only about the amount of money she receives. But an experimental subject may care also about the amount of money her opponent receives. Further, a variant of the ultimatum game in which the players are equity conscious has subgame perfect equilibria in which offers are significant (as you will have discovered if you did Exercise 183.4).

However, if people are equity conscious in the strategic environment of the ultimatum game, they are presumably equity conscious also in related environments; an explanation of the experimental results in the ultimatum game based on the players' preferences' exhibiting equity conscience is not convincing if it applies only to that environment. Several related games have been studied, among them the dictator game and the impunity game (Exercise 183.3). In the subgame perfect equilibria of these games, player 1 offers 0; in a variant in which the players are equity conscious, player 1's offers are no higher than they are in the analogous variant of the ultimatum game, and, for moderate degrees of equity conscience, are lower (see Exercise 183.4). These features of the equilibria are broadly consistent with the experimental evidence on dictator, impunity, and ultimatum games (see, for example, Forsythe, Horowitz, Savin, and Sefton 1994, Bolton and Zwick 1995, and Güth and Huck 1997).

One feature of the experimental results is inconsistent with subgame perfect equilibrium even when players are equity conscious (at least given the form of the payoff functions in Exercise 183.4): positive offers are sometimes rejected. The equilibrium strategy of an equity-conscious player 2 in the ultimatum game rejects inequitable offers, but, knowing this, player 1 does not, in equilibrium, make such an offer. To generate rejections in equilibrium we need to further modify the model by assuming that people differ in their degree of equity conscience, and that player 1 does not know the degree of equity conscience of player 2 (see Exercise 227.1).

An alternative explanation of the experimental results focuses on player 2's behavior. The evidence is consistent with player 1's significant offers in the ultimatum game being driven by a fear that player 2 will reject small offers—a fear that is rational, because small offers are often rejected. Why does player 2 behave in this way? One argument is that in our daily lives, we use "rules of thumb" that work well in the situations in which we are typically involved; we do not calculate our rational actions in each situation. Further, we are not typically involved in one-shot situations with the structure of the ultimatum game. Instead, we usually engage in repeated interactions, where it is advantageous to "punish" a player who makes a paltry offer, and to build a reputation for not accepting such offers. Experimental subjects may apply such rules of thumb rather than carefully thinking through the logic of the game, and thus reject low offers in an ultimatum game but accept them in an impunity game, where rejection does not affect the proposer. The experimental evidence so far collected is broadly consistent with both this explanation and the explanation based on the nature of players' preferences.

> ? EXERCISE 185.1 (Bargaining over two indivisible objects) Consider a variant of the ultimatum game, with indivisible units. Two people use the following procedure to allocate two desirable identical indivisible objects. One person proposes an allocation (both objects go to person 1, both go to person 2, one goes to each person), which the other person then either accepts or rejects. In the event of rejection, neither person receives either object. Each person cares only about the number of objects she obtains. Construct an extensive game that models this situation and find its subgame perfect equilibria. Does the game have any Nash equilibrium that is not a subgame perfect equilibrium? Is there any outcome that is generated by a Nash equilibrium but not by any subgame perfect equilibrium?

> ? EXERCISE 185.2 (Dividing a cake fairly) Two players use the following procedure to divide a cake. Player 1 divides the cake into two pieces, and then player 2 chooses one of the pieces; player 1 obtains the remaining piece. The cake is continuously divisible (no lumps!), and each player likes all parts of it.
>
> a. Suppose that the cake is perfectly homogeneous, so that each player cares only about the size of the piece of cake she obtains. How is the cake divided in a subgame perfect equilibrium?
>
> b. Suppose that the cake is not homogeneous: the players evaluate different parts of it differently. Represent the cake by the set C, so that a piece of the cake is a subset P of C. Assume that if P is a subset of P' not equal to P' (smaller than P'), then each player prefers P' to P. Assume also that the players' preferences are continuous: if player i prefers P to P', then there is a subset of P not equal to P that player i also prefers to P'. Let (P_1, P_2) (where P_1 and P_2 together constitute the whole cake C) be the division chosen by player 1 in a subgame perfect equilibrium of the divide-and-choose game, P_2 being the piece chosen by player 2. Show that player 2 is indifferent between P_1 and P_2, and player 1 likes P_1 at least as much as P_2. Give an example in which player 1 prefers P_1 to P_2.

6.1.2 The holdup game

Before engaging in an ultimatum game in which she may accept or reject an offer of person 1, person 2 takes an action that affects the size c of the pie to be divided. She may exert little effort, resulting in a small pie, of size c_L, or great effort, resulting in a large pie, of size c_H. She dislikes exerting effort. Specifically, assume that her payoff is $x - E$ if her share of the pie is x, where $E = L$ if she exerts little effort and $E = H > L$ if she exerts great effort. The extensive game that models this situation is known as the **holdup game**.

(?) EXERCISE 186.1 (Holdup game) Formulate the holdup game precisely. (Write down the set of players, the set of terminal histories, the player function, and the players' preferences.)

What is the subgame perfect equilibrium of the holdup game? Each subgame that follows person 2's choice of effort is an ultimatum game, and thus has a unique subgame perfect equilibrium, in which person 1 offers 0 and person 2 accepts all offers. Now consider person 2's choice of effort at the start of the game. If she chooses L, then her payoff, given the outcome in the following subgame, is $-L$, whereas if she chooses H, then her payoff is $-H$. Consequently she chooses L. Thus the game has a unique subgame perfect equilibrium, in which person 2 exerts little effort and person 1 obtains all of the resulting small pie.

This equilibrium does not depend on the values of c_L, c_H, L, and H (given that $H > L$). In particular, even if c_H is much larger than c_L, but H is only slightly larger than L, person 2 exerts little effort in the equilibrium, although both players could be much better off if person 2 were to exert great effort (which, in this case, is not very great) and person 2 were to obtain some of the extra pie. No such superior outcome is sustainable in an equilibrium because person 2, having exerted great effort, may be "held up" for the entire pie by person 1.

This result does not depend sensitively on the extreme subgame perfect equilibrium outcome of the ultimatum game. A similar result emerges when the bargaining following person 2's choice of effort generates a more equal division of the pie. By exerting great effort, player 2 increases the size of the pie. The point is that if the negotiation results in some (not necessarily all) of this extra pie going to player 1, then for some values of player 2's cost of exerting great effort less than the value of the extra pie, player 2 prefers to exert little effort. In these circumstances, player 2's exerting great effort generates outcomes in which both players are better off than they are when player 2 exerts little effort, but because the bargaining puts some of the extra pie in the hands of player 1, player 2's incentive is to exert little effort.

6.1.3 Agenda control

In some legislatures, proposals for modifications of the law are formulated by committees. Under a "closed rule", the legislature may either accept or reject a proposed modification, but may not propose an alternative; in the event of rejection, the existing law in unchanged. That is, the committee controls the "agenda". (In Section 10.9 I consider a reason why a legislature might cede such power to a committee.)

Model an outcome as a number y. Assume that the legislature and committee have favorite outcomes that may differ, and that the preferences of each body are represented by a single-peaked payoff function symmetric about its favorite outcome, like the voters' preferences in Hotelling's model of electoral competition (see Figure 71.1). Assign numbers to outcomes so that the legislature's favorite outcome is 0; denote the committee's favorite outcome by $y_c > 0$. Then the following variant of the ultimatum game models the procedure. The players are the committee and the legislature. The committee proposes an outcome y, which the legislature either accepts or rejects. In the event of rejection the outcome is y_0, the "status quo". Note that the main respect in which this game differs from the ultimatum game is that the players' preferences are diametrically opposed only with regard to outcomes between 0 and y_c; if $y' < y'' < 0$ or $y_c < y'' < y'$, then both players prefer y'' to y'.

? EXERCISE 187.1 (Agenda control) Find the subgame perfect equilibrium of this game as a function of the status quo outcome y_0. Show, in particular, that for a range of values of y_0, an increase in the value of y_0 leads to a *decrease* in the value of the equilibrium outcome.

6.2   Stackelberg's model of duopoly

6.2.1   General model

In the models of oligopoly in Sections 3.1 and 3.2, each firm chooses its action not knowing the other firms' actions. How do the conclusions change when the firms move sequentially? Is a firm better off moving before or after the other firms?

In this section I consider a market in which there are two firms, both producing the same good. Firm i's cost of producing q_i units of the good is $C_i(q_i)$; the price at which output is sold when the total output is Q is $P_d(Q)$. (In Section 3.1 I denote this function P; here I add a d subscript to avoid a conflict with the player function of the extensive game.) Each firm's strategic variable is output, as in Cournot's model (Section 3.1), but the firms make their decisions sequentially, rather than simultaneously: one firm chooses its output, then the other firm does so, knowing the output chosen by the first firm.

We can model this situation by the following extensive game, known as **Stackelberg's duopoly game** (after an early analyst of duopoly with asynchronous actions).

Players   The two firms.

Terminal histories   The set of all sequences (q_1, q_2) of outputs for the firms (where each q_i, the output of firm i, is a nonnegative number).

Player function $P(\varnothing) = 1$ and $P(q_1) = 2$ for all q_1.

Preferences   The payoff of firm i to the terminal history (q_1, q_2) is its profit $q_i P_d(q_1 + q_2) - C_i(q_i)$, for $i = 1, 2$.

Firm 1 moves at the start of the game. Thus a strategy of firm 1 is simply an output. Firm 2 moves after every history in which firm 1 chooses an output. Thus a strategy of firm 2 is a *function* that associates an output for firm 2 with each possible output of firm 1.

The game has a finite horizon, so we may use backward induction to find its subgame perfect equilibria.

- First, for any output of firm 1, we find the outputs of firm 2 that maximize its profit. Suppose that for each output q_1 of firm 1 there is one such output of firm 2; denote it $b_2(q_1)$. Then in any subgame perfect equilibrium, firm 2's strategy is b_2.

- Next, we find the outputs of firm 1 that maximize its profit, *given the strategy of firm 2*. When firm 1 chooses the output q_1, firm 2 chooses the output $b_2(q_1)$, resulting in a total output of $q_1 + b_2(q_1)$, and hence a price of $P_d(q_1 + b_2(q_1))$. Thus firm 1's output in a subgame perfect equilibrium is a value of q_1 that maximizes

$$q_1 P_d(q_1 + b_2(q_1)) - C_1(q_1). \tag{188.1}$$

Suppose that there is one such value of q_1; denote it q_1^*.

We conclude that if firm 2 has a unique best response $b_2(q_1)$ to each output q_1 of firm 1, and firm 1 has a unique best action q_1^*, given firm 2's best responses, then the subgame perfect equilibrium of the game is (q_1^*, b_2): firm 1's equilibrium strategy is q_1^* and firm 2's equilibrium strategy is the function b_2. The output chosen by firm 2, given firm 1's equilibrium strategy, is $b_2(q_1^*)$; denote this output q_2^*.

When firm 1 chooses any output q_1, the outcome, given that firm 2 uses its equilibrium strategy, is the pair of outputs $(q_1, b_2(q_1))$. That is, as firm 1 varies its output, the outcome varies along firm 2's best response function b_2. Thus we can characterize the subgame perfect equilibrium outcome (q_1^*, q_2^*) as the point on firm 2's best response function that maximizes firm 1's profit.

6.2.2   Example: constant unit cost and linear inverse demand

Suppose that $C_i(q_i) = cq_i$ for $i = 1, 2$, and

$$P_d(Q) = \begin{cases} \alpha - Q & \text{if } Q \leq \alpha \\ 0 & \text{if } Q > \alpha, \end{cases} \tag{188.2}$$

where $c > 0$ and $c < \alpha$ (as in the example of Cournot's duopoly game in Section 3.1.3). We found that under these assumptions firm 2 has a unique best response to each output q_1 of firm 1, given by

$$b_2(q_1) = \begin{cases} \frac{1}{2}(\alpha - c - q_1) & \text{if } q_1 \leq \alpha - c \\ 0 & \text{if } q_1 > \alpha - c. \end{cases}$$

Thus in a subgame perfect equilibrium of Stackelberg's game firm 2's strategy is this function b_2 and firm 1's strategy is the output q_1 that maximizes

$$q_1(\alpha - c - (q_1 + \tfrac{1}{2}(\alpha - c - q_1))) = \tfrac{1}{2}q_1(\alpha - c - q_1)$$

(refer to (188.1)). This function is a quadratic in q_1 that is zero when $q_1 = 0$ and when $q_1 = \alpha - c$. Thus its maximizer is $q_1 = \tfrac{1}{2}(\alpha - c)$.

We conclude that the game has a unique subgame perfect equilibrium, in which firm 1's strategy is the output $\tfrac{1}{2}(\alpha - c)$ and firm 2's strategy is b_2. The outcome of the equilibrium is that firm 1 produces the output $q_1^* = \tfrac{1}{2}(\alpha - c)$ and firm 2 produces the output $q_2^* = b_2(q_1^*) = b_2(\tfrac{1}{2}(\alpha - c)) = \tfrac{1}{2}(\alpha - c - \tfrac{1}{2}(\alpha - c)) = \tfrac{1}{4}(\alpha - c)$. Firm 1's profit is $q_1^*(P_d(q_1^* + q_2^*) - c) = \tfrac{1}{8}(\alpha - c)^2$, and firm 2's profit is $q_2^*(P_d(q_1^* + q_2^*) - c) = \tfrac{1}{16}(\alpha - c)^2$. By contrast, in the unique Nash equilibrium of Cournot's (simultaneous-move) game under the same assumptions, each firm produces $\tfrac{1}{3}(\alpha - c)$ units of output and obtains the profit $\tfrac{1}{9}(\alpha - c)^2$. Thus under our assumptions firm 1 produces more output and obtains more profit in the subgame perfect equilibrium of the sequential game in which it moves first than it does in the Nash equilibrium of Cournot's game, and firm 2 produces less output and obtains less profit.

? EXERCISE 189.1 (Stackelberg's duopoly game with quadratic costs) Find the subgame perfect equilibrium of Stackelberg's duopoly game when $C_i(q_i) = q_i^2$ for $i = 1, 2$, and $P_d(Q) = \alpha - Q$ for all $Q \leq \alpha$ (with $P_d(Q) = 0$ for $Q > \alpha$). Compare the equilibrium outcome with the Nash equilibrium of Cournot's game under the same assumptions (Exercise 59.1).

6.2.3 Properties of subgame perfect equilibrium

First-mover's equilibrium profit   In the example just studied, the first-mover is better off in the subgame perfect equilibrium of Stackelberg's game than it is in the Nash equilibrium of Cournot's game. A weak version of this result holds under very general conditions: for any cost and inverse demand functions for which firm 2 has a unique best response to each output of firm 1, firm 1 is at least as well off in any subgame perfect equilibrium of Stackelberg's game as it is in any Nash equilibrium of Cournot's game. This result follows from the general result in Exercise 177.3a. The argument is simple. One of firm 1's options in Stackelberg's game is to choose its output in some Nash equilibrium of Cournot's game. If it chooses such an output, then firm 2's best action is to choose its output in the same Nash equilibrium, given the assumption that it has a unique best response to each output of firm 1. Thus by choosing such an output, firm 1 obtains its profit at a Nash equilibrium of Cournot's game; by choosing a different output it may possibly obtain a higher payoff.

Equilibrium outputs   In the example in the previous section (6.2.2), firm 1 produces more output in the subgame perfect equilibrium of Stackelberg's game than it does

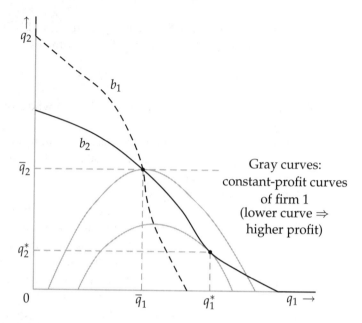

Figure 190.1 The subgame perfect equilibrium outcome (q_1^*, q_2^*) of Stackelberg's game and the Nash equilibrium $(\bar{q}_1, \bar{q}_2)$ of Cournot's game. Along each gray curve, firm 1's profit is constant; the lower curve corresponds to higher profit than does the upper curve. Each curve has a slope of zero where it crosses firm 1's best response function b_1.

in the Nash equilibrium of Cournot's game, and firm 2 produces less. A weak form of this result holds whenever firm 2's best response function is decreasing where it is positive (i.e. a higher output for firm 1 implies a lower optimal output for firm 2).

The argument is illustrated in Figure 190.1. The firms' best response functions are the curves labeled b_1 (dashed) and b_2. The Nash equilibrium of Cournot's game is the intersection $(\bar{q}_1, \bar{q}_2)$ of these curves. Along each gray curve, firm 1's profit is constant; the *lower* curve corresponds to a *higher* profit. (For any given value of firm 1's output, a reduction in the output of firm 2 increases the price and thus increases firm 1's profit.) Each constant-profit curve of firm 1 is horizontal where it crosses firm 1's best response function, because the best response is precisely the output that maximizes firm 1's profit, given firm 2's output. (Cf. Figure 61.1.) Thus the subgame perfect equilibrium outcome—the point on firm 2's best response function that yields the highest profit for firm 1—is the point (q_1^*, q_2^*) in Figure 190.1. In particular, given that the best response function of firm 2 is downward sloping, firm 1 produces at least as much, and firm 2 produces at most as much, in the subgame perfect equilibrium of Stackelberg's game as in the Nash equilibrium of Cournot's game.

For some cost and demand functions, firm 2's output in a subgame perfect equilibrium of Stackelberg's game is zero. An example is shown in Figure 191.1. The discontinuity in firm 2's best response function at q_1^* in this example may arise because firm 2 incurs a "fixed" cost—a cost independent of its output—when it produces a positive output (see Exercise 59.2). When firm 1's output is q_1^*, firm 2's

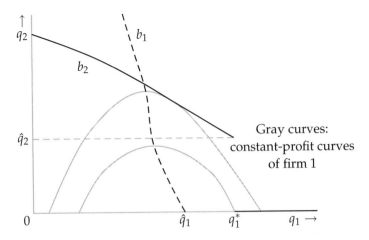

Figure 191.1 The subgame perfect equilibrium output q_1^* of firm 1 in Stackelberg's sequential game when firm 2 incurs a fixed cost. Along each gray curve, firm 1's profit is constant; the lower curve corresponds to higher profit than does the upper curve.

maximal profit is zero, which it obtains both when it produces no output (and does not pay the fixed cost) and when it produces the output $\hat{q}_2$. When firm 1 produces less than q_1^*, firm 2's maximal profit is positive, and firm 2 optimally produces a positive output; when firm 1 produces more than q_1^*, firm 2 optimally produces no output. Given this form of firm 2's best response function and the form of firm 1's constant-profit curves in Figure 190.1, the point on firm 2's best response function that yields firm 1 the highest profit is $(q_1^*, 0)$.

I claim that this example has a unique subgame perfect equilibrium, in which firm 1 produces q_1^* and firm 2's strategy coincides with its best response function except at q_1^*, where the strategy specifies the output 0. The output firm 2's equilibrium strategy specifies after each history must be a best response to firm 1's output, so the only question regarding firm 2's strategy is whether it specifies an output of 0 or $\hat{q}_2$ when firm 1's output is q_1^*. The argument that there is no subgame perfect equilibrium in which firm 2's strategy specifies the output $\hat{q}_2$ is similar to the argument that there is no subgame perfect equilibrium in the ultimatum game in which person 2 rejects the offer 0. If firm 2 produces the output $\hat{q}_2$ in response to firm 1's output q_1^*, then firm 1 has no optimal output: it would like to produce a little more than q_1^*, inducing firm 2 to produce zero, but is better off the closer its output is to q_1^*. Because there is no smallest output greater than q_1^*, no output is *optimal* for firm 1 in this case. Thus the game has no subgame perfect equilibrium in which firm 2's strategy specifies the output $\hat{q}_2$ in response to firm 1's output q_1^*.

Note that if firm 2 were entirely absent from the market, firm 1 would produce $\hat{q}_1$, less than q_1^*. Thus firm 2's presence affects the outcome, even though it produces no output.

? EXERCISE 191.1 (Stackelberg's duopoly game with fixed costs) Suppose that the inverse demand function is given by (188.2) and the cost function of each firm i is given by

$$C_i(q_i) = \begin{cases} 0 & \text{if } q_i = 0 \\ f + cq_i & \text{if } q_i > 0, \end{cases}$$

where $c \geq 0$, $f > 0$, and $c < \alpha$, as in Exercise 59.2. Show that if $c = 0$, $\alpha = 12$, and $f = 4$, Stackelberg's game has a unique subgame perfect equilibrium, in which firm 1's output is 8 and firm 2's output is zero. (Use your results from Exercise 59.2).

The value of commitment   Firm 1's output in a subgame perfect equilibrium of Stackelberg's game is *not* in general a best response to firm 2's output: if firm 1 could adjust its output after firm 2 has chosen its output, then it would do so! (In the case shown in Figure 190.1, it would reduce its output.) However, if firm 1 had this opportunity, and firm 2 knew that it had the opportunity, then firm 2 would choose a different output. Indeed, if we simply add a third stage to the game, in which firm 1 chooses an output, then the first stage is irrelevant, and *firm 2 is effectively the first-mover*; in the subgame perfect equilibrium firm 1 is worse off than it is in the Nash equilibrium of the simultaneous-move game. (In the example in Section 6.2.2, the unique subgame perfect equilibrium has firm 2 choose the output $(\alpha - c)/2$ and firm 1 choose the output $(\alpha - c)/4$.) In summary, even though firm 1 can increase its profit by changing its output after firm 2 has chosen its output, in the game in which it has this opportunity it is worse off than it is in the game in which it must choose its output before firm 2 and cannot subsequently modify this output. That is, firm 1 prefers to be *committed* not to change its mind.

? EXERCISE 192.1 (Sequential variant of Bertrand's duopoly game) Consider the variant of Bertrand's duopoly game (Section 3.2) in which first firm 1 chooses a price, then firm 2 chooses a price. Assume that each firm is restricted to choose a price that is an integral number of cents (as in Exercise 67.2), that each firm's unit cost is constant and equal to c (an integral number of cents), and that the monopoly profit is positive.

   a. Specify an extensive game with perfect information that models this situation.

   b. Give an example of a strategy of firm 1 and an example of a strategy of firm 2.

   c. Find the subgame perfect equilibria of the game.

6.3   Buying votes

A legislature has k members, where k is an odd number. Two rival bills, X and Y, are being considered. The bill that attracts the votes of a majority of legislators will pass. Interest group X favors bill X, whereas interest group Y favors bill Y. Each group wishes to entice a majority of legislators to vote for its favorite bill. First interest group X gives an amount of money (possibly zero) to each legislator, then interest group Y does so. Each interest group wishes to spend as little as possible. Group X values the passing of bill X at $\$V_X > 0$ and the passing of bill Y

at zero, and group Y values the passing of bill Y at $\$V_Y > 0$ and the passing of bill X at zero. (For example, group X is indifferent between an outcome in which it spends V_X and bill X is passed and one in which it spends nothing and bill Y is passed.) Each legislator votes for the favored bill of the interest group that offers her the most money; a legislator to whom both groups offer the same amount of money votes for bill Y (an arbitrary assumption that simplifies the analysis without qualitatively changing the outcome). For example, if $k = 3$, the amounts offered to the legislators by group X are $x = (100, 50, 0)$, and the amounts offered by group Y are $y = (100, 0, 50)$, then legislators 1 and 3 vote for Y and legislator 2 votes for X, so that Y passes. (In some actual legislatures the inducements offered to legislators are more subtle than cash transfers.)

We can model this situation as the following extensive game.

Players   The two interest groups, X and Y.

Terminal histories   The set of all sequences (x, y), where x is a list of payments to legislators made by interest group X and y is a list of payments to legislators made by interest group Y. (That is, both x and y are lists of k nonnegative integers.)

Player function $P(\varnothing) = X$ and $P(x) = Y$ for all x.

Preferences   The preferences of interest group X are represented by the payoff function

$$\begin{cases} V_X - (x_1 + \cdots + x_k) & \text{if bill } X \text{ passes} \\ -(x_1 + \cdots + x_k) & \text{if bill } Y \text{ passes,} \end{cases}$$

where bill Y passes after the terminal history (x, y) if and only if the number of components of y that are at least equal to the corresponding components of x is at least $\frac{1}{2}(k + 1)$ (a bare majority of the k legislators). The preferences of interest group Y are represented by the analogous function (where V_Y replaces V_X, y replaces x, and Y replaces X).

Before studying the subgame perfect equilibria of this game for arbitrary values of the parameters, consider two examples. First suppose that $k = 3$ and $V_X = V_Y = 300$. Under these assumptions, the most group X is willing to pay to get bill X passed is 300. For any payments it makes to the three legislators that sum to at most 300, two of the payments sum to at most 200, so that if group Y matches these payments it spends less than V_Y ($= 300$) and gets bill Y passed. Thus in any subgame perfect equilibrium group X makes no payments, group Y makes no payments, and (given the tie-breaking rule) bill Y is passed.

Now suppose that $k = 3$, $V_X = 300$, and $V_Y = 100$. In this case by paying each legislator more than 50, group X makes matching payments by group Y unprofitable: only by spending more than V_Y ($= 100$) can group Y cause bill Y to be passed. However, there is no subgame perfect equilibrium in which group X pays each legislator more than 50 because it can always pay a little less (as long as the payments still exceed 50) and still prevent group Y from profitably matching. In the only subgame perfect equilibrium group X pays each legislator exactly 50 and group Y makes no payments. Given group X's action, group Y is indifferent between matching X's payments (so that bill Y is passed) and making no payments. However, there is no subgame perfect equilibrium in which group Y matches group X's payments because if this were group Y's response, then group X could increase its payments a little, making matching payments by group Y unprofitable.

For arbitrary values of the parameters, the subgame perfect equilibrium outcome takes one of the forms in these two examples: either no payments are made and bill Y is passed, or group X makes payments that group Y does not wish to match, group Y makes no payments, and bill X is passed.

To find the subgame perfect equilibria in general, we may use backward induction. First consider group Y's best response to an arbitrary strategy x of group X. Let $\mu = \frac{1}{2}(k+1)$, a bare majority of k legislators, and denote by m_x the sum of the smallest μ components of x—the total payments Y needs to make to buy off a bare majority of legislators.

- If $m_x < V_Y$, then group Y can buy off a bare majority of legislators for less than V_Y, so that its best response to x is to match group X's payments to the μ legislators to whom group X's payments are smallest; the outcome is that bill Y is passed.

- If $m_x > V_Y$, then the cost to group Y of buying off any majority of legislators exceeds V_Y, so that group Y's best response to x is to make no payments; the outcome is that bill X is passed.

- If $m_x = V_Y$, then both the actions in the previous two cases are best responses by group Y to x.

We conclude that group Y's strategy in a subgame perfect equilibrium has the following properties.

- After a history x for which $m_x < V_Y$, group Y matches group X's payments to the μ legislators to whom X's payments are smallest.

- After a history x for which $m_x > V_Y$, group Y makes no payments.

- After a history x for which $m_x = V_Y$, group Y either makes no payments or matches group X's payments to the μ legislators to whom X's payments are smallest.

Given that group Y's subgame perfect equilibrium strategy has these properties, what should group X do? If it chooses a list of payments x for which $m_x < V_Y$, then group Y matches its payments to a bare majority of legislators, and bill Y passes. If it reduces all its payments, the same bill is passed. Thus the only list of payments x with $m_x < V_Y$ that may be optimal is $(0, \ldots, 0)$. If it chooses a list of payments x with $m_x > V_Y$, then group Y makes no payments, and bill X passes.

If it reduces all its payments a little (keeping the payments to every bare majority greater than V_Y), the outcome is the same. Thus no list of payments x for which $m_x > V_Y$ is optimal.

We conclude that in any subgame perfect equilibrium we have either $x = (0, \ldots, 0)$ (group X makes no payments) or $m_x = V_Y$ (the smallest sum of group X's payments to a bare majority of legislators is V_Y). Under what conditions does each case occur? If group X needs to spend more than V_X to deter group Y from matching its payments to a bare majority of legislators, then its best strategy is to make no payments ($x = (0, \ldots, 0)$). How much does it need to spend to deter group Y? It needs to pay more than V_Y to every bare majority of legislators, so it needs to pay each legislator more than V_Y/μ, in which case its total payment is more than kV_Y/μ. Thus if $V_X < kV_Y/\mu$, group X is better off making no payments than getting bill X passed by making payments large enough to deter group Y from matching its payments to a bare majority of legislators.

If $V_X > kV_Y/\mu$, on the other hand, group X can afford to make payments large enough to deter group Y from matching. In this case its best strategy is to pay each legislator V_Y/μ, so that its total payment to every bare majority of legislators is V_Y. Given this strategy, group Y is indifferent between matching group X's payments to a bare majority of legislators and making no payments. I claim that the game has no subgame perfect equilibrium in which group Y matches. The argument is similar to the argument that the ultimatum game has no subgame perfect equilibrium in which person 2 rejects the offer 0. Suppose that group Y matches. Then group X can increase its payoff by increasing its payments a little (keeping the total less than V_X), thereby deterring group Y from matching, and ensuring that bill X passes. Thus in any subgame perfect equilibrium group Y makes no payments in response to group X's strategy.

In conclusion, if $V_X \neq kV_Y/\mu$, then the game has a unique subgame perfect equilibrium, in which group Y's strategy is to

- match group X's payments to the μ legislators to whom X's payments are smallest after a history x for which $m_x < V_Y$, and

- make no payments after a history x for which $m_x \geq V_Y$

and group X's strategy depends on the relative sizes of V_X and V_Y:

- if $V_X < kV_Y/\mu$, then group X makes no payments;

- if $V_X > kV_Y/\mu$, then group X pays each legislator V_Y/μ.

If $V_X < kV_Y/\mu$, then the outcome is that neither group makes any payment, and bill Y is passed; if $V_X > kV_Y/\mu$, then the outcome is that group X pays each legislator V_Y/μ, group Y makes no payments, and bill X is passed. (If $V_X = kV_Y/\mu$, then the analysis is more complex.)

Three features of the subgame perfect equilibrium are significant. First, the outcome favors the second-mover in the game (group Y): only if $V_X > kV_Y/\mu$, which is close to $2V_Y$ when k is large, does group X manage to get bill X passed. Second, group Y never makes any payments! According to its equilibrium strategy it is prepared to make payments in response to certain strategies of group X, but given group X's *equilibrium* strategy, it spends not a cent. Third, if group X makes any payments (as it does in the equilibrium for $V_X > kV_Y/\mu$), then it makes a payment to *every* legislator. If there were no competing interest group but nonetheless each legislator would vote for bill X only if she were paid at least some amount, then group X would make payments to only a bare majority of legislators; if it were to act in this way in the presence of group Y, it would supply group Y with almost a majority of legislators who could be induced to vote for bill Y at no cost.

? EXERCISE 196.1 (Three interest groups buying votes) Consider a variant of the model in which there are *three* bills, X, Y, and Z, and *three* interest groups, X, Y, and Z, who choose lists of payments sequentially. Ties are broken in favor of the group moving later. Assume that if each bill obtains the vote of one legislator, then bill X passes. Find the bill passed in any subgame perfect equilibrium when $k = 3$ and (a) $V_X = V_Y = V_Z = 300$, (b) $V_X = 300$, $V_Y = V_Z = 100$, and (c) $V_X = 300$, $V_Y = 202$, $V_Z = 100$. (You may assume that in each case a subgame perfect equilibrium exists; note that you are not asked to find the subgame perfect equilibria themselves.)

? EXERCISE 196.2 (Interest groups buying votes under supermajority rule) Consider another variant of the model in which a supermajority is required to pass a bill. There are two bills, X and Y, and a "default outcome". A bill passes if and only if it receives at least $k^* > \frac{1}{2}(k+1)$ votes; if neither bill passes, the default outcome occurs. There are two interest groups. Both groups attach value 0 to the default outcome. Find the bill that is passed in any subgame perfect equilibrium when $k = 7$, $k^* = 5$, and (a) $V_X = V_Y = 700$ and (b) $V_X = 750$, $V_Y = 400$. In each case, would the legislators be better off or worse off if a simple majority of votes were required to pass a bill?

? EXERCISE 196.3 (Sequential positioning by two political candidates) Consider the variant of Hotelling's model of electoral competition in Section 3.3 in which the n candidates choose their positions sequentially, rather than simultaneously. Model this situation as an extensive game. Find the subgame perfect equilibrium (equilibria?) when $n = 2$.

? EXERCISE 196.4 (Sequential positioning by three political candidates) Consider a further variant of Hotelling's model of electoral competition in which the n candidates choose their positions sequentially and each candidate has the option of staying out of the race. Assume that each candidate prefers to stay out than to enter and lose, prefers to enter and tie with any number of candidates than to stay out, and prefers to tie with as few other candidates as possible. Model the situation as an extensive game and find the subgame perfect equilibrium outcomes when $n = 2$ (easy) and when $n = 3$ and the voters' favorite positions are distributed uniformly from 0 to 1 (i.e. the fraction of the voters' favorite positions less than x is x) (hard).

6.4   A race

6.4.1   General model

Firms compete with each other to develop new technologies; authors compete with each other to write books and film scripts about momentous current events; scientists compete with each other to make discoveries. In each case the winner enjoys a significant advantage over the losers, and each competitor can, at a cost, increase her pace of activity. How do the presence of competitors and size of the prize affect the pace of activity? How does the identity of the winner of the race depend on each competitor's initial distance from the finish line?

We can model a race as an extensive game with perfect information in which the players alternately choose how many "steps" to take. Here I study a simple example of such a game, with two players.

Player i is initially $k_i > 0$ steps from the finish line, for $i = 1, 2$. On each of her turns, a player can either not take any steps (at a cost of 0), or can take one step, at a cost of $c(1)$, or two steps, at a cost of $c(2)$. The first player to reach the finish line wins a prize, worth $v_i > 0$ to player i; the losing player's payoff is 0. To make the game finite, I assume that if, on successive turns, neither player takes any step, the game ends and neither player obtains the prize.

I denote the game in which player i moves first by $G_i(k_1, k_2)$. The game $G_1(k_1, k_2)$ is defined precisely as follows.

Players   The two parties.

Terminal histories   The set of sequences of the form $(x^1, y^1, x^2, y^2, \ldots, x^T)$ or $(x^1, y^1, x^2, y^2, \ldots, y^T)$ for some integer T, where each x^t (the number of steps taken by player 1 on her tth turn) and each y^t (the number of steps taken by player 2 on her tth turn) is 0, 1, or 2, there are never two successive 0's except possibly at the end of a sequence, and either $x^1 + \cdots + x^T = k_1$ and $y^1 + \cdots + y^T < k_2$ (player 1 reaches the finish line first), or $x^1 + \cdots + x^T < k_1$ and $y^1 + \cdots + y^T = k_2$ (player 2 reaches the finish line first).

Player function $P(\varnothing) = 1$, $P(x^1) = 2$ for all x^1, $P(x^1, y^1) = 1$ for all (x^1, y^1), $P(x^1, y^1, x^2) = 2$ for all (x^1, y^1, x^2), and so on.

Preferences   For a terminal history in which player i loses, her payoff is the negative of the sum of the costs of all her moves; for a terminal history in which she wins it is v_i minus the sum of these costs.

6.4.2   Subgame perfect equilibria of an example

A simple example illustrates the features of the subgame perfect equilibria of this game. Suppose that both v_1 and v_2 are between 6 and 7 (their exact values do not affect the equilibria), the cost $c(1)$ of a single step is 1, and the cost $c(2)$ of two steps is 4. (Given that $c(2) > 2c(1)$, each player, in the absence of a competitor, would like to take one step at a time.)

The game has a finite horizon, so we may use backward induction to find its subgame perfect equilibria. Each of its subgames is either a game $G_i(m_1, m_2)$ with $i = 1$ or $i = 2$ and $0 < m_1 \leq k_1$ and $0 < m_2 \leq k_2$, or, if the last player to move before the subgame took no steps, a game that differs from $G_i(m_1, m_2)$ only in that it ends if player i initially takes no steps (i.e. the only terminal history starting with 0 consists only of 0).

First consider the very simplest game, $G_1(1, 1)$, in which each player is initially one step from the finish line. If player 1 takes one step, she wins; if she does not move, then player 2 optimally takes one step (if she does not, the game ends) and wins. We conclude that the game has a unique subgame perfect equilibrium, in which player 1 initially takes one step and wins.

A similar argument applies to the game $G_1(1, 2)$. If player 1 does not move, then player 2 has the option of taking one or two steps. If she takes one step, then play moves to a subgame identical $G_1(1, 1)$, in which we have just concluded that player 1 wins. Thus player 2 takes two steps, and wins, if player 1 does not move at the start of $G_1(1, 2)$. We conclude that the game has a unique subgame perfect equilibrium, in which player 1 initially takes one step and wins.

Now consider player 1's options in the game $G_1(2, 1)$.

- Player 1 takes two steps: she wins, and obtains a payoff of at least $6 - 4 = 2$ (her valuation is more than 6, and the cost of two steps is 4).

- Player 1 takes one step: play moves to a subgame identical to $G_2(1, 1)$; we know that in the equilibrium of this subgame player 2 initially takes one step and wins.

- Player 1 does not move: play moves to a subgame in which player 2 is the first-mover and is one step from the finish line, and, if player 2 does not move, the game ends. In an equilibrium of this subgame, player 2 takes one step and wins.

We conclude that the game $G_1(2, 1)$ has a unique subgame perfect equilibrium, in which player 1 initially takes two steps and wins.

I have spelled out the details of the analysis of these cases to show how we use the result for the game $G_1(1, 1)$ to find the equilibria of the games $G_1(1, 2)$ and $G_1(2, 1)$. In general, the equilibria of the games $G_i(k_1, k_2)$ for all values of k_1 and k_2 up to $\bar{k}$ tell us the consequences of player 1's taking one or two steps in the game $G_1(\bar{k} + 1, \bar{k})$.

⑦ EXERCISE 198.1 (The race $G_1(2, 2)$) Show that the game $G_1(2, 2)$ has a unique subgame perfect equilibrium outcome, in which player 1 initially takes two steps, and wins.

So far we have concluded that in any game in which each player is initially at most two steps from the finish line, the first-mover takes enough steps to reach the finish line, and wins.

Now suppose that player 1 is at most two steps from the finish line, but player 2 is three steps away. Suppose that player 1 takes only *one* step (even if she is initially two steps from the finish line). Then if player 2 takes either one or two steps, play moves to a subgame in which player 1 (the first-mover) wins. Thus player 2 is better off not moving (and not incurring any cost), in which case player 1 takes one step on her next turn, and wins. (Player 1 prefers to move one step at a time than to move two steps initially because the former costs her 2 whereas the latter costs her 4.) We conclude that the outcome of a subgame perfect equilibrium in the game $G_1(2,3)$ is that player 1 takes one step on her first turn, then player 2 does not move, and then player 1 takes another step, and wins.

By a similar argument, in a subgame perfect equilibrium of any game in which player 1 is at most two steps from the finish line and player 2 is three or more steps away, player 1 moves one step at a time, and player 2 does not move; player 1 wins. Symmetrically, in a subgame perfect equilibrium of any game in which player 1 is three or more steps from the finish line and player 2 is at most two steps away, player 1 does not move, and player 2 moves one step at a time, and wins.

Our conclusions so far are illustrated in Figure 200.1, where player 1 moves to the left and player 2 moves down. The values of (k_1, k_2) for which the subgame perfect equilibrium outcome has been determined so far are labeled. The label "1" means that, regardless of who moves first, in a subgame perfect equilibrium player 1 moves one step on each turn, and player 2 does not move; player 1 wins. Similarly, the label "2" means that, regardless of who moves first, player 2 moves one step on each turn, and player 1 does not move; player 2 wins. The label "f" means that the first player to move takes enough steps to reach the finish line, and wins.

Now consider the game $G_1(3,3)$. If player 1 takes one step, we reach the game $G_2(2,3)$. From Figure 200.1 we see that in the subgame perfect equilibrium of this game player 1 wins, and does so by taking one step at a time (the point $(2,3)$ is labeled "1"). If player 1 takes two steps, we reach the game $G_2(1,3)$, in which player 1 also wins. Player 1 prefers not to take two steps unless she has to, so in the subgame perfect equilibrium of $G_1(3,3)$ she takes one step at a time, and wins, and player 2 does not move. Similarly, in a subgame perfect equilibrium of $G_2(3,3)$, player 2 takes one step at a time, and wins, and player 1 does not move.

A similar argument applies to each of the games $G_i(3,4)$, $G_i(4,3)$, and $G_i(4,4)$ for $i = 1, 2$. The argument differs only if the first-mover is four steps from the finish line, in which case she initially takes two steps to reach a game in which she wins. (If she initially takes only one step, the other player wins.)

Now consider the game $G_i(3,5)$ for $i = 1, 2$. By taking one step in $G_1(3,5)$, player 1 reaches a game in which she wins by taking one step at a time. The cost of her taking three steps is less than v_1, so in a subgame perfect equilibrium of $G_1(3,5)$

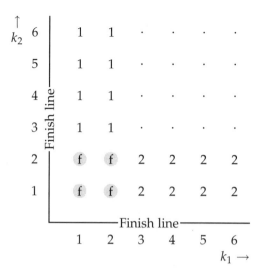

Figure 200.1 The subgame perfect equilibrium outcomes of the race $G_i(k_1, k_2)$. Player 1 moves to the left, and player 2 moves down. The values of (k_1, k_2) for which the subgame perfect equilibrium outcome has been determined so far are labeled; dots represent cases that have not yet been studied. The labels are explained in the text.

she takes one step at a time, and wins, and player 2 does not move. If player 2 takes either one or two steps in $G_2(3, 5)$, she reaches a game (either $G_1(3, 4)$ or $G_1(3, 3)$) in which player 1 wins. Thus whatever she does, she loses, so that in a subgame perfect equilibrium she does not move and player 1 moves one step at a time. We conclude that in a subgame perfect equilibrium of both $G_1(3, 5)$ and $G_2(3, 5)$, player 1 takes one step on each turn and player 2 does not move; player 1 wins.

A similar argument applies to any game in which one player is initially three or four steps from the finish line and the other player is five or more steps from the finish line. We have now made arguments to justify the labeling in Figure 201.1, where the labels have the same meaning as in Figure 200.1, except that "f" means that the first player to move takes enough steps to reach the finish line *or* to reach the closest point labeled with her name, whichever is closer.

A feature of the subgame perfect equilibrium of the game $G_1(4, 4)$ is noteworthy. Suppose that, as planned, player 1 takes two steps, but then player 2 deviates from her equilibrium strategy and takes two steps (rather than not moving). According to our analysis, player 1 should take two steps, to reach the finish line. If she does so, her payoff is negative (less than $7 - 4 - 4 = -1$). Nevertheless she should definitely take the two steps: if she does not, her payoff is even smaller (-4), because player 2 wins. The point is that the cost of her first move is "sunk"; her decision after player 2 deviates must be based on her options from that point on.

The analysis of the games in which each player is initially either five or six steps from the finish line involves arguments similar to those used in the previous cases, with one amendment. A player who is initially six steps from the finish line is

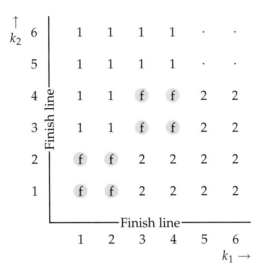

Figure 201.1 The subgame perfect equilibrium outcomes of the race $G_i(k_1, k_2)$. Player 1 moves to the left, and player 2 moves down. The values of (k_1, k_2) for which the subgame perfect equilibrium outcome has been determined so far are labeled; dots represent cases that have not yet been studied. The labels are explained in the text.

better off not moving at all (and obtaining the payoff 0) than she is moving two steps on any turn (and obtaining a negative payoff). An implication is that in the game $G_1(6,5)$, for example, player 1 does not move: if she takes only one step, then player 2 becomes the first-mover and, by taking a single step, moves the play to a game that she wins. We conclude that the first-mover wins in the games $G_i(5,5)$ and $G_i(6,6)$, whereas player 2 wins in $G_i(6,5)$ and player 1 wins in $G_i(5,6)$, for $i = 1, 2$.

A player who is initially more than six steps from the finish line obtains a negative payoff if she moves, even if she wins, so in any subgame perfect equilibrium she does not move. Thus our analysis of the game is complete. The subgame perfect equilibrium outcomes are indicated in Figure 202.1, which shows also the steps taken in the equilibrium of each game when player 1 is the first-mover.

? EXERCISE 201.1 (A race in which the players' valuations of the prize differ) Find the subgame perfect equilibrium outcome of the game in which player 1's valuation of the prize is between 6 and 7, and player 2's valuation is between 4 and 5.

In both of the following exercises, inductive arguments on the length of the game, like the one for $G_i(k_1, k_2)$, can be used.

? EXERCISE 201.2 (Removing stones) Two people take turns removing stones from a pile of n stones. Each person may, on each of her turns, remove either one or two stones. The person who takes the last stone is the winner; she gets $1 from her opponent. Find the subgame perfect equilibria of the games that model this situation for $n = 1$ and $n = 2$. Find the winner in each subgame perfect equilibrium for

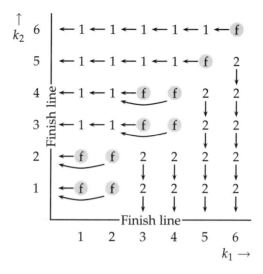

Figure 202.1 The subgame perfect equilibrium outcomes of the race $G_i(k_1, k_2)$. Player 1 moves to the left, and player 2 moves down. The arrows indicate the steps taken in the subgame perfect equilibrium outcome of the games in which player 1 moves first. The labels are explained in the text.

$n = 3$, using the fact that the subgame following player 1's removal of one stone is the game for $n = 2$ in which player 2 is the first-mover, and the subgame following player 1's removal of two stones is the game for $n = 1$ in which player 2 is the first-mover. Use the same technique to find the winner in each subgame perfect equilibrium for $n = 4$, and, if you can, for an arbitrary value of n.

? EXERCISE 202.1 (Hungry lions) The members of a hierarchical group of hungry lions face a piece of prey. If lion 1 does not eat the prey, the prey escapes and the game ends. If it eats the prey, it becomes fat and slow, and lion 2 can eat it. If lion 2 does not eat lion 1, the game ends; if it eats lion 1, then it may be eaten by lion 3, and so on. Each lion prefers to eat than to be hungry, but prefers to be hungry than to be eaten. Find the subgame perfect equilibrium (equilibria?) of the extensive game that models this situation for any number n of lions.

6.4.3 General lessons

Each player's equilibrium strategy involves a "threat" to speed up if the other player deviates. Consider, for example, the game $G_1(3,3)$. Player 1's equilibrium strategy calls for her to take one step at a time, and player 2's equilibrium strategy calls for her not to move. Thus along the equilibrium path player 1's debt climbs to 3 (the cost of her three single steps) before she reaches the finish line.

Now suppose that after player 1 takes her first step, player 2 deviates and takes a step. In this case, player 1's strategy calls for her to take two steps. If she does so, her debt climbs to 5. If at no stage can her debt exceed 3 (its maximal level on the equilibrium path), then her strategy cannot embody such threats.

The general point is that a limit on the debt a player can accumulate may affect the outcome even if it exceeds the player's debt along the equilibrium path in the absence of any limits. You are asked to study an example in the next exercise.

? EXERCISE 203.1 (A race with a liquidity constraint) Find the subgame perfect equilibrium of the variant of the game $G_1(3,3)$ in which player 1's debt may never exceed 3.

In the subgame perfect equilibrium of every game $G_i(k_1, k_2)$, only one player moves; her opponent "gives up". This property of equilibrium holds in more general games. What added ingredient might lead to an equilibrium in which both players are active? A player's uncertainty about the other's characteristics would seem to be such an ingredient: if a player does not know the cost of its opponent's moves, it may assign a positive probability less than one to its winning, at least until it has accumulated some evidence of its opponent's behavior, and while it is optimistic it may be active even though its rival is also active. To build such considerations into the model we need to generalize the model of an extensive game to encompass imperfect information, as we do in Chapter 10.

Another robust feature of the subgame perfect equilibrium of $G_i(k_1, k_2)$ is that the presence of a competitor has little effect on the speed of the player who moves. A lone player would move one step at a time. When there are two players, for most starting points the one that moves does so at the same leisurely pace. Only for a small number of starting points, in all of which the players' initial distances from the starting line are similar, does the presence of a competitor induce the active player to hasten its progress, and then only in the first period.

Notes

The first experiment on the ultimatum game is reported in Güth, Schmittberger, and Schwarze (1982). Grout (1984) is an early analysis of a holdup game. The model of agenda control in legislatures is based on Denzau and Mackay (1983); Romer and Rosenthal (1978) earlier explored a similar idea. The model in Section 6.2 derives its name from the analysis in von Stackelberg (1934, Chapter 4). The vote-buying game in Section 6.3 is taken from Groseclose and Snyder (1996). The model of a race in Section 6.4 is a simplification suggested by Vijay Krishna of a model of Harris and Vickers (1985).

For more discussion of the experimental evidence on the ultimatum game (discussed in the box on page 183), see Roth (1995). Bolton and Ockenfels (2000) study the implications of assuming that players are equity conscious, and relate these implications to the experimental outcomes in various games. The explanation of the experimental results in terms of rules of thumb is discussed by Aumann (1997, 7–8). The problem of fair division, an example of which is given in Exercise 185.2, is studied in detail by Brams and Taylor (1996), who trace the idea of divide-and-choose back to antiquity (p. 10). I have been unable to find the origin of the idea in Exercise 202.1; Barton Lipman suggested the formulation in the exercise.

7 Extensive Games with Perfect Information: Extensions and Discussion

7.1 Allowing for simultaneous moves   205
7.2 Illustration: entry into a monopolized industry   213
7.3 Illustration: electoral competition with strategic voters   215
7.4 Illustration: committee decision-making   217
7.5 Illustration: exit from a declining industry   221
7.6 Allowing for exogenous uncertainty   225
7.7 Discussion: subgame perfect equilibrium and backward induction   231
Prerequisite: Chapter 5

7.1 Allowing for simultaneous moves

7.1.1 Definition

THE model of an extensive game with perfect information (Definition 155.1) assumes that after every sequence of events, a single decision-maker takes an action, knowing every decision-maker's previous actions. I now describe a more general model that allows us to study situations in which, after some sequences of events, the members of a group of decision-makers choose their actions "simultaneously", each member knowing every decision-maker's *previous* actions, but not the contemporaneous actions of the other members of the group.

In the more general model, a terminal history is a sequence of *lists* of actions, each list specifying the actions of a set of players. (A game in which each set contains a single player is an extensive game with perfect information as defined previously.) For example, consider a situation in which player 1 chooses either C or D, then players 2 and 3 simultaneously take actions, each choosing either E or F. In the extensive game that models this situation, $(C, (E, E))$ is a terminal history in which first player 1 chooses C, and then players 2 and 3 both choose E. In the general model, the player function assigns a *set* of players to each nonterminal history. In the example just described, this set consists of the single player 1 for the empty history, and consists of players 2 and 3 for the history C.

An extensive game with perfect information (Definition 155.1) does not specify explicitly the sets of actions available to the players. However, we may derive the set of actions of the player who moves after any nonterminal history from the set of terminal histories and the player function (see (156.1)). When we allow simultaneous moves, the players' sets of actions are conveniently specified in the definition of a game. In the example of the previous paragraph, for instance, we specify the game by giving the eight possible terminal histories (C or D followed by one of the four pairs (E,E), (E,F), (F,E), and (F,F)), the player function defined by $P(\varnothing) = 1$ and $P(C) = P(D) = \{2,3\}$, the sets of actions $\{C,D\}$ for player 1 at the start of the game and $\{E,F\}$ for both player 2 and player 3 after the histories C and D, and each player's preferences over terminal histories.

In any game, the set of terminal histories, player function, and sets of actions for the players must be consistent: the list of actions that follows a subhistory of any terminal history must be a list of actions of the players assigned by the player function to that subhistory. In the game just described, for example, the list of actions following the subhistory C of the terminal history $(C,(E,E))$ is (E,E), which is a pair of actions for the players (2 and 3) assigned by the player function to the history C.

Precisely, an extensive game with perfect information and simultaneous moves is defined as follows.

▶ DEFINITION 206.1 An **extensive game with perfect information and simultaneous moves** consists of

- a set of **players**

- a set of sequences (**terminal histories**) with the property that no sequence is a proper subhistory of any other sequence

- a function (the **player function**) that assigns a set of players to every sequence that is a proper subhistory of some terminal history

- for each proper subhistory h of each terminal history and each player i that is a member of the set of players assigned to h by the player function, a set $A_i(h)$ (the set of **actions** available to player i after the history h)

- for each player, **preferences** over the set of terminal histories

such that the set of terminal histories, player function, and sets of actions are consistent in the sense that h is a terminal history if and only if either (*i*) h takes the form $(a^1, \ldots, a^k)$ for some integer k, the player function is not defined at h, and for every $\ell = 0, \ldots, k-1$, the element $a^{\ell+1}$ is a list of actions of the players assigned by the player function to $(a^1, \ldots, a^\ell)$ (the empty history if $\ell = 0$), or (*ii*) h takes the form $(a^1, a^2, \ldots)$ and for every $\ell = 0, 1, \ldots$, the element $a^{\ell+1}$ is a list of actions of the players assigned by the player function to $(a^1, \ldots, a^\ell)$ (the empty history if $\ell = 0$).

This definition encompasses both extensive games with perfect information as in Definition 155.1 and, in a sense, strategic games. An extensive game with perfect information is an extensive game with perfect information and simultaneous moves in which the set of players assigned to each history consists of exactly one member. (The definition of an extensive game with perfect information and simultaneous moves includes the players' actions, whereas the definition of an extensive game with perfect information does not. However, actions may be derived from the terminal histories and player function of the latter.)

For any strategic game there is an extensive game with perfect information and simultaneous moves in which every terminal history has length 1 that models the same situation. In this extensive game, the set of terminal histories is the set of action profiles in the strategic game, the player function assigns the set of all players to the empty history, and the single set $A_i(\varnothing)$ of actions of each player i is the set of actions of player i in the strategic game.

◆ EXAMPLE 207.1 (Variant of *BoS*) First, person 1 decides whether to stay home and read a book or to attend a concert. If she reads a book, the game ends. If she decides to attend a concert, then, as in *BoS*, she and person 2 independently choose whether to sample the aural delights of Bach or Stravinsky, not knowing the other person's choice. Both people prefer to attend the concert of their favorite composer in the company of the other person to the outcome in which person 1 stays home and reads a book, and prefer this outcome to attending the concert of their less preferred composer in the company of the other person; the worst outcome for both people is that they attend different concerts.

The following extensive game with perfect information and simultaneous moves models this situation.

Players The two people (1 and 2).

Terminal histories *Book*, $(Concert, (B, B))$, $(Concert, (B, S))$, $(Concert, (S, B))$, and $(Concert, (S, S))$.

Player function $P(\varnothing) = 1$ and $P(Concert) = \{1, 2\}$.

Actions The set of player 1's actions at the empty history $\varnothing$ is $A_1(\varnothing) = \{Concert, Book\}$ and the set of her actions after the history *Concert* is $A_1(Concert) = \{B, S\}$; the set of player 2's actions after the history *Concert* is $A_2(Concert) = \{B, S\}$.

Preferences Player 1 prefers $(Concert, (B, B))$ to *Book* to $(Concert, (S, S))$ to $(Concert, (B, S))$, which she regards as indifferent to $(Concert, (S, B))$. Player 2 prefers $(Concert, (S, S))$ to *Book* to $(Concert, (B, B))$ to $(Concert, (B, S))$, which she regards as indifferent to $(Concert, (S, B))$.

This game is illustrated in Figure 208.1, in which I represent the simultaneous choices between B and S in the way that I previously represented a strategic game. (Only a game in which all the simultaneous moves occur at the end of terminal histories may be represented in a diagram like this one. For most other games no convenient diagrammatic representation exists.)

7.1.2 Strategies and Nash equilibrium

As in a game without simultaneous moves, a player's strategy specifies the action she chooses for every history after which it is her turn to move. Definition 159.1

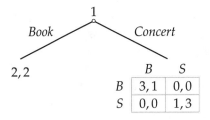

Figure 208.1 The variant of *BoS* described in Example 207.1.

requires only minor rewording to allow for the possibility that players may move simultaneously.

▷ DEFINITION 208.1 (*Strategy in extensive game with perfect information and simultaneous moves*) A **strategy** of player i in an extensive game with perfect information and simultaneous moves is a function that assigns to each history h after which i is one of the players whose turn it is to move (i.e. i is a member of $P(h)$, where P is the player function of the game) an action in $A_i(h)$ (the set of actions available to player i after h).

The definition of a *Nash equilibrium* of an extensive game with perfect information and simultaneous moves is exactly the same as the definition for a game with no simultaneous moves (Definition 161.2): a Nash equilibrium is a strategy profile with the property that no player can induce a better outcome for herself by changing her strategy, given the other players' strategies. Also as before, the *strategic form* of a game is the strategic game in which the players' actions are their strategies in the extensive game (see Section 5.3), and a strategy profile is a Nash equilibrium of the extensive game if and only if it is a Nash equilibrium of the strategic form of the game.

◆ EXAMPLE 208.2 (*Nash equilibria of a variant of BoS*) In the game in Example 207.1, a strategy of player 1 specifies her actions at the start of the game and after the history *Concert*; a strategy of player 2 specifies her action after the history *Concert*. Thus player 1 has four strategies, (*Concert, B*), (*Concert, S*), (*Book, B*), and (*Book, S*), and player 2 has two strategies, *B* and *S*. (Remember that a player's strategy is more than a plan of action; it specifies an action for *every* history after which the player moves, even histories that it precludes. For example, player 1's strategy specifies her action after the history *Concert* even if it specifies that she choose *Book* at the beginning of the game.)

The strategic form of the game is given in Figure 209.1. We see that the game has three pure Nash equilibria: ((*Concert, B*), *B*), ((*Book, B*), *S*), and ((*Book, S*), *S*).

Every extensive game has a unique strategic form. However, some strategic games are the strategic forms of more than one extensive game. Consider, for example, the strategic game in Figure 209.2. This game is the strategic form of the extensive game with perfect information and simultaneous moves in which the two players choose their actions simultaneously; it is also the strategic form of the entry game in Figure 156.1.

	B	S
(Concert, B)	3,1	0,0
(Concert, S)	0,0	1,3
(Book, B)	2,2	2,2
(Book, S)	2,2	2,2

Figure 209.1 The strategic form of the game in Example 207.1.

	L	R
T	1,2	1,2
B	0,0	2,0

Figure 209.2 A strategic game that is the strategic form of more than one extensive game.

7.1.3 Subgame perfect equilibrium

As for a game in which one player moves after each history, the subgame following the history h of an extensive game with perfect information and simultaneous moves is the extensive game "starting at h". (The formal definition is a variant of Definition 164.1.)

For instance, the game in Example 207.1 has two subgames: the whole game, and the game in which the players engage after player 1 chooses *Concert*. In the second subgame, the terminal histories are $(B, B),(B, S)$, (S, B), and (S, S), the player function assigns the set $\{1, 2\}$ consisting of both players to the empty history (the only nonterminal history), the set of actions of each player at the empty history is $\{B, S\}$, and the players' preferences are represented by the payoffs in the table in Figure 208.1. (This subgame models the same situation as *BoS*.)

A subgame perfect equilibrium is defined as before: a *subgame perfect equilibrium* of an extensive game with perfect information and simultaneous moves is a strategy profile with the property that in no subgame can any player increase her payoff by choosing a different strategy, given the other players' strategies. The formal definition differs from that of a subgame perfect equilibrium of a game without simultaneous moves (Definition 166.1) only in that the meaning of "it is player i's turn to move" is that i is a member of $P(h)$, rather than $P(h) = i$.

To find the set of subgame perfect equilibria of an extensive game with perfect information and simultaneous moves that has a finite horizon, we can, as before, use backward induction. The only wrinkle is that some (perhaps all) of the situations we need to analyze are not single-person decision problems, as they are in the absence of simultaneous moves, but problems in which several players choose actions simultaneously. We cannot simply find an optimal action for the player whose turn it is to move at the start of each subgame, given the players' behavior in the remainder of the game. We need to find a *list* of actions for the players who move at the start of each subgame, with the property that each player's action is optimal given the other players' simultaneous actions and the players' behavior in the remainder of the game. That is, the argument we need to make is the same as the one we make when finding a Nash equilibrium of a strategic game. This argument may use any of the techniques discussed in Chapter 2: it may check each action profile in turn, it may construct and study the players' best response functions, or it may show directly that an action profile we have obtained by a combination of intuition and trial and error is an equilibrium.

◆ EXAMPLE 210.1 (Subgame perfect equilibria of a variant of *BoS*) Consider the game in Figure 208.1. Backward induction proceeds as follows.

- In the subgame that follows the history *Concert*, there are two Nash equilibria (in pure strategies), namely (S, S) and (B, B), as we found in Section 2.7.2.

- If the outcome in the subgame that follows *Concert* is (S, S), then the optimal choice of player 1 at the start of the game is *Book*.

- If the outcome in the subgame that follows *Concert* is (B, B), then the optimal choice of player 1 at the start of the game is *Concert*.

We conclude that the game has two subgame perfect equilibria: $((Book, S), S)$ and $((Concert, B), B)$.

Every finite extensive game with perfect information has a (pure) subgame perfect equilibrium (Proposition 173.1). The same is not true of a finite extensive game with perfect information and simultaneous moves because, as we know, a finite strategic game (which corresponds to an extensive game with perfect information and simultaneous moves of length 1) may not possess a pure strategy Nash equilibrium. (Consider *Matching Pennies* (Example 19.1).) If you have studied Chapter 4, you know that some strategic games that lack a pure strategy Nash equilibrium have a "mixed strategy Nash equilibrium", in which each player randomizes. The same is true of extensive games with perfect information and simultaneous moves. However, in this chapter I restrict attention almost exclusively to pure strategy equilibria; the only occasion on which mixed strategy Nash equilibrium appears is Exercise 212.1.

? EXERCISE 210.2 (Extensive game with simultaneous moves) Find the subgame perfect equilibria of the following game. First player 1 chooses either A or B. After either choice, she and player 2 simultaneously choose actions. If player 1 initially chooses A, then she and player 2 subsequently each choose either C or D; if player 1 chooses B initially, then she and player 2 subsequently each choose either E or F. Among the terminal histories, player 1 prefers $(A, (C, C))$ to $(B, (E, E))$ to $(A, (D, D))$ to $(B, (F, F))$, and prefers all these to $(A, (C, D))$, $(A, (D, C))$, $(B, (E, F))$, and $(B, (F, E))$, between which she is indifferent. Player 2 prefers $(A, (D, D))$ to $(B, (F, F))$ to $(A, (C, C))$ to $(B, (E, E))$, and prefers all these to $(A, (C, D))$, $(A, (D, C))$, $(B, (E, F))$, and $(B, (F, E))$, between which she is indifferent.

? EXERCISE 210.3 (Two-period *Prisoner's Dilemma*) Two people simultaneously select actions; each person chooses either Q or F (as in the *Prisoner's Dilemma*). Then they simultaneously select actions again, once again each choosing either Q or F. Each person's preferences are represented by the payoff function that assigns to the terminal history $((W, X), (Y, Z))$ (where each component is either Q or F) a payoff equal to the sum of the person's payoffs to (W, X) and to (Y, Z) in the *Prisoner's Dilemma* given in Figure 15.1. Specify this situation as an extensive game with perfect information and simultaneous moves and find its subgame perfect equilibria.

?) EXERCISE 211.1 (Timing claims on an investment) An amount of money accumulates; in period t $(= 1, 2, \ldots, T)$ its size is \$2t. In each period two people simultaneously decide whether to claim the money. If only one person does so, she gets all the money; if both people do so, they split the money equally; and if neither person does so, both people have the opportunity to do so in the next period. If neither person claims the money in period T, each person obtains \$$T$. Each person cares only about the amount of money she obtains. Formulate this situation as an extensive game with perfect information and simultaneous moves, and find its subgame perfect equilibria). (Start by considering the cases $T = 1$ and $T = 2$.)

?) EXERCISE 211.2 (A market game) A seller owns one indivisible unit of a good, which she does not value. Several potential buyers, each of whom attaches the same positive value v to the good, simultaneously offer prices they are willing to pay for the good. After receiving the offers, the seller decides which, if any, to accept. If she does not accept any offer, then no transaction takes place, and all payoffs are 0. Otherwise, the buyer whose offer the seller accepts pays the amount p she offered and receives the good; the payoff of the seller is p, the payoff of the buyer who obtained the good is $v - p$, and the payoff of every other buyer is 0. Model this situation as an extensive game with perfect information and simultaneous moves and find its subgame perfect equilibria. (Use a combination of intuition and trial and error to find a strategy profile that appears to be an equilibrium, then argue directly that it is. The incentives in the game are closely related to those in Bertrand's oligopoly game (see Exercise 68.1), with the roles of buyers and sellers reversed.) Show, in particular, that in every subgame perfect equilibrium every buyer's payoff is zero.

MORE EXPERIMENTAL EVIDENCE ON SUBGAME PERFECT EQUILIBRIUM

Experiments conducted in 1989 and 1990 among college students (mainly taking economics classes) show that the subgame perfect equilibria of the game in Exercise 211.2 correspond closely to experimental outcomes (Roth, Prasnikar, Okuno-Fujiwara, and Zamir 1991), in contrast to the subgame perfect equilibrium of the ultimatum game (see the box on page 183).

In experiments conducted at four locations (Jerusalem, Ljubljana, Pittsburgh, and Tokyo), nine "buyers" simultaneously bid for the rough equivalent (in terms of local purchasing power) of U.S.\$10, held by a "seller". Each experiment involved a group of 20 participants, which was divided into two markets, each with one seller and nine buyers. Each participant was involved in ten rounds of the market; in each round the sellers and buyers were assigned anew, and in any given round no participant knew who, among the other participants, were sellers and buyers, and who was involved in her market. In every session of the experiment the maximum proposed price was accepted by the seller, and by the seventh round of every experiment the highest bid was at least (the equivalent of) U.S.$9.95.

Experiments involving the ultimatum game, run in the same locations using a similar design, yielded results similar to those of previous experiments (see the box on page 183): proposers kept considerably less than 100% of the pie, and nontrivial offers were rejected.

The box on page 183 discusses two explanations for the experimental results in the ultimatum game. Both explanations are consistent with the results in the market game. One explanation is that people are concerned not only with their own monetary payoffs, but also with other people's payoffs. At least some specifications of such preferences do not affect the subgame perfect equilibria of a market game with many buyers, which still all yield every buyer the payoff of zero. (When there are many buyers, even a seller who cares about the other players' payoffs accepts the highest price offered, because accepting a lower price has little impact on the distribution of monetary payoffs, all but two of which remain zero.) Thus such preferences are consistent with both sets of experimental outcomes. Another explanation is that people incorrectly recognize the ultimatum game as one in which the rule of thumb "don't be a sucker" is advantageously invoked and thus reject a poor offer, "punishing" the person who makes such an offer. In the market game, the players treated poorly in the subgame perfect equilibrium are the buyers, who move first, and hence have no opportunity to punish any other player. Thus the rule of thumb is not relevant in this game, so that this explanation is also consistent with both sets of experimental outcomes.

In the next exercise you are asked to investigate subgame perfect equilibria in which some players use mixed strategies (discussed in Chapter 4).

? EXERCISE 212.1 (Price competition) Extend the model in Exercise 128.1 by having the sellers simultaneously choose their prices before the buyers simultaneously choose which seller to approach. Assume that each seller's preferences are represented by the expected value of a Bernoulli payoff function in which the payoff to not trading is 0 and the payoff to trading at the price p is p. Formulate this model precisely as an extensive game with perfect information and simultaneous moves. Show that for every $p \geq \frac{1}{2}$ the game has a subgame perfect equilibrium in which each seller announces the price p. (You may use the fact that if seller j's price is at least $\frac{1}{2}$, seller i's payoff in the mixed strategy equilibrium of the subgame in which the buyers choose which seller to approach is decreasing in her price p_i when $p_i > p_j$.)

7.2 Illustration: entry into a monopolized industry

7.2.1 General model

An industry is currently monopolized by a single firm (the "incumbent"). A second firm (the "challenger") is considering entry, which entails a positive cost f in addition to its production cost. If the challenger stays out, then its profit is zero, whereas if it enters, the firms simultaneously choose outputs (as in Cournot's model of duopoly (Section 3.1)). The cost to firm i of producing q_i units of output is $C_i(q_i)$. If the firms' total output is Q, then the market price is $P_d(Q)$. (As in Section 6.2, I add a subscript to P to avoid a clash with the player function of the game.)

We can model this situation as the following extensive game with perfect information and simultaneous moves, illustrated in Figure 213.1.

Players The two firms: the incumbent (firm 1) and the challenger (firm 2).

Terminal histories $(In, (q_1, q_2))$ for any pair (q_1, q_2) of outputs (nonnegative numbers), and (Out, q_1) for any output q_1.

Player function $P(\varnothing) = \{2\}$, $P(In) = \{1, 2\}$, and $P(Out) = \{1\}$.

Actions $A_2(\varnothing) = \{In, Out\}$; $A_1(In)$, $A_1(Out)$, and $A_2(In)$ are all equal to the set of possible outputs (nonnegative numbers).

Preferences Each firm's preferences are represented by its profit, which for a terminal history $(In, (q_1, q_2))$ is $q_1 P_d(q_1 + q_2) - C_1(q_1)$ for the incumbent and $q_2 P_d(q_1 + q_2) - C_2(q_2) - f$ for the challenger, and for a terminal history (Out, q_1) is $q_1 P_d(q_1) - C_1(q_1)$ for the incumbent and 0 for the challenger.

7.2.2 Example

Suppose that $C_i(q_i) = cq_i$ for all q_i ("unit cost" is constant, equal to c), and the inverse demand function is linear where it is positive, given by $P_d(Q) = \alpha - Q$ for $Q \leq \alpha$, as in Section 3.1.3. To find the subgame perfect equilibria, first consider the subgame that follows the history In. The strategic form of this subgame is the same as the example of Cournot's duopoly game studied in Section 3.1.3, except that the payoff of the challenger is reduced by f (the fixed cost of entry) regardless of the challenger's output. Thus the subgame has a unique Nash equilibrium, in

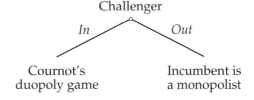

Figure 213.1 An entry game.

which the output of each firm is $\frac{1}{3}(\alpha - c)$; the incumbent's profit is $\frac{1}{9}(\alpha - c)^2$, and the challenger's profit is $\frac{1}{9}(\alpha - c)^2 - f$.

Now consider the subgame that follows the history *Out*. In this subgame the incumbent chooses an output. The incumbent's profit when it chooses the output q_1 is $q_1(\alpha - q_1) - cq_1 = q_1(\alpha - c - q_1)$. This function is a quadratic that increases and then decreases as q_1 increases, and is zero when $q_1 = 0$ and when $q_1 = \alpha - c$. Thus the function is maximized when $q_1 = \frac{1}{2}(\alpha - c)$. We conclude that in any subgame perfect equilibrium the incumbent chooses $q_1 = \frac{1}{2}(\alpha - c)$ in the subgame following the history *Out*.

Finally, consider the challenger's action at the start of the game. If the challenger stays out, then its profit is 0, whereas if it enters, then given the actions chosen in the resulting subgame, its profit is $\frac{1}{9}(\alpha - c)^2 - f$. Thus in any subgame perfect equilibrium the challenger enters if $\frac{1}{9}(\alpha - c)^2 > f$ and stays out if $\frac{1}{9}(\alpha - c)^2 < f$. If $\frac{1}{9}(\alpha - c)^2 = f$, then the game has two subgame perfect equilibria; the challenger enters in one and does not in the other.

In summary, the set of subgame perfect equilibria depends on the value of f. In all equilibria the incumbent's strategy is to produce $\frac{1}{3}(\alpha - c)$ if the challenger enters and $\frac{1}{2}(\alpha - c)$ if it does not, and the challenger's strategy involves its producing $\frac{1}{3}(\alpha - c)$ if it enters.

- If $f < \frac{1}{9}(\alpha - c)^2$ there is a unique subgame perfect equilibrium, in which the challenger enters. The outcome is that the challenger enters and each firm produces the output $\frac{1}{3}(\alpha - c)$.

- If $f > \frac{1}{9}(\alpha - c)^2$ there is a unique subgame perfect equilibrium, in which the challenger stays out. The outcome is that the challenger stays out and the incumbent produces $\frac{1}{2}(\alpha - c)$.

- If $f = \frac{1}{9}(\alpha - c)^2$ the game has two subgame perfect equilibria: the one for the case $f < \frac{1}{9}(\alpha - c)^2$ and the one for the case $f > \frac{1}{9}(\alpha - c)^2$.

Why, if f is small, does the game have no subgame perfect equilibrium in which the incumbent floods the market if the challenger enters, so that the challenger optimally stays out and the incumbent obtains a profit higher than it would have if the challenger had entered? Because the action this strategy prescribes after the history in which the challenger enters is not the incumbent's action in a Nash equilibrium of the subgame: the subgame has a unique Nash equilibrium, in which each firm produces $\frac{1}{3}(\alpha - c)$. Put differently, the incumbent's "threat" to flood the market if the challenger enters is not credible.

? EXERCISE 214.1 (Bertrand's duopoly game with entry) Find the subgame perfect equilibria of the variant of the game studied in this section in which the post-entry competition is a game in which each firm chooses a price, as in the example of Bertrand's duopoly game studied in Section 3.2.2, rather than an output.

7.3 Illustration: electoral competition with strategic voters

The voters in Hotelling's model of electoral competition (Section 3.3) are not play-ers in the game: each citizen is assumed simply to vote for the candidate whose position she most prefers. How do the conclusions of the model change if we assume that each citizen *chooses* the candidate for whom to vote?

Consider the extensive game in which the candidates first simultaneously choose actions, then the citizens simultaneously choose how to vote. As in the variant of Hotelling's game considered on page 74, assume that each candidate may either choose a position (as in Hotelling's original model) or choose to stay out of the race, an option she is assumed to rank between losing and tying for first place with all the other candidates.

   Players   The candidates and the citizens.

   Terminal histories   All sequences (x, v) where x is a list of the candidates' ac-tions, each component of which is either a position (a number) or *Out*, and v is a list of voting decisions for the citizens (i.e. a list of candidates, one for each citizen).

   Player function $P(\varnothing)$ is the set of all the candidates, and $P(x)$, for any list x of positions for the candidates, is the set of all citizens.

   Actions   The set of actions available to each candidate at the start of the game consists of *Out* and the set of possible positions. The set of actions available to each citizen after a history x is the set of candidates.

   Preferences   Each candidate's preferences are represented by a payoff function that assigns n to every terminal history in which she wins outright, k to every terminal history in which she ties for first place with $n - k$ other candidates (for $1 \leq k \leq n - 1$), 0 to every terminal history in which she stays out of the race, and -1 to every terminal history in which she loses, where n is the number of candidates. Each citizen's preferences are represented by a payoff function that assigns to each terminal history the average distance from the citizen's favorite position of the set of winning candidates in that history.

First consider the game in which there are two candidates (and an arbitrary number of citizens). Every subgame following choices of positions by the candi-dates has many Nash equilibria (as you know if you solved Exercise 48.1). For example, any action profile in which *all* citizens vote for the same candidate is a Nash equilibrium. (A citizen's switching her vote to another candidate has no effect on the outcome.)

This plethora of Nash equilibria allows us to construct, for *every* pair of posi-tions, a subgame perfect equilibrium in which the candidates choose those posi-tions! Consider the strategy profile in which the candidates choose the positions x_1 and x_2, and

- all citizens vote for candidate 1 after a history (x_1', x_2') in which $x_1' = x_1$

- all citizens vote for candidate 2 after a history (x_1', x_2') in which $x_1' \neq x_1$.

The outcome is that the candidates choose the positions x_1 and x_2 and candidate 1 wins. The strategy profile is a subgame perfect equilibrium because for every history (x_1, x_2) the profile of the citizens' actions is a Nash equilibrium, and neither candidate can induce an outcome she prefers by deviating: a deviation by candidate 1 to a position different from x_1 leads her to lose, and a deviation by candidate 2 has no effect on the outcome.

However, most of the Nash equilibria of the voting subgames are fragile (as you know if you solved Exercise 48.1): a citizen's voting for her less preferred candidate is weakly dominated (Definition 46.1) by her voting for her favorite candidate. (A citizen who switches from voting for her less preferred candidate to voting for her favorite candidate either does not affect the outcome (if her favorite candidate was three or more votes behind) or causes her favorite candidate either to tie for first place rather than lose, or to win rather than tie.) Thus in the only Nash equilibrium of a voting subgame in which no citizen uses a weakly dominated action, each citizen votes for the candidate whose position is closest to her favorite position.

Hotelling's model (Section 3.3) *assumes* that each citizen votes for the candidate whose position is closest to her favorite position; in its unique Nash equilibrium, each candidate's position is the median of the citizens' favorite positions. Combining this result with the result of the previous paragraph, we conclude that the game we are studying has only one subgame perfect equilibrium in which no player's strategy is weakly dominated: each candidate chooses the median of the citizens' favorite positions, and for every pair of the candidates' positions, each citizen votes for her favorite candidate.

In the game with three or more candidates, not only do many of the voting subgames have many Nash equilibria, with a variety of outcomes, but restricting to voting strategies that are not weakly dominated does not dramatically affect the set of equilibria: a citizen's only weakly dominated strategy is a vote for her least preferred candidate (see Exercise 49.1).

However, the set of equilibrium outcomes is dramatically restricted by the assumption that each candidate prefers to stay out of the race than to enter and lose, as the next two exercises show. The result in the first exercise is that the game has a subgame perfect equilibrium in which no citizen's strategy is weakly dominated and every candidate enters and chooses as her position the median of the citizens' favorite positions. The result in the second exercise is that under an assumption that makes the citizens averse to ties and an assumption that there exist citizens with extreme preferences, in *every* subgame perfect equilibrium all candidates who enter do so at the median of the citizens' favorite positions. The additional assumptions about the citizens' preferences are much stronger that necessary; they are designed to make the argument relatively easy.

? EXERCISE 216.1 (Electoral competition with strategic voters) Assume that there are $n \geq 3$ candidates and q citizens, where $q \geq 2n$ is odd (so that the median of the voters' favorite positions is well defined) and divisible by n. Show that the game has a subgame perfect equilibrium in which no citizen's strategy is weakly dominated and every candidate enters the race and chooses the median of the citizens' favorite positions. (You may use the fact that every voting subgame has a (pure) Nash equilibrium in which no citizen's action is weakly dominated.)

? EXERCISE 217.1 (Electoral competition with strategic voters) Consider the variant of the game in this section in which (*i*) the set of possible positions is the set of numbers x with $0 \le x \le 1$, (*ii*) the favorite position of at least one citizen is 0 and the favorite position of at least one citizen is 1, and (*iii*) each citizen's preferences are represented by a payoff function that assigns to each terminal history the distance from the citizen's favorite position to the position of the candidate in the set of winners whose position is *furthest* from her favorite position. Under the other assumptions of the previous exercise, show that in every subgame perfect equilibrium in which no citizen's action is weakly dominated, the position chosen by every candidate who enters is the median of the citizens' favorite positions. To do so, first show that in any equilibrium each candidate that enters is in the set of winners. Then show that in any Nash equilibrium of any voting subgame in which there are more than two candidates and not all candidates' positions are the same, some candidate loses. (Argue that if all candidates tie for first place, some citizen can increase her payoff by changing her vote.) Finally, show that in any subgame perfect equilibrium in which either only two candidates enter, or all candidates who enter choose the same position, every entering candidates chooses the median of the citizens' favorite positions.

7.4 Illustration: committee decision-making

How does the procedure used by a committee affect the decision it makes? One approach to this question models a decision-making procedure as an extensive game with perfect information and simultaneous moves in which there is a sequence of ballots, in each of which the committee members vote simultaneously; the result of each ballot determines the choices on the next ballot, or, eventually, the decision to be made.

Fix a set of committee members and a set of *alternatives* over which each member has strict preferences (no member is indifferent between any two alternatives). Assume that the number of committee members is odd, to avoid ties in votes. If there are two alternatives, the simplest committee procedure is that in which the members vote simultaneously for one of the alternatives. (We may interpret the game in Section 2.9.3 as a model of this procedure.) In the procedure illustrated in Figure 218.1, there are three alternatives, x, y, and z. The committee first votes whether to choose x (option "*a*") or to eliminate it from consideration (option "*b*"). If it votes to eliminate x, it subsequently votes between y and z.

In these procedures, each vote is between two options. Such procedures are called *binary agendas*. We may define a binary agenda with the aid of an auxiliary one-player extensive game with perfect information in which the set $A(h)$ of ac-

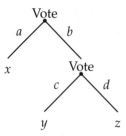

Figure 218.1 A voting procedure, or "binary agenda".

tions following any nonterminal history h has two members, and the number of terminal histories is at least the number of alternatives. We associate with every terminal history h of this auxiliary game an alternative $\alpha(h)$ in such a way that each alternative is associated with at least one terminal history.

In the binary agenda associated with the auxiliary game G, all players vote simultaneously whenever the player in G takes an action. The options on the ballot following the nonterminal history in which a majority of committee members choose option a^1 at the start of the game, then option a^2, and so on, are the members of the set $A(a^1,\ldots,a^k)$ of actions of the player in G after the history $(a^1,\ldots,a^k)$. The alternative selected after the terminal history in which the majority choices are a^1, ..., a^k is the alternative $\alpha(a^1,\ldots,a^k)$ associated with $(a^1,\ldots,a^k)$ in G. For example, in the auxiliary one-person game that defines the structure of the agenda in Figure 218.1, the single player first chooses a or b; if she chooses a the game ends, whereas if she chooses b, she then chooses between c and d. The alternative x is associated with the terminal history a, y is associated with (b,c), and z is associated with (b,d).

Precisely, the **binary agenda** associated with the auxiliary game G is the extensive game with perfect information and simultaneous moves defined as follows.

Players   The set of committee members.

Terminal histories   A sequence $(v^1,\ldots,v^k)$ of action profiles (in which each v^j is a list of the players' votes) is a terminal history if and only if there is a terminal history $(a^1,\ldots,a^k)$ of G such that for every $j = 0,\ldots,k-1$, every element of v^{j+1} is a member of $A(a^1,\ldots,a^j)$ ($A(\varnothing)$ if $j = 0$) and a majority of the players' actions in v^{j+1} are equal to a^{j+1}.

Player function   For every nonterminal history h, $P(h)$ is the set of all players.

Actions   For every player i and every nonterminal history $(v^1,\ldots,v^j)$, player i's set of actions is $A(a^1,\ldots,a^j)$, where $(a^1,\ldots,a^j)$ is the history of G in which, for all ℓ, a^ℓ is the action chosen by the majority of players in v^ℓ.

Preferences   The rank each player assigns to the terminal history $(v^1,\ldots,v^k)$ is equal to the rank she assigns to the alternative $\alpha(a^1,\ldots,a^k)$ associated with the terminal history $(a^1, \ldots, a^k)$ of G in which, for all j, a^j is the action chosen by a majority of players in v^j.

Every binary agenda, like every voting subgame of the model in the previous section, has many subgame perfect equilibria. In fact, in any binary agenda, *every* alternative is the outcome of some subgame perfect equilibrium, because if, in every vote, every player votes for the same option, no player can affect the outcome by changing her strategy. However, if we restrict attention to weakly undominated strategies, we greatly reduce the set of equilibria. As we saw before (Section 2.9.3), in a ballot with two options, a player's action of voting for the option she prefers weakly dominates the action of voting for the other option. Thus in a subgame perfect equilibrium of a binary agenda in which every player's vote on every ballot is weakly undominated, on each ballot every player votes for the option that leads, ultimately (given the outcomes of the later ballots), to the alternative she prefers. The alternative associated with the terminal history generated by such a subgame perfect equilibrium is said to be the outcome of *sophisticated voting*.

Which alternatives are the outcomes of sophisticated voting in binary agendas? Say that alternative x *beats* alternative y if a majority of committee members prefer x to y. An alternative that beats every other alternative is called a *Condorcet winner*. For any preferences, there is either one Condorcet winner or no Condorcet winner (see Exercise 75.3).

First suppose that the players' preferences are such that some alternative, say x^*, is a Condorcet winner. I claim that x^* is the outcome of sophisticated voting in *every* binary agenda. The argument, using backward induction, is simple. First consider a subgame of length 1 in which one option leads to the alternative x^*. In this subgame a majority of the players vote for the option that leads to x^*, because a majority prefers x^* to every other alternative, and each player's only weakly undominated strategy is to vote for the option that leads to the alternative she prefers. Thus in at least one subgame of length 2, at least one option leads ultimately to the decision x^* (given the players' votes in the subgames of length 1). In this subgame, by the same argument as before, the winning option leads to x^*. Continuing backward, we conclude that at least one option on the first ballot leads ultimately to x^* and that consequently the winning option on this ballot leads to x^*.

Thus if the players' preferences are such that a Condorcet winner exists, the agenda does not matter: the outcome of sophisticated voting is always the Condorcet winner. If the players' preferences are such that no alternative is a Condorcet winner, the outcome of sophisticated voting depends on the agenda. Consider, for example, a committee with three members facing three alternatives. Suppose that one member prefers x to y to z, another prefers y to z to x, and the third prefers z to x to y. For these preferences, no alternative is a Condorcet winner. The outcome of sophisticated voting in the binary agenda in Figure 218.1 is the alternative x. (Use backward induction: y beats z, and x beats y.) If the positions of x and y are interchanged, then the outcome is y, and if the positions of x and z are interchanged, then the outcome is z. Thus in this case, for *every* alternative there is a binary agenda for which that alternative is the outcome of sophisticated voting.

Which alternatives are the outcomes of sophisticated voting in binary agendas when no alternative is a Condorcet winner? Consider a committee with arbitrary preferences (not necessarily the ones considered in the previous paragraph) that uses the agenda in Figure 218.1. For x to be the outcome of sophisticated voting it must beat the winner of y and z. It may not beat both y and z directly, but it must beat them both at least "indirectly": either x beats y beats x, or x beats z beats y. Similarly, if y or z is the outcome of sophisticated voting, then it must beat both of the other alternatives at least indirectly.

Precisely, say that alternative x *indirectly beats* alternative y if for some $k \geq 1$ there are alternatives $u_1, \ldots, u_k$ such that x beats u_1, u_j beats u_{j+1} for $j = 1, \ldots, k - 1$, and u_k beats y. The set of alternatives x such that x beats every other alternative either directly or indirectly is called the *top cycle set*. (Note that if alternative x beats any alternative indirectly, it beats at least one alternative directly.) If there is a Condorcet winner, then the top cycle set consists of this single alternative. If there is no Condorcet winner, then the top cycle set contains more than one alternative.

⊘ EXERCISE 220.1 (Top cycle set) A committee has three members.

a. Suppose that there are three alternatives, x, y, and z, and that one member prefers x to y to z, another prefers y to z to x, and the third prefers z to x to y. Find the top cycle set.

b. Suppose that there are four alternatives, w, x, y, and z, and that one member prefers w to z to x to y, one member prefers y to w to z to x, and one member prefers x to y to w to z. Find the top cycle set. Show, in particular, that z is in the top cycle set even though *all* committee members prefer w.

Rephrasing my conclusion for the agenda in Figure 218.1, if an alternative is the outcome of sophisticated voting, then it is in the top cycle set. The argument for this conclusion extends to any binary agenda. In every subgame, the outcome of sophisticated voting must beat the alternative that will be selected if it is rejected. Thus by backward induction, the outcome of sophisticated voting in the whole game must beat every other alternative either directly or indirectly: the outcome of sophisticated voting in any binary agenda is in the top cycle set.

Now consider a converse question: for any given alternative x in the top cycle set, is there a binary agenda for which x is the outcome of sophisticated voting? The answer is affirmative. The idea behind the construction of an appropriate agenda is illustrated by a simple example. Suppose that there are three alternatives, x, y, and z, and x beats y beats z. Then the agenda in Figure 218.1 is one for which x is the outcome of sophisticated voting. Now suppose there are two additional alternatives, u and w, and x beats u beats w. Then we can construct a larger agenda in which x is the outcome of sophisticated voting by replacing the alternative x in Figure 218.1 with a subgame in which a vote is taken for or against x, and, if x is rejected, a vote is subsequently taken between u and w. If there are other chains through which x beats other alternatives, we can similarly add further subgames.

? EXERCISE 221.1 (Designing agendas) A committee has three members; there are five alternatives. One member prefers x to y to v to w to z, another prefers z to x to v to w to y, and the third prefers y to z to w to v to x. Find the top cycle set, and for each alternative a in the set design a binary agenda for which a is the outcome of sophisticated voting. Convince yourself that for no binary agenda is the outcome of sophisticated voting outside the top cycle set.

? EXERCISE 221.2 (An agenda that yields an undesirable outcome) Design a binary agenda for the committee in Exercise 220.1 for which the outcome of sophisticated voting is z (which is worse for all committee members than w).

In summary, (*i*) for any binary agenda, the alternative generated by the subgame perfect equilibrium in which no citizen's action in any ballot is weakly dominated is in the top cycle set, and (*ii*) for every alternative in the top cycle set, there is a binary agenda for which that alternative is generated by the subgame perfect equilibrium in which no citizen's action in any ballot is weakly dominated. In particular, the extent to which the procedure used by a committee affects its decision depends on the nature of the members' preferences. At one extreme, for preferences such that some alternative is a Condorcet winner, the agenda is irrelevant. At another extreme, for preferences for which every alternative is in the top cycle set, the agenda is instrumental in determining the decision. Further, for some preferences there are agendas for which the subgame perfect equilibrium yields an alternative that is unambiguously undesirable in the sense that there is another alternative that *all* committee members prefer.

7.5   Illustration: exit from a declining industry

An industry currently consists of two firms, one with a large capacity, and one with a small capacity. Demand for the firms' output is declining steadily over time. When will the firms leave the industry? Which firm will leave first? Do the firms' financial resources affect the outcome? The analysis of a model that answers these questions illustrates a use of backward induction more sophisticated than that in the previous sections of this chapter.

7.5.1 A model

Take time to be a discrete variable, starting in period 1. Denote by $P_t(Q)$ the market price in period t when the firms' total output is Q, and assume that this price is declining over time: for every value of Q, we have $P_{t+1}(Q) < P_t(Q)$ for all $t \geq 1$. (See Figure 223.1.) We are interested in the firms' decisions to exit, rather than their decisions of how much to produce in the event they stay in the market, so we assume that firm i's only decision is whether to produce some fixed output, denoted k_i, or to produce no output. (You may think of k_i as firm i's capacity.) Once a firm has stopped production, it cannot start up again. Assume that $k_2 < k_1$ (firm 2 is smaller than firm 1) and that each firm's cost of producing q units of output is cq.

The following extensive game with simultaneous moves models this situation.

Players The two firms.

Terminal histories All sequences $(X^1, \ldots, X^t)$ for some $t \geq 1$, where $X^s = (Stay, Stay)$ for $1 \leq s \leq t - 1$ and $X^t = (Exit, Exit)$ (both firms exit in period t), or $X^s = (Stay, Stay)$ for all s with $1 \leq s \leq r - 1$ for some r, $X^r = (Stay, Exit)$ or $(Exit, Stay)$, $X^s = Stay$ for all s with $r + 1 \leq s \leq t - 1$, and $X^t = Exit$ (one firm exits in period r and the other exits in period t), and all infinite sequences $(X^1, X^2, \ldots)$, where $X^r = (Stay, Stay)$ for all r (neither firm ever exits).

Player function $P(h) = \{1, 2\}$ after any history h in which neither firm has exited; $P(h) = 1$ after any history h in which only firm 2 has exited; and $P(h) = 2$ after any history h in which only firm 1 has exited.

Actions Whenever a firm moves, its set of actions is $\{Stay, Exit\}$.

Preferences Each firm's preferences are represented by a payoff function that associates with each terminal history the firm's total profit, where the profit of firm i ($= 1, 2$) in period t is $(P_t(k_i) - c)k_i$ if the other firm has exited and $(P_t(k_1 + k_2) - c)k_i$ if the other firm has not exited.

7.5.2 Subgame perfect equilibrium

In a period in which $P_t(k_i) < c$, firm i makes a loss even if it is the only firm remaining (the market price for its output is less than its unit cost). Denote by t_i the last period in which firm i is profitable if it is the only firm in the market. That is, t_i is the largest value of t for which $P_t(k_i) \geq c$. (Refer to Figure 223.1.) Because $k_1 > k_2$, we have $t_1 \leq t_2$: the time at which the large firm becomes unprofitable as a loner is no later than the time at which the small firm becomes unprofitable as a loner.

The game has an infinite horizon, but after period t_i firm i's profit is negative even if it is the only firm remaining in the market. Thus if firm i is in the market in any period after t_i, it chooses *Exit* in that period in every subgame perfect equilibrium. In particular, both firms choose *Exit* in every period after t_2. We can use backward induction from period t_2 to find the firms' subgame perfect equilibrium actions in earlier periods.

If firm 1 (the larger firm) is in the market in any period from t_1 on, it should exit, regardless of whether firm 2 is still operating. As a consequence, if firm 2 is still operating in any period from $t_1 + 1$ to t_2 it should stay: firm 1 will exit in any such period, and in its absence firm 2's profit is positive.

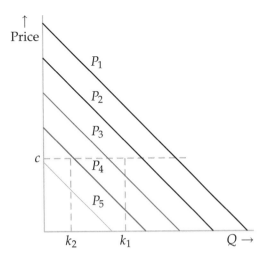

Figure 223.1 The inverse demand curves in a declining industry. In this example, t_1 (the last period in which firm 1 is profitable if it is the only firm in the market) is 2, and t_2 is 4.

So far we have concluded that in every subgame perfect equilibrium, firm 1's strategy is to exit in every period from $t_1 + 1$ on if it has not already done so, and firm 2's strategy is to exit in every period from $t_2 + 1$ on if it has not already done so.

Now consider period t_1, the last period in which firm 1's profit is positive if firm 2 is absent. If firm 2 exits, its profit from then on is zero. If it stays and firm 1 exits, then it earns a profit from period t_1 to period t_2, after which it leaves. If both firms stay, firm 2 sustains a loss in period t_1 but earns a profit in the subsequent periods up to t_2, because in every subgame perfect equilibrium firm 1 exits in period $t_1 + 1$. Thus if firm 2's one-period loss in period t_1 when firm 1 stays in that period is less than the sum of its profits from period $t_1 + 1$ on, then *regardless of whether firm 1 stays or exits in period t_1*, firm 2 stays in every subgame perfect equilibrium. In period $t_1 + 1$, when firm 1 is absent from the industry, the price is relatively high, so that the assumption that firm 2's one-period loss is less than its subsequent multiperiod profit is valid for a significant range of parameters. From now on, I assume that this condition holds.

We conclude that in every subgame perfect equilibrium firm 2 stays in period t_1, so that firm 1 optimally exits. (It definitely exits in the next period, and if it stays in period t_1 it makes a loss, because firm 2 stays.)

Now continue to work backward. If firm 2 stays in period $t_1 - 1$ it earns a profit in periods t_1 through t_2, because in every subgame perfect equilibrium firm 1 exits in period t_1. It may make a loss in period $t_1 - 1$ (if firm 1 stays in that period), but this loss is less than the loss it makes in period t_1 in the company of firm 1, which we have assumed is outweighed by its subsequent profit. Thus regardless of firm 1's action in period $t_1 - 1$, firm 2's best action is to stay in that period. If $t_2 < t_1 - 1$, then firm 1 makes a loss in period $t_1 - 1$ in the company of firm 2, and so should exit.

The same logic applies to all periods back to the first period in which the firms cannot profitably coexist in the industry: in every such period, in every subgame perfect equilibrium firm 1 exits if it has not already done so. Denote by t_0 the last period in which both firms can profitably coexist in the industry: that is, t_0 is the largest value of t for which $P_t(k_1 + k_2) \geq c$.

We conclude that if firm 2's loss in period t_1 when both firms are active is less than the sum of its profits in periods $t_1 + 1$ through t_2 when it alone is active, then the game has a unique subgame perfect equilibrium, in which the large firm exits in period $t_0 + 1$, the first period in which both firms cannot profitably coexist in the industry, and the small firm continues operating until period t_2, after which it alone becomes unprofitable.

⑦ EXERCISE 224.1 (Exit from a declining industry) Assume that $c = 10$, $k_1 = 40$, $k_2 = 20$, and $P_t(Q) = 100 - t - Q$ for all values of t and Q for which $100 - t - Q > 0$, otherwise $P_t(Q) = 0$. Find the values of t_1 and t_2 and check whether firm 2's loss in period t_1 when both firms are active is less than the sum of its profits in periods $t_1 + 1$ through t_2 when it alone is active.

7.5.3   The effect of a constraint on firm 2's debt

When the firms follow their subgame perfect equilibrium strategies, each firm's profit is nonnegative in every period. However, the equilibrium depends on firm 2's ability to go into debt. Firm 2's strategy calls for it to stay in the market if firm 1, contrary to its strategy, does not exit in the first period in which the market cannot profitably sustain both firms. This feature of firm 2's strategy is essential to the equilibrium. If such a deviation by firm 1 induces firm 2 to exit, then firm 1's strategy of exiting may not be optimal, and the equilibrium may consequently fall apart.

Consider an extreme case, in which firm 2 can never go into debt. We can incorporate this assumption into the model by making firm 2's payoff a large negative number for any terminal history in which its profit in any period is negative. (The size of firm 2's profit depends on the contemporaneous action of firm 1, so we cannot easily incorporate the assumption by modifying the choices available to firm 2.) Consider a history in which firm 1 stays in the market after the last period in which the market can profitably sustain both firms. After such a history firm 2's best action is no longer to stay: if it does so its profit is negative, whereas if it exits its profit is zero. Thus if firm 1 deviates from its equilibrium strategy in the absence of a borrowing constraint for firm 2, and stays in the first period in which it is supposed to exit, then firm 2 optimally exits, and firm 1 reaps positive profits for several periods, as the lone firm in the market. Consequently in this case firm 2 exits first; firm 1 stays in the market until period t_1.

How much debt does firm 2 need to be able to bear for the game to have a subgame perfect equilibrium in which firm 1 exits in period t_0 and firm 2 stays until period t_2? Suppose that firm 2 can sustain losses from period $t_0 + 1$ through period $t_0 + k$, but no longer, when both firms stay in the market. For firm 1 to optimally

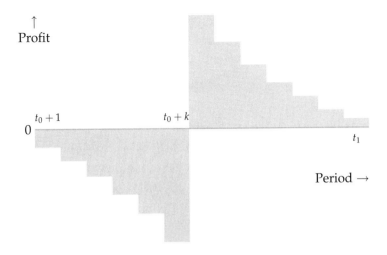

Figure 225.1 Firm 1's profits starting in period $t_0 + 1$ when firm 2 stays in the market until period $t_1 + k$ and firm 1 stays until period t_1.

exit in period $t_0 + 1$, the consequence of its staying in the market must be that firm 2 also stays. Suppose that firm 2's strategy is to stay through period $t_0 + k$, but no longer, if firm 1 does so. Which strategy is best for firm 1 in the subgame starting in period $t_0 + 1$? If it exits, its payoff is zero. If it stays through period $t_0 + k$, its payoff is negative (it makes a loss in every period). If it stays beyond period $t_0 + k$ (when firm 2 exits), it should stay until period t_1, when its payoff is the sum of profits that are negative from period $t_0 + 1$ through period $t_0 + k$ and then positive through period t_1. (See Figure 225.1.) If this payoff is positive it should stay through period t_1; otherwise it should exit immediately.

We conclude that for firm 1 to exit in period $t_0 + 1$, the period until which firm 2 can sustain losses, which I have denoted $t_0 + k$, must be large enough that firm 1's total profit is nonpositive from period $t_0 + 1$ through period t_1 if it shares the market with firm 2 until period $t_0 + k$ and then has the market to itself. This value of k determines the debt that firm 2 must be able to accumulate: the requisite debt equals its total loss when it remains in the market with firm 1 from period $t_0 + 1$ through period $t_0 + k$.

⊘ EXERCISE 225.1 (Effect of borrowing constraint of firms' exit decisions in declining industry) Under the assumptions of Exercise 224.1, how much debt does firm 2 need to be able to bear for the subgame perfect equilibrium outcome in the absence of a debt constraint to remain a subgame perfect equilibrium outcome?

7.6 Allowing for exogenous uncertainty

7.6.1 General model

The model of an extensive game with perfect information (with or without simultaneous moves) does not allow random events to occur during the course of play.

However, we can easily extend the model to cover such situations. The definition of an **extensive game with perfect information and chance moves** is a variant of the definition of an extensive game with perfect information (155.1) in which

- the player function assigns "chance", rather than a set of players, to some histories

- the probabilities that chance uses after any such history are specified

- the players' preferences are defined over the set of lotteries over terminal histories (rather than simply over the set of terminal histories).

(We may similarly add chance moves to an extensive game with perfect information and simultaneous moves by modifying Definition 206.1.) To keep the analysis simple, assume that the random event after any given history is independent of the random event after any other history. (That is, the realization of any random event is not affected by the realization of any other random event.)

The definition of a player's strategy remains the same as before. The outcome of a strategy profile is now a probability distribution over terminal histories. The definition of subgame perfect equilibrium remains the same as before.

◆ EXAMPLE 226.1 (Extensive game with chance moves) Consider a situation involving two players in which player 1 first chooses A or B. If she chooses A the game ends, with (Bernoulli) payoffs $(1, 1)$. If she chooses B, then with probability $\frac{1}{2}$ the game ends, with payoffs $(3, 0)$, and with probability $\frac{1}{2}$ player 2 gets to choose between C, which yields payoffs $(0, 1)$ and D, which yields payoffs $(1, 0)$. An extensive game with perfect information and chance moves that models this situation is shown in Figure 226.1. The label c denotes chance; the number beside each action of chance is the probability with which that action is chosen.

We may use backward induction to find the subgame perfect equilibria of this game. In any equilibrium, player 2 chooses C. Now consider the consequences of player 1's actions. If she chooses A, then she obtains the payoff 1. If she chooses B, then she obtains 3 with probability $\frac{1}{2}$ and 0 with probability $\frac{1}{2}$, yielding an expected payoff of $\frac{3}{2}$. Thus the game has a unique subgame perfect equilibrium, in which player 1 choose B and player 2 chooses C.

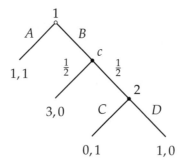

Figure 226.1 An extensive game with perfect information and chance moves. The label c denotes chance; the number beside each action of chance is the probability with which that action is chosen.

⟨?⟩ EXERCISE 227.1 (Variant of ultimatum game with equity-conscious players) Consider a variant of the game in Exercise 183.4 in which $\beta_1 = 0$, and the person 2 whom person 1 faces is drawn randomly from a population in which the fraction p have $\beta_2 = 0$ and the remaining fraction $1 - p$ have $\beta_2 = 1$. When making her offer, person 1 knows only that her opponent's characteristic is $\beta_2 = 0$ with probability p and $\beta_2 = 1$ with probability $1 - p$. Model this situation as an extensive game with perfect information and chance moves in which person 1 makes an offer, then chance determines the type of person 2, and finally person 2 accepts or rejects person 1's offer. Find the subgame perfect equilibria of this game. (Use the fact that if $\beta_2 = 0$, then in any subgame perfect equilibrium of the game in Exercise 183.4, person 2 accepts all offers $x > 0$, rejects all offers $x < 0$, and may accept or reject the offer 0, and if $\beta_2 = 1$, she accepts all offers $x > \frac{1}{3}$, may accept or reject the offer $\frac{1}{3}$, and rejects all offers $x < \frac{1}{3}$.) Are there any values of p for which an offer is rejected in equilibrium?

⟨?⟩ EXERCISE 227.2 (Firm–union bargaining) A firm knows the amount by which its revenue exceeds its outlays on plant and equipment, but a union with which it is bargaining does not. This "surplus", which is to be divided between the firm and the union, is H with probability p and $L < H$ with probability $1 - p$. The bargaining procedure is that of the ultimatum game: the union makes a demand, which the firm either accepts or rejects. We may model this situation as an extensive game in which, between the union's demand and the firm's response, a move of chance determines whether the surplus is H or L. If the size of the surplus is z and the union's demand is x, then the firm's (Bernoulli) payoff is $z - x$ and the union's (Bernoulli) payoff is x if the firm accepts the union's demand and each player's payoff is 0 (there is a strike) if the firm rejects the union's demand. Find the subgame perfect equilibria of this game for each possible value of p. Find the probability of a strike for each equilibrium.

⟨?⟩ EXERCISE 227.3 (Sequential duel) In a sequential duel, two people alternately have the opportunity to shoot each other; each has an infinite supply of bullets. On each of her turns, a person may shoot or refrain from doing so. Each of person i's shots hits (and kills) its intended target with probability p_i (independently of whether any other shots hit their targets). (If you prefer to think about a less violent situation, interpret the players as political candidates who alternately may launch attacks, which may not be successful, against each other.) Each person cares only about her probability of survival (not about the other person's survival). Model this situation as an extensive game with perfect information and chance moves. Show that the strategy pairs in which neither person ever shoots and in which each person always shoots are both subgame perfect equilibria. (Note that the game does not have a finite horizon, so backward induction cannot be used.)

⟨?⟩ EXERCISE 227.4 (Sequential truel) Each of persons A, B, and C has a gun containing a single bullet. Each person, as long as she is alive, may shoot at any surviving person. First A can shoot, then B (if still alive), then C (if still alive). (As in the previous exercise, you may interpret the players as political candidates. In this exercise, each candidate has a budget sufficient to launch a negative campaign to discredit exactly one of its rivals.) Denote by p_i the probability that player i hits her intended target; assume that $0 < p_i < 1$. Assume that each player wishes to maximize her probability of survival; among outcomes in which her survival probability is the same, she wants the danger posed by any other survivors to be as small as possible. (The last assumption is intended to capture the idea that there is some chance that further rounds of shooting may occur, though the possibility of such rounds is not incorporated explicitly into the game.) Model this situation as an extensive game with perfect information and chance moves. (Draw a diagram. Note that the subgames following histories in which A misses her intended target are the same.) Find the subgame perfect equilibria of the game. (Consider only cases in which p_A, p_B, and p_C are all different.) Explain the logic behind A's equilibrium action. Show that "weakness is strength" for C: she is better off if $p_C < p_B$ than if $p_C > p_B$.

Now consider the variant in which each player, on her turn, has the additional option of shooting into the air (in which case she uses a bullet but does not hit anyone). Find the subgame perfect equilibria of this game when $p_A < p_B$. Explain the logic behind A's equilibrium action.

❓ EXERCISE 228.1 (Cohesion in legislatures) The following pair of games is designed to study the implications of different legislative procedures for the cohesion of a governing coalition. In both games a legislature consists of three members. Initially a governing coalition, consisting of two of the legislators, is given. There are two periods. At the start of each period a member of the governing coalition is randomly chosen (i.e. each legislator is chosen with probability $\frac{1}{2}$) to propose a bill, which is a partition of one unit of payoff between the three legislators. Then the legislators simultaneously cast votes; each legislator votes either for or against the bill. If two or more legislators vote for the bill, it is accepted. Otherwise the course of events differs between the two games. In a game that models the current U.S. legislature, rejection of a bill in period t leads to a given partition d^t of the pie, where $0 < d_i^t < \frac{1}{2}$ for $i = 1, 2, 3$; the governing coalition (the set from which the proposer of a bill is drawn) remains the same in period 2 following a rejection in period 1. In a game that models the current U.K. legislature, rejection of a bill brings down the government; a new governing coalition is determined randomly, and no legislator receives any payoff in that period. Specify each game precisely and find its subgame perfect equilibrium outcomes. Study the degree to which the governing coalition is cohesive (i.e. all its members vote in the same way).

7.6.2 Using chance moves to model mistakes

A game with chance moves may be used to model the possibility that players make mistakes. Suppose, for example, that two people simultaneously choose actions.

$$
\begin{array}{c|c|c|}
 & A & B \\
\hline
A & 1,1 & 0,0 \\
\hline
B & 0,0 & 0,0 \\
\hline
\end{array}
$$

Figure 229.1 The players' Bernoulli payoffs to the four pairs of actions in the game studied in Section 7.6.2.

Each person may choose either A or B. Absent the possibility of mistakes, suppose that the situation is modeled by the strategic game in Figure 229.1, in which the numbers in the boxes are Bernoulli payoffs. This game has two Nash equilibria, (A, A) and (B, B).

Now suppose that each person may make a mistake. With probability $1 - p_i > \frac{1}{2}$ the action chosen by person i is the one she intends, and with probability $p_i < \frac{1}{2}$ it is her other action. We can model this situation as the following extensive game with perfect information, simultaneous moves, and chance moves.

Players   The two people.

Terminal histories   All sequences of the form $((W, X), Y, Z)$, where W, X, Y, and Z are all either A or B; in the history $((W, X), Y, Z)$ player 1 chooses W, player 2 chooses X, and then chance chooses Y for player 1 and Z for player 2.

Player function $P(\varnothing) = \{1, 2\}$ (both players move simultaneously at the start of the game), and $P(W, X) = P((W, X), Y) = \{c\}$ (chance moves twice after the players have acted, first selecting player 1's action and then player 2's action).

Actions   The set of actions available to each player at the start of the game, and to chance at each of its moves, is $\{A, B\}$.

Chance probabilities   After any history (W, X), chance chooses W with probability $1 - p_1$ and player 1's other action with probability p_1. After any history $((W, X), Y)$, chance chooses X with probability $1 - p_2$ and player 2's other action with probability p_2.

Preferences   Each player's preferences are represented by the expected value of a Bernoulli payoff function that assigns 1 to any history $((W, X), A, A)$ (in which chance chooses the action A for each player), and 0 to any other history.

The players in this game move simultaneously, so that the subgame perfect equilibria of the game are its Nash equilibria. To find the Nash equilibria, we construct the strategic form of the game. Suppose that each player chooses the action A. Then the outcome is (A, A) with probability $(1 - p_1)(1 - p_2)$ (the probability that neither player makes a mistake). Thus each player's expected payoff is $(1 - p_1)(1 - p_2)$. Similarly, if player 1 chooses A and player 2 chooses B, then the

	A	B
A	$(1-p_1)(1-p_2), (1-p_1)(1-p_2)$	$(1-p_1)p_2, (1-p_1)p_2$
B	$p_1(1-p_2), p_1(1-p_2)$	p_1p_2, p_1p_2

Figure 230.1 The strategic form of the extensive game with chance moves that models the situation in which with probability p_i each player i in the game in Figure 229.1 chooses an action different from the one she intends.

outcome is (A, A) with probability $(1 - p_1)p_2$ (the probability that player 1 does not make a mistake, whereas player 2 does). Making similar computations for the other two cases yields the strategic form in Figure 230.1.

For $p_1 = p_2 = 0$, this game is the same as the original game (Figure 229.1); it has two Nash equilibria, (A, A) and (B, B). If at least one of the probabilities is positive then only (A, A) is a Nash equilibrium: if $p_i > 0$, then $(1 - p_j)p_i > p_jp_i$ (given that each probability is less than $\frac{1}{2}$). That is, only the equilibrium (A, A) of the original game is robust to the possibility that the players make small mistakes.

In the original game, each player's action B is weakly dominated (Definition 46.1). Introducing the possibility of mistakes captures the fragility of the equilibrium (B, B): B is optimal for a player only if she is absolutely certain that the other player will choose B also. The slightest chance that the other player will choose A is enough to make A unambiguously the best choice.

We may use the idea that an equilibrium should survive when the players may make small mistakes to discriminate among the Nash equilibria of any strategic game. For two-player games in which each player has finitely many actions, the equilibria that satisfy this requirement are precisely those in which no player's action is weakly dominated. For games with more than two players, no equilibrium in which any player's action is weakly dominated satisfies the requirement, but equilibria in which no player's action is weakly dominated may fail to satisfy the requirement, as the following exercise shows.

? EXERCISE 230.1 (Nash equilibria when players may make mistakes) Consider the three-player game in Figure 230.2. Show that (A, A, A) is a Nash equilibrium in which no player's action is weakly dominated. Now modify the game by assuming that the outcome of any player i's choosing an action X is that X occurs with probability $1 - p_i$ and the player's other action occurs with probability $p_i > 0$. Show that (A, A, A) is not a Nash equilibrium of the modified game when $p_i < \frac{1}{2}$ for $i = 1, 2, 3$.

	A	B
A	1,1,1	0,0,1
B	1,1,1	1,0,1

A

	A	B
A	0,1,0	1,0,0
B	1,1,0	0,0,0

B

Figure 230.2 A three-player strategic game in which each player has two actions. Player 1 chooses a row, player 2 chooses a column, and player 3 chooses a table.

7.7   Discussion: subgame perfect equilibrium and backward induction

Some of the situations we have studied do not fit well into the idealized setting for the steady state interpretation of a subgame perfect equilibrium discussed in Section 5.4.4, in which each player repeatedly engages in the same game with a variety of randomly selected opponents. In some cases an alternative interpretation fits better: each player deduces her optimal strategy from an analysis of the other players' best actions, given her knowledge of their preferences. Here I discuss a difficulty with this interpretation.

Consider the game in Figure 231.1, in which player 1 moves both before and after player 2. This game has a unique subgame perfect equilibrium, in which player 1's strategy is (B, F) and player 2's strategy is C. Consider player 2's analysis of this game. If she deduces that the only rational action for player 1 at the start of the game is B, then what should she conclude if player 1 chooses A? It seems that she must conclude that something has "gone wrong": perhaps player 1 has made a "mistake", or she misunderstands player 1's preferences, or player 1 is not rational.

If she is convinced that player 1 simply made a mistake, then her analysis of the rest of the game should not be affected. However, if player 1's move induces her to doubt player 1's motivation, she may need to reconsider her analysis of the rest of the game. Suppose, for example, that A and E model similar actions; specifically, suppose that they both correspond to player 1's moving left, whereas B and F both involve her moving right. Then player 1's choice of A at the start of the game may make player 2 wonder whether player 1 confuses left and right, and therefore may choose E after the history (A, C). If so, player 2 should choose D rather than C after player 1 chooses A, giving player 1 an incentive to choose A rather than B at the start of the game.

The next two examples are richer games that more strikingly manifest the difficulty with the alternative interpretation of subgame perfect equilibrium. The first example is an extension of the entry game in Figure 156.1.

◆ EXAMPLE 231.1 (Chain-store game) A chain store operates in K markets. In each market a single challenger must decide whether to compete with it. The chal-

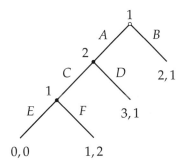

Figure 231.1 An extensive game in which player 1 moves both before and after player 2.

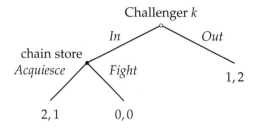

Figure 232.1 The structure of the players' choices in market k in the chain-store game. The first number in each pair is challenger k's profit and the second number is the chain store's profit.

lengers make their decisions sequentially. If any challenger enters, the chain store may acquiesce to its presence (A) or fight it (F). Thus in each period k the outcome is either Out (challenger k does not enter), (In, A) (challenger k enters and the chain store acquiesces), or (In, F) (challenger k enters and is fought). When taking an action, any challenger knows all the actions previously chosen. The profits of challenger k and the chain store in market k are shown in Figure 232.1 (cf. Figure 156.1); the chain store's profit in the whole game is the sum of its profits in the K markets.

We can model this situation as the following extensive game with perfect information.

Players The chain store and the K challengers.

Terminal histories The set of all sequences $(e_1, \ldots, e_K)$, where each e_j is either Out, (In, A), or (In, F).

Player function The chain store is assigned to every history that ends with In, challenger 1 is assigned to the empty history, and challenger k (for $k = 2, \ldots, K$) is assigned to every history $(e_1, \ldots, e_{k-1})$, where each e_j is either Out, (In, A), or (In, F).

Preferences Each player's preferences are represented by its profits.

This game has a finite horizon, so we may find its subgame perfect equilibria by using backward induction. Every subgame at the start of which challenger K moves resembles the game in Figure 232.1 for $k = K$; it differs only in that the chain store's profit after each of the three terminal histories is greater by an amount equal to its profit in the previous $K - 1$ markets. Thus in a subgame perfect equilibrium challenger K chooses In and the incumbent chooses A in market K.

Now consider the subgame faced by challenger $K - 1$. We know that the outcome in market K is independent of the actions of challenger $K - 1$ and the chain store in market $K - 1$: whatever they do, challenger K enters and the chain store acquiesces to its entry. Thus the chain store should choose its action in market $K - 1$ on the basis of its payoffs in that market alone. We conclude that the chain store's optimal action in market $K - 1$ is A, and challenger $K - 1$'s optimal action is In.

We have now concluded that in any subgame perfect equilibrium, the outcome in each of the last two markets is (In, A), regardless of the history. Continuing to work backward to the start of the game we see that the game has a unique subgame perfect equilibrium, in which every challenger enters and the chain store always acquiesces to entry.

? EXERCISE 233.1 (Nash equilibria of chain-store game) Find the set of Nash equilibrium outcomes of the game for an arbitrary value of K. (First think about the case $K = 1$, then generalize your analysis.)

? EXERCISE 233.2 (Subgame perfect equilibrium of chain-store game) Consider the following strategy pair in the game for $K = 100$. For $k = 1, \ldots, 90$, challenger k stays out after any history in which every previous challenger that entered was fought (or no challenger entered), and otherwise enters; challengers 91 through 100 enter. The chain store fights every challenger up to challenger 90 that enters after a history in which it fought every challenger that entered (or no challenger entered), acquiesces to any of these challengers entering after any other history, and acquiesces to challengers 91 through 100 regardless of the history. Find the players' payoffs in this strategy pair. Show that the strategy pair is not a subgame perfect equilibrium: find a player who can increase her payoff in some subgame. By how much can the deviant increase its payoff?

Suppose that $K = 100$. You are in charge of challenger 21. You observe, contrary to the subgame perfect equilibrium, that every previous challenger entered and that the chain store fought each one. What should you do? According to the subgame perfect equilibrium, the chain store will acquiesce to your entry. But should you really regard the chain store's 19 previous decisions as "mistakes"? You might instead read some logic into the chain store's *deliberately* fighting the first 20 entrants: if, by doing so, it persuades more than 20 of the remaining challengers to stay out, then its profit will be higher than it is in the subgame perfect equilibrium. That is, you may imagine that the chain store's aggressive behavior in the earlier markets is an attempt to establish a reputation for being a fighter, which, if successful, will make it better off. By such reasoning you may conclude that your best strategy is to stay out.

Thus, a deviation from the subgame perfect equilibrium by the chain store in which it engages in a long series of fights may not be dismissed by challengers as a series of mistakes, but rather may cause them to doubt the chain store's future behavior. This doubt may lead a challenger who is followed by enough future challengers to stay out.

◆ EXAMPLE 233.3 (Centipede game) The two-player game in Figure 234.1 is known as a "centipede game" because of its shape. (The game, like the arthropod, may have fewer than 100 legs.) The players move alternately; on each move a player can stop the game (S) or continue (C). On any move, a player is better off stopping the game than continuing if the other player stops immediately afterward, but is worse off stopping than continuing if the other player continues, regardless of the subsequent actions. After k periods, the game ends.

This game has a finite horizon, so we may find its subgame perfect equilibria by using backward induction. The last player to move prefers to stop the game

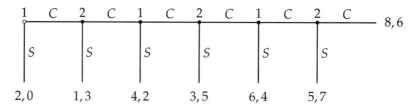

Figure 234.1 A six-period centipede game.

than to continue. Given this player's action, the player who moves before her also prefers to stop the game than to continue. Working backward, we conclude that the game has a unique subgame perfect equilibrium, in which each player's strategy is to stop the game whenever it is her turn to move. The outcome is that player 1 stops the game immediately.

> ? Exercise 234.1 (Nash equilibria of the centipede game) Show that the outcome of every Nash equilibrium of this game is the same as the outcome of the unique subgame perfect equilibrium (i.e. player 1 stops the game immediately).

The logic that in the only steady state player 1 stops the game immediately is unassailable. Yet this pattern of behavior is intuitively unappealing, especially if the number k of periods is large. The optimality of player 1's choosing to stop the game depends on her believing that if she continues, then player 2 will stop the game in period 2. Further, player 2's decision to stop the game in period 2 depends on her believing that if she continues, then player 1 will stop the game in period 3. Each decision to stop the game is based on similar considerations. Consider a player who has to choose an action in period 21 of a 100-period game, after each player has continued in the first 20 periods. Is she likely to consider the first 20 decisions—half of which were hers—"mistakes"? Or will these decisions induce her to doubt that the other player will stop the game in the next period? These questions have no easy answers; some experimental evidence is discussed in the accompanying box.

EXPERIMENTAL EVIDENCE ON THE CENTIPEDE GAME

In experiments conducted in the United States in 1989, each of 58 student subjects played the game shown below (McKelvey and Palfrey 1992). (The payoff of player 1 is the top amount in each pair.) Each subject played the game 9 or 10 times, facing a different opponent each time; in each play of the game, each subject had previously played the same number of games. Each subject knew in advance how many times she would play the game, and knew that she would not play against the same opponent more than once. If each subject cared only about her own monetary payoff, the game induced by the experiment was a six-period centipede.

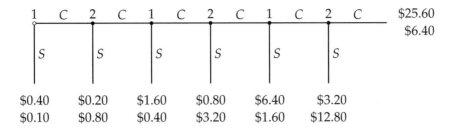

The fraction of plays of the game that ended in each period is shown in the graph below. (A game is counted as ending in period 7 if the last player to move chose C. The graph is computed from McKelvey and Palfrey 1992, Table IIIA.) Results are broken down according to the players' experience (first 5 rounds, last 5 rounds). The game ended earlier when the participants were experienced, but even among experienced participants the outcomes are far from the Nash equilibrium outcome, in which the game ends in period 1.

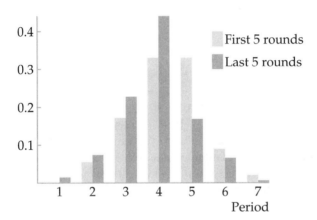

Ten plays of the game may not be enough to achieve convergence to a steady state. But putting aside this limitation of the data, and supposing that convergence was in fact achieved at the end of 10 rounds, how far does the observed behavior differ from a Nash equilibrium (maintaining the assumption that each player cares only about her own monetary payoff)?

The theory of Nash equilibrium has two components: each player optimizes, given her beliefs about the other players, and these beliefs are correct. Some decisions in McKelvey and Palfrey's experiment were patently suboptimal, regardless of the subjects' beliefs: a few subjects in the role of player 2 chose to continue in period 6, obtaining $6.40 with certainty instead of $12.80 with certainty. To assess the departure of the other decisions from optimality we need to assign the subjects beliefs (which were not directly observed). An assumption consistent with the steady state interpretation of Nash equilibrium is that a player's belief is based on her observations of the other players' actions. Even in round 10 of the experiment each player had only nine observations on which to base her belief, and could have used these data in various ways. But suppose that, somehow, at the end of round 4, each player correctly inferred the distribution of her opponents' strategies in the next 5 rounds. What strategy should she subsequently have used? From McKelvey and Palfrey (1992, Table IIIB) we may deduce that the optimal strategy of player 1 stops in period 5 and that of player 2 stops in period 6. That is, each player's best response to the empirical distribution of the other players' strategies differs dramatically from her subgame perfect equilibrium strategy. Other assumptions about the subjects' beliefs rationalize other strategies; the data seem too limited to conclude that the subjects were not optimizing, given the beliefs their experience might reasonably have led them to hold. That is, the experimental data are not strongly inconsistent with the theory of Nash equilibrium as a steady state.

Are the data inconsistent with the theory that rational players, even those with no experience playing the game, will use backward induction to deduce their opponents' rational actions? This theory predicts that the first player immediately stops the game, so certainly the data are inconsistent with it. How inconsistent? One way to approach this question is to consider the implications of each player's thinking that the others are *likely* to be rational, but are not *certainly* so. If, in any period, player 1 thinks that the probability that player 2 will stop the game in the next period is less than $\frac{6}{7}$, continuing yields a higher expected payoff than stopping. Given the limited time the subjects had to analyze the game (and the likelihood that they had never before thought about any related game), even those who understood the implications of backward induction may reasonably have entertained the relatively small doubt about the other players' cognitive abilities required to make stopping the game immediately an unattractive option. Or, alternatively, a player confident of her opponents' logical abilities may have doubted her opponents' assessment of *her own* analytical skills. If player 1 believes that player 2 thinks that the probability that player 1 will continue in period 3 is greater than $\frac{1}{7}$, then she should continue in period 1, because player 2 will continue in period 2. That is, relatively minor departures from the theory yield outcomes close to those observed.

Notes

The idea of regarding games with simultaneous moves as games with perfect information is due to Dubey and Kaneko (1984).

The model in Section 7.3 was first studied by Ledyard (1981, 1984). The approach to voting in committees in Section 7.4 was initiated by Farquharson (1969) (see also Niemi 1983). (The publication of Farquharson's book was delayed; the book was completed in 1958.) The top cycle set was first defined by Ward (1961) (who called it the "majority set"). The characterization of the outcomes of sophisticated voting in binary agendas in terms of the top cycle set is due to Miller (1977) (who calls the top cycle set the "Condorcet set"), McKelvey and Niemi (1978), and

Moulin (1986a, pp. 283–284). Miller (1995) surveys the field (see in particular his pp. 85–86). The model in Section 7.5 is taken from Ghemawat and Nalebuff (1985); the idea is closely related to that of Benoît (1984, Section 1) (see Exercise 174.2). My discussion draws on an unpublished exposition of the model by Vijay Krishna. The idea of discriminating among Nash equilibria by considering the possibility that players make mistakes, briefly discussed in Section 7.6.2, is due to Selten (1975). The chain-store game in Example 231.1 is due to Selten (1978). The centipede game in Example 233.3 is due to Rosenthal (1981).

The experimental results discussed in the box on page 211 are due to Roth, Prasnikar, Okuno-Fujiwara, and Zamir (1991). The subgame perfect equilibria of a variant of the market game in which each player's payoff depends on the other players' monetary payoffs are analyzed by Bolton and Ockenfels (2000). The model in Exercise 212.1 is taken from Peters (1984). The results in Exercises 216.1 and 217.1 are due to Feddersen, Sened, and Wright (1990). The game in Exercise 227.4 is a simplification of an example due to Shubik (1954); the main idea appears in Phillips (1937, 159) and Kinnaird (1946, 246), both of which consist mainly of puzzles previously published in newspapers. Exercise 228.1 is based on Diermeier and Feddersen (1998). The experiment discussed in the box on page 234 is reported in McKelvey and Palfrey (1992).

8 Coalitional Games and the Core

8.1   Coalitional games   239
8.2   The core   243
8.3   Illustration: ownership and the distribution of wealth   247
8.4   Illustration: exchanging homogeneous horses   251
8.5   Illustration: exchanging heterogeneous houses   256
8.6   Illustration: voting   260
8.7   Illustration: matching   263
8.8   Discussion: other solution concepts   269
       Prerequisite: Chapter 1

8.1 Coalitional games

A COALITIONAL GAME is a model of interacting decision-makers that focuses on the behavior of groups of players. It associates a set of actions with every group of players, not only with individual players like the models of a strategic game (Definition 13.1) and extensive game (Definition 155.1). We call each group of players a *coalition*, and the coalition of *all* the players the *grand coalition*.

An outcome of a coalitional game consists of a partition of the set of players into groups, together with an action for each group in the partition. (See Section 17.2 if you are not familiar with the notion of a "partition" of a set.) At one extreme, each group in the partition may consist of a single player, who acts on her own; at another extreme, the partition may consist of a single group containing all the players. The most general model of a coalitional game allows players to care about the action chosen by each group in the partition that defines the outcome. I discuss only the widely studied class of games in which each player cares only about the action chosen by the member of the partition to which she belongs. In such games, each player's preferences rank the actions of all possible groups of players that contain her.

▶ DEFINITION 239.1 (*Coalitional game*) A **coalitional game** consists of

- a set of **players**

- for each coalition, a set of **actions**

- for each player, **preferences** over the set of all actions of all coalitions of which she is a member.

I usually denote the grand coalition (the set of all the players) by N and an arbitrary coalition by S. As before, we may conveniently specify a player's preferences by giving a payoff function that represents them.

Note that the definition does not relate the actions available to a coalition to the actions available to the members of the coalition. The actions available to each coalition are simply taken as given; they are not derived from the actions available to individual players.

◆ EXAMPLE 240.1 (Two-player unanimity game) Two people can together produce one unit of output, which they may share in any way they wish. Neither person by herself can produce any output. Each person cares only about the amount of output she receives, and prefers more to less. The following coalitional game models this situation.

  Players The two people (players 1 and 2).

  Actions Each player by herself has a single action, which yields her no output. The set of actions of the coalition $\{1, 2\}$ of both players is the set of all pairs (x_1, x_2) of nonnegative numbers such that $x_1 + x_2 = 1$ (the set of divisions of one unit of output between the two players).

  Preferences Each player's preferences are represented by the amount of output she obtains.

In this example and in several of the examples that follow, each coalition controls some quantity of a good, which may be distributed among its members. Each action of a coalition S in such a game is a distribution among the members of S of the good that S controls, which I refer to as an S-**allocation** of the good. I refer to an N-allocation simply as an **allocation**.

In the next example the opportunities for producing output are richer than they are in the two-player unanimity game, and the participants are not all symmetric.

◆ EXAMPLE 240.2 (Landowner and workers) A landowner's estate, when used by k workers, produces the output $f(k + 1)$ of food, where f is a increasing function with $f(0) = 0$. The total number of workers is m. The landowner cares only about the amount of output she receives, and prefers more to less; the same is true for each worker. The following coalitional game models this situation.

  Players The landowner and the m workers.

  Actions A coalition consisting solely of workers has a single action in which no member receives any output. The set of actions of a coalition S consisting of the landowner and k workers is the set of all S-allocations of the output $f(k + 1)$ among the members of S.

  Preferences Each player's preferences are represented by the amount of output she obtains.

◆ EXAMPLE 240.3 (Three-player majority game) Three people have access to one unit of output. Any majority—two or three people—may control the allocation of this output. Each person cares only about the amount of output she obtains.

We may model this situation as the following coalitional game.

Players The three people.

Actions Each coalition consisting of a single player has a single action, which yields the player no output. The set of actions of each coalition S with two or three players is the set of S-allocations of one unit of output.

Preferences Each player's preferences are represented by the amount of output she obtains.

In these examples the set of actions of each coalition S is the set of S-allocations of the output that S can obtain, and each player's preferences are represented by the amount of output she obtains. Thus we can summarize each coalition's set of actions by a single number, equal to the total output it can obtain, and we can interpret this number as the total "payoff" that may be distributed among the members of the coalition. Such a game is said to have *transferable payoff*. More generally, we define a game with transferable payoff as follows.

▶ DEFINITION 241.1 (*Coalitional game with transferable payoff*) A coalitional game has **transferable payoff** if there is a collection of payoff functions, one representing each player's preferences, such that for each coalition S, every action of S generates a distribution of payoffs among the members of S that has the same sum.

We refer to the total payoff of a coalition S in a game with transferable payoff as the **worth** of S, and denote it $v(S)$. Such a game is specified by its set of players and its worth function. The games we have studied so far are specified as follows.

Two-player unanimity game $N = \{1, 2\}$, $v(\{1\}) = v(\{2\}) = 0$, and $v(\{1, 2\}) = 1$.

Landowner–worker game $N = \{1, \ldots, m+1\}$ (where the landowner is 1 and the workers are $2, \ldots, m$), and

$$v(S) = \begin{cases} 0 & \text{if 1 is not a member of } S \\ f(k+1) & \text{if } S \text{ consists of 1 and } k \text{ workers.} \end{cases}$$

Three-player majority game $N = \{1, 2, 3\}$, $v(\{i\}) = 0$ for $i = 1, 2, 3$, and $v(S) = 1$ for every other coalition S.

The next exercise invites you to model as a coalitional game a situation modeled in Chapter 2 as a strategic game.

❓ EXERCISE 241.2 (*Stag Hunt*) Consider the situation described in Section 2.5, in which a group of n hunters can catch a stag only if every member remains attentive, and any inattentive member may catch a hare. Assume that a coalition may split its spoils in any way among its members and that each hunter's preferences are represented by the payoff function $\alpha x + y$, where x is the amount of hares and y the amount of a stag she obtains, and $\alpha < 1/n$. Model the situation as a coalitional game, verify that the game has transferable payoff, and specify the worth of each coalition.

In the next two examples, payoff is not transferable.

◆ EXAMPLE 242.1 (House allocation) Each member of a group of n people owns an indivisible good—call it a house. Houses differ. Any subgroup may reallocate its members' houses in any way it wishes (one house to each person). (Time-sharing and other devices to evade the indivisibility of a house are prohibited.) Each person cares only about the house she obtains; the values assigned to houses vary among the people. The following coalitional game models this situation.

   Players The n people.

   Actions The set of actions of a coalition S is the set of all assignments to members of S of the houses initially owned by members of S.

   Preferences Each player prefers one outcome to another according to the house she is assigned.

This game does not have transferable payoff. For example, a coalition of players 1 and 2 can achieve only the two payoff distributions (v_1, w_2) and (v_2, w_1), where v_i is the payoff to player 1 of the house initially owned by player i, and w_i is the payoff to player 2 of this house. The game is studied in Section 8.5.

◆ EXAMPLE 242.2 (Marriage market) A group of men and a group of women may be matched in pairs. Each person cares only about her partner, not about anyone else's partner. A *matching* of the members of a coalition S splits S into pairs, each consisting of a man and woman, and single individuals. The following coalitional game models this situation.

   Players The set of all the men and all the women.

   Actions The set of actions of a coalition S is the set of all matchings of the members of S.

   Preferences Each player prefers one outcome to another according to the partner she is assigned.

This game is studied in Section 8.7.

   A coalitional game is designed to model situations in which players are better off forming groups than acting individually. Most of the theory is oriented to situations in which the incentive to coalesce is extreme, in the sense that there is no disadvantage to the formation of the *single* group consisting of all the players. In considering the action that this single group takes in such a situation, we need to consider the possibility that smaller groups may break away on their own; but when looking for "equilibria" we can restrict attention to outcomes in which all the players coalesce. Such situations are modeled as games in which the grand coalition can achieve outcomes at least as desirable for every player as those achievable by any partition of the players into subgroups. We call such games "cohesive".

▶ DEFINITION 242.3 (*Cohesive coalitional game*) A coalitional game is **cohesive** if, for every partition $\{S_1, \ldots, S_k\}$ of the set of all players and every combination

$(a_{S_1}, \ldots, a_{S_k})$ of actions, one for each coalition in the partition, the grand coalition N has an action at least as desirable for every player i as the action a_{S_j} of the member S_j of the partition to which player i belongs.

The definition implies that a coalitional game with transferable payoff is cohesive if and only if for every partition $\{S_1, \ldots, S_k\}$ of the players we have $v(S_1) + \cdots + v(S_k) \leq v(N)$.

The concepts I subsequently describe may be applied to any game, cohesive or not, but have attractive interpretations only for cohesive games. All the games I have described so far are cohesive. Consider, for example, the two-player unanimity game (Example 240.1). The possible partitions of the set of players are $\{\{1,2\}\}$, consisting of the single coalition of both players, and $\{\{1\}, \{2\}\}$, in which each player acts alone. We have $v(\{1\}) + v(\{2\}) = 0 < v(\{1,2\}) = 1$, so the game is cohesive. To give another example, the house allocation game (Example 242.1) is cohesive because any allocation of the houses that can be achieved by the coalitions in any partition of the set of players can also be achieved by the set of all players.

⊘ EXERCISE 243.1 (*Cohesive games*) Verify that the landowner–worker game (Example 240.2), the three-player majority game (Example 240.3), the *Stag Hunt* (Exercise 241.2), and the marriage market game (Example 242.2) are all cohesive.

8.2 The core

Which action may we expect the grand coalition to choose? We seek an action compatible with the pressures imposed by the opportunities of each coalition, rather than simply those of individual players as in the models of a strategic game (Chapter 2) and an extensive game (Chapter 5). We define an action of the grand coalition to be "stable" if no coalition can break away and choose an action that all its members prefer. The set of all stable actions of the grand coalition is called the *core*, defined precisely as follows.

▶ DEFINITION 243.2 (*Core of coalitional game*) The **core** of a coalitional game is the set of actions a_N of the grand coalition N such that no coalition has an action that all its members prefer to a_N.

If a coalition S has an action that all its members prefer to some action a_N of the grand coalition, we say that S can **improve upon** a_N. Thus we may alternatively define the core to be the set of all actions of the grand coalition upon which no coalition can improve.

Note that the core is defined as a *set* of actions, so it always *exists*; a game cannot fail to have a core, though it may be the empty set, in which case no action of the grand coalition is immune to deviations.

We have restricted attention to games in which, when evaluating an outcome, each player cares only about the action chosen by the coalition in the partition of which she is a member. Thus the members of a coalition do not need to speculate about the remaining players' behavior when considering a deviation.

In a game with transferable payoff, a coalition S can improve upon an action a_N of the grand coalition if and only if its worth $v(S)$ (i.e. the total payoff it can achieve by itself) exceeds the total payoff of its members in a_N. That is,

> a_N *is in the core of a coalitional game with transferable payoff if and only if for every coalition S the total payoff $x_S(a_N)$ it yields the members of S is at least $v(S)$:*

$$x_S(a_N) \geq v(S) \text{ for every coalition } S.$$

In the next example, no coalition can improve upon any action of the grand coalition, so the core consists of *all* actions of the grand coalition.

◆ EXAMPLE 244.1 (Two-player unanimity game) Consider the two-player unanimity game in Example 240.1. An action of the grand coalition is a pair (x_1, x_2) with $x_1 + x_2 = 1$ and $x_i \geq 0$ for $i = 1, 2$ (a division of the one unit of output between the two players). I claim that the core consists of *all* possible divisions:

$$\{(x_1, x_2) : x_1 + x_2 = 1 \text{ and } x_i \geq 0 \text{ for } i = 1, 2\}.$$

Any such division is in the core because if a single player deviates, she obtains no output, and if the grand coalition chooses a different division, then one player is worse off.

In this example no coalition has any action that imposes any restriction on the action of the grand coalition. In most other games the coalitions' opportunities constrain the actions of the grand coalition.

One way to find the core is to check each action of the grand coalition in turn. For each action, we impose the condition that no coalition can make all its members better off; an action is a member of the core if and only if it satisfies these conditions.

Consider, for example, a variant of the two-player unanimity game in which player 1, by herself, can obtain p units of output, and player 2, by herself, can obtain q units of output. The condition that the coalition consisting of player 1 not be able to improve upon the action (x_1, x_2) of the grand coalition is $x_1 \geq p$, and the condition that the coalition consisting of player 2 not be able to improve upon this action is $x_2 \geq q$. As in the original game, the coalition of both players cannot improve upon any action (x_1, x_2), so the core is

$$\{(x_1, x_2) : x_1 + x_2 = 1, x_1 \geq p, \text{ and } x_2 \geq q\}.$$

(An implication is that if $p + q > 1$—in which case the game is not cohesive—the core is empty.)

The landowner–worker game further illustrates this method of finding the core.

◆ EXAMPLE 244.2 (Landowner–worker game with two workers) Consider the game in Example 240.2 in which there are two workers ($k = 2$). Let (x_1, x_2, x_3) be an action of the grand coalition. That is, let (x_1, x_2, x_3) be an allocation of the output

$f(3)$ among the three players. The only coalitions that can obtain a positive amount of output are that consisting of the landowner (player 1), which can obtain the output $f(1)$, those consisting of the landowner and a worker, which can obtain $f(2)$, and the grand coalition. Thus (x_1, x_2, x_3) is in the core if and only if

$$x_1 \geq f(1)$$
$$x_2 \geq 0$$
$$x_3 \geq 0$$
$$x_1 + x_2 \geq f(2)$$
$$x_1 + x_3 \geq f(2)$$
$$x_1 + x_2 + x_3 = f(3),$$

where the last condition ensures that (x_1, x_2, x_3) is an allocation of $f(3)$.

From the last condition we have $x_1 = f(3) - x_2 - x_3$, so that we may rewrite the conditions as

$$0 \leq x_2 \leq f(3) - f(2)$$
$$0 \leq x_3 \leq f(3) - f(2)$$
$$x_2 + x_3 \leq f(3) - f(1)$$
$$x_1 + x_2 + x_3 = f(3).$$

That is, in an action in the core, each worker obtains at most the extra output $f(3) - f(2)$ produced by the third player, and the workers together obtain at most the extra output $f(3) - f(1)$ produced by the second and third players together.

? EXERCISE 245.1 (Three-player majority game) Show that the core of the three-player majority game (Example 240.3) is empty.

? EXERCISE 245.2 (Variant of three-player majority game) Find the core of the variant of the three-player majority game in which player 1 has three votes (and players 2 and 3 each have one vote, as in the original game).

? EXERCISE 245.3 (*Stag Hunt*) Find the core of the *Stag Hunt* in Exercise 241.2. Contrast the coalitional game and the core with the strategic game and Nash equilibria studied in Chapter 2.

? EXERCISE 245.4 (Variant of *Stag Hunt*) Consider the variant of the *Stag Hunt* in Exercise 30.1a. Model the situation as a coalitional game and find the core.

The next example introduces a class of games that model the market for an economic good.

◆ EXAMPLE 245.5 (Market with one owner and two buyers) A person holds one indivisible unit of a good and each of two (potential) buyers has a large amount of money. The owner values money but not the good; each buyer values both money and the good and regards the good as equivalent to one unit of money. Each coalition may assign the good (if owned by one of its members) to any of its members and allocate its members' money in any way it wishes among its members.

We may model this situation as the following coalitional game.

Players The owner and the two buyers.

Actions The set of actions of each coalition S is the set of S-allocations of the money and good (if any) owned by S.

Preferences The owner's preferences are represented by the amount of money she obtains; each buyer's preferences are represented by the amount of the good (either 0 or 1) she obtains plus the amount of money she holds.

I claim that for any action in the core, the owner does not keep the good. Let a_N be an action of the grand coalition in which the owner keeps the good, and let m_i be the amount of money transferred from potential buyer i to the owner in this action. (Transfers of money from the buyers to the owner when the owner keeps the good may not sound sensible, but they are feasible, so that we need to consider them.) Consider the alternative action a'_N of the grand coalition in which the good is allocated to buyer 1, who transfers $m_1 + 2\epsilon$ money to the owner, and buyer 2 transfers $m_2 - \epsilon$ money to the owner, where $0 < \epsilon < \frac{1}{2}$. We see that all the players' payoffs are higher in a'_N than they are in a_N. (The owner's payoff is ϵ higher, buyer 1's payoff is $1 - 2\epsilon$ higher, and buyer 2's payoff is ϵ higher.) Thus a_N is not in the core.

Now consider an action a_N in the core in which buyer 1 obtains the good. I claim that a_N specifies that buyer 1 pays one unit of money to the owner and buyer 2 pays no money to the owner. If buyer 2 pays a positive amount she can improve upon a_N by acting by herself (and making no payment). If buyer 1 pays more than one unit of money to the owner she too can improve upon a_N by acting by herself. Finally, suppose buyer 1 pays $m_1 < 1$ to the owner. Then the owner and buyer 2 can improve upon a_N by allocating the good to buyer 2 and transferring $\frac{1}{2}(1 + m_1)$ units of money from buyer 2 to the owner, yielding the owner a payoff greater than m_1 and buyer 2 a positive payoff.

We conclude that the core contains exactly two actions, in each of which the good is allocated to one of the two buyers and one unit of this buyer's money is allocated to the owner. That is, the good is sold to a buyer at the price of 1, yielding the buyer who obtains the good the same payoff that she obtains if she does not trade. This extreme outcome is a result of the competition between the buyers for the good: any outcome in which the owner trades with buyer i at a price less than 1 can be improved upon by the coalition consisting of the owner and the *other* buyer, who is willing to pay a little more for the good than is buyer i.

❓ EXERCISE 246.1 (Market with one owner and two heterogeneous buyers) Consider the variant of the game in the previous example in which buyer 1's valuation of the good is 1 and buyer 2's valuation is $v < 1$ (i.e. buyer 2 is indifferent between owning the good and owning v units of money). Find the core the game that models this situation.

In the next exercise, the grand coalition has finitely many actions; one way of finding the core is to check each one in turn.

? EXERCISE 247.1 (Vote trading) A legislature with three members decides, by majority vote, the fate of three bills, A, B, and C. Each legislator's preferences are represented by the sum of the values she attaches to the bills that pass. The value attached by each legislator to each bill is indicated in Figure 247.1. For example, if bills A and B pass and C fails, then the three legislators' payoffs are 1, 3, and 0, respectively. Each majority coalition can achieve the passage of any set of bills, whereas each minority is powerless.

	A	B	C
Legislator 1	2	−1	1
Legislator 2	1	2	−1
Legislator 3	−1	1	2

Figure 247.1 The legislators' payoffs to the three bills in Exercise 247.1.

a. Find the core of the coalitional game that models this situation.

b. Find the core of the game in which the values the legislators attach to the passage of each bill differ from those in Figure 247.1 only in that legislator 3 values the passage of bill C at 0.

c. Find the core of the game in which the values the legislators attach to the payoff of each bill differ from those in Figure 247.1 only in that each 1 is replaced by −1.

8.3　Illustration: ownership and the distribution of wealth

The distribution and institutions of landownership differ widely across economies. By studying the cores of coalitional games that model various institutions, we can gain an understanding of the implications of these institutions for the distribution of wealth.

A group of $n \geq 3$ people may work the land to produce food. Denote the output of food when k people work all the land by $f(k)$. Assume that f is an increasing function, $f(0) = 0$, and the output produced by an additional person decreases as the number of workers increases: $f(k) - f(k-1)$ is decreasing in k. An example of such a function f is shown in Figure 248.1. In all the games I study in this section, the set of players is the set of the n people and each person cares only about the amount of food she obtains.

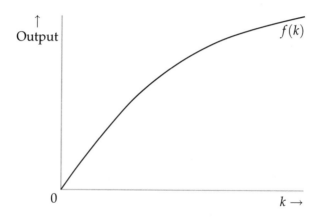

Figure 248.1 The output of food as a function of the number k of workers, under the assumption that the output of an additional worker decreases as the number of workers increases.

8.3.1 Single landowner and landless workers

First suppose that the land is owned by a single person, the *landowner*. I refer to the other people as *workers*. In this case we obtain the game in Example 240.2. In this game the action a_N of the grand coalition in which the landowner obtains all the output $f(n)$ is in the core: all coalitions that can produce any output include the landowner, and none of these coalitions has any action that makes her better off than she is in a_N.

We saw in Example 244.2 that for $n = 3$ the core contains actions in which the workers receive some output. The same is true for any value of n: the workers need the landowner to produce any output, but the landowner also needs the workers to produce more than $f(1)$, so stable actions of the grand coalition exist in which the workers receive some output. Take the landowner to be player 1, and consider the action a_N of the grand coalition in which each player i obtains the output x_i, where $x_1 + \cdots + x_n = f(n)$. Under what conditions on $(x_1, \ldots, x_n)$ is a_N in the core? Because of my assumption about the shape of the function f, the coalitions most capable of profitably deviating from a_N consist of the landowner and every worker but one. Such a coalition can, by itself, produce $f(n-1)$, and it may distribute this output in any way among its members. Thus for a deviation by such a coalition not to be profitable, the sum of x_1 and any collection of $n-2$ other x_i's must be at least $f(n-1)$. That is, $(x_1 + \cdots + x_n) - x_j \geq f(n-1)$ for every $j = 2, \ldots, n$. Because $x_1 + \cdots + x_n = f(n)$, we conclude that $x_j \leq f(n) - f(n-1)$ for every player j with $j \geq 2$ (i.e. every worker). That is, if a_N is in the core, then $0 \leq x_j \leq f(n) - f(n-1)$ for every player $j \geq 2$. In fact, every such action is in the core, as you are asked to verify in the following exercise.

? EXERCISE 248.1 (Core of landowner–worker game) Check that no coalition can improve upon any action of the grand coalition in which the output received by every worker is nonnegative and at most $f(n) - f(n-1)$. (Use the fact that the form of f implies that $f(n) - f(k) \geq (n-k)(f(n) - f(n-1))$ for every $k \leq n$.)

We conclude that the core of the game is the set of all actions of the grand coalition in which the output x_i obtained by each worker i satisfies $0 \leq x_i \leq f(n) - f(n-1)$ and the output obtained by the landowner is the difference between $f(n)$ and the sum of the workers' shares. In economic jargon, $f(n) - f(n-1)$ is a worker's "marginal product". Thus in any action in the core, each worker obtains at most her marginal product.

The workers' shares of output are driven down to at most $f(n) - f(n-1)$ by competition between coalitions consisting of the landowner and workers. If the output received by any worker exceeds $f(n) - f(n-1)$, then the other workers, in cahoots with the landowner, can deviate and increase their share of output. That is, each worker's share of output is limited by her comrades' attempts to obtain more output.

The fact that each worker's share of output is held down by interworker competition suggests that the workers might be better off if they were to agree not to join deviating coalitions *except as a group*. You are asked to check this idea in the following exercise.

? EXERCISE 249.1 (Unionized workers in landowner–worker game) Formulate as a coalitional game the variant of the landowner–worker game in which any group of fewer than $n - 1$ workers refuses to work with the landowner, and find its core.

The core of the original game is closely related to the outcomes predicted by the economic notion of "competitive equilibrium". Suppose that the landowner believes she can hire any number of workers at the fixed wage w (given as an amount of output), and every worker believes that she can obtain employment at this wage. If $w \geq 0$, then every worker wishes to work, and if $w \leq f(n) - f(n-1)$, the landowner wishes to employ all $n - 1$ workers. (Reducing the number of workers by one reduces the output by $f(n) - f(n-1)$; further reducing the number of workers reduces the output by successively larger amounts, given the shape of f.) If $w > f(n) - f(n-1)$, then the landowner wishes to employ fewer than $n - 1$ workers, because the wage exceeds the increase in the total output that results when the $(n-1)$th worker is employed. Thus the demand for workers is equal to the supply if and only if $0 \leq w \leq f(n) - f(n-1)$; every such wage w is a "competitive equilibrium".

A different assumption about the form of f yields a different conclusion about the core. Suppose that each additional worker produces *more* additional output than the previous one. An example of a function f with this form is shown in Figure 250.1. Under this assumption the economy has no competitive equilibrium: for any wage, the landowner wishes to employ an indefinitely large number of workers. The next exercise asks you to study the core of the induced coalitional game.

? EXERCISE 249.2 (Landowner–worker game with increasing marginal products) Consider the variant of the landowner–worker game in which each additional worker produces more additional output than the previous one. (That is, $f(k)/k <$

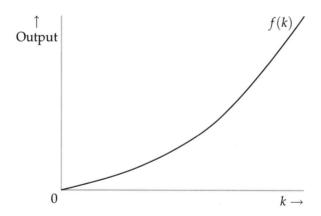

Figure 250.1 The output of food as a function of the number k of workers, under the assumption that the output of an additional worker increases as the number of workers increases.

$f(k+1)/(k+1)$ for all k.) Show that the core of this game contains the action of the grand coalition in which each player obtains an equal share of the total output.

8.3.2 Small landowners

Suppose that the land is distributed equally between all n people, rather than being concentrated in the hands of a single landowner. Assume that a group of k people who pool their land and work together produce $(k/n)f(n)$ units of output. (The output produced by half the people working half the land, for example, is half the output produced by all the people working all the land.)

The following specification of the set of actions available to each coalition models this situation.

> *Actions* The set of actions of a coalition S consisting of k players is the set of all S-allocations of the output $(k/n)f(n)$ between the members of S.

As you might expect, one action in the core of this game is that in which every player obtains an equal share of the total output—that is, $f(n)/n$ units. Under this action, the total amount received by each coalition is precisely the total amount the coalition produces. In fact, no other action is in the core. In any other action, some player receives less than $f(n)/n$, and hence can improve upon the action alone (obtaining $f(n)/n$ for herself). That is, the core consists of the single action in which every player obtains $f(n)/n$ units of output.

8.3.3 Collective ownership

Suppose that the land is owned collectively and the distribution of output is determined by majority voting. Assume that any majority may distribute the output in any way it wishes; any majority may, in particular, take all the output for itself. In this case the set of actions available to each coalition is given as follows.

Actions The set of actions of a coalition S consisting of more than $n/2$ players is the set of all S-allocations of the output $f(n)$ between the members of S. The set of actions of a coalition S consisting of at most $n/2$ players is the single S-allocation in which no player in S receives any output.

The core of the coalitional game defined by this assumption is empty. For every action of the grand coalition, at least one player obtains a positive amount of output. But if player i obtains a positive amount of output, then the coalition of the remaining players, which is a majority, may improve upon the action, distributing the output $f(n)$ among its members (so that player i gets nothing). Thus every action of the grand coalition may be improved upon by some coalition; no distribution of output is stable.

The core of this game is empty because of the extreme power of every majority coalition. If any majority coalition may control how the land is used, but every player owns a "share" that entitles her to the fraction $1/n$ of the output, then a majority coalition with k members can lay claim to only the fraction k/n of the total output, and a stable distribution of output may exist. This alternative ownership institution, which tempers the power of majority coalitions, does not have interesting implications in the model in this section because the control of land use vested in a majority coalition is inconsequential—only one sensible pattern of use exists (all the players work!). If choices exist—if, for example, different crops may be grown, and people differ in their preferences for these crops—then the outcome of collective ownership in which each player is entitled to an equal share of the output may differ from the outcome of individual ownership.

8.4 Illustration: exchanging homogeneous horses

Markets may be modeled as coalitional games in which the set of actions of each coalition S is the set of S-allocations of the good initially owned by the members of S. The core of such a game is the set of allocations of the goods available in the economy that are robust to the trading opportunities of all possible groups of participants: if a_N is in the core, then no group of agents can secede from the economy, trade among themselves, and produce an outcome they all prefer to a_N.

In this section I describe a simple example of a market in which there is money and a single homogeneous good (all units of which are identical). In the next section I describe a market in which there is a single *heterogeneous* good. In both cases the core makes a very precise prediction about the outcome.

8.4.1 Model

Some people own one unit of an indivisible good, whereas others possess only money. Some nonowners value a unit of the good more highly than some owners, so that mutually beneficial trades exist. Which allocation of goods and money will result?

We may address this question with the help of a coalitional game that generalizes the one in Example 245.5. I refer to the goods as "horses" (following the literature on the model, which takes off from an analysis by Eugen von Böhm-Bawerk (1851–1914)). Call each person who owns a horse simply an *owner* and every other person a *nonowner*. Assume that all horses are identical and that no one wishes to own more than one. People value a horse differently; denote player i's valuation by v_i. Assume that there are at least two owners and two nonowners; assume also that some owner's valuation is less than some nonowner's valuation (i.e. for some owner i and nonowner j we have $v_i < v_j$), so that some trade is mutually desirable. Assume also, to avoid some special cases, that some nonowner's valuation is less than some owner's valuation (i.e. for some nonowner i and owner j we have $v_i < v_j$) and that no two players have the same valuation. Further assume that every person has enough money to fully compensate the owner who values a horse most highly, so that no one's behavior is constrained by her cash balance.

As to preferences, assume that each person cares only about the amount of money she has and whether she has a horse. (In particular, no one cares about any other person's holdings.) Specifically, assume that each player i's preferences are represented by the payoff function

$$\begin{cases} v_i + r & \text{if she has a horse and } \$r \text{ more money than she has initially} \\ r & \text{if she has no horse and } \$r \text{ more money than she has initially.} \end{cases}$$

(This assumption does not mean that people do not value the money they have initially. Equivalently we could represent player i's preferences by the functions $v_i + r + m_i$ if she has a horse and $r + m_i$ if she does not, where m_i is the amount of money she has initially.)

The following coalitional game, which I call a **horse trading game**, models the situation.

Players The group of people (owners and nonowners).

Actions The set of actions of each coalition S is the set of S-allocations of the horses and the total amount of money owned by S in which each player obtains at most one horse.

Preferences Each player's preferences are represented by the payoff function described above.

This game incorporates no restriction on the way in which a coalition may distribute its money and horses. In particular, players are not restricted to bilateral trades of money for horses. A coalition of two owners and two nonowners, for example, may, if it wishes, allocate each of the owners' horses to a nonowner and transfer money from *both* nonowners to only one owner, or from one nonowner to the other.

8.4.2 The core

Number the owners in ascending order and the nonowners in descending order of the valuations they attach to a horse. Figure 253.1 illustrates the valuations, ordered in this way. (This diagram should be familiar—perhaps it is a little too familiar—if you have studied economics.) Denote owner i's valuation σ_i and nonowner i's valuation β_i. Denote by k^* the largest number i such that $\beta_i > \sigma_i$ (so that among the owners and nonowners whose indices are k^* or less, every nonowner's valuation is greater than every owner's valuation).

Let a_N be an action in the core. Denote by L^* the set of owners who have no horse in a_N (the set of *sellers*) and by B^* the set of nonowners who have a horse in a_N (the set of *buyers*). These two sets must have the same number of members (by the law of conservation of horses). Denote by r_i the amount of money received by owner i and by p_j the amount paid by nonowner j in a_N.

I claim that $p_j = 0$ for every nonowner j not in B^*. (That is, a nonowner who does not acquire a horse neither pays nor receives any money.)

- If $p_j > 0$ for some nonowner j not in B^*, then her payoff is negative, and she can unilaterally improve upon a_N by retaining her original money.

- If $p_j < 0$ for some nonowner j not in B^*, then the coalition of all players *other than* j has p_j less money than it owned initially, and the same number of horses. Thus this coalition can improve upon a_N by assigning horses in the same way they are assigned in a_N and giving each of its members $p_j/(n-1)$ more units of money than she gets in a_N (where n is the total number of players).

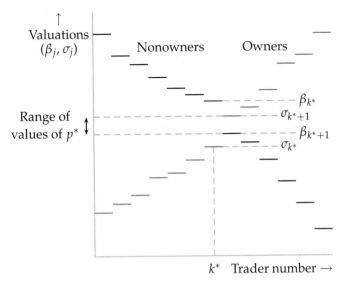

Figure 253.1 An example of the players' valuations in a market with an indivisible good. The buyers' valuations are given in black, the sellers' in gray.

By a similar argument, $r_i = 0$ for every owner not in L^* (an owner who does not sell her horse neither pays nor receives any money.)

I now argue that in a_N every seller (member of L^*) receives the same amount of money, every buyer (member of B^*) pays the same amount of money, and these amounts are equal: $r_i = p_j$ for every seller i and buyer j. That is, all trades occur at the same price.

Suppose that $r_i < p_j$ for seller i and buyer j. I argue that the coalition $\{i, j\}$ can improve upon a_N: i can sell her horse to j at a price between r_i and p_j. Under a_N, seller i's payoff is r_i and buyer j's payoff is $\beta_j - p_j$. If i sells her horse to j at the price $\frac{1}{2}(r_i + p_j)$, then her payoff is $\frac{1}{2}(r_i + p_j) > r_i$ and j's payoff is $\beta_j - \frac{1}{2}(r_i + p_j) > \beta_j - p_j$, so that both i and j are better off than they are in a_N. Thus $r_i \geq p_j$ for every seller i and every buyer j.

Now, the sum of all the amounts r_i received by sellers is equal to the sum of all the amounts p_j paid by buyers (by the law of conservation of money), and L^* and B^* have the same number of members. Thus we have $r_i = p_j$ for every seller i in L^* and buyer j in B^*.

In summary,

> for every action a_N in the core there exists p^* such that $r_i = p_j = p^*$ for every owner i in L^* and every nonowner j in B^*, and $r_i = p_j = 0$ for every owner not in L^* and every nonowner j not in B^*.

I now argue that the common price p^* at which all trades take place lies in a narrow range.

In a_N, every owner i whose valuation of a horse is less than p^* must sell her horse: if she did not, then the coalition consisting of herself and any nonowner j who buys a horse in a_N could improve upon a_N by taking the action in which j buys i's horse at a price between the owner's valuation and p^*. Also, no owner whose valuation exceeds p^* trades, because her payoff from doing so would be negative. Similarly, every nonowner whose valuation is greater than p^* buys a horse, and no nonowner whose valuation is less than p^* does so.

? EXERCISE 254.1 (Range of prices in horse market) Show that the requirement that the number of owners who sell their horses must equal the number of nonowners who buy horses, together with the previous arguments, implies that the common trading price p^* is at least σ_{k^*}, at least β_{k^*+1}, at most β_{k^*}, and at most σ_{k^*+1}. That is, $p^* \geq \max\{\sigma_{k^*}, \beta_{k^*+1}\}$ and $p^* \leq \min\{\beta_{k^*}, \sigma_{k^*+1}\}$.

Finally, I argue that in any action in the core a player whose valuation is equal to p^* trades. Suppose that nonowner i's valuation is equal to p^*. Then owner i's valuation is less than p^* and owner $i + 1$'s valuation is greater than p^* (given my assumption that no two players have the same valuation), so that exactly i owners trade. Thus, given that every trade involves two parties, exactly i nonowners must trade, implying that nonowner i trades. Symmetrically, an owner whose valuation is equal to p^* trades.

In summary, in every action in the core of a horse trading game,

- every nonowner pays the same price for a horse

- the common price is at least $\max\{\sigma_{k^*}, \beta_{k^*+1}\}$ and at most $\min\{\beta_{k^*}, \sigma_{k^*+1}\}$

- every owner whose valuation is at most the price trades her horse

- every nonowner whose valuation is at least the price obtains a horse.

(255.1)

The action satisfying these conditions for the price p^* yields the payoffs

$$\begin{cases} \max\{v_i, p^*\} & \text{for every owner } i \\ \max\{v_i, p^*\} - p^* & \text{for every nonowner } i. \end{cases}$$

The core does not impose any additional restrictions on the actions of the grand coalition: every action that satisfies these conditions is in the core. To establish this result, I need to show that for any action a_N that satisfies the conditions, no coalition has an action that is better for all its members. When a coalition deviates, which of its actions has the best chance of improving upon a_N? The optimal action definitely assigns the coalition's horses to the members who value a horse most highly. (If $v_i < v_j$, then the transfer of a horse from i to j, accompanied by the transfer from j to i of an amount of money between v_i and v_j makes both i and j better off.) No transfer of money makes anyone better off without making someone worse off, so for a coalition to improve upon a_N there must be some distribution of the total amount of money it owns that, given the optimal distribution of horses, makes all its members better off than they are in a_N. For every distribution of a coalition's money, the total payoff of the members of the coalition is the same. Thus a coalition can improve upon a_N if and only if the total payoff of its members under a_N is less than its total payoff when it assigns its horses optimally.

Consider an arbitrary coalition S. Denote by ℓ the total number of owners in S, by b the total number of nonowners in S, and by S^* the set of ℓ members of S whose valuations are highest. Then S's total payoff when it assigns its horses optimally is

$$\sum_{i \in S^*} v_i,$$

whereas its total payoff under a_N is

$$\sum_{i \in S} \max\{v_i, p^*\} - bp^* = \sum_{i \in S^*} \max\{v_i, p^*\} + \sum_{i \in S \setminus S^*} \max\{v_i, p^*\} - bp^*,$$

where $S \setminus S^*$ is the set of members of S *not* in S^*. The former is never higher than the latter because $S \setminus S^*$ has b members, so that $\sum_{i \in S \setminus S^*} \max\{v_i, p^*\} - bp^* \geq 0$.

In summary, the core of a horse trading game is the set of actions of the grand coalition that satisfies the four conditions in (255.1).

❓ EXERCISE 256.1 (Horse trading game with single seller) Find the core of the variant of the horse trading game in which there is a single owner, whose valuation is less than the highest valuation of the nonowners.

If you have studied economics you know that this outcome is the same as the "competitive equilibrium". The theories differ, however. The theory of competitive equilibrium *assumes* that all trades take place at the same price. It defines an equilibrium price to be one at which "demand" (the total number of nonowners whose valuations exceed the price) is equal to "supply" (the total number of owners whose valuations are less than the price). This equilibrium may be justified by the argument that if demand exceeds supply, then the price will tend to rise, and if supply exceeds demand it will tend to fall. Thus in this theory, "market pressures" generate an equilibrium price; no agent in the market chooses a price.

By contrast, the coalitional game we have studied models the players' actions explicitly; each group may exchange its horses and money in any way it wishes. The core is the set of actions of all players that survives the pressures imposed by the trading opportunities of each possible group of players. A uniform price is not assumed, but is shown to be a necessary property of any action in the core.

❓ EXERCISE 256.2 (Horse trading game with large seller) Consider the variant of the horse trading game in which there is a single owner who has two horses. Assume that the owner's payoff is $\sigma_1 + r$ if she keeps one of her horses and $2\sigma_1 + r$ if she keeps both of them, where r is the amount of money she receives. Assume that there are at least two nonowners, both of whose values of a horse exceed σ_1. Find the core of this game. (Do all trades take place at the same price, as they do in a competitive equilibrium?)

8.5 Illustration: exchanging heterogeneous houses

8.5.1 Model

In Example 242.1, the goods that may be exchanged are heterogeneous, unlike the horses of the previous section. Each member of a group of n people owns a single house. Any subgroup may reallocate its members' houses in any way it wishes (one house to each person). Each person cares only about the house she obtains. Assume that each person's ranking of the houses is strict (she is not indifferent between any two houses). I refer to the game defined in Example 242.1, under this assumption, as a **house exchange game**.

Which assignments of houses to people are stable? You may think that without imposing any restrictions on the nature or diversity of preferences, this question is hard to answer, and that for some sufficiently conflicting configurations of preferences no assignment is stable. If so, you are wrong on both counts, at least as far as the core is concerned; remarkably, for *any* preferences, a slight variant of the core yields a *unique* stable outcome.

8.5.2   The top trading cycle procedure and the core

One property of an action in the core is immediate: because every player has the option of simply keeping the house she initially owns, any player who initially owns her favorite house obtains that house in any assignment in the core.

This property allows us to completely analyze the simplest nontrivial example of the game, with two people. Denote the person who initially owns player i's favorite house by $o(i)$.

- If at least one person initially owns her favorite house (i.e. if $o(1) = 1$ or $o(2) = 2$), then the core contains the single assignment in which each person keeps the house she owns.

- If each person prefers the house owned by the other person (i.e. if $o(1) = 2$ and $o(2) = 1$), then the core contains the single assignment in which the two people exchange houses.

In the second case we say that "12 is a 2-cycle". When there are more players, longer cycles are possible. For example, if there are three or more players and $o(i) = j$, $o(j) = k$, and $o(k) = i$, then we say that "ijk is a 3-cycle". (If $o(i) = i$, we can think of i as a "1-cycle".)

The case in which there are three people raises some new possibilities.

- If at least two people initially own their favorite houses, then the core contains the single assignment in which each person keeps the house she initially owns.

- If exactly one person, say player i, initially owns her favorite house, then in any assignment in the core, that person keeps her house. Whether the other two people exchange their houses depends on their preferences over these houses, ignoring player i's house (which has already been assigned); the analysis is the same as that for the two-player game.

- If no person initially owns her favorite house, there are two cases.

  ○ If there is a 2-cycle (i.e. if there exist persons i and j such that j initially owns i's favorite house and i initially owns j's favorite house), then the only assignment in the core is that in which i and j swap houses and the remaining player keeps the house she owns initially.

  ○ Otherwise, suppose that $o(i) = j$. Then $o(j) = k$, where k is the third player (otherwise ij is a 2-cycle), and $o(k) = i$ (otherwise kj is a 2-cycle.) That is, ijk is a 3-cycle. If i gets j's house, j gets k's house, and k gets i's house, then every player is assigned her favorite house, so this assignment is in the core. (This argument does not show that the core contains no other assignments.)

This construction of an assignment in the core can be extended to games with any number of players. First we look for cycles among the houses at the top of

Player 1	Player 2	Player 3	Player 4
h_2	h_1	h_1	h_3
—	—	h_2	h_2
—	—	h_4	h_4
—	—	h_3	—

Figure 258.1 A partial specification of the players' preferences in a game with four players, illustrating the top trading cycle procedure. Each player's ranking is given from best to worst, reading from top to bottom. Dashes indicate irrelevant parts of the rankings.

the players' rankings and assign to each member of each cycle her favorite house. (If there are at most three players, then only one cycle containing more than one player can exist, but if there are more players, many cycles can exist.) Then we eliminate from consideration the players involved in these cycles and the houses they are allocated, look for any cycles at the top of the remains of the players' rankings, and assign to each member of each of these cycles her favorite house among those remaining. We continue in the same manner until all players have been assigned houses. This procedure is called the *top trading cycle procedure*.

To illustrate the procedure, consider the game with four players whose preferences satisfy the specification in Figure 258.1. In this figure, h_i denotes the house owned by player i and the players' rankings are listed from best to worst, starting at the top (player 3 prefers player 1's house to player 2's house to player 4's house, for example). Dashes indicate irrelevant parts of the rankings. We see that 12 is a 2-cycle, so at the first step players 1 and 2 are assigned their favorite houses (h_2 and h_1 respectively). After eliminating these players and their houses, 34 becomes a 2-cycle, so that player 3 is assigned h_4 and player 4 is assigned h_3. If player 3's ranking of h_3 and h_4 were reversed, then at the second stage 3 would be a 1-cycle, so that player 3 would be assigned h_3, and then at the third stage player 4 would be assigned h_4.

? EXERCISE 258.1 (House assignment with identical preferences) Find all the assignments in the core of an n-player house exchange game in which every player ranks the houses in the same way.

I now argue that

> for any (strict) preferences, the core of a house exchange game contains the assignment induced by the top trading cycle procedure.

Every player assigned a house in the first round receives her favorite house, so that no coalition containing such a player can make all its members better off than they are in a_N. Now consider a coalition that contains players assigned houses in the second round, but no players assigned houses in the first round. Such a coalition does not own any of the houses assigned on the first round, so that its members who were assigned in the second round obtain their favorite houses *among the houses the coalition owns.* Thus such a coalition has no action that makes all its members better off than they are in a_N. A similar argument applies to coalitions containing players assigned in later rounds.

8.5.3 The strong core

I remarked that my analysis of a three-player game does not establish the existence of a *unique* assignment in the core. Indeed, consider the preferences in Figure 259.1. We see that 123 is a 3-cycle, so that the top trading cycle procedure generates the assignment in which each player receives her favorite house.

I claim that the alternative assignment a'_N, in which player 1 obtains h_2, player 2 obtains h_1, and player 3 obtains h_3 is also in the core. Player 2 obtains her favorite house, so no coalition containing her can improve upon a'_N. Neither player 1 nor player 3 alone can improve upon a'_N because player 1 prefers h_2 to h_1 and player 3 obtains the house she owns. The only remaining coalition is $\{1,3\}$, which owns h_1 and h_3. If it deviates and assigns h_1 to player 1, then she is worse off than she is in a'_N, and if it deviates and assigns h_1 to player 3, then she is worse off than she is in a'_N. Thus no coalition can improve upon a'_N.

Although no coalition S can achieve any S-allocation that makes all of its members better off than they are in a'_N, the coalition N of all three players *can* make two of its members (players 1 and 3) better off, while keeping the remaining member (player 2) with the same house. That is, it can "weakly" improve upon a'_N.

Define the *strong core* of any game to be the set of actions a_N of the grand coalition N such that no coalition S has an action a_S that some of its members prefer to a_N and all of its members regard to be at least as good as a_N.

The argument I have given shows that the action a'_N is not in the strong core of the game in which the players' preferences are given in Figure 259.1, though it is in the core. In fact,

> *for any (strict) preferences, the strong core of a house exchange game consists of the single assignment defined by the top trading cycle procedure.*

I omit the argument for this result. The result shows that the (strong) core is a highly successful solution for house exchange games; for *any* (strict) preferences, it pinpoints a *single* stable assignment, which is the outcome of a simple, intuitively appealing, procedure.

Player 1	Player 2	Player 3
h_3	h_1	h_2
h_2	h_2	h_3
h_1	h_3	h_1

Figure 259.1 The players' preferences in a game with three players. Each player's ranking is given from best to worst, reading from top to bottom.

Unfortunately, the strengthening of the definition of the core has a side effect: if we depart from the assumption that all preferences are strict, and allow players to be indifferent between houses, then the core may be empty. The next exercise gives an example.

? EXERCISE 260.1 (Emptiness of the strong core when preferences are not strict) Suppose that some players are indifferent between some pairs of houses. Specifically, suppose there are three players, whose preferences are given in Figure 260.1. Find the core and show that the strong core is empty.

Player 1	Player 2	Player 3
h_2	h_1, h_3	h_2
h_1, h_3	h_2	h_1, h_3

Figure 260.1 The players' preferences in the game in Exercise 260.1. A cell containing two houses indicates indifference between these two houses.

8.6 Illustration: voting

A group of people chooses a policy by majority voting. How does the chosen policy depend on the individuals' preferences? In Chapter 2 we studied a strategic game that models this situation and found that the notion of Nash equilibrium admits a very wide range of stable outcomes. In a Nash equilibrium, no single player, by changing her vote, can improve the outcome for herself, but a group of players, by coordinating their votes, may be able to do so. By modeling the situation as a coalitional game and using the notion of the core to identify stable outcomes, we can find the implications of group deviations for the outcome.

To model voting as a coalitional game, the specification I have given of such a game needs to be slightly modified. Recall that an outcome of a coalitional game is a partition of the set of players and an action for each coalition in the partition. So far I have assumed that each player cares only about the action chosen by the coalition in the partition to which she belongs. This assumption means that the payoff of a coalition that deviates from an outcome is determined independently of the action of any other coalition; when deviating, a coalition does not have to consider the action that any other coalition takes. In the situation I now present, a different constellation of conditions has the same implication: every player cares only about the action chosen by the majority coalition (of which there is at most one) in the outcome partition, and only coalitions containing a majority of the players have more than one possible action. In brief, any majority may choose an action that affects everyone, and every minority is powerless.

Precisely, assume that there is an odd number of players, each of whom has preferences over a set of *policies* and prefers the outcome x to the outcome y if and only if either (*i*) there are majority coalitions in the partitions associated with both

x and y and she prefers the action chosen by the majority coalition in x to the action chosen by the majority coalition in y, or (*ii*) there is a majority coalition in x but not in y. (If there is a majority coalition in neither x nor y, she is indifferent between x and y.) The set of actions available to any coalition containing a majority of the players is the set of all policies; every other coalition has a single action. I refer to such a game as a **majority voting game**.

The definition of the core of this variant of a coalitional game is the natural variant of Definition 243.2: the set of actions a_N of the grand coalition N such that no majority coalition has an action that all its members prefer to a_N.

Suppose that the policy x is in the core of the game. Then no policy is preferred to x by any coalition consisting of a majority of the players. Equivalently, for every policy $y \neq x$, the set of players who either prefer x to y or regard x and y to be equally good is a majority. If we assume that every player's preferences are strict—no player is indifferent between any two policies—then for every policy $y \neq x$, the set of players who prefer x to y is a majority. That is, x is a Condorcet winner (see Exercise 75.3). For any preferences, there is at most one Condorcet winner, so we have established that

> *if every player's preferences are strict, the core of a majority voting game is empty if there is no Condorcet winner; otherwise, it is the set consisting of the single Condorcet winner.*

How does the existence and character of a Condorcet winner depend on the players' preferences? First suppose that a policy is a number. Assume that each player i has a favorite policy x_i^*, and that her preferences are *single peaked*: if x and x' are policies for which $x < x' < x_i^*$ or $x_i^* < x' < x$, then she prefers x' to x. Then the median of the players' favorite positions is the Condorcet winner, as you are asked to show in the next exercise, and hence the unique member of the core of the voting game. (The median is well defined because the number of players is odd.)

⑦ EXERCISE 261.1 (Median voter theorem) Show that when the policy space is one-dimensional and the players' preferences are single peaked, the unique Condorcet winner is the median of the players' favorite positions. (This result is known as the *median voter theorem*.)

A one-dimensional space captures some policy choices, but other situations require a higher dimensional space. A two-dimensional space is required, for example, to model a government that has to choose the amounts to spend on health care and defense if not all citizens' preferences are aligned on these issues. Unfortunately, for most configurations of the players' preferences, a Condorcet winner does not exist in a policy space of two or more dimensions, so that the core is empty.

To see why this claim is plausible, suppose the policy space is two-dimensional and there are three players. Place the players' favorite positions at three arbitrary points, like x_1^*, x_2^*, and x_3^* in Figure 262.1. Assume that each player i's distaste for a position x different from her favorite position x_i^* is exactly the distance between x

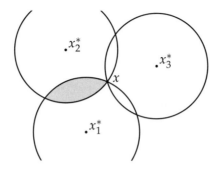

Figure 262.1 A two-dimensional policy space with three players. The point x_i^* is the favorite position of player i for $i = 1, 2, 3$. Every policy in the shaded lens is preferred by players 1 and 2 to x.

and x_i^*, so that for any value of r she is indifferent between all policies on the circle with radius r centered at x_i^*.

Now choose any policy and ask if it is a Condorcet winner. The policy x in the figure is not, because any policy in the shaded area is preferred to x by players 1 and 2, who constitute a majority. The policy x is also beaten in a majority vote by any policy in either of the other lens-shaped areas defined by the intersection of the circles centered at x_1^*, x_2^*, and x_3^*. Is there any policy for which no such lens-shaped area is created? By checking a few other policies, you can convince yourself that the answer is negative. That is, no policy is a Condorcet winner, so that the core of the game is empty.

For *some* configurations of the players' favorite positions, a Condorcet winner exists. If the positions lie on a straight line, for example, then the middle one is a Condorcet winner. But only very special configurations yield a Condorcet winner—in general there is none, so that the core is empty, and our analysis suggests that no policy is stable under majority rule when the policy space is multidimensional.

In some situations in which policies are determined by a vote, a decision requires a positive vote by more than a simple majority. For example, some jury verdicts in the United States require unanimity, and changes in some organizations' and countries' constitutions require a two-thirds majority. To study the implications of these alternative voting rules, fix q with $n/2 \leq q \leq n$ and consider a variant of the majority rule game that I call the *q-rule game*, in which the only coalitions that can choose policies are those containing at least q players. Roughly, the larger is the value of q, the larger is the core. You are invited to explore some examples in the next exercise.

? EXERCISE 262.1 (Cores of q-rule games)

    a. Suppose that the set of policies is one-dimensional and that each player's preferences are single peaked. Find the core of the q-rule game for any value of q with $n/2 \leq q \leq n$.

    b. Find the core of the q-rule game when $q = 3$ in the example in Figure 262.1 (with a two-dimensional policy space and three players).

8.7 Illustration: matching

Applicants must be matched with universities, workers with firms, and football players with teams. Do stable matchings exist? If so, what are their properties, and which institutions generate them?

In this section I analyze the model of two-sided one-to-one matching described in Example 242.2, in which each party on one side must be matched with exactly *one* party on the other side. Most of the main ideas that emerge apply also to many-to-one matching problems. This model is sometimes referred to as one of "marriage", though of course it captures only one dimension of matrimony. Some of the language I use is taken from this interpretation of the model.

8.7.1 Model

I refer to members of the two sides as Xs and Ys. Each X may be matched with at most one Y, and each Y may be matched with at most one X; staying single is an option for each individual. A *matching* of any set of individuals thus splits the set into pairs, each consisting of an X and a Y, and single individuals. I denote the partner of any player i under the matching μ by $\mu(i)$. If i and j are matched, we thus have $\mu(i) = j$ and $\mu(j) = i$; if i is single, then $\mu(i) = i$. Each person cares only about her partner, not about anyone else's partner. Assume that every person's preferences are *strict*: no person is indifferent between any two partners. An example of possible preferences is given in Figure 263.1, in which, for instance, player x_1 ranks y_2 first, then y_1, and finds y_3 unacceptable. I refer to the set of partners that i prefers to the option of remaining single as the set of i's *acceptable* partners, and to the coalitional game as a **two-sided one-to-one matching game**.

8.7.2 The core and the deferred acceptance procedure

A matching in the core of a two-sided one-to-one matching game has the property that no group of players may, by rearranging themselves, produce a matching that they all like better. I claim that when looking for a coalition that can improve upon a matching, we may restrict attention to those consisting either of a single individual or of one X and one Y. Precisely, a matching is in the core if and only if

Xs			Ys		
x_1	x_2	x_3	y_1	y_2	y_3
y_2	y_1	y_1	x_1	x_2	x_1
y_1	y_2	y_2	x_3	x_1	x_3
	y_3		x_2	x_3	x_2

Figure 263.1 An example of the players' preferences in a two-sided one-to-one matching game. Each column gives one player's ranking (from best to worst) of all the players of the other type that she finds acceptable.

> *a.* each player prefers her partner to being single
>
> *b.* for no pair (i, j) consisting of an X and a Y is it the case that i prefers j to $\mu(i)$ and j prefers i to $\mu(j)$.

The following argument establishes this claim. First, any matching μ that does not satisfy the conditions is not in the core: if (*a*) is violated, then some player can improve upon μ by staying single, and if (*b*) is violated, then some pair of players can improve upon μ by matching with each other. Second, suppose that μ is not in the core. Then for some coalition S there is a matching μ' of its members for which every member i prefers $\mu'(i)$ to $\mu(i)$. If S consists of a single individual, then (*a*) is violated. Otherwise, suppose that i is a member of S, and let $j = \mu'(i)$, so that $i = \mu'(j)$. Then i prefers j to $\mu(i)$ and j prefers i to $\mu(j)$. Thus (*b*) is violated.

In the game in which the players' preferences are those given in Figure 263.1, for example, the matching μ in which $\mu(x_1) = y_1$, $\mu(x_2) = y_2$, $\mu(x_3) = x_3$, and $\mu(y_3) = y_3$ (i.e. x_3 and y_3 stay single) is in the core, by the following argument. No single player can improve upon μ because every matched player's partner is acceptable to her. Now consider pairs of players. No pair containing x_3 or y_3 can improve upon μ because x_1 and x_2 are matched with partners they prefer to y_3, and y_1 and y_2 are matched with partners they prefer to x_3. A matched pair cannot improve upon μ either, so the only pairs to consider are $\{x_1, y_2\}$ and $\{x_2, y_1\}$. The first cannot improve upon μ because y_2 prefers x_2, with whom she is matched, to x_1; the second cannot upon μ because y_1 prefers x_1, with whom she is matched, to x_2.

How may matchings in the core be found? As in the case of the market for houses studied in Section 8.5, one member of the core is generated by an intuitively appealing procedure. (In contrast to the core of the house market, however, the core of a two-sided, one-to-one matching game may contain more than one action, as we shall see.)

The procedure comes in two flavors, one in which proposals are made by Xs, and one in which they are made by Ys. The *deferred acceptance procedure with proposals by Xs* is defined as follows. Initially, each X proposes to her favorite Y, and each Y either rejects all the proposals she receives, if none is from an X acceptable to her, or rejects all but the best proposal according to her preferences. Each proposal that is not rejected results in a tentative match between an X and a Y. If every offer is accepted, the process ends, and the tentative matches become definite. Otherwise, there is a second stage in which each X whose proposal was rejected in the first stage proposes to the Y she ranks second, and each Y chooses among the set of Xs who proposed to her *and* the one with whom she was tentatively matched in the first stage, rejecting all but her favorite among these Xs. Again, if every offer is accepted, the process ends, and the tentative matches become definite, whereas if some offer is rejected, there is another round of proposals.

Precisely, each stage has two steps, as follows.

1. Each X whose offer was rejected at the previous stage and for whom some Y is acceptable proposes to her top-ranked Y out of those who have not rejected an offer from her.

2. Each Y rejects the proposal of any X who is unacceptable to her, is "engaged" to the X she likes best in the set consisting of all those who proposed to her and the one (if any) to whom she was previously engaged, and rejects all other proposals.

The procedure stops when the proposal of no X is rejected or when every X whose offer was rejected has run out of acceptable Ys.

Consider, for example, the preferences in Figure 263.1. The progress of the procedure is shown in Figure 265.1, in which "$\to$" stands for "proposes to". First x_1 proposes to y_2, and both x_2 and x_3 propose to y_1; y_1 rejects x_2's proposal. Then x_2 proposes to y_2, so that y_2 may choose between x_2 and x_1 (with whom she was tentatively matched at the first stage). Player y_2 chooses x_2, and rejects x_1, who then proposes to y_1. Player y_1 now chooses between x_1 and x_3 (with whom she was tentatively matched at the first stage), and rejects x_3. Finally, x_3 proposes to y_2, who rejects her offer. The final matching is thus (x_1, y_1), (x_2, y_2), x_3 (alone), and y_3 (alone).

	Stage 1	Stage 2	Stage 3	Stage 4
x_1:	$\to y_2$	Reject $\to y_1$		
x_2:	$\to y_1$	Reject $\to y_2$		
x_3:	$\to y_1$		Reject $\to y_2$ Reject	

Figure 265.1 The progress of the deferred acceptance procedure with proposals by Xs when the players' preferences are those given in Figure 263.1. Each row gives the proposals of one X.

For any preferences, the procedure eventually stops, because there are finitely many players. To show that the matching μ it produces is in the core, we need to consider deviations by coalitions of only one or two players, by an earlier argument.

- No single player may improve upon μ because no X ever proposes to an unacceptable Y, and every Y always rejects every unacceptable X.

- Consider a coalition $\{i, j\}$ of two players, where i is an X and j is a Y. If i prefers j to $\mu(i)$, she must have proposed to j, and been rejected, before proposing to $\mu(i)$. The fact that j rejected her proposal means that j obtained a more desirable proposal. Thus j prefers $\mu(j)$ to i, so that $\{i, j\}$ cannot improve upon μ.

The analogous procedure in which proposals are made by Ys generates a matching in the core, by the same argument. For some preferences the matchings produced by the two procedures are the same, whereas for others they are different.

? EXERCISE 265.1 (Deferred acceptance procedure with proposals by Ys) Find the matching produced by the deferred acceptance procedure with proposals by Ys for the preferences given in Figure 263.1.

In particular, the core may contain more than one matching. It can be shown that the matching generated by the deferred acceptance procedure with proposals by Xs yields each X her most preferred partner among all her partners in matchings in the core, and yields each Y her least preferred partner among all her partners in matchings in the core. Similarly, the matching generated by the deferred acceptance procedure with proposals by Ys yields each Y her most preferred partner among all her partners in matchings in the core, and yields each X her least preferred partner among all her partners in matchings in the core.

? EXERCISE 266.1 (Example of deferred acceptance procedure) Find the matchings produced by the deferred acceptance procedure both with proposals by Xs and with proposals by Ys for the preferences given in Figure 266.1. Verify the results in the previous paragraph. (Argue that the only matchings in the core are the two generated by the procedures.)

x_1	x_2	x_3	y_1	y_2	y_3
y_1	y_1	y_1	x_1	x_1	x_1
y_2	y_2	y_3	x_2	x_3	x_2
y_3	y_3	y_2	x_3	x_2	x_3

Figure 266.1 The players' preferences in the game in Exercise 266.1.

In summary, every two-sided one-to-one matching game has a nonempty core, which contains the matching generated by each deferred acceptance procedure. The matching generated by the procedure is the best one in the core for each player on the side making proposals, and the worst one in the core for each player on the other side. (An implication is that if the two procedures generate the same matching, then, given that every person's preferences are strict, the core contains a single matching.)

8.7.3   Variants

Strategic behavior   So far, I have considered the deferred acceptance procedures only as algorithms that an administrator who *knows* the participants' preferences may use to find matchings in the core. Suppose the participants' preferences are *not* known. We may use the tools developed in Chapter 2 to study whether the participants' interests are served by revealing their true preferences. Consider the strategic game in which each player names a ranking of her possible partners and the outcome is the matching produced by the deferred acceptance procedure with proposals by Xs, given the announced rankings. One can show that in this game each Xs naming her true ranking is a dominant action, and although in a Nash equilibrium the actions of the Ys may *not* be their true rankings, the Nash equilibrium is in the core of the coalitional game defined by the players' *true* rankings. (I omit an argument for this result.)

? EXERCISE 267.1 (Strategic behavior under a deferred acceptance procedure) Consider the preferences in Figure 267.1. Find the matchings produced by the deferred acceptance procedures, and show that the core contains no other matchings. Consider the strategic game described in the previous paragraph that is induced by the procedure with proposals by X's. Take as given that each X's naming her true ranking is a dominant strategy. Show that the game has a Nash equilibrium in which y_1 names the ranking (x_1, x_2, x_3) and every other player names her true ranking.

x_1	x_2	x_3	y_1	y_2	y_3
y_2	y_1	y_1	x_1	x_3	x_1
y_1	y_3	y_2	x_3	x_1	x_3
y_3	y_2	y_3	x_2	x_2	x_2

Figure 267.1 The players' preferences in the game in Exercise 267.1.

Other matching problems I motivated the topic of matching by citing the problems of matching applicants with universities, workers with firms, and football players with teams. All these problems are many-to-one rather than one-to-one. Under mild assumptions about the players' preferences, the results I have presented for one-to-one matching games hold, with minor changes, for many-to-one matching games. In particular, the strong core (defined on page 259) is nonempty, and a variant of the deferred acceptance procedure generates matchings in it.

At this point you may suspect that the nonemptiness of the core in matching games is a very general result. If so, the next exercise shows that your suspicion is incorrect—at least, if "very general" includes the "roommate problem".

? EXERCISE 267.2 (Empty core in roommate problem) An even number of people has to be split into pairs; any person may be matched with any other person. (The matching problem is "one-sided".) Consider an example in which there are four people, i, j, k, and ℓ. Show that if the preferences of i, j, and k are those given in Figure 267.2, then for any preferences of ℓ the core is empty. (Notice that ℓ is the least favorite roommate of every other player.)

i	j	k
j	k	i
k	i	j
ℓ	ℓ	ℓ

Figure 267.2 The preferences of players i, j, and k in the game in Exercise 267.2.

? EXERCISE 267.3 (Spatial preferences in roommate problem) An even number of people has to be split into pairs, to be assigned to rooms. Each person's characteristic is a number; no two characteristics are the same. Each person would like to have a roommate whose characteristic is as close as possible to her own, and prefers to be matched even with the player whose characteristic is most remote from hers to remaining single. Find the set of matchings in the core.

MATCHING DOCTORS WITH HOSPITALS

Around 1900, newly trained doctors in the United States were, for the first time, given the option of working as "interns" (now called "residents") in hospitals, to gain experience in clinical medicine. Initially, hospitals advertised positions, for which newly trained doctors applied. The number of positions exceeded the supply of doctors, and the intense competition between hospitals for interns led the date at which agreements were finalized to get progressively earlier. By 1944, student doctors were finalizing agreements two full years before their internships were to begin. Making agreements at such an early date was undesirable for hospitals, because at that point they lacked extensive information about the students.

The American Association of Medical Colleges attempted to solve the problem by having its members agree not to release any information about students before the end of the third year (of a four-year program). This change prevented hospitals from making earlier appointments, but in doing so brought to the fore the problem of coordinating offers and acceptances. Hospitals wanted their first-choice students to accept quickly, but students wanted to delay as much as possible, hoping to receive better offers. In 1945, hospitals agreed to give students 10 days to consider offers. But there was pressure to reduce this period. In 1949 a 12-hour period was rejected by the American Hospital Association as too long; it was agreed that all offers be made at 12:01 A.M. on November 15, and hospitals could insist on a response within any period. Forcing students to make decisions without having a chance to collect offers from hospitals whose first-choice students had rejected them obviously led to inefficient matches.

These difficulties with efficiently matching doctors with hospitals led to the design of a centralized matching procedure that combines hospitals' rankings of students and students' rankings of hospitals to produce an assignment of students to hospitals. It can be shown that this procedure, designed ten years before game-theoretic work on the deferred acceptance procedure, generates a matching in the core for any stated preferences! It differs from the natural generalization of the deferred acceptance procedure to a many-to-one matching problem, but generates precisely the same matching, namely the one in the core that is best for the hospitals. (The originators of the deferred acceptance procedure, David Gale and Lloyd S. Shapley, and the designers of the student–hospital matching procedure were not aware of each other's work until the mid-1970s, when a physician heard Gale speak on his work.)

In the early years of operation of the procedure, over 95% of students and hospitals participated. In the mid-1970s the participation rate fell to around 85%. Many nonparticipants were married couples who wished to obtain positions in the same city. The matching procedure contained a mechanism for dealing with married couples, but, unlike the mechanism for single students, it could lead to a matching upon which some couple could improve. The difficulty is serious: when couples exist who restrict themselves to accepting positions in the same city, for some preferences the core of the resulting game is empty—no matching is stable.

Further problems arose. In the 1990s, associations of medical students began to argue that changes were needed because the procedure was favorable to hospitals, and possibilities for strategic behavior on the part of students existed. The game theorist Alvin E. Roth was retained by the National Resident Matching Program to design a new procedure to generate stable matchings that are as favorable as possible to applicants. The new procedure was first used in 1998, when it matched around 20,000 new doctors with hospitals.

8.8 Discussion: other solution concepts

In replacing the requirement of a Nash equilibrium that no individual player may profitably deviate with the requirement that no *group* of players may profitably deviate, the notion of the core makes an assumption that is unnecessary in the interpretation of a Nash equilibrium. A single player who deviates from an action profile in a strategic game can be *sure* of her deviant action because she unilaterally chooses it. But a member of a group of players who chooses a deviant action must assume that no subgroup of her comrades will deviate further, or, at least, that she will remain better off if they do.

Consider, for example, the three-player majority game (Example 240.3 and Exercise 245.1). The action $(\frac{1}{2}, \frac{1}{2}, 0)$ of the grand coalition in this game is not in the core because, for example, the coalition consisting of players 1 and 3 can take an action that gives player 1 an amount x with $\frac{1}{2} < x < 1$ and player 3 the amount $1 - x$, which leads to the payoff profile $(x, 0, 1 - x)$. But this profile itself is not stable—the coalition consisting of players 2 and 3, for example, has an action that generates the payoff profile $(0, y, 1 - y)$, where $0 < y < x$, in which both of them are better off than they are in $(x, 0, 1 - x)$. The fact that player 3 will be tempted by an offer of player 2 to deviate from $(x, 0, 1 - x)$ may dampen player 1's enthusiasm for joining player 3 in the deviation from $(\frac{1}{2}, \frac{1}{2}, 0)$. For similar reasons, player 2 may be reluctant to join in a deviation from this action.

Several solution concepts that take into account these considerations have been suggested (see, for example, Osborne and Rubinstein 1994, Chapter 14), though none has so far had anything like the success of the core in illuminating social and economic phenomena.

Notes

The notion of a coalitional game is due to von Neumann and Morgenstern (1944). Shapley and Shubik (1953), Luce and Raiffa (1957, 234–235), and Aumann and Peleg (1960) generalized von Neumann and Morgenstern's notion. The notion of the core was introduced in the early 1950s by Gillies as a tool to study another solution concept (his work is published in Gillies 1959); Shapley and Shubik developed it as a solution concept.

Edgeworth (1881, 35–39) pointed out a connection between the competitive equilibria of a market model and the set of outcomes we now call the core. Von Neumann and Morgenstern (1944, 583–584) first suggested modeling markets as coalitional games; Shubik (1959a) recognized the game-theoretic content of Edgeworth's arguments and, together with Shapley (1959), developed the analysis. Section 8.3 is based on Shapley and Shubik (1967). The core of the market studied in Section 8.4 was first studied by Shapley and Shubik (1971/72). My discussion owes a debt to Moulin (1995, Section 2.3).

The model and result on the nonemptiness of the core in Section 8.5 are due to Shapley and Scarf (1974), who credit David Gale with the top trading cycle procedure. The result that the strong core contains a single action is due to Roth and Postlewaite (1977). The model is discussed in detail by Moulin (1995, Section 3.2).

Voting behavior in committees (Section 8.6) was first studied formally by Black (1958) (written in the mid-1940s), Black and Newing (1951), and Arrow (1951). Black used the core as the solution (before it had been defined generally) and established the median voter theorem (Exercise 261.1). He also noticed that in policy spaces of dimension greater than 1, a Condorcet winner is not likely to exist, a result extended by Plott (1967) and refined by Banks (1995) and others, who find conditions relating the number of voters, the dimension of the policy space, and the value of q for which the core of the q-rule game is generally empty; see Austen-Smith and Banks (1999, Secton 6.1) for details.

The model and main results in Section 8.7 are due to Gale and Shapley (1962). The result about the strategic properties of the deferred acceptance procedures at the end of the section is a combination of results due to Dubins and Freedman (1981) and Roth (1982), and to Roth (1984a). Exercise 267.1 is based on an example in Moulin (1995, 113 and 116). Exercise 267.2 is taken from Gale and Shapley (1962, Example 3). For a comprehensive presentation of results on two-sided matching, see Roth and Sotomayor (1990). The box on page 268 is based on Roth (1984b), Roth and Sotomayor (1990, Section 5.4), and Roth and Peranson (1999).

II   Games with Imperfect Information

9   Bayesian Games   273

10   Extensive Games with Imperfect Information   313

9 Bayesian Games

9.1 Motivational examples 273
9.2 General definitions 278
9.3 Two examples concerning information 282
9.4 Illustration: Cournot's duopoly game with imperfect information 285
9.5 Illustration: providing a public good 289
9.6 Illustration: auctions 291
9.7 Illustration: juries 301
9.8 Appendix: auctions with an arbitrary distribution of valuations 307
Prerequisite: Chapter 2 and Section 4.1.3; Section 9.7 requires Chapter 4

AN ASSUMPTION underlying the notion of Nash equilibrium is that each player holds the correct belief about the other players' actions. To do so, a player must know the game she is playing; in particular, she must know the other players' preferences. In many situations the participants are not perfectly informed about their opponents' characteristics: bargainers may not know each others' valuations of the object of negotiation, firms may not know each others' cost functions, combatants may not know each others' strengths, and jurors may not know their colleagues' interpretations of the evidence in a trial. In some situations, a participant may be well informed about her opponents' characteristics, but may not know how well these opponents are informed about her own characteristics. In this chapter I describe the model of a "Bayesian game", which generalizes the notion of a strategic game to allow us to analyze any situation in which each player is imperfectly informed about an aspect of her environment that is relevant to her choice of an action.

9.1 Motivational examples

I start with two examples that illustrate the main ideas in the model of a Bayesian game. I define the notion of Nash equilibrium separately for each game. In the next section I define the general model of a Bayesian game and the notion of Nash equilibrium for such a game.

◆ EXAMPLE 273.1 (Variant of *BoS* with imperfect information) Consider a variant of the situation modeled by *BoS* (Figure 19.1) in which player 1 is unsure whether

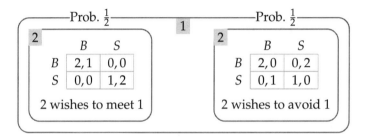

Figure 274.1 A variant of *BoS* in which player 1 is unsure whether player 2 wants to meet her or to avoid her. The frame labeled 2 enclosing each table indicates that player 2 knows the relevant table. The frame labeled 1 enclosing both tables indicates that player 1 does not know the relevant table; the probabilities she assigns to the two tables appear on the frame.

player 2 prefers to go out with her or prefers to avoid her, whereas player 2, as before, knows player 1's preferences. Specifically, suppose player 1 thinks that with probability $\frac{1}{2}$ player 2 wants to got out with her, and with probability $\frac{1}{2}$ player 2 wants to avoid her. (Presumably this assessment comes from player 1's experience: half of the time she is involved in this situation she faces a player who wants to go out with her, and half of the time she faces a player who wants to avoid her.) That is, player 1 thinks that with probability $\frac{1}{2}$ she is playing the game on the left of Figure 274.1 and with probability $\frac{1}{2}$ she is playing the game on the right. Because probabilities are involved, an analysis of the situation requires us to know the players' preferences over lotteries, even if we are interested only in pure strategy equilibria; thus the numbers in the tables are Bernoulli payoffs.

We can think of there being two *states*, one in which the players' Bernoulli payoffs are given in the left table and one in which these payoffs are given in the right table. Player 2 knows the state—she knows whether she wishes to meet or avoid player 1—whereas player 1 does not; player 1 assigns probability $\frac{1}{2}$ to each state.

The notion of Nash equilibrium for a strategic game models a steady state in which each player's beliefs about the other players' actions are correct, and each player acts optimally, given her beliefs. We wish to generalize this notion to the current situation.

From player 1's point of view, player 2 has two possible *types*, one whose preferences are given in the left table of Figure 274.1 and one whose preferences are given in the right table. Player 1 does not know player 2's type, so to choose an action rationally she needs to form a belief about the action of each type. Given these beliefs and her belief about the likelihood of each type, she can calculate her expected payoff to each of her actions. For example, if she thinks that the type who wishes to meet her will choose *B* and the type who wishes to avoid her will choose *S*, then she thinks that *B* will yield her a payoff of 2 with probability $\frac{1}{2}$ and a payoff of 0 with probability $\frac{1}{2}$, so that her expected payoff is $\frac{1}{2} \cdot 2 + \frac{1}{2} \cdot 0 = 1$, and *S* will yield her an expected payoff of $\frac{1}{2} \cdot 0 + \frac{1}{2} \cdot 1 = \frac{1}{2}$. Similar calculations for the other combinations of actions for the two types of player 2 yield the expected payoffs in Figure 275.1. Each column of the table is a pair of actions for the two types of

	(B, B)	(B, S)	(S, B)	(S, S)
B	2	1	1	0
S	0	$\frac{1}{2}$	$\frac{1}{2}$	1

Figure 275.1 The expected payoffs of player 1 for the four possible pairs of actions of the two types of player 2 in Example 273.1. Each row corresponds to an action of player 1, and each column corresponds to a pair of actions of the two types of player 2; the action of the type who wishes to meet player 1 is listed first.

player 2, the first member of each pair being the action of the type who wishes to meet player 1 and the second member being the action of the type who wishes to avoid player 1.

For this situation we define a pure strategy *Nash equilibrium* to be a triple of actions, one for player 1 and one for each type of player 2, with the property that

- the action of player 1 is optimal, given the actions of the two types of player 2 (and player 1's belief about the state)
- the action of each type of player 2 is optimal, given the action of player 1.

That is, we treat the two types of player 2 as separate players and analyze the situation as a three-player strategic game in which player 1's payoffs as a function of the actions of the two other players (i.e. the two types of player 2) are given in Figure 275.1, and the payoff of each type of player 2 is independent of the actions of the other type and depends on the action of player 1 as given in the tables in Figure 274.1 (the left table for the type who wishes to meet player 1, and the right table for the type who wishes to avoid player 1). In a Nash equilibrium, player 1's action is a best response in Figure 275.1 to the pair of actions of the two types of player 2, the action of the type of player 2 who wishes to meet player 1 is a best response in the left table of Figure 274.1 to the action of player 1, and the action of the type of player 2 who wishes to avoid player 1 is a best response in the right table of Figure 274.1 to the action of player 1.

Why should player 2, who knows whether she wants to meet or avoid player 1, have to plan what to do in both cases? She does not have to do so! But we, as analysts, need to consider what she would do in both cases. The reason is that to determine her best action, player 1, who does not know player 2's type, needs to form a belief about the action each type would take, and we wish to impose the equilibrium condition that these beliefs be correct, in the sense that for each type of player 2 they specify a best response to player 1's equilibrium action. Thus the equilibrium action of player 2 for each of her possible types may be interpreted as player 1's (correct) belief about the action that each type of player 2 would take, not as a plan of action for player 2.

I claim that $(B, (B, S))$, where the first component is the action of player 1 and the other component is the pair of actions of the two types of player 2, is a Nash equilibrium. Given that the actions of the two types of player 2 are (B, S), player 1's action B is optimal, from Figure 275.1; given that player 1 chooses B, B is optimal for the type who wishes to meet player 2 and S is optimal for the type who wishes to avoid player 2, from Figure 274.1. Suppose that in fact player 2 wishes to meet player 1. Then we interpret the equilibrium as follows. Both player 1 and player 2 choose B; player 1, who does not know if player 2 wants to meet her or avoid her, believes that if player 2 wishes to meet her she will choose B, and if she wishes to avoid her she will choose S.

? EXERCISE 276.1 (Equilibria of a variant of *BoS* with imperfect information) Show that there is no pure strategy Nash equilibrium of this game in which player 1 chooses S. If you have studied mixed strategy Nash equilibrium (Chapter 4), find the mixed strategy Nash equilibria of the game. (First check whether there is an equilibrium in which both types of player 2 use pure strategies; then look for equilibria in which one or both of these types randomize.)

We can interpret the actions of the two types of player 2 to reflect player 2's intentions in the hypothetical situation *before* she knows the state. We can tell the following story. Initially player 2 does not know the state; she is informed of the state by a *signal* that depends on the state. Before receiving this signal, she plans an action for each possible signal. After receiving the signal she carries out her planned action for that signal. We can tell a similar story for player 1. To be consistent with her not knowing the state when she takes an action, her signal must be uninformative: it must be the same in each state. Given her signal, she is unsure of the state; when choosing an action she takes into account her belief about the likelihood of each state, given her signal. The framework of states, beliefs, and signals, which is unnecessarily baroque in this simple example, comes into its own in the analysis of more complex situations.

◆ EXAMPLE 276.2 (Variant of *BoS* with imperfect information) Consider another variant of the situation modeled by *BoS*, in which neither player knows whether the other wants to go out with her. Specifically, suppose that player 1 thinks that with probability $\frac{1}{2}$ player 2 wants to go out with her, and with probability $\frac{1}{2}$ player 2 wants to avoid her, and player 2 thinks that with probability $\frac{2}{3}$ player 1 wants to go out with her and with probability $\frac{1}{3}$ player 1 wants to avoid her. As before, assume that each player knows her own preferences.

We can model this situation by introducing four states, one for each of the possible configurations of preferences. I refer to these states as yy (each player wants to go out with the other), yn (player 1 wants to go out with player 2, but player 2 wants to avoid player 1), ny, and nn.

The fact that player 1 does not know player 2's preferences means that she cannot distinguish between states yy and yn, or between states ny and nn. Similarly, player 2 cannot distinguish between states yy and ny, and between states yn and nn. We can model the players' information by assuming that each player receives a *signal* before choosing an action. Player 1 receives the same signal, say y_1, in states yy and yn, and a different signal, say n_1, in states ny and nn; player 2 receives the same signal, say y_2, in states yy and ny, and a different signal, say n_2, in states yn and nn. After player 1 receives the signal y_1, she is referred to as *type* y_1

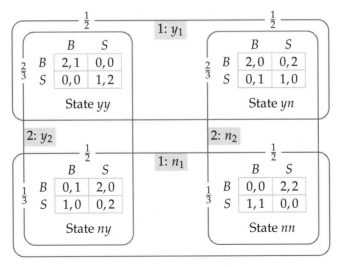

Figure 277.1 A variant of *BoS* in which each player is unsure of the other player's preferences. The frame labeled *i*: *x* encloses the states that generate the signal *x* for player *i*; the numbers appearing over this frame next to each table are the probabilities assigned by type *x* of player *i* to each state she regards to be possible.

of player 1 (who wishes to go out with player 2); after she receives the signal n_1 she is referred to as *type n_1* of player 1 (who wishes to avoid player 2). Similarly, player 2 has two *types*, y_2 and n_2.

Type y_1 of player 1 believes that the probability of each of the states yy and yn is $\frac{1}{2}$; type n_1 of player 1 believes that the probability of each of the states ny and nn is $\frac{1}{2}$. Similarly, type y_2 of player 2 believes that the probability of state yy is $\frac{2}{3}$ and that of state ny is $\frac{1}{3}$; type n_2 of player 2 believes that the probability of state yn is $\frac{2}{3}$ and that of state nn is $\frac{1}{3}$. This model of the situation is illustrated in Figure 277.1.

As in Example 273.1, to study the equilibria of this model we consider the players' plans of action before they receive their signals. That is, each player plans an action for each of the two possible signals she may receive. We may think of there being four players: the two types of player 1 and the two types of player 2. A *Nash equilibrium* consists of four actions, one for each of these players, such that the action of each type of each original player is optimal, given her belief about the state after observing her signal, and given the actions of each type of the other original player.

Consider type y_1 of player 1. Her beliefs about the probabilities of states yy and yn and her payoffs in these states are the same as the beliefs and payoffs of player 1 for the two states in Example 273.1. Thus her expected payoffs for the four pairs of actions of the two types of player 2 are given in Figure 275.1, interpreting each column to represent a pair of actions of types y_2 and n_2 of player 2.

? EXERCISE 277.1 (Expected payoffs in a variant of *BoS* with imperfect information) Construct tables like the one in Figure 275.1 for type n_1 of player 1, and for types y_2 and n_2 of player 2.

I claim that $((B, B), (B, S))$ and $((S, B), (S, S))$ are Nash equilibria of the game, where in each case the first component gives the actions of the two types of player 1 and the second component gives the actions of the two types of player 2. You may use Figure 275.1 to verify that B is a best response of type y_1 of player 1 to the pair (B, S) of actions of player 2, and S is a best response to the pair of actions (S, S). You may use your answer to Exercise 277.1 to verify that in each of the claimed Nash equilibria the action of type n_1 of player 1 and the action of each type of player 2 is a best response to the other players' actions.

In each of these examples a Nash equilibrium is a list of actions, one for each type of each player, such that the action of each type of each player is a best response to the actions of all the types of the other player, given the player's beliefs about the state after she observes her signal. The actions planned by the various types of player i are not relevant to the decision problem of any type of player i, but there is no harm in taking them, as well as the actions of the types of the *other* player, as given when player i is choosing an action. Thus we may define a Nash equilibrium in each example to be a Nash equilibrium of the strategic game in which the set of players is the set of all types of all players in the original situation.

In the next section I define the general notion of a Bayesian game and the notion of Nash equilibrium in such a game. These definitions require significant theoretical development. If you find the theory in the next section heavy going, you may be able to skim the section and then study the subsequent illustrations, relying on the intuition developed in the examples in this section, and returning to the theory only as necessary for clarification.

9.2 General definitions

9.2.1 Bayesian games

A strategic game with imperfect information is called a "Bayesian game". (The reason for this nomenclature will become apparent.) As in a strategic game, the decision-makers are called *players*, and each player is endowed with a set of *actions*.

A key component in the specification of the imperfect information is the set of *states*. Each state is a complete description of one collection of the players' relevant characteristics, including both their preferences and their information. For every collection of characteristics that some player believes to be possible, there must be a state. For instance, suppose in Example 273.1 that player 2 wishes to meet player 1. In this case, the reason for including in the model the state in which player 2 wishes to avoid player 1 is that player 1 believes such a preference to be possible.

At the start of the game a state is realized. The players do not observe this state. Rather, each player receives a *signal* that may give her some information about the state. Denote the signal player i receives in state ω by $\tau_i(\omega)$. The function τ_i is called player i's *signal function*. (Note that the signal is a *deterministic* function of the state: for each state, a definite signal is received.) The states that generate any given signal t_i are said to be *consistent* with t_i. The sizes of the sets of states consistent with each of player i's signals reflect the quality of player i's information. If, for example, $\tau_i(\omega)$ is different for each value of ω, then player i knows, given her signal, the state that has occurred; after receiving her signal, she is perfectly informed about all the players' relevant characteristics. At the other extreme, if $\tau_i(\omega)$ is the same for all states, then player i's signal conveys no information about the state. If $\tau_i(\omega)$ is constant over some subsets of the set of states, but is not the same for all states, then player i's signal conveys partial information. For example, if there are three states, ω_1, ω_2, and ω_3, and $\tau_i(\omega_1) \neq \tau_i(\omega_2) = \tau_i(\omega_3)$, then when the state is ω_1 player i knows that it is ω_1, whereas when it is either ω_2 or ω_3 she knows only that it is one of these two states. (In Figures 274.1 and 277.1, each frame encloses a set of states that yield the same signal for one of the players.)

We refer to player i in the event that she receives the signal t_i as *type t_i* of player i. Each type of each player holds a *belief* about the likelihood of the states consistent with her signal. If, for example, $t_i = \tau_i(\omega_1) = \tau_i(\omega_2)$, then type t_i of player i assigns probabilities to ω_1 and ω_2. (A player who receives a signal consistent with only one state naturally assigns probability 1 to that state.)

Each player may care about the actions chosen by the other players, as in a strategic game with perfect information, and also about the state. The players may be uncertain about the state, so we need to specify their preferences regarding probability distributions over pairs (a, ω) consisting of an action profile a and a state ω. I assume that each player's preferences over such probability distributions are represented by the expected value of a *Bernoulli payoff function*. Thus I specify each player i's preferences by giving a Bernoulli payoff function u_i over pairs (a, ω). (Note that in Examples 273.1 and 276.2, both players care only about the other player's action, not independently about the state.)

In summary, a Bayesian game is defined as follows.

▶ DEFINITION 279.1 (*Bayesian game*) A **Bayesian game** consists of

- a set of **players**
- a set of **states**

and for each player

- a set of **actions**
- a set of **signals** that she may receive and a **signal function** that associates a signal with each state
- for each signal that she may receive, a **belief** about the states consistent with the signal (a probability distribution over the set of states with which the signal is associated)
- a **Bernoulli payoff function** over pairs (a, ω), where a is an action profile and ω is a state, the expected value of which represents the player's preferences among lotteries over the set of such pairs.

Note that the set of actions of each player is independent of the state. Each player may care about the state, but the set of actions available to her is the same in every state.

The eponymous Thomas Bayes (1702–61) first showed how probabilities should be changed in the light of new information. His formula (discussed in Section 17.6.5) is needed when one works with a variant of Definition 279.1 in which each player is endowed with a "prior" belief about the states, from which the belief of each of her types is derived. For the purposes of this chapter, the belief of each type of each player is more conveniently taken as a primitive, rather than being derived from a prior belief.

The game in Example 273.1 fits into this general definition as follows.

Players The pair of people.

States The set of states is $\{meet, avoid\}$.

Actions The set of actions of each player is $\{B, S\}$.

Signals Player 1 may receive a single signal, say z; her signal function τ_1 satisfies $\tau_1(meet) = \tau_1(avoid) = z$. Player 2 receives one of two signals, say m and v; her signal function τ_2 satisfies $\tau_2(meet) = m$ and $\tau_2(avoid) = v$.

Beliefs Player 1 assigns probability $\frac{1}{2}$ to each state after receiving the signal z. Player 2 assigns probability 1 to the state *meet* after receiving the signal m, and probability 1 to the state *avoid* after receiving the signal v.

Payoffs The payoffs $u_i(a, meet)$ of each player i for all possible action pairs are given in the left panel of Figure 274.1, and the payoffs $u_i(a, avoid)$ are given in the right panel.

Similarly, the game in Example 276.2 fits into the definition as follows.

Players The pair of people.

States The set of states is $\{yy, yn, ny, nn\}$.

Actions The set of actions of each player is $\{B, S\}$.

Signals Player 1 receives one of two signals, y_1 and n_1; her signal function τ_1 satisfies $\tau_1(yy) = \tau_1(yn) = y_1$ and $\tau_1(ny) = \tau_1(nn) = n_1$. Player 2 receives one of two signals, y_2 and n_2; her signal function τ_2 satisfies $\tau_2(yy) = \tau_2(ny) = y_2$ and $\tau_2(yn) = \tau_2(nn) = n_2$.

Beliefs Player 1 assigns probability $\frac{1}{2}$ to each of the states yy and yn after receiving the signal y_1 and probability $\frac{1}{2}$ to each of the states ny and nn after receiving the signal n_1. Player 2 assigns probability $\frac{2}{3}$ to the state yy and probability $\frac{1}{3}$ to the state ny after receiving the signal y_2, and probability $\frac{2}{3}$ to the state yn and probability $\frac{1}{3}$ to the state nn after receiving the signal n_2.

Payoffs The payoffs $u_i(a, \omega)$ of each player i for all possible action pairs and states are given in Figure 277.1.

9.2.2   Nash equilibrium

In a strategic game, each player chooses an action. In a Bayesian game, each player chooses a collection of actions, one for each signal she may receive. That is, in a Bayesian game *each type of each player* chooses an action. In a Nash equilibrium of such a game, the action chosen by each type of each player is optimal, given the actions chosen by every type of every other player. (In a steady state, each player's experience teaches her these actions.) Any given type of player i is not affected by the actions chosen by the other types of player i, so there is no harm in thinking that player i takes as given these actions, as well as those of the other players. Thus we may define a Nash equilibrium of a Bayesian game to be a Nash equilibrium of a strategic game in which each player is one of the types of one of the players in the Bayesian game. What is each player's payoff function in this strategic game?

Consider type t_i of player i. For each state ω she knows every other player's type (i.e. she knows the signal received by every other player). This information, together with her belief about the states, allows her to calculate her expected payoff for each of her actions and each collection of actions for the various types of the other players. For instance, in Example 273.1, player 1's belief is that the probability of each state is $\frac{1}{2}$, and she knows that player 2 is type m in the state *meet* and type v in the state *avoid*. Thus if type m of player 2 chooses B and type v of player 2 chooses S, player 1 thinks that if she chooses B then her expected payoff is

$$\tfrac{1}{2}u_1((B,B), meet) + \tfrac{1}{2}u_1((B,S), avoid),$$

where u_1 is her payoff function in the Bayesian game. (In general her payoff may depend on the state, though in this example it does not.) The top box of the second column in Figure 275.1 gives this payoff; the other boxes give player 1's payoffs for her other action and the other combinations of actions for the two types of player 2.

In a general game, denote the probability assigned by the belief of type t_i of player i to state ω by $\Pr(\omega \mid t_i)$. Denote the action taken by each type t_j of each player j by $a(j, t_j)$. Player j's signal in state ω is $\tau_j(\omega)$, so her action in this state is $a(j, \tau_j(\omega))$. For each state ω and each player j, let $\hat{a}_j(\omega) = a(j, \tau_j(\omega))$. Then the expected payoff of type t_i of player i when she chooses the action a_i is

$$\sum_{\omega \in \Omega} \Pr(\omega \mid t_i) u_i((a_i, \hat{a}_{-i}(\omega)), \omega), \tag{281.1}$$

where Ω is the set of states and $(a_i, \hat{a}_{-i}(\omega))$ is the action profile in which player i chooses the action a_i and every other player j chooses $\hat{a}_j(\omega)$. (Note that this expected payoff does not depend on the actions of any other types of player i, but only on the actions of the various types of the *other* players.)

We may now define precisely a Nash equilibrium of a Bayesian game.

▶ DEFINITION 281.2 (*Nash equilibrium of Bayesian game*) A **Nash equilibrium of a Bayesian game** is a Nash equilibrium of the strategic game (with vNM preferences) defined as follows.

Players The set of all pairs (i, t_i) in which i is a player in the Bayesian game and t_i is one of the signals that i may receive.

Actions The set of actions of each player (i, t_i) is the set of actions of player i in the Bayesian game.

Preferences The Bernoulli payoff function of each player (i, t_i) is given by (281.1).

⊘ EXERCISE 282.1 (Fighting an opponent of unknown strength) Two people are involved in a dispute. Person 1 does not know whether person 2 is strong or weak; she assigns probability α to person 2's being strong. Person 2 is fully informed. Each person can either fight or yield. Each person's preferences are represented by the expected value of a Bernoulli payoff function that assigns the payoff of 0 if she yields (regardless of the other person's action) and a payoff of 1 if she fights and her opponent yields; if both people fight, then their payoffs are $(-1, 1)$ if person 2 is strong and $(1, -1)$ if person 2 is weak. Formulate this situation as a Bayesian game and find its Nash equilibria if $\alpha < \frac{1}{2}$ and if $\alpha > \frac{1}{2}$.

⊘ EXERCISE 282.2 (An exchange game) Each of two individuals receives a ticket on which there is an integer from 1 to m indicating the size of a prize she may receive. The individuals' tickets are assigned randomly and independently; the probability of an individual's receiving each possible number is positive. Each individual is given the option of exchanging her prize for the other individual's prize; the individuals are given this option simultaneously. If both individuals wish to exchange, then the prizes are exchanged; otherwise each individual receives her own prize. Each individual's objective is to maximize her expected monetary payoff. Model this situation as a Bayesian game and show that in any Nash equilibrium the highest prize that either individual is willing to exchange is the smallest possible prize.

⊘ EXERCISE 282.3 (Adverse selection) Firm A (the "acquirer") is considering taking over firm T (the "target"). It does not know firm T's value; it believes that this value, when firm T is controlled by its own management, is at least \$0 and at most \$100, and assigns equal probability to each of the 101 dollar values in this range. Firm T will be worth 50% more under firm A's management than it is under its own management. Suppose that firm A bids y to take over firm T, and firm T is worth x (under its own management). Then if T accepts A's offer, A's payoff is $\frac{3}{2}x - y$ and T's payoff is y; if T rejects A's offer, A's payoff is 0 and T's payoff is x. Model this situation as a Bayesian game in which firm A chooses how much to offer and firm T decides the lowest offer to accept. Find the Nash equilibrium (equilibria?) of this game. Explain why the logic behind the equilibrium is called *adverse selection*.

9.3 Two examples concerning information

The notion of a Bayesian game may be used to study how information patterns affect the outcome of strategic interaction. Here are two examples.

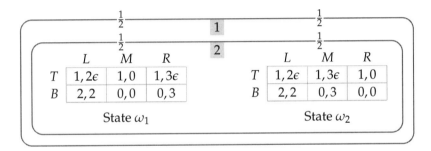

Figure 283.1 The first Bayesian game considered in Section 9.3.1.

9.3.1 More information may hurt

A decision-maker in a single-person decision problem cannot be worse off if she has more information: if she wishes, she can ignore the information. In a game the same is not true: if a player has more information and the other players know that she has more information, then she may be worse off.

Consider, for example, the two-player Bayesian game in Figure 283.1, where $0 < \epsilon < \frac{1}{2}$. In this game there are two states, and neither player knows the state. Player 2's unique best response to each action of player 1 is L. (If player 1 chooses T, L yields 2ϵ, whereas M and R each yield $\frac{3}{2}\epsilon$; if player 1 chooses B, L yields 2, whereas M and R each yield $\frac{3}{2}$.) Further, player 1's unique best response to L is B. Thus (B, L) is the unique Nash equilibrium of the game; it yields each player a payoff of 2. (If you have studied Chapter 4, you will be able to verify that, moreover, the game has no other mixed strategy equilibrium.)

Now consider the variant of this game in which player 2 is informed of the state: player 2's signal function τ_2 satisfies $\tau_2(\omega_1) \neq \tau_2(\omega_2)$. In this game $(T, (R, M))$ is the unique Nash equilibrium. (Each type of player 2 has a strictly dominant action, to which T is player 1's unique best response.)

Player 2's payoff in the unique Nash equilibrium of the original game is 2, whereas her payoff in the unique Nash equilibrium of the game in which she knows the state is 3ϵ in each state. Thus she is worse off when she knows the state than when she does not. To understand this result, notice that among player 2's actions, R is good only in state ω_1, M is good only in state ω_2, and L is a compromise. When she does not know the state she chooses L, inducing player 1 to choose B. When she is fully informed she tailors her action to the state, choosing R in state ω_1 and M in state ω_2, inducing player 1 to choose T. The game has no steady state in which she ignores her information and chooses L because this action leads player 1 to choose B, making R better for player 2 in state ω_1 and M better in state ω_2.

9.3.2 Infection

The notion of a Bayesian game may be used to model not only situations in which players are uncertain about each others' preferences, but also situations in which they are uncertain about each others' *knowledge*. Consider, for example, the Bayesian game in Figure 284.1.

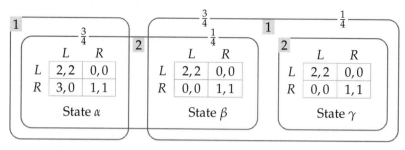

Figure 284.1 The first Bayesian game in Section 9.3.2. In the unique Nash equilibrium of this game, each type of each player chooses R.

Notice that player 2's preferences are the same in all three states, and player 1's preferences are the same in states β and γ. In particular, in state γ, each player knows the other player's preferences, and player 2 knows that player 1 knows her preferences. The shortcoming in the players' information in state γ is that player 1 does not know that player 2 knows her preferences: player 1 knows only that the state is either β or γ, and in state β player 2 does not know whether the state is α or β, and hence does not know player 1's preferences (because player 1's preferences in these two states differ).

This imperfection in player 1's knowledge of player 2's information significantly affects the equilibria of the game. If information were perfect in state γ, then both (L, L) and (R, R) would be Nash equilibria. However, the whole game has a *unique* Nash equilibrium, in which the outcome in state γ is (R, R), as you are asked to show in the next exercise. The argument shows that the incentives faced by player 1 in state α "infect" the remainder of the game.

? EXERCISE 284.1 (Infection) Show that the Bayesian game in Figure 284.1 has a unique Nash equilibrium, in which each player chooses R regardless of her signal. (Start by considering player 1's action in state α. Next consider player 2's action when she gets the signal that the state is α or β. Then consider player 1's action when she gets the signal that the state is β or γ. Finally consider player 2's action in state γ.)

Now extend the game as in Figure 285.1. Consider state δ. In this state, player 2 knows player 1's preferences (because she knows that the state is either γ or δ, and in both states player 1's preferences are the same). What player 2 does not know is whether player 1 knows that player 2 knows player 1's preferences. The reason is that player 2 does not know whether the state is γ or δ; and in state γ player 1 does not know that player 2 knows her preferences, because she does not know whether the state is β or γ, and in state β player 2 (who does not know whether the state is α or β) does not know her preferences. Thus the level of the shortcoming in the players' information is higher than it is in the game in Figure 284.1. Nevertheless, the incentives faced by player 1 in state α again "infect" the remainder of the game, and in the only Nash equilibrium every type of each player chooses R.

The game may be further extended. As it is extended, the level of the imperfection in the players' information in the last state increases. When the number of

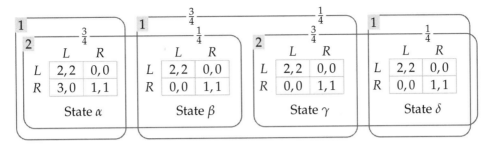

Figure 285.1 The second Bayesian game in Section 9.3.2.

states is large, the players' information in the last state is only very slightly imperfect. Nevertheless, the incentives of player 1 in state α still cause the game to have a unique Nash equilibrium, in which every type of each player chooses R.

In each of these examples, the equilibrium induces an outcome in every state that is worse for both players than another outcome (namely (L, L)); in all states but the first, the alternative outcome is a Nash equilibrium in the game with perfect information. For some other specifications of the payoffs in state α and the players' beliefs, the game has a unique equilibrium in which the "good" outcome (L, L) occurs in every state; the point is only that one of the two Nash equilibria is selected, not that the "bad" equilibrium is necessarily selected. (Modify the payoffs of player 1 in state α so that L strictly dominates R, and change the beliefs to assign probability $\frac{1}{2}$ to each state compatible with each signal.)

9.4 Illustration: Cournot's duopoly game with imperfect information

9.4.1 Imperfect information about cost

Two firms compete in selling a good; one firm does not know the other firm's cost function. How does this lack of information affect the firms' behavior?

Assume that both firms can produce the good at constant unit cost. Assume also that they both know that firm 1's unit cost is c, but only firm 2 knows its own unit cost; firm 1 believes that firm 2's cost is c_L with probability θ and c_H with probability $1 - \theta$, where $0 < \theta < 1$ and $c_L < c_H$.

We may model this situation as a Bayesian game that is a variant of Cournot's game (Section 3.1).

Players Firm 1 and firm 2.

States $\{L, H\}$.

Actions Each firm's set of actions is the set of its possible outputs (nonnegative numbers).

Signals Firm 1's signal function τ_1 satisfies $\tau_1(H) = \tau_1(L)$ (its signal is the same in both states); firm 2's signal function τ_2 satisfies $\tau_2(H) \neq \tau_2(L)$ (its signal is perfectly informative of the state).

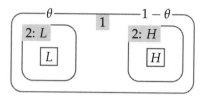

Figure 286.1 The information structure for the model in the variant of Cournot's model in Section 9.4.1, in which firm 1 does not know firm 2's cost. The frame labeled **2: x**, for $x = L$ and $x = H$, encloses the state that generates the signal x for firm 2.

Beliefs The single type of firm 1 assigns probability θ to state L and probability $1 - \theta$ to state H. Each type of firm 2 assigns probability 1 to the single state consistent with its signal.

Payoff functions The firms' Bernoulli payoffs are their profits; if the actions chosen are (q_1, q_2) and the state is I (either L or H), then firm 1's profit is $q_1(P(q_1 + q_2) - c)$ and firm 2's profit is $q_2(P(q_1 + q_2) - c_I)$, where $P(q_1 + q_2)$ is the market price when the firms' outputs are q_1 and q_2.

The information structure in this game is similar to that in Example 273.1; it is illustrated in Figure 286.1.

A Nash equilibrium of this game is a triple (q_1^*, q_L^*, q_H^*), where q_1^* is the output of firm 1, q_L^* is the output of type L of firm 2 (i.e. firm 2 when it receives the signal $\tau_2(L)$), and q_H^* is the output of type H of firm 2 (i.e. firm 2 when it receives the signal $\tau_2(H)$), such that

- q_1^* maximizes firm 1's profit given the output q_L^* of type L of firm 2 and the output q_H^* of type H of firm 2

- q_L^* maximizes the profit of type L of firm 2 given the output q_1^* of firm 1

- q_H^* maximizes the profit of type H of firm 2 given the output q_1^* of firm 1.

To find an equilibrium, we first find the firms' best response functions. Given firm 1's posterior beliefs, its best response $b_1(q_L, q_H)$ to (q_L, q_H) solves

$$\max_{q_1} \left[\theta(P(q_1 + q_L) - c)q_1 + (1 - \theta)(P(q_1 + q_H) - c)q_1 \right].$$

Firm 2's best response $b_L(q_1)$ to q_1 when its cost is c_L solves

$$\max_{q_L} \left[(P(q_1 + q_L) - c_L)q_L \right],$$

and its best response $b_H(q_1)$ to q_1 when its cost is c_H solves

$$\max_{q_H} \left[(P(q_1 + q_H) - c_H)q_H \right].$$

A Nash equilibrium is a triple (q_1^*, q_L^*, q_H^*) such that

$$q_1^* = b_1(q_L^*, q_H^*), \, q_L^* = b_L(q_1^*), \text{ and } q_H^* = b_H(q_1^*).$$

⑦ EXERCISE 287.1 (Cournot's duopoly game with imperfect information) Consider the game when the inverse demand function is given by $P(Q) = \alpha - Q$ for $Q \le \alpha$ and $P(Q) = 0$ for $Q > \alpha$ (see (56.2)). For values of c_H and c_L close enough that there is a Nash equilibrium in which all outputs are positive, find this equilibrium. Compare this equilibrium with the Nash equilibrium of the game in which firm 1 knows that firm 2's unit cost is c_L, and with the Nash equilibrium of the game in which firm 1 knows that firm 2's unit cost is c_H.

9.4.2 Imperfect information about both cost and information

Now suppose that firm 2 does not know whether firm 1 knows its cost. That is, suppose that one circumstance that firm 2 believes to be possible is that firm 1 knows it cost (although in fact it does not). Because firm 2 thinks this circumstance to be possible, we need *four* states to model the situation, which I call $L0$, $H0$, $L1$, and $H1$, with the following interpretations.

$L0$: firm 2's cost is low and firm 1 does not know whether it is low or high

$H0$: firm 2's cost is high and firm 1 does not know whether it is low or high

$L1$: firm 2's cost is low and firm 1 knows it is low

$H1$: firm 2's cost is high and firm 1 knows it is high.

Firm 1 receives one of three possible signals, 0, L, and H. The states $L0$ and $H0$ generate the signal 0 (firm 1 does not know firm 2's cost), the state $L1$ generates the signal L (firm 1 knows firm 2's cost is low), and the state $H1$ generates the signal H (firm 1 knows firm 2's cost is high). Firm 2 receives one of two possible signals, L, in states $L0$ and $L1$, and H, in states $H0$ and $H1$. Denote by θ (as before) the probability assigned by type 0 of firm 1 to firm 2's cost being c_L, and by π the probability assigned by each type of firm 2 to firm 1's knowing firm 2's cost. (The case $\pi = 0$ is equivalent to the one considered in Section 9.4.1.) A Bayesian game that models the situation is defined as follows.

Players Firm 1 and firm 2.

States $\{L0, L1, H0, H1\}$, where the first letter in the name of the state indicates firm 2's cost and the second letter indicates whether firm 1 does (1) or does not (0) know firm 2's cost.

Actions Each firm's set of actions is the set of its possible outputs (nonnegative numbers).

Signals Firm 1 gets one of the signals 0, L, and H, and her signal function τ_1 satisfies $\tau_1(L0) = \tau_1(H0) = 0$, $\tau_1(L1) = L$, and $\tau_1(H1) = H$. Firm 2 gets the signal L or H and her signal function τ_2 satisfies $\tau_2(L0) = \tau_2(L1) = L$ and $\tau_2(H0) = \tau_2(H1) = H$.

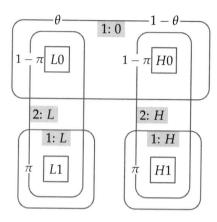

Figure 288.1 The information structure for the model in Section 9.4.2, in which firm 2 does not know whether firm 1 knows its cost. The frame labeled *i: x* encloses the states that generate the signal x for firm i.

Beliefs   Firm 1: type 0 assigns probability θ to state L0 and probability $1 - \theta$ to state H0; type L assigns probability 1 to state L1; type H assigns probability 1 to state H. Firm 2: type L assigns probability π to state L1 and probability $1 - \pi$ to state L0; type H assigns probability π to state H1 and probability $1 - \pi$ to state H0.

Payoff functions   The firms' Bernoulli payoffs are their profits; if the actions chosen are (q_1, q_2), then firm 1's profit is $q_1(P(q_1 + q_2) - c)$ and firm 2's profit is $q_2(P(q_1 + q_2) - c_L)$ in states L0 and L1, and $q_2(P(q_1 + q_2) - c_L)$ in states H0 and H1.

The information structure in this game is illustrated in Figure 288.1. You are asked to investigate its Nash equilibria in the following exercise.

? EXERCISE 288.1 (Cournot's duopoly game with imperfect information) Write down the maximization problems that determine the best response function of each type of each player. (Denote by q_0, q_ℓ, and q_h the outputs of types 0, ℓ, and h of firm 1, and by q_L and q_H the outputs of types L and H of firm 2.) Now suppose that the inverse demand function is given by $P(Q) = \alpha - Q$ for $Q \le \alpha$ and $P(Q) = 0$ for $Q > \alpha$. For values of c_H and c_L close enough that there is a Nash equilibrium in which all outputs are positive, find this equilibrium. Check that when $\pi = 0$ the equilibrium output of type 0 of firm 1 is equal to the equilibrium output of firm 1 you found in Exercise 287.1, and that the equilibrium outputs of the two types of firm 2 are the same as the ones you found in that exercise. Check also that when $\pi = 1$ the equilibrium outputs of type ℓ of firm 1 and type L of firm 2 are the same as the equilibrium outputs when there is perfect information and the costs are c and c_L, and that the equilibrium outputs of type h of firm 1 and type H of firm 2 are the same as the equilibrium outputs when there is perfect information and the costs are c and c_H. Show that for $0 < \pi < 1$, the equilibrium outputs of types L and H of firm 2 lie between their values when $\pi = 0$ and when $\pi = 1$.

9.5 Illustration: providing a public good

Suppose that a public good is provided to a group of people if at least one person is willing to pay the cost of the good (as in the model of crime reporting in Section 4.8). Assume that the people differ in their valuations of the good, and each person knows only her own valuation. Who, if anyone, will pay the cost?

Denote the number of individuals by n, the cost of the good by $c > 0$, and individual i's payoff if the good is provided by v_i. If the good is not provided, then each individual's payoff is 0. Each individual i knows her own valuation v_i. She does not know anyone else's valuation, but she knows that all valuations are at least $\underline{v}$ and at most $\overline{v}$, where $0 \leq \underline{v} < c < \overline{v}$. She believes that the probability that any one individual's valuation is at most v is $F(v)$, independent of all other individuals' valuations, where F is a continuous increasing function. The fact that F is increasing means that the individual does not assign zero probability to any range of values between $\underline{v}$ and $\overline{v}$; the fact that it is continuous means that she does not assign positive probability to any single valuation. (An example of the function F is shown in Figure 289.1.)

The following mechanism determines whether the good is provided. All n individuals simultaneously submit envelopes; the envelope of any individual i may contain either a contribution of c or nothing (no intermediate contributions are allowed). If all individuals submit 0, then the good is not provided and each individual's payoff is 0. If at least one individual submits c, then the good is provided, each individual i who submits c obtains the payoff $v_i - c$, and each individual i who submits 0 obtains the payoff v_i. (The pure strategy Nash equilibria of a variant of this model, in which more than one contribution is needed to provide the good, are considered in Exercise 33.1.)

We can formulate this situation as a Bayesian game as follows.

Players   The set of n individuals.

States   The set of all profiles $(v_1, \ldots, v_n)$ of valuations, where $\underline{v} \leq v_i \leq \overline{v}$ for all i.

Actions   Each player's set of actions is $\{0, c\}$.

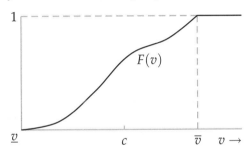

Figure 289.1 An example of the function F for the model in Section 9.5. For each value of v, $F(v)$ is the probability that any given individual's valuation is at most v.

Signals The set of signals that each player may observe is the set of possible valuations. The signal function τ_i of each player i is given by $\tau_i(v_1, \ldots, v_n) = v_i$ (each player knows her own valuation).

Beliefs Every type of player i assigns probability $F(v_1)F(v_2) \cdots F(v_{i-1}) \times F(v_{i+1}) \cdots F(v_n)$ to the event that the valuation of every other player j is at most v_j.

Payoff functions Player i's Bernoulli payoff in state $(v_1, \ldots, v_n)$ is

$$
\begin{cases}
0 & \text{if no one contributes} \\
v_i & \text{if } i \text{ does not contribute but some other player does} \\
v_i - c & \text{if } i \text{ contributes.}
\end{cases}
$$

⑦ EXERCISE 290.1 (Nash equilibria of game of contributing to a public good) Find conditions under which for each value of i this game has a pure strategy Nash equilibrium in which each type v_i of player i with $v_i \geq c$ contributes, whereas every other type of player i, and all types of every other player, do not contribute.

In addition to the Nash equilibria identified in this exercise, the game has a symmetric Nash equilibrium in which every player contributes if and only if her valuation exceeds some critical amount v^*. For such a strategy profile to be an equilibrium, a player whose valuation is less than v^* must optimally not contribute, and a player whose valuation is at least v^* must optimally contribute. Consider player i. Suppose that every other player contributes if and only if her valuation is at least v^*. The probability that at least one of the other players contributes is the probability that at least one of the other players' valuations is at least v^*, which is $1 - (F(v^*))^{n-1}$. (Note that $(F(v^*))^{n-1}$ is the probability that all the other valuations are at most v^*.) Thus if player i's valuation is v_i, her expected payoff is $(1 - (F(v^*))^{n-1})v_i$ if she does not contribute and $v_i - c$ if she does contribute. Hence the conditions for player i to optimally not contribute when $v_i < v^*$ and optimally contribute when $v_i \geq v^*$ are $(1 - (F(v^*))^{n-1})v_i \geq v_i - c$ if $v_i < v^*$, and $(1 - (F(v^*))^{n-1})v_i \leq v_i - c$ if $v_i \geq v^*$, or equivalently

$$
\begin{aligned}
v_i(F(v^*))^{n-1} &\leq c \quad \text{if } v_i < v^* \\
v_i(F(v^*))^{n-1} &\geq c \quad \text{if } v_i \geq v^*.
\end{aligned}
\tag{290.2}
$$

If these inequalities are satisfied, then

$$
v^*(F(v^*))^{n-1} = c.
\tag{290.3}
$$

Conversely, if v^* satisfies (290.3), then it satisfies the two equations in (290.2). Thus the game has a Nash equilibrium in which every player contributes whenever her valuation is at least v^* if and only if v^* satisfies (290.3).

Note that because $F(v) = 1$ only if $v \geq \bar{v}$, and $\bar{v} > c$, we have $v^* > c$. That is, every player's cutoff for contributing exceeds the cost of the public good. When at least one player's valuation exceeds c, all players are better off if the public good is provided and the high-valuation player contributes than if the good is not provided. But in the equilibrium, the good is provided only if at least one player's valuation exceeds v^*, which exceeds c.

As the number of individuals increases, is the good more or less likely to be provided in this equilibrium? The probability that the good is provided is the probability that at least one player's valuation is at least v^*, which is equal to $1 - (F(v^*))^n$. (Note that $(F(v^*))^n$ is the probability that every player's valuation is less than v^*.) From (290.3) this probability is equal to $1 - cF(v^*)/v^*$. How does v^* vary with n? As n increases, for any given value of v^* the value of $(F(v^*))^{n-1}$ decreases, and thus the value of $v^*(F(v^*))^{n-1}$ decreases. Thus to maintain the equality (290.3), the value of v^* must increase as n increases. We conclude that as n increases, the change in the probability that the good is provided depends on the change in $F(v^*)/v^*$ as v^* increases: the probability increases if $F(v^*)/v^*$ is a decreasing function of v^*, whereas it decreases if $F(v^*)/v^*$ is an increasing function of v^*. If F is uniform and $\underline{v} > 0$, for example, $F(v^*)/v^*$ is a decreasing function of v^*, so that the probability that the good is provided increases as the population size increases.

The notion of a Bayesian game may be used to model a situation in which each player is uncertain of the number of other players. In the next exercise you are asked to study another variant of the crime-reporting model of Section 4.8 in which each of the two players does not know whether she is the only witness or whether there is another witness (in which case she knows that witness's valuation). (The exercise requires a knowledge of mixed strategy Nash equilibrium (Chapter 4).)

? EXERCISE 291.1 (Reporting a crime with an unknown number of witnesses) Consider the variant of the model of Section 4.8 in which each of two players does not know whether she is the only witness or whether there is another witness. Denote by π the probability each player assigns to being the sole witness. Model this situation as a Bayesian game with three states: one in which player 1 is the only witness, one in which player 2 is the only witness, and one in which both players are witnesses. Find a condition on π under which the game has a pure Nash equilibrium in which each player chooses *Call* (given the signal that she is a witness). When the condition is violated, find the symmetric mixed strategy Nash equilibrium of the game, and check that when $\pi = 0$ this equilibrium coincides with the one found in Section 4.8 for $n = 2$.

9.6 Illustration: auctions

9.6.1 Introduction

In the analysis of auctions in Section 3.5, every bidder knows every other bidder's valuation of the object for sale. Here I use the notion of a Bayesian game to analyze auctions in which bidders are not perfectly informed about each others' valuations.

Assume that a single object is for sale, and that each bidder independently receives some information—a "signal"—about the value of the object to her. If each bidder's signal is simply her valuation of the object, as assumed in Section 3.5, we say that the bidders' valuations are *private*. If each bidder's valuation depends on other bidders' signals as well as her own, we say that the valuations are *common*.

The assumption of private values is appropriate, for example, for a work of art whose beauty rather than resale value interests the buyers. Each bidder knows her valuation of the object, but not that of any other bidder; the other bidders' valuations have no bearing on her valuation. The assumption of common values is appropriate, for example, for an oil tract containing unknown reserves on which each bidder has conducted a test. Each bidder i's test result gives her some information about the size of the reserves, and hence her valuation of these reserves, but the other bidders' test results, if known to bidder i, would typically improve this information.

As in the analysis of auctions in which the bidders are perfectly informed about each others' valuations, I study models in which bids for a single object are submitted simultaneously (bids are *sealed*), and the participant who submits the highest bid obtains the object. As before I consider both *first-price* auctions, in which the winner pays the price she bid, and *second-price* auctions, in which the winner pays the highest of the remaining bids.

(In Section 3.5 I argue that the first-price rule models an open descending ("Dutch") auction, and the second-price rule models an open ascending ("English") auction. Note that the argument that the second-price rule corresponds to an open ascending auction depends upon the bidders' valuations being private. If a bidder is uncertain of her valuation, which is related to that of other bidders, then in an open ascending auction she may obtain information about her valuation from other participants' bids, information not available in a sealed-bid auction.)

I first consider the case in which the bidders' valuations are private, then the case in which they are common.

9.6.2 Independent private values

In the case in which the bidders' valuations are private, the assumptions about these valuations are similar to those in the previous section (on the provision of a public good). Each bidder knows that all other bidders' valuations are at least $\underline{v}$, where $\underline{v} \geq 0$, and at most $\bar{v}$. She believes that the probability that any given bidder's valuation is at most v is $F(v)$, independent of all other bidders' valuations, where F is a continuous increasing function (as in Figure 289.1).

The preferences of a bidder whose valuation is v are represented by the expected value of the Bernoulli payoff function that assigns 0 to the outcome in which she does not win the object and $v - p$ to the outcome in which she wins the object and pays the price p. (That is, each bidder is risk neutral.) I assume that the expected payoff of a bidder whose bid is tied for first place is $(v - p)/m$, where m is the number of tied winning bids. (The assumption about the outcome when bids are tied for first place has mainly "technical" significance; in Section 3.5, it was convenient to make an assumption different from the one here.)

Denote by $P(b)$ the price paid by the winner of the auction when the profile of bids is b. For a first-price auction $P(b)$ is the winning bid (the largest b_i), whereas for a second-price auction it is the highest bid made by a bidder different from the winner. Given the appropriate specification of P, the following Bayesian game models **first- and second-price auctions with independent private valuations** (and imperfect information about valuations).

Players The set of bidders, say $1, \ldots, n$.

States The set of all profiles $(v_1, \ldots, v_n)$ of valuations, where $\underline{v} \leq v_i \leq \overline{v}$ for all i.

Actions Each player's set of actions is the set of possible bids (nonnegative numbers).

Signals The set of signals that each player may observe is the set of possible valuations. The signal function τ_i of each player i is given by $\tau_i(v_1, \ldots, v_n) = v_i$ (each player knows her own valuation).

Beliefs Every type of player i assigns probability $F(v_1)F(v_2) \cdots F(v_{i-1}) \times F(v_{i+1}) \cdots F(v_n)$ to the event that the valuation of every other player j is at most v_j.

Payoff functions Player i's Bernoulli payoff in state $(v_1, \ldots, v_n)$ is 0 if her bid b_i is not the highest bid, and $(v_i - P(b))/m$ if no bid is higher than b_i and m bids (including b_i) are equal to b_i:

$$u_i(b, (v_1, \ldots, v_n)) = \begin{cases} (v_i - P(b))/m & \text{if } b_j \leq b_i \text{ for all } j \neq i \text{ and} \\ & \qquad b_j = b_i \text{ for } m \text{ players} \\ 0 & \text{if } b_j > b_i \text{ for some } j \neq i. \end{cases}$$

Nash equilibrium in a second-price sealed-bid auction As in a second-price sealed-bid auction in which every bidder knows every other bidder's valuation,

> in a second-price sealed-bid auction with imperfect information about valuations, a player's bid equal to her valuation weakly dominates all her other bids.

Precisely, consider some type v_i of some player i, and let b_i be a bid not equal to v_i. Then for all bids by all types of all the other players, the expected payoff of type v_i of player i is at least as high when she bids v_i as it is when she bids b_i, and for some bids by the various types of the other players, her expected payoff is greater when she bids v_i than it is when she bids b_i.

The argument for this result is similar to the argument in Section 3.5.2 in the case in which the players know each other's valuations. The main difference between the arguments arises because in the case in which the players do not know each others' valuations, any given bids for every type of every player but i leave player i uncertain about the highest of the remaining bids, because she is uncertain of the other players' types. (The difference in the tie-breaking rules between the two cases also necessitates a small change in the argument.) In the next exercise you are asked to fill in the details.

? EXERCISE 294.1 (Weak domination in a second-price sealed-bid auction) Show that for each type v_i of each player i in a second-price sealed-bid auction with imperfect information about valuations the bid v_i weakly dominates all other bids.

We conclude, in particular, that a second-price sealed-bid auction with imperfect information about valuations has a Nash equilibrium in which every type of every player bids her valuation. The game has also other equilibria, some of which you are asked to find in the next exercise.

? EXERCISE 294.2 (Nash equilibria of a second-price sealed-bid auction) For every player i, find a Nash equilibrium of a second-price sealed-bid auction in which player i wins. (Think about the Nash equilibria when the players know each others' valuations, studied in Section 3.5.)

Nash equilibrium in a first-price sealed-bid auction As when the players are perfectly informed about each other's valuations, the bid of v_i by type v_i of player i weakly dominates any bid greater than v_i, does not weakly dominate bids less than v_i, and is itself weakly dominated by any such lower bid. (If type v_i of player i bids v_i, her payoff is certainly 0 (either she wins and pays her valuation, or she loses), whereas if she bids less than v_i, she may win and obtain a positive payoff.)

These facts suggest that the game may have a Nash equilibrium in which each player bids less than her valuation. An analysis of the game for an arbitrary distribution F of valuations requires calculus and is relegated to an appendix (Section 9.8). Here I consider the case in which there are two bidders and each player's valuation is distributed "uniformly" between 0 and 1. This assumption on the distribution of valuations means that the fraction of valuations less than v is exactly v, so that $F(v) = v$ for all v with $0 \leq v \leq 1$.

Denote by $\beta_i(v)$ the bid of type v of player i. I claim that if there are two bidders and the distribution of valuations is uniform between 0 and 1, the game has a (symmetric) Nash equilibrium in which the function β_i is the same for both players, with $\beta_i(v) = \frac{1}{2}v$ for all v. That is, each type of each player bids exactly half her valuation.

To verify this claim, suppose that each type of player 2 bids in this way. Then as far as player 1 is concerned, player 2's bids are distributed uniformly between 0 and $\frac{1}{2}$. Thus if player 1 bids more than $\frac{1}{2}$ she surely wins, whereas if she bids

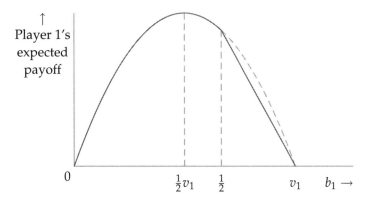

Figure 295.1 Player 1's expected payoff as a function of its bid in a first-price sealed-bid auction in which there are two bidders and the valuations are uniformly distributed from 0 to 1, given that player 2 bids $\frac{1}{2}v_2$.

$b_1 \leq \frac{1}{2}$ the probability that she wins is the probability that player 2's valuation is less than $2b_1$ (in which case player 2 bids less than b_1), which is $2b_1$. Consequently her payoff as a function of her bid b_1 is

$$\begin{cases} 2b_1(v_1 - b_1) & \text{if } 0 \leq b_1 \leq \frac{1}{2} \\ v_1 - b_1 & \text{if } b_1 > \frac{1}{2}. \end{cases}$$

This function is shown in Figure 295.1. Its maximizer is $\frac{1}{2}v_1$ (see Exercise 497.1), so that player 1's optimal bid is half her valuation. Both players are identical, so this argument shows also that given $\beta_1(v) = \frac{1}{2}v$, player 2's optimal bid is half her valuation. Thus, as claimed, the game has a Nash equilibrium in which each type of each player bids half her valuation.

When the number n of bidders exceeds 2, a similar analysis shows that the game has a (symmetric) Nash equilibrium in which every player bids the fraction $1 - 1/n$ of her valuation: $\beta_i(v) = (1 - 1/n)v$ for every player i and every valuation v. (You are asked to verify a claim more general than this one in Exercise 296.1.)

In this example—and, it turns out, for any distribution F satisfying the conditions given at the start of this section—the players' common bidding function in a symmetric Nash equilibrium may be given an illuminating interpretation. Choose $n - 1$ valuations randomly and independently, each according to the cumulative distribution function F. The highest of these $n - 1$ valuations is a "random variable": its value depends on the $n - 1$ valuations that were chosen. Denote it by $\mathbf{X}$. Fix a valuation v. Some values of $\mathbf{X}$ are less than v; others are greater than v. Consider the distribution of $\mathbf{X}$ in those cases in which it is less than v. The expected value of this distribution is denoted $E[\mathbf{X} \mid \mathbf{X} < v]$: the expected value of $\mathbf{X}$ conditional on $\mathbf{X}$ being less than v. We may prove the following result. (See the appendix, Section 9.8, for suggestive arguments.)

If each bidder's valuation is drawn independently from the same continuous and increasing cumulative distribution, a first-price sealed-bid auction (with imperfect information about valuations) has a (symmetric) Nash equilibrium in which each type v of each player bids $E[X \mid X < v]$, the expected value of the highest of the other players' bids conditional on v being higher than all the other valuations.

Put differently, each bidder asks the following question: Over all the cases in which my valuation is the highest, what is the expectation of the highest of the other players' valuations? This expectation is the amount she bids.

If F is uniform from 0 to 1 and $n = 2$, we may verify that indeed the equilibrium we found may be expressed in this way. For any valuation v of player 1, the cases in which player 2's valuation is less than v are distributed uniformly from 0 to v, so that the expected value of player 2's valuation conditional on its being less than v is $\frac{1}{2}v$, which is equal to the equilibrium bidding function that we found.

Comparing equilibria of first- and second-price auctions   Near the end of Section 3.5.3 we saw that first- and second-price auctions are "revenue equivalent" when the players know each others' valuations: their distinguished equilibria yield the same outcome. I now argue that the same is true when the players are uncertain of each others' valuations.

Consider the equilibrium of a second-price auction in which every player bids her valuation. In this equilibrium, the expected price paid by a bidder with valuation v who wins is the expectation of the highest of the other $n - 1$ valuations, conditional on this maximum being less than v, or, in the notation above, $E[X \mid X < v]$. We have just seen that a first-price auction has a symmetric Nash equilibrium in which this amount is precisely the bid of a player with valuation v, and hence the amount paid by such a player. Thus a winning bidder pays the same expected price in the equilibrium of each auction. In both cases, the player with the highest valuation submits the winning bid, so both auctions yield the auctioneer the same revenue:

If each bidder is risk-neutral and each bidder's valuation is drawn independently from the same continuous and increasing cumulative distribution, then the Nash equilibrium of a second-price sealed-bid auction (with imperfect information about valuations) in which each player bids her valuation yields the same revenue as the symmetric Nash equilibrium of the corresponding first-price sealed-bid auction.

This result depends on the assumption that each player's preferences are represented by the expected value of a risk-neutral Bernoulli payoff function. The next exercise asks you to study an example in which each player is risk averse. (See page 103 for a discussion of risk neutrality and risk aversion.)

? EXERCISE 296.1 (Auctions with risk-averse bidders) Consider a variant of the Bayesian game defined earlier in this section in which the players are risk averse.

Specifically, suppose each of the n players' preferences are represented by the expected value of the Bernoulli payoff function $x^{1/m}$, where x is the player's monetary payoff and $m > 1$. Suppose also that each player's valuation is distributed uniformly between 0 and 1, as in the example on page 294. Show that the Bayesian game that models a first-price sealed-bid auction under these assumptions has a (symmetric) Nash equilibrium in which each type v_i of each player i bids $(1 - 1/[m(n-1)+1])v_i$. (You need to use the mathematical fact that the solution of the problem $\max_b[b^k(v-b)^\ell]$ is $kv/(k+\ell)$.) Compare the auctioneer's revenue in this equilibrium with her revenue in the symmetric Nash equilibrium of a second-price sealed-bid auction in which each player bids her valuation. (Note that the equilibrium of the second-price auction does not depend on the players' payoff functions.)

9.6.3 Common valuations

In an auction with common valuations, each player's valuation depends on the other players' signals as well as her own. (As before, I assume that the players' signals are independent.) I denote the function that gives player i's valuation by g_i, and assume that it is increasing in all the signals. Given the appropriate specification of the function P that determines the price $P(b)$ paid by the winner as a function of the profile b of bids, the following Bayesian game models **first- and second-price auctions with common valuations** (and imperfect information about valuations).

Players The set of bidders, say $\{1, \ldots, n\}$.

States The set of all profiles $(t_1, \ldots, t_n)$ of signals that the players may receive.

Actions Each player's set of actions is the set of possible bids (nonnegative numbers).

Signals The signal function τ_i of each player i is given by $\tau_i(t_1, \ldots, t_n) = t_i$ (each player observes her own signal).

Beliefs Each type of each player believes that the signal of every type of every other player is independent of all the other players' signals.

Payoff functions Player i's Bernoulli payoff in state $(t_1, \ldots, t_n)$ is 0 if her bid b_i is not the highest bid, and $(g_i(t_1, \ldots, t_n) - P(b))/m$ if no bid is higher than b_i and m bids (including b_i) are equal to b_i:

$$u_i(b, (t_1, \ldots, t_n)) = \begin{cases} (g_i(t_1, \ldots, t_n) - P(b))/m & \text{if } b_j \leq b_i \text{ for all } j \neq i \text{ and} \\ & \quad b_j = b_i \text{ for } m \text{ players} \\ 0 & \text{if } b_j > b_i \text{ for some } j \neq i. \end{cases}$$

Nash equilibrium in a second-price sealed-bid auction   The main ideas in the analysis of sealed-bid common value auctions are illustrated by an example in which there are two bidders, each bidder's signal is uniformly distributed from 0 to 1, and the valuation of each bidder i is given by $v_i = \alpha t_i + \gamma t_j$, where j is the other player and $\alpha \geq \gamma \geq 0$. The case in which $\alpha = 1$ and $\gamma = 0$ is exactly the one studied in Section 9.6.2: in this case, the bidders' valuations are private. If $\alpha = \gamma$, then for any given signals, each bidder's valuation is the same—a case of "pure common valuations". If, for example, the signal t_i is the number of barrels of oil in a tract, then the expected valuation of a bidder i who knows the signals t_i and t_j is $p \cdot \frac{1}{2}(t_i + t_j)$, where p is the monetary worth of a barrel of oil. Our assumption, of course, is that a bidder does *not* know any other player's signal. However, a key point in the analysis of common value auctions is that the other players' bids contain *some* information about the other players' signals—information that may profitably be used.

I claim that under these assumptions a second-price sealed-bid auction has a Nash equilibrium in which each type t_i of each player i bids $(\alpha + \gamma)t_i$.

To verify this claim, suppose that each type of player 2 bids in this way and type t_1 of player 1 bids b_1. To determine the expected payoff of type t_1 of player 1, we need to find the probability with which she wins, and both the expected price she pays and the expected value of player 2's signal if she wins.

Probability that player 1 wins: Given that player 2's bidding function is $(\alpha + \gamma)t_2$, player 1's bid of b_1 wins only if $b_1 \geq (\alpha + \gamma)t_2$, or if $t_2 \leq b_1/(\alpha + \gamma)$. Now, t_2 is distributed uniformly from 0 to 1, so the probability that it is at most $b_1/(\alpha + \gamma)$ is $b_1/(\alpha + \gamma)$. Thus a bid of b_1 by player 1 wins with probability $b_1/(\alpha + \gamma)$.

Expected price player 1 pays if she wins: The price she pays is equal to player 2's bid, which, *conditional on its being less than b_1*, is distributed uniformly from 0 to b_1. Thus the expected value of player 2's bid, *given that it is less than b_1*, is $\frac{1}{2}b_1$.

Expected value of player 2's signal if player 1 wins: Player 2's bid, given her signal t_2, is $(\alpha + \gamma)t_2$, so that the expected value of signals that yield a bid of less than b_1 is $\frac{1}{2}b_1/(\alpha + \gamma)$ (because of the uniformity of the distribution of t_2).

Now, player 1's expected payoff if she bids b_1 is the difference between her expected valuation, given her signal t_1 and the fact that she wins, and the expected price she pays, multiplied by her probability of winning. Combining the previous calculations, player 1's expected payoff if she bids b_1 is thus $(\alpha t_1 + \frac{1}{2}\gamma b_1/(\alpha + \gamma) - \frac{1}{2}b_1)b_1/(\alpha + \gamma)$, or

$$\frac{\alpha}{2(\alpha + \gamma)^2} \cdot (2(\alpha + \gamma)t_1 - b_1)b_1.$$

This function is maximized at $b_1 = (\alpha + \gamma)t_1$. That is, if each type t_2 of player 2 bids $(\alpha + \gamma)t_2$, any type t_1 of player 1 optimally bids $(\alpha + \gamma)t_1$. Symmetrically, if each type t_1 of player 1 bids $(\alpha + \gamma)t_1$, any type t_2 of player 2 optimally bids $(\alpha + \gamma)t_2$. Hence, as claimed, the game has a Nash equilibrium in which each type t_i of each player i bids $(\alpha + \gamma)t_i$.

? EXERCISE 299.1 (Asymmetric Nash equilibria of second-price sealed-bid common value auctions) Show that when $\alpha = \gamma = 1$, for *any* value of $\lambda > 0$ the game has an (asymmetric) Nash equilibrium in which each type t_1 of player 1 bids $(1 + \lambda)t_1$ and each type t_2 of player 2 bids $(1 + 1/\lambda)t_2$.

Note that when player 1 calculates her expected value of the object, she finds the expected value of player 2's signal *given that her bid wins*. She should not base her bid simply on an estimate of the valuation derived from her own signal and the (unconditional) expectation of the other player's signal. She wins precisely when her bid exceeds those of the other players, so if she bids in this way, then over all the cases in which she wins, she more likely than not overvalues the object. A bidder who incorrectly behaves in this way is said to suffer from the *winner's curse*. (Bidders in real auctions know this problem: when a contractor gives you a quotation to renovate your house, she does not base her price simply on an unbiased estimate out how much it will cost her to do the job; rather, she takes into account that you will select her only if her competitors' estimates are all higher than hers, in which case her estimate may be suspiciously low.)

Nash equilibrium in a first-price sealed-bid auction I claim that under the assumptions on the players' signals and valuations in Section 9.6.2, a first-price sealed-bid auction has a Nash equilibrium in which each type t_i of each player i bids $\frac{1}{2}(\alpha + \gamma)t_i$. This claim may be verified by arguments like those in that section. In the next exercise, you are asked to supply the details.

? EXERCISE 299.2 (First-price sealed-bid auction with common valuations) Verify that under the assumptions on signals and valuations in Section 9.6.2, a first-price sealed-bid auction has a Nash equilibrium in which the bid of each type t_i of each player i is $\frac{1}{2}(\alpha + \gamma)t_i$.

Comparing equilibria of first- and second-price auctions We see that the revenue equivalence of first- and second-price auctions that holds when valuations are private holds also for the symmetric equilibria of the examples in which the valuations are common. That is, the expected price paid by a player of any given type is the same in the symmetric equilibrium of the first-price auction as it is in the symmetric equilibrium of the second-price auction: in each case type t_i of player i pays $\frac{1}{2}(\alpha + \gamma)t_i$ if she wins, and wins with the same probability.

In fact, the revenue equivalence principle holds much more generally. Suppose that each bidder is risk neutral and independently receives a signal from the same distribution, and that this distribution satisfies the conditions in Section 9.6.2. Then the expected payment of a bidder of any given type is the same in the symmetric Nash equilibrium of a second-price sealed-bid auction as it is in the symmetric Nash equilibrium of a first-price sealed-bid auction. Further, this revenue equivalence is not restricted to first- and second-price auctions; a general result, encompassing a wider range of auction forms, is stated at the end of the appendix (Section 9.8).

AUCTIONS OF THE RADIO SPECTRUM

In the 1990s several countries started auctioning the right to use parts of the radio spectrum used for wireless communication (by mobile telephones, for example). Spectrum licenses in the United States were originally allocated on the basis of hearings by the Federal Communications Commission (FCC). This procedure was time-consuming, and a large backlog developed, prompting a switch to lotteries. Licenses awarded by the lotteries could be resold at high prices, attracting many participants. In one case that drew attention, the winner of a license to run cellular telephones in Cape Cod sold it to Southwestern Bell for $41.5 million (*New York Times*, May 30, 1991, page A1). In the early 1990s, the U.S. government was persuaded that auctioning licenses would allocate them more efficiently and might raise nontrivial revenue.

For each interval of the spectrum, many licenses were available, each covering a geographic area. A buyer's valuation of a license could be expected to depend on the other licenses it owned, so many interdependent goods were for sale. In designing an auction mechanism, the FCC had many choices: for example, the bidding could be open, or it could be sealed, with the price equal to either the highest bid or the second-highest bid; the licenses could be sold sequentially, or simultaneously, in which case participants could submit bids for individual licenses or for combinations of licenses. Experts in auction theory were consulted on the design of the mechanism. John McMillan (who advised the FCC), writes that "When theorists met the policy-makers, concepts like Bayes-Nash equilibrium, incentive-compatibility constraints, and order-statistic theorems came to be discussed in the corridors of power" (1994, 146). No theoretical analysis fitted the environment of the auction well, but the experts appealed to some principles from the existing theory, the results of laboratory experiments, and experience in auctions held in New Zealand and Australia in the early 1990s in making their recommendations. The mechanism adopted in 1994 was an open ascending auction for which bids were accepted simultaneously for all licenses in each round. Experts argued that the open (as opposed to sealed-bid) format and the simultaneity of the auctions promoted an efficient outcome because at each stage the bidders could see their rivals' previous bids for all licenses.

The FCC has conducted several auctions, starting with "narrowband" licenses (each covering a sliver of the spectrum, used by paging services) and continuing with "broadband" licenses (used for voice and data communications). These auctions have provided more employment for game theorists, many of whom have advised the companies bidding for licenses. In response to growing congestion of the airwaves and the expectation that a significant part of the rapidly growing Internet traffic will move to wireless devices, in 2000 President Bill Clinton ordered further auctions of large parts of the spectrum (*New York Times*, October 14, 2000). Whether the auctions that have been held have allocated licenses efficiently is hard to tell, though it appears that the winners were able to obtain the sets of licenses they wanted. Certainly the auctions have been successful in generating revenue: the first four generated over $18 billion.

9.7 Illustration: juries

9.7.1 Model

In a trial, jurors are presented with evidence concerning the guilt or innocence of a defendant. Their interpretations of the evidence may differ. Each juror assesses the evidence, and on the basis of her interpretation votes either to convict or acquit the defendant. Assume that a unanimous verdict is required for conviction: the defendant is convicted if and only if every juror votes to convict her. (This rule is used in the United States and Canada, for example.) What can we say about the chance of an innocent defendant's being convicted and a guilty defendant's being acquitted?

In deciding how to vote, each juror must consider the costs of convicting an innocent person and of acquitting a guilty person. She must consider also the likely effect of her vote on the outcome, which depends on the other jurors' votes. For example, a juror who thinks that at least one of her colleagues is likely to vote for acquittal may act differently from one who is sure that all her colleagues will vote for conviction. Thus an answer to the question requires us to consider the strategic interaction between the jurors, which we may model as a Bayesian game.

Assume that each juror comes to the trial with the belief that the defendant is guilty with probability π (the same for every juror), a belief modified by the evidence presented. We model the possibility that jurors interpret the evidence differently by assuming that for each of the defendant's true statuses (guilty and innocent), each juror interprets the evidence to point to guilt with positive probability, and to innocence with positive probability, and that the jurors' interpretations are independent (no juror's interpretation depends on any other juror's interpretation). I assume that the probabilities are the same for all jurors and denote the probability of any given juror's interpreting the evidence to point to guilt when the defendant is guilty by p, and the probability of her interpreting the evidence to point to innocence when the defendant is innocent by q. I assume also that a juror is more likely than not to interpret the evidence correctly, so that $p > \frac{1}{2}$ and $q > \frac{1}{2}$, and hence in particular $p > 1 - q$.

Each juror wishes to convict a guilty defendant and acquit an innocent one. She is indifferent between these two outcomes and prefers each of them to one in which an innocent defendant is convicted or a guilty defendant is acquitted.

Assume specifically that each juror's Bernoulli payoffs are:

$$
\begin{cases}
0 & \text{if guilty defendant convicted or} \\
 & \quad \text{innocent defendant acquitted} \\
-z & \text{if innocent defendant convicted} \\
-(1-z) & \text{if guilty defendant acquitted.}
\end{cases}
\tag{302.1}
$$

The parameter z may be given an appealing interpretation. Denote by r the probability a juror assigns to the defendant's being guilty, given all her information. Then her expected payoff if the defendant is acquitted is $-r(1-z)+(1-r)\cdot 0 = -r(1-z)$ and her expected payoff if the defendant is convicted is $r\cdot 0 - (1-r)z = -(1-r)z$. Thus she prefers the defendant to be acquitted if $-r(1-z) > -(1-r)z$, or $r < z$, and convicted if $r > z$. That is, z is equal to the probability of guilt required for the juror to want the defendant to be convicted. Put differently, for any juror

> acquittal is at least as good as conviction if and only if
> Pr(defendant is guilty, given juror's information) $\leq z$.
> $\tag{302.2}$

We may now formulate a Bayesian game that models the situation. The players are the jurors, and each player's action is a vote to convict (C) or to acquit (Q). We need one state for each configuration of the players' preferences and information. Each player's preferences depend on whether the defendant is guilty or innocent, and each player's information consists of her interpretation of the evidence. Thus we define a state to be a list $(X, s_1, \ldots, s_n)$, where X denotes the defendant's true status, guilty (G) or innocent (I), and s_i represents player i's interpretation of the evidence, which may point to guilt (g) or innocence (b). (I do not use i for "innocence" because I use it to index the players; b stands for "blameless".) The signal that each player i receives is her interpretation of the evidence, s_i. In any state in which $X = G$ (i.e. the defendant is guilty), each player assigns the probability p to any other player's receiving the signal g, and the probability $1 - p$ to her receiving the signal b, independently of all other players' signals. Similarly, in any state in which $X = I$ (i.e. the defendant is innocent), each player assigns the probability q to any other player's receiving the signal b, and the probability $1 - q$ to her receiving the signal g, independently of all other players' signals.

Each player cares about the verdict, which depends on the players' actions and on the defendant's true status. Given the assumption that unanimity is required to convict the defendant, only the action profile $(C, \ldots, C)$ leads to conviction. Thus (302.1) implies that player i's payoff function in the Bayesian game is defined as follows:

$$
u_i(a, \omega) =
\begin{cases}
0 & \text{if } a \neq (C, \ldots, C) \text{ and } \omega_1 = I \text{ or} \\
 & \quad \text{if } a = (C, \ldots, C) \text{ and } \omega_1 = G \\
-z & \text{if } a = (C, \ldots, C) \text{ and } \omega_1 = I \\
-(1-z) & \text{if } a \neq (C, \ldots, C) \text{ and } \omega_1 = G,
\end{cases}
\tag{302.3}
$$

where ω_1 is the first component of the state, giving the defendant's true status.

In summary, the Bayesian game that models the situation has the following components.

Players A set of n jurors.

States The set of states is the set of all lists $(X, s_1, \ldots, s_n)$ where $X \in \{G, I\}$ and $s_j \in \{g, b\}$ for every juror j, where $X = G$ if the defendant is guilty, $X = I$ if she is innocent, $s_j = g$ if player j receives the signal that she is guilty, and $s_j = b$ if player j receives the signal that she is innocent.

Actions The set of actions of each player is $\{C, Q\}$, where C means vote to convict, and Q means vote to acquit.

Signals The set of signals that each player may receive is $\{g, b\}$ and player j's signal function is defined by $\tau_j(X, s_1, \ldots, s_n) = s_j$ (each juror is informed only of her own signal).

Beliefs Type g of any player i believes that the state is $(G, s_1, \ldots, s_n)$ with probability $\Pr(G \mid g) p^{k-1}(1-p)^{n-k}$ and $(I, s_1, \ldots, s_n)$ with probability $\Pr(I \mid g) \times (1-q)^{k-1} q^{n-k}$, where k is the number of players j (including i) for whom $s_j = g$ in each case. Type b of any player i believes that the state is $(G, s_1, \ldots, s_n)$ with probability $\Pr(G \mid b) p^k (1-p)^{n-k-1}$ and $(I, s_1, \ldots, s_n)$ with probability $\Pr(I \mid b)(1-q)^k q^{n-k-1}$, where k is the number of players j for whom $s_j = g$ in each case.

Payoff functions The Bernoulli payoff function of each player i is given in (302.3).

9.7.2 Nash equilibrium

One juror Start by considering the very simplest case, in which there is a single juror. Suppose that her signal is b. To determine whether she prefers conviction or acquittal, we need to find the probability $\Pr(G \mid b)$ she assigns to the defendant's being guilty, given her signal. We can find this probability by using Bayes' rule (see Section 17.6.5, in particular (504.3)), as follows:

$$\Pr(G \mid b) = \frac{\Pr(b \mid G) \Pr(G)}{\Pr(b \mid G) \Pr(G) + \Pr(b \mid I) \Pr(I)}$$

$$= \frac{(1-p)\pi}{(1-p)\pi + q(1-\pi)}.$$

Thus by (302.2), acquittal yields an expected payoff at least as high as does conviction if and only if

$$z \geq \frac{(1-p)\pi}{(1-p)\pi + q(1-\pi)}.$$

That is, after getting the signal that the defendant is innocent, the juror chooses acquittal as long as z is not too small—as long as she is too concerned about acquitting a guilty defendant. If her signal is g, then a similar calculation leads to the conclusion that conviction yields an expected payoff at least as high as does acquittal if

$$z \leq \frac{p\pi}{p\pi + (1-q)(1-\pi)}.$$

Thus if

$$\frac{(1-p)\pi}{(1-p)\pi + q(1-\pi)} \leq z \leq \frac{p\pi}{p\pi + (1-q)(1-\pi)}, \qquad (304.1)$$

then the juror optimally acts according to her signal, acquitting the defendant when her signal is b and convicting her when it is g. (A bit of algebra shows that the term on the left of (304.1) is less than the term on the right, given $p > 1 - q$.)

Two jurors   Now suppose there are two jurors. Are there values for z such that the game has a Nash equilibrium in which each juror votes according to her signal? Suppose that juror 2 acts in this way: type b votes to acquit, and type g votes to convict. Consider type b of juror 1. If juror 2's signal is b, juror 1's vote has no effect on the outcome, because juror 2 votes to acquit and unanimity is required for conviction. Thus when deciding how to vote, juror 1 should ignore the possibility that juror 2's signal is b and assume it is g. That is, juror 1 should take as evidence her signal and the fact that juror 2's signal is g. Hence, given (302.2), for type b of juror 1 acquittal is at least as good as conviction if the probability that the defendant is guilty, given that juror 1's signal is b and juror 2's signal is g, is at most z. This probability is

$$\Pr(G \mid b, g) = \frac{\Pr(b, g \mid G)\Pr(G)}{\Pr(b, g \mid G)\Pr(G) + \Pr(b, g \mid I)\Pr(I)}$$

$$= \frac{(1-p)p\pi}{(1-p)p\pi + q(1-q)(1-\pi)}.$$

Thus type b of juror 1 optimally votes for acquittal if

$$z \geq \frac{(1-p)p\pi}{(1-p)p\pi + q(1-q)(1-\pi)}.$$

By a similar argument, for type g of juror 1 conviction is at least as good as acquittal if

$$z \leq \frac{p^2\pi}{p^2\pi + (1-q)^2(1-\pi)}.$$

Thus when there are two jurors, the game has a Nash equilibrium in which each juror acts according to her signal, voting to acquit the defendant when her signal is b and to convict her when it is g, if

$$\frac{(1-p)p\pi}{(1-p)p\pi + q(1-q)(1-\pi)} \leq z \leq \frac{p^2\pi}{p^2\pi + (1-q)^2(1-\pi)}. \qquad (304.2)$$

Consider the expressions on the left of (304.1) and (304.2). Divide the numerator and denominator of the expression on the left of (304.1) by $1 - p$ and the numerator and denominator of the expression on the left of (304.2) by $(1-p)p$. Then, given $p > 1 - q$, we see that the expression on the left of (304.2) is greater than the expression on the left of (304.1). That is, the lowest value of z for which an equilibrium exists in which each juror votes according to her signal is higher when there are two jurors than when there is only one juror. Why? Because a juror who receives the signal b, knowing that her vote makes a difference only if the other juror votes to convict, makes her decision on the assumption that the other juror's signal is g, and so is less worried about convicting an innocent defendant than is a single juror in isolation.

Many jurors Now suppose the number of jurors is arbitrary, equal to n. Suppose that every juror other than juror 1 votes to acquit when her signal is b and to convict when her signal is g. Consider type b of juror 1. As in the case of two jurors, juror 1's vote has no effect on the outcome unless every other juror's signal is g. Thus when deciding how to vote, juror 1 should assume that all the other signals are g. Hence, given (302.2), for type b of juror 1 acquittal is at least as good as conviction if the probability that the defendant is guilty, given that juror 1's signal is b and every other juror's signal is g, is at most z. This probability is

$$\Pr(G \mid b, g, \ldots, g) = \frac{\Pr(b, g, \ldots, g \mid G)\Pr(G)}{\Pr(b, g, \ldots, g \mid G)\Pr(G) + \Pr(b, g, \ldots, g \mid I)\Pr(I)}$$
$$= \frac{(1-p)p^{n-1}\pi}{(1-p)p^{n-1}\pi + q(1-q)^{n-1}(1-\pi)}.$$

Thus type b of juror 1 optimally votes for acquittal if

$$z \geq \frac{(1-p)p^{n-1}\pi}{(1-p)p^{n-1}\pi + q(1-q)^{n-1}(1-\pi)}$$
$$= \frac{1}{1 + \dfrac{q}{1-p}\left(\dfrac{1-q}{p}\right)^{n-1}\dfrac{1-\pi}{\pi}}.$$

Now, given that $p > 1 - q$, the denominator decreases to 1 as n increases. Thus the lower bound on z for which type b of juror 1 votes for acquittal approaches 1 as n increases. (You may check that if $p = q = 0.8$, $\pi = 0.5$, and $n = 12$, the lower bound on z exceeds 0.999999.) In particular, in a large jury, if jurors care even slightly about acquitting a guilty defendant, then a juror who interprets the evidence to point to innocence will nevertheless vote for conviction. The reason is that the vote of a juror who interprets the evidence to point to innocence makes a difference to the outcome only if every other juror interprets the evidence to point to guilt, in which case the probability that the defendant is in fact guilty is very high.

We conclude that the model of a large jury in which the jurors are concerned about acquitting a guilty defendant has no Nash equilibrium in which every juror votes according to her signal. What *are* its equilibria? You are asked to find the conditions for two equilibria in the next exercise.

⑦ EXERCISE 306.1 (Signal-independent equilibria in a model of a jury) Find conditions under which the game, for an arbitrary number of jurors, has a Nash equilibrium in which every juror votes for acquittal regardless of her signal, and conditions under which every juror votes for conviction regardless of her signal.

Under some conditions on z the game has in addition a symmetric mixed strategy Nash equilibrium in which each type g juror votes for conviction, and each type b juror votes for acquittal and conviction each with positive probability. Denote by β the mixed strategy of each juror of type b. As before, a juror's vote affects the outcome only if all other jurors vote for conviction, so when choosing an action, a juror should assume that all other jurors vote for conviction.

Each type b juror must be indifferent between voting for conviction and voting for acquittal, because she takes each action with positive probability. By (302.2) we thus need the mixed strategy β to be such that the probability that the defendant is guilty, given that all other jurors vote for conviction, is equal to z. Now, the probability of any given juror's voting for conviction is $p + (1-p)\beta(C)$ if the defendant is guilty and $1 - q + q\beta(C)$ if she is innocent. Thus

$\Pr(G \mid \text{signal } b \text{ and } n-1 \text{ votes for } C)$

$$= \frac{\Pr(b \mid G)(\Pr(\text{vote } C \mid G))^{n-1}\Pr(G)}{\Pr(b \mid G)(\Pr(\text{vote } C \mid G))^{n-1}\Pr(G) + \Pr(b \mid I)(\Pr(\text{vote } C \mid I))^{n-1}\Pr(I)}$$

$$= \frac{(1-p)(p + (1-p)\beta(C))^{n-1}\pi}{(1-p)(p + (1-p)\beta(C))^{n-1}\pi + q(1 - q + q\beta(C))^{n-1}(1-\pi)}.$$

The condition that this probability equals z implies

$$(1-p)(p + (1-p)\beta(C))^{n-1}\pi(1-z) = q(1 - q + q\beta(C))^{n-1}(1-\pi)z, \quad (306.2)$$

and hence

$$\beta(C) = \frac{pX - (1-q)}{q - (1-p)X},$$

where $X = [\pi(1-p)(1-z)/((1-\pi)qz)]^{1/(n-1)}$. For a range of parameter values, $0 \leq \beta(C) \leq 1$, so that $\beta(C)$ is indeed a probability. Notice that when n is large, X is close to 1, and hence $\beta(C)$ is close to 1: a juror who interprets the evidence as pointing to innocence very likely nonetheless votes for conviction.

Each type g juror votes for conviction, and so must get an expected payoff at least as high from conviction as from acquittal. From an analysis like that for each type b juror, this condition is

$$p(p + (1-p)\beta(C))^{n-1}\pi(1-z) \geq (1-q)(1 - q + q\beta(C))^{n-1}(1-\pi)z.$$

Given $p > \frac{1}{2}$ and $q > \frac{1}{2}$, this condition follows from (306.2).

An interesting property of this equilibrium is that the probability that an innocent defendant is convicted *increases* as n increases: the larger the jury, the *more* likely an innocent defendant is to be convicted. (The proof of this result is not simple.)

Variants   The key point behind the results is that under unanimity rule a juror's vote makes a difference to the outcome only if every other juror votes for conviction. Consequently, a juror, when deciding how to vote, rationally assesses the defendant's probability of guilt under the assumption that every other juror votes for conviction. The fact that this implication of unanimity rule drives the results suggests that the Nash equilibria might be quite different if less than unanimity were required for conviction. The analysis of such rules is difficult, but indeed the Nash equilibria they generate differ significantly from the Nash equilibria under unanimity rule. In particular, the analogue of the mixed strategy Nash equilibria considered earlier generates a probability that an innocent defendant is convicted that approaches zero as the jury size increases, as Feddersen and Pesendorfer (1998) show.

The idea behind the equilibria of the model in the next exercise is related to the ideas in this section, though the model is different.

? EXERCISE 307.1 (Swing voter's curse) Whether candidate 1 or candidate 2 is elected depends on the votes of two citizens. The economy may be in one of two states, *A* and *B*. The citizens agree that candidate 1 is best if the state is *A* and candidate 2 is best if the state is *B*. Each citizen's preferences are represented by the expected value of a Bernoulli payoff function that assigns a payoff of 1 if the best candidate for the state wins (obtains more votes than the other candidate), a payoff of 0 if the other candidate wins, and payoff of $\frac{1}{2}$ if the candidates tie. Citizen 1 is informed of the state, whereas citizen 2 believes it is *A* with probability 0.9 and *B* with probability 0.1. Each citizen may either vote for candidate 1, vote for candidate 2, or not vote.

a. Formulate this situation as a Bayesian game. (Construct the table of payoffs for each state.)

b. Show that the game has exactly two pure Nash equilibria, in one of which citizen 2 does not vote and in the other of which she votes for 1.

c. Show that an action of one of the players in the second equilibrium is weakly dominated.

d. Why is "swing voter's curse" an appropriate name for the determinant of citizen 2's decision in the first equilibrium?

9.8   Appendix: auctions with an arbitrary distribution of valuations

9.8.1   *First-price sealed-bid auctions*

In this section I construct a symmetric equilibrium of a first-price sealed-bid auction for a distribution *F* of valuations that satisfies the assumptions in Section 9.6.2 and is differentiable on $(\underline{v}, \overline{v})$. (Unlike the remainder of the book, the section uses calculus.)

As before, denote the bid of type *v* of player *i* (i.e. player *i* when her valuation is *v*) by $\beta_i(v)$. In a symmetric equilibrium, every player uses the same bidding function: for some function β we have $\beta_i = \beta$ for every player i. A reasonable guess is that if such an equilibrium exists, β is increasing: the higher a player's valuation, the more she bids. Under the additional assumption that β is differentiable, I derive a condition that it must satisfy in any symmetric equilibrium. Exactly one function satisfies this condition, and this function is in fact increasing (as you are asked to show in an exercise).

Suppose that all $n - 1$ players other than i bid according to the increasing differentiable function β. Then, given the assumptions on F, the probability of a tie is zero, and hence for any bid b, the expected payoff of player i when her valuation is v and she bids b is

$$(v - b)\Pr(\text{Highest bid is } b) = (v - b)\Pr(\text{All } n - 1 \text{ other bids} \le b). \quad (308.1)$$

Now, a player bidding according to the function β bids at most b, for $\beta(\underline{v}) \le b \le \beta(\overline{v})$, if her valuation is at most $\beta^{-1}(b)$ (the inverse of β evaluated at b). Thus the probability that the bids of the $n - 1$ other players are all at most b is the probability that the highest of $n - 1$ randomly selected valuations—a random variable denoted $\mathbf{X}$ in Section 9.6.2—is at most $\beta^{-1}(b)$. Denoting the cumulative distribution function of $\mathbf{X}$ by H, the expected payoff in (308.1) is thus

$$(v - b)H(\beta^{-1}(b)) \text{ if } \beta(\underline{v}) \le b \le \beta(\overline{v})$$

(and 0 if $b < \beta(\underline{v})$, $v - b$ if $b > \beta(\overline{v})$).

I now claim that in a symmetric equilibrium in which every player bids according to β, we have $\beta(v) \le v$ if $v > \underline{v}$ and $\beta(\underline{v}) = \underline{v}$. If $v > \underline{v}$ and $\beta(v) > v$, then a player with valuation v wins with positive probability (players with valuations less than v bid less than $\beta(v)$, because β is increasing) and obtains a negative payoff if she does so. She obtains a payoff of zero by bidding v, so for equilibrium we need $\beta(v) \le v$ whenever $v > \underline{v}$. Given that β satisfies this condition, if $\beta(\underline{v}) > \underline{v}$ then a player with valuation $\underline{v}$ wins with positive probability, and obtains a negative payoff if she does so. Thus $\beta(\underline{v}) \le \underline{v}$. If $\beta(\underline{v}) < \underline{v}$, then players with valuations slightly greater than $\underline{v}$ also bid less than $\underline{v}$ (because β is continuous), so that a player with valuation $\underline{v}$ who increases her bid slightly wins with positive probability and obtains a positive payoff if she does so, rather than obtaining the payoff of zero. We conclude that $\beta(\underline{v}) = \underline{v}$.

Now, the expected payoff of a player of type v when every other player uses the bidding function β is differentiable on $(\underline{v}, \beta(\overline{v}))$ (given that β is increasing and differentiable, and $\beta(\underline{v}) = \underline{v}$) and, if $v > \underline{v}$, is increasing at $\underline{v}$. Thus the derivative of this expected payoff with respect to b is zero at any best response less than $\beta(\overline{v})$:

$$-H(\beta^{-1}(b)) + \frac{(v - b)H'(\beta^{-1}(b))}{\beta'(\beta^{-1}(b))} = 0. \quad (308.2)$$

(The derivative of β^{-1} at the point b is $1/\beta'(\beta^{-1}(b))$.)

In a symmetric equilibrium in which every player bids according to β, the best response of type v of any given player to the other players' strategies is $\beta(v)$. Because β is increasing, we have $\beta(v) < \beta(\overline{v})$ for $v < \overline{v}$, so $\beta(v)$ must satisfy (308.2) whenever $\underline{v} < v < \overline{v}$. If $b = \beta(v)$, then $\beta^{-1}(b) = v$, so that substituting $b = \beta(v)$ into (308.2) and multiplying by $\beta'(v)$ yields

$$\beta'(v)H(v) + \beta(v)H'(v) = vH'(v) \text{ for } \underline{v} < v < \overline{v}.$$

The left-hand side of this differential equation is the derivative with respect to v of $\beta(v)H(v)$. Thus for some constant C we have

$$\beta(v)H(v) = \int_{\underline{v}}^{v} xH'(x)\, dx + C \text{ for } \underline{v} < v < \overline{v}.$$

The function β is bounded, so considering the limit as v approaches $\underline{v}$, we deduce that $C = 0$.

We conclude that if the game has a symmetric Nash equilibrium in which each player's bidding function is increasing and differentiable on $(\underline{v}, \overline{v})$, then this function is defined by

$$\beta^*(v) = \frac{\int_{\underline{v}}^{v} xH'(x)\, dx}{H(v)} \text{ for } \underline{v} < v \leq \overline{v}$$

and $\beta^*(\underline{v}) = \underline{v}$. Now, the function H is the cumulative distribution function of $\mathbf{X}$, the highest of $n - 1$ independently drawn valuations. Thus $\beta^*(v)$ is the expected value of $\mathbf{X}$ conditional on its being less than v: $\beta^*(v) = E[\mathbf{X} \mid \mathbf{X} < v]$, as claimed in Section 9.6.2.

We may alternatively express the numerator in the expression for $\beta^*(v)$ as $vH(v) - \int_{\underline{v}}^{v} H(x)dx$ (using integration by parts), so that given $H(v) = (F(v))^{n-1}$ (the probability that $n - 1$ valuations are at most v), we have

$$\beta^*(v) = v - \frac{\int_{\underline{v}}^{v} H(x)\, dx}{H(v)} = v - \frac{\int_{\underline{v}}^{v} (F(x))^{n-1}\, dx}{(F(v))^{n-1}} \text{ for } \underline{v} < v \leq \overline{v}. \tag{309.1}$$

In particular, $\beta^*(v) < v$ for $\underline{v} < v \leq \overline{v}$.

⁇ EXERCISE 309.2 (Property of the bidding function in a first-price auction) Show that the bidding function β^* defined in (309.1) is increasing.

⁇ EXERCISE 309.3 (Example of Nash equilibrium in a first-price auction) Verify that for the distribution F uniform from 0 to 1 the bidding function defined by (309.1) is $(1 - 1/n)v$.

9.8.2 Revenue equivalence of auctions

I argued in the text that the expected price paid by the winner of a first-price auction is the same as the expected price paid by the winner of a second-price auction. A much more general result may be established.

Suppose that n risk-neutral bidders are involved in a sealed-bid auction in which the price is an arbitrary function of the bids (not necessarily the highest, or second highest). Each player's bid affects the probability p that she wins and the expected amount $e(p)$ that she pays. Thus we can think of each bidder's choosing a value of p, and can formulate the problem of a bidder with valuation v as

$$\max_p (p \cdot v - e(p)).$$

Denote the solution of this problem by $p^*(v)$. Assuming that e is differentiable, the first-order condition for this problem implies that

$$v = e'(p^*(v)) \text{ for all } v.$$

Integrating both sides of this equation, we have

$$e(p^*(v)) = e(p^*(\underline{v})) + \int_{\underline{v}}^{v} x \, dp^*(x). \tag{310.1}$$

Now consider an equilibrium with the property that the object is sold to the bidder with the highest valuation, so that $p^*(v) = \Pr(\mathbf{X} < v)$, and the expected payment $e(p^*(\underline{v}))$ of a bidder with the lowest possible valuation is zero. In any such equilibrium, (310.1) implies that the expected payment $e(p^*(v))$ of a bidder with any given valuation v is equal to $\Pr(\mathbf{X} < v)\mathrm{E}[\mathbf{X} \mid \mathbf{X} < v]$, independent of the price determination rule in the auction.

This result generalizes the earlier observation that the expected payments of bidders in the Nash equilibria of first- and second-price auctions in which the bidders' valuations are independent and private are the same. It is a special case of the more general *revenue equivalence principle*, which applies to a class of common value auctions, as well as private value auctions, and may be stated as follows.

> *Suppose that each bidder (i) is risk neutral, (ii) independently receives a signal from the same continuous and increasing cumulative distribution, and (iii) has a valuation that depends continuously on all the bidders' signals. Consider auction mechanisms in the symmetric Nash equilibria of which the object is sold to the bidder with the highest signal and the expected payoff of a bidder with the lowest possible valuation is zero. In the symmetric Nash equilibrium of any such mechanism, the expected payment of a bidder of any given type is the same, and hence the auctioneer's expected revenue is the same.*

9.8.3 Reserve prices

The following exercise (which requires calculus) asks you to show that, in an example, a seller in a second-price sealed-bid auction can increase the expected selling price by imposing a positive "reserve price".

❓ EXERCISE 310.2 (Reserve prices in second-price sealed-bid auction) Consider a second-price sealed-bid auction with two bidders in which each bidder's valuation is drawn independently from the distribution uniform from 0 to 1. Suppose that the seller imposes the reserve price r. That is, if both bids are less than r, the object is not sold (and neither bidder makes any payment), if one bid is less than r and the other is at least r, the object is sold at the price r, and if both bids are at least r, the object is sold at a price equal to the second highest bid. Show that for each bidder, a bid equal to her valuation weakly dominates all her bids. For the Nash equilibrium in which each bidder submits her valuation, find the reserve price r that maximizes the expected price at which the object is sold.

Notes

The notion of a general Bayesian game was defined and studied by Harsanyi (1967/68). The formulation I describe here is taken (with a minor change) from Osborne and Rubinstein (1994, Section 2.6).

The origin of the observation that more information may hurt (Section 9.3.1) is unclear. The idea of "infection" in Section 9.3.2 was first studied by Rubinstein (1989). The game in Figure 284.1 is a variant suggested by Eddie Dekel of the one analyzed by Morris, Rob, and Shin (1995).

Games modeling voluntary contributions to a public good were first considered by Olson (1965, Section I.D) and have been subsequently much studied. The model in Section 9.5 is a variant of one in an unpublished paper of William F. Samuelson dated 1984.

Vickrey (1961) initiated the study of auctions described in Section 9.6. First-price common value auctions (Section 9.6.3) were first studied by Wilson (1967, 1969, 1977). The "winner's curse" appears to have been first articulated by Capen, Clapp, and Campbell (1971). The general revenue equivalence principle at the end of Section 9.8.2 is due to Myerson (1981). The equilibria in Exercise 299.1 are described by Milgrom (1981, Theorem 6.3). The literature is surveyed by Klemperer (1999). The box on spectrum auctions on page 300 is based on McMillan (1994), Cramton (1995, 1997, 1998), and McAfee and McMillan (1996).

Section 9.7 is based on Austen-Smith and Banks (1996) and Feddersen and Pesendorfer (1998).

Exercise 282.1 was suggested by Ariel Rubinstein. Exercise 282.2 is based on Brams, Kilgour, and Davis (1993). A model of adverse selection was first studied by Akerlof (1970); the model in Exercise 282.3 is taken from Samuelson and Bazerman (1985). Exercise 307.1 is based on Feddersen and Pesendorfer (1996).

10 Extensive Games with Imperfect Information

10.1 Extensive games with imperfect information   313
10.2 Strategies   317
10.3 Nash equilibrium   318
10.4 Beliefs and sequential equilibrium   323
10.5 Signaling games   331
10.6 Illustration: conspicuous expenditure as a signal of quality   336
10.7 Illustration: education as a signal of ability   340
10.8 Illustration: strategic information transmission   343
10.9 Illustration: agenda control with imperfect information   351
Prerequisite: Chapters 4 and 5, and Section 7.6

THE NOTION of an extensive game with perfect information defined in Chapter 5 models situations in which each player, whenever taking an action, is informed of the actions chosen previously by all players. In this chapter I discuss a generalization of this notion that allows us to model situations in which each player, when choosing her action, may not be informed of the other players' previous actions.

10.1 Extensive games with imperfect information

To describe an extensive game with *perfect* information, we need to specify the set of players, the set of terminal histories, the player function, and the players' preferences (see Definition 155.1). To describe an extensive game with *imperfect* information, we need to add a single item to this list: a specification of each player's information about the history at every point at which she moves. Denote by H_i the set of histories after which player i moves. We specify player i's information by partitioning (dividing up) H_i into a collection of *information sets*. (See Section 17.2 for the notion of a partition.) This collection is called player i's *information partition*. When making her decision, player i is informed of the information set that has occurred but not of which history within that set has occurred.

Suppose, for example, that player i moves after the histories C, D, and E (i.e. $H_i = \{C, D, E\}$) and is informed only that the history is C, or that it is either D or E. That is, if the history C has occurred, then she is informed that C has occurred, whereas if either D or E has occurred, then she is informed only that either D or E has occurred and not C—she is not informed whether the history that has occurred was D or E. Then player i's information partition consists of two information sets: $\{C\}$ and $\{D, E\}$. If instead she is not informed at all about which history has occurred, then her information partition consists of a single information set, $\{C, D, E\}$, whereas if she is informed precisely about the history, then her information partition consists of three information sets, $\{C\}$, $\{D\}$, and $\{E\}$.

As before, denote the set of actions available to the player who moves after the history h by $A(h)$ (see (156.1)). We allow two histories h and h' to be in the same information set only if $A(h) = A(h')$. Why? The player who moves after any history must know the set of actions available after that history, so if h and h' are in the same information set and $A(h) \neq A(h')$, then the player who moves at this information set can deduce which of these two histories had occurred by looking at the actions available to her. Only if $A(h) = A(h')$ is the player's knowledge of the set of actions available to her consistent with her not knowing whether the history is h or h'. If the information set that contains h and h' is I_i, the common value of $A(h)$ and $A(h')$ is denoted $A(I_i)$. That is, $A(I_i)$ is the set of actions available to player i at her information set I_i.

Many interesting extensive games with imperfect information contain a move of chance, so my definition of an extensive game, unlike my original definition of an extensive game with perfect information (155.1), allows for such moves. Given the presence of such moves, an outcome is a lottery over the set of terminal histories, so each player's preferences must be defined over such lotteries.

▶ DEFINITION 314.1 (*Extensive game*) An **extensive game** (with imperfect information and chance moves) consists of

- a set of **players**
- a set of sequences (**terminal histories**) having the property that no sequence is a proper subhistory of any other sequence
- a function (the **player function**) that assigns either a player or "chance" to every sequence that is a proper subhistory of some terminal history
- a function that assigns to each history that the player function assigns to chance a probability distribution over the actions available after that history, with the property that each such probability distribution is independent of every other distribution
- for each player, a partition (the player's **information partition**) of the set of histories assigned to that player by the player function
- for each player, **preferences** over the set of lotteries over terminal histories.

The simplest extensive games, in which each player moves once and no player, when moving, is informed of any other player's action, model situations that may alternatively be modeled as strategic games, as illustrated by the next example.

◆ EXAMPLE 314.2 (*BoS as an extensive game*) Section 2.3 considers a situation in which each of two people chooses whether to imbibe the pleasures of Bach or those of Stravinsky, and neither person, when choosing a concert, knows the one chosen by the other person. Example 18.2 models this situation as a strategic game. We may alternatively model it as the following extensive game, in which the players choose their actions sequentially, but the second-mover is not informed of the choice made by the first-mover.

Players The two people, say 1 and 2.

Terminal histories (B, B), (B, S), (S, B), and (S, S).

Player function $P(\varnothing) = 1, P(B) = P(S) = 2$.

Chance moves None.

Information partitions Player 1's information partition contains a single information set, $\varnothing$ (player 1 has a single move, and when moving she is informed that the game is beginning); player 2's information partition also contains a single information set, $\{B, S\}$ (player 2 has a single move, and when moving she is not informed whether the history is B or S).

Preferences As given in the description of the situation.

This game is illustrated in Figure 315.1. As before, the small circle at the top of the figure represents the start of the game and each line represents an action; the numbers below each terminal history are Bernoulli payoffs whose expected values represent the players' preferences over lotteries. The dotted line connecting the histories B and S indicates that these histories are in the same information set of player 2. Note that the condition that player 2's set of actions at every history within her information set be the same is satisfied: after each such history, player 2's set of actions is $\{B, S\}$.

The next example shows how an extensive game may model a situation having a richer information structure and random events. The situation considered in the example is an extremely simple version of the card game poker, in which there are two players, one of whom is dealt a single card.

◆ EXAMPLE 315.1 (Card game) Each of two players begins by putting a dollar in the pot. Player 1 is then dealt a card that is equally likely to be *High* or *Low*; she observes her card, but player 2 does not. Player 1 may *see* or *raise*. If she *sees*, she

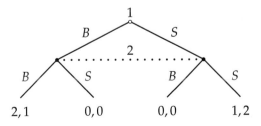

Figure 315.1 The extensive game in Example 314.2. The dotted line (with "2" above it) represents the fact that when moving, player 2 is not informed whether the history is B or S. That is, B and S are in the same information set.

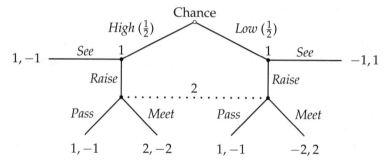

Figure 316.1 An extensive game that models the card game in Example 315.1. The number in parentheses beside each label of the moves of chance is the probability with which that move occurs.

shows her card to player 2. (Player 2 does not have any card for player 1 to see, but you can imagine her holding a fixed card with value between *High* and *Low*. In Exercise 316.1 you are asked to consider a situation in which player 2, like player 1, is dealt a card.) If player 1's card is *High* she takes the money in the pot, and if it is *Low* player 2 takes the money in the pot; in both cases the game ends. If player 1 *raises*, she adds a dollar to the pot and player 2 chooses whether to *pass* or *meet*. If player 2 *passes*, player 1 takes the money in the pot. If player 2 *meets*, she adds a dollar to the pot, and player 1 shows her card. If the card is *High*, player 1 takes the money in the pot, while if it is *Low* player 2 does so.

An extensive game that models this situation is shown in Figure 316.1. Player 1 has two information sets, one containing the single history *High* and one containing the single history *Low*. Player 2 has one information set, consisting of the two histories (*High, Raise*) and (*Low, Raise*). This information set reflects the fact that player 2 cannot observe player 1's card. Note that again the requirement that the set of actions at every history within an information set be the same is satisfied at player 2's information set.

? EXERCISE 316.1 (*Variant of card game*) Consider the following variant of the card game in the previous example. Initially each player puts a dollar in the pot. Then *each* player is dealt a card; each player's card is equally likely to be *High* or *Low*, independent of the other player's card. Each player sees only her own card. Player 1 may *see* or *raise*. If she *sees*, then the players compare their cards. The one with the higher card wins the pot; if the cards are the same, then each player takes back the dollar she had put in the pot. If player 1 *raises*, then she adds k to the pot (where k is a fixed positive number), and player 2 may *pass* or *meet*. If player 2 *passes*, then player 1 takes the money in the pot. If player 2 *meets*, then she adds k to the pot and the players compare cards, the one with the higher card winning the pot; if the cards are the same, then each player takes back the $(1 + k)$ she had put in the pot. Model this card game as an extensive game. (Drawing a diagram is sufficient; you can avoid the need for information sets to cross histories by putting the initial move in the center of your diagram.)

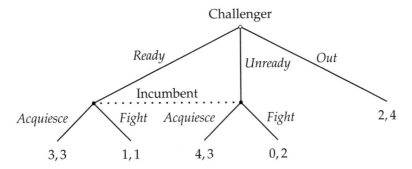

Figure 317.1 An extensive game that models the entry game in Example 317.1. The dotted line indicates that the histories *Ready* and *Unready* are in the same information set. The challenger's payoff is listed first, the incumbent's second.

In these examples, one of the players has an information set that contains more than one history. A game in which every information set of every player contains a single history is equivalent to an extensive game with perfect information. Thus, for instance, the entry game of Example 154.1 can be regarded as a general extensive game in which the challenger has a single information set consisting of the empty history, and the incumbent has a single information set consisting of the history *In*.

The next example is a variant of the entry game in which the challenger, before entering, takes an action that the incumbent does not observe.

◆ EXAMPLE 317.1 (Entry game) An incumbent faces the possibility of entry by a challenger, as in Example 154.1. The challenger has three choices: it may stay out, prepare itself for combat and enter, or enter without making preparations. Preparation is costly but reduces the loss from a fight. The incumbent may either fight or acquiesce to entry. A fight is less costly to the incumbent if the entrant is unprepared; but regardless of the entrant's readiness, the incumbent prefers to acquiesce than to fight. The incumbent observes whether the challenger enters but not whether an entrant is prepared.

An extensive game with imperfect information that models this situation, given some additional assumptions about the players' preferences, is shown in Figure 317.1. Each player has a single information set: the challenger's information set consists of the empty history, and the incumbent's information set consists of the two histories *Ready* (the challenger enters, prepared for combat) and *Unready* (the challenger enters without having made preparations).

10.2 Strategies

As in an extensive game with perfect information, a strategy for a player in a general extensive game specifies the action the player takes whenever it is her turn to move. In a general game, a player takes an action at each of her information sets, so a strategy is defined as follows.

▶ DEFINITION 318.1 (*Strategy in extensive game*) A (pure) **strategy** of player i in an extensive game is a function that assigns to each of i's information sets I_i an action in $A(I_i)$ (the set of actions available to player i at the information set I_i).

Consider, for example, the game in Figure 315.1 (*BoS* as an extensive game). Each player has a single information set, at which two actions, B and S, are available. Thus each player has two strategies, B and S. In the game in Figure 316.1 (the card game), player 1 has two information sets, at each of which she has two actions, *Raise* and *See*. Thus she has four strategies: (*Raise, Raise*) (raise whether her card is *High* or *Low*), (*Raise, See*) (raise if the card is *High*, see if it is *Low*), (*See, Raise*), and (*See, See*). Player 2 has a single information set, at which she has two actions, namely *Meet* and *Pass*; thus she has two strategies, *Meet* and *Pass*.

(?) EXERCISE 318.2 (Strategies in variants of card game and entry game) Find the players' strategies in the games in Exercise 316.1 and Example 317.1.

In some of the games we study, we wish to allow players to choose their actions randomly. One way of doing so is to allow each player to choose a mixed strategy—a probability distribution over her pure strategies—as we did for strategic games (see Definition 107.1).

▶ DEFINITION 318.3 (*Mixed strategy in extensive game*) A **mixed strategy** of a player in an extensive game is a probability distribution over the player's pure strategies.

As before, a pure strategy may be identified with a mixed strategy that assigns probability 1 to the pure strategy. Given this identification, a player's set of mixed strategies contains her pure strategies.

10.3 Nash equilibrium

Having defined a strategy, the definition of a Nash equilibrium is straightforward: a strategy profile is a Nash equilibrium if no player has an alternative strategy that increases her payoff, given the other players' strategies. The following definition closely follows Definition 108.1.

▶ DEFINITION 318.4 (*Nash equilibrium of extensive game*) The mixed strategy profile α^* in an extensive game is a **(mixed strategy) Nash equilibrium** if, for each player i and every mixed strategy α_i of player i, player i's expected payoff to α^* is at least as large as her expected payoff to $(\alpha_i, \alpha^*_{-i})$ according to a payoff function whose expected value represents player i's preferences over lotteries.

As before, I refer to an equilibrium in which no player's strategy entails any randomization (i.e. every player's strategy assigns probability 1 to a single action at each information set) as a *pure Nash equilibrium*.

One way to find a Nash equilibrium of an extensive game is to construct the strategic form of the game and analyze it as a strategic game, as we did for extensive games with perfect information (see Section 5.3).

◆ EXAMPLE 319.1 (*BoS* as an extensive game) Each player in Example 314.2 has two strategies, *B* and *S*. The strategic form of the game is exactly the strategic game *BoS*, as given in Figure 19.1. Thus the game has two pure Nash equilibria, (B, B) and (S, S), and a mixed equilibrium in which player 1 uses *B* with probability $\frac{2}{3}$ and player 2 uses *B* with probability $\frac{1}{3}$.

In this example player 2, when taking an action, is not informed of the action chosen by player 1. This lacuna in player 2's information is reflected in her information set, which contains both the history *B* and the history *S*. However, even though player 2 is not informed of player 1's action, her experience playing the game tells her the history (or probability distribution over histories) to expect. In the steady state in which every person who plays the role of either player chooses *B*, for example, each player knows that the other player will choose *B*. She is not *informed* of this fact, but her long experience playing the game leads her to the (correct) conclusion about the other player's action. Similarly, in the steady state in which *B* is chosen by a third of the people who play the role of player 2, the experience of each person who plays the role of player 1 leads her to expect her adversary to choose *B* with probability $\frac{1}{3}$. The point is that a player's information partition reflects the information obtained from her observations of the other players' actions during a play of the game; her experience playing the game may yield her more information about the other players' steady state actions.

◆ EXAMPLE 319.2 (Card game) The strategic form of the card game in Example 315.1 is given in Figure 320.1. By inspection, we see that the game has no equilibrium in which either player's strategy is pure. Player 1's strategy (*See, See*) is strictly dominated by her mixed strategy that assigns probability $\frac{1}{2}$ to (*Raise, Raise*) and probability $\frac{1}{2}$ to (*Raise, See*). Thus it is not used with positive probability in any Nash equilibrium. Player 1's strategy (*See, Raise*) is not a best response to any mixed strategy of player 2 that assigns positive probability to *Meet*, so given the absence of an equilibrium in pure strategies, in all Nash equilibria player 1 randomizes between (*Raise, Raise*) and (*Raise, See*). The condition that each player receive the same expected payoff from each strategy to which she assigns positive probability generates the conditions $q = \frac{1}{2}(1 - q)$ and $-p = -\frac{1}{2}(1 - p)$, where p is the probability player 1 assigns to (*Raise, Raise*) and q is the probability player 2 assigns to *Pass*. Thus $p = q = \frac{1}{3}$. In conclusion, the game has a unique Nash equilibrium, in which player 1 assigns probability $\frac{1}{3}$ to (*Raise, Raise*) and probability $\frac{2}{3}$ to (*Raise, See*), and player 2 assigns probability $\frac{1}{3}$ to *Pass* and probability $\frac{2}{3}$ to *Meet*. Player 1's equilibrium strategy implies that she always chooses *Raise* if her card is *High*, and chooses *Raise* with probability $\frac{1}{3}$ if her card is *Low*. That is, player 1 "bluffs" with probability $\frac{1}{3}$.

? EXERCISE 319.3 (Nash equilibria of card game) Consider a generalization of the card game in Example 315.1 in which the amount added to the pot when player 1 raises and player 2 meets is k. (In Example 315.1, $k = 1$). Find the Nash equilibrium of this game for any $k \geq 0$. How does player 1's propensity to bluff depend on the value of k?

	Pass	Meet
Raise, Raise	$1, -1$	$0, 0$
Raise, See	$0, 0$	$\frac{1}{2}, -\frac{1}{2}$
See, Raise	$1, -1$	$-\frac{1}{2}, \frac{1}{2}$
See, See	$0, 0$	$0, 0$

Figure 320.1 The strategic form of the card game in Example 315.1.

	X	Y
X	$3, 2$	$1, 1$
Y	$4, 3$	$2, 4$

Figure 320.2 The payoffs in the situation considered in Example 320.2.

? EXERCISE 320.1 (Nash equilibria of variant of card game) Find the Nash equilibria of the game in Exercise 316.1 for $0 < k < 1$ and for $k > 1$. How does player 1's propensity to bluff depend on the value of k?

◆ EXAMPLE 320.2 (Commitment and observability) Two people each have two actions, X and Y. Their payoffs to the four action pairs are shown in Figure 320.2.

First suppose that they choose actions simultaneously. The strategic game that models this situation has a unique Nash equilibrium, in which both players choose Y. (Note that X is strictly dominated by Y for player 1.)

Now suppose that the players choose their actions sequentially, player 1 first, and that player 2 observes player 1's action before choosing her action. That is, player 1 commits to her action before player 2 chooses her action. The extensive game with perfect information that models this situation has a single subgame perfect equilibrium, in which both players choose X. Player 1 is better off in this equilibrium than she is in the equilibrium of the simultaneous-move game.

Finally suppose that player 1 moves first, but her action is not perfectly observed by player 2. If player 1 chooses X, player 2 may think she chose Y, and vice versa. We may model this situation as an extensive game with imperfect information in which player 1's move is followed by a move of chance that selects a signal observed by player 2. Player 2 observes the signal, but not player 1's action. Assume that the probability that the signal is correct is the same for both actions, and less than 1. Denote this probability by $1 - \epsilon$. (Thus if player 1 chooses X, the signal is X with probability $1 - \epsilon$ and Y with probability ϵ, and if player 1 chooses Y, it is Y with probability $1 - \epsilon$ and X with probability ϵ.) Assume that $0 \leq \epsilon < \frac{1}{4}$.

This extensive game, its strategic form, and its Nash equilibria are shown in Figure 321.1. (The strategy IJ of player 2, where I and J are both either X or Y, means choose I after the signal X and J after the signal Y. The mixed strategy equilibria may be found by using the methods of Section 4.10.) We see, in particular, that the game has a pure strategy Nash equilibrium (Y, YY) for all values of ϵ with $0 \leq \epsilon < \frac{1}{4}$.

Extensive game:

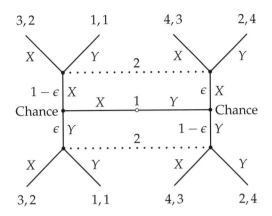

Strategic form:

	XX	XY	YX	YY
X	3, 2	$3 - 2\epsilon, 2 - \epsilon$	$1 + 2\epsilon, 1 + \epsilon$	1, 1
Y	4, 3	$2 + 2\epsilon, 4 - \epsilon$	$4 - 2\epsilon, 3 + \epsilon$	2, 4

Nash equilibrium strategy pairs:

Player 1		Player 2			
X	Y	XX	XY	YX	YY
0	1	0	0	0	1
ϵ	$1 - \epsilon$	0	$\frac{1}{2-4\epsilon}$	0	$\frac{1-4\epsilon}{2-4\epsilon}$
$1 - \epsilon$	ϵ	$\frac{1-4\epsilon}{2-4\epsilon}$	0	$\frac{1}{2-4\epsilon}$	0

Figure 321.1 An extensive game (top) that models a situation in which the payoffs are those in Figure 320.2, player 1 moves first, and player 2 observes an imperfect signal of player 1's action. Note that the empty history is in the center of the game. The strategic form of the game is given in the middle of the figure, followed by its Nash equilibria for $0 \leq \epsilon < \frac{1}{4}$.

In summary, the game in which player 1 moves first and her action is perfectly observable has a unique subgame perfect equilibrium, the outcome of which is that both players choose X, whereas the game in which player 1's action is observable with error has a pure strategy Nash equilibrium in which the outcome is that both players choose Y, regardless of how small the error.

Thus the advantage gained by the commitment entailed in being the first-mover, as reflected in the subgame perfect equilibrium of the game with perfect information, is completely lost in the pure strategy Nash equilibrium of the game in which the second player's observation of the first-mover's action is even slightly imperfect. Why? Suppose both player 1 and player 2 choose Y, and consider the implications of player 1's switching to X. In the game with perfect information, player 2's observation of X is inconsistent with the equilibrium; she interprets it as a deviation, to which she optimally responds by choosing X, making the deviation worthwhile for player 1. In the game with imperfect information, player 2's observation of X is consistent with the equilibrium; she interprets it as an inaccurate signal (regardless of how unlikely such a signal is) and continues to choose Y, making player 1's deviation undesirable for her.

In Chapter 5 we saw that the notion of Nash equilibrium is not adequate in all extensive games with perfect information, and I developed the notion of subgame perfect equilibrium to deal with the problem. How may we extend the idea behind subgame perfect equilibrium to the larger class of extensive games with (possibly) imperfect information?

◆ EXAMPLE 322.1 (Entry game) The strategic form of the entry game in Example 317.1 is shown in Figure 322.1. We see that the game has two Nash equilibria in pure strategies, (*Unready, Acquiesce*) and (*Out, Fight*). (You may verify that it has also mixed strategy Nash equilibria in which the challenger uses the pure strategy *Out* and the probability assigned by the incumbent to *Acquiesce* is at most $\frac{1}{2}$.)

	Acquiesce	*Fight*
Ready	3,3	1,1
Unready	4,3	0,2
Out	2,4	2,4

Figure 322.1 The strategic form of the entry game of Example 317.1.

As in the version of the entry game with perfect information studied in Chapter 5, the Nash equilibrium (*Out, Fight*) is not plausible. If in fact the challenger enters, the incumbent optimally acquiesces, regardless of the history that has occurred (i.e. regardless of whether the challenger is ready for combat). In games with perfect information we eliminated such equilibria by defining the notion of subgame perfect equilibrium, which requires that each player's strategy be optimal, given the other players' strategies, for every history after which she moves, regardless of whether the history occurs if the players adhere to their strategies.

The natural extension of this idea to games with imperfect information requires that each player's strategy be optimal at each of her information sets. In the entry game we are studying, the implementation of this idea is straightforward. The incumbent's action *Fight* is unambiguously suboptimal at its information set because the incumbent prefers *Acquiesce* if the challenger enters, regardless of whether the challenger is ready. Thus the equilibria in which the incumbent assigns positive probability to *Fight* do not satisfy the added requirement. The remaining equilibrium, (*Unready, Acquiesce*), does satisfy the requirement: the incumbent chooses its unambiguously optimal strategy at its information set.

The implementation of the idea in other games is less straightforward because the optimality of an action at an information set may depend on the history that has occurred. Consider a variant of the entry game in which the incumbent prefers to fight than to accommodate an unprepared entrant, as illustrated in Figure 323.1. Like the original game, this game has a Nash equilibrium in which the challenger

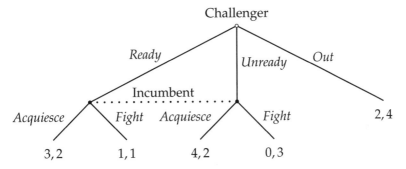

Figure 323.1 A variant of the entry game in Example 317.1 in which the incumbent prefers to fight if the challenger enters unprepared. The challenger's payoff is listed first, the incumbent's second.

stays out and the incumbent fights. But given that fighting is now optimal if the challenger enters unprepared, the reasonableness of the equilibrium in the modified game depends on the history the incumbent believes has occurred if it has to move. The challenger's strategy *Out* gives the incumbent no basis on which to form such a belief, so to pursue the argument we need to consider what this belief might be. In the next section I describe a solution for extensive games that includes the players' beliefs as part of an equilibrium.

10.4 Beliefs and sequential equilibrium

A Nash equilibrium of a strategic game may be characterized by two requirements: that each player choose her best action given her belief about the other players, and that each player's belief be correct (see page 21). The notion of equilibrium I now define for extensive games embodies the same two requirements, and, like the notion of subgame perfect equilibrium for extensive games with perfect information, insists that they hold at each point at which a player has to choose an action. When defining a Nash equilibrium of a strategic game precisely, we do not need to consider the players' beliefs separately from their strategies because the requirement that the beliefs be correct completely determines them: each player's belief about every other player's strategy is simply equal to that strategy. For an extensive game, the players' strategies may not completely determine their beliefs, as we have just seen in the game in Figure 323.1. Thus we are led to define a notion of equilibrium for pairs consisting of a strategy profile and a collection of beliefs.

10.4.1 Beliefs

We assume that at an information set that contains more than one history, the player whose turn it is to move forms a belief about the history that has occurred. We model this belief as a probability distribution over the histories in the information set. (At an information set containing a single history, the only possible belief assigns probability 1 to that history.) We call a collection of beliefs, one for each information set of every player, a *belief system*.

▶ DEFINITION 324.1 A **belief system** in an extensive game is a function that assigns to each information set a probability distribution over the histories in that information set.

Consider, for example, the entry game of Example 317.1. This game has two information sets, one consisting of the empty history, and one consisting of the histories *Ready* and *Unready*. Thus a belief system for the game consists of a pair of probability distributions: one assigns probability 1 to the empty history (the challenger's belief at the start of the game), and the other assigns probabilities to the histories *Ready* and *Unready* (the incumbent's belief after the challenger enters).

10.4.2 Strategies

When studying Nash equilibrium in the previous section we incorporated the possibility of randomization by allowing players to choose mixed strategies. In the current context, a different formulation is convenient. Rather than allowing a player to choose a probability distribution over her pure strategies, we have her assign to each of her information sets a probability distribution over the histories in that set. We refer to such an assignment as a *behavioral strategy*.

▶ DEFINITION 324.2 (*Behavioral strategy in extensive game*) A **behavioral strategy** of player i in an extensive game is a function that assigns to each of i's information sets I_i a probability distribution over the actions in $A(I_i)$, with the property that each probability distribution is independent of every other distribution.

A behavioral strategy in which every probability distribution assigns probability 1 to a single action is equivalent to a pure strategy. In all the games we study, mixed strategies and behavioral strategies are equivalent; I choose to use behavioral strategies now only because they are easier to work with. The relation between the two types of strategy is illustrated by two examples.

In the game in Example 314.2 (*BoS* as an extensive game), each player has a single information set, so a behavioral strategy for each player is a single probability distribution over her actions. Thus in this game each player's set of behavioral strategies is identical to her set of mixed strategies.

In the game in Example 315.1 (the card game), player 1 has two information sets, so a behavioral strategy for her consists of a pair of probability distributions, each over the set {*Raise, See*}. By contrast, a mixed strategy for player 1 in this game is a single probability distribution over the set of her four pure strategies, {(*Raise, Raise*), (*Raise, See*), (*See, Raise*), (*See, See*)}. A behavioral strategy is thus specified by two numbers (the probabilities of *Raise* if player 1's card is *High* and if it is *Low*), while a mixed strategy is specified by three numbers. (Remember that a probability distribution over k actions is determined by $k-1$ numbers, because the k probabilities must sum to 1.) In this sense a behavioral strategy is simpler than a mixed strategy. However, restricting a player to behavioral strategies does not limit her options, in the sense that for every mixed strategy and every list of strategies for the other players there is a behavioral strategy that generates the same probability distribution over outcomes. (This result is not limited to this game—it holds in a very wide class of games that includes all the games studied in this chapter.)

10.4.3 Equilibrium

The notion of equilibrium I define applies to pairs consisting of a profile of behavioral strategies and a belief system; the following piece of terminology is convenient.

▶ DEFINITION 325.1 (*Assessment*) An **assessment** in an extensive game is a pair consisting of a profile of behavioral strategies and a belief system.

An assessment is an equilibrium if it satisfies the following two requirements (which I make precise in the subsequent discussion).

Sequential rationality Each player's strategy is optimal whenever she has to move, given her belief and the other players' strategies.

Consistency of beliefs with strategies Each player's belief is consistent with the strategy profile.

The requirement of sequential rationality generalizes the requirement of subgame perfect equilibrium that each player's strategy be optimal in the part of the game that follows each history after which she moves, given the strategy profile, regardless of whether this history occurs if the players follow their strategies. In the more general context of an extensive game, sequential rationality requires that each player's strategy be optimal *in the part of the game that follows each of her information sets*, given the strategy profile *and given the player's belief about the history in the information set that has occurred*, regardless of whether the information set is reached if the players follow their strategies.

Consider, for example, the game in Figure 326.1. Suppose that player 1's strategy (indicated by the black branches) selects E at the start of the game and J after the history (C, F), and player 2's belief at her information set (indicated by the numbers in brackets) is that the history C has occurred with probability $\frac{2}{3}$ and the history D has occurred with probability $\frac{1}{3}$. Sequential rationality requires that player 2's strategy be optimal at her information set, given the subsequent behavior specified by player 1's strategy, even though this set is not reached if player 1 follows her strategy. Player 2's expected payoff in the part of the game starting at her information set, given her belief, is $\frac{2}{3} \cdot 0 + \frac{1}{3} \cdot 1 = \frac{1}{3}$ to her strategy F and $\frac{2}{3} \cdot 1 + \frac{1}{3} \cdot 0 = \frac{2}{3}$ to her strategy G. Thus sequential rationality requires her to select G. Sequential rationality requires also that player 1's strategy be optimal at each of her two (one element) information sets, given player 2's strategy. Player 1's optimal action after the history (C, F) is J; if player 2's strategy is G, her optimal actions at the start of the game are D and E. Thus given player 2's strategy G, player 1 has two optimal strategies, DJ and EJ.

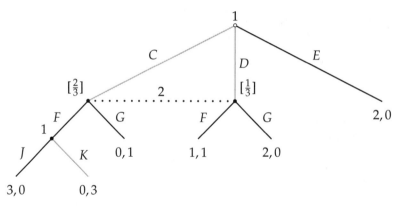

Figure 326.1 A game illustrating the sequential rationality requirement on an assessment. Given player 1's strategy, indicated by the black branches, and player 2's belief, given by the numbers in brackets at the end of the histories C and D, player 2's expected payoff to G exceeds her expected payoff to F, so that her optimal action is G.

Now let (β, μ) be an assessment in an arbitrary game (i.e. let β be a profile of behavioral strategies and μ a belief system), and let I_i be an information set of player i. Denote by $O_{I_i}(\beta, \mu)$ the probability distribution over terminal histories that results if each history in I_i occurs with the probability assigned to it by i's belief μ_i (which is not necessarily the probability with which it occurs if the players adhere to β), and *subsequently* the players adhere to the strategy profile β. (Compare this definition with that of $O_h(s)$ for an extensive game with perfect information (see page 165). For the information set $\{C, D\}$ and the strategy of player 1 and belief of player 2 indicated in the game in Figure 326.1, the probability distribution assigns probability $\frac{2}{3}$ to the terminal history (C, F, J) and probability $\frac{1}{3}$ to (D, F) if player 2 uses the strategy F, and probability $\frac{2}{3}$ to (C, G) and probability $\frac{1}{3}$ to (D, G) if she uses the strategy G.)

We can now state precisely the sequential rationality requirement: for each player i and each of her information sets I_i, her expected payoff to $O_{I_i}(\beta, \mu)$ is at least as large as her expected payoff to $O_{I_i}((\gamma_i, \beta_{-i}), \mu)$ for each of her behavioral strategies γ_i.

The requirement that each player's belief be consistent with the strategy profile is new, though forms of it are implicit in the definitions of Nash equilibrium and subgame perfect equilibrium. The idea is that in a steady state, each player's belief must be correct: the probability it assigns to any history must be the probability with which that history occurs if the players adhere to their strategies. The implementation of this idea is straightforward at an information set reached with positive probability if the players follow their strategies, but is unclear at an information set not reached if the players follow their strategies. *Every* history in such an information set has probability 0 if the players follow their strategies, but if such an information set is reached, the player who moves there must believe that *some* history has occurred. We deal with this difficulty by allowing the player who moves at such an information set to hold *any* belief at that information set.

Thus we formulate the consistency requirement to restrict the belief system only at information sets reached with positive probability if every player adheres to her strategy. Precisely, we require that the probability assigned to every history h^* in such an information set by the belief of the player who moves there be equal to the probability that h^* occurs according to the strategy profile, conditional on the information set's being reached. Denoting the information set by I_i and the strategy profile by β, by Bayes' rule (Section 17.6.5) this probability is

$$\frac{\Pr(h^* \text{ according to } \beta)}{\sum_{h \in I_i} \Pr(h \text{ according to } \beta)}. \tag{327.1}$$

Consider again the game in Figure 326.1. If player 1's behavioral strategy assigns probability 1 to the action E at the start of the game, the consistency requirement places no restriction on player 2's belief because player 2's information set is not reached if player 1 adheres to her strategy. If player 1's action at the start of the game assigns positive probability to C or D, however, the consistency requirement bites. If player 1's strategy assigns probability p to C and probability q to D, so that $\Pr(C \text{ according to } \beta) = p$ and $\Pr(D \text{ according to } \beta) = q$ (where β is the strategy profile), then (327.1) implies that player 2's belief assigns probability $p/(p+q)$ to C and probability $q/(p+q)$ to D. In particular, if player 1 chooses D with probability 1, then player 2's belief must assign probability 0 to C and probability 1 to D.

◆ EXAMPLE 327.2 (Consistent beliefs in *BoS* as an extensive game) In the game in Example 314.2, for every strategy of player 1, player 2's information set is reached with probability 1, so the consistency condition restricts player 2's belief in every assessment. The condition simply requires that player 2's belief assign to B and S the probabilities with which player 1 chooses these actions. That is, in this game consistency requires that player 2's belief always be correct. The same is true for any game in which all the players move simultaneously (no player knows any other player's action when making her move).

◆ EXAMPLE 327.3 (Consistent beliefs in card game) Consider the game in Example 315.1. If player 1's strategy selects *See* whether her card is *High* or *Low*, the consistency condition does not restrict player 2's belief, because player 2's information set is not reached. For every other strategy of player 1, the condition determines player 2's belief. Denote the probability that player 1 chooses *Raise* if her card is *High* by p_H and the probability she chooses *Raise* if her card is *Low* by p_L. Then $\Pr(High \text{ according to } \beta) = p_H$ and $\Pr(Low \text{ according to } \beta) = p_L$, so by (327.1), the consistency requirement is that player 2's belief assign probability $p_H/(p_H + p_L)$ to the history H and probability $p_L/(p_H + p_L)$ to the history L.

◆ EXAMPLE 327.4 (Consistent beliefs in entry game) In the games in Figures 317.1 and 323.1, denote by p_R, p_U, and p_O the probabilities the challenger assigns to *Ready*, *Unready*, and *Out*. If $p_O = 1$, the consistency condition does not restrict the incumbent's belief. Otherwise, the condition requires that the incumbent assign probability $p_R/(p_R + p_U)$ to *Ready* and probability $p_U/(p_R + p_U)$ to *Unready*.

In summary, the notion of equilibrium I use for extensive games is defined precisely as follows.

▶ DEFINITION 328.1 (*Weak sequential equilibrium*) An assessment (β, μ) (consisting of a behavioral strategy profile β and a belief system μ) is a **weak sequential equilibrium** if it satisfies the following two conditions.

Sequential rationality Each player's strategy is optimal in the part of the game that follows each of her information sets, given the strategy profile and her belief about the history in the information set that has occurred. Precisely, for each player i and each information set I_i of player i, player i's expected payoff to the probability distribution $O_{I_i}(\beta, \mu)$ over terminal histories generated by her belief μ_i at I_i and the behavior prescribed subsequently by the strategy profile β is at least as large as her expected payoff to the probability distribution $O_{I_i}((\gamma_i, \beta_{-i}), \mu)$ generated by her belief μ_i at I_i and the behavior prescribed subsequently by the strategy profile (γ_i, β_{-i}), for each of her behavioral strategies γ_i.

Weak consistency of beliefs with strategies For every information set I_i reached with positive probability given the strategy profile β, the probability assigned by the belief system to each history h^* in I_i is given by (327.1).

The game in Figure 326.1 illustrates this notion of equilibrium. As we have seen, in this game player 1's strategy EJ is sequentially rational given player 2's strategy G, and player 2's strategy G is sequentially rational given the beliefs indicated in the figure and player 1's strategy EJ. Further, the belief is consistent with the strategy profile (EJ, G), because this profile does not lead to player 2's information set. Thus the game has a weak sequential equilibrium in which the strategy profile is (EJ, G) and player 2's belief is the one indicated in the figure (or any other belief for which G is optimal). Now consider the strategy profile (DJ, G). Player 1's strategy is sequentially rational given player 2's strategy, and player 2's strategy is sequentially rational given her belief and player 1's strategy. But player 2's belief is not consistent with the strategy profile. The only consistent belief assigns probability 1 to D, which makes player 2's action F, rather than G, optimal. Thus the game has no weak sequential equilibrium in which the strategy profile is (DJ, G).

In an extensive game with perfect information, only one belief system is possible—that in which every player believes at each information set that the single compatible history has occurred with probability 1. Thus the condition of sequential rationality in such a game is the same as the optimality condition on a strategy profile in a subgame perfect equilibrium. Thus

> *in an extensive game with perfect information, the strategy profile in any weak sequential equilibrium is a subgame perfect equilibrium.*

In a general extensive game, the requirement of sequential rationality implies, in particular, that each player's strategy is optimal at the beginning of the game, given the other players' strategies and the player's belief about the history at each information set. Further, the consistency requirement implies that each player's belief about the history is correct at any information set reached with positive probability when the players follow their strategies. Thus if an assessment is a weak sequential equilibrium, then each player's strategy in the assessment is optimal at the beginning of the game, given the other players' strategies. That is,

the strategy profile in any weak sequential equilibrium is a Nash equilibrium.

To find the weak sequential equilibria of a game, we may use a combination of the techniques for finding subgame perfect equilibria of extensive games with perfect information and for finding Nash equilibria of strategic games. Consider, for example, the game in Figure 326.1. The sequential rationality requirement implies that in any weak sequential equilibrium player 1 chooses J after the history (C, F). Now we can consider two cases.

- Does the game have a weak sequential equilibrium in which player 1 chooses E? If player 1 chooses E, player 2's belief is not restricted by consistency, so we need to ask (a) whether any strategy of player 2 makes E optimal for player 1, and, if so, (b) whether there is a belief of player 2 that makes any such strategy optimal. We see that E is optimal if and only if player 2 chooses F with probability at most $\frac{2}{3}$. Any such strategy of player 2 is optimal if player 2 believes the history is C with probability $\frac{1}{2}$, and the strategy of choosing F with probability 0 is optimal if player 2 believes the history is C with any probability of at least $\frac{1}{2}$. We conclude that an assessment is a weak sequential equilibrium if player 1's strategy is EJ and player 2 either chooses F with probability at most $\frac{2}{3}$ and believes that the history is C with probability $\frac{1}{2}$, or chooses G and believes that the history is C with probability at least $\frac{1}{2}$.

- Does the game have a weak sequential equilibrium in which player 1 chooses C and/or D with positive probability? Denote the probability player 1 assigns to C by p and the probability she assigns to D by q. In such an equilibrium, player 2's belief is constrained by consistency to assign probability $p/(p+q)$ to C and probability $q/(p+q)$ to D. Thus G is optimal if $p > q$, F is optimal if $p < q$, and any mixture is optimal if $p = q$. Now, if player 2 chooses G, the only optimal strategy of player 1 that assigns positive probability to C or D assigns probability 1 to D, so that $q = 1$, making G not optimal for player 2. If player 2 chooses F, player 1's only optimal action at the start of the game is C, making F not optimal for player 2. If player 2 chooses a mixture of F and G, then player 1 must assign the same probability to both C and D, and hence must choose D with positive probability, which is incompatible with the fact that her expected payoff to D is less than her expected payoff to E. Thus the game has no weak sequential equilibrium in which player 1 chooses C and/or D with positive probability.

We conclude that in every weak sequential equilibrium of the game, player 1's strategy is EJ and player 2 either chooses F with probability at most $\frac{2}{3}$ and believes that the history is C with probability $\frac{1}{2}$, or chooses G and believes that the history is C with probability at least $\frac{1}{2}$. (Another method of finding these equilibria is to find all the Nash equilibria of the game, and then check which of these equilibria are associated with weak sequential equilibria.)

◆ EXAMPLE 330.1 (Weak sequential equilibria of entry game) As we saw in Example 322.1, the entry game of Example 317.1 has two pure strategy Nash equilibria, (*Unready*, *Acquiesce*) and (*Out*, *Fight*). Consider the first equilibrium. Consistency requires that the incumbent believe that the history is *Unready* at its information set, making *Acquiesce* optimal. Thus the game has a weak sequential equilibrium in which the strategy profile is (*Unready*, *Acquiesce*) and the incumbent's belief is that the history is *Acquiesce*. Now consider the second equilibrium. Regardless of the incumbent's belief at its information set, *Fight* is not an optimal action in the remainder of the game—for every belief, *Acquiesce* yields a higher payoff than does *Fight*. Thus no assessment in which the strategy profile is (*Out*, *Fight*) is both sequentially rational and consistent, so that the game has no weak sequential equilibrium in which the strategy profile is (*Out*, *Fight*).

The games in Examples 314.2 (*BoS* as an extensive game) and 315.1 (the card game) have no Nash equilibria in which some information set is not reached, so that for each game the set of strategy profiles that appear in weak sequential equilibria is equal to the set of Nash equilibria.

Why "weak" sequential equilibrium? The consistency condition's limitation to information sets reached with positive probability generates, in some games, a relatively large set of equilibrium assessments, some of which do not plausibly correspond to steady states. Consider, for example, the game in Figure 331.1, a variant of the entry game in Figure 323.1 in which *Ready* is better than *Unready* for the challenger regardless of the incumbent's action. This game has a weak sequential equilibrium in which the challenger's strategy is *Out*, the incumbent's strategy is F, and the incumbent believes at its information set that the history is *Unready*. In this equilibrium the incumbent believes that the challenger has chosen *Unready*, although this action is dominated (by *Ready*) for the challenger. Thus the incumbent's belief does not seem reasonable.

Notions of equilibrium that impose stronger consistency conditions narrow down the set of equilibrium outcomes in some games. One notion, sequential equilibrium, is widely used. However, the consistency condition it imposes is not straightforward, and the notion does not in any case eliminate all implausible equilibria—for example, it does not eliminate the equilibrium of the game in Figure 331.1 in which the challenger chooses *Out*. Further, in many games the

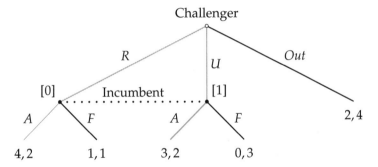

Figure 331.1 A variant of the entry game in Figure 323.1 in which *Ready* is better than *Unready* for the challenger regardless of the incumbent's action and the incumbent prefers *Fight* to *Acquiesce* only if the challenger is unprepared, but there is a weak sequential equilibrium in which the challenger stays out and the incumbent fights. The players' strategies in this equilibrium are indicated by the black lines; the probabilities the incumbent's belief assigns to each history in its information set are shown in brackets.

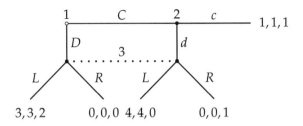

Figure 331.2 The game in Exercise 331.1 (Selten's horse).

set of weak sequential equilibria is not large and does not include implausible assessments. For these reasons I work with weak sequential equilibrium and do not consider "refinements" of this notion.

? EXERCISE 331.1 (Selten's horse) Find the weak sequential equilibria of the game in Figure 331.2 in which each player's strategy is pure. (Find the pure strategy Nash equilibria, then determine which is part of a weak sequential equilibrium. The name of the game comes from the person who first studied it, and its shape.)

? EXERCISE 331.2 (Two similar games with different equilibria) Consider the variant of the game in Figure 331.1 shown in Figure 332.1, in which the challenger's initial move is broken into two steps. Show that this game, unlike the game in Figure 331.1, has no weak sequential equilibrium in which the challenger chooses *Out*. In your opinion, should the games have different equilibria?

10.5 Signaling games

In many interactions, information is "asymmetric": some parties are informed about variables that affect everyone, and some parties are not. In one interesting class of situations, the informed parties have the opportunity to take actions

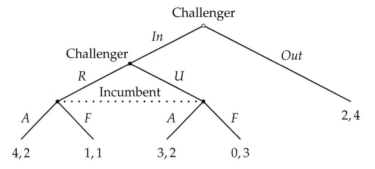

Figure 332.1 A variant of the entry game in Figure 331.1 in which the challenger's decision is broken into two steps.

observed by the uninformed parties before the latter take actions that affect everyone. In some circumstances, the informed parties' actions may "signal" their information.

Suppose, for example, that an employer can observe whether a job applicant has a college degree, but not her ability, and that a person of high ability may obtain a degree at low cost, while one of low ability may do so only at high cost. Then the fact that a person has a degree may signal to an employer that she has high ability—not because college teaches any skills, but because only high-ability individuals find obtaining a degree worthwhile, given the cost. (I return to this example in Section 10.7.)

In a general two-player "signaling game", a *sender* is informed about a variable relevant to both her and a *receiver* (or set of receivers), who is uninformed. The sender takes an action observed by the receiver, who then takes an action that affects them both. Depending on the way in which the message and the receiver's action affect the parties, the sender may want to limit or distort the information her signal conveys.

Such a situation may be modeled as an extensive game in which the sender has several possible "types", each corresponding to a value of the variable about which she is informed. The value she observes, and thus her type, are determined by chance. The receiver does not observe the sender's type, but sees an action she takes, and then herself takes an action. A simple example is given by another variant of the entry game.

◆ EXAMPLE 332.1 (Entry as a signaling game) A challenger contests an incumbent's turf. The challenger is *strong* with probability p and *weak* with probability $1 - p$, where $0 < p < 1$; it knows its type, but the incumbent does not. The challenger may either *ready* itself for battle or remain *unready*. (It does not have the option of staying out.) The incumbent observes the challenger's readiness, but not its type, and chooses whether to *fight* or *acquiesce*. An unready challenger's payoff is 5 if the incumbent acquiesces to its entry. Preparations cost a strong challenger 1 unit of payoff and a weak one 3 units, and fighting entails a loss of 2 units for each type. The incumbent prefers to fight (payoff 1) rather than to acquiesce to (payoff 0) an

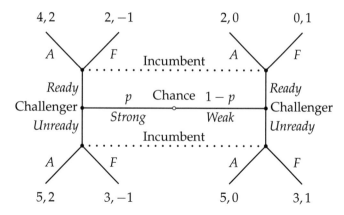

Figure 333.1 The game in Example 332.1. The empty history is in the center of the diagram. The incumbent's actions are A (acquiesce) and F (fight). The challenger's payoff is listed first, the incumbent's second.

unready challenger (who is quickly dispensed with), and prefers to acquiesce to (payoff 2) rather than to fight (payoff -1) a prepared one.

The extensive game in Figure 333.1 models this situation. Note that the empty history is in the center of the diagram. The first move is made by chance, which determines the challenger's type. Both types have two actions, *Ready* and *Unready*, so that the challenger has four strategies. The incumbent has two information sets, at each of which it has two actions (A and F), and thus also has four strategies.

I now find the pure weak sequential equilibria of this game. First note that a weak challenger prefers *Unready* to *Ready* regardless of the incumbent's actions— even if the incumbent acquiesces to a ready challenger and fights an unready one, the challenger prefers to be unready. Thus in any weak sequential equilibrium a weak challenger chooses *Unready*. I consider each possible action of a strong challenger in turn.

Strong challenger chooses *Ready* Both the incumbent's information sets are reached, so the consistency condition restricts its belief at each set. At the top information set, the incumbent must believe that the history was $(Strong, Ready)$, and hence choose A. At the bottom information set it must believe that the history was $(Weak, Unready)$, and hence choose F. Thus if the challenger deviates and chooses *Unready* if it is strong, then it is worse off—it obtains the payoff of 3 rather than 4. We conclude that the game has a weak sequential equilibrium in which the challenger chooses *Ready* when it is strong and *Unready* when it is weak, and the incumbent acquiesces when it sees *Ready* and fights when it sees *Unready*.

Strong challenger choose *Unready* At its bottom information set, the incumbent believes, by consistency, that the history was $(Strong, Unready)$ with probability p and $(Weak, Unready)$ with probability $1 - p$. Thus its expected payoff to A is $2p$ and to F is $-p + 1 - p = 1 - 2p$. Hence A is optimal if $p \geq \frac{1}{4}$ and F is optimal if $p \leq \frac{1}{4}$.

Suppose that $p \geq \frac{1}{4}$ and the incumbent chooses A in response to *Unready*. A strong challenger that chooses *Unready* obtains the payoff of 5. If it switches to *Ready* its payoff is less than 5 regardless of the incumbent's action. Thus if $p \geq \frac{1}{4}$, then the game has weak sequential equilibria in which both types of challenger choose *Unready* and the incumbent acquiesces to an unready challenger. The incumbent may hold any belief about the type of a ready challenger, and, depending on its belief, may fight or acquiesce.

Now suppose that $p \leq \frac{1}{4}$ and that the incumbent chooses F in response to *Unready*. A strong challenger that chooses *Unready* obtains the payoff of 3. If it switches to *Ready* its payoff is 2 if the incumbent fights and 4 if it acquiesces. Thus for an equilibrium the incumbent must fight a ready challenger. If it believes that a ready challenger is weak with high enough probability (at least $\frac{3}{4}$), fighting is indeed optimal. Is such a belief possible in an equilibrium? Yes: the consistency condition does not restrict the incumbent's belief upon observing *Ready* because this action is not taken when the challenger follows its strategy to choose *Unready* regardless of its type. Thus if $p \leq \frac{1}{4}$ the game has a weak sequential equilibrium in which both types of challenger choose *Unready*, the incumbent fights regardless of the challenger's action, and assigns probability of at least $\frac{3}{4}$ to the challenger's being weak if it observes that the challenger is ready for battle.

In summary, the game has two sorts of weak sequential equilibrium.

- The challenger chooses *Ready* if it is strong and *Unready* if it is weak. The incumbent believes that a ready challenger is strong and an unready one is weak and acquiesces to a ready challenger and fights an unready one.

- The challenger chooses *Unready* regardless of its type. The incumbent believes that an unready challenger is strong with probability p. If $p \geq \frac{1}{4}$ the game has equilibria in which the incumbent acquiesces to an unready challenger, holds any belief about the type of a ready challenger, and takes whatever action is optimal, given its belief, if the challenger is ready. If $p \leq \frac{1}{4}$ the game has equilibria in which the incumbent fights all challengers and believes a ready challenger is strong with probability at most $\frac{1}{4}$.

This example illustrates two kinds of pure strategy equilibrium that may exist in signaling games.

Separating equilibrium   Each type of the sender chooses a different action (in the first sort of equilibrium in the example, a strong challenger chooses *Ready* and weak challenger chooses *Unready*), so that upon observing the sender's action, the receiver knows the sender's type.

Pooling equilibrium   All types of the sender choose the same action (in the second sort of equilibrium in the example, both types of challenger choose *Unready*), so that the sender's action gives the receiver no clue to the sender's type.

If the sender has more than two types, mixtures of these types of equilibrium may exist—the set of types may be divided into groups, within each of which all types choose the same action and between which the actions are different.

❓ EXERCISE 335.1 (Pooling and separating equilibria in a signaling game) Consider a game that differs from the one in Figure 333.1 only in the payoffs to the terminal histories (*Weak, Ready, A*) and (*Weak, Ready, F*). For what values of these payoffs, if any, is the *only* weak sequential equilibrium of the game a separating equilibrium in which a strong challenger chooses *Ready* and a weak one chooses *Unready*? For what values of these payoffs, if any, is the *only* weak sequential equilibrium of the game a pooling equilibrium in which both types of challenger choose *Unready*?

❓ EXERCISE 335.2 (Sir Philip Sydney game) Some young animals expend energy begging for food from their parents—they squawk and bleat and scream, sometimes extravagantly. Can we expect these demands to signal their needs accurately? Consider the following signaling game. (The rationale for its name, due to its originator, the distinguished evolutionary biologist John Maynard Smith, is given in the Notes at the end of the chapter.)

A hungry parent has a piece of food that it may give to its offspring, or keep for itself. It does not detect whether its offspring is hungry. In either case, the offspring may signal that it is hungry to its parent (by squawking, for example). An animal is stronger and thus produces more offspring (i.e. has a higher "biological fitness") if it gets the food than if it does not. Normalize the parent's strength if it keeps the food to be 1, and denote its strength if it gives the food to its offspring by $S < 1$. If the offspring does not squawk, its strength is 1 if it gets the food, $V < 1$ if it is not hungry and does not get the food, and 0 if it is hungry and does not get the food. If the offspring squawks, its strength is multiplied by the factor $1 - t$, where $0 \leq t \leq 1$ (i.e. squawking may be costly). Denote the degree to which the parent and offspring are related by r, and take each player's payoff to be its strength plus r times the other player's strength. Evolutionary pressure will lead to behavior for each player that maximizes that player's payoff, given the other player's behavior. (For more on evolutionary games, see Chapter 13.) The game is shown in Figure 336.1.

Find the conditions on r, in terms of S, V, and t, under which the game has a separating equilibrium in which the offspring squawks if and only if it is hungry and the parent gives it the food if and only if it squawks. Show that if the offspring's payoff from obtaining the food exceeds her payoff from not obtaining it, regardless of whether she is hungry (which means that $r < (1 - V)/(1 - S)$), then the game has such an equilibrium only if $t > 0$. That is, in this case an equilibrium exists in which the signal is accurate only if the signal is costly. Show that if $r < (1 - S)/(1 - V)$, then the game has a pooling equilibrium in which the offspring is always quiet and the parent always keeps the food. (For other parameter values, the game has a pooling equilibrium in which the offspring is always quiet and the parent always gives the food.)

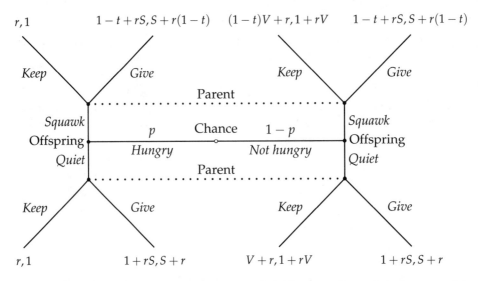

Figure 336.1 The Sir Philip Sydney game (Exercise 335.2). The empty history is in the center of the diagram. The offspring's payoff is listed first, the parent's second.

10.6 Illustration: conspicuous expenditure as a signal of quality

Why do some firms sponsor sporting events? Here is an explanation. The quality of some goods cannot be detected before the goods are consumed, and some firms sell goods of low quality while others sell goods of high quality. A consumer will purchase from a firm repeatedly once she detects goods of high quality, but will not buy low-quality goods more than once. Thus a purveyor of high-quality goods gains more from a consumer's sampling its wares than does a dealer in low-quality merchandise. Consumers may therefore deduce that it is worthwhile only for sellers of high-quality goods to sponsor sporting events—the potential benefit does not exceed the cost for low-quality firms—so that conspicuous expenditure is a sure sign of a high-quality firm, and lack thereof the mark of a low-quality firm. A high-quality firm is thus nudged into sports sponsorship.

Does this argument stand up to careful examination? Suppose that with probability π a firm is one that produces goods of quality $H > 0$ and with probability $1 - \pi$ one that produces goods of quality $L = 0$. (Note that the firm does not choose its quality.) The cost of producing a good of quality H is $c_H > 0$ and that of producing a good of quality 0 is $c_L = 0$.

A consumer interacts with the firm over two periods. In the first period, the firm chooses a price p_1 for its output and an amount $E \geq 0$ to spend conspicuously, for example, sponsoring sporting events. The expenditure E has no effect on the quality of the good. The consumer observes E and p_1, but not the quality of the good, and decides whether to purchase the good. If she makes no purchase, the interaction ends; her payoff is 0 and the firm's is $-E$. If she makes a purchase, she learns the quality of the good, the firm chooses a price p_2 for the second period, and she decides whether to purchase the good again. In any period in which she purchases the good her payoff is $v - p$, where v is the quality of the good and p is the price, and her total payoff is the sum of her payoffs in the two periods. (Thus the consumer is willing to purchase the low-quality good in either period only if its price is zero.) The firm's payoff is $p_1 - E - c_I$, where I is either L or H, if it sells to the consumer only in the first period, and $p_1 + p_2 - E - 2c_I$, if it sells to the consumer in both periods. (Note that the expenditure E occurs only in the first period.)

Assume that $H - c_H > 0$, so that at the highest price the consumer is willing to pay for the high-quality good (namely H), this good yields the firm a positive profit.

The structure of an extensive game that models this situation is shown in Figure 337.1. In this figure only *one* of the possible pairs (p_1, E) of first-period actions for the firm is indicated, and the range of second-period prices p_2 is indicated by the shaded triangles.

Consider the equilibria of this game. In the second period the players are fully informed. Thus the consumer buys the good in this period only if its price is at most equal to its quality. A price equal to H yields the high-quality firm a profit, so in an equilibrium a high-quality firm charges $p_2^H = H$ and the consumer buys the good; the firm's payoff is $H - c_H$ and the consumer's payoff is 0. The profit of a low-quality firm is 0 independent of its price: if the price is positive the consumer does not purchase the good, and if it is zero the firm's profit is zero regardless of whether the consumer purchases the good. Thus any second-period price $p_2^L \geq 0$ for a low-quality firm is compatible with equilibrium.

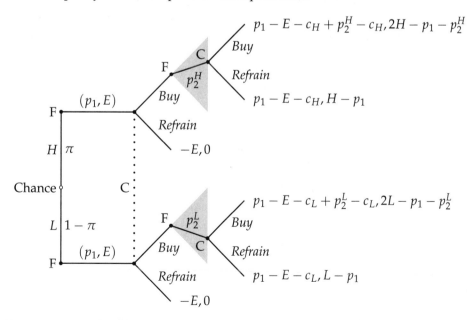

Figure 337.1 An outline of an extensive game that models a firm that signals its quality by sponsoring sporting events. The firm is denoted "F", and the consumer "C". Only *one* of the firm's actions (p_1, E) is shown. The firm's payoffs are listed first, the consumer's second.

I claim that under some conditions the whole game has a (separating) weak sequential equilibrium in which a producer of high-quality goods spends money in the first period, while a producer of low-quality ones does not. Consider the following assessment.

Firm's strategy   Choose (p^{H*}, E^*) in the first period and H in the second period after any history in which chance chooses H, and choose $(0,0)$ in the first period and any nonnegative price in the second period after any history in which chance chooses L.

Consumer's belief   The consumer believes that the history was H if and only if the (price, expenditure) pair (p, E) observed in the first period satisfies $p \leq p^{H*}$ and $E = E^*$.

Consumer's strategy   Buy the good in the first period if and only if the (price, expenditure) pair (p, E) satisfies $p \leq p^{H*}$ and $E = E^*$, and buy it in the second period if and only if either the history starts with H and the second-period price is at most H, or the history starts with L and the second-period price is 0.

Note that the consumer's belief in this assessment is extreme: unless she observes an expenditure of exactly E^* in the first period, she concludes that the firm is low quality. If the firm follows its strategy, the consumer observes a first-period action of either (p^{H*}, E^*) or $(0,0)$. The consistency condition implies that if she observes (p^{H*}, E^*), then she must believe that the firm is high quality, whereas if she observes $(0,0)$, then she must believe that it is low quality but does not restrict her belief after any other observation. The extreme belief I have specified makes a profitable deviation by a high-quality firm as difficult as possible, because any deviation causes the consumer to believe that the firm is low quality.

Under what conditions is this assessment a weak sequential equilibrium? The players' beliefs are consistent by construction, so we need to check only that each player's strategy is sequentially rational.

Firm   The firm's strategy is sequentially rational if and only if neither type of firm can increase its expected payoff, given the consumer's strategy and belief.

>**Type H**   If the firm chooses (p^{H*}, E^*) its profit is $p^{H*} + H - E^* - 2c_H$, if it chooses (p, E^*) with $p < p^{H*}$ its profit is $p + H - E^* - 2c_H$, and if it chooses any other (price, expenditure) pair its profit is 0 (the consumer believes it is low quality and does not purchase the good). Thus for equilibrium we need
>
>$$p^{H*} + H - E^* - 2c_H \geq 0.$$

>**Type L**   If the firm chooses any (p, E) with $E \neq E^*$ or $E = E^*$ and $p > p^{H*}$, then the consumer believes it is low quality, so that its profit is 0. If it chooses any (p, E^*) with $p \leq p^{H*}$, then the consumer believes it is high

quality and purchases the good in the first period, yielding it a profit of $p - E^*$. Thus for equilibrium we need

$$0 \geq p^{H*} - E^*.$$

Consumer If she observes (p, E^*) with $p \leq p^{H*}$, she believes the firm is high quality, so that her expected payoff is $H - p^{H*}$ if she buys the good, and 0 if she does not. Thus for an equilibrium in which she buys the good if and only if the (price, expenditure) pair (p, E^*) satisfies $p \leq p^{H*}$, we need

$$H - p^{H*} \geq 0.$$

If she observes any other (price, expenditure) pair (p, E), she believes the firm is low quality, so that her expected payoff is $0 - p$ if she buys the good and 0 if she does not, so that she optimally does not buy the good.

In summary, the assessment is a weak sequential equilibrium if and only if

$$E^* + 2c_H - H \leq p^{H*} \leq \min\{E^*, H\}. \tag{339.1}$$

If $H \geq 2c_H$, there exist pairs (p^{H*}, E^*) with $E^* > 0$ that satisfy this condition (see Figure 339.1), and thus weak sequential equilibria in which a high-quality firm spends conspicuously (on sporting events, for example). The firm does so because if it does not, then the consumer believes it to be low quality, and hence does not buy its good in the first period, does not find out that it is high quality, and thus does not buy its good in the second period. Eliminating the expenditure saves the firm E^*, but it costs it $H - 2c_H$ in lost profit. Imitating the high-quality firm is not worthwhile for the low-quality one because the cost E^* of doing so exceeds the resulting increase in its profit of p^{H*} (the first-period revenue from selling at the price p^{H*}).

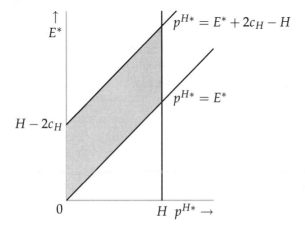

Figure 339.1 The shaded area is the set of pairs (p^{H*}, E^*) satisfying (339.1). For any pair in the set, the game has a weak sequential equilibrium in which a firm of type H chooses (p^{H*}, E^*).

We see that two features of the interaction are important in generating the result. First, a high-quality firm obtains a benefit from attracting a consumer beyond the period in which it makes the expenditure—the consumer purchases the good in the second period. If there were no repeat purchases, then a low-quality firm, by imitating a high-quality one, could induce the consumer to patronize it and thus obtain the same revenue as does a high-quality firm. Given that the low-quality firm's unit cost is lower than that of a high-quality firm, imitation would pay. Second, the consumer does not purchase the good in the first period if it observes the (price, expenditure) pair chosen in equilibrium by a low-quality firm. If it did purchase the good in this case, a high-quality firm could dispense with its conspicuous expenditure and still obtain the benefit of repeat business because the consumer, having purchased its good expecting it to be of low quality, would discover that it is in fact of high quality. If the consumer does not purchase from the low-quality firm, why does this firm exist? The important point is that a high-quality firm loses *some* business when it imitates a low-quality one. If we modify the model by assuming a variety of consumers, some of whom optimally patronize the low-quality firm at the price it charges and some of whom do not, the qualitative feature of the separating equilibria is retained.

Though the game has a separating equilibrium if (339.1) is satisfied, it also has pooling equilibria, which you are invited to study in the following exercise.

? EXERCISE 340.1 (Pooling equilibria of game in which expenditure signals quality) Find weak sequential equilibria of the game in which each type of firm chooses the same (price, expenditure) pair in the first period.

10.7 Illustration: education as a signal of ability

Why are you obtaining a college degree? Because you think that the principles you learn in your courses will prepare you for the day when you run IBM or preside over Italy? Possibly—but there may be another reason. Perhaps nothing you learn in college has any bearing on the job you expect to take, but you need to get a degree to prove to potential employers that your ability is high. How does your obtaining a degree prove this point? Because the cost to persons of low ability of obtaining the degree is much higher than it is for you (they will take longer, and find the process painful), so that such persons cannot profitably imitate you. Thus a college degree signals high ability, even if colleges do nothing to foster that ability: employers know that a recipient of a college degree must have high ability because only for such a person is it worthwhile to obtain a degree. If the cost of achieving high proficiency in freestyle snowboarding were much lower for a person with the skills valued by IBM or the Italian citizenry than for someone without the skills, a certificate attesting to that achievement could be your ticket to a rewarding job. But it is not, so you are in college.

Here is a simple model we can use to study this logic. A worker's ability, which is either H or $L < H$, is known to her but not to either of two potential employers.

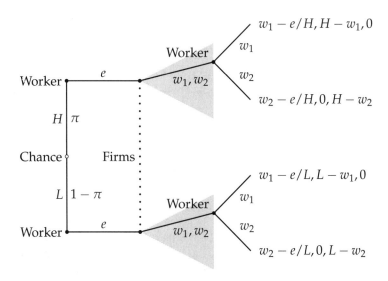

Figure 341.1 An outline of an extensive game that models a worker that signals her ability to a pair of firms by acquiring education. The diagram shows only *one* of the possible education levels e the worker may obtain. The firms' wage offers are made simultaneously. The worker's payoffs are listed first, the firms' second and third.

The worker chooses the amount e of education to obtain, then the firms, observing e, simultaneously offer wages w_1 and w_2, and finally the worker chooses one of the wage offers. Assume that education is less expensive to obtain for a worker of high ability than it is for a worker of low ability. Specifically, assume that the cost to a worker of ability K of obtaining e units of education is e/K, so that the payoff of such a worker who obtains e units of education and takes a job paying w is $w - e/K$. The payoff of a firm that pays a worker of ability K the wage w is $K - w$. The extensive game that corresponds to this model is given in Figure 341.1.

I claim that the game has a weak sequential equilibrium in which a high-ability worker chooses a positive amount of education. Consider the following assessment, in which e^* is a positive number.

Worker's strategy Type H chooses $e = e^*$ and type L chooses $e = 0$; after observing the firms' wage offers, both types choose the highest offer if they differ, and that of firm 1 if they are the same.

Firms' belief Each firm believes that a worker is type H if she chooses e^* and type L otherwise.

Firms' strategies Each firm offers the wage H to a worker who chooses e^* and the wage L to a worker who chooses any other value of e.

The firms' beliefs are consistent with the worker's strategy. (No worker chooses an education level different from e^* and 0, so the consistency condition imposes no restriction on the firms' beliefs after observing such a level.)

I now find conditions on the parameters under which the players' strategies are sequentially rational.

Worker   The worker's strategy of accepting the highest wage offer at the end of the game is clearly optimal. Now consider the worker's initial action.

> **Type H**   A type H worker obtains the payoff $H - e^*/H$ if she follows her strategy and chooses the education level e^*, and the payoff $L - e/H$ if she chooses any other education level e. The education level 0 achieves the highest payoff, of L, for a deviant, so for equilibrium we need $H - e^*/H \geq L$, or
>
> $$e^* \leq H(H - L).$$

> **Type L**   A type L worker obtains the payoff L if she follows her strategy and chooses the education level 0. If she chooses any education level other than e^* she obtains the same wage, and pays a cost, so such a deviation is not profitable. If she chooses the education level e^*, then the firms believe her ability to be H, and she obtains the payoff $H - e^*/L$. Thus for equilibrium we need
>
> $$e^* \geq L(H - L).$$

Firms   Each firm's payoff is 0, given its belief and its strategy. If it raises the wage it offers in response to any value of e, its expected profit is negative, given its belief, and if it lowers the wage its expected profit remains zero (its offer is not accepted).

In summary, the assessment is a weak sequential equilibrium if and only if

$$L(H - L) \leq e^* \leq H(H - L).$$

I have assumed that $H > L$, so the left-hand side of this expression is less than the right-hand side, and hence values of e^* satisfying the expression exist. That is, for any values of H and L, the game has separating equilibria in which high-ability workers obtain some education, whereas low-ability ones do not. Education has no effect on the workers' productivity; a high-ability worker obtains it to avoid being labeled low in ability by potential employers.

Like several of the signaling games we have studied, this game has also pooling equilibria, in which both types of worker obtain the same amount of education. That is, the model is consistent both with a steady state in which only high-ability workers obtain education and with one in which all workers do so.

? EXERCISE 342.1 (Pooling equilibria of game in which education signals ability) Find the range of education levels e for which the game has a weak sequential equilibrium in which both types of worker choose the education level e. Compare these levels with those possible in a separating equilibrium.

10.8 Illustration: strategic information transmission

You research the market for new products and submit a report to your boss, who decides which product to develop. Your preferences differ from those of your boss: you are interested in promoting the interests of your division, whereas she is interested in promoting the interests of the whole firm. What do you tell her?

   If you report the results of your research without distortion, the product she will choose will not be best for you. Can you do better by distorting or obscuring the fruits of your research? If you *systematically* distort your finding, then your boss will be able to unravel your report and deduce your actual findings, so obfuscation seems a more promising route.

   To study the issues precisely, consider the following model. A sender (you) observes the state t, a number from 0 to 1 (the result of your research), that a receiver (your boss) cannot see. Assume that the distribution of the state is uniform: for any number z from 0 to 1, the probability that t is at most z is z. The sender submits a report r, a number, to the receiver, who observes the report and takes an action y, also a number. Both the sender and receiver care about the relation between the state t and the receiver's action y, and neither is affected directly by the value of the sender's report r. Specifically, assume that

$$\text{Sender's payoff function:} \quad -(y - (t + b))^2$$
$$\text{Receiver's payoff function:} \quad -(y - t)^2,$$

where b (the sender's "bias") is a fixed positive number that reflects the divergence between the sender's and receiver's preferences. These functions are shown in Figure 343.1. Note that a receiver who believes that the state is t optimally chooses $y = t$, whereas the best action for the sender in this case is $y = t + b$. The game is illustrated in Figure 344.1.

10.8.1 Perfect information transmission?

Consider the possibility of an equilibrium in which the sender accurately reports the state she observes—that is, her strategy is $r(t) = t$ for all t. Given this strategy, the consistency condition requires that the receiver believe (correctly) that the state is t when the sender reports t, and hence for any report t optimally chooses the

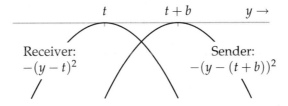

Figure 343.1 The players' payoff functions when the state is t in the game of strategic information transmission. The number b is a positive constant.

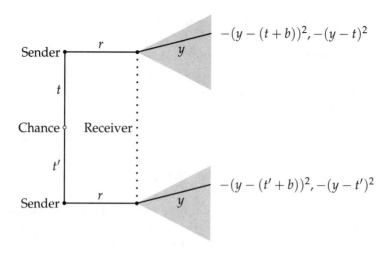

Figure 344.1 An outline of an extensive game that models strategic information transmission. Only *two* of the possible states (t and t') and *one* possible report of the sender are shown. The sender's payoff is listed first, the receiver's second.

action t (the maximizer of $-(y - t)^2$). Is the sender's strategy a best response to this strategy of the receiver? Not if $b > 0$! Suppose the state is t. If the sender reports t, the receiver chooses $y = t$, so that the sender's payoff is $-(t - (t + b))^2 = -b^2$. If instead she reports $t - b$, the receiver believes the state is $t - b$ and chooses $y = t - b$, so that the sender's payoff is $-(t - b - (t - b))^2 = 0$. If $b > 0$ the sender is thus better off reporting $t - b$ when the state is t. So unless the sender's and receiver's preferences are identical, the game has no equilibrium in which the sender accurately reports the state.

A similar argument shows that for $b > 0$ the game has no equilibrium in which the sender's strategy is any increasing function or any decreasing function. If the sender's strategy is such a function r and $r(t) = t'$, the consistency condition requires that upon observing the report t', the receiver believe that the state is t, so that the receiver optimally takes the action t. As before, a sender who observes t is thus better off reporting $t - b$.

10.8.2 No information transmission?

Now consider the possibility of an equilibrium in which the sender's report is constant, independent of the value of the variable she observes—say $r(t) = c$ for all t. Such a report conveys no information; the consistency condition requires that if the receiver observes the report c, her belief must remain the same as it was initially, namely that the state is uniformly distributed from 0 to 1. Given this belief, her optimal action is $y = \frac{1}{2}$. (This claim should be plausible, given the symmetry of the belief and the shape of the receiver's payoff function. If you know calculus, you may verify the claim precisely.)

The consistency condition does not constrain the receiver's belief about the state upon her receiving a report different from c, because such a report does not occur if the sender follows her strategy. Assume that the receiver completely ignores the sender's report: her belief remains the same as it was originally for *every* value of the report. Then the receiver's optimal action is $y = \frac{1}{2}$ whatever report she receives. That is, the sender's report has no effect on the action chosen by the receiver, so that the strategy r for which $r(t) = c$ for all t is optimal for the sender.

In summary, for every value of b the game has a weak sequential equilibrium in which the sender's report conveys no information (it is constant, independent of her type) and the receiver ignores the report (she maintains her initial belief about the state, regardless of the report) and takes the action $y = \frac{1}{2}$. If b is small, then this equilibrium is not very attractive. If $b < \frac{1}{2}$, then for some states there is an action different from $\frac{1}{2}$ that is better for both the sender and the receiver, and the smaller is b, the larger the set of states for which such increases in payoffs are possible. (If $b = \frac{1}{4}$, for example, then for any t with $0 \leq t < \frac{1}{4}$, both the sender and the receiver are better off if the receiver's action is $t + b$ than if it is $\frac{1}{2}$.)

10.8.3 Some information transmission?

Does the game have equilibria in which *some* information is transmitted? Suppose that the sender makes one of two reports, depending on the state. Specifically, suppose that if $0 \leq t < t_1$ she reports r_1 and if $t_1 \leq t \leq 1$ she reports $r_2 \neq r_1$.

Consider the receiver's optimal response to this strategy. If she sees the report r_1, she knows that the state t satisfies $0 \leq t < t_1$; given her initial belief that the state is uniformly distributed from 0 to 1, the consistency condition requires that she now believe that the state is uniformly distributed from 0 to t_1. Her optimal action given this belief is $y = \frac{1}{2}t_1$. (As before, this claim should be plausible given the symmetry and shape of the receiver's payoff function; it may be verified using calculus.) Similarly, if the receiver sees the report r_2 she believes that the state is uniformly distributed from t_1 to 1, and chooses the action $y = \frac{1}{2}(t_1 + 1)$. The consistency condition does not restrict the receiver's belief if she sees a report other than r_1 or r_2. Assume that for each such report the receiver's belief is one of the two beliefs she holds if she sees r_1 or r_2, so that her optimal response to every report is either $\frac{1}{2}t_1$ or $\frac{1}{2}(t_1 + 1)$.

Now, for equilibrium we need the sender's report r_1 to be optimal if $0 \leq t < t_1$ and her report r_2 to be optimal if $t_1 \leq t \leq 1$, given the receiver's strategy. By changing her report, the sender can change the receiver's action from $\frac{1}{2}t_1$ to $\frac{1}{2}(t_1 + 1)$, or vice versa. Thus for the report r_1 to be optimal for the sender in every state t with $0 \leq t \leq t_1$, she must like the action $\frac{1}{2}t_1$ at least as much as the action $\frac{1}{2}(t_1 + 1)$, and for the report r_2 to be optimal in every state t for which $t_1 \leq t \leq 1$ she must like the action $\frac{1}{2}(t_1 + 1)$ at least as much as the action $\frac{1}{2}t_1$. In particular, in state t_1 the sender must be exactly indifferent between the two actions, as in Figure 346.1. This indifference implies that $t_1 + b$ is midway $\frac{1}{2}t_1$ and $\frac{1}{2}(t_1 + 1)$, or $t_1 + b = \frac{1}{2}[\frac{1}{2}t_1 + \frac{1}{2}(t_1 + 1)]$, so that

$$t_1 = \frac{1}{2} - 2b. \tag{345.1}$$

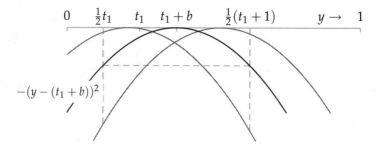

Figure 346.1 A value of t_1 such that in state t_1 the sender is indifferent between the receiver's actions $\frac{1}{2}t_1$ and $\frac{1}{2}(t_1 + 1)$. The black curve is the sender's payoff function in state t_1. The gray curve on the left is the sender's payoff function in a state less than t_1; she prefers $\frac{1}{2}t_1$ to $\frac{1}{2}(t_1 + 1)$. The gray curve on the right is the sender's payoff function in a state greater than t_1; she prefers $\frac{1}{2}(t_1 + 1)$ to $\frac{1}{2}t_1$.

We need $t_1 > 0$, so that this condition can be satisfied only if $b < \frac{1}{4}$. That is, if $b \geq \frac{1}{4}$, then the game has no equilibrium in which the sender makes two different reports, depending on the state. Put differently, there is no point in the receiver's asking the sender to submit a report if her preferences diverge sufficiently from those of the sender—she should simply take the best action for herself given her prior belief.

I claim that (345.1) is not only necessary for an equilibrium, but also sufficient. That is, if t_1 satisfies (345.1), then in every state t with $0 \leq t < t_1$ the sender optimally reports r_1 and in every state t with $t_1 \leq t \leq 1$ she optimally reports $r_2 \neq r_1$. This optimality follows from the shapes of the payoff functions; it is illustrated in Figure 346.1, in which the gray curves are the payoff functions of senders in states less than t_1 (left) and greater than t_1 (right).

In conclusion, if $b < \frac{1}{4}$, then the game has a weak sequential equilibrium in which the sender transmits two different reports, depending on the state: for $0 \leq t < t_1$ she submits one report and the receiver takes the action $\frac{1}{2}t_1$, and for $t_1 \leq t \leq 1$ she submits a different report and the receiver takes the action $\frac{1}{2}(t_1 + 1)$.

This equilibrium is better for both the receiver and the sender (before she observes the state) than the one in which no information is transmitted. Consider the receiver. (An analogous argument may be made for the sender.) In the equilibrium in which no information is transmitted, she takes the action $\frac{1}{2}$ in all states, so that her payoff in each state t is $-(\frac{1}{2} - t)^2$. In the equilibrium we have just found, in which the sender transmits two different reports depending on the state, her payoff is $-(\frac{1}{2}t_1 - t)^2$ for $0 \leq t < t_1$ and $-(\frac{1}{2}(t_1 + 1) - t)^2$ for $t_1 \leq t < 1$.

? EXERCISE 346.1 (Comparing the receiver's expected payoff in two equilibria) Plot the receiver's payoff as a function of t (from 0 to 1) in each equilibrium. Given that the distribution of the state is uniform, the receiver's expected payoff in an equilibrium is the negative of the area between the horizontal axis and the function that gives the payoff in that state. Show that the receiver's payoff is greater in the two-report equilibrium than it is in the equilibrium with no information transmission.

10.8.4 How much information transmission?

For $b < \frac{1}{4}$, does the game have equilibria in which more information is transmitted than in the two-report equilibrium? Consider the possibility of an equilibrium in which the sender makes one of K reports, depending on the state. Specifically, suppose that the sender's report is r_1 if $0 \leq t < t_1$, r_2 if $t_1 \leq t < t_2$, ..., r_K if $t_{K-1} \leq t \leq 1$, where $r_i \neq r_j$ whenever $i \neq j$. For convenience, let $t_0 = 0$ and $t_K = 1$.

The analysis follows the lines of that for the two-report equilibrium. If the receiver observes the report r_k, then the consistency condition requires that she believe the state to be uniformly distributed from t_{k-1} to t_k, so that she optimally takes the action $\frac{1}{2}(t_{k-1} + t_k)$. If she observes a report different from any r_k, the consistency condition does not restrict her belief; assume that her belief in such a case is the belief she holds upon receiving one of the reports r_k.

Now, for equilibrium we need the sender's report r_k to be optimal when the state is t with $t_{k-1} \leq t < t_k$, for $k = 1, \ldots, K$. As before, a sufficient condition for optimality is that in each state t_k, $k = 1, \ldots, K$, the sender be indifferent between the reports r_k and r_{k+1}, and thus between the receiver's actions $\frac{1}{2}(t_{k-1} + t_k)$ and $\frac{1}{2}(t_k + t_{k+1})$. This indifference implies that $t_k + b$ is equal to the average of $\frac{1}{2}(t_{k-1} + t_k)$ and $\frac{1}{2}(t_k + t_{k+1})$:

$$t_k + b = \frac{1}{2}\left[\frac{1}{2}(t_{k-1} + t_k) + \frac{1}{2}(t_k + t_{k+1})\right],$$

which is equivalent to

$$t_{k+1} - t_k = t_k - t_{k-1} + 4b.$$

That is, the interval of states for which the sender's report is r_{k+1} is longer by $4b$ than the interval for which the report is r_k. The length of the first interval, from 0 to t_1, is t_1, and the sum of the lengths of all the intervals must be 1, so we need

$$t_1 + (t_1 + 4b) + \cdots + (t_1 + (K-1)b) = 1$$

or

$$Kt_1 + 4b(1 + 2 + \cdots + (K-1)) = 1.$$

Using the fact that the sum of the first n positive integers is $\frac{1}{2}n(n+1)$, the equation is

$$Kt_1 + 2bK(K-1) = 1. \tag{347.1}$$

If b is small enough that $2bK(K-1) < 1$, there is a positive value of t_1 that satisfies the equation.

Suppose, for example, that $\frac{1}{24} \leq b < \frac{1}{12}$. Then the inequality is satisfied for $K \leq 3$, so that in the equilibrium in which the most information is transmitted the sender chooses one of three reports. From (347.1), we have $t_1 = \frac{1}{3} - 4b$ and hence $t_2 = \frac{2}{3} - 4b$ in this equilibrium. For $b = \frac{1}{24}$, the equilibrium values of t_1 ($\frac{1}{6}$) and t_2 ($\frac{1}{2}$) are illustrated in Figure 348.1, and the equilibrium action y taken by the receiver, as a function of the state t, is shown in Figure 348.2. (I have chosen this

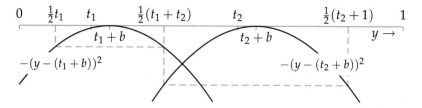

Figure 348.1 The values of t_1 and t_2 in a three-report equilibrium in the model of strategic information transmission for $b = \frac{1}{24}$, the most informative equilibrium for this value of b. In state t_1 the sender is indifferent between the receiver's actions $\frac{1}{2}t_1$ and $\frac{1}{2}(t_1 + t_2)$, and in state t_2 she is indifferent between the receiver's actions $\frac{1}{2}(t_1 + t_2)$ and $\frac{1}{2}(t_1 + 1)$.

value of b because it allows the diagram to clearly show the equilibrium. Note that if b were any smaller, a four-report equilibrium would exist.) The values of the reports r_k do not matter, as long as no two are the same. We may think of them as words in a language; the receiver's long experience playing the game teaches her that r_k means "the state is between t_{k-1} and t_k".

In summary, if there is a positive value of t_1 that satisfies (347.1), then the game has a weak sequential equilibrium in which the sender submits one of K different reports, depending on the state. For any given value of b, the largest value of K for which an equilibrium exists is the largest value for which $2bK(K - 1) < 1$. If $2bK(K - 1) = 1$, then, using the quadratic formula, we have $K = \frac{1}{2}(1 + \sqrt{1 + 2/b})$. Thus, in particular, the larger the value of b, the smaller the largest value of K possible in an equilibrium. That is, the greater the difference between the sender's and receiver's preferences, the coarser the information transmitted in the equilibrium

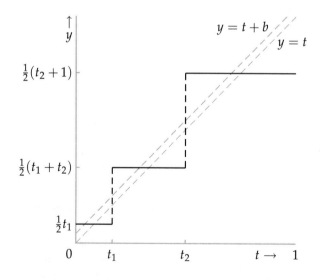

Figure 348.2 The receiver's action y, as a function of the state t, in a three-report equilibrium of the game of strategic information transmission for $b = \frac{1}{24}$, the most informative equilibrium for this value of b. The dashed gray lines show the action optimal in each state for the sender (top) and receiver (bottom).

with the largest number of steps—the "most informative" equilibrium. I claim that the equilibrium that yields the receiver the highest payoff is the most informative one, and this equilibrium is also best for the sender before she observes the state. You should find this claim plausible, though some calculations are needed to verify it.

10.8.5 Summary on strategic information transmission

When a receiver takes an action based on an unverifiable report about the state supplied by a sender, and the sender's and receiver's preferences differ, no equilibrium exists in which the sender accurately reports the state. Regardless of the difference between the sender's and receiver's preferences, an equilibrium exists in which the sender's report is independent of the state, so that no information is transmitted. If the sender's and receiver's preferences are sufficiently similar, there are also equilibria in which the sender makes one of several reports, depending on the state; the maximal number of reports possible in an equilibrium is larger the more similar the parties' preferences. The equilibrium with the maximal number of reports is better for both parties (before the state is known) than all other equilibria.

10.8.6 Delegation

Is there a better way for the receiver to make a decision? Consider the alternative of delegation: the receiver lets the sender choose the action. No reports, no obfuscation; the sender simply chooses the best action for herself—in each state t she chooses the action $t + b$.

Compare this outcome with the outcome of the best equilibrium for the receiver if she acts on the basis of a report by the sender. For $b = \frac{1}{24}$, the outcome, as a function of the state, for the three-report equilibrium (the best equilibrium for this value of b) is given in Figure 348.2, where the dashed line $y = t + b$ indicates the outcome of delegation.

Which outcome does the receiver prefer? Under delegation, the distance between the outcome and the receiver's favorite action is exactly b in every state. Thus the receiver's payoff in every state is $-b^2$. In the three-report equilibrium of the game in which the receiver solicits information from the sender, the outcome for most states is further than b from the receiver's favorite action; only for states within b of $\frac{1}{2}t_1$, $\frac{1}{2}(t_1 + t_2)$, or $\frac{1}{2}(t_2 + 1)$ is it closer to the receiver's favorite action that is the outcome of delegation. If that does not convince you that the receiver prefers the outcome of delegation to the outcome of the three-report equilibrium, take a look at Figure 350.1. This figure plots the receiver's payoffs in the two cases, for each state. The horizontal line labeled $-b^2$, very close to the axis, is the receiver's payoff in each state under delegation. The scalloped curve is her payoff in each state in the three-report equilibrium. The state is distributed uniformly from 0 to 1, so the receiver's expected payoff under delegation is the negative of the area

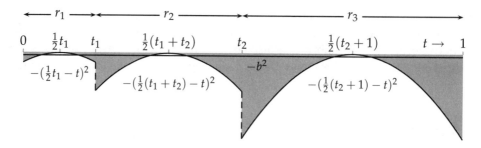

Figure 350.1 The receiver's payoff, as a function of the state t, in a three-report equilibrium of the game of information transmission and under delegation for $b = \frac{1}{24}$. The negative of the shaded area is the receiver's expected payoff in the three-report equilibrium, and the negative of the area between the horizontal line $-b^2$ and the horizontal axis is her expected payoff under delegation.

of the very slim rectangle between the axis and the line $-b^2$, while her expected payoff in the three-report equilibrium is the negative of the shaded area above the scalloped line. Which is larger? You do not need to make an exact calculation to be sure that the receiver prefers the outcome under delegation!

I have analyzed only a single value of b, namely $\frac{1}{24}$. For smaller values of b, the loss from both delegation and the most informative equilibrium of the game of information transmission is smaller, but delegation remains superior. For larger values of b, the loss from both outcomes is larger. Delegation remains better than the most informative equilibrium in the game of information transmission as long as $b < \sqrt{3}/6$ (approximately 0.29). (Calculus is needed to check this cutoff.) As we have seen, for $b \geq \frac{1}{4}$ the most informative equilibrium in the game of information transmission is not informative at all: the sender sends the same report in every state. Thus if the sender's preferences are close enough to the receiver's that the receiver benefits from consulting the sender, she is better off simply delegating the decision rather than soliciting a report. The directive "do what you want" yields a better outcome for the receiver than does "tell me what I should do" because the quality of the information induced by the latter is so low.

? EXERCISE 350.1 (Variant of model with piecewise linear payoff functions) Consider the variant of the game of strategic information transmission in which the sender's payoff function is $-|y - (t + b)|$ and the receiver's payoff function is $-|y - t|$ (where $|x|$ denotes the absolute value of x). That is, in each state t each payoff function has the shape shown in Figure 71.1, with a peak at $t + b$ for the receiver and a peak at t for the sender. How do the k-report weak sequential equilibria of this variant of the model differ from those of the original model?

? EXERCISE 350.2 (Pooling equilibrium in a general model) Consider a generalization of the game of strategic information transmission (Figure 344.1) in which the distribution of states is arbitrary and each player's payoff is an arbitrary function of y and t (but, as before, is independent of r). Assume that there exists an action, say y^*, that maximizes the receiver's expected payoff given the distribution of states. Show that any such game has a weak sequential equilibrium in which the receiver chooses the same action, regardless of the signal.

10.9 Illustration: agenda control with imperfect information

The U.S. House of Representatives assigns to committees the task of formulating modifications of the law. The bills proposed by committees are considered by the legislature under one of several rules, ranging from the "closed rule" (or "gag rule"), under which the legislature may either accept or reject the proposed bill but may not amend it, to the "open rule", under which any amendment may be made. (The Rules Committee determines how each bill is handled.) In general, the preferences of a committee differ from those of the entire legislature. What is the rationale for restricting the actions the legislature may take?

If we treat the legislature and the committee as single players with well-defined preferences, and assume that the legislature is perfectly informed about the environment, an analysis of the open rule is straightforward: the legislature simply chooses the bill that is best according to its preferences, ignoring the committee's proposal. A model of the closed rule is studied in Section 6.1.3. In general, the equilibrium outcome in this case is not the legislature's favorite bill. Thus under perfect information the legislature has no reason to adopt the closed rule.

But of course if the legislature is perfectly informed, it has no reason to assign the drafting of laws to a committee to begin with. If it is not perfectly informed, then a committee has a role: it can discover the "state of the world" and propose legislation to fit. In this environment, a committee whose preferences differ from those of the legislature has an incentive to report distorted information, and the rules under which proposed legislation is considered may affect the degree of distortion. Are there circumstances under which the closed rule produces an outcome better for the legislature than the open rule?

Consider the following model, which follows closely the one in the previous section (10.8). The desirability of a bill depends on the state t, a number from 0 to 1, which the committee, but not the legislature, observes. Assume that the distribution of the state is uniform: for any number z from 0 to 1, the probability that $t \leq z$ is z. After observing the state, the committee recommends a bill r (a number) to the legislature. Under the open rule, the legislature may then choose any bill it wishes. Under the closed rule, it is restricted to either accept r or reject it, in which case the outcome is the status quo y_0. Assume that in state t the legislature's favorite bill is $y = t$, and the committee's favorite bill is $y = t + b$, where b is a fixed positive number. Specifically, assume that

$$\text{Committee's payoff function:} \quad -(y - (t + b))^2$$
$$\text{Legislature's payoff function:} \quad -(y - t)^2,$$

where y is the bill passed by the legislature.

10.9.1 Open rule

Under the open rule, the model is identical to the one in the previous section (10.8), with the committee as sender and the legislature as receiver. Thus we know that if $b > 0$, then in an equilibrium the committee's report obscures its information, the more so the larger b. We also know the character of the best (and most informative) equilibrium for the legislature. In this equilibrium for $b = \frac{1}{24}$, for example, the committee sends one of three different reports, as illustrated in Figures 348.1 and 348.2.

10.9.2 Closed rule

Under the closed rule, the legislature retains the power to veto, but not otherwise to amend, the legislation proposed by the committee, in which case the outcome is the fixed status quo y_0. From Section 10.8.6 we know that if the legislature simply delegates the choice of legislation to the committee, the outcome is better for both the legislature and the committee than the outcome of the best equilibrium under the open rule, assuming that the legislature's and committee's preferences do not diverge so much that the legislature would be better off making the decision itself. The closed rule is close to delegation, but the legislature retains the right to veto the proposed legislation in favor of the status quo. Does the legislature benefit from retaining this vestige of control?

The game for the closed rule is illustrated in Figure 353.1. The legislature optimally exercises its option to choose y_0 if it prefers this outcome to the committee's proposal. In particular, if the committee proposes its favorite bill $y = t + b$ for all values of t (as it does under delegation), then the legislature optimally exercises its option whenever $y_0 - b \le t \le y_0 + b$, or equivalently whenever $t - b \le y_0 \le t + b$. (Refer to Figure 353.2.) Given this response of the legislature, the committee's proposal of $t + b$ is not optimal for t with $y_0 < t < y_0 + b$: the proposal $t + b$ leads to the outcome y_0, and hence the payoff $-(y_0 - (t + b))^2 < -b^2$, but if the committee recommends the bill $t + 2b$, then the legislature accepts it, giving the committee the higher payoff $-(t + 2b - (t + b))^2 = -b^2$. Thus in no equilibrium does the committee propose its favorite bill in all states.

If the status quo y_0 satisfies $b < y_0 < 1 - 3b$, however, I claim that the game has an equilibrium in which the committee recommends its favorite bill in all states except those between $y_0 - b$ and $y_0 + b$, and between $y_0 + b$ and $y_0 + 3b$. The bill proposed by the committee (and accepted by the legislature) in this equilibrium is shown in Figure 354.1. It is defined precisely as follows:

$$
\begin{cases}
t + b & \text{if } t \le y_0 - b \\
y_0 & \text{if } y_0 - b < t \le y_0 \\
y_0 + 2b & \text{if } y_0 < t \le y_0 + 2b \\
y_0 + 4b & \text{if } y_0 + 2b < t \le y_0 + 3b \\
t + b & \text{if } y_0 + 3b < t.
\end{cases}
$$

For any recommendation of less than y_0 or greater than $y_0 + 4b$ the legislature can infer the state precisely. Thus the consistency condition requires that the legislature's belief about the state be correct if the committee makes such a recommendation. For the recommendations y_0, $y_0 + 2b$, and $y_0 + 4b$, the legislature cannot infer the state precisely. The committee makes each of these recommendations for

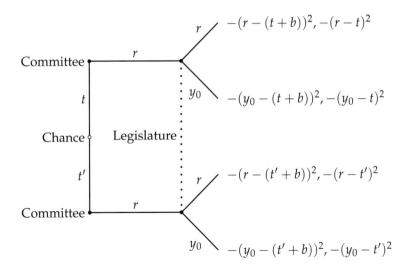

Figure 353.1 An outline of an extensive game that models the closed rule for the consideration of a committee proposal by a legislature. Only *two* of the possible states (t and t') and *one* of the possible reports the committee can make are shown. The committee's payoffs are listed first, the legislature's second.

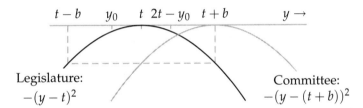

Figure 353.2 For y_0 between $t - b$ and $t + b$, the legislature prefers y_0 to $t + b$, and thus optimally exercises its option to choose y_0 rather than a proposal of $t + b$. For y_0 between $t - b$ and t, it is indifferent between y_0 and $2t - y_0$.

an interval of states, so that given that the initial distribution of states is uniform, the consistency condition requires that the legislature's belief about the state after observing one of these recommendations be uniform on the interval of states that generates the recommendation. In summary, the consistency condition requires that the legislature's belief satisfy the following conditions.

$$\begin{cases} \text{State is } r - b & \text{if } r < y_0 \\ \text{State is uniformly distributed from } y_0 - b \text{ to } y_0 & \text{if } r = y_0 \\ \text{State is uniformly distributed from } y_0 \text{ to } y_0 + 2b & \text{if } r = y_0 + 2b \\ \text{State is uniformly distributed from } y_0 + 2b \text{ to } y_0 + 4b & \text{if } r = y_0 + 4b \\ \text{State is } r - b & \text{if } y_0 + 4b < r. \end{cases}$$

The consistency condition does not restrict the legislature's belief about the state when it observes a recommendation between y_0 and $y_0 + 2b$, or one between $y_0 + 2b$ and $y_0 + 4b$, because the committee does not make such a recommendation if it follows its strategy. Assume that in these cases it believes the state is y_0. Finally,

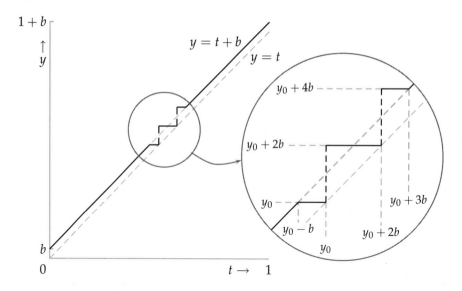

Figure 354.1 The bill y proposed by the committee and accepted by the legislature, as a function of the state t, in an equilibrium of the game of agenda control under the closed rule for $b = \frac{1}{24}$. The 45° dashed gray lines show the action optimal in each state for the committee (top) and legislature (bottom).

the legislature's strategy is to accept all recommendations except those between y_0 and $y_0 + 2b$, and between $y_0 + 2b$ and $y_0 + 4b$ (which are not made if the committee adheres to its equilibrium strategy).

I now argue that this assessment is a weak sequential equilibrium. The legislature's belief satisfies the consistency condition by construction. Consider the optimality of the committee's strategy, given the legislature's strategy. In all states less than $y_0 - b$ or greater than $y_0 + 3b$, the outcome is the committee's favorite bill, so certainly no strategy yields it a higher payoff in these states. Now consider the state y_0, in which its strategy calls for it to recommend the bill y_0, so that it obtains the payoff $-b^2$. If it changes its recommendation, the bill passed by the legislature either remains y_0 (if it recommends between y_0 and $y_0 + 2b$ or between $y_0 + 2b$ and $y_0 + 4b$), changes to less than y_0 (if it recommends less than y_0), or changes to at least $y_0 + 2b$ (if it recommends $y_0 + 2b$ or at least $y_0 + 4b$). None of these changes increases the committee's payoff (refer to Figure 355.1), so its recommendation of y_0 is optimal. In states between $y_0 - b$ and y_0, and between y_0 and $y_0 + 3b$, similar analyses show that the recommendation y_0 is also optimal. (Note that the committee is indifferent between the bills y_0 and $y_0 + 2b$ in state y_0, and between the bills $y_0 + 2b$ and $y_0 + 4b$ in state $y_0 + 2b$.)

Finally consider the legislature's action. A recommendation r from the committee of less than y_0 or greater than $y_0 + 4b$ reveals the state to be $r - b$, so that the legislature prefers r to y_0. Now consider the other possible recommendations the committee may make.

Recommendation of y_0: The outcome is the same, y_0, regardless of the legislature's action.

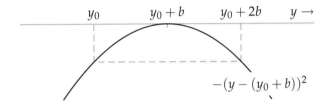

Figure 355.1 In state y_0, the committee prefers the bill y_0 to any bill less than y_0 or greater than $y_0 + 2b$.

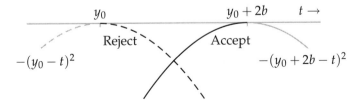

Figure 355.2 The legislature's payoff as a function of the state from y_0 to $y_0 + 2b$ if it accepts the recommended bill $y_0 + 2b$ (solid black curve) and rejects it (dashed black curve).

Recommendation of $y_0 + 2b$: The legislature believes that the state is uniformly distributed from y_0 to $y_0 + 2b$. Its payoff, as a function of the states in this interval, is given by the solid black curve in Figure 355.2 if it accepts the committee's recommendation and by the dashed black curve if it rejects the committee's recommendation. These curves are mirror images of each other, so the legislature is indifferent between accepting and rejecting the committee's recommendation.

Recommendation of $y_0 + 4b$: The legislature believes that the state is uniformly distributed from $y_0 + 2b$ to $y_0 + 3b$. Its payoff, as a function of the states in this interval, is given by the solid black curve in Figure 356.1 if it accepts the committee's recommendation and by the dashed black curve if it rejects the committee's recommendation. (For clarity, the vertical scale in this figure is different from that in Figure 355.2.) The solid curve lies entirely above the dashed one, so the legislature prefers to accept the committee's recommendation than to reject it.

Recommendation between y_0 and $y_0 + 2b$, or between $y_0 + 2b$ and $y_0 + 4b$: The legislature believes that the state is y_0, so it optimally rejects the committee's recommendation.

10.9.3 Comparison of open rule, closed rule, and delegation

The legislature's action, as a function of the state, in the best equilibrium for the legislature under the open rule for $b = \frac{1}{24}$, is given in Figure 348.2. Figure 354.1 is the corresponding figure for the equilibrium found in the previous section (10.9.2) for the closed rule. Which equilibrium does the legislature prefer? Comparing the two

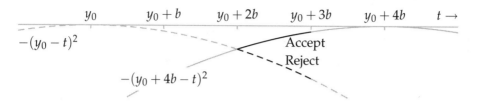

Figure 356.1 The legislature's payoff as a function of the state from $y_0 + 2b$ to $y_0 + 3b$ if it accepts the recommended bill $y_0 + 4b$ (solid black curve) and rejects it (dashed black curve).

figures, it should be plausible that it prefers the equilibrium for the closed rule. In this equilibrium, the difference between the outcome and the legislature's favorite bill is b for most states and is never more than $2b$, whereas for the equilibrium under the open rule the outcome wanders much further afield. The legislature really dislikes large deviations from its favorite bill (its payoff function is quadratic), so the equilibrium under the closed rule is better for it than the equilibrium under the open rule. (Note that I have not argued that the equilibrium found for the closed rule yields the best outcome for the legislature, only that it is better than the best equilibrium under the open rule.)

For other values of b, a comparison of the equilibria under the two rules leads to the same conclusion: if $b < y_0 < 1 - 3b$ and b is small enough that there is an equilibrium under the open rule in which the committee submits at least two different reports, depending on the state, then there is an equilibrium under the closed rule that the legislature prefers to the best equilibrium for it under the open rule.

So in a comparison of the open rule and the closed rule, the analysis provides a rationale for the closed rule: in limiting the legislature's ability to take advantage of the information reported by the committee, the rule gives the committee an incentive to divulge that information, to the ultimate advantage of both the committee and the legislature.

Now compare the outcomes under the closed rule and under delegation. Look carefully at Figure 354.1. In the equilibrium depicted there for the closed rule, the bill proposed by the committee differs from $t + b$ in the region of y_0. The deviations are symmetric about $t + b$, as Figure 357.1 makes clear. Now, the legislature's payoff decreases at an increasing rate away from its favorite bill—its payoff to a bill 2δ from its favorite is more than twice as large a negative number as its payoff to a bill δ from its favorite. Thus it prefers the outcome in which the bill is $t + b$ in every state t to the outcome in the equilibrium we have been studying. That is, for this value of b, delegation is better for it than the equilibrium we found for the closed rule. If it delegates the decision to a committee, the legislature loses control of the outcome; if it retains some control it loses information, because the committee's interest leads to a distorted communication of the state. In the model we have been studying, the loss of information outweighs the loss of control as long as the committee's and legislature's preferences do not differ too much, leading delegation to be the best mechanism for the legislature in this case.

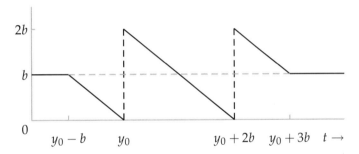

Figure 357.1 The deviation of the bill proposed by the committee from the legislature's favorite bill in an equilibrium in the model of agenda control with the closed rule, as a function of the state around the state y_0.

Thus while the closed rule generates an equilibrium better for the legislature than any equilibrium under the open rule, delegation generates an even better outcome. Assuming the game for the closed rule has no better equilibrium than the one we studied, the conclusion is that if the preferences of the legislature and the committee do not differ so much that the legislature should simply choose the legislation itself, then the legislature's best option is to relinquish all control over the outcome and to cede the choice of legislation to the committee.

Notes

The notion of an extensive game is due to von Neumann and Morgenstern (1944). Kuhn (1950b, 1953) suggested the formulation described in this chapter. The notion of sequential equilibrium, of which weak sequential equilibrium is a variant, is due to Kreps and Wilson (1982); Selten's (1975) notion of "perfect equilibrium" is closely related. (The notion of weak sequential equilibrium is called "assessment equilibrium" by Binmore (1992); it is sometimes called "weak perfect Bayesian equilibrium", though the notion of perfect Bayesian equilibrium (due to Fudenberg and Tirole 1991) is defined only for a restricted set of games.)

The models of poker in Example 315.1 and Exercise 316.1 are variants of models studied by Borel (1938, 91–97) and von Neumann and Morgenstern (1944, 19.14). Von Neumann studied several other models of the game (see von Neumann and Morgenstern 1944, footnote 2 on page 186 and Section 19), as did some of the other pioneers of game theory, including Bellman and Blackwell (1949), Kuhn (1950a), Nash and Shapley (1950), and Karlin (1959b, Chapter 9).

The idea of the model in Section 10.6 is due to Nelson (1970, 1974). The model itself is a simplified version, suggested by Ariel Rubinstein, of the one of Milgrom and Roberts (1986). Section 10.7 is based on Spence (1974), as interpreted by Cho and Kreps (1987). Section 10.8 is based on Crawford and Sobel (1982). The model in Section 10.9 is due to Gilligan and Krehbiel (1987); the equilibrium under the closed rule is taken from Krishna and Morgan (2001). Banks (1991) presents many other applications of signaling games in political science.

Example 320.2 is based on Bagwell (1995). The game in Exercise 331.1 is taken from Selten (1975) and that in Exercise 331.2 is taken from Kohlberg and Mertens (1986). The game in Exercise 335.2 comes from Maynard Smith (1991). In the Battle of Zutphen in 1586, the young British aristocrat and poet Sir Philip Sydney, having been seriously wounded, reportedly gave a water bottle to a dying soldier with the words "Thy necessity is yet greater than mine" (see Greville 1986, 77 and 215). Maynard Smith writes that "This unusual example of altruism by a member of the English upper classes" inspired him to formulate the game. Bergstrom and Lachmann (1997) compare the pooling and separating equilibria of the game. For more discussion of the game, see Godfray and Johnstone (2000).

III Variants and Extensions

11 Strictly Competitive Games and Maxminimization 361

12 Rationalizability 377

13 Evolutionary Equilibrium 393

14 Repeated Games: The *Prisoner's Dilemma* 419

15 Repeated Games: General Results 451

16 Bargaining 465

11 Strictly Competitive Games and Maxminimization

11.1 Maxminimization 361
11.2 Maxminimization and Nash equilibrium 364
11.3 Strictly competitive games 365
11.4 Maxminimization and Nash equilibrium in strictly competitive games 367
Prerequisite: Chapters 2 and 4

THE NOTION of Nash equilibrium (first studied in Chapter 2) models a steady state. It captures the idea that each player, through her experience playing the game against various opponents, forms a correct belief about the actions of every other player and chooses her action in light of this belief.

In this chapter and the next, we study the players' behavior from a different angle. We consider the implications of each player's basing her belief about the other players' actions on her introspective analysis of the game, rather than on her experience.

In this chapter we focus on two-player "strictly competitive" games, in which the players' interests are diametrically opposed. In such games a simple decision-making procedure leads each player to choose a Nash equilibrium action.

11.1 Maxminimization

You are confronted with a game for the first time; you have no idea what actions your opponents will take. How should you choose your action? Here is a very conservative procedure: associate with each of your actions the *worst* outcome for you, as the other players' actions vary, and then choose the action for which this worst outcome is best. This procedure is known as **maxminimization**.

Consider, for example, a game in which player 1's payoffs are those given in Figure 362.1. (Player 2's payoffs are irrelevant to player 1's choice of an action.) Restrict attention to pure strategies (actions). The worst payoff the action T yields is 0 (obtained when player 2 chooses R) and the worst payoff the action B yields is 1 (obtained when player 2 chooses L). Thus maxminimization among the set of pure strategies leads player 1 to choose B.

Many of the interesting examples of maxminimization involve mixed strategies, so from the beginning I define the concept for a strategic game with vNM preferences (Definition 106.1), though the ideas do not depend on the players' randomizing. Let u_i be a Bernoulli payoff function whose expected value represents player i's preferences regarding lotteries over action profiles in a strategic game. Denote player i's expected payoff under u_i to the mixed strategy profile α by $U_i(\alpha)$. For any given mixed strategy α_i of player i, the lowest payoff that player i obtains, for any possible list α_{-i} of the other players' mixed strategies, is

$$\min_{\alpha_{-i}} U_i(\alpha_i, \alpha_{-i}).$$

A maxminimizing mixed strategy for player i is a mixed strategy that maximizes this minimal payoff.

▷ DEFINITION 362.1 (*Maxminimizing mixed strategy in strategic game with vNM preferences*) A **maxminimizing mixed strategy** for player i in a strategic game with vNM preferences is a mixed strategy that solves the problem

$$\max_{\alpha_i} \min_{\alpha_{-i}} U_i(\alpha_i, \alpha_{-i}),$$

where $U_i(\alpha)$ is player i's expected payoff to the strategy profile α. If α_i^* is a maxminimizing mixed strategy for player i, then $\min_{\alpha_{-i}} U_i(\alpha_i^*, \alpha_{-i})$ is her **maxminimized payoff**.

Note that, equivalently, α_i^* is a maxminimizer if and only if $\min_{\alpha_{-i}} U_i(\alpha_i^*, \alpha_{-i}) = \max_{\alpha_i} \min_{\alpha_{-i}} U_i(\alpha_i, \alpha_{-i})$.

In words, a maxminimizing strategy for player i maximizes her expected payoff under the (very pessimistic) assumption that whatever she does the other players will act in a way that minimizes her expected payoff.

A different way of looking at a maxminimizing strategy is useful. Say that a mixed strategy α_i of player i **guarantees** player i the payoff $\overline{U}_i$ if, when player i uses the strategy α_i, her expected payoff is at least $\overline{U}_i$ regardless of the other players' mixed strategies:

$$U_i(\alpha_i, \alpha_{-i}) \geq \overline{U}_i \text{ for every list } \alpha_{-i} \text{ of the other players' mixed strategies.}$$

In the game in Figure 362.1, for example, player 1's strategy T guarantees any payoff of at most 0 and her strategy B guarantees any payoff of at most 1.

A player's maxminimizing mixed strategy guarantees her maxminimized payoff. Further, no strategy guarantees her a higher payoff. That is, if α_i^* is a maxminimizer of player i, then

$$\min_{\alpha_{-i}} U_i(\alpha_i^*, \alpha_{-i}) \geq \min_{\alpha_{-i}} U_i(\alpha_i, \alpha_{-i}) \text{ for every mixed strategy } \alpha_i \text{ of player } i.$$

	L	R
T	3	0
B	1	2

Figure 362.1 Player 1's payoffs in a strategic game. The action of player 1 that maximizes her worst payoff, as player 2's action varies, is B.

② EXERCISE 363.1 (Maxminimizers in a bargaining game) Find each player's max-minimizing strategies, restricting attention to pure strategies (actions), of the game in Exercise 38.2.

A player may be able to guarantee a higher payoff by using a mixed strategy than by using only pure strategies, as the following example shows. The example also illustrates a method of finding a maxminimizing mixed strategy.

◆ EXAMPLE 363.2 (Example of maxminimizers) Consider the game in Figure 363.1. If player 1 chooses T, then the worse that can happen for her is that player 2 chooses R; if player 1 chooses B, then the worst that can happen is that player 2 chooses L. In both cases player 1's payoff is -1, so that if player 1 is restricted to choose either T or B, then she can guarantee no more than -1.

	L	R
T	2, −2	−1, 1
B	−1, 1	1, −1

Figure 363.1 The game in Example 363.2.

Player 1 can do better, however, if she randomizes between T and B. If, for example, she chooses each action with probability $\frac{1}{2}$, then her expected payoff is $\frac{1}{2}$ if player 2 chooses L and 0 if player 2 chooses R, and thus lies between 0 and $\frac{1}{2}$ if player 2 randomizes between L and R. Hence by choosing each of her actions with probability $\frac{1}{2}$, player 1 guarantees the payoff of 0, more than she guarantees if she chooses either T or B.

Can she do better? Let p be the probability she assigns to T. The upward-sloping line in Figure 364.1 indicates her expected payoff, as p varies, if player 2 chooses the action L; the downward-sloping line indicates her expected payoff, as p varies, if player 2 chooses R. Her expected payoff if player 2 randomizes between L and R lies between the two lines, and in particular lies above the lower line. Thus for each value of p, the lower of the two lines indicates player 1's lowest payoff, as the mixed strategy of player 2 varies, if she chooses that value of p. That is, the value of $\min_{\alpha_2} u_1(\alpha_1, \alpha_2)$ for each value of p (which determines α_1) is indicated by the black inverted V. The maxminimizing mixed strategy of player 1 is thus $p = \frac{2}{5}$, which yields her a payoff of $\frac{1}{5}$.

② EXERCISE 363.3 (Finding a maxminimizer) Find the maxminimizing mixed strategy of player 2 in the game in Figure 363.1.

The maxminimizing mixed strategy of player 1 in this example has the property that it yields player 1 the same payoff whether player 2 chooses L or R. Note that this indifference is different from the indifference in a mixed strategy Nash equilibrium, in which player 1's mixed strategy yields *player 2* the same payoff to each of her actions.

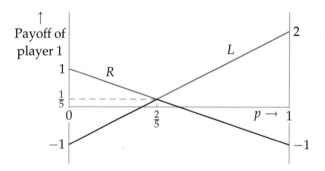

Figure 364.1 The expected payoff of player 1 in the game in Figure 363.1 for each of player 2's actions, as a function of the probability p that player 1 assigns to T.

11.2 Maxminimization and Nash equilibrium

A simple argument establishes that a player's payoff in a mixed strategy Nash equilibrium is at least her maxminimized payoff.

Fix a strategic game, and suppose that α^* is a mixed strategy Nash equilibrium of the game. Consider player i. By definition of equilibrium, her expected payoff when she chooses α_i^* is at least her expected payoff when she chooses any other strategy, given that the remaining players choose their equilibrium strategies:

$$U_i(\alpha_i^*, \alpha_{-i}^*) \geq U_i(\alpha_i, \alpha_{-i}^*) \text{ for every mixed strategy } \alpha_i \text{ of player } i.$$

Now, for any mixed strategy α_i of player i, we have

$$U_i(\alpha_i, \alpha_{-i}^*) \geq \min_{\alpha_{-i}} U_i(\alpha_i, \alpha_{-i}),$$

so that

$$U_i(\alpha_i^*, \alpha_{-i}^*) \geq \min_{\alpha_{-i}} U_i(\alpha_i, \alpha_{-i}) \text{ for every mixed strategy } \alpha_i \text{ of player } i.$$

Given that this inequality holds for any mixed strategy α_i, it holds in particular for the strategy that maximizes the right-hand side, so that

$$U_i(\alpha_i^*, \alpha_{-i}^*) \geq \max_{\alpha_i} \min_{\alpha_{-i}} U_i(\alpha_i, \alpha_{-i}).$$

That is, we have the following result.

■ LEMMA 364.1 *The expected payoff of each player in any mixed strategy Nash equilibrium of a strategic game is at least equal to her maxminimized payoff.*

⍰ EXERCISE 364.2 (Nash equilibrium payoffs and maxminimized payoffs) Give an example of a game with a unique mixed strategy Nash equilibrium in which each player's equilibrium payoff exceeds her maxminimized payoff. (There are examples with two players, each of whom has two actions.)

$$
\begin{array}{c|c|c|}
 & L & R \\
\hline
T & 6,0 & 0,6 \\
\hline
B & 3,2 & 6,0 \\
\hline
\end{array}
$$

Figure 365.1 The strategic game in Exercise 365.1.

? EXERCISE 365.1 (Nash equilibrium payoffs and maxminimized payoffs) Consider the game in Figure 365.1. Find player 1's maxminimizing strategy and her Nash equilibrium strategy. Compare her payoff, as a function of player 2's strategy, when she uses her Nash equilibrium strategy and when she uses her maxminimizing strategy.

11.3 Strictly competitive games

In many games a player has no good reason to believe that the other players will take actions that minimize her payoff. But in a two-player game in which the players' interests are diametrically opposed, the assumption seems reasonable: in maximizing her own payoff in such a game, a player automatically minimizes her opponent's payoff. In this section I define such games precisely. In the next section I argue that in such games the outcome that occurs if each player maxminimizes is very closely related to the Nash equilibrium outcome.

The players' interests in a two-player game are diametrically opposed if whenever one player prefers some outcome a to another outcome b, the other player prefers b to a. We call such a game *strictly competitive*. If we restrict attention to pure strategies, then we have the following definition, in which I assume for convenience that the players' names are "1" and "2".

▶ DEFINITION 365.2 (*Strictly competitive strategic game with ordinal preferences*) A strategic game with ordinal preferences is **strictly competitive** if it has two players and

$$u_1(a_1, a_2) \geq u_1(b_1, b_2) \text{ if and only if } u_2(b_1, b_2) \geq u_2(a_1, a_2),$$

where (a_1, a_2) and (b_1, b_2) are pairs of actions and for $i = 1, 2$, u_i is a payoff function that represents player i's preferences.

Note that an implication of this definition is that in a strictly competitive game

$$u_1(a_1, a_2) = u_1(b_1, b_2) \text{ if and only if } u_2(a_1, a_2) = u_2(b_1, b_2)$$

(because $u_2(a_1, a_2) = u_2(b_1, b_2)$ implies both $u_1(a_1, a_2) \geq u_1(b_1, b_2)$ and $u_1(b_1, b_2) \geq u_1(a_1, a_2)$), and

$$u_1(a_1, a_2) > u_1(b_1, b_2) \text{ if and only if } u_2(b_1, b_2) > u_2(a_1, a_2).$$

Note also that if u_1 is a payoff function that represents player 1's preferences in a strictly competitive game, then the payoff function $-u_1$ represents player 2's

	L	R
T	2,1	0,5
B	1,3	5,0

Figure 366.1 A strategic game that is strictly competitive if attention is restricted to pure strategies but not if mixed strategies are considered.

preferences. That is, in any strictly competitive game there exist payoff functions u_1 and u_2 for the players such that $u_1(a_1, a_2) + u_2(a_1, a_2) = 0$ for every pair (a_1, a_2) of actions. For this reason a strictly competitive game is sometimes called a **zerosum** game.

The *Prisoner's Dilemma* (Figure 15.1) is not strictly competitive because both players prefer *(Quiet, Quiet)* to *(Fink, Fink)*. *BoS* (Figure 19.1) is not strictly competitive either, because (for example) both players prefer (B, B) to (S, B). *Matching Pennies* (Figure 19.2), on the other hand, *is* strictly competitive: player 1's preferences over the four outcomes are precisely the reverse of player 2's. The game in Figure 366.1 is also strictly competitive: player 1 prefers (B, R) to (T, L) to (B, L) to (T, R), whereas player 2's preferences run in the opposite direction.

If we consider mixed strategies, the following definition is appropriate.

▶ DEFINITION 366.1 (*Strictly competitive strategic game with vNM preferences*) A strategic game with vNM preferences is **strictly competitive** if it has two players and

$$U_1(\alpha_1, \alpha_2) \geq U_1(\beta_1, \beta_2) \text{ if and only if } U_2(\beta_1, \beta_2) \geq U_2(\alpha_1, \alpha_2),$$

where (α_1, α_2) and (β_1, β_2) are pairs of mixed strategies and for $i = 1, 2$, U_i is an expected payoff function that represents player i's preferences over lotteries.

As for games with ordinal preferences, there exist payoff functions representing the players' preferences in a strictly competitive game with vNM preferences with the property that the sum of the players' payoffs is zero for every action profile: if u_1 is a Bernoulli payoff function whose expected value represents player 1's preferences regarding lotteries over outcomes, then $-u_1$ is a Bernoulli payoff function whose expected value represents player 2's preferences.

Any game that is strictly competitive when we allow mixed strategies is clearly strictly competitive when we restrict attention to pure strategies, but note that the converse is false. Consider, for example, the game in Figure 366.1, now interpreting the numbers in the boxes as Bernoulli payoffs. In this game player 1 is indifferent between the outcome (T, L) and the lottery in which (T, R) occurs with probability $\frac{3}{5}$ and (B, R) occurs with probability $\frac{2}{5}$ (because $\frac{3}{5} \cdot 0 + \frac{2}{5} \cdot 5 = 2$), but player 2 is not indifferent between these two outcomes (her payoff to (T, L) is 1, whereas her expected payoff to the lottery is $\frac{3}{5} \cdot 5 + \frac{2}{5} \cdot 0 = 3$).

❓ EXERCISE 366.2 (*Determining strict competitiveness*) Is either the game in Exercise 365.1 or the game in Figure 367.1 strictly competitive (*a*) if we restrict attention to pure strategies and (*b*) if we allow mixed strategies?

	L	R
T	$1, -1$	$3, -5$
B	$2, -3$	$1, -1$

Figure 367.1 One of the games in Exercise 366.2.

11.4 Maxminimization and Nash equilibrium in strictly competitive games

We have seen that in any game a player's Nash equilibrium payoff is at least her maxminimized payoff (Lemma 364.1). I now show that in a strictly competitive game that possesses a mixed strategy Nash equilibrium, the two payoffs are the same. In fact,

> *in a strictly competitive game that possesses a mixed strategy Nash equilibrium, a pair of mixed strategies is a mixed strategy Nash equilibrium if and only if each player's strategy is a maxminimizer.*

Though the proof of this result may look complicated, the ideas it entails are very simple; the arguments involve no more than the manipulation of inequalities.

I first establish a preliminary result. Denote player 1's expected payoff function by U_1 and let $U_2 = -U_1$ (so that U_2 is an expected payoff function for player 2). Now, for *any* function f, the minimum of f is equal to the negative of the maximum of $-f$: $\min_x f(x) = -\max_x(-f(x))$ (see Figure 367.2). Thus because $U_2 = -U_1$ we have

$$\max_{\alpha_2} \min_{\alpha_1} U_2(\alpha_1, \alpha_2) = \max_{\alpha_2}\left(-\max_{\alpha_1} U_1(\alpha_1, \alpha_2)\right)$$

or

$$\max_{\alpha_2} \min_{\alpha_1} U_2(\alpha_1, \alpha_2) = -\min_{\alpha_2} \max_{\alpha_1} U_1(\alpha_1, \alpha_2). \tag{367.1}$$

The following proposition is a precise version of the statement at the start of the section.

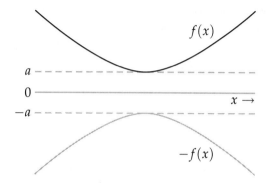

Figure 367.2 The minimum of any function f is equal to the negative of the maximum of $-f$.

■ PROPOSITION 368.1 (Nash equilibrium strategies and maxminimizers of strictly competitive games) *Consider a strictly competitive strategic game with vNM preferences. Let U_1 be an expected payoff function that represents player 1's preferences, and let $U_2 = -U_1$ (so that U_2 represents player 2's preferences).*

  a. *If (α_1^*, α_2^*) is a mixed strategy Nash equilibrium, then α_1^* is a maxminimizer for player 1, α_2^* is a maxminimizer for player 2, and*

$$\max_{\alpha_1} \min_{\alpha_2} U_1(\alpha_1, \alpha_2) = \min_{\alpha_2} \max_{\alpha_1} U_1(\alpha_1, \alpha_2) = U_1(\alpha_1^*, \alpha_2^*).$$

  b. *If $\max_{\alpha_1} \min_{\alpha_2} U_1(\alpha_1, \alpha_2) = \min_{\alpha_2} \max_{\alpha_1} U_1(\alpha_1, \alpha_2)$ (a condition satisfied, in particular, if the game has a mixed strategy Nash equilibrium (see part a)), α_1^* is a maxminimizer for player 1, and α_2^* is a maxminimizer for player 2, then (α_1^*, α_2^*) is a mixed strategy Nash equilibrium.*

Proof. I first prove part *a*. Let (α_1^*, α_2^*) be a mixed strategy Nash equilibrium. By the definition of a Nash equilibrium we have

$$U_2(\alpha_1^*, \alpha_2^*) \geq U_2(\alpha_1^*, \alpha_2) \text{ for every mixed strategy } \alpha_2 \text{ of player 2}$$

or, given $U_2 = -U_1$,

$$U_1(\alpha_1^*, \alpha_2^*) \leq U_1(\alpha_1^*, \alpha_2) \text{ for every mixed strategy } \alpha_2 \text{ of player 2 .}$$

That is,

$$U_1(\alpha_1^*, \alpha_2^*) = \min_{\alpha_2} U_1(\alpha_1^*, \alpha_2). \tag{368.2}$$

Now, define the function g by

$$g(\alpha_1) = \min_{\alpha_2} U_1(\alpha_1, \alpha_2) \text{ for all } \alpha_1.$$

Then the right-hand side of (368.2) is $g(\alpha_1^*)$, which is at most $\max_{\alpha_1} g(\alpha_1)$ (by definition of the maximum!). Thus

$$U_1(\alpha_1^*, \alpha_2^*) \leq \max_{\alpha_1} \min_{\alpha_2} U_1(\alpha_1, \alpha_2).$$

Now, from Lemma 364.1 we have the opposite inequality: a player's Nash equilibrium payoff is at least her maxminimized payoff. Combining the two inequalities we have $U_1(\alpha_1^*, \alpha_2^*) = \max_{\alpha_1} \min_{\alpha_2} U_1(\alpha_1, \alpha_2)$, and hence, using (368.2), $\min_{\alpha_2} U_1(\alpha_1^*, \alpha_2) = \max_{\alpha_1} \min_{\alpha_2} U_1(\alpha_1, \alpha_2)$, so that α_1^* is a maxminimizer for player 1.

An analogous argument establishes that α_2^* is a maxminimizer for player 2 and $U_2(\alpha_1^*, \alpha_2^*) = \max_{\alpha_2} \min_{\alpha_1} U_2(\alpha_1, \alpha_2)$. From (367.1) we deduce that $U_1(\alpha_1^*, \alpha_2^*) = \min_{\alpha_2} \max_{\alpha_1} U_1(\alpha_1, \alpha_2)$, completing the proof of part *a*.

To prove part *b*, let α_1^* be a maxminimizer for player 1, let α_2^* be a maxminimizer for player 2, and assume that $\max_{\alpha_1} \min_{\alpha_2} U_1(\alpha_1, \alpha_2) = \min_{\alpha_2} \max_{\alpha_1} U_1(\alpha_1, \alpha_2)$. Define

$$v^* = \max_{\alpha_1} \min_{\alpha_2} U_1(\alpha_1, \alpha_2) = \min_{\alpha_2} \max_{\alpha_1} U_1(\alpha_1, \alpha_2).$$

From (367.1) we have $\max_{\alpha_2} \min_{\alpha_1} U_2(\alpha_1, \alpha_2) = -v^*$. Because α_1^* is a maxmini-mizer for player 1 we have $U_1(\alpha_1^*, \alpha_2) \geq v^*$ for every mixed strategy α_2 of player 2, and because α_2^* is a maxminimizer for player 2 we have $U_2(\alpha_1, \alpha_2^*) \geq -v^*$ for every mixed strategy α_1 of player 1. Letting $\alpha_2 = \alpha_2^*$ and $\alpha_1 = \alpha_1^*$ in these two inequali-ties we obtain $U_1(\alpha_1^*, \alpha_2^*) \geq v^*$ and $U_2(\alpha_1^*, \alpha_2^*) \geq -v^*$. Given $U_2 = -U_1$, the latter inequality is $U_1(\alpha_1^*, \alpha_2^*) \leq v^*$, so that we have $U_1(\alpha_1^*, \alpha_2^*) = v^*$. Thus

$$U_1(\alpha_1^*, \alpha_2) \geq U_1(\alpha_1^*, \alpha_2^*) \text{ for every mixed strategy } \alpha_2 \text{ of player 2,}$$

or, using $U_2 = -U_1$ again,

$$U_2(\alpha_1^*, \alpha_2) \leq U_2(\alpha_1^*, \alpha_2^*) \text{ for every mixed strategy } \alpha_2 \text{ of player 2,}$$

so that α_2^* is a best response of player 2 to α_1^*. Similarly,

$$U_2(\alpha_1, \alpha_2^*) \geq U_2(\alpha_1^*, \alpha_2^*) \text{ for every mixed strategy } \alpha_1 \text{ of player 1,}$$

or

$$U_1(\alpha_1, \alpha_2^*) \leq U_1(\alpha_1^*, \alpha_2^*) \text{ for every mixed strategy } \alpha_1 \text{ of player 1,}$$

so that α_1^* is a best response of player 1 to α_2^*.

We conclude that (α_1^*, α_2^*) is a Nash equilibrium of the game. $\qquad\square$

This result is of interest not only because it shows the close relation between Nash equilibrium strategies and maxminimizers in strictly competitive games, but also because it reveals properties of the equilibria of such games.

First, part *a* of the result implies that the mixed strategy Nash equilibrium payoff of each player in a strictly competitive game is unique.

■ COROLLARY 369.1 *Every mixed strategy Nash equilibrium of a strictly competitive game yields the same pair of expected payoffs.*

As we have seen, in games that are not strictly competitive, not all Nash equi-libria necessarily yield the same pair of payoffs (consider *BoS* (Figure 19.1), for example).

? EXERCISE 369.2 (Equilibrium payoffs in symmetric game) Show that in any sym-metric (see Definition 129.1) strictly competitive game in which $U_2 = -U_1$, where U_i is player i's expected payoff function for $i = 1, 2$, each player's payoff in every mixed strategy Nash equilibrium is 0.

Second, suppose that (α_1, α_2) and (α_1', α_2') are mixed strategy Nash equilibria of a strictly competitive game. Then by part *a* of Proposition 368.1 the strategies α_1 and α_1' are maxminimizers for player 1, and the strategies α_2 and α_2' are maxmin-imizers for player 2. But then by part *b* of the result both (α_1, α_2') and (α_1', α_2) are mixed strategy Nash equilibria of the game. That is, we have the following result.

■ COROLLARY 369.3 *The mixed strategy Nash equilibria of a strictly competitive game are interchangeable: if (α_1, α_2) and (α_1', α_2') are mixed strategy Nash equilibria, then so are (α_1, α_2') and (α_1', α_2).*

The game *BoS* shows that the Nash equilibria of a game that is not strictly competitive are not necessarily interchangeable.

Third, denote player 1's equilibrium payoff in a strictly competitive game by U_1^*. Part *a* of Proposition 368.1 implies that any Nash equilibrium strategy of player 1 *guarantees* that her payoff is at least U_1^*, and any Nash equilibrium strategy of player 2 *guarantees* that her payoff is at least $-U_1^*$. The second implication means that any Nash equilibrium strategy of player 2 *guarantees* that player 1's payoff is at most U_1^*. That is, we have the following result.

■ COROLLARY 370.1 *Any Nash equilibrium strategy of player 1 in a strictly competitive game guarantees that her payoff is at least her equilibrium payoff, and any Nash equilibrium strategy of player 2 guarantees that player 1's payoff is at most her equilibrium payoff.*

In a game that is not strictly competitive the equality in part *a* of Proposition 368.1 does not generally hold, and a player's equilibrium strategy does not in general have these properties, as the following exercise shows.

⑦ EXERCISE 370.2 (Maxminimizers in *BoS*) For the game *BoS* (Figure 19.1), find the maxminimizer of each player. For each mixed strategy Nash equilibrium, show that the strategy of neither player guarantees her equilibrium payoff.

However, in *any* game (whether strictly competitive or not), the inequality

$$\max_{\alpha_1} \min_{\alpha_2} U_1(\alpha_1, \alpha_2) \le \min_{\alpha_2} \max_{\alpha_1} U_1(\alpha_1, \alpha_2)$$

holds. In words, the highest payoff that player 1 can guarantee herself is *at most* the lowest value that player 2 can guarantee player 1's payoff does not exceed. The argument is simple: for any mixed strategy α_1' of player 1 we have $U_1(\alpha_1', \alpha_2) \le \max_{\alpha_1} U_1(\alpha_1, \alpha_2)$ for each strategy α_2 of player 2, and hence $\min_{\alpha_2} U_1(\alpha_1', \alpha_2) \le \min_{\alpha_2} \max_{\alpha_1} U_1(\alpha_1, \alpha_2)$. This inequality holds for all values of α_1', and thus in particular holds for the value that maximizes the left-hand side.

MAXMINIMIZATION: SOME HISTORY

The theory of maxminimization in general strictly competitive games was developed by John von Neumann in the late 1920s. The idea of maxminimization in the context of a specific game, however, appeared two centuries earlier. In 1713 or 1714 Pierre Rémond de Montmort, a major figure in the history of probability theory (see, for example, Hald 1990) published *Essay d'analyse sur les jeux de hazard* (Analytical essay on games of chance), in which he reports correspondence with Nikolaus Bernoulli (a member of the Swiss family of scientists and mathematicians). Montmort describes a letter dated November 13, 1713, that he received from "M. de Waldegrave" (probably Baron Waldegrave of Chewton, a British noble born and educated in France, according to Kuhn 1968). Montmort,

Bernoulli, and Waldegrave had been corresponding about the card game *le Her* ("the gentleman").

This two-player game uses an ordinary deck of cards. Each player is first dealt a single card, which she alone sees. Each player's object is to hold a card whose value is higher than that of the card held by her opponent, with the ace counted as 1 and the jack, queen, and king counted as 11, 12, and 13, respectively. After each player has received her card, player 1 can, if she wishes, exchange her card with that of player 2, who must make the exchange unless she holds a king, in which case she is automatically the winner. Then, regardless of whether player 1 exchanges her card, player 2 has the option of exchanging hers for a card randomly selected from the cards remaining in the deck. If the randomly selected card is a king, she automatically loses; otherwise she makes the exchange. Finally, the players compare their cards, and the one whose card has the higher value wins; if both cards have the same value, then player 2 wins.

We can model this situation as a strategic game in which an action for player 1 is a rule that says, for each possible card that she may receive, whether she *keeps* or *exchanges* the card. For example, one possible action is to *exchange* any card with value up to 5 and to *keep* any card with higher value; another possible action is to *exchange* any even card and to *keep* any odd card. There are 13 different values of cards, so player 1 has 2^{13} (8,192) actions. If player 1 exchanges her card, then player 2 knows both cards being held, and she should clearly exchange with a random card from the deck if and only if the card she holds would otherwise lose. If player 1 does not exchange her card, then player 2's decision of whether to exchange is not as clear. Like an action of player 1 at the start of the game, an action of player 2 is a rule that says, for each possible card that she holds, whether she *keeps* or *exchanges* the card. Like player 1, player 2 has 2^{13} actions.

Montmort, Bernoulli, and Waldegrave argued that the only actions that could possibly be optimal are "*exchange* up to 6 and *keep* 7 and over" or "*exchange* up to 7 and *keep* 8 and over" for player 1, and "*exchange* up to 7 and *keep* 8 and over" or "*exchange* up to 8 and *keep* 9 and over" for player 2. When the players are restricted to use only these actions, the game is equivalent to

0, 0	5, −5
3, −3	0, 0

The three scholars had corresponded about which action each player should choose. As you can see, the best action for each player depends on the other player's action, and the game has no pure strategy Nash equilibrium. Waldegrave made the key conceptual leap of considering the possibility that the players randomize. He observed that player 1's mixed strategy $(\frac{3}{8}, \frac{5}{8})$ yields her the same payoff regardless of player 2's action and guarantees her a payoff of $\frac{15}{8}$, and, further, that player 2's mixed strategy $(\frac{5}{8}, \frac{3}{8})$ ensures that player 1's payoff is no more than $\frac{15}{8}$.

That is, Waldegrave found the maxminimizers for each player and appreciated their significance. Montmort wrote to Bernoulli that "it seems to me that [Waldegrave's letter] exhausts everything that one can say on [the players' behavior in *le Her*]."

⊘ EXERCISE 372.1 (Increasing payoffs and eliminating actions in strictly competitive games) Let G be a strictly competitive game that has a Nash equilibrium.

    a. Suppose that the strictly competitive game G' differs from G only in that some of player 1's payoffs in G' are higher than the corresponding payoffs in G. Show that G' has no equilibrium in which player 1 is worse off than she is in an equilibrium of G. (Use part a of Proposition 368.1.)

    b. Suppose that the game G' differs from G only in that one of player 1's actions in G is absent from her set of actions in G'. Show that G' has no equilibrium in which player 1's payoff is higher than it is in any equilibrium of G.

    c. Give examples to show that neither of the above properties necessarily holds for a game that is not strictly competitive.

⊘ EXERCISE 372.2 (Equilibrium in strictly competitive games) Either prove or give a counterexample to the claim that if the equilibrium payoff of player 1 in a strictly competitive game is v, then any strategy pair that gives player 1 a payoff of v is an equilibrium.

⊘ EXERCISE 372.3 (*Morra*) In the two-player game "Morra", the players simultaneously hold up some fingers and each guesses the total number of fingers held up. If exactly one player guesses correctly, then the other player pays her the amount of her guess (in dollars, say). If either both players guess correctly or neither does so, then no payments are made. (The game was played in ancient Rome, where it was known as "micatio" (Carcopino 1940, 251–252).) Consider a version of the game in which the number of fingers each player may hold up is restricted to be either one or two.

    a. Model this situation as a (strictly competitive) strategic game.

    b. Given the symmetry of the game, each player's equilibrium payoff is 0 by the result in Exercise 369.2. Find the mixed strategies of player 1 that guarantee that her payoff is at least 0 (i.e. the strategies such that her payoff is at least 0 for each pure strategy of player 2), and hence find all the mixed strategy equilibria of the game.

⊘ EXERCISE 372.4 (O'Neill's game) Consider the game in Figure 373.1.

    a. Find a mixed strategy Nash equilibrium in which each player assigns positive probability to each of her actions and assigns the same probability to the actions 1, 2, and 3.

	1	2	3	J
1	$-1,\ \ 1$	$1, -1$	$1, -1$	$-1,\ \ 1$
2	$1, -1$	$-1,\ \ 1$	$1, -1$	$-1,\ \ 1$
3	$1, -1$	$1, -1$	$-1,\ \ 1$	$-1,\ \ 1$
J	$-1,\ \ 1$	$-1,\ \ 1$	$-1,\ \ 1$	$1, -1$

Figure 373.1 The game in Exercise 372.4.

b. Use Corollaries 369.1 and 370.1 to show that the equilibrium you found in part *a* is the only equilibrium of the game.

EMPIRICAL TESTS: EXPERIMENTS, TENNIS, AND SOCCER

The theory of maxminimization makes a sharp prediction about the players' strategies in a strictly competitive game. Does human behavior bear out this prediction?

Experiments

To test whether experimental subjects choose maxminimizers (or Nash equilibrium strategies) in a specific strictly competitive game, we need to know their preferences given the monetary payoffs with which we confront them. When working with mixed strategies, not only do we have to be sure that the subjects care only about their own payoffs (see the discussion on page 24), but also we need, in general, to know their attitudes to risk (see Section 4.1.3). However, in games with only two outcomes, risk attitudes play no role. If each player in such a game cares only about the amount of money she receives, her preferences are represented by the expected value of the Bernoulli payoff function that assigns to each outcome this amount of money. This fact makes two-outcome games attractive for experiments.

One experiment used the game in Exercise 372.4 (O'Neill 1987). Each player's unique maxminimizing (and hence Nash equilibrium) mixed strategy in this game is $(0.2, 0.2, 0.2, 0.4)$ (with the actions ordered 1, 2, 3, J, as in Figure 373.1). In the experiment, each of 25 pairs of people played the game 105 times. This design raises two issues. First, when the same two players confront each other repeatedly, strategic possibilities absent from a one-shot game emerge: each player may condition her current action on her opponent's past actions. However, an analysis that takes into account these strategic options leads to the conclusion that, for the game used in the experiment, the players will eschew them. Second, because of the repeated play in the experiment, each subject faced more than two possible outcomes. However, under the hypothesis that each player's preferences are separable between the different trials, each player's preferences in the whole experiment may be represented by her expected total monetary payoff.

Each subject was given \$2.50 in cash at the start of the game, was paid \$0.05 for every win, and paid her opponent \$0.05 for every loss. On average, subjects in the role of player 1 chose the actions with probabilities $(0.221, 0.215, 0.203, 0.362)$ and subjects in the role of player 2 chose them with probabilities $(0.226, 0.179, 0.169, 0.426)$. These observed frequencies seem close to those predicted by the theory of maxminimization. Are they close enough to be consistent with the theory? A standard statistical test (χ^2) asks the question: If each player uses her maxminimizer, what is the probability that the observed frequencies deviate at least as much from the predicted ones? Applying this test to the aggregate data on the frequencies of the 16 possible outcomes of the game leads to the decisive *rejection* of the hypothesis that the subjects were using their maxminimizing strategies. (The probability of a deviation from the prediction at least as large as that observed is less than 1 in 1,000.) However, this statistical test is severe: for a game in which a player has a pure strategy maxminimizer, for example, it would reject the hypothesis that the player is using the maxminimizer if there were a *single* instance in which she used another strategy. Nevertheless, a variety of other tests suggest also that the observations are not closely consistent with the theory of maxminimization (Brown and Rosenthal 1990), so that at best the experiment appears to offer only limited support for the theory.

Tennis and soccer

One explanation for the relatively poor performance of the theory of maxminimization in the experiment using the game in Figure 373.1 is that because the subjects had insufficient time to gain experience playing the game, their play had not reached a steady state. This explanation suggests that the behavior of professional game players might yield better results. Professional athletes, for example, spend their lives gaining experience and have huge monetary incentives to optimize. Most games played professionally are too complex to test straightforwardly, but parts of tennis and soccer have been successfully isolated for scrutiny.

The server in tennis would like to hit the ball as close as possible to one of the sides of the receiver's court. The receiver must decide whether to prepare for a serve to the left or to the right. Assuming that the receiver must make her decision before the ball is served, we may model the play of a point as a strategic game in which the server's actions are "play to the left" and "play to the right", and the receiver's actions are "prepare for a serve to the left" and "prepare for a serve to the right". The serve does not fully determine the outcome of a point, but significantly influences it: the probability of the server's ultimately winning the point depends on the initial actions of the server and the receiver.

The server's action on each point is easily observable. The receiver's action and the probabilities that the server wins the point for each of the four action pairs are, however, not observable, so we cannot directly test whether the server is playing an equilibrium strategy. We can, however, check two implications of the theory of maxminimization (and Nash equilibrium): the equality of the server's payoff (probability of winning) to her two actions, and the statistical independence of her actions over a series of points. Walker and Wooders (2000) use data from ten matches in major tournaments between top players who had played each other many times. They find that the probabilities of the server's winning a point played to the left and to the right are close enough to be consistent with their being equal, as the theory implies, but the server's choices from point to point are not statistically independent. These results thus support the theory, but not without qualification.

Penalty kicks in soccer matches provide another set of data to test the theory. A penalty kick may be modeled as a two-player strictly competitive game between a kicker and a goalkeeper. To have a good chance of scoring a goal, the kicker must propel the ball to one of the two sides of the goal; to prevent a goal's being scored, the goalkeeper must move to the side the kicker chooses. Given the speed of the ball and human reaction times, the goalkeeper must act simultaneously with the kicker; waiting to see at which side the kicker is aiming is not practical. Both players' actions—the side to which the ball is kicked and the direction in which the goalkeeper jumps—are observable. Using data on highly skilled players who often faced each other, Palacios-Huerta (2003) performs tests like those used on the tennis data. He finds that the data are consistent, for almost all kickers, with the probability of scoring a goal when the ball is kicked to the left being equal to the probability of scoring a goal when the ball is kicked to the right, and, for almost all goalkeepers, with the probability of preventing a goal by jumping to the left being equal to the probability of preventing a goal by jumping to the right. Further, the players' actions from one penalty kick to the next are consistent with their choices being statistically independent. Thus these data are consistent with both implications of the theory.

In conclusion, the theory of maxminimization appears to perform well in situations in which players are experienced; it performs much less well, as we would expect, in games between inexperienced players.

Notes

The main ideas and results in this chapter are due to von Neumann (1928); the theory was developed by von Neumann and Morgenstern (1944).

The material in the box on page 370 is based on Todhunter (1865) and Kuhn (1968). Guilbaud (1961) rediscovered Montmort's report of Waldegrave's work.

The box on page 373 is based on O'Neill (1987), Brown and Rosenthal (1990), Walker and Wooders (2000), and Palacios-Huerta (2003).

The game in Exercise 365.1 is taken from Aumann (1989, Example 2.21), and the one in Exercise 372.4 is taken from O'Neill (1987).

12 Rationalizability

12.1 Rationalizability 377
12.2 Iterated elimination of strictly dominated actions 385
12.3 Iterated elimination of weakly dominated actions 388
12.4 Dominance solvability 391
Prerequisite: Chapters 2 and 4; Chapter 5 for Section 12.3

W HAT outcomes in a strategic game are consistent with the players' introspective analyses of each others' rational behavior? The main solution notion we have studied so far, Nash equilibrium, is not designed to address this question; rather, it models a steady state in which each player has learned the other players' actions from her long experience playing the game. In this chapter I discuss an approach to the question that considers rational players who attempt to deduce their opponents' rational actions from their opponents' preferences and from analyses of their opponents' reasoning about their own rational actions.

12.1 Rationalizability

12.1.1 Introductory examples

We say that a player's action is *rational* if it maximizes her payoff, given *some* belief about the other players' actions. (Note that we place no restriction on the player's belief.)

In some games, the assumption of rationality significantly restricts the players' actions. Consider, for example, the *Prisoner's Dilemma* (Example 14.1). For *any* belief about the other player's action, *Fink* yields a payoff higher than does *Quiet* (*Fink* is better than *Quiet regardless* of the other player's action), so that *Fink* is the only rational action for each player. (This action is also of course the only Nash equilibrium action.)

In other games, the assumption of rationality is less restrictive. Consider the variant of the *Prisoner's Dilemma* in Figure 378.1. If player 1 believes that player 2 will choose Q, then she should choose Q, whereas if she believes that player 2 will choose F, then she should choose F. Thus both Q and F are rational for player 1. Are the beliefs that support these actions reasonable? Suppose we restrict player 1's belief to be consistent with player 2's rationality. The only rational action of player 2 is F (as in the *Prisoner's Dilemma*), and player 1's only rational action given the belief that player 2 chooses F is F. Thus F is the only action of

$$\begin{array}{c|c|c|}
 & Q & F \\
\hline
Q & 3,2 & 0,3 \\
\hline
F & 2,0 & 1,1 \\
\hline
\end{array}$$

Figure 378.1 A variant of the *Prisoner's Dilemma*.

player 1 that is both rational and supported by a belief consistent with player 2's action being rational.

In yet other games, the outcome is not significantly restricted by the assumptions that each player's action is rational and that her belief is consistent with her opponents' rationality but is restricted by further steps in the players' reasoning process. Consider the game in Figure 378.2. The action Q of player 1 is rational (supported by the belief that player 2 chooses Q) and the action F is also rational (supported by the belief that player 2 chooses F). Further, both Q and F are rational for player 2 (supported respectively by the beliefs that player 1 chooses X and either Q or F). Thus player 1's assuming that player 2's action is rational does not rule out either of player 2's actions, so that player 1's actions Q and F are both consistent with her rationality and her assuming that player 2's action is rational.

Now for an additional step: suppose that player 1 assumes that player 2 assumes that player 1's action is rational. Player 2's assumption that player 1's action is rational leads her to conclude that player 1 will not choose X (because this action is not a best response to any belief of player 1 about player 2). But then player 2's rationality leads her to choose F, because Q is not a best response to any belief of player 2 that assigns probability zero to X. Finally, if player 1 assumes that player 2 assumes that her action is rational, she knows that player 2 will chooses F, and thus rationally chooses F herself. Thus for this game, (F, F) is the only pair of actions consistent with (*i*) each player's assuming that the other player assumes that her action is rational, (*ii*) each player's assuming that the other player's action is rational, and (*iii*) each player's action being rational.

For each of these three games I have argued that the only action for each player consistent with the players' rationality and up to two levels of introspective reasoning about each other's rationality is F. I further claim that, in each game, the action F for each player survives all higher level reasoning of the same type. That is, for each player i in each game, (*i*) there is a belief about the other player's action (she will choose F) under which F is optimal, (*ii*) there is a belief about i's action (she will choose F) under which the action hypothesized for the other player in (*i*) is optimal, (*iii*) there is a belief about the other player's action (she will choose F)

$$\begin{array}{c|c|c|}
 & Q & F \\
\hline
Q & 4,2 & 0,3 \\
\hline
X & 1,1 & 1,0 \\
\hline
F & 3,0 & 2,2 \\
\hline
\end{array}$$

Figure 378.2 A further variant of the *Prisoner's Dilemma*.

under which the action hypothesized for the other player in (*ii*) is optimal, and so on indefinitely. At each stage, we can find a belief that justifies the action assumed in the previous stage. We say that an action that can be supported in this way is "rationalizable".

I now formulate these ideas precisely and describe their implications. We shall see that in some games (like the three examples), the players' introspective reasoning about each other's actions significantly restricts the outcome, while in others it does not.

12.1.2 Definitions

A "rational" player forms a probabilistic belief about the other players' actions and chooses her action (or mixed strategy) to maximize her expected payoff given this belief. (Throughout this chapter I work with strategic games with vNM preferences.)

▶ DEFINITION 379.1 (*Player's belief and rationality in strategic game*) A **belief** of player i about the other players' actions in a strategic game with vNM preferences is a probability distribution over the set A_{-i} of lists of the other players' actions. Player i's mixed strategy α_i is **rational** if there exists a belief μ_i of player i about the other players' actions under which α_i maximizes player i's expected payoff

$$\sum_{a_{-i} \in A_{-i}} \mu_i(a_{-i}) U_i(\alpha_i, a_{-i}),$$

where $U_i(\alpha_i, a_{-i})$ is player i's expected payoff when she uses the mixed strategy α_i and the other players' actions are a_{-i}. In this case we say that α_i is **rational for the belief** μ_i, or a **best response to** μ_i.

? EXERCISE 379.2 (Best responses to beliefs) Give an example of an action that is a best response to a belief but is not a best response to any belief that assigns probability 1 to a single action.

Note that the definition allows a player to hold a belief that is *not* derived from independent mixed strategies of the other players: a belief of player i may be any probability distribution over A_{-i}, regardless of whether the probabilities this distribution assigns to lists of actions are products of the probabilities assigned by mixed strategies of the other players. That is, the definition allows a player to believe that the other players' actions are "correlated". For example, in a three-player game in which the actions of player 2 are A and B, and those of player 3 are X and Y, player 1 may hold the belief that the actions of players 2 and 3 will be (A, X) with probability $\frac{1}{2}$ and (B, Y) with probability $\frac{1}{2}$, a probability distribution that is not possible if players 2 and 3 independently randomize.

In the terminology of the definition, the notion of Nash equilibrium requires not only that each player's strategy be rational but also that each player's belief be correct. Precisely, a mixed strategy profile α^* is a Nash equilibrium if, for each player i,

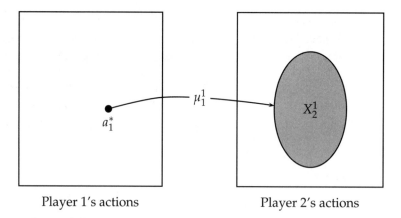

Player 1's actions   Player 2's actions

Figure 380.1 An illustration of the condition that player 1's action a_1^* is rational. The action a_1^* is a best response to the belief μ_1^1; the set of actions of player 2 to which this belief assigns positive probability is X_2^1.

- α_i^* is rational for the belief μ_i

- for every list a_{-i} of the other players' actions, the probability $\mu_i(a_{-i})$ that i's belief μ_i assigns to a_{-i} is equal to the product of $\alpha_j^*(a_j)$ over all $j \neq i$, the probability under α^* that the list of the other players' actions is a_{-i}.

The requirement of Nash equilibrium that each player's belief about the other players be correct is not appealing for a player who confronts a game in which she has little or no experience. In the previous section (12.1.1) we considered the implications in some examples of the alternative requirement that each player knows (or at least assumes) that the other players' actions are rational, that the other players assume that her action is rational, that the other players assume that she assumes that their actions are rational, and so on.

I now formulate these requirements precisely, initially restricting attention to a two-player game.

Suppose that the action a_1^* of player 1 is rational. Then a_1^* is a best response to some belief, say μ_1^1, of player 1 about player 2's actions. This condition is illustrated in Figure 380.1, where the rectangles represent the players' action sets and the shaded set X_2^1 on the right is the set of player 2's actions assigned positive probability by μ_1^1.

Now suppose that not only is the action a_1^* of player 1 rational, but

- there is a belief μ_1^1 of player 1 to which a_1^* is a best response such that every action of player 2 assigned positive probability by μ_1^1 is rational for player 2.

This condition is illustrated in Figure 381.1, which shows two representative actions a_2' and a_2'' to which μ_1^1 assigns positive probability, together with beliefs of player 2, $\mu_2^2(a_2')$ and $\mu_2^2(a_2'')$, to which these actions are best responses. The sets of actions of player 1 to which these two beliefs assign positive probability are the sets inside the black ellipses on the left. (These sets may or may not intersect; in

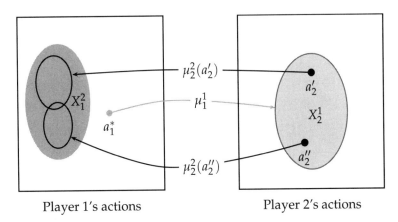

$\mu_2^2(a_2')$

μ_1^1

$\mu_2^2(a_2'')$

Player 1's actions

Player 2's actions

Figure 381.1 An illustration of an action a_1^* of player 1 that is both rational and supported by a belief μ_1^1 with the property that every action of player 2 assigned positive probability by μ_1^1 is rational for player 2.

the diagram, they do.) The shaded set of player 1's actions consists of all actions assigned positive probability by a belief that supports *some* member of X_2^1. That is, the shaded set is the union over all members a_2 of X_2^1 of the sets of actions assigned positive probability by $\mu_2^2(a_2)$.

Taking the argument one step further, suppose that not only is the action a_1^* of player 1 rational, but

- there is a belief μ_1^1 of player 1 to which a_1^* is a best response such that

  - for every action a_2 of player 2 assigned positive probability by μ_1^1 there is a belief $\mu_2^2(a_2)$ to which a_2 is a best response such that every action of player 1 assigned positive probability by $\mu_2^2(a_2)$ is rational for player 1.

This condition is illustrated in Figure 382.1. The beliefs under which a_1' and a_1'' are rational are $\mu_1^3(a_1')$ and $\mu_1^3(a_1'')$ respectively, and the actions of player 2 to which these beliefs assign positive probability are enclosed in the black ellipses on the right. The dark gray set on the right, X_2^3, is the set of all actions of player 2 assigned positive probability by a belief that supports some member of X_1^2. (The sets X_2^1 and X_2^3 may or may not intersect.)

We may be able to continue the process further, at each stage t finding, for each action a_j in X_i^{t-1}, beliefs of player j under which a_j is rational. If we can continue the process indefinitely, we say that a_i^* is *rationalizable*. That is, an action a_i^* of player i is rationalizable if player i can say to herself "I should choose a_i^* because (*i*) it is rational, (*ii*) there is a belief that makes it rational that assigns positive probability only to rational actions of player j, (*iii*) there are beliefs of player j that make each of these actions rational that assign positive probability only to rational actions of mine", and so on indefinitely.

In the game in Figure 378.2, for example, the action Q of player 1 is *not* rationalizable. It is rational, and there is a belief μ_1^1 that supports it that assigns positive probability only to rational actions of player 2 (μ_1^1 assigns probability 1 to Q, which

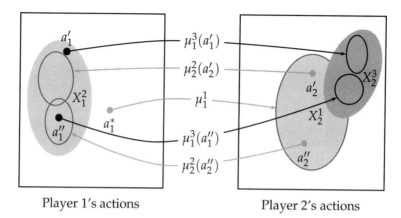

Player 1's actions   Player 2's actions

Figure 382.1 An illustration of an action a_1^* of player 1 that (*a*) is rational and (*b*) is supported by a belief μ_1^1 with the property that every action of player 2 assigned positive probability by μ_1^1 is (*i*) rational for player 2 and (*ii*) supported by a belief with the property that every action of player 1 assigned positive probability by this belief is rational for player 1.

is rational for player 2 if she believes that player 1 chooses X with probability 1). But no belief that supports it assigns positive probability to actions of player 2 that are themselves supported by beliefs that assign positive probability only to rational actions of player 1. The point is that player 1 rationally chooses Q only if she believes that player 2 is sufficiently likely to choose Q, an action that is optimal for player 2 only if she believes that player 1 is sufficiently likely to chooses X, an action that is not rational for player 1.

In this game, the action F of player 1, however, *is* rationalizable, supported by beliefs for each player that assign probability 1 to F. That is, player 1 thinks that player 2 will choose F, and thinks that player 2 thinks that she will choose F, and thinks that player 2 thinks that she thinks that player 2 will choose F, and so on indefinitely.

We could now define rationalizability precisely by formulating the infinite sequence of conditions. But alternatively, the informal discussion suggests a much simpler definition that circumvents the infinite sequence. Suppose that there are sets Z_1 and Z_2 of actions of players 1 and 2, respectively, such that Z_1 contains a_1^*, every action in Z_1 is a best response to a belief of player 1 that assigns positive probability only to actions in Z_2, and every action in Z_2 is a best response to a belief of player 2 that assigns positive probability only to actions in Z_1. (Refer to Figure 383.1.) Then we can construct sequences satisfying the conditions discussed above: simply set $X_1^t = Z_1$ for all even values of t, and $X_2^t = Z_2$ for all odd values of t. Thus a_1^* is rationalizable.

Conversely, suppose that we can find an infinite sequence of beliefs and sets of actions as described above. Let Z_1 be the union of $\{a_1^*\}$ with the union of the sets X_1^t for all even values of t, and let Z_2 be the union of the sets X_2^t for all odd values of t. Then every action in Z_i is a best response to a belief that assigns positive probability only to actions in Z_j for $i = 1$ and $j = 2$, and for $i = 2$ and $j = 1$.

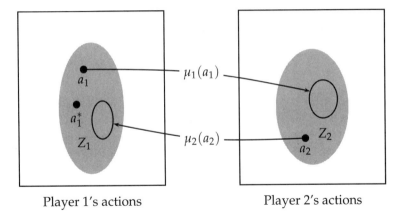

Player 1's actions   Player 2's actions

Figure 383.1 An illustration of the definition of a rationalizable action a_1^*. Each action in Z_1 is a best response to a belief that assigns positive probability only to members of Z_2, and each action in Z_2 is a best response to a belief that assigns positive probability only to members of Z_1. The figure shows an example of a member a_1 of Z_1 and the set of actions of player 2 to which the belief $\mu_1(a_1)$ that supports it assigns positive probability, together with an example of a member a_2 of Z_2 and the set of actions of player 2 to which the belief $\mu_2(a_2)$ that supports it assigns positive probability.

Thus we define an action to be rationalizable as follows, where Z_{-i} denotes the set of all collections a_{-i} of actions for the players other than i for which $a_j \in Z_j$ for all j.

▷ DEFINITION 383.1 (*Rationalizable action in strategic game*) The action a_i^* of player i in a strategic game with vNM preferences is **rationalizable** if for each player j there exists a set Z_j of actions such that

- Z_i contains a_i^*
- for every player j, every action a_j in Z_j is a best response to a belief of player j that assigns positive probability only to lists of actions in Z_{-j}.

12.1.3   Properties of rationalizable actions

Suppose that a^* is a pure strategy Nash equilibrium. Then for each player i the action a_i^* is a best response to a belief that assigns probability one to a_{-i}^*. Setting $Z_i = \{a_i^*\}$ for each i, we see that a^* is rationalizable. In fact, we have the following stronger result, which follows from the fact that in a mixed strategy Nash equilibrium, any action a player uses with positive probability is a best response to the list of the other players' strategies.

∎ PROPOSITION 383.2 *Every action used with positive probability in some mixed strategy Nash equilibrium is rationalizable.*

Proof. Let α^* be a mixed strategy Nash equilibrium, and for each player i let Z_i be the set of actions to which player i's strategy α_i^* assigns positive probability. By Proposition 116.2, every action in Z_i is a best response to the belief of player i generated by the other players' strategies (i.e. the belief that assigns to the list of

	L	C	R
T	0,7	2,5	7,0
M	5,2	3,3	5,2
B	7,0	2,5	0,7

Figure 384.1 A game in which the actions T and B of player 1 and L and R of player 2 are not used with positive probability in any Nash equilibrium, but are rationalizable.

actions a_{-i} a probability equal to the product of $\alpha_j^*(a_j)$ over all $j \neq i$), and this belief by definition assigns positive probability only to lists of actions in Z_{-i}. Hence every action in Z_i is rationalizable.   □

Actions not used with positive probability in any Nash equilibrium may also be rationalizable. First consider a game in which each action of every player is a best response to *some* list of strategies of the other players. For such a game, the conditions in Definition 383.1 are satisfied when, for every player i, Z_i is equal to the set of *all* player i's actions. Thus *every* action of every player in such a game is rationalizable.

I claim that the game in Figure 384.1 (a) is such a game and (b) has a unique Nash equilibrium, (M, C).

❓ EXERCISE 384.1 (Mixed strategy equilibrium of game in Figure 384.1) Show that the game in Figure 384.1 has no mixed strategy equilibrium in which any player's strategy assigns positive probability to more than one action.

Each action of each player is a best response to some action of the other player (for example, T is a best response of player 1 to R, M is a best response to C, and B is a best response to L), so by the argument of the previous paragraph, all actions of both players are rationalizable. In particular, the actions T and B of player 1 are rationalizable, though they are not used with positive probability in any Nash equilibrium. For example, the action T is rational for player 1 if she believes that player 2 will choose R, which is rational for player 2 if she believes that player 1 will choose B, which is rational for player 1 if she thinks that player 2 will choose L, which in turn is rational for player 2 if she thinks that player 1 will choose T, at which point we are back to the beginning of the cycle.

Even in games in which every rationalizable action is used with positive probability in some Nash equilibrium, the implications of rationalizability differ from those of Nash equilibrium. The reason is that the notion of Nash equilibrium isolates a set of strategy *profiles*, while the notion of rationalizability isolates a set of actions for each player. Consider, for example, the game in Figure 385.1. This game has exactly two Nash equilibria, both in pure strategies: (T, T) and (B, B). The notion of rationalizability, however, does not restrict the outcome at all: both T and B are rationalizable for both players, so that all four pure outcomes are consistent with each player's action being rationalizable.

Finding a collection of sets Z_i of actions that satisfies Definition 383.1 can be difficult. In the next section I describe an alternative concept that is easier to work with and is equivalent to rationalizability.

$$
\begin{array}{c|cc}
 & T & B \\
\hline
T & 2,2 & 1,0 \\
B & 0,1 & 1,1 \\
\end{array}
$$

Figure 385.1 A game with two Nash equilibria, (T,T) and (B,B).

12.2 Iterated elimination of strictly dominated actions

The notion of rationalizability, in requiring that a player act rationally, eliminates from consideration actions that are not best responses to any belief. Such actions are called *never-best responses*.

▷ DEFINITION 385.1 (*Never-best response in strategic game*) The action a'_i of player i in a strategic game with vNM preferences is a **never-best response** if for every belief μ_i of player i about the other players' actions there exists a mixed strategy α_i of player i such that player i's expected payoff to α_i exceeds her expected payoff to a'_i:

$$
\sum_{a_{-i} \in A_{-i}} \mu_i(a_{-i}) U_i(\alpha_i, a_{-i}) > \sum_{a_{-i} \in A_{-i}} \mu_i(a_{-i}) u_i(a'_i, a_{-i}), \tag{385.2}
$$

where $U_i(\alpha_i, a_{-i})$ is player i's expected payoff when she uses the mixed strategy α_i and the other players' actions are a_{-i}, u_i is her Bernoulli payoff function, and A_{-i} is the set of lists of the other players' actions.

Another criterion that we might use to eliminate an action from consideration is *domination*. Recall that an action a_i of player i in a strategic game with vNM preferences is *strictly dominated* if player i has a mixed strategy that yields her a higher payoff than does a_i *regardless* of the other players' actions (Definition 120.1).

An argument on page 121 shows that a strictly dominated action is a never-best response (a result you should find unsurprising). Here is an argument using the current terminology: if a'_i is strictly dominated by the mixed strategy α_i, then $U_i(\alpha_i, a_{-i}) > u_i(a'_i, a_{-i})$ for all a_{-i}, so that (385.2) is satisfied for any belief μ_i of player i about the other players' actions, and hence a'_i is a never-best response.

In a game in which each player has finitely many actions, the converse of this result is also true: every never-best response is strictly dominated. Although you may be able to convince yourself that this result is plausible, the proof (which I omit) is not trivial. In summary, we have the following result.

■ LEMMA 385.3 *A player's action in a strategic game with vNM preferences in which each player has finitely many actions is a never-best response if and only if it is strictly dominated.*

Now reconsider the argument behind the notion of rationalizability. First we argue that a player will not use a never-best response, or equivalently, a strictly dominated action. Next we argue that if she works under the assumption that her opponents are rational, then her belief should not assign positive probability to any of her opponents' actions that are never-best responses. Putting these two arguments together, a player should not choose an action that is strictly dominated in the game that results when we eliminate all her opponents' strictly dominated actions. We argue further that a player who works under the assumption that her opponents assume that she is rational will assume that her opponents' actions are best responses to beliefs that assign positive probability only to actions of hers that are best responses to some belief. That is, she will assume that her opponents' actions are not strictly dominated in the game that results when all of her strictly dominated actions are eliminated. Thus she will choose an action that is not strictly dominated in the game that results when, first, all of her strictly dominated actions are eliminated, and then all of the other players' strictly dominated actions are eliminated.

We see that given Lemma 385.3, each step in the argument for rationalizability is equivalent to an additional round of elimination of strictly dominated strategies, so that the rationalizable actions are those that remain no matter how many rounds of elimination we perform. That is, an action profile is rationalizable if and only if it survives *iterated elimination of strictly dominated actions*.

Precisely, we define a set of action profiles to survive iterated elimination of strictly dominated actions as follows.

▶ DEFINITION 386.1 (*Iterated elimination of strictly dominated actions*) Suppose that for each player i in a strategic game and each $t = 1, \ldots, T$ there is a set X_i^t of actions of player i (the set of actions remaining at the start of round t of elimination) such that

- $X_i^1 = A_i$ (we start with the set of all possible actions)
- X_i^{t+1} is a subset of X_i^t for each $t = 1, \ldots, T-1$ (at each stage we may eliminate actions)
- for each $t = 1, \ldots, T-1$, every action of player i in X_i^t but not in X_i^{t+1} is strictly dominated in the game in which the set of actions of each player j is X_j^t (we eliminate only strictly dominated actions)
- no action in X_i^T is strictly dominated in the game in which the set of actions of each player j is X_j^T (at the end of the process no action of any player is strictly dominated).

Then the set of action profiles a such that $a_i \in X_i^T$ for every player i **survives iterated elimination of strictly dominated actions**.

This definition admits the possibility that more than one set of action profiles survives iterated elimination of strictly dominated actions: that different orders and rates of elimination lead to different sets of surviving action profiles. But in fact we can show that the set of survivors is independent of the order and rate of elimination, and, as I have argued informally, coincides with the set of profiles of rationalizable actions (I omit the proof).

■ PROPOSITION 386.2 *For any strategic game with vNM preferences in which each player has finitely many actions, a unique set of action profiles survives iterated elimination of strictly dominated actions, and this set is equal to the set of profiles of rationalizable actions.*

	B	S	X
B	3,1	0,0	−1,2
S	0,0	1,3	0,2

	B	S	X
B	4,3	0,0	2,1
S	0,0	3,4	1,1

Figure 387.1 Two variants of *BoS*.

◆ EXAMPLE 387.1 (Rationalizable actions in two variants of *BoS*) Consider the game in the left panel of Figure 387.1. Neither action of player 1 is strictly dominated, but the action *B* of player 2 is strictly dominated by *X*. In the game obtained by eliminating *B* for player 2, the action *B* of player 1 is strictly dominated. Finally, in the game obtained by eliminating *B* for player 2 and *B* for player 1 the action *X* for player 2 is strictly dominated. We conclude that the only rationalizable action of each player is *S*.

Now consider the game in the right panel of Figure 387.1. I claim that the action *X* of player 2 is strictly dominated by mixed strategies that assign positive probabilities to *B* and *S*. To establish this claim, denote by α_2^* the strategy of player 2 that assigns probability p to *B* and probability $1 - p$ to *S*. For α_2^* to strictly dominate the action *X*, we need $3p > 1$ (the expected payoff to α_2^* exceeds the expected payoff to *X* when player 1 chooses *B*) and $4(1 - p) > 1$ (the expected payoff to α_2^* exceeds the expected payoff to *X* when player 1 chooses *S*). These two conditions are satisfied if $\frac{1}{3} < p < \frac{3}{4}$. Now consider the game that results when *X* is eliminated. In this game, for each player the action *B* is a best response to the belief that assigns probability 1 to *B*, and the action *S* is a best response to the belief that assigns probability 1 to *S*, so that neither action of either player is strictly dominated. Hence both *B* and *S* are rationalizable for each player in the whole game.

? EXERCISE 387.2 (Finding rationalizable actions) Find the set of rationalizable actions of each player in the game in Figure 387.2.

? EXERCISE 387.3 (*Morra*) Find the rationalizable actions of each player in the game *Morra* (Exercise 372.3).

? EXERCISE 387.4 (Guessing two-thirds of the average) Find the rationalizable actions of each player in the game in Exercise 34.1.

? EXERCISE 387.5 (Hotelling's model of electoral competition) Consider a variant of Hotelling's model of electoral competition (Section 3.3) in which there are two candidates and the set of possible positions is $\{0, 1, 2, \ldots, \ell\}$, where ℓ is even. Assume that there is only one position m with the property that exactly half of the voters' favorite positions are at most m, and half of the voters' favorite positions are at least m. Show that this position is the unique rationalizable action of each player.

	L	C	R
T	2,1	1,4	0,3
B	1,8	0,2	1,3

Figure 387.2 The game in Exercise 387.2

In the games on which the following exercise and example are based, each player has infinitely many actions. In each case I describe a finite variant, so that Lemma 385.3 and Proposition 386.2 can be applied.

⁇ EXERCISE 388.1 (Contributing to a public good) Show the following results for the variant of the game in Exercise 44.1 in which the number of players is an arbitrary positive integer n and the contribution of each player i is restricted to be a nonnegative multiple of some small amount $\delta > 0$ that is at most w_i. Assume that δ is such that all the specific contribution levels you need in your argument are multiples of δ (so that you do not need to worry about the finiteness of the action sets).

    a. Any contribution of more than $w_i/2$ is strictly dominated for player i by a contribution of $w_i/2$.

    b. If $n = 3$ and $w_1 = w_2 = w_3 = w$, then every contribution of at most $w/2$ is rationalizable. [Show that every such contribution is a best response to a belief that assigns probability 1 to each of the other players' contributing some amount at most equal to $w/2$.]

    c. If $n = 3$ and $w_1 = w_2 < \frac{1}{3}w_3$, then the unique rationalizable contribution of players 1 and 2 is 0 and the unique rationalizable contribution of player 3 is w_3. [Eliminate strictly dominated actions iteratively. After eliminating a contribution of more than $w_i/2$ for each player i (by part *a*), you can eliminate small contributions by player 3. Subsequently you can eliminate any positive contribution by players 1 and 2.]

? EXERCISE 388.2 (Cournot's duopoly game) Consider the example of Cournot's duopoly game with constant unit cost and linear inverse demand studied in Section 3.1.3. Restrict each firm's output to be a nonnegative multiple of a small amount $\delta > 0$ and to be at most α; assume that $\frac{1}{3}(\alpha - c)$ is a multiple of δ. Use Figure 58.1 to argue that every output greater than $\frac{1}{2}(\alpha - c)$ is strictly dominated by the output $\frac{1}{2}(\alpha - c)$. Then use a similar argument to show that when all such outputs are eliminated from the game, every output less than $\frac{1}{4}(\alpha - c)$ is strictly dominated by the output $\frac{1}{4}(\alpha - c)$. Continue along similar lines, using Figure 59.1 to obtain the cutoff outputs, to reach the conclusion that the only rationalizable output for each firm is the Nash equilibrium output $\frac{1}{3}(\alpha - c)$.

12.3 Iterated elimination of weakly dominated actions

Recall that we say that an action a_i of player i is *weakly dominated* if player i has a mixed strategy that yields her *at least as high* a payoff as does a_i whatever the other players' actions and a higher payoff than does a_i for some actions of the other players (Definition 121.1).

    We may define a set of action profiles to survive iterated elimination of weakly dominated actions by replacing "strictly" with "weakly" in Definition 386.1. That is, we obtain a set of action profiles that survives iterated elimination of weakly dominated actions as follows. First we mark actions of each player that are weakly

	L	C	R
T	1,1	1,1	0,0
B	0,0	1,2	1,2

Figure 389.1 A game in which the set of actions that survive iterated elimination of weakly dominated actions depends on the order in which actions are eliminated.

dominated. Then we remove all the marked actions, and again mark weakly dominated actions for every player. Once again, we remove all the marked actions. We repeat the process until no more actions can be eliminated for any player.

This procedure has less appeal than that of iteratively eliminating strictly dominated actions. First, in some games the set of actions that survives iterated elimination of weakly dominated actions depends on the order in which actions are eliminated. Consider the game in Figure 389.1. If we first eliminate L (weakly dominated by C) and then T (weakly dominated by B), the outcomes that survive are (B, C) and (B, R), yielding the payoff profile $(1, 2)$. But if we first eliminate R (weakly dominated by C) and then B (weakly dominated by T), the outcomes that survive are (T, L) and (T, C), yielding the payoff profile $(1, 1)$, and if we first eliminate both L and R, the outcomes that survive are (T, C) and (B, C), yielding the payoff profiles $(1, 1)$ and $(1, 2)$, respectively.

Second, a weakly dominated action that is not strictly dominated, unlike a strictly dominated action, is not an unambiguously poor choice: by Lemma 385.3 such an action is a best response to *some* belief. Thus, whereas a strictly dominated action remains strictly dominated in any game obtained by deleting any actions of the other players, a weakly (but not strictly) dominated action does not necessarily remain weakly dominated in a game obtained by deleting some actions of the other players. In the game in Figure 389.2, for example, the action B of player 1 is weakly dominated by T but is not weakly dominated in the game obtained by deleting the action R of player 2.

This feature of a weakly (but not strictly) dominated action means that the removal of an action at some stage in the iterative procedure may eliminate the rationale for the removal of some other action at an earlier stage. Suppose that in the game in Figure 389.2, for example, we first eliminate B and then eliminate R. In the absence of R, player 1 no longer has a reason not to choose B.

Despite these difficulties with the iterated elimination of weakly dominated actions, the procedure retains some appeal. One reason is a connection between the subgame perfect equilibrium outcomes of a class of extensive games with per-

	L	M	R
T	2,2	2,1	1,0
B	2,1	2,2	0,2

Figure 389.2 A game illustrating the iterated elimination of weakly dominated actions. The action B of player 1 is weakly dominated by T but is not weakly dominated in the game obtained by deleting the action R of player 2.

fect information and the action profiles that survive iterated elimination of weakly dominated actions in the strategic form of such games. Specifically, let Γ be a finite extensive game with perfect information in which no player is indifferent between any two terminal histories (so that, in particular, Γ has a unique subgame perfect equilibrium). We can argue straightforwardly that there is an order of elimination of weakly dominated actions in the strategic form of Γ for which every member of the surviving set of action profiles generates the subgame perfect equilibrium outcome of Γ. (Note that I do not assert that the surviving set of action profiles contains only subgame perfect equilibria: every surviving action profile generates the unique subgame perfect equilibrium *outcome*, but may not itself be a subgame perfect equilibrium.)

The order of elimination that yields the result corresponds to the steps in the procedure of backward induction. First consider subgames of length 1. Take one such subgame. Denote by h the history that precedes the subgame, by i the player who moves, and by a_i^* player i's equilibrium action in the subgame. We eliminate every strategy of player i that (*a*) chooses actions consistent with h and (*b*) chooses an action different from a_i^* in the subgame. Every such strategy is weakly dominated by the strategy that differs only in that in the subgame it chooses a_i^*. After eliminating these strategies, we replace each subgame of length 1 with the outcome that results from the subgame perfect equilibrium action in the subgame. Then, in the second stage, we repeat the exercise with the subgames of length 1 in the remaining game. We continue until we arrive at the start of the game.

The game in Figure 391.1 illustrates the procedure. Assume that player 1 prefers d to a to b and player 2 prefers a to c and d to e, so that the subgame perfect equilibrium actions are those indicated by black line segments. Denote the strategic form of the game, shown in the right panel of the figure, by G. We first look at the subgames of length 1, namely those following the histories (A, C) and B. In the subgame following (A, C), player 1 moves, and the fact that she prefers a to b means that in the strategic form her strategy AH weakly dominates her strategy AI. (Her strategies BH and BI are inconsistent with the history (A, C), so we do not consider them.) In the other subgame of length 1, following the history B, player 2 moves. She prefers d to e, so that in G her strategy CE weakly dominates CF, and DE weakly dominates DF. Thus in the first round we eliminate from G the strategy AI of player 1 and the strategies CF and DF of player 2. Call the resulting strategic game G^1. We now replace the subgame following (A, C) with the outcome a and the subgame following the history B with the outcome d. The resulting game has a single subgame of length 1, following the history A. In this subgame player 2 moves and prefers a to c, so that in G^1 her strategy CE weakly dominates her strategy DE, and we thus eliminate DE to create G^2. Finally, we replace the subgame following A with the outcome a. The resulting game has length 1; player 1 moves and prefers d to a. Thus in G^2 player 1's strategy BH weakly dominates her strategy AH, so that in the third stage we eliminate AH. The strategy pairs that remain are (BH, CE) and (BI, CE); both generate the subgame perfect equilibrium outcome d (though (BI, CE) is not a subgame perfect equilibrium).

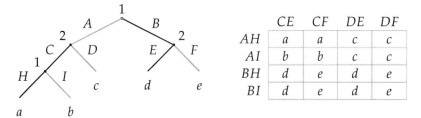

	CE	CF	DE	DF
AH	a	a	c	c
AI	b	b	c	c
BH	d	e	d	e
BI	d	e	d	e

Figure 391.1 An extensive game with perfect information (left) and its strategic form (right). The actions taken in the unique subgame perfect equilibrium are shown in black.

12.4 Dominance solvability

A version of the procedure of iterated elimination of weakly dominated actions of particular interest is that in which *all* weakly dominated actions of each player are eliminated at each stage. If all the players are indifferent between all action profiles that survive when we perform such iterated elimination, we say that the game is *dominance solvable*.

The game in Figure 389.1 is not dominance solvable, because at the first stage the weakly dominated actions are L and R for player 2 (neither action of player 1 is weakly dominated), and once these are eliminated, no action is weakly dominated, and player 2 is not indifferent between the two remaining action pairs. The game in Figure 389.2, however, *is* dominance solvable: B are R are the weakly dominated actions at the first stage, and M is the weakly dominated action at the second stage, leaving the single outcome (T, L).

In the following exercises you need to find, at each round, the set of all weakly dominated actions. Note that a player's action is *not* weakly dominated if it is a strict best response to some list of the other players' actions.

? EXERCISE 391.1 (Example of dominance-solvable game) Find the set of Nash equilibria (mixed as well as pure) of the game in Figure 391.2. Show that the game is dominance solvable, and find the pair of payoffs that survives. Find an order of elimination such that more than one outcome survives.

? EXERCISE 391.2 (Dividing money) Show that the game in Exercise 38.2 is dominance solvable and find the set of surviving action pairs.

? EXERCISE 391.3 (Voting) Consider the model of voting in Section 2.9.3. Suppose there are three candidates and assume that the conditions in Exercise 49.1 are satisfied. Show that if more than two-thirds of the citizens rank the same candidate last, then the game is dominance solvable.

	L	C	R
T	2,2	0,2	0,1
M	2,0	1,1	0,2
B	1,0	2,0	0,0

Figure 391.2 The game for Exercise 391.1.

⑦ EXERCISE 392.1 (Bertrand's duopoly game) Consider the variant of Bertrand's duopoly game in Exercise 67.2, in which each firm is restricted to choose a price that is an integral number of cents. Assume that the profit function $(p - c)D(p)$ has a single maximizer and is increasing up to this maximizer. Show that the game is dominance solvable and find the set of surviving outcomes.

⑦ EXERCISE 392.2 (Strictly competitive extensive games with perfect information) Show that a finite strictly competitive extensive game with perfect information in which there are two possible outcomes is dominance solvable in (at most) a single step.

Notes

The notion of rationalizability is due to Bernheim (1984) and Pearce (1984); Spohn (1982) is a precursor. Gale (1953) and Luce and Raiffa (1957, 108–109, 173) first studied in detail versions of the procedure of iterated elimination of dominated strategies. The formulation here is due to Moulin (1979). Lemma 385.3 is due to Pearce (1984); it is closely related to Lemma 3.2.1 of van Damme (1983). Proposition 386.2 is due to Pearce (1984, 1035). Aumann and Brandenburger (1995) make precise the idea that rationalizability is equivalent to each player's being rational, assuming the other players are rational, assuming that the other players assume that the first player is rational, and so on. The notion of dominance solvability is due to Moulin (1979; it is closely related to the notion of "solvability in the complete weak sense" of Luce and Raiffa (1957, 109).

The game in Exercise 387.4 is taken from Moulin (1986b, 72), Exercise 388.1 was suggested by Stuart Mestelman, the result in Exercise 388.2 is due to Gabay and Moulin (1980), Bernheim (1984), and Moulin (1984), and the result in Exercise 391.3 is due to Dhillon and Lockwood (2004). Ewerhart (2000) shows that every finite strictly competitive extensive game with perfect information that has three possible outcomes (like chess, in which the outcome may be a win for Black, a win for White, or a tie) is dominance solvable in at most two steps, extending the result in Exercise 392.2.

13 Evolutionary Equilibrium

13.1 Monomorphic pure strategy equilibrium 394
13.2 Mixed strategies and polymorphic equilibrium 400
13.3 Asymmetric contests 406
13.4 Variation on a theme: sibling behavior 411
13.5 Variation on a theme: the nesting behavior of wasps 414
13.6 Variation on a theme: the evolution of the sex ratio 416
Prerequisite: Chapters 2 and 4

A CCORDING to the Darwinian theory of evolution, a mode of behavior survives only if no other mode is more successful at producing offspring. In an environment in which organisms interact, the reproductive success of a mode of behavior may depend on the behavior of other organisms. If all organisms act aggressively, for example, then an organism may be able to survive only if it is aggressive, whereas if all organisms are passive, then an organism's reproductive success may be greater if it acts passively than if it acts aggressively. Game theory provides tools with which to study evolution in such an environment.

In this chapter I describe models based on the notion of a strategic game. The players are interpreted to be members of an evolving population of organisms (humans, animals, plants, bacteria, . . .), pairs of whom interact. Each player's set of actions consists of the modes of behavior an organism could acquire through mutation, and its payoffs measure its biological *fitness*, or reproductive success (expected number of healthy offspring).

We do not interpret the players' payoffs as reflections of their subjective feelings, nor their actions as conscious choices. Rather, each player's payoff is a concrete measure of its fitness, and we assume that each player is programmed to follow a certain mode of behavior, which comes from one of two sources: with high probability it is inherited from the player's parent (or parents), and with low (but positive) probability it is assigned to the player as the result of a mutation. For most of the models in this chapter, inheritance is conceived very simply: each player has a single parent, and, unless it is a mutant, simply takes the same action as does its parent. This model of inheritance captures the essential features of both genetic inheritance and social inheritance: players either follow the programs encoded in their genes, which come from their parents, or learn how to behave by imitating their parents.

If, given the modes of behavior of all other organisms, an organism's biological fitness associated with the action a exceeds its fitness associated with the action a', then adherents of a reproduce faster than adherents of a', causing the composition of actions in the population to change. Thus, roughly, a configuration of actions is stable only if each organism's action is a best response to the environment, which suggests that evolutionarily stable outcomes are related to Nash equilibria.

13.1 Monomorphic pure strategy equilibrium

13.1.1 Introduction

We consider a population of organisms whose members are repeatedly randomly matched in pairs. The population is large enough that the probability of an organism's being matched with the same opponent more than once is negligible. The set of possible modes of behavior of every organism is the same, and the consequence of an interaction for an organism depends only on its action and that of its opponent, not on its name. Each organism regularly produces offspring (reproduction is asexual). An organism's mode of behavior is, with high probability, that of its parent, and with low probability a randomly chosen "mutant" mode of behavior.

As an example, think of a population of identical animals, pairs of which are periodically engaged in conflicts over prey. The actions available to each animal could correspond to various degrees of aggression, and we could reasonably assume that the outcome for each animal depends only on its degree of aggression and that of its opponent.

We may model the interaction between each pair of organisms as a two-player symmetric strategic game. In this context, such a game consists of a common set A of actions and a payoff function u, where for any pair of actions (a, a'), the payoff $u(a, a')$ is interpreted as the fitness (expected number of offspring) of an organism that takes the action a when its opponent takes the action a'. (Note that each function u gives rise to a different game; no two payoff functions give rise to the same game, as they do when the game is specified by the players' preferences.) We assume that the adherents of each mode of behavior multiply at a rate proportional to their payoff and look for a configuration of modes of behavior in the population that is stable in the sense it cannot be "invaded" by any other mode: if a small fraction of the population consists of identical mutants, every mutant obtains an expected payoff lower than that of any nonmutant. (We ignore the case in which mutants taking different actions are present in the population at the same time.)

In this section I restrict attention to situations in which all organisms, except those resulting from by mutation, follow the *same* mode of behavior, which has no random component. That is, I consider only *monomorphic pure strategy* equilibria ("monomorphic" = "one form").

13.1.2 Examples

To get an idea of the implications of evolutionary stability, consider two examples. First suppose that the game between each pair of organisms is the one in

	X	Y
X	2,2	0,0
Y	0,0	1,1

Figure 395.1 A strategic game in which both actions of each player are evolutionarily stable.

Figure 395.1. Suppose that every organism normally takes the action X. Suppose the population contains the small fraction ϵ of mutants who take the action Y. The population is large, so the probability of any given normal organism's being matched with a mutant is approximately ϵ; I take it to be exactly ϵ. Thus a normal organism's opponent is another normal organism with probability $1 - \epsilon$ and a mutant with probability ϵ, so that a normal organism's expected payoff is

$$2 \cdot (1 - \epsilon) + 0 \cdot \epsilon = 2(1 - \epsilon).$$

Similarly, a mutant's expected payoff is

$$0 \cdot (1 - \epsilon) + 1 \cdot \epsilon = \epsilon.$$

If ϵ is small (less than $\frac{2}{3}$), then the first payoff exceeds the second, so that the entry of a *small* fraction of mutants leads to a situation in which the expected payoff (fitness) of every mutant is lower than the expected payoff of every normal organism. Thus normal organisms reproduce faster than do mutants, and the action X is evolutionarily stable.

Now suppose that every organism normally takes the action Y. Mutants taking the action X who meet each other obtain a payoff higher than that of normal organisms who meet each other. But when ϵ is small, a mutant is likely to be paired with a normal organism, in which case its payoff is 0. Making a calculation like that in the previous case, a normal organism's expected payoff is $1 - \epsilon$, whereas a mutant's expected payoff is 2ϵ, so that if ϵ is small (less than $\frac{1}{3}$ in this case), the first payoff exceeds the second, and the action Y is evolutionarily stable. The value of ϵ for which a normal organism does better than a mutant is smaller in this case than it is in the case that the normal action is X. However, the significant point is that in both cases there is *some* value of ϵ such that for smaller values no mutant can invade: we wish to capture the idea that mutation is extremely rare, relative to normal behavior, so we are satisfied with the existence of *some* value of ϵ that prevents invasion by mutants.

Now consider the game in Figure 396.1. By an argument like those above, the action X is evolutionarily stable. Is the action Y also evolutionarily stable? In a population containing the fraction ϵ of mutants choosing X, the expected payoff of a normal organism choosing Y is 0 (it obtains 0 whether its opponent is normal or a mutant), whereas the expected payoff of a mutant is 2ϵ (it obtains 2 against another mutant and 0 against a normal organism). Thus the action Y is *not* evolutionarily stable: for *any* value of ϵ the expected payoff of a mutant exceeds that of a normal organism.

	X	Y
X	2,2	0,0
Y	0,0	0,0

Figure 396.1 A strategic game in which only the action X of each player is evolutionarily stable.

In both games, both (X, X) and (Y, Y) are Nash equilibria, but whereas X is an evolutionarily stable action in both games, Y is evolutionarily stable only in the first game. What is the essential difference between the games? If the normal action is Y, then in the first game a mutant that chooses X is worse off than a normal organism in encounters with normal organisms, whereas in the second game such a mutant obtains the *same* expected payoff as does a normal organism in encounters with normal organisms. Thus in the first game, for ϵ small enough, the gain (relative to the payoff of a normal organism) that a mutant obtains with probability ϵ when it faces another mutant does not cancel out the loss it incurs with probability $1 - \epsilon$ when it faces a normal organism. In the second game, however, a mutant loses nothing relative to a normal organism, so no matter how small ϵ is, a mutant is better off than a normal organism. That is, the essential difference between the games is that $u(X, Y) < u(Y, Y)$ in the game in Figure 395.1, but $u(X, Y) = u(Y, Y)$ in the game in Figure 396.1.

13.1.3 General definitions

Consider now an arbitrary symmetric two-player strategic game in which each player has finitely many actions. Under what circumstances is the action a^* evolutionarily stable?

Suppose that a small group of mutants choosing an action different from a^* enters the population. The notion of evolutionary stability requires that each such mutant obtain an expected payoff less than that of each normal organism, so that the mutants die out. (If the mutants obtained a payoff higher than that of the normal organisms, then they would eventually come to dominate the population; if they obtained the same payoff as that of the normal organisms, then they would neither multiply nor decline. Our notion of stability excludes the latter case: it requires that mutants be driven out of the population.)

Denote the fraction of mutants in the population by ϵ. First consider a mutant that adopts the action b. In a random encounter, the probability of its facing an organism that adopts the action a^* is approximately $1 - \epsilon$, and the probability of its facing a mutant, which adopts b, is approximately ϵ. Thus its expected payoff is

$$(1 - \epsilon)u(b, a^*) + \epsilon u(b, b).$$

Similarly, the expected payoff of an organism that adopts the action a^* is

$$(1 - \epsilon)u(a^*, a^*) + \epsilon u(a^*, b).$$

For any mutation to be driven out of the population, we need the expected payoff of any mutant to be less than the expected payoff of a normal organism:

$$(1 - \epsilon)u(a^*, a^*) + \epsilon u(a^*, b) > (1 - \epsilon)u(b, a^*) + \epsilon u(b, b) \text{ for all } b \neq a^*. \quad (397.1)$$

To capture the idea that mutation is extremely rare, the notion of evolutionary stability requires only that there be *some* number $\bar{\epsilon}$ such that the inequality holds whenever $\epsilon < \bar{\epsilon}$. That is, we make the following definition.

> The action a^* is *evolutionarily stable* if there exists $\bar{\epsilon} > 0$ such that (397.1) is satisfied for all ϵ with $0 < \epsilon < \bar{\epsilon}$.

Intuitively, the larger is $\bar{\epsilon}$, the "more stable" is the action a^*, because larger mutations are resisted. However, in the current discussion I do not attach any significance to the value of $\bar{\epsilon}$; for an action to be evolutionarily stable, I require only that there be *some* value of $\bar{\epsilon}$ such that all smaller mutations are resisted.

The condition in this definition of evolutionary stability is a little awkward to work with because whenever we apply it, we need to check whether we can find a suitable value of $\bar{\epsilon}$. It can be reformulated to avoid the variable $\bar{\epsilon}$, making it easier to use.

I first claim that

> if there exists $\bar{\epsilon} > 0$ such that a^* satisfies (397.1) for all ϵ with $0 < \epsilon < \bar{\epsilon}$, then (a^*, a^*) is a Nash equilibrium.

To reach this conclusion, suppose that (a^*, a^*) is not a Nash equilibrium. Then there exists an action b such that $u(b, a^*) > u(a^*, a^*)$. Hence (397.1) is strictly violated when $\epsilon = 0$, and thus remains violated for all sufficiently small positive values of ϵ. (If $w < x$, and y and z are any numbers, then $(1 - \epsilon)w + \epsilon y < (1 - \epsilon)x + \epsilon z$ whenever ϵ is small enough.) Thus there is no value of $\bar{\epsilon} > 0$ such that the inequality holds whenever $\epsilon < \bar{\epsilon}$. We conclude that if the action a^* is evolutionarily stable, then (a^*, a^*) is a Nash equilibrium.

I now claim that

> if (a^*, a^*) is a *strict* Nash equilibrium, then there exists $\bar{\epsilon} > 0$ such that a^* satisfies (397.1) for all ϵ with $0 < \epsilon < \bar{\epsilon}$.

The argument is that if (a^*, a^*) is a strict Nash equilibrium, then $u(b, a^*) < u(a^*, a^*)$ for all b, so that the strict inequality in (397.1) is satisfied for $\epsilon = 0$, and hence also for sufficiently small positive values of ϵ.

What if (a^*, a^*) is a Nash equilibrium but is not strict? Then some action $b \neq a^*$ is a best response to a^*: $u(b, a^*) = u(a^*, a^*)$. Thus (397.1) reduces to the condition $u(a^*, b) > u(b, b)$.

We conclude that the action a^* is evolutionarily stable if and only if (*i*) (a^*, a^*) is a Nash equilibrium, and (*ii*) $u(a^*, b) > u(b, b)$ for every $b \neq a^*$ that is a best response to a^*. Intuitively, for mutant behavior to die out, (*i*) no mutant can do better than an organism using a^* in encounters with organisms using a^*, and (*ii*) any mutant that does as well as an organism using a^* in such encounters must do worse than an organism using a^* in encounters with mutants.

To summarize, the definition of evolutionary stability based on (397.1) is equivalent to the following definition.

▶ DEFINITION 398.1 (*Evolutionarily stable action in strategic game*) An action a^* of a player in a symmetric two-player strategic game in which the payoff of each player is $u(a, a')$ when the player's action is a and her opponent's action is a' is **evolutionarily stable** with respect to mutants using pure strategies if

- (a^*, a^*) is a Nash equilibrium, and
- $u(b, b) < u(a^*, b)$ for every action $b \neq a^*$ that is a best response to a^*.

Note that if (a^*, a^*) is a strict Nash equilibrium, then the second condition is automatically satisfied, because no action $b \neq a^*$ is a best response to a^*. Note also that the inequality in the second condition is strict. If it were weak, then situations in which mutants neither multiply nor die out, but reproduce at the same rate as the normal population, would be included as stable.

13.1.4   Examples

Both symmetric pure Nash equilibria of the game in Figure 395.1 are strict, so that both X and Y are evolutionarily stable (confirming our previous analysis). In the game in Figure 396.1, (X, X) and (Y, Y) are symmetric pure Nash equilibria also. But in this case (X, X) is strict whereas (Y, Y) is not. Further, because $u(X, X) > u(Y, X)$, the second condition in the definition of evolutionary stability is not satisfied by Y. Thus in this game only X is evolutionarily stable (again confirming our previous analysis).

The *Prisoner's Dilemma* (Figure 15.1) has a unique symmetric Nash equilibrium (F, F), and this Nash equilibrium is strict. Thus the action F is the only evolutionarily stable action. The game *BoS* (Figure 19.1) has no symmetric pure Nash equilibrium, and hence no evolutionarily stable action. (I consider mixed strategies in the next section.)

The following game, which generalizes the ideas of the game in Exercise 31.2, presents a richer range of possibilities for evolutionarily stable actions.

◆ EXAMPLE 398.2 (*Hawk–Dove*) Two animals of the same species compete for a resource (e.g. food, or a good nesting site) whose value (in units of "fitness") is $v > 0$. (That is, v measures the increase in the expected number of offspring due to control of the resource.) Each animal can be either *aggressive* or *passive*. If both animals are aggressive, they fight until one is seriously injured; the winner obtains the resource without sustaining any injury, whereas the loser suffers a loss of c. The two animals are equally likely to win, so each one's expected payoff is $\frac{1}{2}v + \frac{1}{2}(-c)$. If both animals are passive, then each obtains the resource with probability $\frac{1}{2}$, with-

EVOLUTIONARY GAME THEORY: SOME HISTORY

In his book *The Descent of Man*, Charles Darwin gives a game-theoretic argument that in sexually reproducing species, the only evolutionarily stable sex ratio is 50:50 (1871, Vol. I, 316). Darwin's argument is game theoretic in appealing to the fact that the number of an animal's descendants depends on the "behavior" of the other members of the population (the sex ratio of their offspring; see Exercise 416.1). Coming 50 years before the language and methods of game theory began to develop, however, it is not couched in game-theoretic terms. In the late 1960s, two decades after the appearance of von Neumann and Morgenstern's (1944) seminal book, Hamilton (1967) proposed an explicitly game-theoretic model of the evolution of the sex ratio that applies to situations more general than that considered by Darwin.

But the key figure in the application of game theory to evolutionary biology is John Maynard Smith. Maynard Smith (1972a) and Maynard Smith and Price (1973) propose the notion of an evolutionarily stable strategy, and Maynard Smith's subsequent research develops the field in many directions. (Maynard Smith gives significant credit to Price: he writes that he would probably not have had the idea of using game theory had he not seen unpublished work by Price. "Unfortunately", Maynard Smith writes, "Dr. Price is better at having ideas than at publishing them" (1972b, vii).)

Since Maynard Smith and Price's seminal work, evolutionary game theory has blossomed. Biological models abound, and the methods of the theory have made their way into economics and other social sciences.

out a fight. Finally, if one animal is aggressive while the other is passive, then the aggressor obtains the resource without a fight. The game is shown in Figure 399.1.

If $v > c$, then the game has a unique Nash equilibrium (A, A), which is strict, so that A is the unique evolutionarily stable action.

If $v = c$, then also the game has a unique symmetric Nash equilibrium (A, A). But in this case the equilibrium is not strict: against an opponent that chooses A, a player obtains the same payoff whether it chooses A or P. However, the second condition in Definition 398.1 is satisfied: $\frac{1}{2}v = u(P, P) < u(A, P) = v$. Thus A is the unique evolutionarily stable action in this case also.

In both cases, a population of passive players can be invaded by aggressive players: an aggressive mutant does better than a passive player when its op-

	A	P
A	$\frac{1}{2}(v-c), \frac{1}{2}(v-c)$	$v, 0$
P	$0, v$	$\frac{1}{2}v, \frac{1}{2}v$

Figure 399.1 The game *Hawk–Dove*.

ponent is passive, and at least as well as a passive player when its opponent is aggressive.

If $v < c$, then the game has no symmetric Nash equilibrium in pure strategies: neither (A, A) nor (P, P) is a Nash equilibrium. Thus in this case the game has no evolutionarily stable action. (The game has only *asymmetric* Nash equilibria in this case.)

⊘ EXERCISE 400.1 (*Evolutionary stability and weak domination*) Let a^* be an evolutionarily stable action. Does a^* necessarily weakly dominate every other action? Is it possible that some action weakly dominates a^*?

⊘ EXERCISE 400.2 (*Example of evolutionarily stable actions*) Pairs of members of a single population engage in the following game. Each player has three actions, corresponding to demands of 1, 2, or 3 units of payoff. If both players in a pair make the same demand, each player obtains her demand. Otherwise the player who demands less obtains the amount demanded by her opponent, whereas the player who demands more obtains $a\delta$, where a is her demand and δ is a number less than $\frac{1}{3}$. Find the set of pure strategy symmetric Nash equilibria of the game, and the set of pure evolutionarily stable strategies. What happens if each player has n actions, corresponding to demands of 1, 2, ..., n units of payoff (and $\delta < 1/n$)?

To gain an understanding of the outcome that evolutionary pressure might induce in games that have no evolutionarily stable action (e.g. *BoS*, and *Hawk–Dove* when $v < c$), we can take several routes. One is to consider mixed strategies as well as pure strategies; another is to allow for the possibility of several types of behavior coexisting in the population; a third is to consider interpretations of asymmetric equilibria. In the next section I discuss the first two approaches; in the section after that I consider the third approach.

13.2   Mixed strategies and polymorphic equilibrium

13.2.1   Definition

So far we have considered only situations in which both "normal" organisms and mutants use pure strategies. If we assume that mixed strategies, as well as pure strategies, are passed from parents to their offspring and may be thrown up by mutation, then an argument analogous to the one in the previous section leads to the conclusion that an evolutionarily stable mixed strategy satisfies conditions like those in Definition 398.1. Precisely, we can define an evolutionarily stable (mixed) strategy, known briefly as an ESS, as follows.

▶ DEFINITION 400.3 (*Evolutionarily stable mixed strategy*) An **evolutionarily stable strategy** (**ESS**) in a symmetric two-player strategic game in which the expected payoff of each player is $U(\alpha, \alpha')$ when the player's mixed strategy is α and her opponent's mixed strategy is α' is a mixed strategy α^* such that

- (α^*, α^*) is a Nash equilibrium

- $U(\beta, \beta) < U(\alpha^*, \beta)$ for every mixed strategy $\beta \neq \alpha^*$ that is a best response to α^*.

Can animals really use mixed strategies? John Maynard Smith, the originator of the notion of an ESS, argues as follows.

> "If it were selectively advantageous, a randomising device could surely evolve, either as an entirely neuronal process or by dependence on functionally irrelevant external stimuli. Perhaps the one undoubted example of a mixed ESS is the production of equal numbers of X and Y gametes by the heterogametic sex: if the gonads can do it, why not the brain?" (1982, 76).

Evidence that some animals randomize is presented by Brockmann, Grafen, and Dawkins (1979), who argue that certain wasps pursue mixed strategies. (For a discussion of Brockmann et al.'s model, see Section 13.5.)

13.2.2   Pure strategies and mixed strategies

Definition 400.3 does not, of course, preclude the use of pure strategies: every pure strategy is a special case of a mixed strategy. Thus Definitions 398.1 and 400.3 both apply to pure strategies. Do they yield the same conclusions?

Suppose that a^* is an evolutionarily stable action in the sense of Definition 398.1, and let α^* be the mixed strategy that assigns probability 1 to the action a^*. Because a^* is evolutionarily stable, (a^*, a^*) is a Nash equilibrium, so (α^*, α^*) is a mixed strategy Nash equilibrium (Proposition 122.2). Is α^* necessarily an ESS in the sense of Definition 400.3? No: the second condition in the definition of an ESS may be violated. That is, a pure strategy may be immune to invasion by mutants that follow any *pure* strategy but may not be immune to invasion by mutants that follow some *mixed* strategy. Stated briefly, though a pure strategy Nash equilibrium is a mixed strategy Nash equilibrium, an action that is evolutionarily stable in the sense of Definition 398.1 is *not* necessarily an ESS in the sense of Definition 400.3.

The game in Figure 402.1 illustrates this point. In studying this game, it may help to think of pairs of players working on a project. Two type Xs work well together, and both a type Y and a type Z work well with an X, although the X suffers in each case. However, a pair of type Ys or type Zs is a disaster, whereas a Y and a Z are a great combination.

The action X is evolutionarily stable in the sense of Definition 398.1: (X, X) is a Nash equilibrium, both Y and Z are best responses to X, $u(Y, Y) < u(X, Y)$, and $u(Z, Z) < u(X, Z)$. However, the action X is *not* an ESS in the sense of Definition 400.3. Precisely, the mixed strategy α^* that assigns probability 1 to X is not an ESS. To establish this claim we need only find a mixed strategy β that is a best response to α^* and satisfies $U(\beta, \beta) \geq U(\alpha^*, \beta)$ (in which case a mutant that uses β

	X	Y	Z
X	2,2	1,2	1,2
Y	2,1	0,0	3,3
Z	2,1	3,3	0,0

Figure 402.1 A game illustrating the difference between Definition 398.1 (which considers only pure strategies) and Definition 400.3 (which considers mixed strategies). The action X is an evolutionarily stable action in the sense of the first definition but not in the sense of the second.

will not die out of the population). Let β be the mixed strategy that assigns probability $\frac{1}{2}$ to Y and probability $\frac{1}{2}$ to Z. Because both Y and Z are best responses to X, so is β. Further, $U(\alpha^*, \beta) = 1 < \frac{3}{2} = U(\beta, \beta)$. (When both players use β, the outcome is (Y, Y) with probability $\frac{1}{4}$, (Y, Z) with probability $\frac{1}{4}$, (Z, Y) with probability $\frac{1}{4}$, and (Z, Z) with probability $\frac{1}{4}$.) Thus even though a population of adherents to α^* cannot be invaded by any mutant using a pure strategy, it *can* be invaded by mutants using the mixed strategy β. The point is that Y types do poorly against each other and so do Z types, but the match of a Y and a Z is very productive. Thus if all mutants either invariably choose Y or invariably choose Z, then they fare badly when they meet each other; but if all mutants follow the mixed strategy that chooses Y and Z with equal probability, then with probability $\frac{1}{2}$ two mutants that are matched are of different types and are very productive.

? EXERCISE 402.1 (Mixed strategy ESSs) Suppose that α^* is a mixed ESS, and let a be an action to which α^* assigns positive probability. Show that if α^* assigns positive probability to an action different from a, then (a, a) is not a pure strategy Nash equilibrium (and hence a is not an ESS).

13.2.3 Strict equilibria

As I noted after Definition 398.1, a *strict* pure Nash equilibrium is evolutionarily stable. Any strict Nash equilibrium is also an ESS, because the second condition in Definition 400.3 is vacuously satisfied (there are no best responses to α^*). However, in the context of mixed strategy Nash equilibria the usefulness of this observation is limited because no mixed strategy Nash equilibrium in which positive probability is assigned to two or more actions is strict. (If (α^*, α^*) is a mixed strategy equilibrium, then every action to which α^* assigns positive probability is a best response to α^*, and so too is any mixed strategy that assigns positive probability to the same pure strategies as does α^* (Proposition 116.2).)

13.2.4 Polymorphic steady states

A mixed strategy ESS corresponds to a monomorphic steady state in which each organism randomly chooses an action in each play of the game, according to the probabilities in the mixed strategy. Alternatively, it corresponds to a *polymorphic* steady state, in which a variety of pure strategies is in use in the population, the fraction of the population using each pure strategy being given by the probability the mixed strategy assigns to that pure strategy. (Cf. the interpretation of a mixed strategy equilibrium discussed in Section 4.1, in which different members of the population from which each player is drawn choose different actions.) I argue in Section 13.1.3 that for a monomorphic steady state in which each player's strategy is pure, the two conditions in the definition of an ESS are equivalent to the requirement that any mutant die out. The same argument applies also to a monomorphic steady state in which every player's strategy is mixed, but it does not apply directly to a polymorphic steady state. However, a different argument, based on similar ideas, shows that in this case too the conditions in the definition of an ESS are necessary and sufficient for the local stability of a steady state (see Hammerstein and Selten 1994, 948–951): mutations that slightly change the fractions of the population using each pure strategy generate changes in payoffs that cause the fractions to return to their equilibrium values.

13.2.5 Examples

◆ EXAMPLE 403.1 (*Bach or Stravinsky?*) The members of a single population are randomly matched in pairs, and play *BoS*, with payoffs given in Figure 403.1. (In this presentation of the game, L means "choose favorite concert" (B for player 1, S for player 2), and D means "choose less preferred concert".) This game has no symmetric pure strategy equilibrium. It has a unique symmetric mixed strategy equilibrium, in which the strategy α^* of each player assigns probability $\frac{2}{3}$ to L. As in any mixed strategy equilibrium, any mixed strategy that assigns positive probabilities to the same pure strategies as does the equilibrium strategy (α^*) are best responses to the equilibrium strategy. Let $\beta = (p, 1 - p)$ be such a mixed strategy. For α^* to be an ESS we need $U(\beta, \beta) < U(\alpha^*, \beta)$ whenever $\beta \neq \alpha^*$. The payoffs in the game are low when the players choose the same action, so it seems possible that this condition is satisfied. To check the condition precisely, we need to find $U(\beta, \beta)$ and $U(\alpha^*, \beta)$. If both players use the strategy β, then the outcome is (L, L) with probability p^2, (L, D) and (D, L) each with probability $p(1 - p)$, and (D, D) with probability $(1 - p)^2$. Thus $U(\beta, \beta) = 3p(1 - p)$. Similarly, $U(\alpha^*, \beta) = \frac{4}{3} - p$. Thus for α^* to be an ESS we need

$$3p(1 - p) < \tfrac{4}{3} - p$$

for all $p \neq \frac{2}{3}$. This inequality is equivalent to $(p - \frac{2}{3})^2 > 0$, so the strategy $\alpha^* = (\frac{2}{3}, \frac{1}{3})$ is an ESS.

	L	D
L	0,0	2,1
D	1,2	0,0

Figure 403.1 The game *BoS*.

	X	Y
X	2,2	0,0
Y	0,0	1,1

Figure 404.1 The game in Example 404.1.

◆ EXAMPLE 404.1 (A coordination game) The members of a single population are randomly matched in pairs, and play the game in Figure 404.1. In this game both (X, X) and (Y, Y) are strict pure Nash equilibria (as we noted previously), so that both X and Y are ESSs. The game also has a symmetric mixed strategy equilibrium (α^*, α^*), in which $\alpha^* = (\frac{1}{3}, \frac{2}{3})$. Every mixed strategy $\beta = (p, 1 - p)$ is a best response to α^*, so for α^* to be an ESS we need $U(\beta, \beta) < U(\alpha^*, \beta)$ whenever $\beta \neq \alpha^*$. In this game the players are better off choosing the same action as each other than they are choosing different actions, so plausibly the condition is not satisfied. The β that seems most likely to violate the condition is the pure strategy X (i.e. $\beta = (1, 0)$). In this case we have $U(\beta, \beta) = 2$ and $U(\alpha^*, \beta) = \frac{2}{3}$, so indeed the condition is violated. Thus the game has no mixed strategy ESS.

The intuition for this result is that a mutant that uses the pure strategy X is better off than a normal organism that uses the mixed strategy $(\frac{1}{3}, \frac{2}{3})$ when it encounters a mutant, and it obtains the same payoff as does a normal organism when it encounters a normal organism. Thus such a mutant invades a population of organisms using the mixed strategy $(\frac{1}{3}, \frac{2}{3})$. (In fact, a mutant following *any* strategy different from α^* invades the population: for $\beta = (p, 1 - p)$ we have $U(\beta, \beta) = 2p^2 + (1 - p)^2$, which exceeds $\frac{2}{3}$ if $p \neq \frac{1}{3}$.)

◆ EXAMPLE 404.2 (Mixed strategies in *Hawk–Dove*) Consider again the game *Hawk–Dove* (Example 398.2). If $v > c$, then the only symmetric Nash equilibrium is the strict pure equilibrium (A, A), so that the only ESS is A.

If $v \leq c$, the game has a unique symmetric mixed strategy equilibrium, in which the strategy of each player is $(v/c, 1 - v/c)$. To determine whether this strategy is an ESS, we need to check the second condition in Definition 400.3. Let $\beta = (p, 1 - p)$ be any mixed strategy. We need to determine whether $U(\beta, \beta) < U(\alpha^*, \beta)$ for $\beta \neq \alpha^*$, where $\alpha^* = (v/c, 1 - v/c)$. If each player uses the strategy β, then the outcome is (A, A) with probability p^2, (A, P) and (P, A) each with probability $p(1 - p)$, and (P, P) with probability $(1 - p)^2$. Thus

$$U(\beta, \beta) = p^2 \cdot \tfrac{1}{2}(v - c) + p(1 - p) \cdot v + p(1 - p) \cdot 0 + (1 - p)^2 \cdot \tfrac{1}{2}v.$$

Similarly, if a player uses the strategy α^* and its opponent uses the strategy β, then its expected payoff is

$$U(\alpha^*, \beta) = (v/c)p \cdot \tfrac{1}{2}(v - c) + (v/c)(1 - p) \cdot v + (1 - v/c)(1 - p) \cdot \tfrac{1}{2}v.$$

Upon simplification we find that $U(\alpha^*, \beta) - U(\beta, \beta) = \tfrac{1}{2}c(v/c - p)^2$, which is positive if $p \neq v/c$. Thus $U(\beta, \beta) < U(\alpha^*, \beta)$ for any $\beta \neq \alpha^*$. We conclude that if $v \leq c$, then the game has a unique ESS, namely the mixed strategy $\alpha^* = (v/c, 1 - v/c)$.

	A	P	R
A	$\frac{1}{2}(v-c),\frac{1}{2}(v-c)$	$v,0$	$\frac{1}{2}(v-c),\frac{1}{2}(v-c)$
P	$0,v$	$\frac{1}{2}v,\frac{1}{2}v$	$\frac{1}{2}v-\delta,\frac{1}{2}v+\delta$
R	$\frac{1}{2}(v-c),\frac{1}{2}(v-c)$	$\frac{1}{2}v+\delta,\frac{1}{2}v-\delta$	$\frac{1}{2}v,\frac{1}{2}v$

Figure 405.1 The game *Hawk–Dove–Retaliator*.

To summarize, if injury is not costly ($v \geq c$), then only aggressive behavior survives. In this case, a passive mutant is doomed: it is worse off than an aggressive organism in encounters with other mutants and does no better than an aggressive organism in encounters with aggressive organisms. If injury costs more than the value of the resource ($v < c$), then aggression is not universal in an ESS. A population containing exclusively aggressive organisms is not evolutionarily stable in this case, because passive mutants do better than aggressive organisms against aggressive opponents. Nor is a population containing exclusively passive organisms evolutionarily stable, because aggressive pays against a passive opponent. The only ESS is a mixed strategy, which may be interpreted as corresponding to a situation in which the fraction v/c of organisms are aggressive and the fraction $1 - v/c$ are passive. As the cost of injury increases, the fraction of aggressive organisms declines; the incidence of fights decreases, and an increasing number of encounters end without a fight (the dispute is settled "conventionally", in the language of biologists).

⑦ EXERCISE 405.1 (*Hawk–Dove–Retaliator*) Consider the variant of *Hawk–Dove* in which a third strategy is available: "retaliator", which fights only if the opponent does so. Assume that a retaliator has a slight advantage over a passive animal against a passive opponent. The game is shown in Figure 405.1; assume $\delta < \frac{1}{2}v$. Find the ESSs. (Consider the cases $v \geq c$ and $v < c$ separately.)

? EXERCISE 405.2 (Variant of *BoS*) Find all the ESSs, in pure and mixed strategies, of the game in Figure 405.2.

⑦ EXERCISE 405.3 (Bargaining) For each of the equilibria you found in Exercise 130.3, determine whether the equilibrium strategy is an ESS.

13.2.6 Games that have no ESS

Every game we have studied so far possesses an ESS. But some games do not. A very simple example is the trivial game in the left-hand panel of Figure 406.1. Let

	A	B	C
A	$0,0$	$3,1$	$0,0$
B	$1,3$	$0,0$	$0,0$
C	$0,0$	$0,0$	$1,1$

Figure 405.2 The game in Exercise 405.2.

	X	Y
X	1,1	1,1
Y	1,1	1,1

	A	B	C
A	$\gamma,\ \gamma$	$-1,\ 1$	$1,-1$
B	$1,-1$	$\gamma,\ \gamma$	$-1,\ 1$
C	$-1,\ 1$	$1,-1$	$\gamma,\ \gamma$

Figure 406.1 Games with no ESS. In the unique symmetric Nash equilibrium of the right-hand game, each player's mixed strategy is $(\frac{1}{3}, \frac{1}{3}, \frac{1}{3})$, which is not an ESS.

α be *any* mixed strategy. Then the strategy pair (α, α) is a Nash equilibrium. However, because $U(X, X) = 1 = U(\alpha, X)$, the mixed strategy α does not satisfy the second condition in the definition of an ESS. In a population in which all players use α, a mutant who uses X reproduces at the same rate as the other players (its fitness is the same) and thus does not die out. At the same time, such a mutant does not come to dominate the population. Thus, although the game has no ESS, every mixed strategy is only weakly unstable.

In some games, however, every mixed strategy is seriously unstable. Consider, for example, the game in the right-hand panel of Figure 406.1 with $\gamma > 0$. (If γ were zero, then the game would be *Rock, Paper, Scissors* (Exercise 141.2).) This game has a unique symmetric Nash equilibrium, in which each player's mixed strategy is $\alpha^* = (\frac{1}{3}, \frac{1}{3}, \frac{1}{3})$. To see that this strategy is not an ESS, note that any pure strategy a is a best response to α^* and $U(a, a) = \gamma > \gamma/3 = U(\alpha^*, a)$, strictly violating the second requirement for an ESS. That is, if all members of the population use the unique symmetric mixed strategy Nash equilibrium strategy α^*, then a mutant using any of the three pure strategies invades the population.

13.3 Asymmetric contests

The situations we have studied so far are symmetric: the players are identical and their roles in each match are the same. If the players are not identical, or their roles in a match differ, each player can condition its action on its characteristics, the characteristics of its opponent, and its role. If, for example, the players are the owner of a nesting site and an intruder, who may differ in size, then each player's action may depend upon its size, the size of its opponent, and its ownership status.

One approach to modeling such asymmetric contests assumes that each organism inherits a "conditional" strategy that specifies its action in each of the situations it may face. In the example of the previous paragraph, the strategy each organism inherits specifies its action for each possible combination of its size, its opponent's size, and its ownership status. The idea is that all organisms are fundamentally the same; their specific characteristics (e.g. size) and the situations they face are only incidental, and their genetic makeup specifies their behavior in all possible cases. The assumption that conditional strategies are inherited allows us to model an asymmetric contest as a *symmetric* game in which each player's set of actions consists of her conditional strategies.

In this section I illustrate this approach for the case in which the players differ only in the roles they play. As before, pairs of players are selected randomly from a

SIDE-BLOTCHED LIZARDS

Side-blotched lizards (*Uta stansburiana*), residents of the inner Coast Range of California, show that the game in the right-hand panel of Figure 406.1 is not simply a theoretical curiosity. Male lizards follow one of three reproductive strategies, each associated with a distinctive throat coloration. Lizards with orange throats are very aggressive and defend large territories; those with blue throats are less aggressive and defend smaller territories; and those with yellow stripes on their throats do not defend any territory, but rather depend on their similarity in coloration to females to sneak unnoticed into another male's territory to mate. The lizards breed annually, and throat color is largely genetically determined. Sinervo and Lively (1996) estimate the fitness associated with each of the three strategies, based on their observation of a population of lizards between 1990 and 1995. The sneaky strategy of the yellow-throated lizards works well against their aggressive orange-throated comrades—a yellow-throated lizard can slip unnoticed into the large group of females—but is not effective against the blue-throated strategy. Further, the orange strategy defeats the blue strategy. Thus the structure of the fitness payoffs resembles that in the right-hand panel of Figure 406.1: yellow (*A*) beats orange (*C*) beats blue (*B*) beats yellow. The absence of an ESS in this game suggests that we should see continual changes in the frequencies of the three morphs in the population. Sinervo and Lively observed substantial variation during their study: in 1990 and 1991 blue-throated males predominated, while in 1992 their numbers fell significantly and the number of orange-throated males reached a peak; in 1993 and 1994 the most common coloration was yellow, and in 1995 the composition of the population was roughly the same as it was in 1990. This variation appears to be driven by the relative fitnesses of the three strategies and is consistent with the absence of an ESS in the game in the right-hand panel of Figure 406.1.

large population of identical organisms. Each interaction between a pair of organisms may be modeled as a two-player (not necessarily symmetric) strategic game C (the "contest game"). Denote player i's set of actions in C by A_i. Each organism may play the role of either player 1 or player 2 in C (e.g. "owner" or "intruder"), and knows its role, so that it can condition its action on this role. A *conditional strategy* of an organism is a pair (σ_1, σ_2) in which σ_j is a probability distribution over A_j for $j = 1, 2$, with the interpretation that the organism chooses the mixed strategy σ_1 when it plays the role of player 1 in C and the mixed strategy σ_2 when it plays the role of player 2.

We study the evolution of the organisms' behavior by considering the two-player *symmetric* strategic game G in which each player's set of actions is the set of conditional strategies and its payoff when its action (conditional strategy) is (σ_1, σ_2) and its opponent's action is (τ_1, τ_2) is

$$u((\sigma_1, \sigma_2), (\tau_1, \tau_2)) = \tfrac{1}{2} U_1(\sigma_1, \tau_2) + \tfrac{1}{2} U_2(\tau_1, \sigma_2),$$

where $U_i(\alpha, \beta)$ is player i's expected payoff (fitness) in the game C when player 1's mixed strategy is α and player 2's is β. The rationale for the payoff function u is that in each contest one participant is player 1 and the other is player 2, so given the random assignment of roles, the probability of an organism's playing each role is $\frac{1}{2}$.[1]

The equilibria of the games C and G are closely related, as you are asked to demonstrate in the following exercise.

? EXERCISE 408.1 (Equilibria of C and of G) Show that a mixed strategy pair (α_1, α_2) is a mixed strategy Nash equilibrium of C if and only if $((\alpha_1, \alpha_2), (\alpha_1, \alpha_2))$ is a Nash equilibrium of G, and that if (α_1, α_2) is a strict Nash equilibrium of C, then $((\alpha_1, \alpha_2), (\alpha_1, \alpha_2))$ is a strict Nash equilibrium of G.

A conditional strategy is evolutionarily stable if it is an ESS of G. That is, the conditional strategy (σ_1, σ_2) is evolutionarily stable if

- $((\sigma_1, \sigma_2), (\sigma_1, \sigma_2))$ is a Nash equilibrium of G, and

- $u((\tau_1, \tau_2), (\tau_1, \tau_2)) < u((\sigma_1, \sigma_2), (\tau_1, \tau_2))$ for every conditional strategy (τ_1, τ_2) different from (σ_1, σ_2) that is a best response to (σ_1, σ_2).

If $((\alpha_1, \alpha_2), (\alpha_1, \alpha_2))$ is a strict Nash equilibrium of G, then, as before, the second condition is vacuously satisfied, so that (α_1, α_2) is evolutionarily stable. Thus by the previous exercise, any strict Nash equilibrium of C is evolutionarily stable. Also, by definition, if (α_1, α_2) is evolutionarily stable, then $((\alpha_1, \alpha_2), (\alpha_1, \alpha_2))$ is a Nash equilibrium of G, so by the exercise every evolutionarily stable conditional strategy is a Nash equilibrium of C. In fact, we can show that every evolutionarily stable conditional strategy is a *strict* Nash equilibrium of C. To do so, suppose that (α_1, α_2) is a Nash equilibrium but not a strict Nash equilibrium of C. Specifically, suppose that $U_1(\beta_1, \alpha_2) = U_1(\alpha_1, \alpha_2)$ for some mixed strategy β_1 of player 1. Then

$$u((\beta_1, \alpha_2), (\beta_1, \alpha_2)) = \tfrac{1}{2}U_1(\beta_1, \alpha_2) + \tfrac{1}{2}U_2(\beta_1, \alpha_2)$$
$$= \tfrac{1}{2}U_1(\alpha_1, \alpha_2) + \tfrac{1}{2}U_2(\beta_1, \alpha_2)$$
$$= u((\alpha_1, \alpha_2), (\beta_1, \alpha_2)),$$

so that the second condition in the definition of an evolutionarily stable conditional strategy is not satisfied. A similar argument applies if player 2 has a mixed strategy different from α_2 that is a best response to α_1.

No mixed strategy equilibrium of a strategic game is strict, as noted on page 118, so we have the following result.

■ PROPOSITION 408.2 *A conditional strategy is evolutionarily stable if and only if it is a strict (and hence pure) Nash equilibrium of the contest game C.*

---

[1] You may wonder why we do not define a conditional strategy to be a pair of *actions* in C (rather than a pair of mixed strategies), and allow for randomization by studying the mixed strategy Nash equilibria of the game in which the players' actions are these conditional strategies. The reason is that the resulting set of mixed strategies contains redundancies (many strategies generate the same pattern of behavior), which causes difficulties in the definition of an evolutionarily stable pattern of behavior.

◆ EXAMPLE 409.1 (*Hawk–Dove*) Consider a variant of *Hawk–Dove* (Example 398.2) in which the resource being contested is a nesting site, and one animal is the (current) owner whereas the other is an intruder. Suppose that the value of the site may be different for an owner than for an intruder. Specifically, assume that contest game is the game in Figure 409.1, where V is the value of the site to an owner, v is the value to an intruder, and c is the loss suffered by a loser.

Intruder

		A	P
Owner	A	$\frac{1}{2}(V-c), \frac{1}{2}(v-c)$	$V, 0$
	P	$0, v$	$\frac{1}{2}V, \frac{1}{2}v$

Figure 409.1 An asymmetric variant of *Hawk–Dove*.

We see that if $V < c$ and $v < c$, then the game has two strict Nash equilibria, namely (A, P) and (P, A). Thus by Proposition 408.2 these are the two evolutionarily stable conditional strategies. In both cases the dispute is resolved without a fight. The first strategy, in which an intruder concedes to an owner without a fight, is known as the *bourgeois strategy*; the second, in which the owner concedes to an intruder, is known as the *paradoxical strategy*. There are many examples in nature of the bourgeois strategy. The paradoxical strategy is so named because it leads the members of a population to constantly change roles: whenever there is an encounter, the intruder becomes the owner, and the owner becomes a potential intruder. Examples of this strategy are hard to come by. Maynard Smith (1982, 96) writes that the only example he knows in which the resource being contested is of long-lasting value involves the spider *Oecibus civitas*; Burgess (1976, 105) reports that this spider abandons its retreat without a fight when an intruder arrives.

? EXERCISE 409.2 (*Variant of BoS*) Members of a population are randomly matched and play *BoS* (Figure 403.1). Each player in any given match can condition her action on whether she was the first to suggest getting together. Assume that for any given player, the probability of being the first is $\frac{1}{2}$. Find the evolutionarily stable conditional strategies of this game.

EXPLAINING THE OUTCOMES OF CONTESTS IN NATURE

Hawk–Dove and its variants give us insights into the way in which animal conflicts are resolved. Before the development of evolutionary game theory, one explanation of the observation that animal conflicts are often settled without a fight was that it is not in the interest of a species for its members to be killed or injured. This explanation leaves open the question of how evolution can lead the members of a species to act in a way that benefits the species as a whole. Further, by no means are all animal conflicts resolved peacefully, and the explanation has nothing to say about the conditions under which peaceful resolution is likely to be the norm. As we have seen, a game-theoretic analysis in which the unit of analysis is the individual member of the species suggests that in a symmetric contest, the relation between the value of the resource under contention and the cost of an escalated contest determines the incidence of escalation. In an asymmetric contest the theory predicts that no escalation will occur, regardless of the value of the resource and the cost of injury. Both the convention that the owner always wins (the *bourgeois strategy*) and the convention that the intruder always wins (the *paradoxical strategy*) are evolutionarily stable.

Animal contests have been widely studied by biologists. Many instances of the bourgeois strategy have been found. To take one example, an experiment suggests that competitions for a mate between male Ethiopian hamadryas baboons (*Papio hamadryas*) from the same troop are won by the current "owner" of the female. Kummer, Götz, and Angst (1974) sampled groups of two males and a female. In each group, the female was previously unknown to the males. One of the males was initially allowed to interact with the female while the other male watched in a cage. After fifteen minutes the caged male was released. In each case, the female was retained by the first male. Later, the same two males took part in another trial, with a different female, with their roles reversed: the one who had been caged previously was the first to interact with the female, while the other watched from a cage. Again, the male given the chance to establish initial "ownership" was not challenged by the second male. When males from different troops were involved in the same experiment, fights sometimes took place, and in some cases the ownership of the female changed. One interpretation of these results is that when the males are similar, each uses the bourgeois strategy, while when they are different, their behavior may be determined by other asymmetries (like size).

A study of two populations of the funnel web spider *Agelenopsis aperta* in New Mexico and Arizona links the evidence more tightly to the theory by estimating payoffs. The spiders compete for web sites; the owner of a site periodically has to react to an intruder. Spiders differ in their weight, and web sites differ greatly in their expected supply of prey. Hammerstein and Riechert (1988), who model a spider's options "escalate" (threaten and fight), "display" (to scare off opponent), and "withdraw", estimate, from field data, the effect on a spider's egg production of each possible outcome as a function of the contestants' attributes (e.g. owner larger than intruder) and web site quality. They find that for a population in a harsh environment with little prey, an ESS entails a spider's escalating if it is larger than its opponent and displaying if it is smaller, regardless of its ownership status, and, when it is the same size as its opponent, either escalating when it is the owner and displaying when it is the intruder, or, at a site of average quality, the reverse. The evidence on the spiders' behavior is broadly consistent with these strategies: withdrawal is rare, escalation is much more likely than display for a spider that is larger than its opponent or of the same size and an owner, and display is much more likely in the remaining cases. In a population in a more favorable prey-filled environment, similar calculations predict that a larger spider or an equal-sized owner will display and a smaller spider or equal-sized intruder will withdraw, or the reverse. Here the theory is less successful—in particular, the incidence of escalation is significant.

13.4 Variation on a theme: sibling behavior

In the models we have studied so far, the players in each match are unrelated. The model I describe in this section illustrates how we may analyze the evolutionarily stable behavior of related individuals. It specifically concerns the behavior of siblings.

13.4.1 Asexual reproduction

Consider siblings who interact in pairs. First suppose, as before, that reproduction is asexual: each individual, on its own, produces offspring, who inherit its behavior. Suppose that every individual in the population uses the action a^* in its interactions with its siblings, obtaining the payoff $u(a^*, a^*)$. If a mutant using the action b appears, its fitness is determined by its interactions with its siblings, who use a^*. But, assuming that it has *some* offspring and ignoring further mutations, all these offspring inherit the behavior b and obtain the payoff $u(b, b)$ in their interactions with each other. In the absence of further mutations, all the descendants of any of these offspring also obtain the payoff $u(b, b)$ in their interaction with each other. Thus the mutant behavior b invades the population if and only if $u(b, b) > u(a^*, a^*)$; it is driven out of the population if and only if $u(b, b) < u(a^*, a^*)$. We conclude that

> if an action a^* is evolutionarily stable, then $u(a^*, a^*) \geq u(b, b)$ for every action b; if $u(a^*, a^*) > u(b, b)$ for every action b, then a^* is evolutionarily stable.

A necessary condition for an action a^* to be evolutionarily stable in a population of unrelated individuals is that (a^*, a^*) be a Nash equilibrium (Definition 398.1). In intrasibling interaction no such requirement appears: only actions a^* for which $u(a^*, a^*)$ is as high as possible can be evolutionarily stable. For example, if the game the siblings play is the *Prisoner's Dilemma* (Figure 411.1), then the only evolutionarily stable action is C (because $u(C, C) > u(D, D)$); if this game is played between unrelated organisms, then the only evolutionarily stable action is D.

	C	D
C	2,2	0,3
D	3,0	1,1

Figure 411.1 The *Prisoner's Dilemma*.

In words, an evolutionarily stable action is the result of a player's following the maxim "act toward your sibling as would be in your own best interest if your sibling's [action] would mimic your own" (to quote Bergstrom 1995, 61). An important assumption in reaching this conclusion is that reproduction is asexual. As Bergstrom succinctly puts it, "Careful observers of human siblings will not be surprised to find that in sexually reproducing species, equilibrium behavior is not so perfectly cooperative."

13.4.2 Sexual reproduction

Suppose that each individual has two parents and inherits its behavior from each parent with probability $\frac{1}{2}$. (The inheritance could be genetic or social.) Assume that all mating is monogamous: all siblings share the same two parents.

Under what circumstances is a population of individuals all choosing the action a^* evolutionarily stable? Suppose that a mutant choosing the action b emerges. Almost all individuals choose a^*, so, under the assumption that each individual chooses a mate randomly, almost every mutant mates with such an individual. Each of the offspring of such a pair chooses a^* with probability $\frac{1}{2}$ and b with probability $\frac{1}{2}$, and thus obtains the expected payoff

$$\tfrac{1}{2}u(b,a^*) + \tfrac{1}{2}u(b,b)$$

in its interactions with its siblings. Individuals choosing a^* are present both in ("normal") families with two a^* parents and in families with one a^* parent and one b parent, but when b is rare, the vast majority of such individuals are in normal families. Thus to determine whether b, when it is rare, multiplies faster than does a^*, we need to consider only the payoff of an individual choosing b in an a^*–b family relative to that of an individual choosing a^* in a normal family. All the siblings of an a^* in a normal family choose a^*, and hence obtain the payoff

$$u(a^*, a^*).$$

We conclude that b is driven out of the population if

$$\tfrac{1}{2}u(b,a^*) + \tfrac{1}{2}u(b,b) < u(a^*, a^*)$$

and invades the population if the inequality is reversed.

Define the function v by

$$v(b,a) = \tfrac{1}{2}u(b,a) + \tfrac{1}{2}u(b,b).$$

The payoff $v(b,a)$ is the average of an individual's payoff in the original game and its payoff when its sibling mimics its own behavior. That is, this payoff lies midway between the payoff in the original game and the payoff relevant in the case of asexual reproduction.

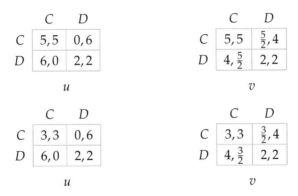

Figure 413.1 Two versions of the *Prisoner's Dilemma*. On the left are the basic games, with payoff function u, and on the right are the corresponding games with payoff function v.

We have $v(a, a) = u(a, a)$ for every action a, so the sufficient condition for a^* to be evolutionarily stable is

$$v(b, a^*) < v(a^*, a^*) \text{ for every action } b.$$

That is, (a^*, a^*) is a strict Nash equilibrium *of the game with payoff function v*. If the inequality is reversed for any action b, then a^* is not evolutionarily stable, so that a necessary condition for a^* to be evolutionarily stable is that (a^*, a^*) be a Nash equilibrium of the game with payoff function v.

In summary,

> if an action a^* is evolutionarily stable, then (a^*, a^*) is a Nash equilibrium of the game with payoff function v; if (a^*, a^*) is a strict Nash equilibrium of the game with payoff function v, then a^* is evolutionarily stable.

That is, in this case an evolutionarily stable action is the result of a player's following the maxim "act toward your sibling as would be in your own best interest if with probability $\frac{1}{2}$ your sibling's action would mimic your own" (again quoting Bergstrom 1995, 62).

Consider the implications for the *Prisoner's Dilemma*. First consider the payoff function at the top left of Figure 413.1. The game with payoff function v is shown at the top right. We see that (C, C) is the only Nash equilibrium of the game with payoff function v, so that C is the only evolutionarily stable strategy when the game with payoff function u is played between siblings.

Now consider the payoff function at the bottom left of the figure. In this case the only Nash equilibrium of the game with payoff function v is (D, D), so that D is the only evolutionarily stable strategy when the game with payoff function u is played between siblings.

Thus in the *Prisoner's Dilemma*, whether siblings in a sexually reproducing species are cooperative depends on the gain from being uncooperative. When this gain is small, the cooperative outcome is evolutionarily stable. Even though

$$\begin{array}{c|c|c|} & X & Y \\ \hline X & x,x & 0,0 \\ \hline Y & 0,0 & 1,1 \\ \hline \end{array}$$

Figure 414.1 The game in Exercise 414.1.

purely selfish behavior fails to sustain cooperation, the behavioral similarity of siblings causes cooperative behavior to be evolutionarily stable. When the gain is large enough, however, the relatedness of siblings is not enough to overcome the pressure to defect, and the only evolutionarily stable outcome is joint defection.

? EXERCISE 414.1 (A coordination game between siblings) Consider the game in Figure 414.1. For what values of $x > 1$ is X the unique evolutionarily stable action when the game is played between siblings and reproduction is sexual, modeled as in this section?

? EXERCISE 414.2 (Assortative mating) Assume that all mating is assortative, in the sense that every individual mates with an individual who chooses the same action. How does the analysis change?

13.5 Variation on a theme: the nesting behavior of wasps

In the models we have studied so far, the players interact in pairs. In many situations the result of a player's action depends on the behavior of several other players. In this section I describe a model of a population engaged in contests for nesting sites that takes into account that intruding is less time-consuming than building a nest, so that an invader potentially interacts with several builders while a builder is constructing her nest.

Female great golden digger wasps (*Sphex ichneumoneus*) lay their eggs in burrows, which must be stocked with katydids for the larva to eat when they hatch. In a simple model, each wasp decides, when ready to lay an egg, whether to dig a burrow or to invade another wasp's burrow. A wasp that invades a burrow fights with the occupant, and may win or lose. If invaders are sufficiently scarce, then not all diggers are invaded, so that although digging takes time, it offers the possibility of laying an egg without a fight. The higher the proportion of invaders, the worse off is a digger, because it is more likely to be invaded.

Each wasp's fitness is measured by the number of eggs it lays. Assuming that the length of a wasp's life is independent of its behavior, we can work with payoffs equal to the number of eggs laid per unit time. Let T_d be the time it takes for a wasp to build a burrow and stock it with katydids; let T_i be the time spent on a nest by an invader (T_i is not zero, because fighting takes time) and assume $T_i < T_d$. Assume that all wasps lay the same number of eggs in a nest; choose the units in which eggs are measured so that this number is 1.

Suppose that the fraction of the population that digs is p and the fraction that invades is $1 - p$. To determine the probability of a digger's being invaded, we need

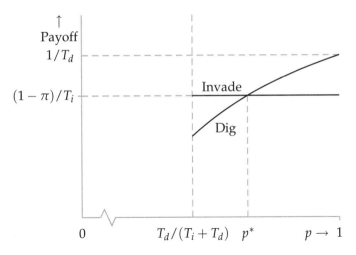

Figure 415.1 The payoffs to digging and invading as a function of p, the fraction of diggers in the population, for values of p for which the model is defined. The figure shows a case in which $1/T_d > (1 - \pi)/T_i$. The value of p^* is $(1 - \pi)T_d/T_i$.

to take into account the fact that because invading takes less time than digging, an invader can invade more than one nest in the time that it takes a digger to dig. If invading takes half the time of digging, for example, and there are only half as many invaders as there are diggers in the population, then *all* diggers will be invaded—the probability of a digger's being invaded is 1. In general, a wasp can invade T_d/T_i burrows during a period of length T_d. For every digger there are $(1 - p)/p$ invaders, so the probability that a digger is invaded is $q = [(1 - p)/p]T_d/T_i = (1 - p)T_d/(pT_i)$. If this number exceeds 1, the number of nests that can be invaded per unit time exceeds the number that exist. I evade specifying what happens in this case by restricting attention to values of p for which $(1 - p)T_d \le pT_i$ (i.e. $p \ge T_d/(T_i + T_d)$), so that $q \le 1$.

Denote by π the probability of an invader's losing a fight with an owner. A wasp that digs its own burrow succeeds in laying its eggs unless it is invaded and loses the fight (in which case I assume that the whole time T_d is wasted), an event with probability $q(1 - \pi)$. Thus the payoff—the expected number of eggs laid per unit time—of such a wasp is

$$\frac{1 - q(1 - \pi)}{T_d} = \frac{1}{T_d} - \frac{(1 - \pi)(1 - p)}{pT_i}.$$

The expected number of eggs laid per unit time by an invader is $(1 - \pi)/T_i$, independent of p. These payoffs are shown as functions of p in Figure 415.1.

We see that if $T_i > (1 - \pi)T_d$, as in the figure, there are two equilibria. In one equilibrium $p = 1$ (every wasp digs its own burrow); the expected payoff to digging, $1/T_d$, exceeds the expected payoff to invading, $(1 - \pi)/T_i$. In the other equilibrium the payoffs to digging and to invading are equal, which requires $p = (1 - \pi)T_d/T_i$ (labeled p^* in the figure). If $T_i = (1 - \pi)T_d$ there is a single equilibrium, with $p = 1$, and if $T_i < (1 - \pi)T_d$ there is no equilibrium.

Are these equilibria evolutionarily stable? First consider the equilibrium in which every wasp digs its own burrow. If $T_i > (1 - \pi)T_d$, then mutants that invade obtain a smaller payoff than the normal wasps, and hence die out. Thus the equilibrium is evolutionarily stable.

Now consider the equilibrium in which diggers and invaders coexist in the population, with the fraction of diggers equal to $(1 - \pi)T_d/T_i$. Suppose that a small mutation increases slightly the fraction of diggers in the population. That is, p rises slightly. Then q, the probability of being invaded, falls, and the expected payoff to digging increases; the expected payoff to invading does not change. Thus the slight increase in p leads to an increase in the relative attractiveness of digging; diggers prosper relative to invaders, further increasing the value of p. We conclude that the equilibrium is not evolutionarily stable.

The polymorphic equilibrium (with $p = (1 - \pi)T_d/T_i$) can alternatively be interpreted as a mixed strategy equilibrium, in which each individual wasp randomizes between digging and invading, digging with probability p. Brockmann et al. (1979) conclude, based on careful observations of wasps at two locations, that not only do digging and invading coexist, but in fact individual wasps pursue mixed strategies—sometimes they dig and sometimes they invade. This evidence is consistent with the existence of a mixed strategy equilibrium, but at odds with our conclusion that this equilibrium is not evolutionarily stable. Brockmann et al., who propose a variant of the model in which the mixed strategy equilibrium *is* evolutionarily stable, find that at one of their two sites, the wasps' behavior closely approximates the equilibrium.

13.6 Variation on a theme: the evolution of the sex ratio

A final variant of the models we have studied takes us back to the starting point of the chapter: Darwin. The following exercise asks you to find an evolutionarily stable strategy in Darwin's model of the sex ratio.

? EXERCISE 416.1 (Darwin's theory of the sex ratio) A population of males and females mate pairwise to produce offspring. Suppose that each offspring is male with probability p and female with probability $1 - p$. Then there is a steady state in which the fraction p of the population is male and the fraction $1 - p$ is female. For what values of p is such an equilibrium evolutionarily stable? If $p \neq \frac{1}{2}$, then males and females have different numbers of offspring (on average). Denote the number of children born to each female by n, so that the number of children born to each male is $((1 - p)/p)n$. Suppose a mutation occurs that produces boys and girls each with probability $\frac{1}{2}$. Assume for simplicity that the mutant trait is dominant: if one partner in a couple has it, then all the offspring of the couple have it. Assume also that the number of children produced by a female with the trait is n, the same as for "normal" members of the population. Both normal and mutant females produce the same number of children, so it might seem that the fitness of a mutant is the same as that of a normal organism. But compare the number of *grand*children of mutants and normal organisms. How many female offspring does a normal organism produce? How many male offspring? Use your answers to find the number of grandchildren born to each mutant and to each normal organism. Does the mutant invade the population? Which value (values?) of p is evolutionarily stable?

Notes

The idea of an evolutionarily stable strategy is due to Maynard Smith and Price (see Maynard Smith 1972a, 1974, 1982 and Maynard Smith and Price 1973). The chapter draws also on Hammerstein and Selten (1994), van Damme (1987, Chapter 9), and Weibull (1995). Asymmetric contests (Section 13.3) are considered by Maynard Smith and Parker (1976) and Selten (1980), who establishes Proposition 408.2. Section 13.4 is based on Bergstrom (1995), and Section 13.5 is based on Brockmann, Grafen, and Dawkins (1979), simplified along the lines of Bergstrom and Varian (1987, 324–327). Darwin's theory of the evolution of the sex ratio (see the box on page 399 and Section 13.6) was independently discovered by Ronald A. Fisher (1930, 141–143) and is often referred to as "Fisher's theory". In the second edition of *The Descent of Man* (1874, 256), Darwin retracts his theory for reasons that are not apparent, and Fisher appears to have been aware of only the retraction, not of the original theory. Bulmer (1994, 207–208) appears to have been the first to notice that "Fisher's theory" was given by Darwin.

The result in Exercise 402.1 is a special case of Lemma 9.2.4 of van Damme (1987). The *Hawk–Dove–Retaliator* game in Exercise 405.1 is taken from Maynard Smith (1982, 18); it is a variant of a game studied by Maynard Smith and Price (1973). The box on side-blotched lizards on page 407 is based on Sinervo and Lively (1996). The box on contests in nature on page 409 is based on Kummer, Götz, and Angst (1974) and Hammerstein and Riechert (1988). See Pool (1995) for an informal discussion of some other applications of the theory.

14 Repeated Games: The *Prisoner's Dilemma*

14.1 The main idea 419

14.2 Preferences 421

14.3 Repeated games 423

14.4 Finitely repeated *Prisoner's Dilemma* 424

14.5 Infinitely repeated *Prisoner's Dilemma* 426

14.6 Strategies in an infinitely repeated *Prisoner's Dilemma* 426

14.7 Some Nash equilibria of an infinitely repeated *Prisoner's Dilemma* 428

14.8 Nash equilibrium payoffs of an infinitely repeated *Prisoner's Dilemma* 431

14.9 Subgame perfect equilibria and the one-deviation property 437

14.10 Some subgame perfect equilibria of an infinitely repeated *Prisoner's Dilemma* 441

14.11 Subgame perfect equilibrium payoffs of an infinitely repeated *Prisoner's Dilemma* 446

14.12 Concluding remarks 449

Prerequisite: Chapters 5 and 7

WHEN a group of players interacts repeatedly, each member can condition her action at each point in time on the other players' previous actions. The model of an extensive game (Chapters 5–7) allows us to think precisely about the implications of this possibility. In this chapter and the next we study a class of extensive games in which these implications are striking. In these games, a set of players repeatedly engages in the same strategic game. In this chapter the strategic game is the *Prisoner's Dilemma*, an example that illustrates many of the key points. The next chapter extends the analysis to an arbitrary strategic game.

14.1 The main idea

The main idea of the theory is that a player may be deterred from exploiting her short-term advantage by the "threat" of "punishment" that reduces her long-term payoff. Suppose, for example, that two people repeatedly play the *Prisoner's Dilemma* (Section 2.2), with payoffs as in Figure 420.1. Think of C as "cooperation" and D as "defection".

$$
\begin{array}{c|c|c}
 & C & D \\
\hline
C & 2,2 & 0,3 \\
\hline
D & 3,0 & 1,1 \\
\end{array}
$$

Figure 420.1 A *Prisoner's Dilemma*.

As we know, this strategic game has a unique Nash equilibrium, in which each player chooses D. Now consider the following strategy in the repeated game, known as the *grim trigger strategy*:

- choose C as long as the other player chooses C

- if in any period the other player chooses D, then choose D in *every subsequent period*.

This strategy begins by playing cooperatively and continues doing so until the other player defects; a single defection by the opponent triggers relentless ("grim") defection, which we may interpret as retaliatory "punishment" of the opponent. How should a player respond if her opponent uses this strategy? If she chooses C in every period, then the outcome is (C, C) and her payoff is 2 in every period. If she switches to D in some period, then she obtains a payoff of 3 in that period (a short-term gain) and a payoff of 1 in every subsequent period (a long-term loss). She may value the present more highly than the future—she may be *impatient*—but as long as the value she attaches to future payoffs is not too small compared with the value she attaches to her current payoff, the stream of payoffs $(3, 1, 1, \ldots)$ is worse for her than the stream $(2, 2, 2, \ldots)$, so that she is better off choosing C in every period than she is switching to D in some period.

This argument shows that if a player is sufficiently patient, the strategy that chooses C after every history is a best response to the grim trigger strategy. I claim that another best response is this same grim trigger strategy. If your opponent uses the grim trigger strategy, then the outcome of your using the grim trigger strategy is the same as the outcome of your using the strategy that chooses C after every history. In both cases, the outcome in every period is (C, C) (the other player never defects, so the grim trigger strategy never switches to punishment). And a deviation from the grim trigger strategy involving the unprovoked use of D has the same implications as a similar deviation from the always-C strategy.

Thus when the players are sufficiently patient, the strategy pair in which both players use the grim trigger strategy is a Nash equilibrium of the repeated *Prisoner's Dilemma*: neither player can do better by adopting another strategy in the repeated game. The outcome of this equilibrium is (C, C) in every period. This conclusion accords with our intuition that in long-term relationships there is scope for mutually supportive strategies that do not exploit short-term gain.

This strategy pair is, however, not the only Nash equilibrium of the repeated game. Another Nash equilibrium is the strategy pair in which each player chooses D after every history: if one player adopts this strategy, then the other player can do no better than to adopt the strategy herself, regardless of how she values the future, because choosing D is in her short-term interest and choosing C has no effect on the other player's future behavior.

This analysis raises many questions.

- Exactly how patient do the players have to be for the repeated *Prisoner's Dilemma* to have a Nash equilibrium in which the outcome is (C, C) in every period?

- What other outcomes are generated by Nash equilibria?

- We saw in Chapter 5 that Nash equilibria of extensive games are not always intuitively appealing because the actions they prescribe after histories that result from deviations may not be optimal. The notion of subgame perfect equilibrium, which requires strategies to be optimal after every possible history, not only those reached if the players adhere to their strategies, may be more appealing. Is the strategy pair in which each player uses the grim trigger strategy a subgame perfect equilibrium? That is, does each player optimally punish the other player for deviating? If not, does the game have a subgame perfect equilibrium that supports desirable outcomes?

- The grim trigger strategy prescribes rather severe retaliation. Are there Nash equilibria or subgame perfect equilibria in which the players' strategies punish deviations less severely?

- How do the arguments apply to games other than the *Prisoner's Dilemma*?

This chapter addresses all questions but the last, which is tackled in the next chapter. I begin by formulating the model of a repeated game precisely, starting with the players' preferences.

14.2 Preferences

14.2.1 Discounting

The outcome of a repeated game is a sequence of outcomes of a strategic game. How does a player evaluate such sequences? I assume that she associates a payoff with each outcome of the strategic game and evaluates each sequence of outcomes in the repeated game by the **discounted sum** of the associated sequence of payoffs. More precisely, each player i has a payoff function u_i for the strategic game and a discount factor δ_i between 0 and 1 such that she evaluates the sequence $(a^1, a^2, \ldots, a^T)$ of outcomes of the strategic game by the sum

$$u_i(a^1) + \delta_i u_i(a^2) + \delta_i^2 u_i(a^3) + \cdots + \delta_i^{T-1} u_i(a^T) = \sum_{t=1}^{T} \delta_i^{t-1} u_i(a^t).$$

(Note that the superscripts in this expression are used for two purposes: a^t is the action profile in period t, while δ_i^t is the discount factor δ_i raised to the power t.)

If δ_i is close to 0, then the player cares very little about the future—she is very impatient; if δ_i is close to 1 she is very patient. I assume throughout that all players have the same discount factor: $\delta_i = \delta$ for all i.

Why should a person value future payoffs less than current ones? Possibly she is simply impatient. (Perhaps the hazard of death has favored those who reproduce early, leading to the evolution of people with impatient preferences.) Or, possibly, though her underlying preferences do not display impatience, she takes into account the positive probability with which she may die in any given period. Or, if the outcome in each period involves her receiving some amount of money, possibly she is induced to behave as if she were impatient by the fact that she can borrow and lend at a positive interest rate. If she can borrow and lend at the interest rate r and her underlying preferences over streams of monetary payoffs do not display impatience, then she is indifferent, for example, between the sequence ($100, $100) and the sequence ($100 + $100/(1 + r), 0), because by lending $100/(1 + r) of the amount she obtains in the first period she obtains $100 in the second period. In fact, under these assumptions her preferences are represented precisely by the discounted sum of her payoffs with the discount factor $1/(1 + r)$: any stream can be obtained from any other stream with the same discounted sum by borrowing and lending.

The assumption that everyone's preferences over sequences of outcomes are represented by a discounted sum of payoffs is restrictive: people's preferences do not *necessarily* take this form. However, the discounted sum captures simply the idea that people may value the present more highly than the future, and it appears not to obscure any other feature of preferences significant to the problem we are considering.

Suppose that a player's preferences over streams $(w^1, w^2, \ldots)$ of payoffs are represented by the discounted sum $\sum_{t=1}^{\infty} \delta^{t-1} w^t$ of these payoffs, where $0 < \delta < 1$. For any given stream $(w^1, w^2, \ldots)$, is there a value of c such that the player is indifferent between the stream $(w^1, w^2, \ldots)$ and the constant stream $(c, c, \ldots)$? Denote the discounted sum of the stream $(w^1, w^2, \ldots)$ by V. The discounted sum of the stream $(c, c, \ldots)$ is $c/(1 - \delta)$ (consult Section 17.5 if you do not know how to calculate the sum of a geometric series), so the player is indifferent between the two streams if $c = (1 - \delta)V$. This fact makes it reasonable to call $(1 - \delta)V$ the *discounted average* of the stream $(w^1, w^2, \ldots)$.

Precisely, the **discounted average** of any stream $(w^1, w^2, \ldots)$ of payoffs for the discount factor δ is $(1 - \delta) \sum_{t=1}^{\infty} \delta^{t-1} w^t$. The factor $1 - \delta$ is a constant, so for a given value of δ the discounted sum and discounted average represent the same preferences. Note that for any discount factor δ between 0 and 1, and any number c, the discounted average of the constant stream of payoffs $(c, c, \ldots)$ is equal to c.

14.2.2 Equivalent payoff functions

When we considered preferences over deterministic atemporal outcomes, we found that many payoff functions represent the same preferences. Specifically, if u is a payoff function that represents a person's preferences over deterministic outcomes, then any increasing function of u also represents her preferences (Section 1.2.2). When we considered preferences over atemporal lotteries, we found that the equivalence of payoff functions is more restrictive: if u is a Bernoulli payoff function whose expected value represents a person's preferences over lotteries, then every other payoff function whose expected value represents her preferences is an increasing *linear* function of u (Section 4.12.2).

In the current context also, many payoff functions represent the same preferences. As in the case of preferences over atemporal lotteries, equivalent payoff functions are linear functions of each other. Specifically, if a person's preferences are represented by the discounted average of payoffs with payoff function u and discount factor δ, then they are also represented by the discounted average of payoffs with payoff function $\alpha + \beta u$ and discount factor δ, where α and β are numbers with $\beta > 0$.

(?) EXERCISE 423.1 (Equivalence of payoff functions) Demonstrate the claim in the previous sentence.

Further, linear transformations of u are the only ones that preserve preferences: if discounted averages using the payoff functions u and v and the same discount factor represent the same preferences, then $v = \alpha + \beta u$ for some numbers α and $\beta > 0$.

The significance of this result is that different payoffs for the same strategic game may generate different preferences in the repeated game, even if we restrict attention to deterministic outcomes. For example, the players' preferences in the repeated game based on a *Prisoner's Dilemma* with the payoffs given in Figure 420.1 are different from the players' preferences in the repeated game based on a *Prisoner's Dilemma* in which the payoff pairs $(0,3)$ and $(3,0)$ in Figure 420.1 are replaced by $(0,5)$ and $(5,0)$. When the discount factor is close enough to 1, for instance, each player prefers the sequence of outcomes $((C,C),(C,C))$ to the sequence of outcomes $((D,C),(C,D))$ in the first case, but not in the second case. Thus I refer to *a* repeated *Prisoner's Dilemma*, rather than *the* repeated *Prisoner's Dilemma*. More generally, throughout this chapter and the next I define strategic games in terms of payoff functions rather than preferences: a **strategic game** consists of a set of players, and, for each player, a set of actions and a payoff function. Any game in which the payoffs are ranked as they are in Figure 420.1 is called a *Prisoner's Dilemma*.

14.3 Repeated games

Given a strategic game G, a repeated game of G is an extensive game with perfect information and simultaneous moves (Definition 206.1) in which a history is a sequence of action profiles in G. After every nonterminal history, *every* player chooses an action in G. The length of every history is either some positive integer

T, in which case we have a *finitely repeated game*, or infinite, in which case we have an *infinitely repeated game*.

▶ DEFINITION 424.1 (*Repeated game*) Let *G* be a strategic game. Denote the set of players by *N* and the set of actions and payoff function of each player *i* by A_i and u_i respectively. The *T*-**period repeated game of** *G* for the discount factor δ is the extensive game with perfect information and simultaneous moves in which

- the set of players is *N*
- the set of terminal histories is the set of sequences $(a^1, a^2, \dots, a^T)$ of action profiles in *G*
- the player function assigns the set of all players to every history $(a^1, \dots, a^t)$ (for every value of *t*)
- the set of actions available to any player *i* after any history is A_i
- each player *i* evaluates each terminal history $(a^1, a^2, \dots, a^T)$ according to its discounted average $(1 - \delta) \sum_{t=1}^{T} \delta^{t-1} u_i(a^t)$.

The **infinitely repeated game of** *G* for the discount factor δ differs only in that the set of terminal histories is the set of infinite sequences $(a^1, a^2, \dots)$ and the payoff of each player *i* to the terminal history $(a^1, a^2, \dots)$ is the discounted average $(1 - \delta) \sum_{t=1}^{\infty} \delta^{t-1} u_i(a^t)$. In both cases a terminal history is also called an **outcome path**.

14.4 Finitely repeated *Prisoner's Dilemma*

14.4.1 Nash equilibrium

A player's strategy in an extensive game specifies her action for all possible histories after which it is her turn to move, including histories that are inconsistent with her strategy (Definition 208.1). Thus a strategy of player *i* in a *T*-period repeated game of the strategic game *G* specifies an action of player *i* (a member of A_i) at the start of the game (i.e. after the initial history ∅) and for every sequence $(a^1, \dots, a^t)$ of outcomes of *G* with $1 \leq t \leq T - 1$.

Consider the *T*-period repeated game of the *Prisoner's Dilemma*. Suppose that one player's strategy chooses *D* in every period, for every possible history. What can the other player do? Whatever she does, her opponent will choose *D* in every period, so she can do no better than choose *D* in every period. Thus the strategy pair in which each player's strategy chooses *D* in every period for every possible history is a Nash equilibrium of the *T*-period game. This strategy pair generates the outcome path in which the outcome is (D, D) in every period.

I claim that *every* Nash equilibrium generates the same outcome path, so that the game does not capture the idea discussed in the introduction to the chapter that cooperative outcomes can be sustained by the threat of punishment for deviations. The argument is simple: a deviation from *C* to *D* in the last period that either player chooses *C* cannot be punished—the outcome in every subsequent period is

Period:	1	...	$t-1$	t	$t+1$	...	T
(s_1, s_2):	a^1	...	a^{t-1}	(C, X)	(D, D)	...	(D, D)
Relation between player 1's payoffs:	$\parallel$	...	$\parallel$	$\wedge$	$\wedge\mid$	...	$\wedge\mid$
(s_1', s_2):	a^1	...	a^{t-1}	(D, X)	$(D, ?)$	...	$(D, ?)$

Figure 425.1 The outcome paths generated by the strategy pairs (s_1, s_2) and (s_1', s_2) in the T-period repeated game of the *Prisoner's Dilemma*, and the relation between player 1's payoffs in each period in the two outcome paths.

(D, D) in any case—so that no player optimally chooses C in any period. More precisely, suppose the strategy pair (s_1, s_2) generates an outcome path in which at least one player's action is different from D in at least one period. Denote by t the last period in which the outcome is not (D, D), and suppose that player 1's action is C in this period. I claim that player 1 can deviate from s_1 and increase her payoff. Suppose she switches to a strategy s_1' that differs from s_1 only in that from period t on it chooses D for every history. The outcome path generated by the strategy pair (s_1', s_2) differs from the outcome path generated by (s_1, s_2) only in player 1's action in period t, which is D rather than C, and, possibly, in player 2's actions in period $t+1$ and later. In period t, player 2's action is the same under (s_1', s_2) as it is under (s_1, s_2), because s_1' differs from s_1 only in its prescriptions for period t and later. In period $t+1$ and later, player 1's action in both cases is D. Thus player 1's payoff is the same under both strategy pairs through period $t-1$, is higher under (s_1', s_2) than it is under (s_1, s_2) in period t, and is at least as high under (s_1', s_2) as it is under (s_1, s_2) from period $t+1$ through period T. Figure 425.1 shows the outcome path generated by each strategy pair and the relation between the payoff of player 1 in each period.

We conclude that every Nash equilibrium of a finitely repeated *Prisoner's Dilemma* generates the outcome (D, D) in every period. A player's strategy may specify an action other than D for histories for which the outcome in some period is not (D, D)—it may promise to be cooperative if the other player is cooperative—but the outcome generated by any equilibrium strategy pair is (D, D) in every period (no player ever chooses C, so no cooperation is ever induced). In particular, the notion of Nash equilibrium does not capture the idea discussed at the start of the chapter.

14.4.2 Subgame perfect equilibrium

Every subgame perfect equilibrium of an extensive game is a Nash equilibrium, so we know that every subgame perfect equilibrium of a finitely repeated *Prisoner's Dilemma*, like every Nash equilibrium, generates the outcome (D, D) in every period. But for a subgame perfect equilibrium we can further restrict the strategies.

⑦ EXERCISE 426.1 (Subgame perfect equilibrium of finitely repeated *Prisoner's Dilemma*) Show that a finitely repeated *Prisoner's Dilemma* has a unique subgame perfect equilibrium, in which each player's strategy chooses D in every period, regardless of the history.

14.5 Infinitely repeated *Prisoner's Dilemma*

The argument that in every Nash equilibrium of a finitely repeated *Prisoner's Dilemma* each player's action is D in every period depends on the fact that every outcome path in such a game has a last period in which at least one player chooses C. A game in which play may go on indefinitely has outcome paths in which, for each player and every period t, there is a future period in which the player's action is C, so that by choosing D instead of C she can punish the other player for a deviation in period t. This fact suggests that an infinitely repeated game may be a suitable model in which to capture the idea that cooperation may be sustained by "punishment" strategies when players interact repeatedly.

Most interactions neither last for a predetermined finite number of periods (as in the model of a finitely repeated game) nor continue indefinitely. Which assumption better captures the participants' strategic reasoning? As we have seen, in the model of a finitely repeated *Prisoner's Dilemma* the fixed finite horizon exerts an overpowering influence on the players' behavior. Intuition suggests that in many long-lasting interactions, the termination date may play little role in the participants' strategic calculations until it is imminent. In such cases, a model in which play may continue indefinitely may better capture the considerations relevant to a participant's choice of a strategy than the model of a finitely repeated game.

Before studying the equilibria of an infinitely repeated *Prisoner's Dilemma*, I discuss a convenient way of describing a strategy.

14.6 Strategies in an infinitely repeated *Prisoner's Dilemma*

A strategy of player i in an infinitely repeated game of the strategic game G specifies an action of player i (a member of A_i) for every sequence $(a^1, \ldots, a^T)$ of outcomes of G.

For example, the *grim trigger strategy* for an infinitely repeated *Prisoner's Dilemma* discussed in Section 14.1 is defined as follows: $s_i(\varnothing) = C$ and

$$s_i(a^1, \ldots, a^t) = \begin{cases} C & \text{if } (a_j^1, \ldots, a_j^t) = (C, \ldots, C) \\ D & \text{otherwise,} \end{cases} \quad (426.2)$$

for every history $(a^1, \ldots, a^t)$, where j is the other player. That is, player i chooses C at the start of the game (after the initial history $\varnothing$) and after any history in which every previous action of player j was C, and D after every other history.

We can think of this strategy as having two *states*: one, call it $\mathcal{C}$, in which C is chosen, and another, call it $\mathcal{D}$, in which D is chosen. Initially the state is $\mathcal{C}$. If,

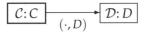

Figure 427.1 The grim trigger strategy for an infinitely repeated *Prisoner's Dilemma*.

when the state is C, the other player chooses D, then the state changes to D, where it stays forever. Figure 427.1 gives a natural representation of the strategy when we think of it in these terms. The box on the left, with a bold outline, represents the initial state, C, in which the player chooses the action C. The state remains C unless the other player chooses D (indicated by the $(\cdot, D)$ under the arrow), in which case the state changes to D, and the player chooses D. (I use the convention that the state remains the same unless an event occurs that is a label for one of the arrows emanating from the state.) Once state D is reached, it is never left: no arrow emanates from the box for state D.

Any strategy can be represented in a diagram like Figure 427.1. In many cases, such a diagram is easier to interpret than a symbolic specification of the action taken after each history like (426.2).

Figure 427.2 shows a strategy that entails punishment less draconian than does the grim trigger strategy. This strategy punishes deviations for only three periods: it responds to a deviation by choosing the action D for three periods, then reverting to C, no matter how the other player behaves during her punishment. (Note that in this strategy, as in the grim trigger strategy, a transition occurs from the initial state only if the *other* player chooses D. Later (Section 14.10) we encounter strategies in which a transition may be caused by a player's own action.)

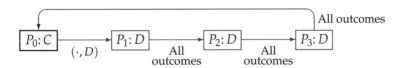

Figure 427.2 A strategy for an infinitely repeated *Prisoner's Dilemma* that punishes deviations for three periods.

In the strategy *tit-for-tat*, the length of the punishment depends on the behavior of the player being punished. If she continues to choose D, then *tit-for-tat* continues to do so; if she reverts to C, then *tit-for-tat* reverts to C also. The strategy can be given a very compact description: do whatever the other player did in the previous period. It is illustrated in Figure 427.3.

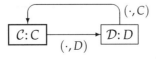

Figure 427.3 The strategy *tit-for-tat* in an infinitely repeated *Prisoner's Dilemma*.

⏺ EXERCISE 428.1 (*Strategies in an infinitely repeated Prisoner's Dilemma*) Represent each of the following strategies for an infinitely repeated *Prisoner's Dilemma* in a diagram like Figure 427.1.

  a. Choose *C* in period 1 and after any history in which the other player chose *C* in every period except, possibly, the previous period; choose *D* after any other history. (That is, punishment is grim, but its initiation is delayed by one period.)

  b. Choose *C* in period 1 and after any history in which the other player chose *D* in at most one period; choose *D* after any other history. (That is, punishment is grim, but a single lapse is forgiven.)

  c. (*Pavlov*, or *win–stay, lose–shift*) Choose *C* in period 1 and after any history in which the outcome in the last period is either (C, C) or (D, D); choose *D* after any other history. (That is, choose the same action again if the outcome was relatively good for you, and switch actions if it was not.)

14.7   Some Nash equilibria of an infinitely repeated *Prisoner's Dilemma*

If one player chooses *D* after every history in an infinitely repeated *Prisoner's Dilemma*, then the other player optimally does the same (because (D, D) is a Nash equilibrium of the *Prisoner's Dilemma*). Thus the strategy pair in which each player chooses *D* after every history is a Nash equilibrium of the infinitely repeated game.

   The argument at the start of the chapter suggests that if the players are sufficiently patient, then an infinitely repeated *Prisoner's Dilemma* has other, less dismal, equilibria—for example, the strategy pair in which each player uses the grim trigger strategy defined in Figure 427.1. I now make this argument precise. Throughout I consider the infinitely repeated *Prisoner's Dilemma* in which each player's discount factor is δ and the one-shot payoffs are given in Figure 420.1.

14.7.1   Grim trigger strategies

Suppose that player 1 uses the grim trigger strategy. If player 2 uses the same strategy, then the outcome is (C, C) in every period, so that she obtains the stream of payoffs $(2, 2, \ldots)$, whose discounted average is 2.

   If player 2 adopts a strategy that generates a different sequence of outcomes, then in at least one period her action is *D*. In all subsequent periods player 1 chooses *D* (player 2's choice of *D* triggers the grim punishment), so the best deviation for player 2 chooses *D* in every subsequent period (because *D* is her unique best response to *D*). Up to the first period in which player 2 chooses *D*, she obtains the payoff 2 in each period, as she does when she uses the grim trigger strategy. Subsequently she obtains the stream of payoffs $(3, 1, 1, \ldots)$ (she gains one unit of payoff in the period of her deviation and loses one unit in every subsequent

$$
\begin{array}{c|cc}
 & C & D \\
\hline
C & x, x & 0, y \\
D & y, 0 & 1, 1
\end{array}
$$

Figure 429.1 The general *Prisoner's Dilemma* in Exercise 429.1. The parameters x and y satisfy $1 < x < y$.

period), whose discounted average is

$$(1 - \delta)(3 + \delta + \delta^2 + \delta^3 + \cdots) = (1 - \delta)\left(3 + \frac{\delta}{1 - \delta}\right)$$
$$= 3(1 - \delta) + \delta.$$

Thus she cannot increase her payoff by deviating if and only if

$$3(1 - \delta) + \delta \leq 2,$$

or $\delta \geq \frac{1}{2}$. We conclude that if $\delta \geq \frac{1}{2}$, then the strategy pair in which each player's strategy is the grim trigger strategy defined in Figure 427.1 is a Nash equilibrium of the infinitely repeated *Prisoner's Dilemma* with one-shot payoffs as in Figure 420.1.

? EXERCISE 429.1 (Grim trigger strategies in a general *Prisoner's Dilemma*) Find the condition on the discount factor δ under which the strategy pair in which each player uses the grim trigger strategy is a Nash equilibrium of the infinitely repeated game of the *Prisoner's Dilemma* in Figure 429.1.

14.7.2 Limited punishment

Consider a generalization of the limited punishment strategy in Figure 427.2 in which a player who chooses D is punished for k periods. (In the strategy in Figure 427.2, we have $k = 3$; in the grim trigger strategy, k is infinitely large.) Denote the strategy $s^P(k)$. If one player adopts this strategy, does the other optimally do so? Suppose that player 1 uses it. If $s^P(k)$ is not a best response for player 2, then her best response chooses D in some period (otherwise the outcome is (C, C) in every period, as it is when she uses $s^P(k)$). Denote by t the first period in which player 2 chooses D. Then player 1 chooses D from period $t + 1$ through period $t + k$, regardless of player 2's choices, so that player 2 also should choose D in these periods. In period $t + k + 1$ player 1 switches back to C (regardless of player 2's action in period $t + k$), and player 2 faces precisely the situation she faced at the beginning of the game. Thus if her best response to $s^P(k)$ yields her a payoff greater than does $s^P(k)$, it does so from period t to period $t + k + 1$, during which it yields her the discounted average payoff

$$(1 - \delta)(3 + \delta + \delta^2 + \cdots + \delta^k) = 3(1 - \delta) + \delta(1 - \delta^k)$$

(see (499.1) for the formula for the sum of a finite geometric series). The strategy $s^P(k)$ yields her the payoff 2 in each of these periods, and thus the discounted average payoff from period t to period $t + k + 1$ of

$$(1 - \delta)(2 + 2\delta + 2\delta^2 + \cdots + 2\delta^k) = 2(1 - \delta^{k+1}).$$

Hence the strategy $s^P(k)$ is a best response to itself if and only if

$$2(1 - \delta^{k+1}) \geq 3(1 - \delta) + \delta(1 - \delta^k),$$

or $\delta^{k+1} - 2\delta + 1 \leq 0$. If $k = 1$, then no value of δ less than 1 satisfies the inequality: one period of punishment is not severe enough to discourage a deviation, however patient the players are. If $k = 2$, then the inequality is satisfied for $\delta \geq 0.62$ (approximately), and if $k = 3$ it is satisfied for $\delta \geq 0.55$. As k increases, the lower bound on δ approaches $\frac{1}{2}$, the lower bound for the grim strategy.

We conclude that the strategy pair in which each player punishes the other for k periods in the event of a deviation is a Nash equilibrium of the infinitely repeated game as long as $k \geq 2$ and δ is large enough; the larger k, the smaller the lower bound on δ. Thus short punishment is effective in sustaining the mutually desirable outcome (C, C) only if the players are very patient.

? EXERCISE 430.1 (Limited punishment strategies in an infinitely repeated *Prisoner's Dilemma*) Find conditions on k, x, y, and the discount factor δ under which the strategy pair in which each player punishes a deviation by choosing D for k periods is a Nash equilibrium of the infinitely repeated game of the *Prisoner's Dilemma* in Figure 429.1.

14.7.3 Tit-for-tat

Under what conditions is the strategy pair in which each player uses the strategy *tit-for-tat* (Figure 427.3) a Nash equilibrium? Suppose that player 1 adheres to this strategy. Denote by t the first period in which player 2 chooses D. Then player 1 chooses D in period $t + 1$, and continues to choose D until player 2 reverts to C. Thus player 2 has two options from period $t + 1$: she can revert to C, in which case in period $t + 2$ she faces the same situation she faced at the start of the game, or she can continue to choose D, in which case player 1 will continue to do so too. We conclude that if player 2's best response to *tit-for-tat* chooses D in some period, then it either alternates between D and C, or chooses D in every period.

If player 2 alternates between D and C, then her stream of payoffs is $(3, 0, 3, 0, \ldots)$, with a discounted average of $(1 - \delta) \cdot 3/(1 - \delta^2) = 3/(1 + \delta)$, while if she chooses D in every period her stream of payoffs is $(3, 1, 1, \ldots)$, with a discounted average of $3(1 - \delta) + \delta = 3 - 2\delta$. Her discounted average payoff to using the strategy *tit-for-tat* (which generates the outcome (C, C) in every period) is 2, so we conclude that *tit-for-tat* is a best response to *tit-for-tat* if and only if

$$2 \geq \frac{3}{1 + \delta} \quad \text{and} \quad 2 \geq 3 - 2\delta.$$

Both of these conditions are equivalent to $\delta \geq \frac{1}{2}$.

Thus if $\delta \geq \frac{1}{2}$, then the strategy pair in which each player uses *tit-for-tat* is a Nash equilibrium of the infinitely repeated *Prisoner's Dilemma* with payoffs as in Figure 420.1.

? EXERCISE 431.1 (*Tit-for-tat in an infinitely repeated Prisoner's Dilemma*) Find conditions on x, y, and the discount factor δ under which the strategy pair in which each player uses *tit-for-tat* is a Nash equilibrium of the infinitely repeated game of the *Prisoner's Dilemma* in Figure 429.1. Show, in particular, that if $y \geq 2x$, then the strategy pair is not a Nash equilibrium for any value of $\delta < 1$.

? EXERCISE 431.2 (Nash equilibria of an infinitely repeated *Prisoner's Dilemma*) For each of the three strategies s in Exercise 428.1 determine the values of δ, if any, for which the strategy pair (s,s) is a Nash equilibrium of the infinitely repeated *Prisoner's Dilemma* in Figure 420.1 with discount factor δ. For each strategy s for which there is no value of δ such that (s,s) is a Nash equilibrium of this game, determine whether there are any other payoffs for the *Prisoner's Dilemma* such that for some δ the strategy pair (s,s) is a Nash equilibrium of the infinitely repeated game with discount factor δ.

14.8   Nash equilibrium payoffs of an infinitely repeated *Prisoner's Dilemma*

The Nash equilibria of an infinitely repeated *Prisoner's Dilemma* that I have discussed so far generate either the outcome (C,C) in every period or the outcome (D,D) in every period. The first outcome path yields the discounted average payoff of 2 to each player, whereas the second one yields the discounted average payoff of 1 to each player. What other discounted average payoffs are generated by Nash equilibria? This question is hard to answer for an arbitrary discount factor but relatively straightforward to answer for a discount factor close to 1 (i.e. when the players are very patient). Before tackling it, we need to determine the set of discounted average pairs of payoffs that can be achieved by some outcome path, regardless of whether the path is generated by an equilibrium.

14.8.1   Feasible discounted average payoffs

For any outcome (X,Y) of the strategic game, the outcome path in which (X,Y) occurs in every period yields the pair $(u_1(X,Y), u_2(X,Y))$ of discounted average payoffs. Thus $(2,2)$, $(3,0)$, $(0,3)$, and $(1,1)$ can all be achieved as pairs of discounted average payoffs in the infinitely repeated *Prisoner's Dilemma* with payoffs as in Figure 420.1.

Now consider the path in which the outcome alternates between (C,C) and (C,D). Along this path player 1's payoff alternates between 2 and 0, and player 2's alternates between 2 and 3. Thus the players' average payoffs along the path are 1 and $\frac{5}{2}$, respectively. Player 1 receives more of her payoff in the first period of each two-period cycle than in the second period (in fact, she obtains nothing in the second period), so her *discounted* average payoff exceeds 1, whatever the discount factor. But if the discount factor is close to 1, then her discounted average payoff is close to 1: the fact that more payoff is obtained in the first period of each two-period cycle is insignificant in this case. Similarly, because player 2 receives most of her payoff in the second period of each two-period cycle, her discounted average payoff is less than $\frac{5}{2}$, whatever the discount factor, but is close to $\frac{5}{2}$ when the discount factor is close to 1. Thus $(1, \frac{5}{2})$ can approximately be achieved as a pair of discounted average payoffs when the discount factor is close to 1.

This argument can be extended to any outcome path in which a finite sequence of outcomes is repeated. If the discount factor is close to 1, then a player's discounted average payoff on such a path is close to her average payoff in the sequence. For example, the outcome path that consists of repetitions of the sequence $((C, C), (D, C), (D, C))$ yields player 1 a discounted average payoff close to $\frac{1}{3}(2 + 3 + 3) = \frac{8}{3}$ and player 2 a discounted average payoff close to $\frac{1}{3}(2 + 0 + 0) = \frac{2}{3}$.

In summary, if the discount factor is close to 1, then for any finite sequence of outcomes of the strategic game, the infinitely repeated game has an outcome path (consisting of repetitions of the sequence) for which the players' discounted average payoffs are close to the averages of their payoffs to the outcomes in the sequence. I claim further that, conversely, if the discount factor is close to 1, then for any outcome path of the infinitely repeated game, the players' discounted average payoffs are close to their average payoffs to a (possibly very long) finite sequence of outcomes.

Now, a player's average payoff to a finite sequence of outcomes is a weighted average of her payoffs to the four outcomes in the game, where the weight attached to each outcome is proportional to the number of times the outcome occurs in the sequence. Thus if the discount factor is close to 1, the set of discounted average payoff pairs that may be achieved in the infinitely repeated game is approximately equal to the set of all pairs of weighted averages of payoffs in the component strategic game. This result may be stated concisely with the aid of a new piece of terminology.

▶ DEFINITION 432.1 (*Feasible payoff profiles in strategic game*) The set of **feasible** payoff profiles of a strategic game is the set of all weighted averages of payoff profiles in the game.

The result, valid for any strategic game (not only the *Prisoner's Dilemma*), may now be stated as follows.

> If the discount factor is close to 1, the set of discounted average payoff profiles generated by the outcome paths of an infinitely repeated game is approximately equal to the set of feasible payoff profiles in the component strategic game.

The set of feasible payoff pairs in a two-player strategic game may usefully be represented geometrically. The set of weighted averages of the points (x_1, x_2) and (y_1, y_2) in two-dimensional space consists of the line segment connecting (x_1, x_2) and (y_1, y_2). Thus the set of feasible payoff pairs in the *Prisoner's Dilemma* with payoffs as in Figure 420.1 is the shaded set in Figure 433.1 (including the boundary).

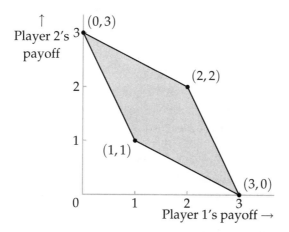

Figure 433.1 The set of feasible payoff pairs in the *Prisoner's Dilemma* with payoffs as in Figure 420.1. Any pair of payoffs in this set can approximately be achieved as a pair of discounted average payoffs in the infinitely repeated game when the discount factor is close to 1.

? EXERCISE 433.1 (Feasible payoff pairs in a *Prisoner's Dilemma*) Draw a diagram like Figure 433.1 showing the set of feasible payoff pairs for the *Prisoner's Dilemma* in Figure 429.1 when $y = 5$ and $x = 2$.

14.8.2 Nash equilibrium discounted average payoffs

We have seen that the feasible payoff pairs $(2, 2)$ and $(1, 1)$ can be achieved as discounted average payoffs pairs in Nash equilibria of the infinitely repeated *Prisoner's Dilemma* with payoffs as in Figure 420.1. Which other payoff pairs can be achieved in Nash equilibria when the discount factor is close to 1? Which pairs can be achieved in Nash equilibria of the infinitely repeated game of an arbitrary *Prisoner's Dilemma*?

By choosing D in every period of the infinitely repeated game, each player i can obtain a payoff of at least $u_i(D, D)$ in each period, and hence a discounted average payoff of at least $u_i(D, D)$. Thus in any Nash equilibrium of an infinitely repeated *Prisoner's Dilemma*, each player's discounted average payoff is at least $u_i(D, D)$.

I claim that the set of Nash equilibrium payoffs is essentially not otherwise restricted: if the discount factor is close enough to 1, then *every* feasible pair of payoffs in which each player's payoff is greater than $u_i(D, D)$ is close to the discounted average payoff pair of a Nash equilibrium.

To demonstrate this claim, let (x_1, x_2) be a feasible pair of payoffs in a *Prisoner's Dilemma* with $x_i > u_i(D, D)$ for $i = 1, 2$. Then by the definition of feasibility we can find a finite sequence $(a^1, \ldots, a^k)$ of outcomes of the game for which player i's average payoff approximates x_i, for $i = 1, 2$, as closely as we wish. (If the pair (x_1, x_2) of payoffs is a weighted average of pairs of payoffs to outcomes in which the weights are irrational numbers, we may not be able to find a finite sequence for which the average payoff of each player i is *exactly* x_i.)

Now consider the outcome path of the infinitely repeated game that consists of repetitions of the sequence $(a^1, \ldots, a^k)$. Denote this outcome path by $(b^1, b^2, \ldots)$. (That is, $b^{qk+t} = a^t$ for $q = 0, 1, \ldots$ and $t = 1, \ldots, k$.) For a discount factor close to 1, the discounted average payoff of each player i along this path is close to x_i.

I construct a strategy pair that generates the outcome path $(b^1, b^2, \ldots)$ and, for a discount factor close enough to 1, is a Nash equilibrium of the infinitely repeated game. The structure of each player's strategy resembles that of a grim trigger strategy: the player adheres to the path until the other player deviates, at which point she switches to "grim" punishment, choosing D in every subsequent period. Once punishment starts, the payoff of the other player, say j, is at most $u_j(D, D)$ in every period, so that for a discount factor close enough to 1, the threat of such punishment deters deviations, and the strategy pair is a Nash equilibrium.

Precisely, player i's strategy s_i chooses the action b_i^1 in the first period and, after any other history $(h^1, \ldots, h^{t-1})$, chooses the action

$$s_i(h^1, \ldots, h^{t-1}) = \begin{cases} b_i^t & \text{if } h_j^r = b_j^r \text{ for } r = 1, \ldots, t-1 \\ D & \text{otherwise,} \end{cases} \tag{434.1}$$

where j is the other player. If every player adheres to this strategy, then the outcome in each period t is b^t.

Why is (s_1, s_2) a Nash equilibrium when the discount factor is close to 1? Suppose that player 1 uses a strategy that, given s_2, deviates from the path $(b^1, b^2, \ldots)$ in some period, say t. Then from period $t+1$ on, player 1's payoff is at most $u_1(D, D)$. Now, $(b^1, b^2, \ldots)$ consists of repetitions of the sequence $(a^1, \ldots, a^k)$; suppose that period t is the ℓth period of this sequence. (Refer to Figure 434.1, where $w_1 = u_1(D, D)$.) In the period of her deviation, and in the following $k - \ell$ periods until the end of the sequence, player 1's payoff may be higher under her deviant strategy than it is under s_1. (The outcomes $a^{\ell+1}, \ldots, a^k$ may entail payoffs of less than $u_1(D, D)$ for her.) However, her average payoff in every subsequent $(a^1, \ldots, a^k)$ cycle is definitely less than her payoff when she uses s_1: her payoff in every period of every such cycle is at most $u_1(D, D)$, while her average payoff over each cycle under s_1 is greater than $u_1(D, D)$. If her discount factor is close enough to 1, these losses outweigh her (finite) gain in the period of her deviation and the following $k - \ell$ periods. The same logic applies to a deviation by player 2.

This argument establishes that for any feasible pair (x_1, x_2) of payoffs in a *Prisoner's Dilemma*, for a discount factor close enough to 1 the infinitely repeated game has a Nash equilibrium for which the pair of discounted average payoffs is approx-

	1 ... $\ell - 1$	ℓ	$\ell + 1$	...	k	1	...	k	1	...	k	...
s_1	Same	$u_1(a^\ell)$	$u_1(a^{\ell+1})$	...	$u_1(a^k)$	Average $> w_1$			Average $> w_1$			...
Dev.	outcome	v^ℓ	$\leq w_1$	...	$\leq w_1$	$\leq w_1$	...	$\leq w_1$	$\leq w_1$	...	$\leq w_1$	...

Figure 434.1 Player 1's payoffs when she uses the strategy s_1 and when she uses a strategy that, given that player 2 uses the strategy s_2, deviates from the path $(b^1, b^2, \ldots)$ for the first time in period ℓ, with $\ell \leq k$. Player 1's payoff in period ℓ, when she deviates, is v^ℓ; $w_1 = u_1(D, D)$.

imately (x_1, x_2). In fact, with more work we can dispense with the approximation and obtain the following result, one of several results known as "folk theorems" because their basic structure was understood long before proofs were published.

■ PROPOSITION 435.1 (Nash folk theorem for infinitely repeated *Prisoner's Dilemma*) *Let G be a Prisoner's Dilemma.*

- *For any discount factor δ with $0 < \delta < 1$, the discounted average payoff of each player i in any Nash equilibrium of the infinitely repeated game of G is at least $u_i(D, D)$.*

- *Let (x_1, x_2) be a feasible pair of payoffs in G for which $x_i > u_i(D, D)$ for each player i. There exists $\overline{\delta} < 1$ such that if the discount factor exceeds $\overline{\delta}$, then the infinitely repeated game of G has a Nash equilibrium in which the discounted average payoff of each player i is x_i.*

- *For any value of the discount factor, the infinitely repeated game of G has a Nash equilibrium in which the discounted average payoff of each player i is $u_i(D, D)$.*

You may wonder why the second part of this statement is not simpler: why do I not claim that any outcome path in which each player's discounted average payoff exceeds her payoff to (D, D) can be generated by a Nash equilibrium? The reason is simple: this claim is not true! Consider, for example, the outcome path $((C, C), (D, D), (D, D), \ldots)$ in which the outcome in every period but the first is (D, D). For any discount factor less than 1, each player's discounted average payoff exceeds her payoff to (D, D) on this path. However, no Nash equilibrium generates the path: a player who deviates to D in the first period obtains a higher payoff in the first period and at least the *same* payoff in every subsequent period, however her opponent behaves. (This argument is the same as the argument for the nonexistence of a Nash equilibrium in which either player chooses C in any period in a finitely repeated game (see Section 14.4.1).)

Figure 436.1 illustrates the set of discounted average payoffs generated by Nash equilibria of the infinitely repeated game of the *Prisoner's Dilemma* with payoffs as in Figure 420.1, as specified by Proposition 435.1. For every point (x_1, x_2) in the shaded set, by choosing the discount factor close enough to 1 we can ensure that there is a point as close as we want to (x_1, x_2) that is the pair of discounted average payoffs to a Nash equilibrium of the infinitely repeated game. The diagram makes it clear that the set of Nash equilibrium payoffs of the repeated game is large. The *Prisoner's Dilemma* has a unique Nash equilibrium, and hence a unique pair of Nash equilibrium payoffs, but the Nash equilibrium payoff pairs of the infinitely repeated game vary from dismal to jointly maximal.

The result does not say anything about the equilibrium *strategies*. The proof shows that the strategy pair in which each player "punishes" deviations by switching permanently to D is a Nash equilibrium but does not otherwise shed light on the equilibria. In any equilibrium in which a player chooses C in some period, the other player's strategy must deter a deviation to D by choosing D in some future

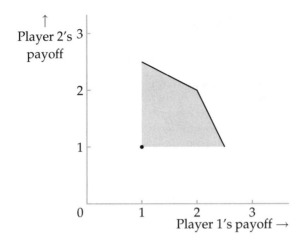

Figure 436.1 The approximate set of Nash equilibrium discounted average payoffs for the infinitely repeated *Prisoner's Dilemma* with payoffs as in Figure 420.1 when the discount factor is close to 1.

period in which, absent the deviation, it would have chosen C. In this sense, any equilibrium strategy entails "punishment". But as we saw in Section 14.7, when the players are patient, cooperative outcomes may be sustained by punishment considerably less harsh than "grim".

EXPERIMENTAL EVIDENCE

In January 1950, when John Nash was still a graduate student, Melvin Dresher and Merrill Flood devised the game now known as the *Prisoner's Dilemma* and conducted an experiment in which two of their friends played it 100 times in succession (see Flood 1958/59, 11). Dresher and Flood intended to test the notion of Nash equilibrium by viewing the 100 rounds as independent observations of an outcome of a *Prisoner's Dilemma* and looking at the number of periods in which the outcome was the unique equilibrium (D, D). Nash, in a comment reported on page 16 of Flood's paper, points out that the experiment should be viewed not as 100 independent plays of the *Prisoner's Dilemma*, but as a single 100-fold repeated game. He notes that in every Nash equilibrium of this finitely repeated game each player chooses D in every period (as we saw in Section 14.4.1). But he argues that the strategy pair in which each player uses the grim trigger strategy is "very nearly" an equilibrium, and *is* an equilibrium of a variant of the game with an infinite horizon. He goes on to argue that having 100 trials makes the game long enough that "one should expect an approximation to [the grim trigger strategy] . . . , with a little flurry of aggressiveness at the end and perhaps a few sallies, to test the opponent's mettle during the game." The subjects' behavior in the experiment seems to fit the framework Nash proposes. In 60 of the last 89 periods the outcome is (C, C). In all but two of these periods the outcome is consistent with player 2's using a "limited punishment" strategy in which the number of periods of punishment varies from 0 to 4, and player 1's using a strategy that chooses C most of the time but occasionally tries to get away with a one-period deviation to D which, if punished, is followed by plays of D until player 2 stops the punishment.

In this experiment, the two subjects played the game only once. Would experienced subjects have behaved differently? An experiment conducted among economics and business administration students at the University of Bielefeld, Germany, in the early 1980s examines one aspect of this question: As subjects gain experience playing a finitely repeated *Prisoner's Dilemma*, does the outcome approach the unique Nash equilibrium, in which (D, D) is played every period? Each of 35 subjects played a 10-period repeated *Prisoner's Dilemma* 25 times against changing opponents (Selten and Stoecker 1986). Almost all (96%) of the outcome paths of the last five repeated games played by each subject consist of at least four periods of (C, C), followed by a deviation to D by either one or both of the players, and then (D, D) in the remaining periods. Thus plausibly most subjects plan to play C initially, to play D once their opponent does so, and have in mind a period in which they intend to deviate to D if their opponent has not already done so. The experimenters deduce the intended deviation period for each player by studying the observed plays and the subjects' written comments during the game. They find that in the last 13 plays of the repeated game the mean intended period of deviation falls steadily from 9.2 to 7.4. As in the experiments on the "centipede game" discussed on page 234, the subjects' behavior is initially far from the unique Nash equilibrium, but slowly moves in the direction of this equilibrium. The results suggest that having 25 plays of the repeated game is not enough for the subjects' behavior to have stabilized and unfortunately does not give us any clue about the nature of stable behavior. Experiments involving more plays of the game are difficult (and expensive) to run, and the questions raised by Dresher and Flood's first experiment remain largely unanswered.

14.9 Subgame perfect equilibria and the one-deviation property

We know from our study of extensive games (Chapter 5) that a Nash equilibrium may entail threats that are not credible. The notion of subgame perfect equilibrium rules out such threats. The Nash equilibria of an infinitely repeated *Prisoner's Dilemma* studied in Section 14.7 that generate the outcome (C, C) in every period certainly entail threats. Indeed, their efficacy rests entirely on threats to "punish" the other player for a deviation from (C, C). Are these threats credible?

A strategy pair in an extensive game is a subgame perfect equilibrium if the strategy pair it induces in every subgame is a Nash equilibrium of the subgame. To check whether this condition is satisfied in a game with an arbitrary finite or infinite horizon can be difficult. In this section I describe a result that substantially simplifies the task. In the next section I use the result to study the subgame perfect equilibria of an infinitely repeated *Prisoner's Dilemma*.

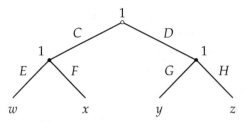

Figure 438.1 A one-player extensive game illustrating the result that a strategy profile satisfying the one-deviation property is a subgame perfect equilibrium.

I claim that a strategy profile in an extensive game with a finite horizon or in an infinitely repeated game with discounting is a subgame perfect equilibrium if and only if it satisfies the following condition.

> *One-deviation property*: no player can increase her payoff by changing her action at the start of any subgame in which she is the first-mover, *given* the other player's strategies *and* the rest of her own strategy.

If a strategy profile is a subgame perfect equilibrium, then certainly it satisfies the one-deviation property because no player can increase her payoff by *any* change in her strategy. To establish my claim, I need to show the converse: if a strategy profile satisfies the one-deviation property, then it is a subgame perfect equilibrium.

The main idea of the argument is illustrated by the one-player two-period game in Figure 438.1. Suppose that the strategy CEG satisfies the one-deviation property. Then the player cannot increase her payoff by switching from E to F in the subgame following C (this subgame is only one period long), so that $w \geq x$, and similarly cannot increase her payoff by switching from G to H in the subgame following D, so that $y \geq z$. Further, she cannot increase her payoff in the whole game (the subgame following $\varnothing$) by switching from C to D at the start of the game, while holding the rest of her strategy fixed (and hence choosing G after the history D). Thus $w \geq y$. We conclude that $w \geq z$, so that the remaining possible changes in her strategy, from CEG to DEH or DFH (which involve deviations in both periods) are not profitable. Thus CEG is a subgame perfect equilibrium. We see that the assumption that the player cannot increase her payoff by changing her action only at the beginning of any subgame leads to the conclusion that she cannot increase her payoff by any change in her strategy, because any change in her strategy can be broken into a sequence of one-period changes.

This argument does not depend on the presence of a single player, because the notion of subgame perfect equilibrium (like the notion of Nash equilibrium) involves the consideration only of deviations by a single player *given* the other players' strategies. It also does not depend on the length of the game's being 2, but applies to any game with a finite horizon. Thus we have the following result (for which I omit a precise proof).

■ PROPOSITION 438.1 (One-deviation property of subgame perfect equilibria of finite horizon games) *A strategy profile in an extensive game with perfect information and a finite horizon is a subgame perfect equilibrium if and only if it satisfies the one-deviation property.*

⑦ EXERCISE 439.1 (Finitely repeated *Prisoner's Dilemma* with switching cost) Use this result to study the subgame perfect equilibria of the variant of the model of a *finitely* repeated *Prisoner's Dilemma* with discount factor 1 in which a player incurs the cost $\epsilon > 0$ in any period in which her action differs from her action in the previous period. Consider a *Prisoner's Dilemma* in which the payoffs are $(3,3)$ to (C,C), $(0,4)$ to (C,D), $(4,0)$ to (D,C), and $(2,2)$ to (D,D).

    a. Show that the strategy pair in which each player chooses C at the start of the game and after any history that ends with (C,C), and otherwise chooses D, is a subgame perfect equilibrium of the finitely repeated game when $1 < \epsilon < 2$.

    b. Find a subgame perfect equilibrium of the finitely repeated game that generates the outcome (C,C) in every period when $2 < \epsilon < 3$.

In working back from the last period, the argument for Proposition 438.1 does, however, rely on the finiteness of the horizon and does not immediately apply to infinitely repeated games. But given a discount factor less than 1, it can be modified to cover such games. The modification consists of arguing that if some player i has a strategy s_i' that yields her a payoff larger than her payoff to her strategy s_i, given the other players' strategies, then she also has a strategy s_i'' that yields her a payoff larger than her payoff to s_i *and*, for some large enough value of T, coincides with s_i after period T. The reason is that given that the discount factor is less than 1, payoffs in the sufficiently distant future are worth very little, so even if s_i' induces the best possible outcome for player i in every period after T and s_i induces the worst possible outcome in every such period, for T sufficiently large the difference between their contributions to the player's discounted average payoff in the game is arbitrarily small. The coincidence of s_i'' and s_i after period T allows us to work back from period T as we worked back from the end of the game in Figure 438.1.

A precise statement of the result for infinitely repeated games follows. (I omit a precise proof.)

∎ PROPOSITION 439.2 (One-deviation property of subgame perfect equilibria of infinitely repeated games) *A strategy profile in an infinitely repeated game with a discount factor less than 1 is a subgame perfect equilibrium if and only if it satisfies the one-deviation property.*

AXELROD'S TOURNAMENTS

In the late 1970s, Robert Axelrod (a political scientist at the University of Michigan) invited some economists, psychologists, mathematicians, and sociologists familiar with the repeated *Prisoner's Dilemma* to submit strategies (written in computer code) for a finitely repeated *Prisoner's Dilemma* with payoffs of $(3,3)$ for

(C,C), $(5,0)$ for (D,C), $(0,5)$ for (C,D), and $(1,1)$ for (D,D). He received 14 entries, which he pitted against each other and against a strategy that randomly chooses C and D each with probability $\frac{1}{2}$, in 200-fold repetitions of the game. He paired each strategy against each of the others five times. (Strategies could involve random choices, so a pair of strategies could generate different outcomes when paired repeatedly.) The strategy with the highest payoff was *tit-for-tat* (submitted by Anatol Rapoport, a member of the Department of Psychology of the University of Toronto). (See Axelrod 1980a, 1984.)

Axelrod subsequently ran a second tournament. He invited the participants in the first tournament to compete again and also recruited entrants by advertising in journals read by microcomputer users (a relatively small crowd in the early 1980s). Contestants were informed of the results of the first round. Sixty-two strategies were submitted. The contest was run slightly differently this time: the length of each game was determined probabilistically. Again *tit-for-tat* (again submitted by Anatol Rapoport) won. (See Axelrod 1980b, 1984.)

Axelrod used the strategies submitted in his second tournament to simulate an evolutionary environment in which strategies that do well reproduce faster than other strategies. He repeatedly matched the strategies against each other, increasing the number of representatives of strategies that achieved high payoffs. A strategy that obtained a high payoff initially might, under these conditions, have obtained a low one subsequently if the opponents against which it did well became less numerous. Axelrod found that after a large number of "generations", *tit-for-tat* had the most representatives in the population.

Intriguing as they are, Axelrod's results are not robust. A theoretical result shows that any limit point of a dynamic process like Axelrod's is a Nash equilibrium of the game in which each player's strategy set consists of all the strategies in the initial population (Nachbar 1992, Proposition 1). Thus the limit point of such a dynamic process for a finitely repeated *Prisoner's Dilemma* is the strategy pair in which each player chooses D after every history whenever this strategy is in the initial population. Only if this strategy is absent from the initial population (as in Axelrod's tournament) can another strategy come to dominate. Axelrod's simulation is also limited in not allowing for mutation. Variants of his simulation show that a variety of strategies other than *tit-for-tat* can come to dominate a population in evolutionary competition, depending on the assumptions (see, for example, Hirshleifer and Martinez Coll 1988, Linster 1992, 1994, and Nowak and Sigmund 1992). The work of Nachbar (1992) suggests, however, that these simulations must be treated with caution. Nachbar simulates the evolution of the strategies used in a six-period *Prisoner's Dilemma*. He includes in the initial population the strategy that always defects, so that this strategy is the only possible limit point of his process. Yet the path that leads to this limit point is far from monotone and includes long stretches in which another strategy comes extremely close to dominating the population. If the same behavior occurred in an environment in which we had no theoretical result concerning the limit point, we might reach various false conclusions, depending on the number of periods used in the simulation.

As we have seen, an *infinitely* repeated *Prisoner's Dilemma* has a wide range of Nash equilibrium payoff pairs. Does the theory of evolutionary games (Chapter 13) offer insights into the strategies that might be expected to survive in an evolutionary competition? Unfortunately, the standard notion of an evolutionarily stable strategy cannot be straightforwardly applied to an infinitely repeated game, and well-defined variants of the notion yield a variety of results: either an infinitely repeated *Prisoner's Dilemma* has no ESS, or the only ESS is the strategy that chooses *D* in every period regardless of history, or every feasible pair of payoffs can be sustained by some pair of ESSs (Kim 1994).

14.10 Some subgame perfect equilibria of an infinitely repeated *Prisoner's Dilemma*

Are the Nash equilibria of an infinitely repeated *Prisoner's Dilemma* we considered in Section 14.7 subgame perfect equilibria? Clearly the Nash equilibrium in which each player chooses *D* after every history is a subgame perfect equilibrium: whatever happens, each player chooses *D*, so it is optimal for the other player to do likewise.

In the other Nash equilibria we studied, each player is induced to choose *C* by the other player's "threat" to punish a deviation from *C* by choosing *D* subsequently. For the equilibria to be subgame perfect, these threats must be credible: each player must have an incentive to punish the other player if she deviates.

14.10.1   Grim trigger strategies

I claim that the strategy pair in which each player uses the grim trigger strategy (Figure 427.1) is *not* a subgame perfect equilibrium of the infinitely repeated game of the *Prisoner's Dilemma* in Figure 420.1 for any value of the discount factor.

Consider the subgame following the outcome (C, D) in the first period. Suppose that player 1 adheres to the grim trigger strategy in the subgame. I argue that subsequent adherence to the grim trigger strategy is not optimal for player 2.

- If player 2 also adheres to the grim trigger strategy, then the outcome is (D, C) in the first period of the subgame (player 1 initiates punishment of player 2, while player 2 sticks with *C*, given that player 1 did not deviate in the first period). In every subsequent period of the subgame the outcome is (D, D), so that player 2's discounted average payoff in the subgame is

$$(1 - \delta)(0 + \delta + \delta^2 + \delta^3 + \cdots) = \delta.$$

- If player 2 deviates from the grim trigger strategy and chooses *D* in every period of the subgame, then the outcome is (D, D) in every period of the subgame, and her discounted average payoff is 1.

Thus player 2, having deviated to D, and knowing that this deviation will induce player 1 to punish her subsequently by playing D, prefers to choose D in every period of the subgame, rather than choosing C in the first period. Hence the strategy pair in which both players adhere to the grim trigger strategy is not a subgame perfect equilibrium.

In fact, in the subgame following a deviation by a single player, *both* players have an incentive to deviate if the discount factor is high enough. As we have seen, the deviator has an incentive to continue to choose D rather than C in the period after her deviation. In addition, if $\delta > \frac{1}{2}$, the other player is better off ignoring the deviation and continuing to choose C, with the result that the deviator also reverts to C, rather than initiating punishment. The following exercise asks you to verify this fact.

? EXERCISE 442.1 (Deviations from grim trigger strategy) Show that in the subgame following the outcome (C, D) in the first period of an infinitely repeated *Prisoner's Dilemma* with payoffs as in Figure 420.1 and $\delta > \frac{1}{2}$, player 1 is better off choosing C in every subsequent period than she is adhering to the grim trigger strategy.

However, a variant of the grim trigger strategy *is* a subgame perfect equilibrium strategy if $\delta \geq \frac{1}{2}$. Consider the strategy in which a player chooses D after any history in which *either* player chose D in some period. This strategy is illustrated in Figure 442.1. If both players adopt this strategy, then in the subgame following a deviation, the miscreant chooses D in every period (she does not wait for the other player to deviate), so that her opponent is better off "punishing" her by choosing D than she is choosing C. The point is that (D, D) is a Nash equilibrium of a *Prisoner's Dilemma*, so that neither player has any quarrel with the prescription to choose D after any history in which some player chose D. The fact that the strategy specifies that a player choose D after any history in which she deviated means that the other player optimally punishes her, and because she is punished she optimally chooses D. Effectively, a player's strategy "punishes" her opponent—by choosing D—if her opponent does not "punish" her for deviating.

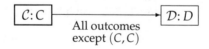

Figure 442.1 The modified grim trigger strategy for an infinitely repeated *Prisoner's Dilemma*.

To show precisely that the strategy pair in which each player uses the modified grim trigger strategy in Figure 442.1 is a subgame perfect equilibrium if $\delta \geq \frac{1}{2}$, we can use Proposition 439.2. Given that both players use this strategy, the outcome path in any subgame consists of either (C, C) in every period (if the subgame follows the initial history or a history in which the outcome was (C, C) in every period) or (D, D) in every period (otherwise). The following arguments show that in each case neither player has an incentive to change her action in the first period of the subgame, given the remainder of her strategy and her opponent's strategy, so that by Proposition 439.2 the strategy pair is a subgame perfect equilibrium.

Subgame following the initial history or a history consisting of (C,C) in each period When both players follow the modified grim trigger strategy in the subgame, the outcome is (C,C) in every period, yielding each player a discounted average payoff of 2. If player 1 deviates from the strategy and chooses D in the first period of the subgame, but otherwise follows the strategy, then the outcome is (D,C) in the first period of the subgame and (D,D) subsequently. This outcome path yields player 1 the discounted average payoff of $(1-\delta)(3+\delta+\delta^2+\delta^3+\cdots) = 3-2\delta$. Thus the deviation is not profitable if $3-2\delta \leq 2$, or $\delta \geq \frac{1}{2}$. A similar argument applies to a deviation by player 2.

Any other subgame When both players follow the modified grim trigger strategy in any other subgame, the outcome is (D,D) in every period, yielding each player a discounted average payoff of 1. For any discount factor, no player can profitably deviate from the strategy and choose C in the first period of the subgame because (D,D) is a Nash equilibrium of the game, and choosing C rather than D has no effect on the subsequent outcomes.

? EXERCISE 443.1 (Delayed modified grim trigger strategies) Choose a positive integer k and consider the strategy that chooses D in the first k periods of the game, regardless of the history, and then follows the modified grim trigger strategy, starting in state C. Find the range of values for the discount factor for which the strategy pair in which each player uses this strategy is a subgame perfect equilibrium.

14.10.2 Limited punishment

The strategy pair in which each player uses the limited punishment strategy studied in Section 14.7.2 is not a subgame perfect equilibrium of the infinitely repeated *Prisoner's Dilemma* for the same reason that a pair of grim trigger strategies is not a subgame perfect equilibrium. However, we can modify the limited punishment strategy in the same way that we modified the grim trigger strategy to obtain a subgame perfect equilibrium for high enough values of δ. Specifically, we need the transition from state P_0 to state P_1 in Figure 427.2 to occur whenever *either* player chooses D (not just whenever the *other* player chooses D). A player using this modified strategy chooses D during her punishment, which both is optimal for her and makes the other player's choice to punish optimal if δ is large enough. When the punishment ends, she, like her punisher, reverts to C.

? EXERCISE 443.2 (Different punishment lengths in subgame perfect equilibrium) Does an infinitely repeated *Prisoner's Dilemma* (with payoffs as in Figure 420.1) have any subgame perfect equilibrium, for any value of δ, in which each player's strategy involves limited punishment but the lengths of the punishment are different for each player? If so, describe such a subgame perfect equilibrium; if not, argue why not.

14.10.3 Tit-for-tat

The behavior in a subgame of a player who uses the strategy *tit-for-tat* depends only on the last outcome in the history that precedes the subgame. Thus to examine whether the strategy pair in which both players use the strategy *tit-for-tat* is a subgame perfect equilibrium, we need to consider four types of subgame, following histories in which the last outcome is (C, C), (C, D), (D, C), and (D, D).

The optimality of *tit-for-tat* for each player in a subgame following a history ending in (C, C), given that the other player uses *tit-for-tat*, is covered by our analysis of Nash equilibrium: *tit-for-tat* is a best response to *tit-for-tat* in such a subgame if and only if $\delta \geq \frac{1}{2}$.

To study subgames following histories ending in other outcomes, I appeal, as before, to the fact that a strategy pair is a subgame perfect equilibrium if and only if it satisfies the one-deviation property (Proposition 439.2).

History ending in (C, D) Suppose that player 2 adheres to *tit-for-tat*. If player 1 also adheres to *tit-for-tat*, then the outcome alternates between (D, C) and (C, D), and player 1's discounted average payoff in the subgame is

$$(1 - \delta)(3 + 3\delta^2 + 3\delta^4 + \cdots) = (1 - \delta)\left(\frac{3}{1 - \delta^2}\right) = \frac{3}{1 + \delta}.$$

If player 1 instead chooses C in the first period of the subgame, and subsequently adheres to *tit-for-tat*, then the outcome is (C, C) in every period of the subgame, so that player 1's discounted average payoff is 2. Thus a single deviation from *tit-for-tat* in the first period of such a subgame is unprofitable for player 1 if and only if

$$\frac{3}{1 + \delta} \geq 2, \text{ or } \delta \leq \tfrac{1}{2}.$$

Now suppose that player 1 adheres to *tit-for-tat*. If player 2 also adheres to *tit-for-tat*, the outcome alternates between (D, C) and (C, D), and player 2's discounted average payoff in the subgame is

$$(1 - \delta)(3\delta + 3\delta^3 + 3\delta^5 + \cdots) = (1 - \delta)\left(\frac{3\delta}{1 - \delta^2}\right) = \frac{3\delta}{1 + \delta}.$$

If player 2 instead chooses D in the first period of the subgame, and subsequently adheres to *tit-for-tat*, then the outcome is (D, D) in every period of the subgame, so that player 2's discounted average payoff is 1. Thus a single deviation from *tit-for-tat* in the first period of such a subgame is unprofitable for player 2 if and only if

$$\frac{3\delta}{1 + \delta} \geq 1, \text{ or } \delta \geq \tfrac{1}{2}.$$

History ending in (D, C)   The argument is the same as for a history ending in (C, D), except that the roles of the players are reversed. Thus a single deviation from *tit-for-tat* in the first period of such a subgame is unprofitable for each player if and only if $\delta = \frac{1}{2}$.

History ending in (D, D)   The outcome is (D, D) in every period if both players adhere to *tit-for-tat*, yielding each player a discounted average payoff of 1. If either player deviates to C in the first period of the subgame, and subsequently adheres to *tit-for-tat*, the outcome alternates between (C, D) and (D, C), yielding the deviant a discounted average payoff of $3\delta/(1+\delta)$. Thus a single deviation from *tit-for-tat* in the first period of such a subgame is unprofitable for each player if and only if $\delta \leq \frac{1}{2}$.

We conclude that (*tit-for-tat*, *tit-for-tat*) is a subgame perfect equilibrium of the infinitely repeated *Prisoner's Dilemma* with payoffs as in Figure 420.1 if and only if $\delta = \frac{1}{2}$.

We can easily find other payoffs for the *Prisoner's Dilemma* such that (*tit-for-tat*, *tit-for-tat*) is not a subgame perfect equilibrium of the infinitely repeated game for *any* value of δ. The next exercise asks you to establish a precise result to this effect.

⑦ EXERCISE 445.1 (*Tit-for-tat* as a subgame perfect equilibrium) Consider the infinitely repeated *Prisoner's Dilemma* in which the payoffs of the component game are those given in Figure 429.1. Show that (*tit-for-tat*, *tit-for-tat*) is a subgame perfect equilibrium of this infinitely repeated game with discount factor δ if and only if $y - x = 1$ and $\delta = 1/x$. (Use Proposition 439.2.)

RECIPROCAL ALTRUISM AMONG STICKLEBACKS

Perhaps more than any other idea in game theory, the possibility of sustaining cooperation in repeated interactions by retaliatory strategies has caught the interest of students of human and animal behavior. Some biologists, in particular, have embraced the theory as an explanation for "altruistic" behavior in animals.

Robert L. Trivers first argued that cooperative outcomes, supported by what he termed "reciprocal altruism", can result from evolutionary pressure; he credits William D. Hamilton with proposing a game-theoretic implementation of this idea (see Trivers 1971, 39). Axelrod's tournaments (see the box on page 439) interested researchers in the field in the strategy *tit-for-tat*. Nowak and Sigmund (1993) write that "The Prisoner's Dilemma is the leading metaphor for the evolution of cooperative behavior in populations of selfish agents", and after Axelrod's tournaments, *tit-for-tat* "became the major paradigm for reciprocal altruism."

A much discussed example involves predator inspection by sticklebacks (*Gasterosteus aculeatus*). Sticklebacks often approach a predator in pairs, the members of a pair taking turns to be the first to move forward a few centimeters. (Approaching a predator closely is advantageous because it allows a stickleback to obtain information about the predator.) The process can be modeled as a repeated *Prisoner's Dilemma*, in which moving forward is analogous to cooperating and holding back is like defecting. Milinski (1987) reports an experiment in which he put a stickleback into one compartment of a tank and a cichlid, which resembles a perch, a common predator of sticklebacks, in another compartment, separated by glass. In one condition he placed a mirror along one side of the tank (a "cooperating mirror"), so that as the stickleback approached the predator it had the impression that there was another stickleback mimicking its actions, as if following the strategy *tit-for-tat*. In a second condition he placed the mirror at an angle (a "defecting mirror"), so that a stickleback that approached the cichlid had the impression that there was another stickleback that was increasingly holding back. He found that the stickleback approached the cichlid much more closely with a cooperating mirror than it did with a defecting mirror. With a defecting mirror, the apparent second stickleback held back when the real one moved forward, and disappeared entirely when the real stickleback moved into the front half of the tank—that is, it tended to defect. Milinski interprets the behavior of the real stickleback as consistent with the strategy *tit-for-tat*. The same behavior has subsequently been observed in guppies (*Poecilia reticulata*) approaching a pumpkinseed sunfish (Dugatkin 1988, 1991).

This evidence, while not strong, suggests that the fish might at least be following some retaliatory strategy. Milinski (1993) suggests that further evidence indicates that the strategy may be closer to *Pavlov* (see Exercise 431.2) than to *tit-for-tat*.

14.11 Subgame perfect equilibrium payoffs of an infinitely repeated *Prisoner's Dilemma*

In Section 14.8 we saw that the set of Nash equilibrium payoffs of an infinitely repeated *Prisoner's Dilemma* is large. Specifically, for every feasible pair (x_1, x_2) of payoffs in the *Prisoner's Dilemma* for which $x_i > u_i(D, D)$ for each player i, the infinitely repeated game has a Nash equilibrium in which the discounted average payoffs are close to (x_1, x_2) when the players are sufficiently patient (Proposition 435.1).

Every subgame perfect equilibrium is a Nash equilibrium, so the set of subgame perfect equilibrium payoff pairs is a subset of the set of Nash equilibrium payoff pairs. We have seen that the grim trigger strategy, while not itself a subgame perfect equilibrium strategy, can be modified to make credible the punishments it imposes. This strategy is the key element in the proof of the Nash equilibrium folk theorem (Proposition 435.1), so we might conjecture that the set of subgame perfect equilibrium payoff pairs is exactly the same as the set of Nash equilibrium payoff pairs. I now argue that this conjecture is correct.

As in the argument for Proposition 435.1, let (x_1, x_2) be a feasible pair of payoffs in the *Prisoner's Dilemma* with $x_i > u_i(D, D)$ for $i = 1, 2$, let $(a^1, \ldots, a^k)$ be a finite sequence of outcomes of the *Prisoner's Dilemma* for which player i's average payoff approximates x_i for $i = 1, 2$, and denote the outcome path of the infinitely repeated game that consists of repetitions of the sequence $(a^1, \ldots, a^k)$ by $(b^1, b^2, \ldots)$. Denote by s_i the strategy of player i that adheres to the path $(b^1, b^2, \ldots)$ until either she or the other player deviates, at which point she switches to "grim" punishment, choosing D in every subsequent period. Neither player i has an incentive to deviate from the path because her payoff during the punishment phase is at most $u_i(D, D)$ in every period. Further, neither player has an incentive to deviate during the punishment phase because during this phase *both* players choose D, regardless of history.

Precisely, s_i chooses the action b_i^1 in the first period and, after any other history $(h^1, \ldots, h^{t-1})$, chooses the action

$$
s_i(h^1, \ldots, h^{t-1}) = \begin{cases} b_i^t & \text{if } h^r = b^r \text{ for } r = 1, \ldots, t-1 \\ D & \text{otherwise,} \end{cases}
$$

where j is the other player. (Note that the condition for this strategy to choose b^t in period t is that in every previous period r we have $h^r = b^r$, not merely $h_j^r = b_j^r$ as in (434.1).) If every player adheres to this strategy, then the outcome in each period t is b^t.

I claim that (s_1, s_2) is a subgame perfect equilibrium of the infinitely repeated game when the discount factor is close to 1. By Proposition 439.2 we need to show that neither player can gain by deviating only in the first period of any subgame. The game has two types of subgame.

Subgames following a history $(b^1, \ldots, b^{t-1})$ for some t The argument that player i cannot profitably deviate from the prescription of s_i to choose b_i^t after such a history is the same as the argument in the proof of Proposition 435.1 that player i cannot profitably deviate from the strategy defined in (434.1).

Subgames following other histories In any other history of length $t - 1$, at least one of the players deviated from the path $(b^1, \ldots, b^{t-1})$ at some point. Thus each player's strategy calls for her to choose D in every subsequent period. Because (D, D) is a Nash equilibrium of the *Prisoner's Dilemma*, neither player can gain by deviating from s_i in the first period of such a subgame: a deviation entails a loss in the period it is carried out, and no subsequent gain.

As in the case of Nash equilibrium, additional arguments allow us to dispense with the approximation, yielding the following result.

■ PROPOSITION 447.1 (Subgame perfect folk theorem for infinitely repeated *Prisoner's Dilemma*) *Let G be a Prisoner's Dilemma.*

- *For any discount factor δ with $0 < \delta < 1$, the discounted average payoff of each player i in any subgame perfect equilibrium of the infinitely repeated game of G is at least $u_i(D, D)$.*

- Let (x_1, x_2) be a feasible pair of payoffs in G for which $x_i > u_i(D, D)$ for each player i. There exists $\bar{\delta} < 1$ such that if the discount factor exceeds $\bar{\delta}$, then the infinitely repeated game of G has a subgame perfect equilibrium in which the discounted average payoff of each player i is x_i.

- For any value of the discount factor, the infinitely repeated game of G has a subgame perfect equilibrium in which the discounted average payoff of each player i is $u_i(D, D)$.

MEDIEVAL TRADE FAIRS

In 12th and 13th century Europe, most long distance-trade took place at "fairs". A transaction between merchants from regions with different currencies typically involved a transfer of goods in exchange for a promissory note to be paid at the next fair. For such trade to flourish in the absence of a well-developed legal system, mechanisms had to exist to give buyers incentives to live up to their promises.

Our analysis of a repeated game shows that if two parties interact repeatedly, mutually beneficial outcomes can be supported by strategies that "punish" cheaters. This model, however, is not well suited to a medieval trade fair, in which no party traded repeatedly with any other given party. But the ideas can be adapted to fit this situation. Consider a set of traders who are matched into pairs each period. If each trader knows the history of her partner's actions, then she can "punish" this partner for past transgressions, even transgressions that were directed against some other trader. Precisely, suppose that we model the game between each pair of traders as a *Prisoner's Dilemma*, with every player using the strategy that chooses C initially and in any period t for which both she and her partners in all periods through t chose C in all previous periods, and otherwise chooses D. Then no player has an incentive to deviate from the strategy after any history, by the argument we used to show that the modified grim trigger strategy is a subgame perfect equilibrium strategy in a standard infinitely repeated game. Further, the outcome is (C, C) in every period.

This argument shows that "community enforcement" can support the cooperative outcome in an environment in which no player interacts repeatedly with any other given player. But it makes a demanding informational assumption: each player must know the entire history of each of her partner's actions. This assumption seems unreasonable in the context of medieval trade fairs.

Milgrom, North, and Weingast (1990) show that the basic idea, however, can be used to drive a model with more more meager informational demands. They introduce an additional actor, L, who keeps track of traders' records and awards damages to aggrieved parties. This additional actor plays the role of one of the courts that adjudicated disputes at medieval fairs within the framework of the code of procedures known as the *Law Merchant* (or *Lex Mercatoria*). In Milgrom et al.'s model, no trader is required to know any other trader's history. In each period, after traders are matched, each trader may pay L to check whether her current partner has any unpaid damages assessed against her. Then the traders play a *Prisoner's Dilemma*, and a trader whose partner chose D may appeal, at a cost, to L if she initially submitted a query. If exactly one trader chooses D and at least one of them appeals, L asks the trader who chose D to pay damages to her partner. Finally, a trader who is assessed a penalty decides whether to pay up; if she does not, L notes the nonpayment in her records.

Milgrom et al. show that if the costs of querying and appealing to L are not too high and the players are sufficiently patient, there is a strategy that supports honest trade: each trader chooses C in every period. Under the strategy, a trader who chooses D is assessed a penalty by L; if she does not pay this penalty, her future trading partners will find out when they query L, and will choose D when they trade with her. The strategy induces traders to query L by specifying D to be the action of partners of ones who fail to submit a query.

The actor L in this model collects just enough information to allow effective punishment strategies to be implemented. The model nicely illuminates the role of the institution of the courts, which were much more effective at publicizing dishonest behavior than they were at punishing it, in allowing mutually beneficial decentralized trade to take place. Milgrom et al. give several examples of other mechanisms for spreading information that played a role in maintaining socially desirable outcomes. They write that "the use of the 'hue and cry' to identify cheaters in medieval England; the famed 'Scarlett Letter', described in Hawthorne's famous story; and the public stocks and pillories of 17th century New England ... are all examples of institutions and practices in which a principal aim is to convey information to the community about who has violated its norms" (1990, 19).

14.12 Concluding remarks

Our analysis confirms the intuition that when patient decision-makers repeatedly play the *Prisoner's Dilemma*, mutually retaliatory strategies support as an equilibrium the outcome path consisting of the repeated play of the desirable outcome (C, C). We have seen that these strategies can be designed so that each decision-maker has an incentive to carry out the "punishment" for deviations necessary to sustain cooperation—that is, the cooperative outcome path can be supported as a subgame perfect equilibrium. We have also seen that many other outcome paths may be supported as subgame perfect equilibria. In the next chapter, we see that similar results hold for general repeated games.

Notes

In a comment on an experiment of Dresher and Flood (see page 436), Nash argues that a finitely repeated *Prisoner's Dilemma* has a unique Nash equilibrium and that the strategy pair in which each player uses the grim trigger strategy is a Nash equilibrium of an infinitely repeated game (see Flood 1958/59, note 11 on page 16). Luce and Raiffa (1957, pages 97–105 and Appendix 8) elaborate on Nash's arguments, as does Shubik (1959b, Chapter 10, especially page 226), who points to the key idea of the Nash folk theorem (Proposition 435.1). Friedman (1971) further develops the theory. The subgame perfect folk theorem (Proposition 447.1) is an implication of the results of Fudenberg and Maskin (1986, 1991), which build on results established by Aumann and Shapley and by Rubinstein in the mid-1970s (see Aumann and Shapley 1994 and Rubinstein 1979, 1994).

The box on page 436 is based on Flood (1958/59) and Selten and Stoecker (1986), the box on page 439 is based on Axelrod (1980a, 1980b, 1984), Hirshleifer and Martinez Coll (1988), Linster (1992, 1994), Nachbar (1992), Nowak and Sigmund (1992), and Kim (1994), the box on page 445 is based on Milinski (1987, 1993), and the box on page 448 is based on Milgrom, North, and Weingast (1990) and conversations with John Munro.

The strategy *Pavlov* (Exercise 428.1) is studied from an evolutionary perspective by Nowak and Sigmund (1993). The implications of switching costs in finitely repeated games, of which Exercise 439.1 is an example, are studied by Lipman and Wang (2000). The result in Exercise 445.1 is an implication of the more general results of Kalai, Samet, and Stanford (1988).

15 Repeated Games: General Results

15.1 Nash equilibria of general infinitely repeated games   451
15.2 Subgame perfect equilibria of general infinitely repeated
     games   455
15.3 Finitely repeated games   460
15.4 Variation on a theme: imperfect observability   461
     Prerequisite: Chapter 14

THE BASIC IDEA explored in the previous chapter is that "cooperative" outcome paths may be generated by equilibria of an infinitely repeated *Prisoner's Dilemma* that involve strategies that impose "punishments" for deviations. In this chapter I discuss extensions of this result to a large class of infinitely repeated games and consider also general finitely repeated games.

15.1 Nash equilibria of general infinitely repeated games

In an infinitely repeated *Prisoner's Dilemma*, player i cannot be deterred from deviating from a path that yields her a discounted average payoff of less than $u_i(D,D)$ starting in some period t. Why not? Because she can *guarantee* herself a payoff of at least $u_i(D,D)$ in period t and subsequently by choosing D regardless of history: no strategy of the other player can force her payoff below $u_i(D,D)$ in any period.

Conversely, if player i is sufficiently patient, then she *can* be deterred from deviating from any path that, for each period t, yields her a discounted average payoff of more than $u_i(D,D)$ starting in period t. One strategy of her opponent that provides the necessary deterrence is the grim trigger strategy, which starts by following the path and switches permanently to D in the first period in which player i deviates from this path. If player j follows this strategy, then a deviation by player i that yields her the payoff v_i in period t generates for her a discounted average payoff in the subgame starting in period t equal to at most

$$(1-\delta)(v_i + \delta u_i(D,D) + \delta^2 u_i(D,D) + \cdots) = (1-\delta)v_i + \delta u_i(D,D),$$

which can be made as close as we wish to $u_i(D,D)$ by taking δ close enough to 1. By assumption, the path yields her more than $u_i(D,D)$, so if she is sufficiently patient the deviation makes her worse off.

We see that the twofold significance of $u_i(D,D)$ in the infinitely repeated *Prisoner's Dilemma* is that (*a*) player i can ensure that her payoff is at least $u_i(D,D)$ in every period, and (*b*) the other player can ensure (by choosing *D*) that player *i*'s payoff in any period does not exceed $u_i(D, D)$. That is, $u_i(D, D)$ is the lowest payoff that the other player can force upon player *i*.

This argument suggests that to generalize the Nash folk theorem (Proposition 435.1) to the infinitely repeated game of an arbitrary strategic game, we need to define the lowest payoff that can be forced upon each player in any strategic game. Denote the set of actions of each player *j* by A_j. For any collection a_{-i} of actions for the players other than *i*, player *i*'s highest possible payoff is her payoff when she chooses a best response to a_{-i}, namely

$$\max_{a_i \in A_i} u_i(a_i, a_{-i}).$$

As a_{-i} varies, this maximal payoff varies. We seek a collection a_{-i} of actions that make this maximum as small as possible. That is, we seek a solution to the problem

$$\min_{a_{-i} \in A_{-i}} \left(\max_{a_i \in A_i} u_i(a_i, a_{-i}) \right).$$

This payoff is known as player *i*'s *minmax* payoff.

▷ DEFINITION 452.1 (*Minmax payoff in strategic game*) Player *i*'s **minmax** payoff in a strategic game is

$$\min_{a_{-i} \in A_{-i}} \left(\max_{a_i \in A_i} u_i(a_i, a_{-i}) \right), \tag{452.2}$$

where for each player *j*, A_j is *j*'s set of actions and u_j is her payoff function.

(Note that this definition involves only actions, not mixed strategies.)

In the *Prisoner's Dilemma* with the payoffs in Figure 420.1, for example, each player's minmax payoff is 1; in *BoS* (Example 18.2) each player's minmax payoff is also 1.

❓ EXERCISE 452.3 (Minmax payoffs) Find each player's minmax payoff in each of the following games.

a. The game of dividing money in Exercise 38.2.

b. Cournot's oligopoly game (Section 3.1) when $C_i(0) = 0$ for each firm *i* and $P(Q) = 0$ for some sufficiently large value of *Q*.

c. Hotelling's model of electoral competition (Section 3.3) when (*i*) there are two candidates and (*ii*) there are three candidates, under the assumptions that the set of possible positions is the interval $[0, 1]$, the distribution of the candidates' favorite positions has a unique median, a tie results in each candidate's winning with probability $\frac{1}{2}$, and each candidate's payoff is her probability of winning.

I claim that for any strategic game *G*, in no Nash equilibrium of the infinitely repeated game of *G* is any player's discounted average payoff less than her minmax payoff. The argument is simple: any player *i* can ensure that her payoff in every period is at least her minmax payoff by using a strategy that, after every history h, chooses a best response to $s_{-i}(h)$, the collection of actions prescribed by the other players' strategies after the history h.

Our argument for the infinitely repeated *Prisoner's Dilemma* suggests that, conversely, for any strategic game G, any outcome path that, for each period t, yields each player a discounted average payoff of more than her minmax payoff in the path starting in period t can be supported as a Nash equilibrium of the infinitely repeated game of G if the players are sufficiently patient.

I now prove this result for an outcome path that consists of the *same* outcome of G in every period. Precisely, I argue that if a is an action profile of G for which $u_i(a)$ exceeds i's minmax payoff for every player i, then for a discount factor close enough to 1, the path $(a, a, a, \ldots)$ is the outcome of a Nash equilibrium of the infinitely repeated game of G in which each player uses a grim trigger strategy that imposes permanent punishment on the first player to deviate from the path in a period in which exactly one player deviated.

For each player i, let p_{-i} be a collection of actions for the players other than i that holds player i down to her minmax payoff. (That is, p_{-i} is a solution of the minimization problem (452.2).) Define a strategy for each player i as follows. Choose a_i following any history in which every other player j chose a_j in every previous period, and otherwise choose the action $(p_{-j})_i$, where j is the player who deviated in the first period in which exactly one player deviated. Precisely, let H^* be the set of terminal histories in which there is at least one period in which the action of exactly one player j is different from a_j. Refer to such a player as a *lone deviant*. The strategy s_i of player i is defined by $s_i(\varnothing) = a_i$ (her action at the start of the game is a_i) and

$$s_i(h) = \begin{cases} a_i & \text{if } h \text{ is not in } H^* \\ (p_{-j})_i & \text{if } h \in H^* \text{ and } j \text{ is the first lone deviant in } h. \end{cases}$$

The strategy profile s is a Nash equilibrium of the infinitely repeated game by the following argument. Suppose that every player $j \neq i$ adheres to s_j.

- If player i adheres to s_i, then her payoff is $u_i(a)$ in every period.

- If player i deviates from s_i, then she may gain in the period in which she deviates, but she loses in every subsequent period, obtaining at most her minmax payoff.

Thus for a discount factor close enough to 1, s_i is a best response to s_{-i} for every player i, so that s is a Nash equilibrium.

Note that the strategy s_i does not react when more than one player deviates in any given period. It does not need to, because the notion of Nash equilibrium requires only that no *single* player has an incentive to deviate.

For any strategic game in which each player has finitely many actions, the argument can be extended to any outcome path for which each player's discounted average payoff exceeds her minmax payoff, along the lines of the argument for the *Prisoner's Dilemma* in the previous chapter.

The Nash folk theorem for the infinitely repeated *Prisoner's Dilemma* (Proposition 435.1) includes the assertion that the infinitely repeated game has a Nash equilibrium in which the discounted average payoff of each player i is $u_i(D, D)$, her minmax payoff. This assertion is true because (D, D) is a Nash equilibrium (indeed, the only Nash equilibrium) of the *Prisoner's Dilemma*, so that the strategy profile in which each player chooses D regardless of history is a Nash equilibrium of the infinitely repeated game that yields each player her minmax payoff. A strategic game does not necessarily have a Nash equilibrium in which each player's payoff is her minmax payoff, but for a game that does, the strategy profile in which each player chooses her action in this Nash equilibrium regardless of history is a Nash equilibrium of the infinitely repeated game in which each player's payoff is her minmax payoff.

■ PROPOSITION 454.1 (Nash folk theorem for infinitely repeated games) *Let G be a strategic game in which each player has finitely many actions.*

- *For any discount factor δ with $0 < \delta < 1$, the discounted average payoff of each player in any Nash equilibrium of the infinitely repeated game of G is at least her minmax payoff.*

- *Let w be a feasible payoff profile of G for which each player's payoff exceeds her minmax payoff. There exists $\bar{\delta} < 1$ such that if the discount factor exceeds $\bar{\delta}$, then the infinitely repeated game of G has a Nash equilibrium in which the discounted average payoff of each player i is w_i.*

- *If G has a Nash equilibrium in which each player's payoff is her minmax payoff, then for any value of the discount factor the infinitely repeated game of G has a Nash equilibrium in which the discounted average payoff of each player i is her minmax payoff.*

The strategies I used to prove Proposition 454.1 are grim trigger strategies: any transgression leads to interminable punishment. As in the case of the *Prisoner's Dilemma*, less draconian punishment is sufficient to deter deviations. The punishment embedded in a strategy has only to be severe enough to ensure that any deviation ultimately results in a net loss for its perpetrator.

② EXERCISE 454.2 (Nash equilibrium payoffs in infinitely repeated games) For the infinitely repeated game generated by each of the following strategic games, find the set of discounted average payoffs to Nash equilibria when the discount factor is close to 1, as given by Proposition 454.1. (This result applies to the game in part *b*, even though each player has infinitely many actions; Exercise 452.3c is relevant.)

a. *BoS* (Example 18.2).

b. Hotelling's model of electoral competition (Section 3.3) when there are two candidates, under the assumptions of Exercise 452.3c.

② EXERCISE 454.3 (Repeated Bertrand duopoly) Consider Bertrand's duopoly game (Section 3.2) in the case that each firm's unit cost is constant, equal to c. Denote the total demand for the good at the price p by $D(p)$, let $\pi(p) = (p - c)D(p)$ for every price p, and assume that D is such that the function π is continuous and has a single maximizer, denoted p^m (the "monopoly price").

a. Let s_i be the strategy of firm i in the infinitely repeated game of this strategic game that charges p^m in the first period and subsequently as long as the other firm continues to charge p^m and punishes any deviation from p^m by the other firm by choosing the price c for k periods, then reverting to p^m. Given any value of δ, for what values of k is the strategy pair (s_1, s_2) a Nash equilibrium of the infinitely repeated game?

b. Let s_i be the following strategy for firm i in the infinitely repeated game:

   • in the first period charge the price p^m
   • in every subsequent period charge the lowest of all the prices charged by the other firm in all previous periods.

   (That is, firm i matches the other firm's lowest price.) Is the strategy pair (s_1, s_2) a Nash equilibrium of the infinitely repeated game for any discount factor less than 1?

15.2   Subgame perfect equilibria of general infinitely repeated games

15.2.1   Setting

A feature of the *Prisoner's Dilemma* makes it easy to construct a subgame perfect equilibrium of the infinitely repeated game to prove the subgame perfect folk theorem (Proposition 447.1): it has a Nash equilibrium in which each player's payoff is her minmax payoff. This feature means that each player has an incentive to participate in punishment involving the Nash equilibrium if the other player does so.

In any game, each player's payoff is at least her minmax payoff, but, as we know, a game does not generally possess a Nash equilibrium in which each player's payoff is exactly her minmax payoff. In the absence of such a Nash equilibrium, is credible punishment possible for a deviator from an outcome path that yields her a payoff between her minmax payoff and her Nash equilibrium payoff? The answer in most games, including all two-player games, is, perhaps surprisingly, affirmative. A carefully designed strategy profile can give each player an incentive to punish a deviation, even when the punishment yields her a payoff lower than her payoff in any Nash equilibrium.

15.2.2   Example

The game in the left panel of Figure 456.1 has a unique Nash equilibrium (A, A), with payoffs $(4, 4)$; each player's minmax payoff is 1. Consider the strategy s in the right panel of the figure for a player in the infinitely repeated game. The outcome path generated by (s, s) consists of (B, B) in every period. Deviators from

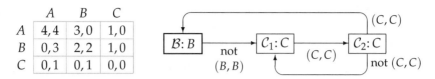

Figure 456.1 *Left*: a strategic game with a unique Nash equilibrium, in which each player's payoff exceeds her minmax payoff. *Right*: a subgame perfect equilibrium strategy for a player in the infinitely repeated game of the game on the left.

this path are subjected to punishment in which the action pair is (C, C). If both players adhere to this punishment, it lasts only two periods. If, however, one of them deviates from the punishment, then the punishment phase starts again: the transition from the first punishment state C_1 to the second punishment state C_2 does not occur unless both players choose C, and there is also a transition from C_2 back to C_1 unless both players choose C. Thus built into the strategy is punishment for a player who does not carry out a punishment.

I claim that if the discount factor is close enough to 1, then the strategy pair (s, s) is a subgame perfect equilibrium of the infinitely repeated game of the strategic game in Figure 456.1. A strategy pair is a subgame perfect equilibrium if and only if it satisfies the one-deviation property (Proposition 439.2), so we need to check only whether either player can increase her payoff by changing her action at the start of some subgame, given the other player's strategy and the remainder of her own strategy. The players' behavior in any period is determined only by the current state, so we need to consider only three subgames, one starting in each state. Suppose that player 2 adheres to the strategy, and consider whether player 1 can increase her payoff by deviating, holding the rest of her strategy fixed.

State B: If player 1 adheres to the strategy, then her payoffs in the next three periods are $(2, 2, 2)$, whereas if she deviates they are at most $(3, 0, 0)$. In both cases her payoff is subsequently 2. Thus adhering to the strategy is optimal if $2 + 2\delta + 2\delta^2 \geq 3$, or $\delta \geq \frac{1}{2}(\sqrt{3} - 1)$.

State C_1: If player 1 adheres to the strategy, then her payoffs in the next three periods are $(0, 0, 2)$, whereas if she deviates they are at most $(1, 0, 0)$. In both cases, her payoff is subsequently 2. Thus adhering to the strategy is optimal if $2\delta^2 \geq 1$, or $\delta \geq \frac{1}{2}\sqrt{2}$.

State C_2: If player 1 adheres to the strategy, then her payoffs in the next three periods are $(0, 2, 2)$, whereas if she deviates they are at most $(1, 0, 0)$. In both cases, her payoff is subsequently 2. Thus adhering to the strategy is optimal if $2\delta + 2\delta^2 \geq 1$, or certainly if $2\delta^2 \geq 1$, as required by the previous case.

The same arguments apply to deviations by player 2, given player 1's strategy, so that given $\sqrt{3} - 1 < \sqrt{2}$, we conclude that (s, s) is a subgame perfect equilibrium if $\delta \geq \frac{1}{2}\sqrt{2}$.

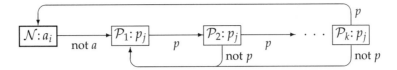

Figure 457.1 A subgame perfect equilibrium strategy for player i in a two-player infinitely repeated game. The pair of actions p holds each player down to her minmax payoff.

15.2.3 General two-player games

The idea behind this example can be extended to any two-player game. Consider an outcome a of such a game G in which both players' payoffs exceed their minmax payoffs. I construct a subgame perfect equilibrium of the infinitely repeated game of G in which the outcome is a in every period. Let p_j be an action of player i that holds player j down to her minmax payoff. (That is, p_j is a solution of the minimization problem (452.2).) Let $p = (p_2, p_1)$ (each player punishes the other), and let s_i be a strategy of player i of the form shown in Figure 457.1, for some value of k. This strategy starts off choosing a_i, and continues to choose a_i as long as the outcome is a; otherwise, it chooses the action p_j that holds player j to her minmax payoff. Once punishment begins, it continues for k periods as long as both players choose their punishment actions. If any player deviates from her punishment action, then the punishments are restarted (from each state $\mathcal{P}_\ell$ there is a transition to state $\mathcal{P}_1$ if the outcome in the previous period is not p).

I claim that we can find a number $\underline{\delta} < 1$ and a function $\underline{k}$ such that if $\delta > \underline{\delta}$, then the strategy pair (s_1, s_2) in which $k = \underline{k}(\delta)$ is a subgame perfect equilibrium of the infinitely repeated game of G. As in the example, I appeal to the result that a strategy pair is a subgame perfect equilibrium if and only if it satisfies the one-deviation property, and consider whether player i can profitably deviate at the start of any subgame, given player j's strategy.

State $\mathcal{N}$: If player i adheres to s_i, then her payoff in each of the next $k + 1$ periods is $u_i(a)$. If she deviates, she obtains at most her maximal payoff in the game, say $\bar{u}_i$, in the period of her deviation, and then $u_i(p)$ for k periods. In both cases, her payoff in every subsequent period is $u_i(a)$. Thus her adherence to the strategy is optimal if

$$(1 + \delta + \cdots + \delta^k)u_i(a) \geq \bar{u}_i + (\delta + \cdots + \delta^k)u_i(p),$$

or, rearranging the terms, if

$$(\delta + \cdots + \delta^k)(u_i(a) - u_i(p)) \geq \bar{u}_i - u_i(a). \tag{457.1}$$

State $\mathcal{P}_\ell$: If player i adheres to s_i in any state $\mathcal{P}_\ell$ ($\ell = 1, \ldots, k$), then her payoff is $u_i(p)$ in the next $k - \ell$ periods and $u_i(a)$ subsequently. If she deviates, then she obtains at most her minmax payoff m_i in the period of her deviation, followed by k periods of $u_i(p)$, and then $u_i(a)$ subsequently. Thus for $\ell = 1$ her adherence to the strategy is optimal if

$$(1 + \delta + \cdots + \delta^{k-1})u_i(p) + \delta^k u_i(a) \geq m_i + (\delta + \cdots + \delta^k)u_i(p),$$

and, given $u_i(a) > m_i \geq u_i(p)$, this condition ensures that adherence is optimal also for $\ell > 1$. The condition is equivalent to

$$\delta^k(u_i(a) - u_i(p)) \geq m_i - u_i(p). \tag{458.1}$$

Now, given $u_i(a) > u_i(p)$, there is an integer k^* large enough that for $\delta = 1$ inequality (457.1) is strictly satisfied. Thus there exists $\delta' < 1$ such that for $k = k^*$ this inequality is satisfied also for all $\delta > \delta'$. Further, because $u_i(a) > m_i$, for $k = k^*$ there exists $\delta'' < 1$ large enough that (458.1) is satisfied for all $\delta > \delta''$. Thus for $k = k^*$ and $\delta > \max\{\delta', \delta''\}$ both inequalities are satisfied, so that the strategy pair (s_1, s_2) is a subgame perfect equilibrium.

This argument shows that for any outcome a of a strategic game G in which each player's payoff exceeds her minmax payoff, the infinitely repeated game of G has a subgame perfect equilibrium that yields the outcome path in which the outcome is a every period. As in the case of Nash equilibrium in Section 15.2.2, for a game in which each player has finitely many actions the argument can be extended to any outcome path in which each player's discounted average payoff exceeds her minmax payoff, to yield the following result.

■ PROPOSITION 458.2 (Subgame perfect folk theorem for two-player infinitely re-peated games) *Let G be a two-player strategic game in which each player has finitely many actions.*

- *For any discount factor δ with $0 < \delta < 1$, the discounted average payoff of each player in any subgame perfect equilibrium of the infinitely repeated game of G is at least her minmax payoff.*

- *Let w be a feasible payoff profile of G for which each player's payoff exceeds her min-max payoff. There exists $\bar{\delta} < 1$ such that if the discount factor exceeds $\bar{\delta}$, then the infinitely repeated game of G has a subgame perfect equilibrium in which the discounted average payoff of each player i is w_i.*

- *If G has a Nash equilibrium in which each player's payoff is her minmax payoff, then for any value of the discount factor the infinitely repeated game of G has a subgame perfect equilibrium in which the discounted average payoff of each player i is her minmax payoff.*

The conclusion of this result holds for any multiplayer game in which each player has finitely many actions and no player's payoff function is equivalent to any other's (see Section 14.2.2 for the definition of equivalence). In multiplayer games that do not satisfy this condition, the lower bound on each player's payoff is a variant of her minmax payoff that takes into account the relations between the players' payoff functions. (For the precise result, see Wen 1994.)

⁇ EXERCISE 459.1 (Costly price changing) Consider the infinitely repeated game of Bertrand's duopoly game (Section 3.2) under the assumptions of Exercise 454.3. Assume that each firm incurs the cost $\epsilon > 0$ in period t whenever its price in period t is different from its price in period $t - 1$ for $t \geq 2$. Consider the following strategy s.

- In the first period, and following every history in which the pair of prices is (p^m, p^m) in every period, charge the price p^m.

- After any other history, charge the price c.

  a. Is the strategy pair (s, s) a Nash equilibrium of the game for any value of $\delta < 1$? If so, find the values of δ.

  b. Is the strategy pair (s, s) a subgame perfect equilibrium of the game for any value of $\delta < 1$? If so, find the values of δ.

⁇ EXERCISE 459.2 (Detection lags) Consider again the infinitely repeated game of Bertrand's duopoly game (Section 3.2) under the assumptions of Exercise 454.3. Suppose that firm i cannot detect a deviation until $k_i \geq 1$ periods have passed (for $i = 1, 2$). Let s_i be the strategy of firm i that charges the price p^* until a deviation is detected, and the price c subsequently.

  a. Find, as a function of δ, the most profitable price p^* for which the strategy pair (s_1, s_2) is a subgame perfect equilibrium.

  b. Suppose that before the firms start choosing prices they simultaneously choose detection technologies. Each firm i may choose any positive integer k_i, or θ, meaning no detection at all. The cost of choosing θ is zero, while the cost of choosing a positive integer is positive and decreasing in the value of the integer. Study the subgame perfect equilibria of the entire game in which each firm i uses either s_i or the strategy that chooses c in every period regardless of history. Does a promise to beat the price charged by another firm promote or inhibit competition?

⁇ EXERCISE 459.3 (Alternating moves) Suppose that two players *alternately* choose actions in the game in Figure 460.1. First player 1 chooses an action, which she carries out in period 1. Subsequently, in every odd period player 2 chooses an action, and in every even period player 1 chooses an action. Each action persists for two periods. Thus if, for example, player 1 chooses X initially, player 2 chooses X in period 1, player 1 chooses Y in period 2, and player 2 chooses Y in period 3, then the outcomes in the first three periods are (X, X), (Y, X), and (Y, Y). The game goes on forever, and each player discounts payoffs using the factor δ. Is the strategy pair in which each player always chooses Y a Nash equilibrium? Is it a subgame perfect equilibrium? (A strategy pair in the game is a subgame perfect equilibrium if and only if it satisfies the one-deviation property.)

$$
\begin{array}{c c}
 & X \quad\ Y \\
\begin{array}{c} X \\ Y \end{array} &
\begin{array}{|c|c|}
\hline
2,2 & 0,0 \\
\hline
0,0 & 1,1 \\
\hline
\end{array}
\end{array}
$$

Figure 460.1 The game in Exercise 459.3.

15.3 Finitely repeated games

The previous two sections (15.1 and 15.2) show that the key properties of the equilibria of an infinitely repeated *Prisoner's Dilemma* carry over to general infinitely repeated games. The same is not true of the properties of the equilibria of a *finitely* repeated *Prisoner's Dilemma*.

15.3.1 Nash equilibrium

As we saw in Section 14.4, every Nash equilibrium of a finitely repeated *Prisoner's Dilemma* generates the same outcome path, in which the outcome in every period is a Nash equilibrium (in fact the only Nash equilibrium) of the *Prisoner's Dilemma*. The same is true of the finitely repeated game of any strategic game for which the profile of payoffs to every Nash equilibrium is the profile of the players' minmax payoffs. (The argument is a variant of the argument for the *Prisoner's Dilemma*.) But the set of such strategic games is small: many games have a Nash equilibrium in which at least some player's payoff exceeds her minmax payoff. If for every player the strategic game G has a Nash equilibrium in which that player's payoff exceeds her minmax payoff, then for $\delta = 1$ and large values of T, the T-period finitely repeated game of G has a wide range of Nash equilibrium payoffs. Precisely, we obtain the following result (cf. Proposition 454.1).

■ PROPOSITION 460.1 (Nash folk theorem for finitely repeated games) *Let G be a strategic game that, for each player, has a Nash equilibrium in which that player's payoff exceeds her minmax payoff. Let w be a feasible payoff profile of G for which each player's payoff exceeds her minmax payoff. For every $\epsilon > 0$ there exists an integer T^* such that if $T > T^*$, then the T-period repeated game of G with discount factor 1 has a Nash equilibrium in which the average payoff of each player i is within ϵ of w_i.*

The idea behind the proof of this result can be understood by considering the case in which w is a profile of payoffs to an action profile a in G and G has a single Nash equilibrium a^* in which every player's payoff exceeds her minmax payoff. In this case we can find a number L such that for any integer $T > L$ the T-period finitely repeated game of G has a Nash equilibrium in which the outcome is a in each of the first $T - L$ periods and a^* in each remaining period. A player who deviates from a in one of the first $T - L$ periods induces the other players to subsequently hold her down to her minmax payoff; the number L is large enough that even a deviation in period $T - L$ is unprofitable. A player who deviates from a^* in the last L periods does not need to be punished, because a^*

is a Nash equilibrium. By choosing T large enough, each player's payoff in the outcome path can be made as close to w as we wish.

15.3.2 Subgame perfect equilibrium

For any strategic game G that, like the *Prisoner's Dilemma*, has a unique Nash equilibrium, the finitely repeated game of G has a unique subgame perfect equilibrium. The argument is a generalization of the argument for the *Prisoner's Dilemma* (see Exercise 426.1). But for a strategic game G with more than one Nash equilibrium payoff profile, the finitely repeated game of G may have many subgame perfect equilibria, with a range of payoffs. In fact, in most such games we can support in a subgame perfect equilibrium any feasible payoff profile in which each player's payoff exceeds her minmax payoff. As for infinitely repeated games, the result most easily stated is for two-player games; I omit a proof.

■ PROPOSITION 461.1 (Subgame perfect folk theorem for two-player finitely repeated games) *Let G be a two-player strategic game that, for each player i, has two Nash equilibria in which player i's payoff differs. Let w be a feasible payoff profile of G for which each player's payoff exceeds her minmax payoff. For every $\epsilon > 0$ there exists an integer T^* such that if $T > T^*$, then the T-period repeated game of G with discount factor 1 has a subgame perfect equilibrium in which the average payoff of each player i is within ϵ of w_i.*

15.4   Variation on a theme: imperfect observability

We have seen that outcomes desirable for all players can be achieved as equilibria of repeated games when the players use strategies that threaten to "punish" deviations. In the worlds we have studied, the threats deter all deviations, and no punishment is ever carried out, so that the severity of the threatened punishment has no direct impact on the players' payoffs. In less perfect worlds, punishment is sometimes carried out, so that its severity entails a tradeoff: more drastic punishment may allow more desirable outcomes to be sustained, but at the same time may entail low payoffs during its implementation.

In this section I study an example that illustrates these issues. Consider a variant of the infinitely repeated Bertrand duopoly game in Exercise 454.3 in which (*a*) each firm observes only the demand it faces, not the other firm's price, and (*b*) the demand each firm faces depends on its price, the other firm's price, and factors that we model as random. Specifically, each firm's unit cost is constant, equal to c, and the total demand at the price p in each period is

$$\begin{cases} 0 & \text{with probability } \rho \\ D(p) & \text{with probability } 1 - \rho, \end{cases}$$

where $D(p) > 0$ for some price $p > c$, and $(p - c)D(p)$ has a single maximizer, the "monopoly price" p^m. Assume that each firm evaluates a stream of payoffs by its expected discounted average value.

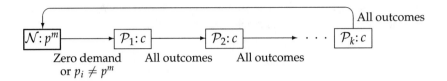

Figure 462.1 A strategy for firm i in an infinitely repeated Bertrand duopoly game.

Under these assumptions a firm that faces no demand in some period does not know whether the cause of its lack of custom is that business is generally bad (total demand is zero) or that the other firm is charging a lower price. In this environment grim trigger strategies are not sensible: if a period of zero demand—which will surely occur eventually—causes each firm to subsequently charge the price c, then from some point on—the sooner, the larger is ρ—both firms' profits are surely zero. Suppose that instead each firm i uses the limited punishment strategy s_i^k in Figure 462.1, charging the monopoly price p^m until it faces zero demand, then switching to the price c for k periods, and subsequently reverting to p^m. The pair (c,c) of prices is a Nash equilibrium of the strategic game, so the argument in Section 14.10.2 suggests that we can find a value of k for which the strategy pair in which each firm i uses the strategy s_i^k is a subgame perfect equilibrium.

The strategy pair (s_1^k, s_2^k) induces only a finite number of periods of zero profit after a period of no demand, so each firm's profit is higher than it is if both firms use the grim trigger strategy. Further, each firm's expected profit is clearly higher the smaller is k. At the same time, for the strategy pair to be a subgame perfect equilibrium, k must be large enough, otherwise a deviation from the monopoly price is profitable. Thus among all strategy pairs (s_1^k, s_2^k), the one that yields each firm the highest expected discounted average payoff has k just large enough to make it a subgame perfect equilibrium.

We can calculate this value of k as follows. First find each firm's expected discounted average payoff to the strategy pair (s_1^k, s_2^k). This strategy pair leads to many possible outcome paths, depending on the realization of demand in each period, and one way to find the firms' payoffs is to study all these paths. A much easier method exploits the relation between the paths starting from each state. Denote by V^N and V^{P_1} the expected discounted sums of payoffs for a firm in states $\mathcal{N}$ and $\mathcal{P}_1$ respectively, when each firm i uses the strategy s_i^k, and by π^m the monopoly profit $(p^m - c)D(p^m)$.

Suppose the state is currently $\mathcal{N}$. Demand is high with probability $1 - \rho$, in which case each firm earns the profit $\frac{1}{2}\pi^m$ and the state remains $\mathcal{N}$, so that in the next period each firm gets V^N, which is worth δV^N now. Demand is zero with probability ρ, in which case each firm earns zero profit, and the state becomes $\mathcal{P}_1$, yielding each firm V^{P_1} with one period of delay. Thus we have

$$V^N = (1-\rho)(\tfrac{1}{2}\pi^m + \delta V^N) + \rho\delta V^{P_1}.$$

Similarly

$$V^{P_1} = \delta^k V^N,$$

because during the k periods of punishment both firms earn zero profit, and at the end of this phase they return to state $\mathcal{N}$. Solving these two equations, we obtain

$$V^N = \frac{\frac{1}{2}(1-\rho)\pi^m}{1 - \delta(1-\rho) - \rho\delta^{k+1}} \tag{463.1}$$

and $V^{P_1} = \delta^k V^N$. As k increases, V^N decreases, confirming the earlier informal argument.

For the strategy pair (s_1^k, s_2^k) to be a subgame perfect equilibrium, neither firm must be able to increase its profit by deviating in the first period of any subgame. In any state P_j neither firm can profitably deviate because (c, c) is a Nash equilibrium of the one-shot game. Now consider state $\mathcal{N}$. A firm's best deviation is to slightly undercut its rival. Its profit is then close to π^m in the period in which it deviates, and the deviation induces a punishment phase, so that for the deviation not to be profitable we need

$$V^N \geq (1-\rho)(\pi^m + \delta V^{P_1}) + \rho\delta V^{P_1},$$

or, using the values we found for V^N and V^{P_1},

$$2\delta(1-\rho) + (2\rho - 1)\delta^{k+1} \geq 1. \tag{463.2}$$

If $\rho \geq \frac{1}{2}$, then the left-hand side of (463.2) is nonincreasing in k, so that if the inequality holds for any value of k it must hold for $k = 0$, which it does not. (*Some punishment is required.*) Thus if $\rho \geq \frac{1}{2}$, there is no value of k for which the strategy pair is a subgame perfect equilibrium. If $\rho < \frac{1}{2}$, then the left-hand side is increasing in k. As k increases without bound, the left-hand side approaches $2\delta(1-\rho)$, so if $2\delta(1-\rho) > 1$, or $\delta > 1/(2(1-\rho))$, there is a value of k such that for any larger value the inequality (463.2) is satisfied. Precisely, this value is

$$\frac{\log\left(\frac{1 - 2\delta(1-\rho)}{2\rho - 1}\right)}{\log \delta} - 1.$$

In summary, if bad times are not too likely and the firms are sufficiently patient ($\rho < 1/2$ and δ is large enough), then there is a value of k such that for any larger value the strategy pair (s_1^k, s_2^k) is a subgame perfect equilibrium. As we have seen, the equilibrium with the smallest value of k maximizes each firm's profit.

Notes

The origins of the theory of repeated games are discussed in the notes at the end of the previous chapter (page 449). The subgame perfect folk theorem for infinitely repeated two-player games (Proposition 458.2) is due to Fudenberg and

Maskin (1986, 1991), who establish also a result for a class of multiplayer games. A result of Wen (1994) covers all multiplayer games.

The folk theorems for finitely repeated games, Propositions 460.1 and 461.1, are due to Benoît and Krishna (1985, 1987).

Games in which the players alternate moves, like the one in Exercise 459.3, are studied by Lagunoff and Matsui (1997); Rubinstein and Wolinsky (1995) study a closely related class of games.

The idea in Section 15.4 is due to Green and Porter (1984), who study a variant of Cournot's oligopoly game. The formulation I use is taken from Tirole (1988, Section 6.7.1.1).

16 Bargaining

16.1 Bargaining as an extensive game   465
16.2 Illustration: trade in a market   477
16.3 Nash's axiomatic model   481
16.4 Relation between strategic and axiomatic models   489
Prerequisite: Chapter 5 and Sections 4.1.3, 6.1.1, and 7.6

I N MANY situations, parties divide a "pie". A capitalist and the workers she hires divide the total revenue generated by the output produced; legislators divide tax revenue among spending programs valued by their constituents; a buyer of an object and a seller divide the amount by which the buyer's valuation of the object exceeds the seller's. In this chapter I discuss two very different models that are intended to capture "bargaining" between the parties in such situations. One model is an extensive game (see Chapter 5). The other model takes an approach not previously used in this book: it considers the outcomes compatible with a list of apparently sensible properties. Though the models are very different, the outcomes they isolate are closely related.

16.1 Bargaining as an extensive game

16.1.1 Extensions of the ultimatum game

One point of departure for a theory of bargaining is the "ultimatum game" studied in Section 6.1.1. In this game, two players split a pie of size c that they both value. Throughout this section I take $c = 1$. Player 1 proposes a division (x_1, x_2) of the pie, where $x_1 + x_2 = 1$ and $0 \leq x_i \leq 1$ for $i = 1, 2$. Player 2 either accepts this division, in which case she receives x_2 and player 1 receives x_1, or rejects it, in which case neither player receives any pie. This game has a unique subgame perfect equilibrium, in which player 1 proposes the division $(1, 0)$, and player 2 accepts all offers. The outcome of the equilibrium is that player 1 receives all the pie.

What accounts for this one-sided outcome? Player 2 is powerless because her only alternative to the acceptance of player 1's proposal is rejection, which yields her no pie. Suppose, instead, that we give player 2 the option of making a counterproposal after rejecting player 1's proposal, which player 1 may accept or reject. Then we have the game illustrated in Figure 466.1, where Y means "accept" and N means "reject".

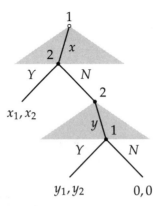

Figure 466.1 An extension of the ultimatum game in which player 2, after rejecting player 1's offer, may make a counteroffer. The top gray triangle represents the continuum of possible proposals of player 1; the bottom gray triangle represents the continuum of possible counterproposals of player 2 after she rejects player 1's proposal x. The black lines indicate three of the infinitely many terminal histories (namely (x, Y), (x, N, y, Y), and (x, N, y, N)).

In this game, *player 1* is powerless; her proposal at the start of the game is irrelevant. Every subgame following player 2's rejection of a proposal of player 1 is a variant of the ultimatum game in which player 2 moves first. Thus every such subgame has a unique subgame perfect equilibrium, in which player 2 offers nothing to player 1, and player 1 accepts all proposals. Using backward induction, player 2's optimal action after any offer (x_1, x_2) of player 1 with $x_2 < 1$ is rejection (N). Hence in every subgame perfect equilibrium player 2 obtains all the pie.

In the extension of this game in which the players alternate offers over many periods, a similar result holds: in every subgame perfect equilibrium, the player who makes the offer in the last period obtains all the pie. The feature of the model responsible for this result is the players' indifference about the timing of an agreement. Real-life bargaining takes time, and time is valuable, so we may reasonably assume that the players' preferences do not have this characteristic, but rather exhibit a bias toward early agreements. The next section explores the consequences of a particular form of impatience.

16.1.2 A finite horizon game with alternating offers and impatient players

Suppose that the players alternate proposals, one per "period", and that each player i regards the outcome in which she receives all of the pie after t periods of delay as equivalent to the outcome in which she receives the fraction δ_i^t of the pie immediately, where $0 < \delta_i < 1$ for $i = 1, 2$. That is, suppose that each player i "discounts" the future using the constant *discount factor* δ_i. (See Section 14.2 for a discussion of preferences with discounting.)

Two-period deadline Consider the game in which two periods are possible: if player 2 rejects player 1's initial proposal, player 2 may make a counterproposal which, if rejected by player 1, ends the game with a payoff of 0 for each player. This game is illustrated in Figure 467.1.

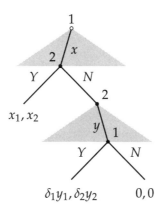

Figure 467.1 A two-period bargaining game of alternating offers in which each player i uses the factor δ_i to discount future payoffs.

We may find the subgame perfect equilibria of this game by using backward induction, as in Section 16.1.1. The subgame starting after a history in which player 2 has rejected an initial proposal of player 1 is similar to an ultimatum game. It has a unique subgame perfect equilibrium, in which player 2 proposes $(0, 1)$ and player 1 accepts all proposals. This equilibrium results in payoffs, viewed from the start of the game, of 0 for player 1 and δ_2 for player 2.

Now consider the subgame following an initial proposal of player 1. If player 2 rejects the proposal, her payoff is δ_2, as we have just found. Thus she optimally rejects any proposal that gives her less than δ_2 and accepts any proposal that gives her more than δ_2; she is indifferent between accepting and rejecting the proposal $(1 - \delta_2, \delta_2)$.

Finally consider player 1's initial proposal. Player 2 accepts any proposal (x_1, x_2) with $x_2 > \delta_2$. Thus no such proposal is optimal: player 2 will accept slightly less, as long as the amount she gets exceeds δ_2, so that player 1 can increase the amount she receives by offering player 2 less. No proposal that gives player 2 less than δ_2 is optimal either: player 2 rejects such a proposal and in the following subgame proposes $(0, 1)$, which player 1 accepts, giving player 1 the payoff 0. Thus the only proposal of player 1 possible in a subgame perfect equilibrium is $(1 - \delta_2, \delta_2)$. I claim that the game indeed has a subgame perfect equilibrium in which player 1 makes this proposal, and in this equilibrium player 2 accepts the proposal. If player 2 were to reject it, player 1's payoff would ultimately be 0, so that player 1 could increase her payoff by raising the amount she initially offers to player 2 above δ_2, inducing player 2 to accept her proposal.

In conclusion, the game has a unique subgame perfect equilibrium in which

- player 1's initial proposal is $(1 - \delta_2, \delta_2)$

- player 2 accepts all proposals in which she receives at least δ_2 and rejects all proposals in which she receives less than δ_2

- player 2 proposes $(0, 1)$ after any history in which she rejects a proposal of player 1

- player 1 accepts all proposals of player 2 at the end of the game (after a history in which player 2 rejects player 1's opening proposal).

The outcome of this equilibrium is that player 1 proposes $(1 - \delta_2, \delta_2)$, which player 2 accepts; player 1's payoff is $1 - \delta_2$ and player 2's is δ_2. This finding is consistent with the intuition that the incentive to reach an early agreement embodied in the players' impatience leads to an outcome in which player 1's payoff is positive. Player 2's "threat" to reject player 1's initial proposal is credible only if the proposal gives player 2 less than δ_2, because rejection leads to a delay that reduces her value of the pie to δ_2.

⁇ EXERCISE 468.1 (Two-period bargaining with constant cost of delay) Find the subgame perfect equilibrium (equilibria?) of the variant of the game in this section in which player i's payoff when she accepts the proposal (y_1, y_2) in period 2 is $y_i - c_i$, where $0 < c_i < 1$ (rather than $\delta_i y_i$), and her payoff to any terminal history that ends in rejection is $-c_i$ (rather than 0), for $i = 1, 2$. (Payoffs can be negative, but a proposal must still be a pair of nonnegative numbers.)

Many-period deadline We may extend the game by allowing the players to alternate proposals over many periods, rather than only two. For any given deadline, the game has a finite horizon, so we may use backward induction to find its set of subgame perfect equilibria. As for a two-period deadline, the game has a unique subgame perfect equilibrium, in which player 2 immediately accepts the initial proposal of player 1. This proposal depends on the deadline.

Consider, for example, a three-period deadline.

- By our analysis of the two-period game, any subgame following a history in which player 1's opening proposal is rejected has a unique subgame perfect equilibrium, in which player 2's proposal is $(\delta_1, 1 - \delta_1)$, which player 1 accepts, resulting in the pair of payoffs $(\delta_1^2, \delta_2(1 - \delta_1))$.

- The whole game has a unique subgame perfect equilibrium, in which player 1 offers player 2 the amount $\delta_2(1 - \delta_1)$ at the start of the game (making her indifferent between acceptance and rejection). Player 2 accepts this offer, generating the pair of payoffs $(1 - \delta_2(1 - \delta_1), \delta_2(1 - \delta_1))$.

⁇ EXERCISE 468.2 (Three-period bargaining with constant cost of delay) Find the subgame perfect equilibrium (equilibria?) of the variant of the game in Exercise 468.1 in which the game may last for three periods, and the cost to each player i of each period of delay is c_i. (Treat the cases $c_1 \geq c_2$ and $c_1 < c_2$ separately.)

16.1.3 An infinite horizon game with alternating offers and impatient players

Definition An appealing version of the model assumes that each player, after rejecting an offer, always has the opportunity to make a counteroffer. That is, there is no deadline; the players may alternate offers indefinitely. This game does not have a finite horizon: every infinite sequence $(x^1, N, x^2, N, \ldots)$ in which every offer x^t

for $t = 1, 2, \ldots$ is rejected is a possible terminal history. Every other terminal history is finite and takes the form $(x^1, N, x^2, N, \ldots, x^t, Y)$: for some value of t, all proposals through period $t - 1$ are rejected, and the proposal in period t is accepted. The game is called the *bargaining game of alternating offers*.

▶ DEFINITION 469.1 (*Bargaining game of alternating offers*) The **bargaining game of alternating offers** is the following extensive game with perfect information.

Players Two negotiators, say 1 and 2.

Terminal histories Every sequence of the form $(x^1, N, x^2, N, \ldots, x^t, Y)$ for $t \geq 1$, and every (infinite) sequence of the form $(x^1, N, x^2, N, \ldots)$, where each x^r is a division of the pie (a pair of numbers that sums to 1).

Player function $P(\varnothing) = 1$ (player 1 makes the first offer), and

$$P(x^1, N, x^2, N, \ldots, x^t) = P(x^1, N, x^2, N, \ldots, x^t, N) = \begin{cases} 1 & \text{if } t \text{ is even} \\ 2 & \text{if } t \text{ is odd.} \end{cases}$$

Preferences For $i = 1, 2$, player i's payoff to the terminal history $(x^1, N, x^2, N, \ldots, x^t, Y)$ is $\delta_i^{t-1} x_i^t$, where $0 < \delta_i < 1$, and her payoff to every (infinite) terminal history $(x^1, N, x^2, N, \ldots)$ is 0.

The first two periods of this game look like the two-period game in Figure 467.1, except that player 1's rejection of an offer in the second period leads not to the end of the game (with payoffs $(0,0)$), but to a subgame in which the first move is a proposal of player 1. The structure of this subgame is the same as the structure of the whole game: player 1 makes a proposal, which player 2 either accepts or rejects; then, if player 2 rejects the proposal, she makes a proposal, which player 1 either accepts or rejects; and so on. In fact, the subgame is *identical* to the whole game. That is, not only are the players, terminal histories, and player function the same in the subgame as they are in the game, but so too are the players' preferences. The players' *payoffs* differ in the game and the subgame. For example, player 2's acceptance of player 1's offer (x_1, x_2) in the first period of the game generates the payoffs (x_1, x_2), while her acceptance of player 1's offer (x_1, x_2) in the first period of the subgame generates the payoffs $(\delta_1^2 x_1, \delta_1^2 x_2)$. But the players' *preferences* are the same in the game and the subgame: for any number k, each player i is indifferent between receiving k units of payoff with t periods of delay and receiving $\delta_i^t k$ units of payoff immediately.

Similarly, *all* subgames starting with a proposal of player 1 (including the whole game) are identical to each other. Further, all subgames starting with a proposal of player 2 are identical to each other. For this reason, we say that the structure of the game is *stationary*.

Subgame perfect equilibrium Because the game does not have a finite horizon, we cannot use backward induction to find its subgame perfect equilibria. Instead, I argue that the stationary structure of the game suggests a certain form for an equilibrium, and then check that an equilibrium of such a form exists.

A player's strategy in the game is complicated. A strategy of player 1, for example, specifies an offer in period 1; a response (accept or reject) to every history of the form (x, N, y), where x is an offer (of player 1) in the first period and y is an offer (of player 2) in the second period; a counteroffer following every history of the form (x, N, y, N); and so on. In particular, although each player faces the same subgame whenever she makes an offer, she certainly is not restricted to making the same offer whenever it is her turn to propose. Player 1's offer at the start of the game, for example, may differ from her offer after a history (x, N, y, N), which may depend arbitrarily on the values of x and y.

However, the stationary structure of the game makes it reasonable to guess that the game has a subgame perfect equilibrium in which each player always makes the same proposal and always accepts the same set of proposals—that is, each player's strategy is *stationary*. The fact that the structure of the game is stationary implies neither that the game necessarily has an equilibrium in stationary strategies, nor that it does not have equilibria in strategies that are not stationary. But stationary strategies definitely provide a reasonable starting point in the search for an equilibrium.

A stationary strategy is specified by giving the offer the player always makes and the criterion she always uses to accept offers. Intuition suggests that in an equilibrium each player accepts offers that give her a sufficiently high payoff and rejects all other offers. A pair of stationary strategies in which each player uses such a criterion for accepting offers takes the form

- player 1 always proposes x^* and accepts a proposal y if and only if $y_1 \geq y_1^*$

- player 2 always proposes z^* and accepts a proposal w if and only if $w_2 \geq w_2^*$

for some proposals w^*, x^*, y^*, and z^*.

Can we find values of these proposals such that the strategy pair is a subgame perfect equilibrium? We found that in a finite horizon game every proposal is accepted in equilibrium. A reasonable guess is that the same is true in the infinite game, so that $x_2^* \geq w_2^*$ and $z_1^* \geq y_1^*$. If either of these inequalities is strict, one of the players is willing to accept less than she is offered, so that the proposer can increase her payoff by reducing her offer. Thus for equilibrium we need $x_2^* = w_2^*$ and $z_1^* = y_1^*$. Under these conditions, the strategy pair we are considering is one in which

- player 1 always proposes x^* and accepts a proposal y if and only if $y_1 \geq y_1^*$

- player 2 always proposes y^* and accepts a proposal x if and only if $x_2 \geq x_2^*$.

Now consider a subgame in which the first move is a response by player 2 to a proposal of player 1. If player 2 rejects player 1's proposal, her strategy calls for her to propose y^*, which player 1 accepts, yielding player 2 the payoff y_2^* with one period of delay. Thus player 2 optimally rejects any proposal x for which $x_2 < \delta_2 y_2^*$, accepts any proposal x for which $x_2 > \delta_2 y_2^*$, and is indifferent between accepting and rejecting a proposal x for which $x_2 = \delta_2 y_2^*$. Hence we need

$$x_2^* = \delta_2 y_2^* \tag{471.1}$$

for the strategy pair to be a subgame perfect equilibrium. By a symmetric argument for a subgame in which the first move is a response by player 1 to a proposal of player 2 we need

$$y_1^* = \delta_1 x_1^*. \tag{471.2}$$

We have $x_2^* = 1 - x_1^*$ and $y_2^* = 1 - y_1^*$, so these two inequalities imply that

$$x_1^* = \frac{1 - \delta_2}{1 - \delta_1 \delta_2}$$

$$y_1^* = \frac{\delta_1(1 - \delta_2)}{1 - \delta_1 \delta_2}.$$

This argument shows that if the strategy pair we are considering is a subgame perfect equilibrium, then x_1^* and y_1^* are given in these two equations.

In fact, the strategy pair thus defined is indeed a subgame perfect equilibrium, as I show below. Further, it is the only subgame perfect equilibrium (so that, in particular, the game has no subgame perfect equilibrium in which the players' strategies are not stationary). That is, we have the following result.

■ PROPOSITION 471.3 (Subgame perfect equilibrium of bargaining game of alternating offers) *The bargaining game of alternating offers has a unique subgame perfect equilibrium, in which*

- *player 1 always proposes x^* and accepts a proposal y if and only if $y_1 \geq y_1^*$*
- *player 2 always proposes y^* and accepts a proposal x if and only if $x_2 \geq x_2^*$,*

where

$$x^* = \left(\frac{1 - \delta_2}{1 - \delta_1 \delta_2}, \frac{\delta_2(1 - \delta_1)}{1 - \delta_1 \delta_2} \right)$$

$$y^* = \left(\frac{\delta_1(1 - \delta_2)}{1 - \delta_1 \delta_2}, \frac{1 - \delta_1}{1 - \delta_1 \delta_2} \right).$$

The outcome of the equilibrium strategy pair is that player 1 proposes x^* at the start of the game, and player 2 immediately accepts this proposal.

I have argued that if a pair of stationary strategies in which every offer is accepted is a subgame perfect equilibrium, then it takes the form given in the result. I now argue that this strategy pair is in fact a subgame perfect equilibrium.

I first claim without proof the following result, the argument for which follows the lines of the argument for Proposition 439.2. (For a statement of the one-deviation property, see page 438.)

■ PROPOSITION 471.4 (One-deviation property of subgame perfect equilibria of bargaining game of alternating offers) *A strategy profile in the bargaining game of alternating offers is a subgame perfect equilibrium if and only if it satisfies the one-deviation property.*

Denote the strategy pair in Proposition 471.3 by s^*. The game has two types of subgame: one in which the first move is an offer, and one in which the first move is a response to an offer.

First consider a subgame in which the first move is an offer. Suppose the offer is made by player 1, and fix player 2's strategy to be s_2^*. If player 1 uses the strategy s_1^*, her payoff is x_1^*. If she deviates from s_1^* in the first period of the subgame, she is worse off by the following arguments.

- If she offers player 2 more than x_2^* in the first period, then player 2 accepts her proposal, and her payoff is less than x_1^*.

- If she offers player 2 less than x_2^* in the first period, then player 2 rejects her proposal and proposes (y_1^*, y_2^*). Player 1 accepts this proposal, obtaining the payoff $\delta_1 y_1^*$, which is less than x_1^*.

A symmetric argument shows that player 2 cannot profitably deviate in the first period of a subgame that starts with her making an offer.

Now consider a subgame in which the first move is a response to an offer. Suppose that the responder is player 1, and fix player 2's strategy to be s_2^*. Denote by (y_1, y_2) the offer to which player 1 is responding. Player 1's strategy s_1^* calls for her to accept the proposal if and only if $y_1 \geq y_1^*$. If she rejects the proposal, she proposes x^*, which player 2 accepts, so that her payoff is $\delta_1 x_1^*$, which is equal to y_1^*. Thus no deviation in the first period of the subgame increases player 1's payoff. A symmetric argument shows that player 2 cannot profitably deviate in the first period of a subgame in which she responds to a proposal.

We conclude that s^* is a subgame perfect equilibrium. The proof that it is the *unique* subgame perfect equilibrium (so that, in particular, the game has no subgame perfect equilibrium in which the players' strategies are not stationary) is a little intricate, and I do not present it.

Properties of subgame perfect equilibrium   The equilibrium s^* has some noteworthy properties.

Efficiency   Player 2 accepts player 1's first offer, so that agreement is reached immediately; no resources are wasted in delay. This feature of the equilibrium is intuitively appealing, given that the players are perfectly informed about each other's preferences. If the outcome were not reached immediately, there would be an alternative outcome that both players prefer; given their perfect information, one might expect the players to both perceive and pursue this alternative outcome. Nevertheless, some variants of the model that maintain the players' perfect information have subgame perfect equilibria in which agreement is *not* reached immediately (the case $c_1 = c_2 = c$ in Exercise 473.2 yields such equilibria when $c < \frac{1}{3}$).

Effect of changes in patience   For a given value of δ_2, the value of x_1^*, the equilibrium payoff of player 1, increases as δ_1 increases to 1. That is, fixing the patience of player 2, player 1's share increases as she becomes more patient. Further, as player 1 becomes extremely patient (δ_1 close to 1), her share approaches 1. Symmetrically, fixing the patience of player 1, player 2's share increases to 1 as she becomes more patient.

First-mover advantage If $\delta_1 = \delta_2 = \delta$, then the only asymmetry in the game is that player 1 moves first. Player 1's equilibrium payoff is $(1 - \delta)/(1 - \delta^2) = 1/(1 + \delta)$, which exceeds $\frac{1}{2}$, but approaches $\frac{1}{2}$ as δ approaches 1. Thus if the players are equally and only slightly impatient, player 1's first-mover advantage is small and the outcome is almost symmetric.

? EXERCISE 473.1 (One-sided offers) Consider the variant of the bargaining game of alternating offers in which only player 1 makes proposals: in every period, player 1 makes a proposal, which player 2 either accepts, ending the game, or rejects, leading to the next period, in which player 1 makes another proposal. Consider the strategy pair in which player 1 always proposes $(x_1, 1 - x_1)$ and player 2 always accepts a proposal (y_1, y_2) if and only if $y_2 \geq 1 - x_1$. Find the value(s) of x_1 for which this strategy pair is a subgame perfect equilibrium. (A strategy pair is a subgame perfect equilibrium of this game if and only if it satisfies the one-deviation property.)

? EXERCISE 473.2 (Alternating offer bargaining with constant cost of delay) Marx (1973, 65) writes that "Wages are determined by the antagonistic struggle between capitalist and worker. Victory goes necessarily to the capitalist. The capitalist can live longer without the worker than can the worker without the capitalist." Perhaps he has in mind the variant of the bargaining game of alternating offers in which each player i loses c_i during each period of delay (rather than discounting her payoff), as in Exercises 468.1 and 468.2. Show that if $c_1 < c_2$, then this game has a subgame perfect equilibrium in which player 1 always proposes $(1, 0)$. (In this case, in fact, the game has no other subgame perfect equilibrium.) Show also that if $c_1 = c_2 = c$, then for every value of z_1 with $c \leq z_1 \leq 1$ the game has a subgame perfect equilibrium in which player 1 always proposes $(z_1, 1 - z_1)$. (In both cases, a strategy pair is a subgame perfect equilibrium if and only if it satisfies the one-deviation property.)

16.1.4 Risk of breakdown

In some situations, a negotiator is motivated to reach agreement because she thinks there is a chance, independent of her behavior and that of her adversary, that negotiations will end prematurely. She may fear, for example, that the pie that is currently available will at some point disappear because of the actions of third parties, or that her adversary will happen upon a more appealing venture and lose interest in bargaining with her.

We may capture this idea in a variant of the bargaining game of alternating offers in which after any offer is rejected, a move of chance terminates negotiations

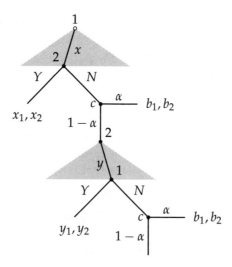

Figure 474.1 The first two periods of a variant of the bargaining game of alternating offers in which negotiations break down with probability α after an offer is rejected.

with probability $\alpha > 0$. Given the presence of this randomness, we need to endow the players with preferences regarding lotteries over divisions of the pie. Assume that the preferences of each player i are represented by the expected value of the Bernoulli payoff function u_i defined over the amount of the pie she receives (so that her valuation of the division (x_1, x_2) is $u_i(x_i)$). Denote by (b_1, b_2) the players' Bernoulli payoffs in the event negotiations terminate, and assume that there is some division (x_1, x_2) of the pie such that $0 \leq b_i < u_i(x_i)$ for each player i. (That is, some division of the pie is preferred by both players to breakdown, and for each player breakdown is no worse than receiving no pie.) The possibility of breakdown puts pressure on the parties to reach agreement even if they are not impatient; I assume that $\delta_1 = \delta_2 = 1$. The first two periods of the game are illustrated in Figure 474.1.

By logic similar to that for the bargaining game of alternating offers, this game has a unique subgame perfect equilibrium. In this equilibrium,

- player 1 always proposes $\hat{x}(\alpha)$ and accepts a proposal y if and only if $y_1 \geq \hat{y}_1(\alpha)$

- player 2 always proposes $\hat{y}(\alpha)$ and accepts a proposal x if and only if $x_2 \geq \hat{x}_2(\alpha)$,

where each player is indifferent between accepting and rejecting the other player's equilibrium proposal, so that

$$
\begin{aligned}
u_1(\hat{y}_1(\alpha)) &= (1 - \alpha)u_1(\hat{x}_1(\alpha)) + \alpha b_1 \\
u_2(\hat{x}_2(\alpha)) &= (1 - \alpha)u_2(\hat{y}_2(\alpha)) + \alpha b_2.
\end{aligned}
\tag{474.1}
$$

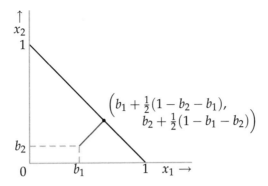

Figure 475.1 An illustration of the approximate proposal made by each player (and accepted by the other player) in a variant of the bargaining game of alternating offers in which there is a very small positive probability that after the rejection of any offer, negotiations break down.

If, for example, both players are risk neutral, with $u_i(x_i) = x_i$ for each player i, then

$$\hat{x}_1 = \frac{1 - b_2 + (1 - \alpha)b_1}{2 - \alpha}$$

$$\hat{y}_1 = \frac{(1 - \alpha)(1 - b_2) + b_1}{2 - \alpha}.$$

When the value of α is close to zero, player 1's advantage in being the first to make a proposal, before chance possibly intervenes and terminates negotiations, is small. In this case $\hat{x}_1$ and $\hat{y}_1$ are both close to $\frac{1}{2}(1 - b_2 + b_1)$, or $b_1 + \frac{1}{2}(1 - b_1 - b_2)$. Thus the proposals made in the unique subgame perfect equilibrium when the probability of breakdown is close to zero and the players are risk neutral are both close to

$$\left(b_1 + \tfrac{1}{2}(1 - b_2 - b_1), b_2 + \tfrac{1}{2}(1 - b_1 - b_2)\right). \tag{475.1}$$

That is, the players split equally the excess of the pie over the sum $b_1 + b_2$ of the amounts they obtain in the event of breakdown (see Figure 475.1).

16.1.5 Outside options

In some situations, a bargaining party has the *option* of breaking off negotiations and pursuing some other activity at various points during negotiations. For example, a buyer negotiating with a seller may have the option of starting to bargain with another seller; a firm negotiating with a union may have the option of closing down and selling its assets.

Consider a simple variant of the bargaining game of alternating offers in which one of the parties, say player 2, may, when responding to an offer, pursue an *outside option* that yields her the fixed payoff v_2. Assume that if she pursues this option, player 1's payoff is 0. The first two periods of the game are illustrated in Figure 476.1, in which O is player 2's action of opting out.

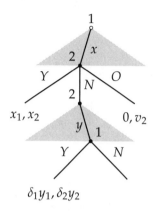

Figure 476.1 The first two periods of a variant of the bargaining game of alternating offers in which player 2 may opt out when responding to an offer.

Before studying this game, consider variants of it with finite horizons. In a one-period version (a variant of the ultimatum game), player 1 must offer player 2 at least v_2 to stop her opting out, which yields player 1 the payoff of 0. By an argument like that for the ultimatum game, in the unique subgame perfect equilibrium player 1 offers exactly v_2, so that her payoff is $1 - v_2$.

In a two-period version, the existence of an outside option does not change player 2's offer in the second period—she still takes all the pie—but implies that player 1 needs to offer her at least v_2 in the first period to stop her opting out. Thus if $\delta_2 < v_2$, so that opting out is better for player 2 than obtaining all the pie in the second period, the equilibrium opening offer of player 1 is $(1 - v_2, v_2)$. If $\delta_2 > v_2$, however, player 2's outside option is irrelevant: the subgame perfect equilibrium of the subgame that results if player 2 does not opt out yields her more than her outside option, and player 1 needs to offer her δ_2 in the first period, as in the game without the outside option.

The lesson is that if player 2's outside option yields her a payoff higher than her equilibrium payoff in the subgame that follows a decision to forgo the option, the existence of the option constrains player 1's offers; otherwise it does not affect her offers. Precisely, let x^* be player 1's opening proposal in the bargaining game of alternating offers (without any outside option), as in Proposition 471.3. Then we have the following result for the infinite horizon game.

- If $v_2 < x_2^*$, then the strategy pair defined in Proposition 471.3 is the unique subgame perfect equilibrium of the game. (Player 2 never opts out.)

- If $v_2 > x_2^*$, then the game has a unique subgame perfect equilibrium, in which

  ○ player 1 always proposes $(1 - v_2, v_2)$ and accepts a proposal y if and only if $y_1 \geq \delta_1(1 - v_2)$

  ○ player 2 always proposes $(\delta_1(1 - v_2), 1 - \delta_1(1 - v_2))$ and accepts a proposal x if and only if $x_2 \geq v_2$.

This result neatly captures the intuition that a player's outside option has value only if it is worth more than her equilibrium payoff in its absence. It depends, however, upon the assumption that a player can opt out only when responding to an offer. If, for example, a player can opt out after her opponent rejects an offer, or both when responding to an offer and after her opponent rejects an offer, then for some values of v_2 less than x_2^* the game has subgame perfect equilibria in which player 2's payoff exceeds x_2^*. (For details, see Shaked 1994 and Osborne and Rubinstein 1990, 60–62.)

16.1.6 Exogenous breakdown versus outside options

In Section 16.1.4 we saw the effect on the outcome of bargaining of the possibility that, after any rejection, negotiations are terminated with a probability out of the control of either party. In particular, an increase in a party's breakdown payoff always increases her equilibrium payoff, even if the breakdown payoff is less than her equilibrium payoff. The reason is that an increase in the breakdown payoff increases the player's expected payoff in the subgame following the rejection of an offer. If a player can *choose* to break off negotiations, we obtain a different result. Under the temporal assumption in Section 16.1.5, a player's outside option affects her equilibrium payoff only if the payoff it yields exceeds her equilibrium payoff in its absence. The point is that a player rationally takes an option only when it benefits her, so an option worse than the player's equilibrium payoff in its absence is irrelevant. (This logic is subject to the caveat in the last paragraph of Section 16.1.5.)

An implication of these results is that when one is using a bargaining model to capture an economic or social phenomenon, the game must be specified appropriately, either as one in which bargaining may be terminated by events out of the control of either player, or as one in which one or both of the players may choose to break off negotiations.

16.1.7 More than two players

The bargaining game of alternating offers may be extended to three or more players in several ways. We may, for example, require all players, or only a majority, to accept an offer before it is final. In each case, we may easily find a subgame perfect equilibrium in which each player's strategy is stationary. In one major respect, however, these extensions are less successful than the two-player game: they have many nonstationary subgame perfect equilibria, with a wide range of equilibrium payoffs. An example is discussed in Osborne and Rubinstein (1994, 130–131).

16.2 Illustration: trade in a market

In the bargaining game of alternating offers, the two parties are restricted to negotiate only with each other. When trading in a market, an agent typically has the option to abandon her current partner and start negotiating with someone else. In this section I present some very simple models in which a single seller has the opportunity to trade with one of two buyers. In each case, the seller initially owns one indivisible unit of a good, and receives the payoff p if she trades at the price p and the payoff 0 if she does not trade. The buyers attach the values L and $H \geq L$ to the good; a buyer with value v receives the payoff $v - p$ if she obtains the good at the price p and the payoff 0 if she does not trade. Each party uses the factor δ to discount future payoffs. We are interested in how the presence of a second buyer affects the negotiated price.

16.2.1 Random matching

In the first model I discuss, in each period the seller is matched randomly with one of the buyers, and the proposer in the matched pair is determined randomly. Before studying this model, consider the implications of assuming that the proposer is chosen randomly in a model with a *single* buyer. That is, consider a variant of the bargaining game of alternating offers in which, at the start of the game and after any offer is rejected, each player is selected randomly with probability $\frac{1}{2}$ to make a proposal, to which the other player responds. This game, like the bargaining game of alternating offers, has a unique subgame perfect equilibrium, in which each player makes the same offer whenever she is the proposer and uses the same rule to accept an offer whenever she is the responder. Also as before, in the equilibrium a responder is indifferent between accepting a proposal and rejecting it. Denote the prices proposed by the seller and buyer in equilibrium by s and b. If the seller accepts b her payoff is b. If she rejects b, then play moves to the next period, in which with probability $\frac{1}{2}$ she is the proposer, so that her payoff is δs, and with probability $\frac{1}{2}$ the buyer is the proposer, so that her payoff is δb. Thus in an equilibrium we have

$$b = \tfrac{1}{2}\delta s + \tfrac{1}{2}\delta b.$$

By a similar argument for the buyer with value v we have

$$v - s = \tfrac{1}{2}\delta(v - s) + \tfrac{1}{2}\delta(v - b).$$

Solving these equations (which are analogues of (471.1) and (471.2)), we obtain

$$b = \tfrac{1}{2}\delta v \quad \text{and} \quad s = \tfrac{1}{2}(2 - \delta)v.$$

In particular, if δ is close to 1 (the players are very patient), then both prices are close to $\frac{1}{2}v$: in equilibrium, the surplus v is split almost equally between the seller and the buyer.

Now suppose there are two identical buyers ($H = L = v$). Consider the game in which in every period the seller is first randomly matched with one of the buyers, then one of the matched parties is randomly chosen to make an offer. The responder either accepts the offer, in which case trade occurs and the game ends, or rejects the offer, in which case play moves to the next period, in which the seller is again randomly matched with one of the buyers. This game has a unique sub-game perfect equilibrium, in which, as before, a responder is indifferent between accepting a proposal and rejecting it.

? EXERCISE 479.1 (One seller–two buyer bargaining with random matching) Find the prices proposed by the seller and by each buyer in a subgame perfect equilibrium of the game described in the previous paragraph. Show that when δ is close to 1, both these prices are close to v.

The result in this exercise shows that when the players are patient, the seller obtains almost all the surplus: the addition of a second potential buyer raises the price from close to $\frac{1}{2}v$ to close to v. The seller's power comes from the fact that a buyer knows that if she rejects an offer, with probability $\frac{1}{2}$ the other buyer will be matched with the seller in the next period, and she will not trade.

16.2.2 Choice of partner

Suppose that whenever the seller makes an offer, she *chooses* the buyer with whom to negotiate. That is, consider the following game. First, the seller chooses a buyer. Then the seller makes an offer to the buyer she chose. The chosen buyer either accepts the offer, in which case the game ends, or rejects it, in which case she makes a counteroffer to the seller. If the seller rejects this counteroffer, then the seller chooses the buyer with whom to negotiate in the next period. The buyers' valuations, H and L, may differ; refer to the buyer with valuation H as B_H, and to the buyer with valuation L as B_L.

How does the seller's ability to trade the buyers off against each other affect the equilibrium? A key question is whether a "threat" by the seller to switch to the other buyer if her current partner rejects her offer is credible. Given our analysis of the impact of an outside option in Section 16.1.5, we might correctly guess that it is not. The next exercise asks you to check that a strategy profile in which the seller bargains with buyer B_H as if the other buyer did not exist is a subgame perfect equilibrium. All subgame perfect equilibria, in fact, yield the same payoffs as does this one.

? EXERCISE 479.2 (One seller–two buyer bargaining with choice of partner) Show that the following strategy profile is a subgame perfect equilibrium of the game defined in this section. (A strategy profile in the game is a subgame perfect equilibrium if and only if it satisfies the one-deviation property.) The seller always chooses buyer B_H, proposes the price $H/(1+\delta)$ (to either buyer), and accepts a price if and only if it is at least $\delta H/(1+\delta)$. Buyer B_H always proposes $\delta H/(1+\delta)$ and accepts a price if and only if it is at most $H/(1+\delta)$. Buyer B_L always proposes $\min\{L, \delta H/(1+\delta)\}$ and accepts a price if and only if it is at most $\min\{L, H/(1+\delta)\}$.

The point is that if $H > L$, then the seller is in a stronger position with buyer B_H than she is with B_L, so that the threat, while bargaining with B_H, to switch to B_L, is not credible.

As when we add outside options to the bargaining game of alternating offers, this result depends on the timing of the game. The game in which the seller can switch partners just before a buyer makes an offer has many subgame perfect equilibria, in some of which the seller's payoff exceeds her payoff in the absence of buyer B_L.

16.2.3 Public price announcements

In the model in Section 16.2.1 (random matching), the presence of two buyers leads each of them to accept offers she otherwise would not because of the risk, if she rejects an offer, of the seller's being matched with, and subsequently trading with, the other buyer. In this sense, the buyers compete with each other. In the following game, the competition between the buyers is more direct.

First the seller announces a price. Buyer B_H either accepts or rejects this price. If she accepts it, she trades with the seller, and the game ends. If she rejects it, buyer B_L may either accept or reject it. If buyer B_L accepts it, she trades with the seller and the game ends. If buyer B_L rejects the price, the buyers simultaneously announce counteroffers in the next period. The seller may accept one of these offers, or reject them both. If she rejects them both, then in the next period she once again announces a price, and play continues as before.

If B_L did not exist, and the seller and buyer B_H played the bargaining game of alternating offers, in the unique subgame perfect equilibrium the seller would always propose the price $H/(1+\delta)$ and accept a price of at least $\delta H/(1+\delta)$, and B_H would always propose the price $\delta H/(1+\delta)$ and accept a price of at most $H/(1+\delta)$. Does the three-player game that includes B_L have a subgame perfect equilibrium in which the seller and B_H use these strategies?

Consider a subgame starting with the buyers' simultaneous offers. Buyer B_L can affect the outcome only if she proposes a price greater than $\delta H/(1+\delta)$, the price proposed by B_H. If $L < \delta H/(1+\delta)$, her payoff from trading at such a price is negative, so she optimally proposes a price of at most $\delta H/(1+\delta)$ and is content not to trade. In this case, the three-player game has a subgame perfect equilibrium in which the seller and B_H act as they do in the absence of B_L.

If $L > \delta H/(1+\delta)$, however, B_L has an interest in competing with B_H by proposing a price between $\delta H/(1+\delta)$ and L, and thus trading with the seller. Consequently the three-player game has no subgame perfect equilibrium in which the seller and B_H behave as if B_L did not exist. In this case, in fact, the competition between the buyers drives up to L the price they both propose and raises the price the seller proposes to $\delta L + (1-\delta)H$. The next exercise invites you to check that the game has a subgame perfect equilibrium with these properties; in fact, in every subgame perfect equilibrium the seller obtains the same price.

? EXERCISE 480.1 (One seller–two buyer bargaining with public price announcements) Show that if $\delta H/(1+\delta) < L$, then the following strategy profile is a subgame perfect equilibrium of the three-player game in this section. The seller always proposes the price $p^* = \delta L + (1-\delta)H$ (which exceeds $\delta H/(1+\delta)$). If the proposed prices of the buyers differ, the seller accepts the higher proposed price if this price is at least δp^*; if the proposed prices of the buyers are the same and at least δp^*, she accepts the proposal of buyer B_H; otherwise she rejects the buyers' proposals. Both buyers propose the price L. Buyer B_H accepts any price of at most p^*, and buyer B_L accepts any price less than L.

16.3 Nash's axiomatic model

A completely different approach to the study of bargaining considers the set of outcomes that satisfy some "reasonable" properties. It does not model the bargaining procedure—the sequence of possible offers and counteroffers—but rather studies the set of outcomes consistent with some assumptions about the character of the outcome and how it depends on the players' preferences and opportunities.

Suppose, as before, that two players must split one unit of a desirable good and that if they fail to reach agreement, neither receives anything. If their preferences are identical, we might reasonably predict that each player will obtain half of the unit. This prediction embodies two principles. First, the outcome is *efficient*. That is, none of the good is wasted; in particular, the parties do not fail to reach agreement. Second, the outcome is *symmetric*. Absent any differences between the players, there is no reason for the split to be anything but equal. The only outcome satisfying both of these principles is the equal split.

What if the players' preferences are not identical? This question forces us to think about the specification of preferences. Denote by X the set of possible *agreements* the players may reach and by D the outcome that they fail to agree—the *disagreement outcome*. If, for example, the players have to split one unit of a good, and failure to agree means that neither player receives anything, X is the set of possible divisions of the good, and D is the outcome in which neither player receives any of the good. In general, X may be any set; it could, for example, consist of contracts that specify the players' actions in many contingencies. Whatever its nature, we assume that each player has preferences over $X \cup \{D\}$ (the set of all members of X, together with D).

The players' preferences over deterministic outcomes do not seem to contain enough information to allow us to analyze the outcome of negotiation because risk appears to be inherent in bargaining: a negotiator is uncertain about her adversary's behavior and in particular must consider the possibility that negotiations will break down. Thus we take as given the players' preferences regarding *lotteries* over $X \cup \{D\}$. We assume, following convention, that each player's preferences are represented by the expected value of a Bernoulli payoff function (see Section 4.1.3). That is, player i has a payoff function u_i defined on $X \cup \{D\}$ such that she likes the lottery z over $X \cup \{D\}$ at least as much as the lottery z' over $X \cup \{D\}$ if and only if the expected value of u_i is at least as large for z as it is for z'.

Given payoff functions u_1 and u_2, the set X of possible agreements generates a set U of possible pairs of payoffs, defined by

$$U = \{(v_1, v_2) : u_1(x) = v_1 \text{ and } u_2(x) = v_2 \text{ for some } x \in X\},$$

and the disagreement outcome D generates the pair of payoffs $d = (u_1(D), u_2(D))$.

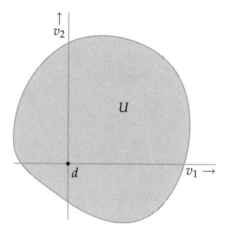

Figure 482.1 An illustration of a bargaining problem (U, d).

From now on, we work exclusively with the set U and the pair of payoffs d, rather than with X and D. In doing so, we assume that the outcome of bargaining depends only on the players' preferences, not independently on any feature of the set of possible agreements. Our aim is to isolate, for every possible set U and pair of payoffs d, the pair of payoffs to the outcome of negotiation.

We restrict attention to pairs (U, d) that satisfy the conditions in the following definition.

▶ DEFINITION 482.1 (*Bargaining problem*) A **bargaining problem** is a pair (U, d), where U is a set of pairs of numbers (the set of pairs of payoffs to agreements) and d is a pair of numbers (the pair of payoffs to disagreement), satisfying the following conditions.

- d is a member of U. (Disagreement is a possible outcome of bargaining—the players may "agree to disagree".)
- For some member (v_1, v_2) of U we have $v_1 > d_1$ and $v_2 > d_2$. (Some agreement is better for both players than disagreement.)
- If (v_1, v_2) and (w_1, w_2) are both in U, then for every α with $0 \leq \alpha \leq 1$ the pair of payoffs $(\alpha v_1 + (1 - \alpha)w_1, \alpha v_2 + (1 - \alpha)w_2)$ is also in U. (The set U is "convex".)
- U is bounded (i.e. it is a subset of a sufficiently large disk) and closed (i.e. the limit of every convergent sequence $(v^1, v^2, \ldots)$ of members of U is in U).

An example of a bargaining problem is shown in Figure 482.1. The geometric interpretation of the condition that U be convex is that if (v_1, v_2) and (w_1, w_2) are in U, then all points on the line segment joining (v_1, v_2) and (w_1, w_2) are in U. (A heart shape is not convex, for example, because the line segment joining the top of the left half with the top of the right half passes outside the shape.)

A *bargaining solution* associates with every bargaining problem (U, d) a member of U.

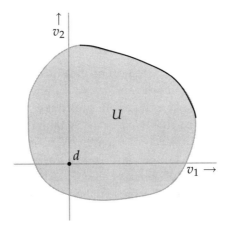

Figure 483.1 An illustration of the axiom of Pareto efficiency (PAR) for bargaining solutions. This axiom requires that the bargaining solution assign to the bargaining solution (U, d) a pair of payoffs on the black line segment.

▶ DEFINITION 483.1 (*Bargaining solution*) A **bargaining solution** is a function that associates with every bargaining problem (U, d) a member of U.

We can now state our objective: to study the bargaining solutions that satisfy a list of "reasonable" conditions, or "axioms". At the beginning of the section, I suggested two axioms for an environment in which the players split a pie. For the more general environment we are now studying, these axioms may be stated as follows.

First, the outcome should be efficient, in the sense that no other agreement yields both players higher payoffs. This type of efficiency is known as *Pareto efficiency* (after Vilfredo Pareto, 1848–1923), and the axiom may be stated precisely as follows.

Pareto efficiency (PAR) Let (U, d) be a bargaining problem, and let (v_1, v_2) and (v_1', v_2') be members of U. If $v_1 > v_1'$ and $v_2 > v_2'$, then the bargaining solution does not assign (v_1', v_2') to (U, d).

This axiom is illustrated in Figure 483.1. It restricts the possible agreements for the set U to those on the upper right boundary, indicated by the black curve. For any member of U not on this upper right boundary, there is another member in which both players' payoffs are higher.

Second, in the absence of any asymmetry between the players, the outcome should give both players the same payoff. That is, if the set U is perfectly symmetric, and d gives both players the same payoff, then the outcome of bargaining should give each player the same payoff.

Symmetry (SYM) Let (U, d) be a bargaining problem for which (v_1, v_2) is in U if and only if (v_2, v_1) is in U, and $d_1 = d_2$. Then the pair (v_1^*, v_2^*) of payoffs the bargaining solution assigns to (U, d) satisfies $v_1^* = v_2^*$.

This axiom is illustrated in Figure 484.1. Note that it imposes no restriction whatsoever on the outcome the bargaining solution assigns to bargaining problems (U, d) in which U is not symmetric or $d_1 \neq d_2$.

These two axioms immediately determine the outcome of any bargaining problem (U, d) in which U is symmetric and $d_1 = d_2$: the point on the upper right boundary of U in which the players' payoffs are equal.

We may extend the scope of the two axioms by taking into account the meaning of a member of U as a pair of Bernoulli payoffs. We know from Section 4.12.2 that a Bernoulli payoff function is unique only up to a linear transformation. Precisely, if there are numbers $\alpha > 0$ and β such that $w(x) = \alpha u(x) + \beta$ for all $x \in X$, then the Bernoulli payoff functions u and w represent the same preferences. An implication is that if $u_i'(x) = \alpha_i u_i(x) + \beta_i$ for $i = 1, 2$, then the bargaining problems (U, d) and (U', d') in which

$$U = \{(v_1, v_2) : u_1(x) = v_1 \text{ and } u_2(x) = v_2 \text{ for some } x \in X\}$$
$$d = (u_1(D), u_2(D))$$

and

$$U' = \{(v_1', v_2') : u_1'(x) = v_1' \text{ and } u_2'(x) = v_2' \text{ for some } x \in X\}$$
$$d' = (u_1'(D), u_2'(D))$$

represent the same situation: only the payoff representations differ, not the underlying preferences. A transparent example is shown in Figure 485.1. A pair (v_1', v_2') of payoffs is a member of the set U' on the right if and only if $v_1' - d_1' = 2(v_1 - d_1)$ and $v_2' - d_2' = v_2 - d_2$ for a member (v_1, v_2) of the set U on the left. We may rewrite the relations between the payoffs as $v_1' = 2v_1 - 2d_1 + d_1'$ and $v_2' = v_2 - d_2 + d_2'$, allowing us to see that each player's payoff in one problem is a linear function of

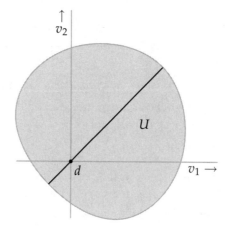

Figure 484.1 An illustration of the axiom of symmetry (SYM) for bargaining solutions. This axiom requires that the bargaining solution assign a point on the 45° line (indicated in black) to the bargaining problem (U, d), in which U is symmetric about the 45° line and d is on this line.

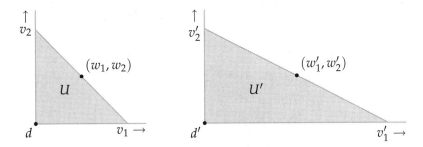

Figure 485.1 Two equivalent bargaining problems. The problem on the right may be obtained from the one on the left by applying linear transformations to the players' payoff functions.

her payoff in the other problem. Thus in the two bargaining problems, the players' preferences are the same; the problems differ only in the payoff representations of these preferences.

A basic assumption of our approach is that the outcome of bargaining depends only on the players' preferences, not on the payoff functions used to represent these preferences. Thus a bargaining solution should yield the same agreement when applied to bargaining problems that differ only in the payoff functions used to represent the players' preferences. A bargaining solution that yields the pair of payoffs (w_1, w_2) for the left-hand problem in Figure 485.1, for example, should yield the pair (w'_1, w'_2) for the right-hand problem, where $w'_1 = 2w_1 - 2d_1 + d'_1$ and $w'_2 = w_2 - d_2 + d'_2$

We may state the condition that a bargaining solution depend only on preferences, not on their payoff representation, precisely as follows.

Invariance to equivalent payoff representations (INV) Let (U, d) be a bargaining problem, let α_i and β_i be numbers with $\alpha_i > 0$ for $i = 1, 2$, let U' be the set of all pairs $(\alpha_1 v_1 + \beta_1, \alpha_2 v_2 + \beta_2)$, where (v_1, v_2) is a member of U, and let $d' = (\alpha_1 d_1 + \beta_1, \alpha_2 d_2 + \beta_2)$. If the bargaining solution assigns (w_1, w_2) to (U, d), then it assigns $(\alpha_1 w_1 + \beta_1, \alpha_2 w_2 + \beta_2)$ to (U', d').

This axiom, when combined with PAR and SYM, pins down the bargaining solution of any bargaining problem derived from a symmetric problem by linear transformations of the players' payoffs. Consider, for example, the bargaining problems in Figure 485.1. The axioms PAR and SYM, as we have seen, lead to the conclusion that the bargaining solution of the problem on the left, which is symmetric, is the point (w_1, w_2) indicated, where $w_1 - d_1 = w_2 - d_2$. The axiom INV thus implies that the bargaining solution of the problem on the right is (w'_1, w'_2).

Not all bargaining problems can be derived from symmetric problems by applying linear transformations to the players' payoffs, so the axioms PAR, SYM, and INV do not suffice to determine a unique solution for all problems. A single additional axiom, however, is enough to fully determine the outcome. This axiom ("independence of irrelevant alternatives") says that if we have two bargaining problems (U, d) and (U', d') for which U' is a subset of U and $d = d'$, and the pair of payoffs assigned by the bargaining solution to (U, d) is in U', then this pair of

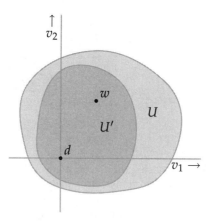

Figure 486.1 An illustration of the axiom of independence of irrelevant alternatives (IIA) for bargaining solutions. This axiom requires that if the bargaining solution assigns to the bargaining problem (U, d) the pair of payoffs w, and $w \in U'$, then it assigns w to the bargaining problem (U', d).

payoffs is assigned by the bargaining solution also to (U', d'). More loosely, if the solution of a large set is a member of a smaller set, then this solution is also the solution of the smaller set. The axiom is illustrated in Figure 486.1. The idea behind it is that in selecting a pair of payoffs to be the outcome of the bargaining problem (U, d), we have discarded all other members of U. Thus as long as U' includes the outcome we selected for (U, d), the fact that it excludes some of the pairs we discarded is not relevant to the outcome of (U', d).

Independence of irrelevant alternatives (IIA) Let (U, d) and (U', d') be bargaining problems for which U' is a subset of U and $d = d'$. If the agreement the bargaining solution assigns to (U, d) is in U', then the bargaining solution assigns the same agreement to (U', d').

? EXERCISE 486.1 (Implications of PAR, SYM, and IIA) Find the agreement (agreements?) compatible with PAR, SYM, and IIA for the bargaining problem (U, d) in which U is the triangle with corners at $(0,0)$, $(1,1)$, and $(2,0)$, and $d = (0,0)$.

The four axioms PAR, SYM, INV, and IIA are sufficient to determine a unique bargaining solution, as described in the following result.

▪ PROPOSITION 486.2 (Nash bargaining solution) *A unique bargaining solution satisfies the axioms INV, SYM, IIA, and PAR. This solution assigns to the bargaining problem (U, d) the pair of payoffs that solves the problem*

$$\max_{(v_1, v_2)} (v_1 - d_1)(v_2 - d_2) \text{ subject to } (v_1, v_2) \in U \text{ and } (v_1, v_2) \geq (d_1, d_2). \quad (486.3)$$

The bargaining solution defined in (486.3) is known as the **Nash bargaining solution**. I denote the Nash bargaining solution of the bargaining problem (U, d) by $\mathcal{N}(U, d)$. For any value of c, the set of points (v_1, v_2) such that $(v_1 - d_1)(v_2 - d_2) =$

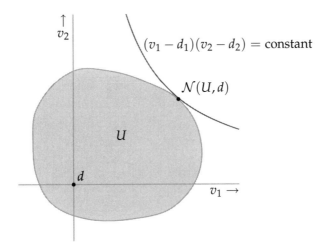

Figure 487.1 An illustration of the Nash bargaining solution $\mathcal{N}(U,d)$ of the bargaining problem (U,d).

c is a rectangular hyperbola relative to axes through the point (d_1, d_2); the hyperbola for c lies to the northeast of the hyperbola for any $c' < c$. Thus $\mathcal{N}(U,d)$ is the pair (v_1, v_2) of payoffs on the highest such hyperbola that has a point in common with U, as illustrated in Figure 487.1.

I do not give a full proof of the result, but outline some of the elements of the argument. First I argue that the bargaining solution $\mathcal{N}$ defined in the result satisfies the four axioms. The properties of the rectangular hyperbola defined by $(v_1 - d_1)(v_2 - d_2) = c$ imply that $\mathcal{N}$ satisfies PAR and SYM. The fact that $\mathcal{N}$ is the solution of a maximization problem implies that it satisfies IIA. Finally, I argue that $\mathcal{N}$ satisfies INV. Fix $\alpha_1 > 0$, $\alpha_2 > 0$, β_1, and β_2. Let

$$U' = \{(v_1', v_2') : v_1' = \alpha_1 v_1 + \beta_1 \text{ and } v_2' = \alpha_2 v_2 + \beta_2 \text{ for some } (v_1, v_2) \in U\},$$

and let $d' = (\alpha_1 d_1 + \beta_1, \alpha_2 d_2 + \beta_2)$. Then the maximizer of $(v_1' - d_1')(v_2' - d_1')$ over U' is $(\alpha_1 v_1^* + \beta_1, \alpha_1 v_1^* + \beta_1)$, where (v_1^*, v_2^*) is the maximizer of $(\alpha_1 v_1 + \beta_1 - d_1')(\alpha_2 v_2 + \beta_2 - d_1')$ over U. But

$$(\alpha_1 v_1 + \beta_1 - d_1')(\alpha_2 v_2 + \beta_2 - d_1') = \alpha_1 \alpha_2 (v_1 - d_1)(v_2 - d_1),$$

so its maximizer is $\mathcal{N}(U,d)$, the Nash solution of (U,d).

Second, I outline an argument that $\mathcal{N}$ is the only bargaining solution that satisfies the four axioms. Take an arbitrary bargaining problem (U,d) and a member (z_1, z_2) of U that is Pareto efficient, as in the left panel of Figure 488.1. Transform the players' payoffs in this problem, using linear functions $\alpha_i v_i + \beta_i$ for $i = 1, 2$, to obtain a new bargaining problem (U',d') in which $d' = (0,0)$ and (z_1, z_2) is transformed into $(\frac{1}{2}, \frac{1}{2})$, as in the right panel of Figure 488.1. (The transformations that yield this result satisfy $\alpha_i d_i + \beta_i = 0$ and $\alpha_i z_i + \beta_i = \frac{1}{2}$ for $i = 1, 2$.)

Suppose that no point in U' lies above a line with slope -1 through $(\frac{1}{2}, \frac{1}{2})$. We have no reason to think this condition is satisfied, but suppose it is. Then U' is

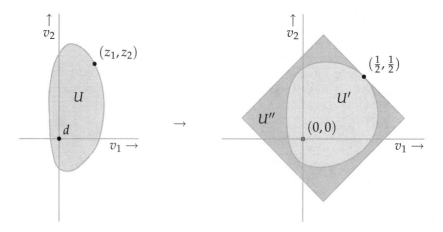

Figure 488.1 An illustration of a step in the argument that a bargaining solution satisfying PAR, SYM, INV, and IIA is the Nash bargaining solution.

contained in the symmetric rectangle U'' shown in the right panel of Figure 488.1, and we can argue as follows. Any bargaining solution that satisfies SYM and PAR assigns the agreement $(\frac{1}{2}, \frac{1}{2})$ to the bargaining problem (U'', d'), so any bargaining solution that in addition satisfies IIA assigns this same agreement to the bargaining problem (U', d'). Finally, the bargaining problem (U', d') is the result of applying linear transformations to (U, d) that map (z_1, z_2) into $(\frac{1}{2}, \frac{1}{2})$. Thus any bargaining solution that in addition satisfies INV assigns the agreement (z_1, z_2) to (U, d).

We are now left with the task of determining the point (z_1, z_2) in an arbitrary set U with the property that no point in the set U' generated from U by transformations that move d to $(0, 0)$ and (z_1, z_2) to $(\frac{1}{2}, \frac{1}{2})$ lies above a line with slope -1 through $(\frac{1}{2}, \frac{1}{2})$. The point with this property, it turns out, is the maximizer of the function $(v_1 - d_1)(v_2 - d_2)$ over U.

The result says that the only bargaining solution that satisfies the axioms PAR, SYM, INV, and IIA is the Nash bargaining solution $\mathcal{N}$. Thus any other bargaining solution fails to satisfy at least one of these axioms. The bargaining solution defined by $f(U, d) = d$ for any bargaining problem (U, d), for example, clearly satisfies SYM, INV, and IIA, but not PAR.

? EXERCISE 488.1 (Bargaining solutions)

a. For any bargaining problem (U, d), let $f(U, d)$ be the point in U on the 45° line through d for which v_1 (and v_2) is as large as possible. Show that the bargaining solution f does not satisfy INV.

b. For any bargaining problem (U, d), denote by b^1 the member of U for which $b_2^1 \geq d_2$ and b_1^1 is as large as possible, and by b^2 the member of U for which $b_1^2 \geq d_1$ and b_2^2 is as large as possible. Let $f(U, d)$ be the member of U on the line through d and (b_1^1, b_2^2) for which v_1 (and v_2) is as large as possible. Show that the bargaining solution f does not satisfy IIA. (It satisfies the other three axioms.)

? EXERCISE 489.1 (Wage bargaining) A firm and a union representing L workers negotiate a wage–employment contract. The firm produces $f(\ell)$ units of output when it employs ℓ workers, where f is an increasing function. Each worker not hired by the firm obtains the payoff w_0 (the wage in another job, or perhaps the unemployment benefit). The contract (w, ℓ), in which the firm pays the wage w and employs ℓ workers, yields payoffs of $f(\ell) - w\ell$ to the firm and $\ell w + (L - \ell)w_0$ to the union. In the event of disagreement, the firm's payoff is 0 and that of the union is Lw_0; let $d = (0, Lw_0)$. Assume that f is such that the set U of possible pairs of payoffs to agreements satisfies the assumptions on a bargaining problem (Definition 482.1). (In particular, assume that U is convex.) The Nash bargaining solution of (U, d) involves the employment level ℓ^* that maximizes $f(\ell) + (L - \ell)w_0$. (For any other value of ℓ the resulting pair of payoffs is not Pareto efficient.) Find the wage level in the Nash bargaining solution of (U, d).

16.4 Relation between strategic and axiomatic models

Consider the variant of the bargaining game of alternating offers considered in Section 16.1.4, in which after any proposal is rejected, negotiation breaks down with probability α. We found that if the Bernoulli payoff of each player i for the agreement (x_1, x_2) is x_i and α is small, then the agreement reached, and hence the pair of the players' payoffs in this agreement, is close to

$$\left(b_1 + \tfrac{1}{2}(1 - b_2 - b_1), b_2 + \tfrac{1}{2}(1 - b_1 - b_2) \right)$$

(see (475.1)). This pair of payoffs is precisely the Nash solution of the bargaining problem (U, d) in which U is the set of all pairs of payoffs to divisions of the pie (pairs (v_1, v_2) such that $v_1 + v_2 = 1$) and $d_i = b_i$ for $i = 1, 2$. (Refer to Figure 490.1.) That is, the variant of the bargaining game of alternating offers with probabilistic breakdown and Nash's axiomatic model, though built of entirely different components, yield the same outcome.

This remarkable relationship between the subgame perfect equilibrium outcome of a variant of the bargaining game of alternating offers and the Nash solution of an associated bargaining problem does not depend on the players' being risk neutral. Suppose that player i's Bernoulli payoff function is u_i, with $u_i(0) = 0$ for $i = 1, 2$. Define

$$U = \{(u_1(x_1), u_2(x_2)) : x_1 + x_2 \leq 1\}. \tag{489.2}$$

If each player i is risk averse (u_i is "concave"), then U is convex (see the definition of a bargaining problem, 482.1). Under the assumptions in Section 16.1.4, U is also bounded, contains $b = (b_1, b_2)$, and contains a pair of payoffs (v_1, v_2) such that $v_i > b_i$ for each player i. Thus (U, b) is a bargaining problem. The Nash bargaining solution $\mathcal{N}(U, b)$ of this problem is shown in Figure 491.1.

Now consider the variant of the bargaining game of alternating offers in which negotiation breaks down with probability α after each rejection. As we saw in Section 16.1.4, this game has a unique subgame perfect equilibrium, in which player 1

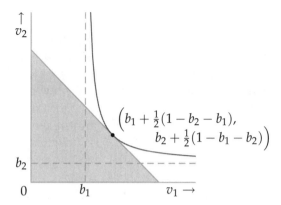

Figure 490.1 The Nash bargaining solution for the bargaining problem associated with the variant of the bargaining game of alternating offers in which there is a small probability of breakdown and the Bernoulli payoff function u_i of each player i is given by $u_i(x_i) = x_i$ for all x_i.

always proposes $\hat{x}(\alpha)$, player 2 always proposes $\hat{y}(\alpha)$, and player 2 immediately accepts player 1's first proposal, where $\hat{x}(\alpha)$ and $\hat{y}(\alpha)$ satisfy (474.1). This characterization of $\hat{x}(\alpha)$ and $\hat{y}(\alpha)$ has two key implications. First, as α converges to zero, the difference between $x(\alpha)$ and $y(\alpha)$ converges to zero. (Consider the equations when α is close to zero.) Second, $(u_1(\hat{y}_1(\alpha)), u_2(\hat{y}_2(\alpha)))$ and $(u_1(\hat{x}_1(\alpha)), u_2(\hat{x}_2(\alpha)))$ lie on the same rectangular hyperbola relative to the axes through (b_1, b_2). To reach this conclusion, subtract b_1 from the top equation and b_2 from the bottom equation in (474.1), to get

$$u_1(\hat{y}_1(\alpha)) - b_1 = (1 - \alpha)(u_1(\hat{x}_1(\alpha)) - b_1)$$
$$u_2(\hat{x}_2(\alpha)) - b_2 = (1 - \alpha)(u_2(\hat{y}_2(\alpha)) - b_2).$$

Now, multiply the left-hand side of the first equation by the right-hand side of the second equation, and the right-hand side of the first equation by the left-hand side of the second equation, and divide by $1 - \alpha$, to get

$$(u_1(\hat{x}_1(\alpha)) - b_1)(u_2(\hat{x}_2(\alpha)) - b_2) = (u_1(\hat{y}_1(\alpha)) - b_1)(u_2(\hat{y}_2(\alpha)) - b_2).$$

These two implications of (474.1) imply that the agreement $\hat{z}$ to which both $\hat{x}(\alpha)$ and $\hat{y}(\alpha)$ converge as α converges to 0 is the Nash solution of (U, b), as illustrated in Figure 491.1.

In summary, we have the following result.

■ PROPOSITION 490.1 *The subgame perfect equilibrium outcome of the variant of the bargaining game of alternating offers with risk of breakdown (and discount factors of 1 for each player) converges to the Nash bargaining solution of the associated bargaining problem as the probability of breakdown converges to 0.*

This result implies that when we use the Nash bargaining solution in a situation in which the main pressure on the players to reach an agreement is the possibility that bargaining will break down because of some exogenous event, we

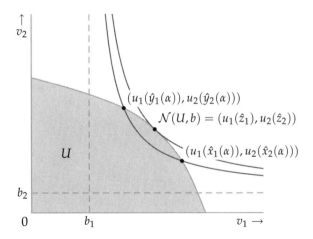

Figure 491.1 An illustration of the argument that the subgame perfect equilibrium outcome of the variant of the bargaining game of alternating offers with risk of breakdown converges to the Nash bargaining solution of the associated bargaining problem as the probability of breakdown converges to 0. When the probability of breakdown is α, the agreement proposed by player 1 in the subgame perfect equilibrium of the bargaining game of alternating offers is $x(\alpha)$, and the agreement proposed by player 2 is $y(\alpha)$; each of these agreements converges to $\hat{z}$ as α converges to 0.

should choose the disagreement point to be the players' payoffs in the event of breakdown. In particular, we should definitely not choose the disagreement point to be the players' payoffs in the event that one of the player's exercises an outside option, if she has one. As we saw in Section 16.1.5, the presence of an outside option *constrains* the subgame perfect equilibrium outcome of the bargaining game of alternating offers. A change in the outside option has no effect on the outcome of bargaining as long as the payoff of the player who may exercise the option remains below her equilibrium payoff in the absence of the option. By contrast, a change in a player's payoff in the event of a breakdown in negotiations affects her equilibrium payoff even when it remains below her equilibrium payoff in the absence of the possibility of breakdown.

Notes

Ståhl (1972, 1977) studies the alternating offer bargaining procedure in situations in which the horizon is effectively finite. The infinite horizon bargaining game of alternating offers in Section 16.1.3 was formulated and studied by Rubinstein (1982), who established Proposition 471.3.

The models in Section 16.2 are taken from Rubinstein and Wolinsky (1990) (random matching), and Binmore (1985) and unpublished notes of Robert B. Wilson (choice of partner, public price announcements). The presentation of the models follows Osborne and Rubinstein (1990, Chapter 9).

Section 16.3 is based on Nash (1950c), which originated axiomatic bargaining theory, and in particular establishes Proposition 486.2.

The close relation between the strategic and axiomatic models discussed in Section 16.4 was first noticed by Binmore (1987) and further explored by Binmore, Rubinstein, and Wolinsky (1986).

The model in Exercise 489.1 is standard; the specific assumptions are taken from Osborne and Rubinstein (1990, 19–20).

17 Appendix: Mathematics

17.1 Numbers 493
17.2 Sets 494
17.3 Functions 495
17.4 Profiles 498
17.5 Sequences 499
17.6 Probability 499
17.7 Proofs 505

THIS CHAPTER presents informal definitions and discussions of the mathematical concepts used in the text. Much of the material should be familiar to you, though a few concepts may be new.

17.1 Numbers

I take the concept of a **number** as basic; 3, -7.4, $\frac{1}{2}$, and $\sqrt{2}$ are all numbers. The whole numbers $\ldots, -3, -2, -1, 0, 1, 2, 3, \ldots$ are called **integers**. Let x be a number. If $x > 0$, then x is **positive**; if $x \geq 0$, then x is **nonnegative**; if $x < 0$, then x is **negative**; and if $x \leq 0$, then x is **nonpositive**. Note that 0 is both nonnegative and nonpositive, but neither positive nor negative.

When working with sums of numbers, a shorthand that uses the symbol $\sum$ (a large uppercase Greek sigma) is handy. Instead of writing $x_1 + x_2 + x_3 + x_4$, for example, where x_1, x_2, x_3, and x_4 are numbers, we can write

$$\sum_{i=1}^{4} x_i.$$

This expression is read as "the sum from $i = 1$ to $i = 4$ of x_i". The name we give the indexing variable is arbitrary; we frequently use i or j, but may alternatively use any other letter. If the number of items in the sum is a variable, say n, the notation is even more useful. Instead of writing $x_k + \cdots + x_n$, which leaves in doubt the variables indicated by the ellipsis, we can write

$$\sum_{i=k}^{n} x_i,$$

which has a precise meaning: first set $i = k$ and take x_i; then increase i by one and add the new x_i; continue increasing i by one at a time and adding x_i to the sum at each step, until $i = n$.

17.2 Sets

A **set** is a collection of objects. If we can count the members of a set, and, when we do so, we eventually exhaust the set, then the set is **finite**. We can specify a finite set by listing the names of its members within braces: {Paris, Venice, Havana} is a set of (beautiful) cities, for example. Neither the order in which the members of the set are listed nor the number of times each one appears has any significance: {Paris, Venice, Havana} is the same set as {Venice, Paris, Havana}, which is the same set as {Paris, Venice, Paris, Havana} (and has three members).

The symbol $\in$ is used to denote set membership: for example, Havana $\in$ {Paris, Venice, Havana}. We read the statement "$a \in A$" as "a is in A".

If every member of the set B is a member of the set A, we say that B is a **subset** of A. For example, the set {Paris}, consisting of the single city Paris, is a subset of the set {Paris, Venice, Havana} because Paris is a member of this set. The set {Paris, Havana} is also a subset of {Paris, Venice, Havana} because both Paris and Havana are members of the set. Further, the set {Paris, Venice, Havana} is a subset of itself: saying that A is a subset of B does *not* rule out the possibility that A and B are equal.

Given two sets A and B, the set consisting of all the members of both sets is called the **union** of A and B, and is denoted $A \cup B$. If, for example, $A =$ {Paris, Venice} and $B =$ {Havana, Kyoto, Paris}, then $A \cup B =$ {Paris, Venice, Havana, Kyoto}.

A **partition** of a set A is a collection $\{A_1, \ldots, A_k\}$ of subsets of A such that every member of A is in exactly one of the sets A_j. The set {Paris, Venice, Havana}, for example, has five possible partitions:

$$\{\{\text{Paris}\}, \{\text{Venice}\}, \{\text{Havana}\}\}$$
$$\{\{\text{Paris}, \text{Venice}\}, \{\text{Havana}\}\}$$
$$\{\{\text{Paris}, \text{Havana}\}, \{\text{Venice}\}\}$$
$$\{\{\text{Paris}\}, \{\text{Venice}, \text{Havana}\}\}$$
$$\{\{\text{Paris}, \text{Venice}, \text{Havana}\}\}.$$

Some sets are not finite. We can divide such sets into two groups. The members of some sets can be counted, but if we count them, then we go on counting forever. The set of positive integers is in this group. The members of other sets cannot be counted. For example, the set of all numbers between 0 and 1 cannot be counted. (Of course, one can arbitrarily choose one number in this set, then arbitrarily choose another number, and so on. But there is no systematic way of counting all the numbers.) We say that both types of sets have **infinitely many** members.

A set with infinitely many members obviously cannot be described by listing all its members. One way to describe such a set is to state a property that characterizes its members. For example, if a person's set of actions is a set A of numbers, then we can describe the subset of her actions that exceed 1 as

$$\{a \in A : a > 1\}.$$

We read this as "the set of all a in A such that a exceeds 1". If the set from which the objects come—in this case, the set A—is the set of all numbers, I do not specify it explicitly. Thus

$$\{p : 0 \leq p \leq 1\}$$

is the set of all nonnegative numbers that are at most 1.

Sometimes we wish to calculate the sum of the numbers x_i for every i in some set S. If S is a set of consecutive numbers of the form $\{1, \ldots, k\}$, then we can write this sum as

$$\sum_{i=1}^{k} x_i,$$

as described in Section 17.1. If S is not a set of consecutive numbers, then we can use a variant of this notation to denote the sum

$$\sum_{i \in S} x_i,$$

which means "the sum of all values of x_i for i in the set S". For example, if $S = \{\text{Paris, Venice, Havana}\}$ and the population of city i is x_i, then the total population of the cities in S is

$$\sum_{i \in S} x_i.$$

17.3 Functions

A **function** is a rule defining a relationship between two variables. We usually specify a function by giving the formula that defines it. For example, the function, say f, that associates with every number twice that number is defined by $f(x) = 2x$ for each number x, and the function, say g, that associates with every number its square is defined by $g(x) = x^2$.

If the variables that a function relates are both numbers, then the function can be represented in a graph, like the one in Figure 496.1. We usually put the independent variable (denoted x in the examples above) on the horizontal axis and the value of the function, $f(x)$, on the vertical axis. To read the graph, find a value of x on the horizontal axis, go vertically up to the graph, then horizontally to the vertical axis; the number on this axis is the value $f(x)$ of the function at x.

Two classes of functions figure prominently in the examples in this book: linear functions and quadratic functions. A function f defining a relationship between two numbers is **linear** (or, more properly, **affine**) if it takes the form $f(x) = ax + b$, where a and b are constants. For example, the functions $-3x + 1$ and $4x$ are both linear. (Sometimes the term "linear" is reserved for functions of the form $f(x) = ax$. However, it is widely used as a synonym for "affine", an informal convention

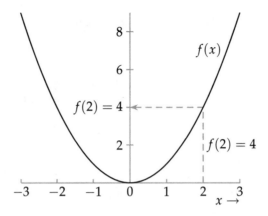

Figure 496.1 The graph of the function f defined by $f(x) = x^2$, for $-3 \le x \le 3$.

that I follow.) The graph of a general linear function $ax + b$ is a straight line with slope a that goes through the points $(0, b)$ and $(-b/a, 0)$ (because $a \cdot 0 + b = b$ and $a \cdot (-b/a) + b = 0$). In particular, if $a > 0$, then the slope is positive and if $a < 0$, then the slope is negative. An example with $a > 0$ and $b < 0$ is given in Figure 496.2.

A function f defining a relationship between two numbers is **quadratic** if it takes the form $f(x) = ax^2 + bx + c$, where a, b, and c are constants. If $a > 0$, then the graph of a quadratic function is U shaped, as in the left-hand panel of Figure 497.1; if $a < 0$, then the shape of the graph is an inverted U, as in the right-hand panel of this figure.

In both cases the graph is symmetric about a vertical line through the extremum of the function (the minimum when the graph of the function is U shaped and the maximum when it is an inverted U). Thus if we know the points x_0 and x_1 at which the graph of the function intersects some horizontal line (e.g. the horizontal axis), then we know that its extremum occurs at the midpoint of x_0 and x_1, namely $\frac{1}{2}(x_0 + x_1)$.

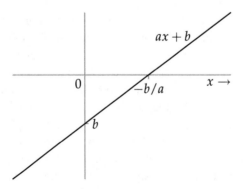

Figure 496.2 The graph of the linear function $ax + b$ (with $a > 0$ and $b < 0$).

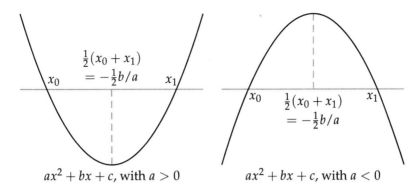

Figure 497.1 The graphs of two quadratic functions.

We can write the quadratic function $ax^2 + bx + c$ as $x(ax + b) + c$. Doing so allows us to see that the value of the function is c when $x = 0$ and when $x = -b/a$. That is, the function crosses the horizontal line of height c when $x = 0$ and when $x = -b/a$, so that its maximum (if $a < 0$) or minimum (if $a > 0$) occurs at $-\frac{1}{2}b/a$ (the midpoint of 0 and $-b/a$).

⊘ EXERCISE 497.1 (Maximizer of quadratic function) Find the maximizer of the function $x(\alpha - x)$ for any value of the constant α.

The graphs of the functions in Figures 496.1 and 497.1 do not have any jumps in them: for every point x, by choosing x' close enough to x we can ensure that the values $f(x)$ and $f(x')$ of the function at x and x' are as close as we wish. A function with this property is **continuous**. The graph of a continuous function does not have any holes in it. For example, the function whose graph is shown in the left panel of Figure 497.2 is continuous, whereas the function whose graph is shown in the right panel is not continuous. In graphs of discontinuous functions I use the convention that a small disk indicates a point that is included and a small circle indicates a point that is excluded.

For all the functions I have described so far, the value $f(x)$ of the function is a single number for every value of x. We sometimes need to work with functions

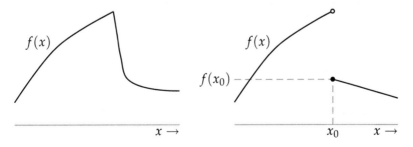

Figure 497.2 The function in the left panel is continuous, while the function in the right panel is not. The small disk indicates a point that is included in the graph, while the small circle indicates a point that is excluded.

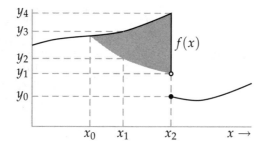

Figure 498.1 The graph of a set-valued function. For $x_0 < x \leq x_2$ the set $f(x)$ consists of more than one point. For example, $f(x_1) = \{y : y_2 < y \leq y_3\}$ and $f(x_2) = \{y: y = y_0$ or $y_1 < y \leq y_4\}$.

whose values are sets rather than points. Suppose, for example, that we need a function that assigns to each starting point x in some city the best route from x to city hall. For some values of x there may be a single best route, but for other values of x there are quite possibly several routes that are best, all equally good. At these latter values of x, the value of our function is a *set* of routes. It is convenient for our function to assign the same "type" of object to every value of x, so in this case we take all the values to be sets; if the single route A is optimal from the starting point $x_{,,}$ then we take the value of the function to be the set $\{A\}$ consisting of the single route A.

A set-valued function, like a point-valued function, may be specified by giving its graph. I indicate values of the function that consist of more than a single point by shading in gray, with boundaries that are included indicated by black lines. For example, for the function in Figure 498.1, $f(x_1) = \{y : y_2 < y \leq y_3\}$ and $f(x_2) = \{y: y = y_0$ or $y_1 < y \leq y_4\}$.

17.4 Profiles

Frequently in this book we wish to associate an object with each member of a set of players. For example, we often need to refer to the action chosen by each player. We can describe the correspondence between players and actions by specifying the function that associates each player with the action she takes. For example, if the players are Ernesto, whose action is R, and Hilda, whose action is S, then we may describe the correspondence between players and actions by the function a defined by $a(\text{Ernesto}) = R$ and $a(\text{Hilda}) = S$. We may alternatively present the function a by writing $(a_{\text{Ernesto}}, a_{\text{Hilda}}) = (R, S)$. We call such a function a a **profile**. The order in which we write the elements is irrelevant: we can alternatively write the profile as $(a_{\text{Hilda}}, a_{\text{Ernesto}}) = (S, R)$.

In most of the book I sacrifice color for convenience and name the players 1, 2, 3, and so on. Doing so allows me to write a profile of actions as a list like (R, S), without saying explicitly which action belongs to which player: the convention is that the first action is that of player 1, the second is that of player 2, and so on. When the number of players is arbitrary, equal to say n, I follow convention and write an action profile as $(a_1, \ldots, a_n)$, where the ellipsis stands for the actions of players 2 through $n - 1$.

I frequently need to refer to the action profile that differs from $(a_1, \ldots, a_n)$ only in that the action of player i is b_i (say) rather than a_i. I denote this variant of $(a_1, \ldots, a_n)$ by (b_i, a_{-i}). The $-i$ subscript on a stands for "except i": every player except i chooses her component of a. If $(a_1, a_2, a_3) = (T, L, M)$ and $b_2 = R$, for example, then $(b_2, a_{-2}) = (T, R, M)$.

17.5   Sequences

A **sequence** is an ordered list. The sequences used in this book consist of events that unfold over time; the first element of a sequence is an event that occurs before the second element of the sequence, and so on. A sequence that continues indefinitely is **infinite**; one that ends eventually is **finite**.

In Chapters 14 and 15 the formula for the sum of a sequence of numbers of the form $a, ar, ar^2, ar^3, \ldots$ (a "geometric series") is useful. First consider a finite sequence. Let $s_T = a + ar + ar^2 + \cdots + ar^T$. Then $rs_T = ar + ar^2 + \cdots + ar^T + ar^{T+1}$, so that $s_T - rs_T = a - ar^{T+1}$ (all the intermediate terms cancel out). Thus $s_T = a(1 - r^{T+1})/(1 - r)$ if $r \neq 1$, or

$$a + ar + ar^2 + \cdots + ar^T = \frac{a(1 - r^{T+1})}{1 - r} \qquad \text{if } r \neq 1. \qquad (499.1)$$

(Note that the exponent $T + 1$ of r in the numerator of the formula is the number of terms in the sequence.) If $-1 < r < 1$, then r^{T+1} converges to 0 as T increases without bound, so for an infinite sequence we have

$$a + ar + ar^2 + \cdots = \frac{a}{1 - r} \qquad \text{if } -1 < r < 1. \qquad (499.2)$$

⑦ EXERCISE 499.3 (Sums of sequences) Find the sums $1 + \delta^2 + \delta^4 + \cdots$ and $1 + 2\delta + \delta^2 + 2\delta^3 + \cdots$, where δ is a constant with $0 < \delta < 1$. (Split the second sum into two parts.)

17.6   Probability

17.6.1   Basic concepts

We may sometimes conveniently model an event as "random". Rather than modeling the causes of such an event, we assume that if the event occurs many times, then sometimes it takes one value, sometimes another value, in no regular pattern. We refer to the proportion of times it takes any given value as the **probability** of its taking that value.

A simple example is the outcome of a coin toss. We could model this outcome as a function of the initial position of the coin, the speed and direction in which it is tossed, the nature of the air currents, and so on. But it is simpler, and for many purposes satisfactory, to model the outcome as a head with probability $\frac{1}{2}$ and a tail with probability $\frac{1}{2}$. Given the sensitivity of the outcome to tiny changes in the initial position of the coin and the speed and direction in which it is tossed, and the inability of a person to precisely control these factors, the probabilistic theory is likely to work very well over many tosses: if the coin is tossed a large number n of times, then the number of heads is likely to be close to $n/2$.

We refer to an assignment of probabilities to events as a **probability distribution**. If, for example, there are three possible events, A, B, and C, then one probability distribution assigns probability $\frac{1}{3}$ to A, probability $\frac{1}{2}$ to B, and probability $\frac{1}{6}$ to C. In any probability distribution, the sum of the probabilities of all possible events is 1 (on any given occasion, *one* of the events must occur), and each probability is nonnegative and at most 1. Saying that an event occurs with positive probability is equivalent to saying that there is some chance that it may occur; saying that an event occurs with probability zero is equivalent to saying that it will never occur. Similarly, saying that an event occurs with probability less than one is equivalent to saying that there is some chance that it may not occur; saying that an event occurs with probability one is equivalent to saying that it is certain to occur. We sometimes denote the probability of an event E by $\Pr(E)$.

If the events E and F cannot both occur, then the probability that *either E or F* occurs is the sum $\Pr(E) + \Pr(F)$. For example, suppose we model the outcome of the toss of a die as random, with the probability of each side equal to $\frac{1}{6}$. Then the probability that the side is either 3 or 4 is $\Pr(3) + \Pr(4) = \frac{1}{6} + \frac{1}{6} = \frac{1}{3}$.

17.6.2 Independence

Two events E and F are **independent** if the probability $\Pr(E \text{ and } F)$ that they both occur is the product $\Pr(E)\Pr(F)$ of the probabilities that each occurs. Events may sensibly be modeled as independent if the occurrence of one has no bearing on the occurrence of the other. For example, the outcome of an election may sensibly be modeled as independent of the outcome of a coin toss, but not independent of the weather on the polling day (which may affect the candidates' supporters differently). In a strategic game, we usually model the players' choices of actions as independent: the probability that player 1 chooses action a_1 and player 2 chooses action a_2 is assumed to be the product of the probability that player 1 chooses a_1 and the probability that player 2 chooses a_2.

17.6.3 Lotteries and expected values

The material in this section is used only in Chapter 4 (Mixed Strategy Equilibrium), Section 7.6 (Allowing for exogenous uncertainty), Chapter 9 (Bayesian Games), Chapter 10 (Extensive Games with Imperfect Information), Chapter 11 (Strictly Competitive Games and Maxminimization), and Chapter 12 (Rationalizability).

Consider a decision-maker who faces a situation in which there are probabilistic elements. Each action that she chooses induces a probability distribution over outcomes. If you make an offer for an item in a classified advertisement, for example, then given the behavior of other potential buyers, your offer may be accepted with probability $\frac{1}{3}$ and rejected with probability $\frac{2}{3}$. We refer to a probability distribution over outcomes as a **lottery** over outcomes.

If the outcomes of a lottery are numerical (for example, amounts of money), we may be interested in their average value—the value we should expect to get if we found the total of the values on a large number n of trials and divided by n. For the lottery that yields the amount x_i with probability p_i, for $i = 1, \ldots, n$, this average value is

$$p_1 x_1 + \cdots + p_n x_n$$

or, more compactly, $\sum_{i=1}^{n} p_n x_n$. It is called the **expected value** of the lottery. A lottery that yields \$12 with probability $\frac{1}{3}$, \$4 with probability $\frac{1}{2}$, and \$6 with probability $\frac{1}{6}$, for example, has an expected value of $\frac{1}{3} \cdot 12 + \frac{1}{2} \cdot 4 + \frac{1}{6} \cdot 6 = 7$. On no single occasion does the lottery yield \$7, but over a large number of occasions the average amount that it yields is likely to be close to \$7 (the more likely, the larger the number of occasions).

17.6.4 Cumulative probability distributions

The material in this section is used only in Section 4.11 (Extension: games in which each player has a continuum of actions) and Chapter 9 (Bayesian Games).

If the events in our model are associated with numbers, we can describe the probabilities assigned to them by giving the **cumulative probability distribution**, which assigns to each number x the total of the probabilities of all numbers at most equal to x. The cumulative probability distribution of the number of dots on the top of a die, for example, is the function F for which $F(1) = \frac{1}{6}$, $F(2) = \frac{1}{3}$, $F(3) = \frac{1}{2}$, and so on. Given a cumulative probability distribution, we can recover the probabilities of the events by calculating the differences between values of F: the probability of x is $F(x) - F(x')$, where x' is the next smaller event.

When the number of events is finite, we can represent the assignment of probabilities to events either by a probability distribution or by a cumulative probability distribution. When the number of events is infinite, we can usefully represent the probabilities only by a cumulative probability distribution, because the probability of any single event is typically zero. If the set of events is the set of numbers from $\underline{a}$ to $\bar{a}$, then a cumulative probability distribution is a nondecreasing function, say F, for which $F(x) = 0$ if $x < \underline{a}$ (the probability of a number less than $\underline{a}$ is 0) and $F(\bar{a}) = 1$ (the probability of a number at most equal to $\bar{a}$ is 1). The number $F(x)$ is the probability of an event at most equal to x.

For example, if $\underline{a} = 0$ and $\bar{a} = 1$, then the function $F(x) = x$ (shown in the left panel of Figure 502.1) is a cumulative probability distribution. This distribution represents uniform randomization over the interval (sets of the same size have the same probability). Another cumulative probability distribution is given by the function $F(x) = x^2$ (shown in the right panel of Figure 502.1). In this distribution

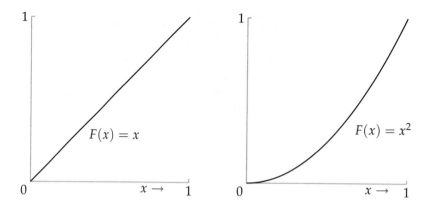

Figure 502.1 Two cumulative probability distributions.

the probabilities of sets of numbers close to 0 are lower than the probabilities of sets of numbers close to 1.

17.6.5 Conditional probability and Bayes' rule

The material in this section is used only in Section 9.7 (Illustration: juries) and Chapter 10 (Extensive Games with Imperfect Information).

Sometimes, when there is no possibility of an event's being repeated, we use the notion of probability to refer to the character of a person's belief. For example, a jury in a civil case is asked to determine whether the probability of a person's being guilty is greater than or less than one-half; you may form a belief about the probability of your carrying a particular gene or of your getting into graduate school. In some cases, these beliefs may be tightly linked to numerical evidence. If, for example, the only information you have about the prevalence of a particular gene is that it is carried by 10% of the population, then it is reasonable for you to believe that your probability of carrying the gene is 0.1. In other cases, beliefs may be at most loosely linked to numerical evidence. The evidence presented to a jury, for example, is likely to be qualitative, and open to alternative interpretations.

Whatever the basis for probabilistic beliefs, the theory of probability gives a specific rule for how such beliefs should be modified in the light of new probabilistic evidence. In this context, the initial belief is called the **prior belief**, and the belief modified by the evidence is called the **posterior belief**.

Suppose that 10% of the population carries the gene X, so that in the absence of any other information, your prior belief is that you carry the gene with probability 0.1. An imperfect test for the presence of X is available. The test is positive in 90% of subjects who carry X and in 20% of subjects who do not carry X. The test on you is positive. What should be your posterior belief about your carrying X? The probabilities are illustrated in Figure 503.1.

Consider a random group of 100 people from the population. Of these, on average 10 carry X and 90 do not. If all these 100 people were tested, then, on

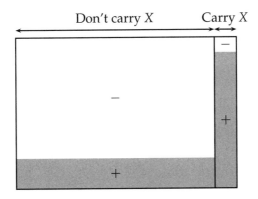

Figure 503.1 The outer box represents the set of people. People to the right of the vertical line carry gene X, while people to the left of this line do not. People in the shaded areas test positive for the gene.

average, 9 of the 10 (90%) who carry X and 18 of the 90 (20%) who do not carry X would test positive. These sets are represented by the shaded areas in Figure 503.1. Of all the people who test positive, what fraction of them carry the gene? That is, what fraction of the total shaded area in Figure 503.1 lies to the right of the vertical line? Of the 100 people, a total of $9 + 18 = 27$ test positive, and one-third of these (9/27) carry the gene. Thus after testing positive, your posterior belief that you carry the gene is $\frac{1}{3}$: the positive test raises the probability you assign to your carrying X from $\frac{1}{10}$ to $\frac{1}{3}$.

To generalize the analysis in this example, we introduce the concept of conditional probability. Let E and F be two events that may be related; assume that $\Pr(F) > 0$. Suppose that F is true. Define the **probability** $\Pr(E \mid F)$ **of** E **conditional on** F by

$$\Pr(E \mid F) = \frac{\Pr(E \text{ and } F)}{\Pr(F)}. \tag{503.1}$$

This number makes sense as the probability that E is true *given that F is true*. One way to see that it makes sense is to consider Figure 503.1 again. Let E be the event that you carry X and let F be the event that you test positive. If you test positive, then we know you lie in the shaded area. Given that you lie in this area, what is the probability $\Pr(E \mid F)$ that you lie to the right of the vertical line? This probability is the ratio of the shaded area to the right of the vertical line—the probability $\Pr(E \text{ and } F)$ that you carry the gene and test positive—to the total shaded area—the probability $\Pr(F)$ that you test positive.

If the events E and F are independent, then

$$\Pr(E \mid F) = \Pr(E) \text{ and } \Pr(F) > 0$$

or, alternatively,

$$\Pr(F \mid E) = \Pr(F) \text{ and } \Pr(E) > 0.$$

These conditions express directly the idea that the occurrence of one event has no bearing on the occurrence of the other event.

In using the expression for conditional probability to find the posterior belief in this case, we needed to calculate $\Pr(E \text{ and } F)$ and $\Pr(F)$, which were not given directly as data in the problem. The data we were given were the prior belief $\Pr(E)$, the probability $\Pr(F \mid E)$ of a person who carries the gene testing positive, and the probability $\Pr(F \mid \text{not } E)$ of a person who does not carry the gene testing positive.

Bayes' rule expresses the conditional probability $\Pr(E \mid F)$ in terms of $\Pr(E)$, $\Pr(F \mid E)$, and $\Pr(F \mid \text{not } E)$:

$$\Pr(E \mid F) = \frac{\Pr(E)\Pr(F \mid E)}{\Pr(E)\Pr(F \mid E) + \Pr(\text{not } E)\Pr(F \mid \text{not } E)}. \tag{504.1}$$

(The probability $\Pr(\text{not } E)$ is of course equal to $1 - \Pr(E)$; recall that I have assumed that $\Pr(F) > 0$.) This formula follows from the definition of conditional probability (503.1) and the properties of probabilities. First, interchanging E and F in (503.1) we deduce $\Pr(E)\Pr(F \mid E) = \Pr(E \text{ and } F)$. Thus the numerator of (504.1) is equal to $\Pr(E \text{ and } F)$. Second, again using (503.1) we see that the denominator of (504.1) is equal to $\Pr(E \text{ and } F) + \Pr((\text{not } E) \text{ and } F)$. Now, either the event E or the event not E occurs, but not both. Thus $\Pr(E \text{ and } F) + \Pr((\text{not } E) \text{ and } F) = \Pr(F)$. (The probability that either "it rains and you carry an umbrella" or "it rains and you do not carry an umbrella" is equal to the probability that "it rains".)

? EXERCISE 504.2 (Bayes' rule) Consider a generalization of the example of testing positive for a gene in which the fraction p of the population carries the gene. Verify that as p decreases, the posterior probability that you carry X given that you test positive decreases. What value does this posterior probability take when p is 0.001? What value does it take when p is 0.001 and the test is positive for 99% of those who carry X and is negative for 99% of those who do not carry X? (Are you surprised?)

In the cases I have described so far, the event about which we form a belief takes two possible values (E, or not E). More generally, this event may take many values. For example, we may form a belief about the quality of an item, or its price. In general, let F be an event and let $E_1, \ldots, E_n$ be a collection of events, exactly one of which must occur. (In my gene example, F is the event that you test positive, $n = 2$, E_1 is the event you carry the gene, and E_2 is the event you do not carry the gene.) Then the probability of E_k conditional on F is

$$\Pr(E_k \mid F) = \frac{\Pr(F \mid E_k)\Pr(E_k)}{\sum_{j=1}^{n}\Pr(F \mid E_j)\Pr(E_j)}. \tag{504.3}$$

This formula is known as **Bayes' rule**, after Thomas Bayes (1702–61). In the context in which we use this rule in a Bayesian game to find the probability of a state given the observed signal, the events $E_1, \ldots, E_n$ are the states, the event F is a signal, and every probability $\Pr(F \mid E_k)$ is either one or zero, depending on whether the state E_k generates the signal F or does not.

17.7 Proofs

This book focuses on concepts, but it contains precise arguments, and, in some cases, proofs of results. The results are given three names: lemma, proposition, and corollary. These names have no formal significance—they do not have any implications for the type of logic used—but are intended to convey the role of the result in the analysis. Lemmas are results whose importance lies mainly in their being steps on the way to proving further results. Propositions are the main results. Corollaries are more or less direct implications of the main results.

A result consists of a series of statements of the form "if A is true, then B is true". Frequently the series contains only one such statement, which may not be explicitly rendered as "if A, then B". For example, "all prime numbers are odd" is a result; it can be transformed into the "if ..., then" form: "if a number is prime, then it is odd". A result that makes the two claims "if A is true, then B is true" and "if B is true, then A is true" is sometimes stated compactly as "A is true if and only if B is true".

A proof of the result "if A, then B" is a series of arguments that lead from A to B, each member of which follows from a known fact, including an earlier member of the series. Except for the proofs of very simple results, most proofs are not, and should not sensibly be, "complete". To spell out how each step follows from the basic principles of mathematics would make a proof extremely long and very difficult to read. Some facts must be taken for granted; judging which to put in and which to leave out is an art. A good proof should contain just enough detail to convince readers that the result is true and to give them some understanding of *why* it is true (the features of A that are significant in establishing B, and those that are not significant). The author of a proof, like the author of a book, has to know when to stop adding material.

References

The page numbers on which the references are cited are given in brackets after each item.

Akerlof, George A. (1970), "The market for 'lemons': quality uncertainty and the market mechanism", *Quarterly Journal of Economics* **84**, 488–500. [311]

Allais, Maurice (1953), "Le comportement de l'homme rationnel devant le risque: critique des postulats et axiomes de l'école Américaine", *Econometrica* **21**, 503–546. [151]

Andreau, Jean (1999), *Banking and business in the Roman world*. Cambridge: Cambridge University Press. [97]

Aronson, Elliot (1995), *The social animal*, 7th ed. New York: Freeman. [151]

Arrow, Kenneth J. (1951), *Social choice and individual values*. New York: Wiley. [270]

Aumann, Robert J. (1985), "What is game theory trying to accomplish?", in *Frontiers of economics* (Kenneth J. Arrow and Seppo Honkapohja, eds.), 28–76. Oxford: Blackwell. [9]

Aumann, Robert J. (1989), *Lectures on game theory*. Boulder, CO: Westview Press. [375]

Aumann, Robert J. (1997), "Rationality and bounded rationality", *Games and Economic Behavior* **21**, 2–14. [203]

Aumann, Robert J., and Adam Brandenburger (1995), "Epistemic conditions for Nash equilibrium", *Econometrica* **63**, 1161–1180. [392]

Aumann, Robert J., and Bezalel Peleg (1960), "Von Neumann–Morgenstern solutions to cooperative games without side payments", *Bulletin of the American Mathematical Society* **66**, 173–179. [270]

Aumann, Robert J., and Lloyd S. Shapley (1994), "Long-term competition—a game-theoretic analysis", in *Essays in game theory* (Nimrod Megiddo, ed.), 1–15. New York: Springer-Verlag. [450]

Austen-Smith, David, and Jeffrey S. Banks (1996), "Information aggregation, rationality, and the Condorcet jury theorem", *American Political Science Review* **90**, 34–45. [311]

Austen-Smith, David, and Jeffrey S. Banks (1999), *Positive political theory I*. Ann Arbor: University of Michigan Press. [270]

Axelrod, Robert (1980a), "Effective choice in the Prisoner's Dilemma", *Journal of Conflict Resolution* **24**, 3–25. [440, 450]

Axelrod, Robert (1980b), "More effective choice in the Prisoner's Dilemma", *Journal of Conflict Resolution* **24**, 379–403. [440, 450]

Axelrod, Robert (1984), *The evolution of cooperation*. New York: Basic Books. [440, 450]

Bagwell, Kyle (1995), "Commitment and observability in games", *Games and Economic Behavior* **8**, 271–280. [358]

Banks, Jeffrey S. (1991), *Signaling games in political science*. Chur, Switzerland: Harwood Academic Publishers. [357]

Banks, Jeffrey S. (1995), "Singularity theory and core existence in the spatial model", *Journal of Mathematical Economics* **24**, 523–536. [270]

Baye, Michael R., Dan Kovenock, and Casper G. de Vries (1996), "The all-pay auction with complete information", *Economic Theory* **8**, 291–305. [151]

Baye, Michael R., and John Morgan (1999), "A folk theorem for one-shot Bertrand games", *Economic Letters* **65**, 59–65. [151]

Becker, Gary S. (1974), "A theory of social interactions", *Journal of Political Economy* **82**, 1063–1093. [180]

Bellman, Richard (1957), *Dynamic programming*. Princeton, NJ: Princeton University Press. [179]

Bellman, Richard, and David Blackwell (1949), "Some two-person games involving bluffing", *Proceedings of the National Academy of Sciences of the United States of America* **35**, 600–605. [357]

Benoît, Jean-Pierre (1984), "Financially constrained entry in a game of incomplete information", *Rand Journal of Economics* **15**, 490–499. [179, 237]

Benoît, Jean-Pierre, and Lewis A. Kornhauser (2002), "Game-theoretic analysis of legal rules and institutions", in *Handbook of Game Theory with Economic Applications*, Volume 3 (Robert J. Aumann and Sergiu Hart, eds.), 2229–2269. Amsterdam: Elsevier. [97]

Benoît, Jean-Pierre, and Vijay Krishna (1985), "Finitely repeated games", *Econometrica* **53**, 905–922. [464]

Benoît, Jean-Pierre, and Vijay Krishna (1987), "Nash equilibria of finitely repeated games", *International Journal of Game Theory* **16**, 197–204. [464]

Bergstrom, Carl T., and Michael Lachmann (1997), "Signalling among relatives. I. Is costly signalling *too* costly?", *Philosophical Transactions of the Royal Society of London, Series B (Biological Sciences)* **352**, 609–617. [358]

Bergstrom, Theodore C. (1989), "A fresh look at the rotten kid theorem—and other household mysteries", *Journal of Political Economy* **97**, 1138–1159. [180]

Bergstrom, Theodore C. (1995), "On the evolution of altruistic ethical rules for siblings", *American Economic Review* **85**, 58–81. [412, 413, 417]

Bergstrom, Theodore C., Lawrence E. Blume, and Hal R. Varian (1986), "On the private provision of public goods", *Journal of Public Economics* **29**, 25–49. [53]

Bergstrom, Theodore C., and Hal R. Varian (1987), *Workouts in intermediate microeconomics*, 3rd ed. New York: Norton. [417]

Bernheim, B. Douglas (1984), "Rationalizable strategic behavior", *Econometrica* **52**, 1007–1028. [392]

Bernoulli, Daniel (1738), "Specimen theoriae novae de mensura sortis", translated by Louise Sommer as "Exposition of a new theory on the measurement of risk", *Econometrica* **22** (1954), 23-36. [150]

Bertrand, Joseph (1883), "Review of 'Théorie mathématique de la richesse sociale' by Léon Walras and 'Recherches sur les principes mathématiques de la théorie des richesses' by Augustin Cournot", *Journal des Savants*, September, 499–508. (Translated by Margaret Chevaillier as "Review by Joseph Bertrand of two books", *History of Political Economy* **24** (1992), 646–653.) [63, 70, 97]

Binmore, Kenneth G. (1985), "Bargaining and coalitions", in *Game-theoretic models of bargaining* (Alvin E. Roth, ed.), 269–304. Cambridge: Cambridge University Press. [491]

Binmore, Kenneth G. (1987), "Nash bargaining theory II", in *The economics of bargaining* (Kenneth G. Binmore and Partha Dasgupta, eds.), 61–76. Oxford: Blackwell. [492]

Binmore, Kenneth G. (1992), *Fun and games*. Lexington, MA: Heath. [357]

Binmore, Kenneth G., Ariel Rubinstein, and Asher Wolinsky (1986), "The Nash bargaining solution in economic modelling", *Rand Journal of Economics* **17**, 176–188. [492]

Black, Duncan (1958), *The theory of committees and elections*. Cambridge: Cambridge University Press. [270]

Black, Duncan, and R. A. Newing (1951), *Committee decisions with complementary valuation*. London: Hodge. [270]

Blackwell, David, and M. A. Girshick (1954), *Theory of games and statistical decisions*. New York: Wiley. [97]

Bolton, Gary E, and Axel Ockenfels (2000), "ERC: a theory of equity, reciprocity, and competition", *American Economic Review* **90**, 166–193. [203, 237]

Bolton, Gary E, and Rami Zwick (1995), "Anonymity versus punishment in ultimatum bargaining", *Games and Economic Behavior* **10**, 95–121. [184]

Borel, Émile (1921), "La théorie du jeu et les equations intégrales à noyau symétrique", *Comptes Rendus Hebdomadaires des Séances de l'Académie des Sciences (Paris)* **173**, 1304–1308. (Translated by Leonard J. Savage as "The theory of play and integral equations with skew symmetric kernels", *Econometrica* **21** (1953), 97–100.) [53, 150]

Borel, Émile (1924), *Eléments de la théorie des probabilités*, 3rd ed. Paris: Hermann. (Pages 204–221 translated by Leonard J. Savage as "On games that involve chance and the skill of the players", *Econometrica* **21** (1953), 101–115.) [150, 151]

Borel, Émile (1927), "Sur les systèmes de formes linéaires à déterminant symétrique gauche et la théorie générale du jeu", *Comptes Rendus Hebdomadaires des Séances de l'Académie des Sciences (Paris)* **184**, 52–54. (Translated by Leonard J. Savage as "On systems of linear forms of skew symmetric determinant and the general theory of play", *Econometrica* **21** (1953), 116–117.) [150]

Borel, Émile (1938), *Traité du calcul des probabilités et de ses applications*, Volume IV, Part II (*Applications aux jeux de hasard*) (Lectures by Émile Borel, transcribed by Jean Ville). Paris: Gauthier-Villars. [357]

Boylan, Richard T. (2000), "An optimal auction perspective on lobbying", *Social Choice and Welfare* **17**, 55–68. [97]

Braess, Dietrich (1968), "Über ein Paradoxon der Verkehrsplanung", *Unternehmensforschung* **12**, 258–268. [54]

Brams, Steven J., and Peter C. Fishburn (1978), "Approval voting", *American Political Science Review* **72**, 831–847. [53]

Brams, Steven J., and Peter C. Fishburn (1983), *Approval voting.* Boston: Birkhäuser. [53]

Brams, Steven J., D. Marc Kilgour, and Morton D. Davis (1993), "Unraveling in games of sharing and exchange", in *Frontiers of Game Theory* (Kenneth G. Binmore, Alan Kirman, and Piero Tani, eds.), 195–212. Cambridge, MA: MIT Press. [54, 311]

Brams, Steven J., and Philip D. Straffin, Jr. (1979), "Prisoners' Dilemma and professional sports drafts", *American Mathematical Monthly* **86**, 80–88. [174, 179]

Brams, Steven J., and Alan D. Taylor (1996), *Fair division.* Cambridge University Press: Cambridge. [203]

Brockmann, H. Jane, Alan Grafen, and Richard Dawkins (1979), "Evolutionarily stable nesting strategy in a digger wasp", *Journal of Theoretical Biology* **77**, 473–496. [401, 416, 417]

Brown, George W. (1951), "Iterative solution of games by fictitious play", in *Activity analysis of production and allocation* (Tjalling C. Koopmans, ed.), 374–376. New York: Wiley. [151]

Brown, James N., and Robert W. Rosenthal (1990), "Testing the minimax hypothesis: a re-examination of O'Neill's game experiment", *Econometrica* **58**, 1065–1081. [374, 375]

Brown, John P. (1973), "Toward an economic theory of liability", *Journal of Legal Studies* **2**, 323–349. [97]

Brown, Roger (1986), *Social psychology, the second edition.* New York: Free Press. [151]

Bryant, John (1983), "A simple rational expectations Keynes-type model", *Quarterly Journal of Economics* **98**, 525–528. [30]

Bryant, John (1994), "Coordination theory, the stag hunt and macroeconomics", in *Problems of coordination in economic activity* (James W. Friedman, ed.), 207–225. Boston, MA: Kluwer. [30]

Bulmer, Michael G. (1994), *Theoretical evolutionary ecology.* Sunderland, MA: Sinauer Associates. [417]

Burgess, J. Wesley (1976), "Social spiders", *Scientific American* **234 (3)**, 100–106. [409]

Camerer, Colin (1995), "Individual decision making", in *The handbook of experimental economics* (John H. Kagel and Alvin E. Roth, eds.), 587–703. Princeton, NJ: Princeton University Press. [104]

Capen, E. C., R. V. Clapp, and W. M. Campbell (1971), "Competitive bidding in high-risk situations", *Journal of Petroleum Technology* **23**, 641–653. [311]

Carcopino, Jérôme (1940), *Daily life in ancient Rome* (edited with bibliography and notes by Henry T. Rowell, translated by E. O. Lorimer). New Haven, CT: Yale University Press. [372]

Cassady, Ralph, Jr. (1967), *Auctions and auctioneering*. Berkeley: University of California Press. [81, 97]

Cho, In-Koo, and David M. Kreps (1987), "Signaling games and stable equilibria", *Quarterly Journal of Economics* **102**, 179–221. [357]

Conlisk, John (1989), "Three variants on the Allais example", *American Economic Review* **79**, 392–407. [104, 105, 151]

Cooper, Russell, Douglas V. DeJong, Robert Forsythe, and Thomas W. Ross (1996), "Cooperation without reputation: experimental evidence from Prisoner's Dilemma games", *Games and Economic Behavior* **12**, 187–218. [28]

Cournot, Antoine A. (1838), *Recherches sur les principes mathématiques de la théorie des richesses*. Paris: Hachette. (Translated by Nathaniel T. Bacon as "Researches into the mathematical principles of the theory of wealth", New York: Macmillan, 1897.) [53, 55, 97, 151]

Court, Gordon S. (1996), "The seal's own skin game", *Natural History* **105 (8)**, 36–41. [114]

Cramton, Peter C. (1995), "Money out of thin air: the nationwide narrowband PCS auction", *Journal of Economics and Management Strategy* **4**, 267–343. [311]

Cramton, Peter C. (1997), "The FCC spectrum auctions: an early assessment", *Journal of Economics and Management Strategy* **6**, 431–495. [311]

Cramton, Peter C. (1998), "The efficiency of the FCC spectrum auctions", *Journal of Law and Economics* **41**, 727–736. [311]

Crawford, Vincent P., and Joel Sobel (1982), "Strategic information transmission", *Econometrica* **50**, 1431–1451. [357]

Darwin, Charles (1871), *The descent of man, and selection in relation to sex*. London: Murray. [399]

Darwin, Charles (1874), *The descent of man, and selection in relation to sex*, 2nd ed. (revised and augmented). London: Murray. [417]

Denzau, Arthur T., and Robert J. Mackay (1983), "Gatekeeping and monopoly power of committees: an analysis of sincere and sophisticated behavior", *American Journal of Political Science* **27**, 740–761. [203]

Deutsch, Morton (1958), "Trust and suspicion", *Journal of Conflict Resolution* **2**, 265–279. [28]

Dhillon, Amrita, and Ben Lockwood (2004), "When are plurality rule voting games dominance-solvable?", *Games and Economic Behavior* **46**, 55–75. [392]

Diamond, Peter A. (1974), "Accident law and resource allocation", *Bell Journal of Economics and Management Science* **5**, 366–405. [97]

Diermeier, Daniel, and Timothy J. Feddersen (1998), "Cohesion in legislatures and the vote of confidence procedure", *American Political Science Review* **92**, 611–621. [237]

Downs, Anthony (1957), *An economic theory of democracy*. New York: Harper & Row. [97]

Dubey, Pradeep, and Mamoru Kaneko (1984), "Information patterns and Nash equilibria in extensive games: I", *Mathematical Social Sciences* **8**, 111–139. [236]

Dubins, Lester E., and David A. Freedman (1981), "Machiavelli and the Gale–Shapley algorithm", *American Mathematical Monthly* **88**, 485–494. [270]

Dugatkin, Lee Alan (1991), "Dynamics of the tit for tat strategy during predator inspection in the guppy (*Poecilia reticulata*)", *Behavioral Ecology and Sociobiology* **29**, 127–132. [446]

Edgeworth, Francis Y. (1881), *Mathematical psychics*. London: Kegan Paul. [270]

Elster, Jon (1998), "Emotions and economic theory", *Journal of Economic Literature* **36**, 47–74. [9]

Ewerhart, Christian (2000), "Chess-like games are dominance solvable in at most two steps", *Games and Economic Behavior* **33**, 41–47. [392]

Farquharson, Robin (1969), *Theory of voting*. New Haven, CT: Yale University Press. [53, 236]

Feddersen, Timothy J., and Wolfgang Pesendorfer (1996), "The swing voter's curse", *American Economic Review* **86**, 408–424. (See also Mark Fey and Jaehoon Kim (2002), "The swing voter's curse: comment", *American Economic Review* **92**, 1264–1268.) [311]

Feddersen, Timothy J., and Wolfgang Pesendorfer (1998), "Convicting the innocent: the inferiority of unanimous jury verdicts under strategic voting", *American Political Science Review* **92**, 23–35. [307, 311]

Feddersen, Timothy J., Itai Sened, and Stephen G. Wright (1990), "Rational voting and candidate entry under plurality rule", *American Journal of Political Science* **34**, 1005–1016. [237]

Fellner, William (1949), *Competition among the few*. New York: Knopf. [70]

Fisher, Ronald A. (1930), *The genetical theory of natural selection*. Oxford: Clarendon Press. [417]

Flood, Merrill M. (1958/59), "Some experimental games", *Management Science* **5**, 5–26. [53, 436, 449, 450]

Forsythe, Robert, Joel L. Horowitz, N. E. Savin, and Martin Sefton (1994), "Fairness in simple bargaining experiments", *Games and Economic Behavior* **6**, 347–369. [184]

Frank, Robert H., Thomas Gilovich, and Dennis T. Regan (1993), "Does studying economics inhibit cooperation?", *Journal of Economic Perspectives* **7 (2)**, 159–171. [28]

Friedman, James W. (1971), "A non-cooperative equilibrium for supergames", *Review of Economic Studies* **38**, 1–12. [450]

Fudenberg, Drew, and David K. Levine (1998), *The theory of learning in games*. Cambridge, MA: MIT Press. [151]

Fudenberg, Drew, and Eric S. Maskin (1986), "The folk theorem in repeated games with discounting or with incomplete information", *Econometrica* **54**, 533–554. [450, 464]

Fudenberg, Drew, and Eric S. Maskin (1991), "On the dispensability of public randomization in discounted repeated games", *Journal of Economic Theory* **53**, 428–438. [450, 464]

Fudenberg, Drew, and Jean Tirole (1991), "Perfect Bayesian equilibrium and sequential equilibrium", *Journal of Economic Theory* **53**, 236–260. [357]

Gabay, Daniel, and Hervé Moulin (1980), "On the uniqueness and stability of Nash-equilibria in noncooperative games", in *Applied stochastic control in econometrics and management science* (Alain Bensoussan, Paul Kleindorfer, and Charles S. Tapiero, eds.), 271–293. Amsterdam: North-Holland. [392]

Gale, David (1953), "A theory of *N*-person games with perfect information", *Proceedings of the National Academy of Sciences of the United States of America* **39**, 496–501. [392]

Gale, David, and Lloyd S. Shapley (1962), "College admissions and the stability of marriage", *American Mathematical Monthly* **69**, 9–15. [270]

Gardner, Martin (1959), *The Scientific American book of mathematical puzzles and diversions*. New York: Simon & Schuster. [180]

Ghemawat, Pankaj, and Barry Nalebuff (1985), "Exit", *Rand Journal of Economics* **16**, 184–194. [237]

Gillies, Donald B. (1959), "Solutions to general non-zero-sum games", in *Contributions to the theory of games*, Volume IV (*Annals of Mathematics Studies*, 40) (A. W. Tucker and R. D. Luce, eds.), 47–85. Princeton, NJ: Princeton University Press. [270]

Gilligan, Thomas W., and Keith Krehbiel (1987), "Collective decisionmaking and standing committees: an informational rationale for restrictive amendment procedures", *Journal of Law, Economics, and Organization* **3**, 287–335. [357]

Godfray, H. Charles J., and Rufus A. Johnstone (2000), "Begging and bleating: the evolution of parent–offspring signalling", *Philosophical Transactions of the Royal Society of London, Series B (Biological Sciences)* **355**, 1581–1591. [358]

Gordon, H. Scott (1954), "The economic theory of a common-property resource: the fishery", *Journal of Political Economy* **62**, 124–142. [53]

Green, Edward J., and Robert H. Porter (1984), "Noncooperative collusion under imperfect price information", *Econometrica* **52**, 87–100. [464]

Greville, Fulke (1986), *The prose works of Fulke Greville, Lord Brooke* (John Gouws, ed.). Oxford: Clarendon Press. [358]

Groseclose, Tim, and James M. Snyder, Jr. (1996), "Buying supermajorities", *American Political Science Review* **90**, 303–315. [203]

Grout, Paul A. (1984), "Investment and wages in the absence of binding contracts: a Nash bargaining approach", *Econometrica* **52**, 449–460. [203]

Guilbaud, Georges T. (1961), "Faut-il jouer au plus fin? (notes sur l'histoire de la théorie des jeux)", in *La décision*, 171–182. Paris: Éditions du Centre National de la Recherche Scientifique. [150, 375]

Güth, Werner, and Steffen Huck (1997), "From ultimatum bargaining to dictatorship—an experimental study of four games varying in veto power", *Metroeconomica* **48**, 262–279. [184]

Güth, Werner, Rolf Schmittberger, and Bernd Schwarze (1982), "An experimental analysis of ultimatum bargaining", *Journal of Economic Behavior and Organization* **3**, 367–388. [184, 203]

Hald, Anders (1990), *A history of probability and statistics and their applications before 1750*. New York: Wiley. [370]

Halmos, Paul R. (1973), "The legend of John von Neumann", *American Mathematical Monthly* **80**, 382–394. [3, 9]

Hamilton, W. D. (1967), "Extraordinary sex ratios", *Science* **156**, 477–488. [399]

Hammerstein, Peter, and Susan E. Riechert (1988), "Payoffs and strategies in territorial contests: ESS analyses of two ecotypes of the spider *Agelenopsis aperta*", *Evolutionary Ecology* **2**, 115–138. [410, 417]

Hammerstein, Peter, and Reinhard Selten (1994), "Game theory and evolutionary biology", in *Handbook of Game Theory*, Volume 2 (Robert J. Aumann and Sergiu Hart, eds.), 929–993. Amsterdam: Elsevier. [403, 417]

Hardin, Garrett (1968), "The tragedy of the commons", *Science* **162**, 1243–1248. [53]

Harris, Christopher, and John Vickers (1985), "Perfect equilibrium in a model of a race", *Review of Economic Studies* **52**, 193–209. [203]

Harsanyi, John C. (1967/68), "Games with incomplete information played by 'Bayesian' players, Parts I, II, and III", *Management Science* **14**, 159–182, 320–334, and 486–502. [311]

Herodotus (1998), *The histories* (translated by Robin Waterfield). Oxford: Oxford University Press. [97]

Heuer, Gerald A. (1995), "Solution to problem 1069", *Journal of Recreational Mathematics* **27**, 146–158. [Author's middle initial incorrectly given as "N" in journal.] [151]

Hey, John D. (1997), "Experiments and the economics of individual decision making under risk and uncertainty", in *Advances in economics and econometrics: theory and applications (Seventh World Congress)*, Volume I (David M. Kreps and Kenneth F. Wallis, eds.), 173–205. Cambridge: Cambridge University Press. [151]

Hirshleifer, Jack, and Juan Carlos Martinez Coll (1988), "What strategies can support the evolutionary emergence of cooperation?", *Journal of Conflict Resolution* **32**, 367–398. [440, 450]

Hoffman, Elizabeth, Kevin A. McCabe, and Vernon L. Smith (1996), "On expectations and the monetary stakes in ultimatum games", *International Journal of Game Theory* **25**, 289–301. [184]

Holt, Charles A., Jr., and Roger Sherman (1982), "Waiting-line auctions", *Journal of Economic Perspectives* **90**, 280–294. [98]

Hotelling, Harold (1929), "Stability in competition", *Economic Journal* **39**, 41–57. [73, 97]

Jervis, Robert (1977/78), "Cooperation under the security dilemma", *World Politics* **30**, 167–214. [53]

Kalai, Ehud, Dov Samet, and William Stanford (1988), "A note on reactive equilibria in the discounted Prisoner's Dilemma and associated games", *International Journal of Game Theory* **17**, 177–186. [450]

Karlin, Samuel (1959a), *Mathematical methods and theory in games, programming, and economics*, Volume I. Reading, MA: Addison-Wesley. [151]

Karlin, Samuel (1959b), *Mathematical methods and theory in games, programming, and economics*, Volume II. Reading, MA: Addison-Wesley. [97, 357]

Kim, Yong-Gwan (1994), "Evolutionarily stable strategies in the repeated Prisoner's Dilemma", *Mathematical Social Sciences* **28**, 167–197. [441, 450]

Kinnaird, Clark (1946), *Encyclopedia of puzzles and pastimes*. New York: Citadel Press. [237]

Klemperer, Paul (1999), "Auction theory: a guide to the literature", *Journal of Economic Surveys* **13**, 227–286. [311]

Kohlberg, Elon, and Jean-François Mertens (1986), "On the strategic stability of equilibria", *Econometrica* **54**, 1003–1037. [358]

Kohler, David A., and R. Chandrasekaran (1971), "A class of sequential games", *Operations Research* **19**, 270–277. [179]

Kreps, David M., and Robert B. Wilson (1982), "Sequential equilibria", *Econometrica* **50**, 863–894. [357]

Krishna, Vijay, and John Morgan (2001), "Asymmetric information and legislative rules: some amendments", *American Political Science Review* **95**, 435–452. [357]

Kuhn, Harold W. (1950a), "A simplified two-person poker", in *Contributions to the theory of games*, Volume I (*Annals of Mathematics Studies*, 24) (Harold W. Kuhn and Albert W. Tucker, eds.), 97–103. Princeton, NJ: Princeton University Press. [357]

Kuhn, Harold W. (1950b), "Extensive games", *Proceedings of the National Academy of Sciences of the United States of America* **36**, 570–576. [179, 357]

Kuhn, Harold W. (1953), "Extensive games and the problem of information", in *Contributions to the theory of games*, Volume II (*Annals of Mathematics Studies*, 28) (Harold W. Kuhn and A. W Tucker, eds.), 193–216. Princeton, NJ: Princeton University Press. [179, 357]

Kuhn, Harold W. (1968), "Preface" and "Waldegrave's comments: excerpt from Montmort's letter to Nicholas Bernoulli", in *Precursors in mathematical economics: an anthology* (Series of Reprints of Scarce Works on Political Economy, 19) (William J. Baumol and Stephen M. Goldfeld, eds.), 3–9. London: London School of Economics and Political Science. [150, 370, 375]

Kuhn, Harold W. (1996), "Introduction", *Duke Mathematical Journal* **81**, i–v. [23, 53]

Kuhn, Harold W., John C. Harsanyi, Reinhard Selten, Jörgen W. Weibull, Eric van Damme, John F. Nash, Jr., and Peter Hammerstein (1995), "The work of John Nash in game theory", in *Les prix Nobel 1994*, 280–310. Stockholm: Almqvist & Wiksell. (Reprinted in *Journal of Economic Theory* **69** (1996), 153–185.) [23, 53]

Kummer, H., W. Götz, and W. Angst (1974), "Triadic differentiation: an inhibitory process protecting pair bonds in baboons", *Behaviour* **49**, 62–87. [410, 417]

Lagunoff, Roger, and Akihiko Matsui (1997), "Asynchronous choice in repeated coordination games", *Econometrica* **65**, 1467–1477. [464]

Langdon, Merle (1994), "Public auctions in ancient Athens", in *Ritual, finance, politics* (Robin Osborne and Simon Hornblower, eds.), 253–265. Oxford: Clarendon Press. [81, 97]

Latané, Bibb, and Steve Nida (1981), "Ten years of research on group size and helping", *Psychological Bulletin* **89**, 308–324. [151]

Ledyard, John O. (1981), "The paradox of voting and candidate competition: a general equilibrium analysis", in *Essays in contemporary fields of economics* (George Horwich and James P. Quirk, eds.), 54–80. West Lafayette, IN: Purdue University Press. [236]

Ledyard, John O. (1984), "The pure theory of large two-candidate elections", *Public Choice* **44**, 7–41. [236]

Leininger, Wolfgang (1989), "Escalation and cooperation in conflict situations: the dollar auction revisited", *Journal of Conflict Resolution* **33**, 231–254. [179]

Leonard, Janet L. (1990), "The hermaphrodite's dilemma", *Journal of Theoretical Biology* **147**, 361–371. [53]

Leonard, Robert J. (1994), "Reading Cournot, reading Nash: the creation and stabilisation of the Nash equilibrium", *Economic Journal* **104**, 492–511. [53, 70, 97]

Leonard, Robert J. (1995), "From parlor games to social science: von Neumann, Morgenstern, and the creation of game theory 1928–1944", *Journal of Economic Literature* **33**, 730–761. [9]

Lewis, David K. (1969), *Convention*. Cambridge, MA: Harvard University Press. [53]

Linster, Bruce G. (1992), "Evolutionary stability in the infinitely repeated Prisoners' Dilemma played by two-state Moore machines", *Southern Economic Journal* **58**, 880–903. [440, 450]

Linster, Bruce G. (1994), "Stochastic evolutionary dynamics in the repeated Prisoners' Dilemma", *Economic Inquiry* **32**, 342–357. [440, 450]

Lipman, Barton L., and Ruqu Wang (2000), "Switching costs in frequently repeated games", *Journal of Economic Theory* **93**, 149–190. [450]

Luce, R. Duncan, and Howard Raiffa (1957), *Games and decisions*. New York: Wiley. [53, 270, 392, 449]

Machina, Mark J. (1987), "Choice under uncertainty: problems solved and unsolved", *Journal of Economic Perspectives* **1(1)**, 121–154. [151]

MacKie-Mason, Jeffrey K., and Hal R. Varian (1995), "Pricing the Internet", in *Public access to the Internet* (Brian Kahin and James Keller, eds.), 269–314. Cambridge, MA: MIT Press. [98]

Magnan de Bornier, Jean (1992), "The 'Cournot–Bertrand debate': a historical perspective", *History of Political Economy* **24**, 623–656. [97]

Marx, Karl (1973), *Economic and philosophic manuscripts of 1844* (edited with an introduction by Dirk J. Struik, translated by Martin Milligan). London: Lawrence and Wishart. [473]

Maynard Smith, John (1972a), "Game theory and the evolution of fighting", in *On evolution* (John Maynard Smith), 8–28. Edinburgh: Edinburgh University Press. [399, 417]

Maynard Smith, John (1972b), *On evolution*. Edinburgh: Edinburgh University Press. [399]

Maynard Smith, John (1974), "The theory of games and the evolution of animal conflicts", *Journal of Theoretical Biology* **47**, 209–221. [97, 417]

Maynard Smith, John (1982), *Evolution and the theory of games*. Cambridge: Cambridge University Press. [401, 409, 417]

Maynard Smith, John (1991), "Honest signalling: the Philip Sydney game", *Animal Behaviour* **42**, 1034–1035. [358]

Maynard Smith, John, and G. A. Parker (1976), "The logic of asymmetric contests", *Animal Behaviour* **24**, 159–175. [417]

Maynard Smith, John, and G. R. Price (1973), "The logic of animal conflict", *Nature* **246**, 15–18. [53, 399, 417]

McAfee, R. Preston, and John McMillan (1996), "Analyzing the airwaves auction", *Journal of Economic Perspectives* **10 (1)**, 159–175. [311]

McKelvey, Richard D., and Richard G. Niemi (1978), "A multistage game representation of sophisticated voting and binary procedures", *Journal of Economic Theory* **18**, 1–22. [236]

McKelvey, Richard D., and Thomas R. Palfrey (1992), "An experimental study of the centipede game", *Econometrica* **60**, 803–836. [234, 235, 236, 237]

McMillan, John (1994), "Selling spectrum rights", *Journal of Economic Perspectives* **8 (3)**, 145–162. [300, 311]

Milgrom, Paul R. (1981), "Rational expectations, information acquisition, and competitive bidding", *Econometrica* **49**, 921–943. [311]

Milgrom, Paul R., Douglass C. North, and Barry R. Weingast (1990), "The role of institutions in the revival of trade: the Law Merchant, private judges, and the Champagne fairs", *Economics and Politics* **2**, 1–23. [448, 449, 450]

Milgrom, Paul R., and D. John Roberts (1986), "Price and advertising signals of product quality", *Journal of Political Economy* **94**, 796–821. [357]

Milinski, Manfred (1987), "Tit for tat in sticklebacks and the evolution of cooperation", *Nature* **325**, 433–435. [446, 450]

Milinski, Manfred (1993), "Cooperation wins and stays", *Nature* **364**, 12–13. [446, 450]

Miller, Nicholas R. (1977), "Graph-theoretical approaches to the theory of voting", *American Journal of Political Science* **21**, 769–803. [236]

Miller, Nicholas R. (1995), *Committees, agendas, and voting*. Chur, Switzerland: Harwood Academic Publishers. [237]

Milnor, John W. (1995), "A Nobel prize for John Nash", *Mathematical Intelligencer* **17 (3)**, 11–17. [23]

Morris, Stephen, Rafael Rob, and Hyun Song Shin (1995), "*p*-Dominance and belief potential", *Econometrica* **63**, 145–157. [311]

Moulin, Hervé (1979), "Dominance solvable voting schemes", *Econometrica* **47**, 1337–1351. [392]

Moulin, Hervé (1981), "Prudence versus sophistication in voting strategy", *Journal of Economic Theory* **24**, 398–412. [179]

Moulin, Hervé (1984), "Dominance solvability and Cournot stability", *Mathematical Social Sciences* **7**, 83–102. [392]

Moulin, Hervé (1986a), "Choosing from a tournament", *Social Choice and Welfare* **3**, 271–291. [237]

Moulin, Hervé (1986b), *Game theory for the social sciences*, 2nd ed. New York: New York University Press. [54, 151, 392]

Moulin, Hervé (1995), *Cooperative microeconomics*. Princeton, NJ: Princeton University Press. [270]

Mueller, Dennis C. (1978), "Voting by veto", *Journal of Public Economics* **10**, 57–75. [179]

Murchland, J. D. (1970), "Braess's paradox of traffic flow", *Transportation Research* **4**, 391–394. [54]

Myerson, Roger B. (1981), "Optimal auction design", *Mathematics of Operations Research* **6**, 58–73. [311]

Myerson, Roger B. (1996), "John Nash's contribution to economics", *Games and Economic Behavior* **14**, 287–295. [53]

Nachbar, John H. (1992), "Evolution in the finitely repeated Prisoner's Dilemma", *Journal of Economic Behavior and Organization* **19**, 307–326. [440, 450]

Nasar, Sylvia (1998), *A beautiful mind*. New York: Simon & Schuster. [53]

Nash, John F., Jr. (1950a), "Equilibrium points in *N*-person games", *Proceedings of the National Academy of Sciences of the United States of America* **36**, 48–49. [53, 151]

Nash, John F., Jr. (1950b), "Non-cooperative games", Doctoral dissertation, Princeton University. (Reprinted in *The essential John Nash* (Harold W. Kuhn and Sylvia Nasar, eds.), 53–84. Princeton, NJ: Princeton University Press, 2002.) [23, 53]

Nash, John F., Jr. (1950c), "The bargaining problem", *Econometrica* **18**, 155–162. [23, 491]

Nash, John F., Jr. (1951), "Non-cooperative games", *Annals of Mathematics* **54**, 286–295. [151]

Nash, John F., Jr. (1995), "John F. Nash, Jr.", in *Les prix Nobel 1994*, 275–279. Stockholm: Almqvist & Wiksell. [53]

Nash, John F., Jr., and Lloyd S. Shapley (1950), "A simple three-person poker game", in *Contributions to the theory of games*, Volume I (*Annals of Mathematics Studies*, 24) (Harold W. Kuhn and Albert W. Tucker, eds.), 105–116. Princeton, NJ: Princeton University Press. [357]

Nelson, Phillip (1970), "Information and consumer behavior", *Journal of Political Economy* **78**, 311–329. [357]

Nelson, Phillip (1974), "Advertising as information", *Journal of Political Economy* **82**, 729–754. [357]

Niemi, Richard G. (1983), "An exegesis of Farquharson's 'Theory of voting' ", *Public Choice* **40**, 323–328. [53, 236]

Novshek, William, and Hugo Sonnenschein (1978), "Cournot and Walras equilibrium", *Journal of Economic Theory* **19**, 223–266. [97]

Nowak, Martin A., and Karl Sigmund (1992), "Tit for tat in heterogeneous populations", *Nature* **355**, 250–253. [440, 450]

Nowak, Martin A., and Karl Sigmund (1993), "A strategy of win-stay, lose-shift that outperforms tit-for-tat in the Prisoner's Dilemma", *Nature* **364**, 56–58. [445, 450]

Olson, Mancur, Jr. (1965), *The logic of collective action.* Cambridge, MA: Harvard University Press. [53, 311]

O'Neill, Barry (1986), "International escalation and the dollar auction", *Journal of Conflict Resolution* **30**, 33–50. [179]

O'Neill, Barry (1987), "Nonmetric test of the minimax theory of two-person zero-sum games", *Proceedings of the National Academy of Sciences of the United States of America* **84**, 2106–2109. [373, 375]

O'Neill, Barry (1994), "Game theory models of peace and war", in *Handbook of game theory with economic applications*, Volume 2 (Robert J. Aumann and Sergiu Hart, eds.), 995–1053. Amsterdam: Elsevier. [53]

Osborne, Martin J. (1995), "Spatial models of political competition under plurality rule: a survey of some explanations of the number of candidates and the positions they take", *Canadian Journal of Economics* **28**, 261–301. [97]

Osborne, Martin J., and Ariel Rubinstein (1990), *Bargaining and markets.* San Diego, CA: Academic Press. [477, 491, 492]

Osborne, Martin J., and Ariel Rubinstein (1994), *A course in game theory.* Cambridge, MA: MIT Press. [xiii, 119, 269, 311, 477]

Osborne, Martin J., and Al Slivinski (1996), "A model of political competition with citizen-candidates", *Quarterly Journal of Economics* **111**, 65–96. [97]

Palacios-Huerta, Ignacio (2003), "Professionals play minimax", *Review of Economic Studies* **70**, 395–415. [375]

Palfrey, Thomas R., and Howard Rosenthal (1983), "A strategic calculus of voting", *Public Choice* **41**, 7–53. [54, 151]

Palfrey, Thomas R., and Howard Rosenthal (1984), "Participation and the provision of discrete public goods: a strategic analysis", *Journal of Public Economics* **24**, 171–193. [53, 151]

Pearce, David G. (1984), "Rationalizable strategic behavior and the problem of perfection", *Econometrica* **52**, 1029–1050. [392]

Pepys, Samuel (1970), *The diary of Samuel Pepys*, Volume III (Robert Latham and William Matthews, eds.). Berkeley: University of California Press. [81]

Peters, Michael (1984), "Bertrand equilibrium with capacity constraints and restricted mobility", *Econometrica* **52**, 1117–1127. [151, 237]

Phillips, Hubert (1937), *Question time.* London: Dent. [237]

Pitchik, Carolyn, and Andrew Schotter (1987), "Honesty in a model of strategic information transmission", *American Economic Review* **77**, 1032–1036 (see also **78**, 1164). [151]

Plott, Charles R. (1967), "A notion of equilibrium and its possibility under majority rule", *American Economic Review* **57**, 787–806. [270]

Pool, Robert (1995), "Putting game theory to the test", *Science* **267**, 1591–1593. [417]

Poundstone, William (1992), *Prisoner's dilemma*. New York: Doubleday. [9, 180]

Rabin, Matthew (1998), "Psychology and economics", *Journal of Economic Literature* **36**, 11–46. [7, 9]

Rapoport, Anatol, Melvin J. Guyer, and David G. Gordon (1976), *The* 2×2 *game*. Ann Arbor: University of Michigan Press. [28]

Robinson, Julia (1951), "An iterative method of solving a game", *Annals of Mathematics* **54**, 296–301. [151]

Romer, Thomas, and Howard Rosenthal (1978), "Political resource allocation, controlled agendas, and the status quo", *Public Choice* **33 (4)**, 27–43. [203]

Rosenthal, A. M. (1964), *Thirty-eight witnesses*. New York: McGraw-Hill. [133, 151]

Rosenthal, Robert W. (1981), "Games of perfect information, predatory pricing and the chain-store paradox", *Journal of Economic Theory* **25**, 92–100. [237]

Roth, Alvin E. (1982), "The economics of matching: stability and incentives", *Mathematics of Operations Research* **7**, 617–628. [270]

Roth, Alvin E. (1984a), "Misrepresentation and stability in the marriage problem", *Journal of Economic Theory* **34**, 383–387. [270]

Roth, Alvin E. (1984b), "The evolution of the labor market for medical interns and residents: a case study in game theory", *Journal of Political Economy* **92**, 991–1016. [270]

Roth, Alvin E. (1995), "Bargaining experiments", in *The handbook of experimental economics* (John H. Kagel and Alvin E. Roth, eds.), 253–348. Princeton, NJ: Princeton University Press. [203]

Roth, Alvin E., and Axel Ockenfels (2002), "Last-minute bidding and the rules for ending second-price auctions: evidence from eBay and Amazon auctions on the Internet", *American Economic Review* **92**, 1093–1103. [82, 97]

Roth, Alvin E., and Elliott Peranson (1999), "The redesign of the matching market for American physicians: some engineering aspects of economic design", *American Economic Review* **89**, 748–780. [270]

Roth, Alvin E., and Andrew Postlewaite (1977), "Weak versus strong domination in a market with indivisible goods", *Journal of Mathematical Economics* **4**, 131–137. [270]

Roth, Alvin E., Vesna Prasnikar, Masahiro Okuno-Fujiwara, and Shmuel Zamir (1991), "Bargaining and market behavior in Jerusalem, Ljubljana, Pittsburgh, and Tokyo: an experimental study", *American Economic Review* **81**, 1068–1095. [211, 237]

Roth, Alvin E., and Marilda A. Oliveira Sotomayor (1990), *Two-sided matching*. Cambridge: Cambridge University Press. [270]

Rousseau, Jean-Jacques (1988), "Discourse on the origin and foundations of inequality among men", in *Rousseau's political writings* (Alan Ritter and Julia Conaway Bondanella, eds.), 3–57. New York: Norton. [20]

Rubinstein, Ariel (1979), "Equilibrium in supergames with the overtaking criterion", *Journal of Economic Theory* **21**, 1–9. [450]

Rubinstein, Ariel (1982), "Perfect equilibrium in a bargaining model", *Econometrica* **50**, 97–109. [491]

Rubinstein, Ariel (1989), "The electronic mail game: strategic behavior under 'almost common knowledge'", *American Economic Review* **79**, 385–391. [311]

Rubinstein, Ariel (1991), "Comments on the interpretation of game theory", *Econometrica* **59**, 909–924. [179]

Rubinstein, Ariel (1994), "Equilibrium in supergames", in *Essays in game theory* (Nimrod Megiddo, ed.), 17–27. New York: Springer-Verlag. [450]

Rubinstein, Ariel, and Asher Wolinsky (1990), "Decentralized trading, strategic behaviour and the Walrasian outcome", *Review of Economic Studies* **57**, 63–78. [491]

Rubinstein, Ariel, and Asher Wolinsky (1995), "Remarks on infinitely repeated extensive-form games", *Games and Economic Behavior* **9**, 110–115. [464]

Samuelson, William F., and Max H. Bazerman (1985), "The winner's curse in bilateral negotiations", in *Research in experimental economics*, Volume 3 (Vernon L. Smith, ed.), 105–137. Greenwich, CT: JAI Press. [311]

Schelling, Thomas C. (1960), *The strategy of conflict.* Cambridge, MA: Harvard University. [32, 53]

Schelling, Thomas C. (1966), *Arms and influence.* New Haven, CT: Yale University Press. [179]

Schwalbe, Ulrich, and Paul Walker (2001), "Zermelo and the early history of game theory", *Games and Economic Behavior* **34**, 123–137. [180]

Selten, Reinhard (1965), "Spieltheoretische Behandlung eines Oligopolmodells mit Nachfrageträgheit", *Zeitschrift für die gesamte Staatswissenschaft* **121**, 301–324 and 667–689. [179]

Selten, Reinhard (1975), "Reexamination of the perfectness concept for equilibrium points in extensive games", *International Journal of Game Theory* **4**, 25–55. [151, 237, 357, 358]

Selten, Reinhard (1978), "The chain store paradox", *Theory and Decision* **9**, 127–159. [237]

Selten, Reinhard (1980), "A note on evolutionarily stable strategies in asymmetric animal conflicts", *Journal of Theoretical Biology* **84**, 93–101. [417]

Selten, Reinhard, and Rolf Stoecker (1986), "End behavior in sequences of finite Prisoner's Dilemma supergames: a learning theory approach", *Journal of Economic Behavior and Organization* **7**, 47–70. [437, 450]

Shaked, Avner (1994), "Opting out: bazaars versus 'hi tech' markets", *Investigaciones Económicas* **18**, 421–432. [477]

Shapiro, Carl (1989), "Theories of oligopoly behavior", in *Handbook of industrial organization*, Volume 1 (Richard Schmalensee and Robert D. Willig, eds.), 329–414. Amsterdam: North-Holland. [97]

Shapley, Lloyd S. (1959), "The solutions of a symmetric market game", in *Contributions to the theory of games*, Volume IV (*Annals of Mathematics Studies*, 40) (A. W. Tucker and R. D. Luce, eds.), 145–162. Princeton, NJ: Princeton University Press. [270]

Shapley, Lloyd S. (1964), "Some topics in two-person games", in *Advances in game theory* (*Annals of Mathematics Studies*, 52) (M. Dresher, Lloyd S. Shapley, and A. W. Tucker, eds.), 1–28. Princeton, NJ: Princeton University Press. [151]

Shapley, Lloyd S., and Herbert Scarf (1974), "On cores and indivisibility", *Journal of Mathematical Economics* **1**, 23–37. [270]

Shapley, Lloyd S., and Martin Shubik (1953), "Solutions of *N*-person games with ordinal utilities", *Econometrica* **21**, 348–349. (Abstract of a paper presented at a conference.) [270]

Shapley, Lloyd S., and Martin Shubik (1967), "Ownership and the production function", *Quarterly Journal of Economics* **81**, 88–111. [270]

Shapley, Lloyd S., and Martin Shubik (1971/72), "The assignment game I: the core", *International Journal of Game Theory* **1**, 111–130. [270]

Shepsle, Kenneth A. (1991), *Models of multiparty electoral competition*. Chur, Switzerland: Harwood Academic Publishers. [97]

Shubik, Martin (1954), "Does the fittest necessarily survive?", in *Readings in game theory and political behavior* (Martin Shubik, ed.), 43–46. Garden City, NY: Doubleday. [237]

Shubik, Martin (1959a), "Edgeworth market games", in *Contributions to the theory of games*, Volume IV (*Annals of Mathematics Studies*, 40) (A. W. Tucker and R. D. Luce, eds.), 267–278. Princeton, NJ: Princeton University Press. [270]

Shubik, Martin (1959b), *Strategy and market structure*. New York: Wiley. [450]

Shubik, Martin (1971), "The dollar auction game: a paradox in noncooperative behavior and escalation", *Journal of Conflict Resolution* **15**, 109–111. [97, 175, 179]

Shubik, Martin (1982), *Game theory in the social sciences*. Cambridge, MA: MIT Press. [151]

Shubik, Martin (1983), "Auctions, bidding, and markets: an historical sketch", in *Auctions, bidding, and contracting* (Richard Engelbrecht-Wiggans, Martin Shubik, and Robert M. Stark, eds.), 33–52. New York: New York University Press. [97]

Silverman, David L. (1981–82), "*N*-gumbo (Problem 1069)", *Journal of Recreational Mathematics* **14**, 139. [151]

Simon, Leo K., and William R. Zame (1990), "Discontinuous games and endogenous sharing rules", *Econometrica* **58**, 861–872. [97]

Sinervo, B., and C. M. Lively (1996), "The rock-paper-scissors game and the evolution of alternative male strategies", *Nature* **380**, 240–243. [407, 417]

Spence, A. Michael (1974), *Market signaling*. Cambridge, MA: Harvard University Press. [357]

Spohn, Wolfgang (1982), "How to make sense of game theory", in *Philosophy of economics* (Wolfgang Stegmüller, Wolfgang Balzer, and Wolfgang Spohn, eds.), 239–270. Berlin: Springer-Verlag. [392]

Ståhl, Ingolf (1972), *Bargaining theory*. Stockholm: Economics Research Institute at the Stockholm School of Economics. [491]

Ståhl, Ingolf (1977), "An *N*-person bargaining game in the extensive form", in *Mathematical economics and game theory* (Lecture notes in economics and mathematical systems, Volume 141) (R. Henn and O. Moeschlin, eds.), 156–172. Berlin: Springer-Verlag. [491]

Straffin, Philip D., Jr. (1980), "The Prisoner's Dilemma", *UMAP Journal* **1**, 102–103. [53]

Sun-tzu (1993), *The art of warfare* (translated, with an introduction and commentary, by Roger T. Ames). New York: Ballantine Books. [179]

Taylor, Alan D. (1995), *Mathematics and politics*. New York: Springer-Verlag. [179]

Thompson, Gerald L. (1987), "John von Neumann", in *The new Palgrave*, Volume 4 (John Eatwell, Murray Milgate, and Peter Newman, eds.), 818–822. London: Macmillan. [9]

Tirole, Jean (1988), *The theory of industrial organization*. Cambridge, MA: MIT Press. [179, 464]

Todhunter, Isaac (1865), *A history of the mathematical theory of probability from the time of Pascal to that of Laplace*. Cambridge: Macmillan. [375]

Trivers, Robert L. (1971), "The evolution of reciprocal altruism", *Quarterly Review of Biology* **46**, 35–57. [445]

Tucker, Albert W. (1950), "A two-person dilemma", unpublished paper, Stanford University. (Reprinted in *UMAP Journal* **1** (1980), 101.) [53]

Ulam, S. (1958), "John von Neumann, 1903–1957", *Bulletin of the American Mathematical Society* **64**, 1–49 of special issue on von Neumann. [9]

Ullmann-Margalit, Edna (1977), *The emergence of norms*. Oxford: Clarendon Press. [53]

van Damme, Eric (1983), *Refinements of the Nash equilibrium concept* (Lecture notes in economics and mathematical systems, Volume 219). Berlin: Springer-Verlag. [392]

van Damme, Eric (1987), *Stability and perfection of Nash equilibria*. Berlin: Springer-Verlag. [417]

Van Huyck, John B., Raymond C. Battalio, and Richard O. Beil (1990), "Tacit coordination games, strategic uncertainty, and coordination failure", *American Economic Review* **80**, 234–248. [54]

Vickrey, William (1961), "Counterspeculation, auctions, and competitive sealed tenders", *Journal of Finance* **16**, 8–37. [97, 311]

von Neumann, John (1928), "Zur Theorie der Gesellschaftsspiele", *Mathematische Annalen* **100**, 295–320. (Translated by Sonya Bargmann as "On the theory of games of strategy" in *Contributions to the theory of games*, Volume IV (*Annals of Mathematics Studies*, 40) (A. W. Tucker and R. D. Luce, eds.), 13–42. Princeton, NJ: Princeton University Press, 1959.) [3, 53, 151, 375] von Neumann, John, and Oskar Morgenstern (1944), *Theory of games and economic behavior*. Princeton, NJ: Princeton University Press. [2, 9, 24, 102, 146, 150, 179, 270, 357, 375, 399]

von Neumann, John, and Oskar Morgenstern (1947), *Theory of games and economic behavior*, 2nd ed. Princeton, NJ: Princeton University Press. [150]

von Stackelberg, Heinrich (1934), *Marktform und Gleichgewicht*. Vienna: Julius Springer. [203]

Walker, Mark, and John Wooders (2001), "Minimax play at Wimbledon", *American Economic Review* **91**, 1521–1538. [375]

Waltz, Kenneth N. (1959), *Man, the state and war*. New York: Columbia University Press. [53]

Ward, Benjamin (1961), "Majority rule and allocation", *Journal of Conflict Resolution* **5**, 379–389. [236]

Warr, Peter G. (1983), "The private provision of a public good is independent of the distribution of income", *Economic Letters* **13**, 207–211. [53]

Weibull, Jörgen W. (1995), *Evolutionary game theory*. Cambridge, MA: MIT Press. [417]

Wen, Quan (1994), "The 'folk theorem' for repeated games with complete information", *Econometrica* **62**, 949–954. [458, 464]

Wilson, Robert B. (1967), "Competitive bidding with asymmetric information", *Management Science (Series A)* **13**, 816–820. [311]

Wilson, Robert B. (1969), "Competitive bidding with disparate information", *Management Science (Theory)* **15**, 446–448. [311]

Wilson, Robert B. (1977), "A bidding model of perfect competition", *Review of Economic Studies* **44**, 511–518. [311]

Wilson, Robert B. (1992), "Strategic analysis of auctions", in *Handbook of game theory with economic applications*, Volume 1 (Robert J. Aumann and Sergiu Hart, eds.), 227–279. Amsterdam: North-Holland. [97]

Wittman, Donald (1977), "Candidates with policy preferences: a dynamic model", *Journal of Economic Theory* **14**, 180–189. [97]

Zermelo, Ernst (1913), "Über eine Anwendung der Mengenlehre auf die Theorie des Schachspiels", in *Proceedings of the fifth international congress of mathematicians* (Volume II) (E. W. Hobson and A. E. H. Love, eds.), 501–504. Cambridge: Cambridge University Press. (Translated by Ulrich Schwalbe and Paul Walker as "On an application of set theory to the theory of the game of chess", *Games and Economic Behavior* **34** (2001), 133–136.) [180]

Index

Page numbers in boldface indicate pages on which objects are defined. See the References for the pages on which books and papers are cited. The text of the book may be searched electronically at `http://www.economics.utoronto.ca/osborne/igt`*.*

⊘ = Exercise   ▶ = Definition   ▪ = Result   ◆ = Example

A

Ability signaled by education, 340–342
Accident law, 91–97
Actions, 4
  Bayesian game, ▶ **279.1**
  coalitional game, ▶ **239.1**
  extensive game with perfect information, 156
  rational, 377, ▶ **379.1**
  strategic game with ordinal preferences, ▶ **13.1**
  strategic game with vNM preferences, ▶ **106.1**
Adverse selection, ⊘ 282.3
Affine function, **495**
Agenda
  binary, **218**
  control, 186–187, 351–357
  design, ⊘ 221.1
Allocation (coalitional game), **240**
Alternating move repeated game, ⊘ 459.3
Alternating offer bargaining, *see* Bargaining
Altruism, reciprocal, 445–446
Altruistic preferences, ⊘ 5.3
  and social behavior, ⊘ 27.2
  in variant of *Prisoner's Dilemma*, ⊘ 27.1
Animals
  begging for food, ⊘ 335.2
  fighting over prey, 77
Approval voting, ⊘ 49.2
Arms race, 17, ◆ 20.2
Assessment (extensive game), ▶ **325.1**
Assortative mating, ⊘ 414.2
Asymmetric contests, 406–409
Asymmetric information, 331–335
Auction
  dollar, ◆ 175.1
  history, 81
  imperfect information, 88, 291–301, 307–311
    common valuations, 89, 297–300
    independent private values, 292–297
    reserve prices, 310–311
    revenue equivalence, 296–297, 299–300, 309–310
    risk-averse bidders, ⊘ 296.1
  perfect information, 80–91
    all-pay, ⊘ 89.1, ◆ 143.1
    first-price, 86–88
    multiunit, 89
    second-price, 82–86
    third-price, ⊘ 88.1
  radio spectrum, 300–301
  sniping, 82
Axelrod, Robert, 439–441, 445
Axiomatic bargaining model, 481–491

B

Baboon, Ethiopian hamadryas, 410
Babylonia, 81
Bach or Stravinsky?, *see BoS*
Backward induction, 158, 169–178
  discussion, 231–236
Bargaining
  alternating offers
    finite horizon, 466–468, 489–491
    infinite horizon, 468–473
    many players, 477
    market trade, 477–481
    outside options, 475–477
    risk of breakdown, 473–475, 477, 489–491
  axiomatic model, 481–491
  disagreement outcome, 481
  example (mixed strategies), ⊘ 130.3
    evolutionary stability, ⊘ 405.3
  firm–union, ⊘ 177.1, ⊘ 227.2, ⊘ 489.1
  one-sided offers, ⊘ 473.1
  two indivisible units, ⊘ 185.1
  ultimatum game, 181–187
Bargaining problem, ▶ **482.1**
Bargaining solution, ▶ **483.1**
Battle of the Sexes, ◆ 18.2
Bayes, Thomas, 280, 504
Bayes' rule, **504**
Bayesian game, ▶ **279.1**
  Nash equilibrium, ▶ **281.2**
Behavioral strategy, ▶ **324.2**
Belief
  Bayesian game, 279
  extensive game with imperfect information, ▶ **324.1**
  formation in strategic game, 134–137

Belief (*continued*)
  posterior, 502
  prior, 502
  strategic game, ▶ **379.1**
Bernoulli, Daniel, 102
Bernoulli, Nikolaus, 370
Bernoulli payoff function, **102**
  equivalence, 148–149
Bertrand oligopoly, 63–70
  dominance solvability, ⑦ 392.1
  infinitely repeated, ⑦ 454.3
    costly price changing, ⑦ 459.1
    detection lags, ⑦ 459.2
    imperfect observability, 461–463
  mixed strategies, ⑦ 146.1
  sequential variant, ⑦ 192.1
Best response dynamics, 135–136
Best response function, **36**
  Bertrand duopoly, 65
  Cournot duopoly, 57
  electoral competition, 72
  mixed strategies, 108–115
  War of Attrition, 78
Best response to belief, ▶ **379.1**
Binary agenda, **218**
Böhm-Bawerk, Eugen von, 252
Borel, Émile, 2
BoS, 18–19
  evolutionarily stable actions, 398, ◆ 403.1
  extensive game, ◆ 314.2
    consistent beliefs, ◆ 327.2
    Nash equilibrium, ◆ 319.1
  infinitely repeated game, ⑦ 454.2
  maxminimizer, ⑦ 370.2
  mixed strategy Nash equilibrium, 113–114
  pure strategy Nash equilibrium, 29
  variant (evolution), ⑦ 405.2, ⑦ 409.2
  variant with book option, ◆ 207.1
    Nash equilibrium, ◆ 208.2
    subgame perfect equilibrium, ◆ 210.1
  variant with imperfect information, ◆ 273.1,
      ◆ 276.2
    as Bayesian game, 280
  variants (rationalizable actions), ◆ 387.1
  with vNM preferences, ⑦ 106.2
Bourgeois strategy (evolution), 410
Breakdown risk in bargaining, 473–475, 477,
      489–491
Burning a bridge, ⑦ 173.4
Buyer–seller game, ⑦ 128.1, ⑦ 212.1; *see also*
      Market game
Buying votes, 192–196

C

Cake division, fair, ⑦ 185.2
Card game (extensive), ◆ 315.1, ⑦ 316.1

  consistent beliefs, ◆ 327.3
  Nash equilibrium, ◆ 319.2
  strategies, ⑦ 318.2
Cars approaching, ⑦ 130.2
Centipede game, ◆ 233.3
  experiments, 234–236
Chain-store game, ◆ 231.1
Chance moves in extensive game, 225–231
  modeling mistakes, 228–230
Chess, 178
Choosing numbers, ⑦ 117.2
Citizen-candidates, ⑦ 75.2
Closed rule (legislatures), 186, 352–355
Coalition, 239
Coalitional game, ▶ **239.1**
  cohesive, ▶ **242.3**
  core, ▶ **243.2**
  other solutions, 269
  transferable payoff, ▶ **241.1**
Cohesive coalitional game, ▶ **242.3**
Collective decision-making, 49–50
Collective ownership
  landowner–worker game, 250–251
Collusion in duopoly, ⑦ 60.2
Commitment and observability, ◆ 320.2
Commitment value, 192
Committee decision-making, 217–221
Common property, 18
  Cournot game, 62–63
Competitive equilibrium, 256
Conditional probability, 503
Condorcet winner, ⑦ 75.3, 219
  coalitional voting, 261
Consistency (extensive), 325, ▶ **328.1**
Conspicuous expenditure as quality signal,
      336–340
Continuous function, **497**
Coordination game
  evolutionarily stable actions, ◆ 404.1
  mixed strategy Nash equilibrium, ⑦ 114.3
  played by siblings, ⑦ 414.1
  pure strategy Nash equilibrium, 31
Core of coalitional game, ▶ **243.2**
  strong, **259**
Cournot oligopoly, 55–63, 69–70
  imperfect information, 285–288
  minmax payoff, ⑦ 452.3
  rationalizable actions, ⑦ 388.2
Crime reporting, 131–134

D

Darwin, Charles, 399
  model of sex ratio, ⑦ 416.1
Decision-making
  collective, 49–50
  by committee, 217–221

Declining industry exit, 221–225
Defending territory, ⑦ 118.3
Deferred acceptance procedure, 263–266
  strategic behavior, ⑦ 267.1
Delegation
  agenda control, 355–357
  information transmission, 349–350
Detection lags (repeated game), ⑦ 459.2
Dictator game, ⑦ 183.3
Disagreement outcome, 481
Discounted average of payoffs, 422
Discounted sum of payoffs, 421
Dividing money, ⑦ 38.2
  dominance solvability, ⑦ 391.2
  maxminimizers, ⑦ 363.1
  minmax payoff, ⑦ 452.3
Dollar auction, ◆ 175.1
Dominance solvability, 391–392
Domination
  strict
    elimination, ▶ 386.1
    mixed strategies, ▶ **120.1**, 385
    pure strategies, ▶ **45.1**
  weak
    elimination, 388
    and evolutionary stability, ⑦ 400.1
    mixed strategies, ▶ **121.1**, 388
    pure strategies, ▶ **46.1**
Duel, sequential, ⑦ 227.3
Duopoly, 16–17
  Bertrand, 63–70
    dominance solvability, ⑦ 392.1
    mixed strategies, ⑦ 146.1
    repeated, ⑦ 454.3, ⑦ 459.1, ⑦ 459.2, 461–463
    sequential variant, ⑦ 192.1
  Cournot, 55–63
    imperfect information, 285–288
    rationalizable actions, ⑦ 388.2
    repeated, ⑦ 452.3
  Stackelberg, 187–192
    with fixed costs, ⑦ 191.1
    value of commitment, 192

E

eBay, 81
Education signaling ability, 340–342
Election campaigns, ⑦ 141.3
Electoral competition, 70–76
  sequential model, ⑦ 196.3, ⑦ 196.4
  with strategic votes, 215–217
Empty history, **154**
Entry game, ◆ 154.1
  backward induction, 158
  with Bertrand competition, ⑦ 214.1
  with Cournot competition, 213–214
  as extensive game, ◆ 155.2

with financially constrained firm, ⑦ 174.2
  imperfect information, ◆ 317.1
    consistent beliefs, ◆ 327.4
    Nash equilibrium, ◆ 322.1
    weak sequential equilibrium, ◆ 330.1
  Nash equilibrium, ◆ 162.1
  signaling, ◆ 332.1
  subgame perfect equilibrium, ◆ 167.1
  variant, 158
    subgame perfect equilibrium, ◆ 167.2
Evolutionarily stable action, ▶ **398.1**
Evolutionarily stable strategy (ESS), ▶ **400.3**
  games without, 405–406
  repeated game, 441
Exchange game, ⑦ 282.2
Existence
  mixed strategy equilibrium, ■119.1
    symmetric, ■130.1
  subgame perfect equilibrium, ■173.1
Exit from declining industry, 221–225
Expected payoffs, 101–105
  evidence, 104
  as representation of preferences, 146–150
Expected value of lottery, **501**
Experiments
  centipede game, 234–236
  market game, 211–212
  maxminimization, 373–375
  Nash equilibrium (general discussion), 24–26
  Prisoner's Dilemma, 28
  repeated games, 436–437
  subgame perfect equilibrium, 211–212
  ultimatum game, 183–185
Expert diagnosis, 123–128
Extensive game
  imperfect information, ▶ **314.1**
    behavioral strategy, ▶ **324.2**
    belief system, ▶ **324.1**
    mixed strategy, ▶ **318.3**
    Nash equilibrium, ▶ **318.4**
    pure strategy, ▶ **318.1**
  perfect information, ▶ **155.1**
    backward induction, 169–178
    chance moves, **226**
    finite, 157
    finite horizon, 157
    Nash equilibrium, ▶ **161.2**
    outcome, **161**
    strategic form, **162**
    strategy, ▶ **159.1**
    subgame, ▶ **164.1**
    subgame perfect equilibrium, ▶ **166.1**
  perfect information and simultaneous
    moves, ▶ **206.1**
    Nash equilibrium, **208**
    strategic form, **208**

⑦ = Exercise   ▶ = Definition   ■ = Result   ◆ = Example

Extensive game (*continued*)
  perfect information and simultaneous
    moves (*continued*)
      strategy, ▶ **208.1**
      subgame perfect equilibrium, **209**

F

Fair division, ❓ 185.2
Feasible payoffs (repeated game), ▶ 432.1
  Prisoner's Dilemma, 432
Fictitious play, 136–137
Fighting, 77, ❓ 80.2
  opponent of unknown strength, ❓ 282.1
Finite extensive game, 157
Finite horizon extensive game, 157
Finitely repeated game, ▶ **424.1**
  general, 460–461
    Nash equilibrium, 460–461
    subgame perfect equilibrium, 461
  Prisoner's Dilemma, 424–426
Firm–union bargaining, ❓ 177.1, ❓ 227.2, ❓ 489.1
First-mover advantage
  bargaining, 473
  oligopoly, 189
Fish
  hermaphroditic, ❓ 18.1
  reciprocal altruism, 445–446
Fitness (biological), 393
Focal points, 32
Folk theorem
  Nash
    finitely repeated games, ▪460.1
    infinitely repeated games, ▪454.1
    infinitely repeated *Prisoner's Dilemma*, ▪435.1
  subgame perfect
    infinitely repeated *Prisoner's Dilemma*, ▪447.1
    infinitely repeated two-player games, ▪458.2
    two-player finitely repeated games, ▪461.1
Function (mathematical), **495**
  affine, **495**
  continuous, **497**
  linear, **495**
  quadratic, **496**
  set-valued, **498**

G

Game of timing, 79
Genovese, Catherine, 133
Grand coalition, 239
Grim trigger strategy, 420, 426, 428–429, 441–443
Guaranteed payoff, 362
  in strictly competitive game, ▪370.1
Guessing two-thirds of average, ❓ 34.1
  rationalizable actions, ❓ 387.4

H

Harsanyi, John C., 2, 23
Hawk–Dove
  asymmetric variant, ◆ 409.1–409
  evolutionarily stable actions, ◆ 398.2, ◆ 404.2
    variant, ❓ 405.1
  mixed strategy Nash equilibrium, ❓ 114.1
  Nash equilibrium, ❓ 31.2
  and *War of Attrition*, 77
Her, le (game), 371
Herodotus, 81
History (extensive game), **154**
  empty, **154**
Holdup game, 186
Horse (extensive game), ❓ 331.1
Horse market (coalitional game), 251–256
Hospital–resident matching, 268–269
Hotelling's model, 70–76
  infinitely repeated, ❓ 454.2
  minmax payoff, ❓ 452.3
  rationalizable actions, ❓ 387.5
  sequential variant, ❓ 196.3, ❓ 196.4
  with strategic voters, 215–217
House allocation, ◆ 242.1
House market, 256–260
Hungry lions, ❓ 202.1

I

Imperfect information extensive game, *see*
    Extensive game, imperfect information
Imperfect observability (repeated game), 461–463
Improve upon, 243
Impunity game, ❓ 183.3
  with equity-conscious players, ❓ 183.4
Independence of irrelevant alternatives
    (bargaining), **486**
Independent events, **500**
Infection (Bayesian game), 283–285
Infinitely repeated game, ▶ **424.1**
  alternating moves, ❓ 459.3
  imperfect observability, 461–463
  Nash equilibrium, 451–455
  Prisoner's Dilemma, 426–449
    Nash equilibrium, 428–437
    strategies, 426–428
    subgame perfect equilibrium, 441–449
  subgame perfect equilibrium, 455–459
Information
  asymmetric, 331–335
  modeled in Bayesian game, 282–285
  partition, ▶ 314.1
  set, 313
  transmission, 343–350
Interchangeable equilibria, ▪369.3
Internet pricing, ❓ 90.3

❓ = Exercise   ▶ = Definition   ▪ = Result   ◆ = Example

Interpretation
    Nash equilibrium, 22
    subgame perfect equilibrium, 168–169
Invariance to equivalent payoff transformations
        (bargaining), **485**
Iterated elimination
    strictly dominated actions, 134–135, ▷ **386.1**
        and rationalizability, ■386.2
    weakly dominated actions, **388**
        and subgame perfect equilibrium, 389

J

Joint project, 15–16, ② 42.2
Jury (Bayesian game), 301–307
    Nash equilibrium, 303–307

L

Landowner–worker game, ◆ 240.2
    core, ◆ 244.2
    general model, 247–251
Law, accident, 91–97
Law Merchant, 448
Learning (strategic game), 135
Legislatures
    agenda control, 186–187, 351–357
    cohesion, ② 228.1
    vote buying, 192–196
    vote trading, ② 247.1
Limited punishment strategy, 427
    Nash equilibrium, 429–430
    subgame perfect equilibrium, 443–444
Linear function, **495**
Lions, hungry, ② 202.1
Lizards, side-blotched, 407
Lobbying, 91
Lottery, 146, **501**
    expected value, **501**

M

Majority game, ◆ 240.3
    core, ② 245.1
    variant, ② 245.2
    voting, **261**
Market game
    bargaining, 477–481
    coalitional, ◆ 245.5
        heterogeneous goods, 256–260
        homogeneous goods, 251–256
    extensive, ② 211.2
        experiments, 211–212
Marriage market, ◆ 242.2
    general model, 263–269
Matching, ◆ 242.2, 263–269
Matching Pennies, 19–20
    fictitious play, 137

mixed strategy Nash equilibrium, 111–112
Nash equilibrium, 29
stochastic steady state, 100–101
Maxminimizer, ▷ **362.1**
    experimental tests, 373–375
    history, 370–372
    relation with Nash equilibrium, 364–365
        strictly competitive games, 367–370
Median favorite position, 71
Median voter theorem, ② 261.1
Medieval trade fairs, 448–449
Menu auction, ② 91.1
Mill (game), ② 179.3
Minmax payoff, ▷ **452.1**
    BoS, 452
Mistakes modeled as chance moves, 228–230
Mixed strategy
    animals and, 401
    extensive game with imperfect information,
        ▷ **318.3**
    strategic game, ▷ **107.1**
Mixed strategy Nash equilibrium
    extensive game with imperfect information,
        ▷ **318.4**
    strategic game, ▷ **108.1**
        characterization (continuum of actions), ■142.2
        characterization (finite actions), 115–119
        continuum of actions, 142–146
        existence, ■119.1
        existence in symmetric game, ■130.1
        finding all, 137–142
Model (abstract notion), 1–2
Monomorphic pure strategy equilibrium,
    394–400
Monopoly, entry into, 213–214
Montmort, Pierre Rémond de, 370
Morra, ② 372.3
    rationalizable actions, ② 387.3

N

Nash, John F., Jr., 2, **23**
Nash bargaining solution, **486**
Nash equilibrium
    Bayesian game, ▷ 281.2
    defined by best responses, ■36.1
    experiments (general discussion), 24–26
    extensive game
        general, ▷ **318.4**
        perfect information, ▷ **161.2**
        perfect information and simultaneous moves,
            208
    finding, 37–42
    idealized circumstances, 21
    mixed strategy, ▷ 108.1
        characterization, 115–119, ■142.2
        extensive game, ▷ **318.4**

② = Exercise   ▷ = Definition   ■ = Result   ◆ = Example

Nash equilibrium (*continued*)
  mixed strategy (*continued*)
    finding all, 137–142
    in games with continuum of actions, 142–146
  pure and mixed related, 122–123
  as steady state, 22
  strategic game, ▶ **23.1**
    examples, 26
    mixed strategy, ▶ **108.1**
    symmetric, ▶ **52.1**, ▶ **129.2**
    and weak domination, ⊘ 47.2
    strict, **33**, ⊘ 41.1
    and dominated actions, ⊘ 47.1
National Resident Matching Program, 269
Nesting behavior of wasps, 414–416
Neumann, John von, 3
Never-best response, ▶ **385.1**
  and strict domination, ■385.3
Nobel Prize, 2, 23

O

Observability and commitment, ◆ 320.2
Oligopoly
  Bertrand, 63–70
    dominance solvability, ⊘ 392.1
    mixed strategies, ⊘ 146.1
    repeated, ⊘ 454.3, ⊘ 459.1, ⊘ 459.2, 461–463
    sequential variant, ⊘ 192.1
  Cournot, 55–63, 69–70
    imperfect information, 285–288
    minmax payoff, ⊘ 452.3
    rationalizable actions, ⊘ 388.2
  Cournot and Bertrand, 69–70
  Stackelberg, 187–192
One-deviation property
  bargaining game of alternating offers, ■471.4
  repeated game, 437–439
O'Neill's game, ⊘ 372.4
Open rule (legislatures), 351–352
Outcome
  coalitional game, 239
  extensive game
    imperfect information, 314
    perfect information, **161**
  path (repeated game), ▶ **424.1**
Outside options in bargaining, 475–477
Ownership and wealth distribution, 247–251

P

Paradoxical strategy (evolution), 410
Pareto, Vilfredo, 483
Pareto efficiency (bargaining), **483**
Partition of set, **494**
Pavlov strategy, ⊘ 428.1
Payoff function, 5
  Bernoulli, **102**

Bernoulli equivalence, 148–149
discounted equivalence, 422–423
extensive game, 155
strategic game, 14
Pedestrians approaching, 52, 129
Pepys, Samuel, 81
Perfect information extensive game, *see* Extensive game, perfect information
Philip Sydney game, ⊘ 335.2
Player function in extensive game
  imperfect information, ▶ **314.1**
  perfect information, ▶ **155.1**
  perfect information and simultaneous moves, ▶ 206.1
Players
  Bayesian game, ▶ **279.1**
  coalitional game, ▶ **239.1**
  extensive game
    imperfect information, ▶ **314.1**
    perfect information, ▶ **155.1**
  strategic game with ordinal preferences, ▶ **13.1**
  strategic game with vNM preferences, ▶ **106.1**
Polymorphic steady state, 402–403
Pooling equilibria, 334
Posterior belief, 502
Preferences, 4
  coalitional game, ▶ **239.1**
  extensive game
    imperfect information, ▶ **314.1**
    perfect information, ▶ **155.1**
  repeated game, 421–423
  represented by expected payoffs, 146–150
  strategic game with ordinal preferences, ▶ **13.1**
  strategic game with vNM preferences, ▶ **106.1**
  vNM, **102**
Prior belief, 502
Prisoner's Dilemma, 14–18
  evolutionarily stable actions, 398
  experimental evidence, 28
  finitely repeated, 424–426
    switching cost, ⊘ 439.1
  infinitely repeated, 426–449
  minmax payoff, 452
  Nash equilibrium, 26–28
  played by siblings, 413–414
  rational actions, 377
  two-period, ⊘ 210.3
  variant with altruistic preferences, ⊘ 27.1
  variants (rationalizability), 377–379
  with vNM preferences, 106
    equivalent games, ⊘ 150.1
Probability, conditional, 503
Probability distribution, **500**
  cumulative, 501
Product differentiation, ⊘ 76.1
Profile, 498

⊘ = Exercise   ▶ = Definition   ■ = Result   ◆ = Example

Public good provision
  Bayesian game, 289–291
  rationalizable actions, ⑦ 388.1
  strategic game, 32, 42–45, ⑦ 132.3
Pure strategy, 108

Q

q-Rule game, 262
  core, ⑦ 262.1
Quadratic function, 496
  maximizer, 497

R

Race, 197–203
  with liquidity constraint, ⑦ 203.1
Radio spectrum auctions, 300–301
Rapoport, Anatol, 440
Rational action, 377, ▷ **379.1**
Rational choice, theory of, 4–7
Rationalizable action, ▷ **383.1**
  and Nash equilibrium, ■383.2
Reciprocal altruism, 445–446
Removing stones, ⑦ 201.2
Repeated game, ▷ **424.1**; *see also* Finitely repeated
      game, Infinitely repeated game
  experiments, 436–437
Reporting crime, 131–134
Resident–hospital matching, 268–269
Risk preferences, 103
Rock, paper, scissors, ⑦ 141.2
  variant (evolutionary stability), 406
Roommate problem
  empty core, ⑦ 267.2
  spatial preferences, ⑦ 267.3
Rotten kid theorem, ⑦ 177.2
Rousseau, Jean-Jacques, 20
Route-choosing game, ⑦ 34.3

S

Security dilemma, ◆ 20.2
Selten, Reinhard, 2, 23
Selten's horse, ⑦ 331.1
Separating equilibria, 334
Sequence, **499**
Sequential equilibrium, ▷ **328.1**
Sequential rationality, 325, ▷ **328.1**
Sex ratio, stable, 399, ⑦ 416.1
Sharing heterogeneous objects, ⑦ 174.1
Sibling behavior (evolution), 411–414
Side-blotched lizards, 407
Signal function (Bayesian game), 278
Signaling games, 331–335
  pooling equilibria, 334
  separating equilibria, 334

Signaling quality by conspicuous expenditure,
      336–340
Silverman's game, ⑦ 118.1
Simultaneous versus sequential games, ⑦ 177.3
Sir Philip Sydney game, ⑦ 335.2
Smith, John Maynard, 399
Soccer, 374–375
Social norm, 22
Social psychology and game theory, 133
Solution
  for Bayesian game
    Nash equilibrium, ▷ **281.2**
  for coalitional game
    core, ▷ **243.2**
    other, 269
  for extensive game with imperfect information
    Nash equilibrium, ▷ **318.4**
    weak sequential equilibrium, ▷ **328.1**
  for extensive game with perfect information
    Nash equilibrium, ▷ **161.2**
    subgame perfect equilibrium, ▷ **166.1**, 209
  for strategic game
    evolutionary stability, ▷ **398.1**
    maxminimizer, ▷ **362.1**
    Nash equilibrium, ▷ **23.1**
    rationalizability, ▷ **383.1**
Sophisticated voting, 219
Spider, funnel web, 410
Stackelberg duopoly, 187–192
  with fixed costs, ⑦ 191.1
  value of commitment, 192
Stag Hunt, 20–21
  coalitional game, ⑦ 241.2
    core, ⑦ 245.3, ⑦ 245.4
  Nash equilibrium, 29–31
States (Bayesian game), ▷ **279.1**
Steady state
  deterministic, 22
  perturbed, 163
  stochastic, 99–100
Sticklebacks, 445–446
Strategic form of extensive game
  perfect information, **162**
  perfect information and simultaneous moves,
      208
Strategic game
  best response function, **36**
  without conflict, ⑦ 20.1
  form of extensive game, 162
  Nash equilibrium
    defined by best responses, ■36.1
    examples, 26
    finding, 37–42
    strict, 33
    symmetric, ▷ **52.1**, ▷ **129.2**
    weak domination, ⑦ 47.2

Strategic game (*continued*)
  with ordinal preferences, ▶ **13.1**
    Nash equilibrium, ▶ **23.1**
    strictly competitive, ▶ **365.2**
    symmetric, ▶ **51.1**
  strictly competitive, 19
  three-player, ⑦ 142.1
  with vNM preferences, ▶ 106.1
    equivalence, 149–150
    rationalizable action, ▶ **383.1**
    strictly competitive, ▶ **366.1**
    symmetric, ▶ **129.1**
Strategic information transmission, 343–350
Strategy
  bourgeois (evolution), 410
  extensive game
    imperfect information, ▶ **318.1**, ▶ **324.2**
    perfect information, ▶ **159.1**
    perfect information and simultaneous moves,
      ▶ 208.1
  grim trigger, 420, 426, 428–429, 441–443
  limited punishment, 427
    Nash equilibrium, 429–430
    subgame perfect equilibrium, 443–444
  mixed
    extensive game with imperfect information,
      ▶ **318.3**
    strategic game, ▶ **107.1**
  paradoxical (evolution), 410
  Pavlov, ⑦ 428.1
  tit-for-tat, 427, 440
    Nash equilibrium, 430–431
    subgame perfect equilibrium, 444–446
  win–stay, lose–shift, ⑦ 428.1
Strategy, conditional (evolution), 407
Strict domination
  mixed strategies, ▶ **120.1**
  pure strategies, ▶ **45.1**
Strict Nash equilibrium, **33**, ⑦ 41.1
  and dominated actions, ⑦ 47.1
  not mixed, 118
Strictly competitive strategic game, 19, ▶ **365.2**,
    ▶ **366.1**
  dominance solvability, ⑦ 392.2
Strong core, **259**
Subgame of extensive game, ▶ **164.1**
  length, **169**
  proper, 164
Subgame perfect equilibrium
  discussion, 231–236
  experiments, 211–212
  extensive game with perfect information,
    ▶ **166.1**
    backward induction, 169–178
    continuum of actions, 176–178
    existence, ■173.1

  interpretation, 168–169
  and Nash equilibrium, 166–167
  extensive game with perfect information and
    simultaneous moves, **209**
Subhistory, **154**
Subset of set, **494**
Sun-tzu, 179
Swimming with sharks, ⑦ 114.4
Swing voter's curse, ⑦ 307.1
Symmetric Nash equilibrium, ▶ **52.1**, ▶ **129.2**
  existence, ■130.1
Symmetric strategic game
  ordinal, ▶ **51.1**
  vNM preferences, ▶ **129.1**
Symmetry (bargaining), **483**
Synergistic relationship, ◆ 39.1

T

Takeover (Bayesian game), ⑦ 282.3
Tennis, 374–375
Terminal history
  extensive game with imperfect information,
    ▶ **314.1**
  extensive game with perfect information,
    ▶ **155.1**
Three Men's Morris, ⑦ 179.3
Ticktacktoe, 178
Timing claims on investment, ⑦ 211.1
Timing product release, ⑦ 80.1
Tit-for-tat strategy, 427, 440
  Nash equilibrium, 430–431
  subgame perfect equilibrium, 444–446
Top cycle set, **220**
Top cycle trading procedure, **258**
Tournaments of Axelrod, 439–441, 445
Trade fairs, medieval, 448–449
Transferable payoff, ▶ **241.1**
Trigger strategy, grim, 420, 426, 428–429, 441–443
Truel, sequential, ⑦ 227.4
Type (Bayesian game), 279

U

Ultimatum game, 181–187
  with equity-conscious players, ⑦ 183.4, ⑦ 227.1
  experiments, 183–185
  extensions, 465–466
  indivisible units, ⑦ 183.2
  variant with two indivisible objects, ⑦ 185.1
Unanimity game, ◆ 240.1
  core, ◆ 244.1
Union
  bargaining with firm, ⑦ 177.1, ⑦ 227.2, ⑦ 489.1
  landowner–worker game, ⑦ 249.1
Union of sets, **494**
utility function, 5

V

Vickrey auction, 89
vNM preferences, **102**
von Böhm-Bawerk, Eugen, 252
von Neumann, John, 3
Vote trading, ⑦ 247.1
Voting
  by alternating veto, ⑦ 163.2
    subgame perfect equilibrium, ⑦ 173.3
  approval, ⑦ 49.2
  buying votes, 192–196
  coalitional game, 260–262
  dominance solvability, ⑦ 391.3
  median voter theorem, ⑦ 261.1
  participation, ⑦ 34.2
    mixed strategy Nash equilibrium, ⑦ 118.2
  sophisticated, 219
  strategic (in Hotelling's model), 215–217
  strategic game, 48–49
  swing voter's curse, ⑦ 307.1

W

Wage bargaining, ⑦ 489.1
Waiting in line, ⑦ 90.2
Waldegrave, 370
War of Attrition, 77–80
Wasps' nesting behavior, 414–416
Weak domination
  and evolutionary stability, ⑦ 400.1
  mixed strategies, ▶ **121.1**
  pure strategies, ▶ **46.1**
  second-price auction, ⑦ 294.1
Weak sequential equilibrium, ▶ **328.1**
Wealth distribution and ownership, 247–251
Win–stay, lose–shift strategy, ⑦ 428.1
Worker–landowner game, *see*
    Landowner–worker game
Worth of coalition, **241**

Z

Zerosum game, 366